KERUX COMMENTARIES

COLOSSIANS AND PHILEMON

KERUX COMMENTARIES

COLOSSIANS AND PHILEMON

A Commentary for Biblical Preaching and Teaching

ADAM COPENHAVER
JEFFREY D. ARTHURS

Colossians and Philemon: A Commentary for Biblical Preaching and Teaching

Published by Kregel Ministry, an imprint of Kregel Publications, 2450 Oak Industrial Dr. NE, Grand Rapids, MI 49505-6020.

Unless otherwise indicated, the translation of the Scripture quotations used throughout the exegetical portions of this volume are the authors' own English rendering of the original biblical languages.

Italics in Scripture quotations indicate emphasis added by the authors.

The Hebrew font, NewJerusalemU, and the Greek font, GraecaU, are available from www.linguistsoftware.com/lgku.htm, +1-425-775-1130.

All photos are under Creative Commons licensing, and contributors are indicated in the captions of the photos.

Maps on pages 38, 40, and 114 were designed by Shawn Vander Lugt, Managing Editor for Academic and Ministry Books at Kregel Publications.

ISBN 978-0-8254-5836-1

Printed in the United States of America
22 23 24 25 26 / 5 4 3 2 1

Contents

PUBLISHER'S PREFACE TO THE SERIES

Since words were first uttered, people have struggled to understand one another and to know the main meaning in any verbal exchange.

The answer to what God is talking about must be understood in every context and generation; that is why Kerux (KAY-rukes) emphasizes text-based truths and bridges from the context of the original hearers and readers to the twenty-first-century world. Kerux values the message of the text, thus its name taken from the Greek *kērux*, a messenger or herald who announced the proclamations of a ruler or magistrate.

Biblical authors trumpeted all kinds of important messages in very specific situations, but a big biblical idea, grasped in its original setting and place, can transcend time. This specific, big biblical idea taken from the biblical passage embodies a single concept that transcends time and bridges the gap between the author's contemporary context and the reader's world. How do the prophets perceive the writings of Moses? How does the writer of Hebrews make sense of the Old Testament? How does Clement in his second epistle, which may be the earliest sermon known outside the New Testament, adapt verses from Isaiah and also ones from the Gospels? Or what about Luther's bold use of Romans 1:17? How does Jonathan Edwards allude to Genesis 19? Who can forget Martin Luther King Jr.'s "I Have a Dream" speech and his appropriation of Amos 5:24: "No, no, we are not satisfied, and we will not be satisfied until 'justice rolls down like waters, and righteousness like a mighty stream'"? How does a preacher in your local church today apply the words of Hosea in a meaningful and life-transforming way?

WHAT IS PRIME IN GOD'S MIND, AND HOW IS THAT EXPRESSED TO A GIVEN GENERATION IN THE UNITS OF THOUGHT THROUGHOUT THE BIBLE?

Answering those questions is what Kerux authors do. Based on the popular "big idea" preaching model, Kerux commentaries uniquely combine the insights of experienced Bible exegetes (trained in interpretation) and homileticians (trained in preaching). Their collaboration provides for every Bible book:

- A detailed introduction and outline
- A summary of all preaching sections with their primary exegetical, theological, and preaching ideas
- Preaching pointers that join the original context with the contemporary one
- Insights from the Hebrew and Greek text
- A thorough exposition of the text
- Sidebars of pertinent information for further background
- Appropriate charts and photographs
- A theological focus to passages

- A contemporary big idea for every preaching unit
- Present-day meaning, validity, and application of a main idea
- Creative presentations for each primary idea
- Key questions about the text for study groups

Many thanks to Jim Weaver, Kregel's former acquisitions editor, who conceived of this commentary series and further developed it with the team of Jeffrey D. Arthurs, Robert B. Chisholm, David M. Howard Jr., Darrel L. Bock, Roy E. Ciampa, and Michael J. Wilkins. We also recognize with gratitude the significant contributions of Dennis Hillman, Fred Mabie, Paul Hillman, Herbert W. Bateman IV, and Shawn Vander Lugt who have been instrumental in the development of the series.

—Kregel Publications

PREFACE TO COLOSSIANS AND PHILEMON

As commentators, we certainly had great material with which to work. Colossians and Philemon are little gems that sparkle with many facets of the person and work of Christ and the composition and character of the church. Or to mix the metaphor, they are poems so compact in language and density of thought that they reward only those who give them their full attention. That's what writing this book has been for us: a chance to slow down and give the little books our full attention. Adam had a leg up on Jeffrey because he wrote his dissertation on Colossians, so Jeffrey had to catch up by slowing down. Adam was always out front cheering as he handed his exegetical analyses to Jeffrey the homiletician.

That handoff is the foundation of the Kerux series and the conviction held by the authors of this volume: God has taken the initiative to reveal himself through his inspired Word, so the preacher's job is first of all to understand with the mind, and imagine with the heart, what God has communicated. Then the preacher can cross the bridge of relevance to ask how the text can be contextualized in his or her particular milieu. Adam and Jeffrey have been of one accord with that conviction since day one, and that has made the writing of this volume a delight and not just a labor.

EXEGETICAL AUTHOR'S ACKNOWLEDGMENTS

For all who labor
as shepherds of the local church
in the spirit of Epaphras

This commentary grows out of a decade-long love affair with Colossians and Philemon, both in various writing endeavors as well as multiple sermon series. These two letters from Paul are exciting and richly rewarding to preach. All congregations can relate to the story of conflict and reconciliation that hovers over both letters, as Paul aims to reconcile the slave Onesimus with his master Philemon through these two letters. The letters surely had a deep and lasting impact upon the young church in Colossae and they continue to have a similar impact upon the churches in which they are preached today—both in in my own church and now, Lord willing, in your church as well.

Thanks are due to Kregel Publishers for their work in bringing this series to fruition, as well as to Herb Bateman, who has championed it for many years. Further thanks go to my congregation, Mabton Grace Brethren Church, and especially to my wife, Susie, and to my boys, Simon and Calvin, all of whom have endured countless sermons and lessons derived from Colossians and Philemon. Their questions, discussions, and reactions have shaped this commentary as much or more than my own study and reflection. Finally, thank you to Jeff Arthurs for being a true coauthor and a companion in this project. It has been a joy to write this volume together.

—Adam Copenhaver

PREACHING AUTHOR'S ACKNOWLEDGMENTS

For Pastor Robert Nitz,
my first pastor,
the first man to preach the gospel to me,
a true herald of the Word

With thanks to God for giving us his inspired Word, especially the rich books of Colossians and Philemon, I dedicate this commentary to my fellow preachers worldwide.

For this engagement with Colossians and, for me, the unplowed field of Philemon, I have really enjoyed collaborating with Adam. From our first meeting in 2015 and through many email exchanges, phone calls, and face-to-face meetings at conferences, I have found Adam to be a kindred spirit. He has been encouraging, flexible, and insightful. I love the fact that Adam is a pastor, so he knows what will preach! I am also grateful for the editors at Kregel who kept the vision for the Kerux series front and center. My colleagues at Gordon-Conwell Theological Seminary have checked in with me regularly to spur me on to love and good works. This has truly been a team effort.

—Jeffrey Arthurs

OVERVIEW OF ALL PREACHING PASSAGES

Colossians 1:1–8

EXEGETICAL IDEA
Paul thanked God for the Colossians because they had heard and received the gospel message from Epaphras and because the gospel was now actively reaching more people and bearing fruit, even as their hope was producing faith toward Christ and love toward the saints.

THEOLOGICAL FOCUS
When people hear and receive the gospel, their lives are transformed as they grow in their faith in Christ, love for one another, and hope for eternity.

PREACHING IDEA
Let's thank God for the good news that changes us.

PREACHING POINTERS
Although Paul had not visited the small town of Colossae, his faithful companion Epaphras preached the good news there, and the first text of Colossians depicts a marvelous real-life picture of the power of the gospel. Greco-Roman culture promoted polytheism and licentiousness, but when some of the people of Colossae heard and understood the gospel, it took root, grew, and bore fruit. No wonder Paul thanked God for the Colossians (v. 3). For these converts, the gospel was more than a stripped-down message of sin and salvation (although it was not *less* than that). It was a full-orbed but shorthand way that Paul used to capture all that God is doing to save his people from sin and redeem this broken world. For Paul, the good news announced how the Colossians had been made blameless in the eyes of God through Jesus; it also produced the fruit of Christlike attitudes and behaviors, as with the Colossians.

The good news has the same power to produce the same results today as well. Too often a "profession of faith" produces little moral change. It has been said that Christianity in North America is a mile wide and an inch deep. The same is also true for many parts of Africa and South America. The "health-and-wealth gospel" produces "converts" who use God as their errand boy and genie. On the other hand, salvation can be framed in a way that implies a burdensome and guilt-producing obligation to please God lest he disown us. That doesn't sound like good news! The first passage in Colossians steers between these shoals, or rather, it rejects both and finds deep water elsewhere—in the good news of the gospel. There we learn how much God loves us and has done for us, and this produces the fruit of faith, hope, and love (vv. 4–6). So, let's thank God for the good news that changes us.

Colossians 1:9–14

EXEGETICAL IDEA
Paul prayed for the Colossians to know God's will in order that they might live worthy of the Lord and fully please him by doing good works, by growing in knowledge, by persevering, and by joyfully thanking the Father, who had delivered them into the kingdom of the Son.

THEOLOGICAL FOCUS
Believers will walk worthy of the Lord and aim to please him in every way when they know his will and the salvation they have received.

PREACHING IDEA
By experiencing God and understanding what he wants, we can live lives of good works that please him.

PREACHING POINTERS
The apostle Paul lifts up a soaring prayer for the believers in Colossae with intercession following thanksgiving (a good pattern for any prayer meeting!). In one long, magnificent sentence that continues through verse 23, Paul and his team pray for the saints living in the small town of the Roman province of southwest Asia Minor, that they would know God's desire—namely, that they would live for God even as they were empowered by God. In this passage, Paul likely has in view concerns that emerge later in the letter, including the pressure the Colossian believers experienced from false teachings and the unresolved situation between Onesimus and Philemon. Here he prays for them in a general sense that they would know God's will and walk in it. The prayer asks for knowledge, strength, and joy.

Those qualities seem to be in short supply today. For instance, consider joy. The "World Happiness Report" found that in 2018, Americans were less happy than they were the year before and ranked nineteenth, behind Australia and Canada. According to *The New Republic*, psychologists reported in 2019 that anxiety was on the rise.

Closely connected to joy is the issue of strength. Christians often feel powerless to overcome bad habits and besetting sins. Depending on willpower alone to break those habits turns into drudgery and leads only to short-term change, but when we are motivated by joy, strength follows. Obedience becomes a delight.

Where are strength and joy to be found? This rich passage tells us: in deep, experiential knowledge of the salvation Jesus Christ provides. By experiencing God and understanding what he wants, we can exhibit lives of good works that please him.

Colossians 1:15–23

EXEGETICAL IDEA
Paul used poetic language to describe the surpassing nature of Christ because of his great work in creation and redemption, and therefore Paul appealed for the Colossian believers to

remain faithful to Christ until they are presented blameless with him before God, for there is no one more exalted than Christ.

THEOLOGICAL FOCUS
Believers must remain in the faith they learned in the gospel, for Christ is exalted over all things in creation and redemption, and he has even reconciled believers to God in order to present them perfect before God.

PREACHING IDEA
Christ is above all, he has done it all, and now we have it all—so don't move at all.

PREACHING POINTERS
In a soaring "hymn," the apostle Paul reminds the believers in the little town of Colossae that Jesus is, as theological formulations would later summarize, the exalted second person of the Trinity. That message hit home because in the Greco-Roman world, multiple gods vied for attention. If people had heard about Jesus, he was probably seen as just the newest deity on the block. The Christ-followers in Colossae knew differently, but the pressure of culture was strong, so Paul reminds them who Jesus is: the firstborn from the dead in whom the fullness of God dwells.

Today the situation is similar. People choose religious beliefs from multiple options. One of the options is even "none," which James Emery White claims is the fastest-growing religious demographic (*The Rise of the Nones*, Baker, 2014). A 2020 report from Religion News Service indicates that the "nones" are as numerous as evangelicals or Catholics: 23.1%. Many people are attracted to Jesus (even while they are turned off by organized religion), but they may be creating their own version of the Son of God. Views about Jesus abound: he is a good man, a revolutionary, a sage, and so forth. This passage from Colossians sets the record straight. In the face of religious pluralism, the modern preacher can follow the apostle Paul: lift up Jesus Christ as the eternal Son of God and urge listeners to remain steadfast in their faith because Christ is above all, has done it all, and now we have it all—so we should not move at all.

Colossians 1:24–29

EXEGETICAL IDEA
As an apostle, Paul was entrusted by God with an obligation to proclaim the mystery of Christ to all people, including the Gentiles, that all people might be united to Christ and brought to maturity in Christ. Toward this end, Paul labored exhaustively and suffered extensively.

THEOLOGICAL FOCUS
In Christ, God's mysterious plan has been made known, so that all people are invited into saving union with Christ, exhorted to grow to maturity in Christ, and called to embrace the mission of making Christ known to all people.

PREACHING IDEA
The mystery of Christ concealed is now revealed.

PREACHING POINTERS

With a touch of autobiography Paul returns to the theme of his own ministry as an apostle—how he suffered and labored to present everyone mature in Christ. Yet even as he speaks of his afflictions, there is also joy and confidence because the suffering came in his role as a minister of the mystery that was hidden for ages. That mystery is summarized as the "gospel," or "good news," the whole magnificent story about the person and work of Jesus—his divinity, incarnation, sacrificial death, resurrection, intercession, and imminent return. By making peace through the cross, Jesus broke down the wall to include Gentiles as part of his covenant people, so that his righteousness and honored standing before God became theirs also. Thus, the Gentiles experienced the "hope of glory" (v. 27). That is the good news, and ministers like Paul made it known.

The same good news operates today as well. And God still uses spokespeople like Paul to steward the message. Yet some followers of Christ find it difficult to manage their stewardship. We tend to be reticent in sharing the good news, the hope of glory. Perhaps we find it easier to talk about current events or personal ailments. This is understandable in our pluralistic culture, where certainty can be seen as close-minded and sharing might be seen as proselytizing. This passage challenges and encourages us to work hard in evangelism with the inspiration and courage God provides to make the good news known, because the mystery that was once concealed is now revealed.

Colossians 2:1–5

EXEGETICAL IDEA

Paul described how he worked specifically for the Colossians: that they would be able to stand against deception because they were a tight-knit church community, and because they stood firm in the full treasures of knowledge in Christ.

THEOLOGICAL FOCUS

To avoid being deceived and led astray in our faith, God's people need strong relationships with other believers and good teaching about Christ.

PREACHING IDEA

When we're knit together in love and knowledge, deception won't unravel us.

PREACHING POINTERS

Paul was laboring to protect the little church in Colossae from false teachers. He called this a "great struggle" (v. 1). The problem of false teachers and teaching is described on many pages of the New Testament such as Galatians where some people were propounding a combination of grace and legalism; and 1, 2, 3 John, which battled the "antichrists." Heresies continued to plague the early church, and the problem has not abated since then. The message of the false teachers will be discussed later in Colossians (2:16–23), but in this text Paul rings the warning bell about their "plausible arguments" (v. 4).

Today false teachers continue to offer plausible arguments through print media, blogs, podcasts, and television. The teachers might say that Jesus is just a man or that God is an impersonal "force." A brilliant scientist like Richard Dawkins uses interviews, articles, and books to sound his shrill message of atheism. In *The God Delusion* (2006) he says: "The God of the Old Testament is arguably the most unpleasant character in all fiction: jealous and proud of it; a petty, unjust, unforgiving control-freak; a vindictive, bloodthirsty ethnic cleanser; a misogynistic, homophobic, racist, infanticidal, genocidal, filicidal, pestilential, megalomaniacal, sadomasochistic, capriciously malevolent bully." A white witch named Starhawk calls nature "the Goddess." In *The Spiral Dance* (1979) she opines, "The Mysteries are teachings that cannot be grasped by the intellect alone, but only by the deep mind made accessible in trance. They may be conveyed by an object . . . by a key phrase, or symbol. . . . Only within the framework of the ritual does it take on its illuminating power."

Colossians 2:6–15

EXEGETICAL IDEA

Paul appealed to the Colossians to live faithfully with Christ as their Lord, resisting all teachings and powers contrary to Christ, for by faith they have been united to Christ in his death and resurrection, so that they shared in the full blessings of Christ.

THEOLOGICAL FOCUS

When believers understand the fullness of blessings they have received by union with Christ, they will hold fast to Christ and not be captured by false teachings or defeated spiritual powers.

PREACHING IDEA

Jesus is better than religion, so don't let religion take you captive.

PREACHING POINTERS

Paul was concerned about the false teachings that circulated in the Greco-Roman world. Some of those philosophies made their way into the church in Colossae, or at least threatened to infiltrate it. The church in Colossae was surrounded by a culture that worshipped many gods. In the ancient world shrines dotted the landscape, and feasts and festivals punctuated the yearly calendar. The philosophies of the day offered their own take on values, personhood, the afterlife, community, knowledge, and theology, and the teachings tempted the Colossians to stray from Christ.

Today in the West, the worship of idols is not as overt as it was in the first century with shrines and temples, although neo-paganism seems to be on the rise. James Emery White (2019) summarizes the present situation: "Most Americans mix traditional faith with beliefs in psychics, reincarnation and spiritual energy that they say can be found in physical objects such as mountains, trees and crystals." In addition to the mainstreaming of such ideas, the more traditional "isms" of nationalism, materialism, and agnosticism are magnets that try to draw the hearts of Christ-followers. The rise in both neo-pagan and secular philosophies prompted Pope Francis in 2019 to state starkly that "we are not in Christianity anymore."[1] The United

1 Francis X. Rocca, "Pope Francis, in Christmas Message, Says Church Must Adapt to Post-Christian West," *The Wall Street Journal*, December 21, 2019.

States and Canada should now be considered mission fields. Whether the philosophies are religious or secular, this text from Paul to the Colossians warns, "Don't be led astray!" Jesus is better than religion, so we are on our guard to not let it capture us.

Colossians 2:16–23

EXEGETICAL IDEA
Paul warned the Colossian believers against submitting themselves to teachings and practices that were unable to save them from the sinful flesh, whether Jewish laws that were outdated in light of Christ or pagan religions that were the vain fruit of human imagination.

THEOLOGICAL FOCUS
Believers must be on their guard against false teachings and religious practices that purport to offer something better than Christ when in reality they are empty, vain, and useless for conquering the flesh.

PREACHING IDEA
Shadows can't save us, but the Son can.

PREACHING POINTERS
In Paul's day, the Jewish and pagan teachers counseled, "Touch not, taste not, handle not—that's the way to conquer sinful desires!" But the apostle said: "Wrong!" Neither Jewish regulations nor the rituals of pagan worship could curb sinful desires and change the heart. Furthermore, the teachers in Paul's day were judging the members of the Colossian church for failing to follow Jewish and pagan rules, and Paul responded: "Don't let them do it!" Returning to the old practices, whether Jewish or polytheistic, is tantamount to abandoning Christ, and doing so would disqualify the Christ-followers in Colossae from receiving their reward.

Asceticism and legalism are alive today too: crawl up the towering flight of stairs on your knees, and you will earn God's favor; fast until your bones protrude, and you will get God's attention; deny yourself sex with your spouse because that's what the cult leader says to do, and then you will be free from carnal desire. This passage addresses people who have been saved from heavy-handed, false religions. Ironically, some Christians are tempted to return to those old ways. Legalism goads them: do more, do better, and then God will give you grace. But religious rules are just a shadow of the deeper reality that is Christ. He has already defeated the flesh, so we must cling to him alone. Making an idol out of anything—even spiritual practices like fasting, prayer, and self-denial—leads to shame and withdrawal when we fail, or pride and scoffing when we succeed. Legalistic rules and man-made religious ideas are just a shadow, and shadows can't save us, but the Son can.

Colossians 3:1–4

EXEGETICAL IDEA
Paul exhorted the Colossians to seek to live in light of heaven, where Jesus reigns as Lord, and in light of their identity in Christ—for they have died and been raised with Christ in the

past, their lives now belong to Christ in the present, and they will in the future be revealed with Christ in glory.

THEOLOGICAL FOCUS
Believers must reorient their present lives on earth around the heavenly reality that Jesus lives as the exalted Lord in heaven and that they have a new identity in Christ and will one day share in his eternal glory.

PREACHING IDEA
Live on earth by thinking of Christ in heaven.

PREACHING POINTERS
Having lifted up Christ and put down the false teachers in the previous sections of Colossians, Paul now turns toward application to daily life. But before becoming intensely practical, Paul has a few more words to say about the mind: fix it on "things that are above, not on things that are on earth" (v. 2). The mind was valued highly in Greco-Roman culture. When he was in Athens, he debated in the marketplace every day and then gave an extended address on the Areopagus (Acts 17:17, 19–31); in Ephesus, not far from Colossae, he reasoned daily for two years in the lecture hall of Tyrannus (Acts 19:9), presumably a venue for the TED Talks of the day.

The mind matters today just as it did then. How we think, and what we think about, have an enormous influence on how we live. Like "garbage in, garbage out," poor thoughts in, poor actions out. This cause-effect dynamic may be reflected in the dramatic increase in the suicides in rural areas of the United States. The Center for Disease Control recorded 1.4 million total attempts and 47,173 suicides in 2017. The highest rates were in Montana, Alaska, Wyoming, New Mexico, Idaho, and Utah. Poverty, isolation, and the easy availability of guns were key factors, but according to one researcher, the men's mentality was also a factor. As quoted in Stephen Rodrick's *Rolling Stone* article "All-American Despair," Dr. Craig Bryan of the University of Utah, who studies military and rural suicide, put it this way: "There's been an increase in the 'every-man-for-himself mentality.'"

Positive thinking is also beneficial: heavenly thoughts in, God-honoring actions out. In this text, the Lord commands us to "set our minds on things above" and to "seek the things above." We live on earth by thinking of Christ in heaven.

Colossians 3:5–11

EXEGETICAL IDEA
Paul exhorted the Colossians to stop living in their former way of life apart from Christ, by putting to death the practices of that former life and embracing their identity as new persons being transformed into the image of Christ, as members together in the body of Christ.

THEOLOGICAL FOCUS
Believers must be transformed into the image of Christ by putting off their old habits of sin, and by living out of the new nature and identity they have received in Christ and in the body of Christ.

PREACHING IDEA
Now that we are spiritually alive in Christ, let's put to death the old ways.

PREACHING POINTERS
In the previous passages of Colossians, Paul focused on pagan beliefs, and in this passage he focuses on pagan lifestyle. The church in the village of Colossae was an island in a sea of paganism. The Colossians should no longer display the old habits of paganism because they were now alive in Christ. That spiritual reality was to be demonstrated in daily living: no sins of passion such as sexual immorality; no sins of anger such as slander; and no sins regarding material wealth such as greed. The Colossians knew well the old ways because they used to drift in the stream of their culture, but then they became new in Christ. Impurity, malice, and greed must be put to death and put off like a dirty garment

The lists of sins Paul gave the Colossians could have been gleaned from today's talk radio, evening news, advertisements, schools, and workplaces. Little has changed in two thousand years. Politicians slander each other with vituperative malice; sitcoms parade obscene talk with a wink and a titter; and websites make sexual impurity just a click away. The Pew Research Center found that in 2019, more Americans cohabited than were married: 59% and 50%. (In 2002 the figures were 54% and 60%.) Sixty-nine percent of Americans say that it is okay to cohabit even if they don't plan to marry, and 78% of respondents under the age of thirty say it's okay. (These statistics can be found at Pew Research.) With sins like polyamory and virtual sex with robots on the rise, this passage has much to say today.

Christ-followers have been made new, so they must act like it by putting to death impurity, greed, and anger, along with factions. All of that belongs to the old way, but we are now spiritually alive in Christ, so let's put to death the old ways.

Colossians 3:12–17

EXEGETICAL IDEA
Paul exhorted the Colossians to put on the virtues of Christ, especially love, that they might have peace and unity together as the body of Christ, where the word of Christ dwells richly among them and they bring honor to the name of the Lord Jesus in all that they do.

THEOLOGICAL FOCUS
Believers must put on the virtues of Christ that will allow them to live in peaceful unity with one another as the body of Christ, to grow together through the word of Christ, and to honor the Lord Jesus in all things.

PREACHING IDEA
Only Jesus can dress you for church.

PREACHING POINTERS
When Paul spoke to the church in the little town of Colossae, he addressed a surprisingly diverse group of people: Jew and Gentile, slave and free, barbarian, and Scythian. Christ had

called and regenerated people from many backgrounds and strata of society. That diversity testified to the power of Christ's call. The door to his kingdom is narrow, but all who desire to enter may do so. But this inclusivity was not only inspiring; it was also challenging, because diversity easily brings disunity. That was the challenge this first-century church faced, and percolating beneath the surface of Colossians is a particularly divisive issue—Philemon and his slave, Onesimus. How could master and runaway slave, brothers in Christ, demonstrate the unity of their spiritual standing?

Today we also face the issue of divisiveness. Racial, economic, cultural, and political diversity must not be allowed to divide Christ's body. One member of the church tunes in to a conservative news station and another to a progressive station. One member works at manual labor and another works in the world of ideas. Still another speaks with an accent and sometimes feels left out. Cultural differences and personal preferences, not to mention the daily irritations of living in community, must not trump the fact that we are one in Christ. How is this ideal to be actualized? By putting on love and the qualities that flesh out love: kindness, humility, meekness, patience, forgiveness, and thankfulness. Now that we've put off the dirty clothes associated with life before believing in Jesus, it's time to dress in those beautiful garments. Let's let Jesus dress us for church.

Colossians 3:18–4:1

EXEGETICAL IDEA

Paul instructed the Colossians regarding how they ought to live out their new life of Christ within their former household roles in a transformed manner, so that they will please the Lord Jesus in whatever they do as wives and husbands, children and fathers, and slaves and masters.

THEOLOGICAL FOCUS

Believers must learn to serve Jesus as Lord within every aspect of their lives in the world, including their household roles and other circumstances that they are powerless to change, for the Lord Jesus is more concerned with their internal transformation than he is with their external situation.

PREACHING IDEA

In the Christian household, we have different roles but the same Lord.

PREACHING POINTERS

Although Paul was not married and lived as an itinerant missionary, he wrote often about home life. In this passage, he takes up that theme and draws out the practical implications of being "in Christ" in the home. Households in Colossae, including Christian households, followed traditional Greco-Roman codes that specified how husbands and wives, fathers and children, and masters and slaves were to treat each other. This passage is similar to those household codes, so in one sense, Christianity in Colossae was traditional and conservative, but Paul also introduces a progressive, even revolutionary, approach to family life. Wives, children, and slaves are elevated, while husbands, fathers, and masters are tempered. Paul treats all members of the household as responsible moral agents.

In a day when the concept of family is being redefined, Colossians 3:18–4:1 takes Christ-followers back to their roots and shows them what it looks like to be in Christ under one roof. Our spirituality rises no higher than the way we treat our families. As the old Firestone tire commercial says, this is "where the rubber meets the road." In this passage theology is put into practice in the most mundane and constant of our environments, the home. Christianity is neither exclusively traditional nor exclusively radical. The Christian home transcends those categories because all members of the household dethrone self and enthrone Christ. The theology of the first three chapters walks into our homes and arranges things in surprising ways because in the Christian household, we have different roles but the same Lord.

Colossians 4:2–6

EXEGETICAL IDEA

Paul instructed the Colossians to make the gospel known by praying for him in his global mission of proclaiming the gospel in new places, and by embracing their local mission in Colossae of answering knowledgably about the gospel when asked about their transformed speech and conduct.

THEOLOGICAL FOCUS

All Christians bear the responsibility to make the gospel known, not only by persistently praying for preachers and missionaries but also by faithfully honoring Christ in how they live, by speaking graciously in every situation, and by answering the inevitable questions that arise about their faith.

PREACHING IDEA

To spread the good news, pray for the preachers and salt your own speech.

PREACHING POINTERS

Writing from jail, Paul asks the Colossians to pray that a door would be opened, so that he could return to his work as an apostle, declaring the mystery of Christ. He also asks them to pray that he would make that message clear. Working in conjunction with the public ministry of preaching was the interpersonal witness of church members. Paul exhorts them to walk in wisdom toward "outsiders," use gracious speech, and then be ready to explain why they lived differently than the people of the Greco-Roman world. In this passage, Paul puts evangelism on center stage.

The same emphasis is needed today. Few churches in North America are growing from conversions, but partnership between public proclamation and interpersonal witness is a timeless combination, as effective in our day as in the first century. Thom Rainer observes that excellent preaching is crucial to what he calls "breakout churches," congregations that are growing because of conversions. He states that preaching is the "number one correlated factor related to the evangelistic growth of the church. . . . It is hard to overstate how important the centrality of preaching was in these breakout churches" (Rainer, n.d.). I suspect that behind the clear, passionate, and relevant expository preaching that Rainer discovered in these churches there is also a host of members who have formed relationships with "outsiders," to use Paul's term (v. 5). They witness by their words and lifestyle and invite their friends to church to hear the Word of God. Public proclamation and interpersonal witness is a winning combination, so to spread the good news we pray for the preachers and partner with them by salting our own speech.

Colossians 4:7–18

EXEGETICAL IDEA

Paul closed his letter with a series of greetings and instructions that connected the Colossian church with the broader body of Christ, for the purpose of mutual encouragement and regional partnership together in the global mission of proclaiming the gospel and strengthening believers in Christ.

THEOLOGICAL FOCUS

When local churches partner together and strive to encourage one another and work together for the gospel, they are mutually strengthened and together they accomplish the mission of living and proclaiming the gospel.

PREACHING IDEA

To spread the good news, work locally and partner globally.

PREACHING POINTERS

Paul wraps up his epistle with the standard form of first-century letters. He sends greetings from his team, makes a few "announcements," and gives a few directives. That was the conventional way to conclude, but Paul uses the convention to drive home some of the key themes of Colossians one more time. Those themes are the advance of the gospel and the nature of the church. With references to house churches such as the one that met at Nympha's (v. 15) and the citywide church in towns like Laodicea (vv. 15–16), we see that the church was a regional body. Paul and his team had a vision to reach the whole district.

Today that vision is needed as well. The legacy of the Protestant Reformation is separation more than unification. According to the authoritative *World Christian Encyclopedia*, there are more than thirty-three thousand denominations, so Jesus's prayer rings urgently today: "that they may all be one" (John 17:21). A vision of unity and partnership between churches is the heart beneath Colossians 4:7–18 and perhaps by preaching on this final section, it can become the heart of our churches too. Evangelism is best done when churches partner with each other. To spread the good news, the church should work locally and partner globally.

Philemon 1–7

EXEGETICAL IDEA

Paul addressed his letter to Philemon and the church in Colossae, and rather than malign Philemon's character because of his conflict with Onesimus, he gave thanks to God for Philemon's genuine Christian faith and love that had benefited many Christians, including even Paul himself.

THEOLOGICAL FOCUS
Believers must discipline themselves to give thanks to God for one another and acknowledge the positive work of Christ in one another's lives, including and especially in the context of conflict that must be addressed.

PREACHING IDEA
When there's a conflict, what you share is better than what you win.

PREACHING POINTERS
Paul opened this letter, the most personal one he wrote, by greeting and blessing Philemon, a well-to-do patron of a house church. That kind of opening was typical in ancient letters, yet in the introduction of this letter to Philemon, Paul goes far beyond convention. The introduction cultivates the soil for the seeds to be planted later—a command and appeal to receive back the runaway slave, Onesimus. Paul cultivates the soil by emphasizing his interpersonal relationship with Philemon, full of genuine affection and sincere admiration. But cultivation was more than a rhetorical device designed to put Philemon in a receptive state of mind, because Paul meant every word.

Thus, Paul sets a good model for us today when dealing with conflict. At a tense board meeting or when the family can't get along or when the congregation is divided, before planting seeds of exhortation, cultivate the soil with prayer, thanks, and encouragement. Before trying to persuade someone, begin by affirming them. Unfortunately, today persuasion is often carried on with rancor. Accusations, overstatement, sarcasm, and one-sided arguments may win applause from those who already agree with our position, but those tactics do nothing to persuade skeptics or heal divisions. A better way, the one modeled by Philemon 1–7, is to begin with humility, prayer, thanks, and praise. Conflict is unavoidable in the world and in the church, so to bind together what has come loose. Let us first remember the tie that binds. When there's a conflict, what you share is better than what you win.

Philemon 8–16

EXEGETICAL IDEA
Paul appealed on the basis of love for Philemon to do the proper thing toward Onesimus, for God had perhaps superintended the entire situation so that Philemon would embrace Onesimus no longer *merely* as a slave, but as *more than* a slave, as a beloved brother.

THEOLOGICAL FOCUS
Believers must recognize the work of Christ in one another's lives and thereby come to no longer view one another in worldly terms, *merely* as objects to be utilized or rejected for personal gain, but must learn to embrace one another as *more than* such objects, as beloved brothers and sisters in Christ.

PREACHING IDEA
Before believing, we were "merely"—but now we are "more than."

PREACHING POINTERS

Tension pulses under the surface of Paul's seemingly simple letter—the tension of a runaway slave and his offended master. Roman law was clear that Onesimus should be returned to his master, but the situation was more complex than that, because God had arranged things so that Onesimus came under the ministry of Paul and was converted. Onesimus and Philemon now had a new relationship in Christ. The one who was "useless" in Philemon's estimation had become a disciple and was now "useful." Paul wants to make him part of his church planting team, helping the old apostle especially while he is still in jail, so he writes to Philemon to receive his new brother in the Lord. The church that met in Philemon's house probably leaned in to hear Paul address his friend. How would the old veteran address Philemon, his fellow-soldier? Would he command him or shame him? Would he abandon Onesimus, his spiritual child? No. All three of the men were brothers, so Paul appealed to Philemon, not commanded him. Onesimus is no longer what he was, "merely" a slave; he is now "much more" and should be treated as such.

The same reasoning is needed today. We see a propensity to dehumanize people by reducing them to hits on social media. A better propensity is based on the theological sociology modeled in Philemon. Everyone (including slaves!) is made in the image of God, and all followers of Christ have one Father. In the church, we are not "merely" objects or statistics, we are "more than" that; we are fellow workers in God's vineyard (v. 1), fellow soldiers in the fight (v. 2), brothers and sisters (vv. 7, 16), spiritual children (v. 10), formerly perceived as useless, but now useful in the Lord's work (v. 11). Before believing, we were "merely"—but now we are "more than."

Philemon 17–25

EXEGETICAL IDEA

Paul instructed Philemon to welcome Onesimus as if he were Paul himself, and if Philemon will embrace Paul's theological vision and do what Paul asks—and more!—then Philemon will have refreshed Paul's heart and prepared the way for Paul to visit Colossae, so they could have fellowship as mates together in Christ.

THEOLOGICAL FOCUS

When believers develop a Christ-centered theological vision through which they see the world, then they are equipped not only to obey the direct commands of Christ but also to discern how to honor Christ in every situation, so that they are mutually refreshed as they welcome one another as mates together in Christ.

PREACHING IDEA

Let's refresh one another by welcoming one another.

PREACHING POINTERS

Paul wraps up the letter to Philemon by finally delivering some imperatives. The old apostle has taken a long on-ramp to these imperatives, but in this passage he pulls into the fast lane with four commands in quick succession: *welcome* Onesimus (v. 17), *charge* his debts to my account (v. 18), *refresh* my heart in Christ (v. 20), and *prepare* a room for me (v. 22). Welcome

Onesimus? Easier said than done. Onesimus had shirked his duty, broken their relationship, and shamed his master in the process. But the command was still given: welcome him as you would welcome me. Grace like that would refresh the old apostle.

In the church there are no Greeks or Jews, barbarian, Scythian, slave or free (Col. 3:11). Today we might say that in the church there are no employers or employees, young or old, male or female, Filipino or Japanese, British-Canadian or French-Canadian. Every member of Christ's body is there because of grace, not merit, and all members love and fear the Lord, our master in heaven (Col. 3:22–4:1). That theological vision is the basis of Paul's command to welcome Onesimus who has become part of the body. So, let's refresh one another by welcoming one another.

Today in our polarized culture, welcome is offered to people we agree with—those who vote the way we vote, scoff at the things we scoff at, and dress the ways we dress. But to be part of the church, one does not need to know the "secret handshake." One simply has to confess that Jesus is Lord. That is the basis for why we welcome one another to the family.

ABBREVIATIONS

GENERAL ABBREVIATIONS

A.D.	in the year of our Lord (*anno Domini*)
B.C.	before Christ
B.C.E.	before the Common Era
C.E.	Common Era
NT	New Testament
OT	Old Testament

TECHNICAL ABBREVIATIONS

ca.	circa
ch(s).	chapter(s)
cf.	*confer* (compare)
ed.	edition
e.g.	*exempli gratia* (for example)
et al.	*et alii* (and others)
etc.	*et cetera* (and so forth, and the rest)
fn.	footnote
gen.	genitive
idem	the same
i.e.	*id est* (that is)
inf.	infinitive
instr.	instrumental
p(p).	page(s)
pass.	passive
perf.	perfect
pres.	present
ptc.	participle
sbjv.	subjunctive
subj.	subject
s.v.	*sub verbo* (under the word)
temp.	temporal
trans.	translation
v(v).	verse(s)
vol(s).	volume(s)

BIBLICAL SOURCES

Old Testament

Gen.	Genesis
Exod.	Exodus
Lev.	Leviticus
Num.	Numbers
Deut.	Deuteronomy
Josh.	Joshua
Judg.	Judges
Ruth	Ruth
1 Sam.	1 Samuel
2 Sam.	2 Samuel
1 Kings	1 Kings
2 Kings	2 Kings
1 Chron.	1 Chronicles
2 Chron.	2 Chronicles
Ezra	Ezra
Neh.	Nehemiah
Esther	Esther
Job	Job
Ps./Pss.	Psalm(s)
Prov.	Proverbs
Eccl.	Ecclesiastes
Song	Song of Songs
Isa.	Isaiah
Jer.	Jeremiah
Lam.	Lamentations
Ezek.	Ezekiel
Dan.	Daniel
Hos.	Hosea
Joel	Joel
Amos	Amos
Obad.	Obadiah
Jonah	Jonah
Mic.	Micah
Nah.	Nahum

Old Testament (continued)

Hab.	Habakkuk
Zeph.	Zephaniah
Hag.	Haggai
Zech.	Zechariah
Mal.	Malachi

New Testament

Matt.	Matthew
Mark	Mark
Luke	Luke
John	John
Acts	Acts
Rom.	Romans
1 Cor.	1 Corinthians
2 Cor.	2 Corinthians
Gal.	Galatians
Eph.	Ephesians
Phil.	Philippians
Col.	Colossians
1 Thess.	1 Thessalonians
2 Thess.	2 Thessalonians
1 Tim.	1 Timothy
2 Tim.	2 Timothy
Titus	Titus
Philem.	Philemon
Heb.	Hebrews
James	James
1 Peter	1 Peter
2 Peter	2 Peter
1 John	1 John
2 John	2 John
3 John	3 John
Jude	Jude
Rev.	Revelation

EXTRABIBLICAL SOURCES

Apocrypha

Sir	Wisdom of Jesus the Son of Sirach (Ecclesiastucs)
Bar	Baruch
3 Macc	3 Maccabees
4 Esd	4 Esdras

Old Testament Pseudepigrapha

2 Bar.	2 Baruch (Syriac Apocalypse)
4 Ezra	4 Ezra

Papyrii

P. Oxy.	*The Oxyrhynchus Papyri*
P. Par.	*The Paris Papyri*
P. Wisc.	*The Wisconsin Papyri*

Apostolic Fathers

Did	*Didache*
Diogn	*Diognetus*
Ignatius (of Antioch)	Syrian bishop, church father; ca. A.D. 50–ca. 110
Eph	*To the Ephesians*

Other Sources

Apuleius	
Metam.	*The Golden Ass (Metamorphoses)*
Aristotle	
Eth. nic.	*Nichomachean Ethics (Ethica nichomachea)*
Metaph.	*Metaphysics (Metaphysica)*
Pol.	*Politics (Politica)*
Cicero	
Rep.	*On the Commonwealth (De Republica)*
Verr.	*Against Verres (In Verrem)*
[Cicero]	
Rhet. Her.	*Rhetoric: For Herennius (Rhetorical ad Herennium)*
Clement of Alexandria	
Strom.	*Miscellanies (Stromata)*
Columella	
Rust.	*On Agriculture (De re rustica)*
Dio Chrysostom	
Troj.	*Trojan Discourse (Trojana [Or. 11])*
Dionysius of Halicarnassus	
Ant. rom.	*Roman Antiquities (Antiquitates romanae)*
Epictetus	
Diatr.	*Discourses (Diatribai [Dissertationes])*
Eusebius (of Caesarea)	
Hist. eccl.	*Ecclesiastical History (Historia ecclesiastica)*
Herodotus	
Hist.	*Histories (Historiae)*
Iamblichus	
Myst.	*On the Mysteries (De mysteriis)*
Josephus	
C. Ap.	*Against Apion (Contra Apionem)*

A.J.	*Jewish Antiquities (Antiquitates judaicae)*
B.J.	*Jewish War (Bellum judaicum)*
Justin	
Dial.	*Dialogue with Trypho (Dialogus cum Tryphone)*
Justinian	
Dig.	*Digest (Digesta)*
Longinus	
[Subl.]	*On the Sublime (De sublimitate)*
Philo (of Alexandria)	
Leg.	*Allegorical Interpretation (Legum allegoriae)*
Spec. Leg.	*On the Special Laws (De specialibus legibus)*
Plato	
Theaet.	*Theaetetus*
Pliny (the Younger)	
Ep.	*Letters (Epistulae)*
Plutarch	
Aem.	*Aemilius Paullus*
Quintilian	
Decl.	*Declamations (Declamationes)*
Seneca	
Ep.	*Moral Epistles (Epistulae morales)*
Strabo	
Geogr.	*Geography (Geographica)*
Suetonius	
Claud.	*Divine Clausius (Divus Claudius)*
Tacitus	
Ann.	*Annals (Annales)*
Xenophon	
Anab.	*Expedition (Anabasis)*
Mem.	*Memoirs (Memorabilia)*
Oec.	*Economics (Oeconomicus)*

PERIODICALS

AJA	*American Journal of Archaeology*
BSac	*Bibliotheca Sacra*
BT	*The Bible Translator*
EvQ	*Evangelical Quarterly*
Int	*Interpretation*
JETS	*Journal of the Evangelical Theological Society*
JSNT	*Journal for the Study of the New Testament*
JSPL	*Journal for the Study of Paul and His Letters*
JTS	*Journal of Theological Studies*

NTS	*New Testament Studies*
ST	*Studia Theologica*
WTJ	*Westminster Theological Journal*

SERIES

AB	Anchor Bible
ASBT	Acadia Studies in Biblical Theology
BNTC	Black's New Testament Commentaries
EGGNT	Exegetical Guide to the Greek New Testament
ICC	International Critical Commentary
JRASS	Journal of Roman Archaeology Supplementary Series
JSNTSup	Journal for the Study of the New Testament Supplement Series
KEK	Kritisch-exegetischer Kommentar über das Neue Testament (Meyer-Kommentar)
LCL	Loeb Classical Library
LNTS	Library of New Testament Studies
NCC	New Covenant Commentary
NICNT	The New International Commentary on the New Testament
NIGTC	The New International Greek Testament Commentary
NTL	The New Testament Library
PCNT	Paideia: Commentaries on the New Testament
PNTC	The Pillar New Testament Commentary
PPS	Popular Patristic Series
SP	Sacra Pagina
THNTC	Two Horizons New Testament Commentary
TNTC	Tyndale New Testament Commentaries
WBC	Word Biblical Commentary
WEC	The Wycliffe Exegetical Commentary

REFERENCE

ANRW	*Aufstieg und Niedergang der römischen Welt*
BDAG	Danker, F. W., W. Bauer, W. F. Arndt, and F. W. Gingrich. *Greek-English Lexicon of the New Testament and Other Early Christian Literature.* 3rd ed.
BDB	F. Brown, S. Driver, and C. Briggs, *The Brown-Driver-Briggs Hebrew and English Lexicon.*
HALOT	L. Koehler, and W. Baumgartner, *Hebrew and Aramaic Lexicon of the Old Testament*
LSJ	H.G. Liddell, R. Scott, and H.S. Jones, *A Greek-English Lexicon.* 9th ed.

PGM	K. Preisendanz, ed. *Papyri Graecae Magicae: Die Griechischen Zauberpapyri.*
TDNT	Kittel, G., and G. Friedrich, eds. *Theological Dictionary of the New Testament.* Trans. G. W. Bromiley. 10 vols.

Bible Translations

ESV	English Standard Version
HCSB	Holman Christian Standard Bible
KJV	King James Version
LXX	Septuagint
NASB	New American Standard Bible
NET	New English Translation
NIV	New International Version
NLT	New Living Translation
NRSV	New Revised Standard Version

INTRODUCTION

OVERVIEW OF COLOSSIANS AND PHILEMON

Author: Paul

Coauthor: Timothy

Provenance: Ephesian imprisonment

Date: A.D. 52–55

Readers: The church in Colossae and especially Philemon

Historical Setting: Colossae

Occasion: Paul sent the slave Onesimus back to his master Philemon and to the church in his house, and he appealed for them all to be reconciled and united together as the one body of Christ.

Genre: Letter

Theological Emphasis: When Christians know the supremacy of Christ in his person and work, they will be transformed and learn to live in his ways as the body of Christ, including forgiving and being reconciled with one another.

AUTHORSHIP OF COLOSSIANS AND PHILEMON

Both Colossians and Philemon begin with Paul identifying himself as the author in accordance with the standard Greco-Roman epistolary convention of his day. Colossians begins, "Paul, an apostle of Christ Jesus by the will of God, and Timothy our brother" (Col. 1:1 ESV). Similarly, Philemon begins, "Paul, a prisoner for Christ Jesus, and Timothy our brother" (Philem. 1 ESV). For some modern readers, this self-attestation of authorship is sufficient to establish that the apostle Paul did indeed write the letter, perhaps with the secretarial support of his coworker, Timothy. However, some scholars have questioned whether we should take for granted these claims of Pauline authorship. The letter to Philemon is almost universally considered to be authentically Pauline because of its personal and occasional nature, for it is highly unlikely that someone seeking to forge a letter in Paul's name would choose such a specific and identifiable situation as the theme of the letter. With Colossians, however, modern scholars have divided almost evenly over its authenticity.[1]

Those who argue against Colossians' authenticity generally do so on the basis of unique features in the Greek text and unusual theological themes (e.g., Bujard, 1973). The Greek text of Colossians includes sixty-two words that do not appear elsewhere in Paul's letters (Lohse, 1971, 85–87), and Colossians lacks several common Pauline terms, such as righteousness (δικαιοσύνη), law (νόμος), and salvation (σωτηρία). Colossians also contains various expressions and grammatical structures (e.g., series of dependent genitives) that are otherwise unusual to Paul (Lohse, 1971, 88–89). However, such linguistic arguments are not persuasive in the end, for similar disparities appear across the Pauline corpus (for example, Philippians uses seventy-nine words that do not appear in the undisputed Pauline letters; cf. Moo, 2008, 30) and the corpus is simply too small to make definitive conclusions regarding the kind of vocabulary and grammar Paul was and was not capable of utilizing. Further, all of Paul's letters are intrinsically occasional and reflect the unique historical context in which they were written. Finally, much of the unique material in Colossians may have been cited rather than composed by Paul, whether as traditional Christian material (e.g., the Christ-hymn of Col. 1:15–20) or as the language of his opponents (e.g., Col. 2:16–23).

Other scholars argue against authenticity on the basis of unique theological themes contained within Colossians. For example, the Christology of Colossians presents Christ and his work in a more exalted way than the other letters, and with particular relevance for the entire cosmos (e.g., Col. 1:15–20). The ecclesiology of Colossians presents the church not only as a local congregation but also as the universal body of Christ incorporating all believers worldwide into the one church (Col. 1:18, 24, 28; 3:15). The eschatology of Colossians brings the future work of Christ into the present as if believers have already realized some aspects of what remains future elsewhere in Paul's writings, namely their resurrection and new life with Christ (3:1–4). At the same time, central theological concepts of Paul are missing from Colossians, especially the law, justification, and the Holy Spirit. For some scholars, these theological perspectives are inconsistent enough with Paul's own thought that they must reflect later developments either by Paul himself or, more likely, Paul's associates shortly after his death.[2]

However, none of these themes are in fact unique to Colossians, even if they do receive more emphasis in Colossians. A cosmic Christology in which Christ is the agent of creation also appears clearly in 1 Corinthians 8:5–6, and his future exaltation is declared in cosmic terms in Philippians 2:9–11. The ecclesiology of the broader union of believers together in what could be called a universal church appears also in Paul's other letters (e.g., the greetings in various letters, such as Romans 16; cf. 1 Cor. 10:16–17; 12:12–13), and Colossians still retains a very strong sense of the local church, even identifying individual churches in terms of the town and home in which they meet (Col. 4:15–16; cf. Philem. 2). Regarding eschatology, the realized elements of Colossians emphasize the resurrection believers have already experienced by their

1 In 1974, Perrin estimated most scholars favored authenticity (Perrin, 1974, 124), but in 1997, Brown concluded that 60 percent of scholars at that time viewed Colossians as post-Pauline (Brown, 1997, 610). However, there may be a trend among scholars back toward authenticity in one form or another (see Foster, 2016, 67, 73–78).

2 Eduard Lohse, for example, sees such profound changes to Paul's theology that "Paul cannot be considered to be the direct or indirect author" of Colossians; rather, "a theologian schooled in Pauline thought composed the letter" (Lohse, 1971, 181). Brown goes a step farther and postulates a school of Pauline disciples in Ephesus composed Colossians using the letter to Philemon as a guide (Brown, 1997, 616).

union with Christ. But similar language appears in Romans 6:1–14, and as in Romans, Colossians does not bring all eschatological promises into the present, for believers still await the return of Christ and future glory (Col. 3:4), as well as the coming wrath of God (Col. 3:6). And as we will see throughout this commentary, all of these theological themes play particular roles in Paul's argument for why these particular believers in this particular place must act in a particular way as they face particular false teaching (Col. 2:16–23) and a particular interpersonal situation demanding reconciliation (i.e., Philemon and Onesimus). In other words, the occasion of the letter accounts for these variations in theological themes far better than arguments for non-Pauline authorship.

Thus, the arguments against Pauline authorship ultimately fail to persuade that Paul could not have written the letter. At the same time, additional evidence further supports that Paul did indeed write the letter. From the perspective of church history, the letter was consistently regarded as Pauline, with all of the church fathers recognizing Paul as the author when they cited the letter. The early church was aware of spurious letters and exercised care in recognizing them as such and rejecting them, yet no evidence exists that Colossians was ever questioned. One scholar has surveyed how the church fathers used Colossians as authoritative Scripture with no apparent concern that it might be pseudepigraphal, and he famously concluded, "The external evidence for the genuineness of the letter is in no wise defective" (Abbott, 1897, li; cited by Moo, 2008, 30) Indeed, the authenticity of Colossians was only questioned with the rise of higher criticism in the nineteenth century.[3] Therefore, we conclude that we are on secure grounds to recognize Paul as the genuine author of Colossians.

Apostle Paul by Jan Lievens. Public domain.

The Relationship of Colossians and Philemon

Paul's letters to Colossians and Philemon intersect in the following ways, indicating they were likely written at the same time:

(1) In both letters, Onesimus traveled from Paul to Colossae. In Colossians 4:7–9, Onesimus was listed as letter carrier alongside Tychicus, while in Philemon 12 he was being sent to reconcile with Philemon.

(2) Paul was careful not to regard Onesimus as a slave in either letter. In Colossians, Paul described Tychicus as "the beloved brother and faithful servant and fellow slave in the Lord" (ὁ ἀγαπητὸς ἀδελφὸς καὶ πιστὸς διάκονος καὶ σύνδουλος ἐν κυρίῳ; Col. 4:7), but when he offered a similar description of Onesimus, he eliminated the language of slavery, calling him "our faithful and beloved brother who is one of

3 Lohse suggests the authenticity of Colossians was first challenged in 1838 by Ernst Mayerhoff and then reached full steam through Ferdinand Baur and his school in the late nineteenth century (Lohse, 1971, 90; cf. Mayerhoff, 1838).

you" (τῷ πιστῷ καὶ ἀγαπητῷ ἀδελφῷ, ὅς ἐστιν ἐξ ὑμῶν; Col. 4:9). Likewise, Paul appealed to Philemon to receive Onesimus no longer as a "slave" (δοῦλος) but as a "beloved brother" (ἀδελφὸν ἀγαπητόν; Philem. 16).

(3) The list of people who were with Paul and send their greetings overlap significantly. Both letters include Epaphras, Mark, Aristarchus, Demas, and Luke, while only Colossians mentions Jesus who is called Justus (Col. 4:10–14; Philem. 23–24).

(4) Both letters give Epaphras a central role, for Epaphras is from Colossae, has evangelized Colossae, but now remains with Paul at the time both letters were written. Thus, Paul feels it necessary to justify Epaphras's ongoing absence from Colossae and to pass along Epaphras's ongoing concern for the Colossian believers (Col. 1:7; 4:12; Philem. 23).

(5) Archippus appears at the end of Colossians and at the beginning of Philemon (Col. 4:17; Philem. 2), providing a point of transition and continuity between the letters.

(6) Paul is in prison at the time of writing both letters (Col. 4:3, 18; Philem. 1, 22).

(7) Both letters envision being read aloud in a gathering of the entire church in Colossae. Colossians explicitly addresses the church in Colossae (Col. 1:2) and anticipates a public reading of the letter to the church (Col. 4:16). The letter to Philemon is addressed not only to Philemon but also to Apphia, Archippus, and the entire church that meets in Philemon's house (Phil. 1–2).

(8) Colossians includes various theological themes common to Paul but expressed in a manner particularly relevant to the situation in the letter to Philemon. For example, in the household code, Paul offers extended discussion on the relationship of slaves and masters but only minimal discussion of husbands and wives, when compared with the household code in Ephesians (Col. 3:22–4:1; cf. Eph 5:22–33). Reconciliation and peace also emerge as themes in Colossians, as does the unity of the body of Christ (Col. 1:20–22; 3:13, 15). These themes are foundational to Paul's appeal in the letter to Philemon.

These points of connection suggest a close relationship between the two letters, in which the situation between Onesimus and Philemon overshadows them both. They were likely written within a close proximity of time and sent simultaneously to Colossae with Tychicus and Onesimus.

PLACE AND DATE OF WRITING

Paul wrote both Colossians and Philemon from prison (Col. 4:3, 18; Philem. 1), but he was imprisoned on multiple occasions (see 2 Cor. 11:23). Scholars have identified the following three primary options for when and where the letter was written: first, that Paul wrote from Rome in A.D. 60–62; second, that Paul wrote from Caesarea in A.D. 57–59; or third, that Paul wrote from Ephesus in A.D. 52–55.[4] All three arguments have their strengths and weaknesses, which we will survey here, and in the end, deciding between them largely depends on which seems the most likely place for Onesimus to have traveled in his flight as a runaway slave.

Rome

Paul may have written during his well-known and lengthy imprisonment in Rome near the end of his life (A.D. 60–62; cf. Acts 27:16–31). The location of Rome is supported by early manuscripts of Colossians which include subscriptions stating that Paul was writing from

4 F. F. Bruce provides a full timeline of Paul's life and ministry, including the dates referenced here (Bruce, 1977, 475).

Rome (Metzger, 1994, 589–90). The late date proves favorable for those modern scholars who see Colossians as the apex of Paul's theology and who understand his theology to have developed linearly over the course of his life. Further, Rome may have been an optimal destination for Onesimus if he was fleeing from Philemon without intention of returning, for in Rome Onesimus could have easily blended into the diverse melting pot of the immense population.[5] Aristarchus was also with Paul in Rome (Acts 27:2; cf. Col. 4:10; Philem. 24). For these reasons, Rome has been a popular choice of provenance for many scholars (Foster, 2016, 73–78).

However, a Roman provenance does not solve every problem. In the first place, when Paul arrived in Rome, he desired to travel west to Spain (Rom. 15:22–29) rather than east to Colossae, as in Philemon 22. Also, Luke describes Paul having great freedom during his Roman imprisonment—which was really more of a house arrest—for preaching the gospel (Acts 28:16, 30), but in his letters Paul describes himself in chains that are restricting his ability to proclaim the gospel (Col. 1:24; 4:3, 9, 18; Philem. 1, 9, 22). We may further wonder whether Rome really served as a probable destination for Onesimus, considering the arduous length of such a journey. And if Onesimus did intend to disappear into Rome, then his encounter with Paul under house arrest seems all the more improbable, since a runaway slave would hardly have happened upon Paul, a Roman citizen, in his house arrest.

Caesarea

Paul may have written during his previous imprisonment in Caesarea (A.D. 57–59). Bo Reicke suggests this provenance makes the best sense of several features of the letters (Reicke, 1970). First, Paul was traveling with several Gentile believers when he was arrested in Jerusalem and transferred to Caesarea, and he was arrested partially because he had brought them into the temple in Jerusalem (Acts 21:27–29). Some of his companions at the time of this arrest overlap with those mentioned in Colossians and Philemon, including Aristarchus, Timothy, and Tychicus (Acts 20:4; Col. 1:1; 4:7, 10; Philem. 1, 23–24) as well as Luke, who is the presumed author of Acts writing in the first person at this point (cf. Col. 4:14; Philem. 24). Second, Paul intended to travel to Rome from Caesarea, a journey that would have taken him through Asia Minor, from where he could have easily made the trip to Colossae as he hopes in Philemon 22. Finally, Paul seems to suggest he has only recently become a prisoner (Philem. 9), and Caesarea was the beginning of his long imprisonment.

However, this view creates additional challenges regarding the story of Onesimus. Like Rome, Caesarea was a very long journey by land, or an expensive and exposed journey by sea, where capture was likely. If Onesimus was going to undertake such a long journey, he was more likely to head east toward Rome, where he had a better chance of blending into obscurity. In the end, beyond the fact that some of Paul's companions overlap with the time of this imprisonment, the Caesarean provenance has relatively little additional evidence to argue for it (so Pao, 2012, 23).

Ephesus

Third, Paul may have written the letters during an imprisonment in Ephesus. The primary problem with this view emerges immediately,

5 To this end, Lightfoot colorfully describes why a runaway thief and slave such as Onesimus would flee to Rome. "Rome was the natural cesspool for these offscourings of humanity. In the thronging crowds of the metropolis was his best hope of secrecy. In the dregs of the city rabble he would find the society of congenial spirits" (Lightfoot, 1981, 312).

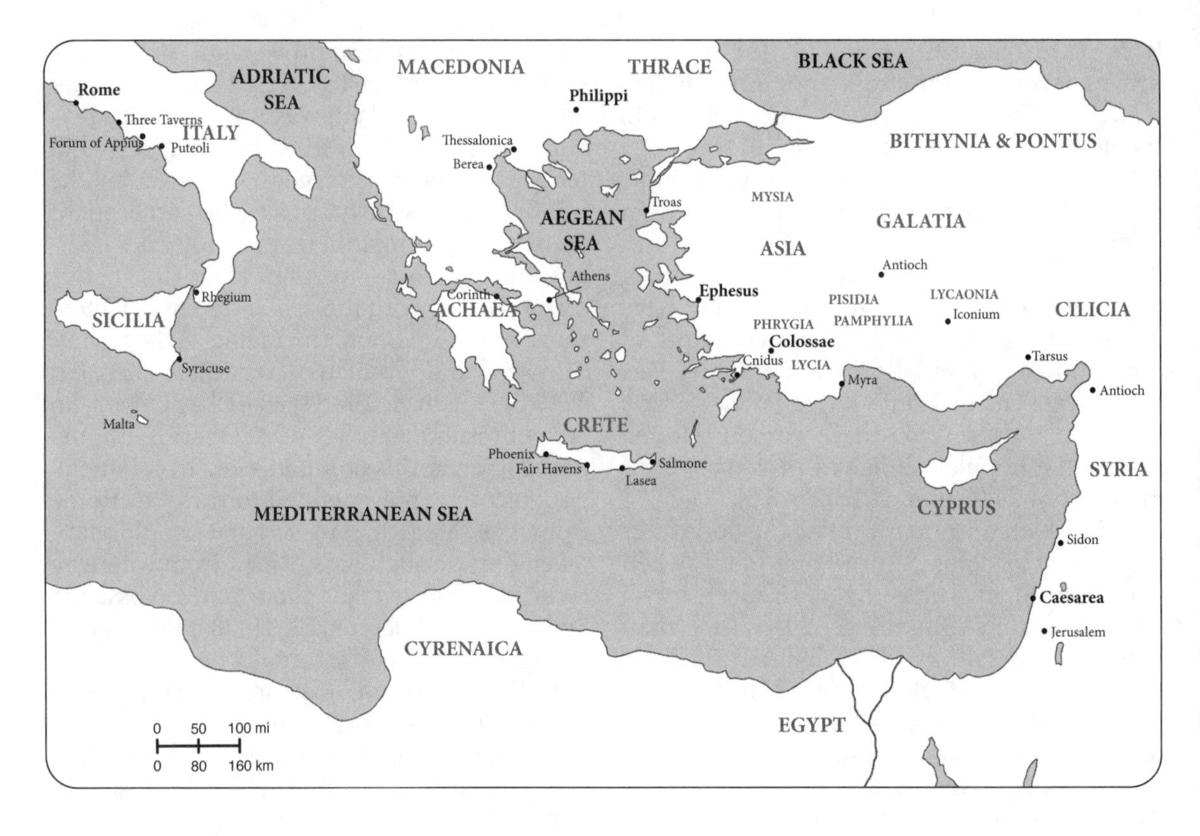

namely that such an imprisonment is never explicitly mentioned in Acts or Paul's letters. However, Paul does mention additional afflictions and perhaps even imprisonments that he experienced in and around Ephesus (2 Cor. 1:8–9; cf. 1 Cor. 15:32), and we know that the time he spent in Ephesus resulted in riots and conflict with city officials (Acts 19:21–41). We may easily presume that he was arrested on occasion and may have served one or more terms of imprisonment while in Ephesus.

An Ephesian provenance resolves some key problems related to the letter. First and most importantly, this view best accounts for the success of Onesimus's flight. He only had to travel about 100 miles to Ephesus, and this would have been a reasonable trip for a runaway slave. Further, because Luke does not mention an Ephesian imprisonment in Acts, we may presume any such imprisonment was likely short in duration, and this would explain Paul's optimism about being released and visiting Colossae (Philem. 22), even as he suffered in chains (Col. 4:18; Philem. 9, 22). Finally, the movements of Paul's coworkers back and forth between Paul and Colossae are best explained if Paul was in Ephesus, especially since Aristarchus, Paul's "co-prisoner" (Col. 4:10), also ran afoul of legal authorities there (Acts 19:29). Paul seems to presume a close proximity between himself and Colossae, so that Epaphras has traveled to and from Paul with reports (Col. 1:7–8) and Tychicus and Onesimus can travel at Paul's behest without apparent trouble (Col. 4:7–9).

However, weighing most heavily against this view is the stubborn fact that no direct evidence attests to Paul actually being imprisoned in Ephesus. Also, a presumably short incarceration may not have afforded enough time for all that Paul has accomplished, including bringing

Onesimus to faith in Christ (Philem. 10), establishing a close relationship with him (Philem. 12–13), and convincing him to return with two newly written letters.

Conclusion

Fortunately for us, the provenance of the letter has only minimal bearing upon the interpretation of the letter. In the end, we find the proximity of Ephesus to be the most compelling argument in that it best explains the various movements of Paul's associates as well as Paul's own desire to soon visit Colossae, and it also seems most plausible that Onesimus would have successfully reached Paul in Ephesus and was intentionally seeking him. Therefore, we cautiously conclude that Paul most likely wrote from Ephesus during an otherwise unspecified and likely brief imprisonment during his time there in A.D. 52–55.

ORIGINAL READERS

Both Colossians and Philemon have complex audiences. The letter to the Colossians begins by identifying the audience as "holy and faithful brothers" who dwell in Colossae (Col. 1:2). Later in the letter, however, Paul gives instructions for the letter to be read also by the church in Laodicea (Col. 4:16). The cities of Laodicea and Colossae, together with Hierapolis, were located within ten miles of one another in the Lycus Valley. They were closely associated also as one region of ministry for which Epaphras was responsible (Col. 4:13), and Paul also seems to meld them together into one geographical region he has never personally visited (Col. 2:1). On the one hand, therefore, the audience is simply the church in Colossae, but on the other hand, Paul envisions his letter being read and applied among churches across the region. He writes *to* the Colossians but *for* a wider audience (Copenhaver, 2018, 73–75, 96–98; cf. Stirewalt, 1991).

Similarly, Paul's letter to Philemon also has a broader audience including not only Philemon, but also Apphia, Archippus, and "the church in your home" (Philem. 1–2). His audience is both personal and corporate, and the letter reflects both layers of audience. Through most of the letter, Paul uses the second person singular pronoun ("you") with reference to Philemon, refers to him as a singular "brother" (e.g., Philem. 7, 20), and uses second person singular imperatives, even as he also writes very personally about his personal relationship with Philemon. But on occasion, Paul also uses the second person plural pronoun ("you *all*") to speak also to his broader audience of Apphia, Archippus, and the rest of the church (e.g., Philem. 3, 22, 25). Paul writes directly to Philemon while also presuming these other folks will hear the letter along with Philemon.

The audiences of these two are connected by Onesimus. Onesimus is both the slave who belongs to the household of Philemon, and he is "one of you" (*ἐξ ὑμῶν*; Col. 4:9), meaning he is from Colossae in the same way Epaphras is from Colossae (Col. 4:12). Philemon's household, in other words, is in Colossae. So, when Paul writes his letter to Philemon and the church in his home, he is writing to the church in Colossae, and when Paul writes to the church in Colossae, he is writing to Philemon and his household. The audiences of both letters overlap, with the letter to the Colossians being intended also for a broader audience of churches beyond Colossae, while the letter to Philemon was written personally to Philemon with implications for the church in Colossae.

HISTORICAL SETTING

About the Roman Empire

When Paul wrote his letter to the Colossians and Philemon, the Roman Empire controlled the entire Mediterranean world, including the region of Asia Minor where Colossae was located. The beginnings of this empire date back as far as the seventh or eighth century

B.C., when the city of Rome was founded (Beard, 2015, 21). The empire expanded through both military conquest and the subsequent absorption of conquered peoples. The Roman system allowed all kinds of people to become citizens, including even freed slaves, and it absorbed foreign cultures and religions (Ferguson, 1993, 20). As a result, by the first century A.D., the Roman Empire had become a diverse melting pot.

Also, by this time, the emperor Augustus had ushered in a time of relative peace and prosperity known as the *pax Romana* ("Roman peace"). However, this peace was only a thin veneer covering over the heavy military hand through which Rome expanded and maintained its rule. All peoples were forced to submit to Rome and to her emperor, including participating in the worship of Roman gods and even the emperor himself. Those who opposed Rome could expect punishment from Rome, and in certain situations, Rome would even torture her enemies in the arena or through crucifixion. The emperor Nero, who reigned A.D. 54–68, may have been in power when Paul wrote these letters, and he was known for exercising such violence with minimal restraint. Submit to Rome and enjoy her peace and prosperity, or resist Rome and suffer the consequences.

About Colossae

Colossae was a relatively small town located in the interior of Asia Minor, about one hundred miles east of Ephesus, in the Lycus Valley. Like many small towns still today, Colossae appears to have experienced significant reversals of fortune throughout its history. The earliest references to the city suggest it was a sizeable town with considerable resources able to host large armies. In the fifth century B.C., Herodotus (*Hist.* 7.30) called Colossae a "great city of Phrygia" (πόλιν μεγάλην θρυγίης) through which Xerxes passed with his army, and Xenophon (*Anab.* 1.2.6) referred to it

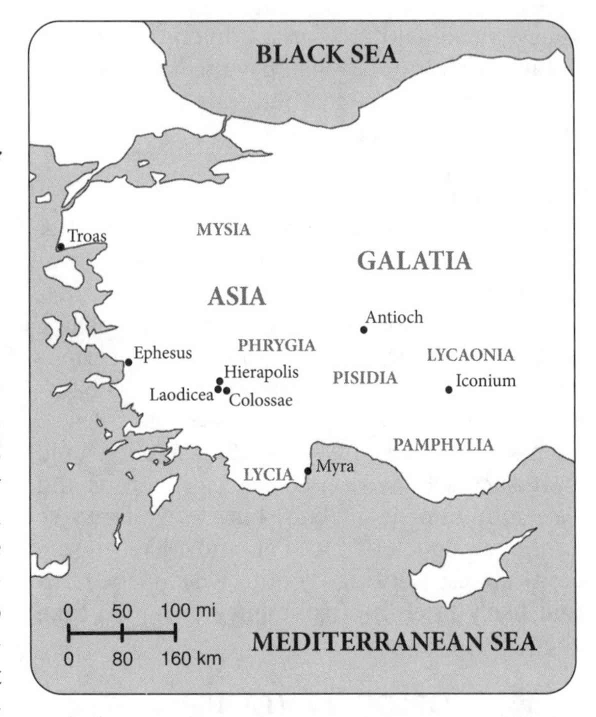

as a "city being inhabited and fortunate and great" (πόλιν οἰκουμένον καὶ εὐδαίμονα και μεγάλην) where Cyrus lodged with his army. At one point in history, Colossae was capable of accommodating an army encampment of 15,000 soldiers for multiple days.

However, by the second century B.C., Colossae had apparently declined and become overshadowed by the neighboring cities of Laodicea and Hierapolis. Strabo (*Geogr.* 12.8.13; cf. Copenhaver, 2018, 146) describes Colossae as a "small town" (πολίσματα), unlike its neighbor, Laodicea, which is one of the "great cities of Phrygia" (μέγισται τῶν κατὰ τὴν θρυγίαν πόλεων). The decline of Colossae was likely the result of two economic factors. First, Laodicea's fertile fields proved more profitable than Colossae's industry of wool. Second, Laodicea was situated at the intersection of two roads that became increasingly important, so that most travelers were effectively steered around Colossae but through Laodicea (Hemer, 1986, 180).

Little mention is made of Colossae after this time, prompting some scholars to presume the town was abandoned sometime in the second half of the first century. This view has been fueled by the ancient historian Tacitus (*Ann.* 14.27) who records a devastating earthquake in the region in A.D. 61, but though he describes the reconstruction of Laodicea afterward, he makes no mention of Colossae. However, more recent studies argue that Colossae was continuously inhabited throughout the first century and for many centuries to come. One inscription, in fact, describes the rebuilding of a bath at the end of the first century, perhaps because it had been damaged in the earthquake, and Colossae also continued to mint coins for decades to come (Cadwallader, 2011, 162–65, 171–74). Pottery fragments discovered upon the mound attest the site may have been consistently occupied from 3500 B.C. all the way to A.D. 1100 (Duman and Konakçi, 2011, 252). If and when the site is finally excavated, we have every reason to presume more evidence will be discovered affirming its ongoing habitation.

Though it was indeed inhabited, Colossae was nevertheless a diminished town of relative insignificance at the time of Paul's writing. The economy was primarily agrarian, and they were known especially for the vibrant colors of wool they produced. They bred their sheep to grow dark wools, and the minerals of the Lycus River enabled them to grow roots from which high-quality dyes (especially purple) were extracted and used for producing linens and clothing (Cadwallader, 2015, 111–34). Colossae may not have been the epicenter of global commerce, but it was able to maintain a stable economy through which its residents could achieve a sustainable standard of living.

Though various attempts have been made to procure permits and gather archaeological teams, none have yet been successful, and the site of Colossae remains unexcavated. Sadly, however, it does not remain untouched, as many of the stones and artifacts that once rested upon the surface have since been relocated and even repurposed.

However, the fact that Colossae was a small town rather than a major city should not lead to the assumption that its residents were small in mind or uniform in culture or religion. On the contrary, the population of Colossae represented a cross-section of the broader cosmopolitan population of Asia Minor, and even of the Roman Empire. The recently discovered inscription describing the reconstruction of the baths also records sixty-six diverse names that are largely Greek but also include Thracian, Scythian, Phrygian, and possibly Lycian, Lydian and Carian ethnicities (Cadwallader, 2012, 170). The cemetery in the neighboring city of Hierapolis has yielded inscriptions indicating Jews have been buried there and this serves as further evidence of Jews residing throughout Asia Minor, likely including Colossae (Ritti and Arthur, 2006, 26). There were also slaves like Onesimus, who lived and died in obscurity and left behind no trace of their existence, let alone their identity.

The religious atmosphere of Colossae was also as variegated as the rest of the Roman Empire (Copenhaver, 2018, 144–194). The people continued to venerate local deities such as Men and Cybele. The goddess Artemis was prominent in the region and even appears on some Colossian coins, perhaps due to the influence of the famous temple of Artemis in nearby Ephesus. The mystery religions of Egypt, and especially of Isis, were making inroads in the region at this time, and the worship of the Roman emperor as a god was also on the rise. The

Roman god Apollo was honored in Laodicea and Hierapolis. Some Jews also resided in the Lycus Valley and some of them surely called Colossae home. Colossae may not have been prominent, but the population was diverse and the people were complex.

About Slavery

Slavery, though repulsive to modern culture, was ubiquitous in the ancient world, when a world without slavery was as unimaginable as a world without employment today. Slaves constituted perhaps 20 percent of the Roman population (Ferguson, 1993, 56), and in some areas their population may have reached as high as 35 percent (McKnight, 2018, 14). Aristotle regarded slaves as "living property" who were of a different and lesser nature than their masters (Aristotle, *Pol.* 1.2.4–7). He effectively dehumanized slaves as living tools incapable of friendship with their masters, saying, "There can be no friendship, nor justice, towards inanimate things; indeed not even towards a horse or an ox, nor yet towards a slave as slave. For master and slave have nothing in common: a slave is a living tool, just as a tool is an inanimate slave" (Aristotle, *Nic. Ethics* 1161b; trans. Rackham 1934)." This perspective of slaves was widely adopted in the ancient world and it in turn led to the various kinds of abuse perpetuated against them.

How an individual slave was treated could vary widely depending upon their master. Some masters ruled their households with fear and abuse, and their slaves were under constant threat of corporal punishment and worse. For example, Cicero said a master should "coerce and break" his slaves with the whip (Cicero, *Rep.* 3.37). Other masters exercised goodwill toward their slaves in order to maximize productivity. In this vein, Columella advised masters to treat their slaves justly because this "contributes greatly to the increase of his estate" (Columella, *Rust.* 1.8.18; Thompson and Longenecker, 2016, 155, 158). Some masters even allowed their slaves to work toward their freedom as an incentive for good behavior or gifted freedom to slaves in their wills (Dill, 1956, 116–19). Even in the best of households, slaves naturally desired their freedom, but the opportunity for freedom depended entirely upon the benevolence of their master.

Slaves Desire Freedom

One young African slave, Mary Prince, in her 1831 memoir *The History of Mary Prince*, reminds us that all slaves desire their freedom: "All slaves want to be free—to be free is very sweet . . . I have been a slave myself—and I know what slaves feel—I can tell by myself what other slaves feel, and by what they have told me. The man that says slaves be quite happy in slavery—that they don't want to be free—that man is either ignorant or a lying person. I never heard a slave say so" (Prince, 2002, 263).

OCCASION FOR WRITING

Occasion of Philemon

The occasion of Philemon centers around Paul's command to Philemon to "receive" (προσλαμβάνω; Philem. 17) Onesimus as he would receive Paul. The command itself would be simple enough were it not for the situation behind the command. Philemon is a master, and Onesimus is his slave, so they have the kind of dehumanized relationship typical of a master and slave. Further, the two have become estranged through what was likely a series of grievances, whereby Philemon came to regard Onesimus as useless (Philem. 11); and Onesimus ultimately departed from Philemon without permission and unjustly became indebted to Philemon in the process, perhaps by stealing from him (Philem. 18–19). Based on these past events, Philemon would have been expected to receive Onesimus as a fugitive slave in need of redress, which is hardly the way he would receive Paul.

Reconstructing the Storyline behind Philemon

The letter to Philemon contains various details that can be rearranged into the core elements of the narrative behind the letter. With some additional details from Colossians, and with some interpretation and basic deduction, we reconstruct the storyline as follows:

1. Philemon acquired Onesimus as a slave.
2. Philemon and Onesimus live in Colossae (Col. 4:9).
3. Philemon traveled outside Colossae and was converted by Paul (Philem. 19).
4. Philemon became a partner of Paul in his gospel ministry (Philem. 17).
5. Philemon returned to Colossae.
6. Philemon began hosting the Colossian church (started by Epaphras) in his home (Philem. 2).
7. The relationship between Philemon and Onesimus became estranged.
8. Philemon *perhaps* determined Onesimus was useless as a slave (Philem. 11).
9. Onesimus *perhaps* was deficient in his duties and *perhaps* stole from Philemon (Philem. 11, 18).
10. Onesimus departed from Philemon without permission.
11. Onesimus encountered Paul in prison (Philem. 10).
12. Onesimus was converted by Paul (Philem. 10).
13. Onesimus became dear and useful to Paul (Philem. 11–13).
14. Paul wrote letters to Philemon and to the church in Colossae.
15. Paul sent Onesimus back to Philemon along with Tychicus (Philem. 12; Col. 4:7–9).
16. Onesimus and Tychicus arrived in Colossae.
17. The church gathered in Philemon's home and heard the letters read.
18. Paul intends for Philemon to receive Onesimus as he would Paul (Philem. 17).
19. Paul intends for Philemon to do "even more" than Paul asks (Philem. 21).
20. Paul intends to visit Philemon in Colossae (Philem. 22).

Paul, however, bases his instruction for how Onesimus should be received by Philemon on their mutual relationship in Christ. Paul is an apostle of Jesus Christ, Philemon is Paul's partner in Christ who owes a spiritual debt to Paul (Philem. 17, 19), and Onesimus has now become Paul's spiritual son in Christ (Philem. 10). All three of them are brothers in Christ, and therefore Paul calls both Onesimus and Philemon to establish a new relationship centered upon Christ. This is why Paul has sent Onesimus back to Philemon with this letter, and this is why he appeals to Philemon to welcome Onesimus no longer as a slave but as a beloved brother (Philem. 3:16). Paul does not directly command Philemon because he wants more than simple obedience; he wants Philemon's heart and his thinking to be so genuinely transformed by the love of Christ that he will do what Paul asks of his own accord, and indeed, to do even more than Paul asks (Philem. 8–9, 14, 21). Paul is confident that Philemon will do the right thing (Philem. 21)—so confident, in fact, that he sends Onesimus with the letter rather than first seeking a response from Philemon.[6] Nevertheless, Paul also brings the entire church into the situation (Philem. 2) and writes to them a second letter that will provide the theological underpinnings for Paul's appeal.

6 In the first century, slaves could appeal to a friend of their master for help mediating a dispute. In one instance, Pliny appeals to his friend Sabinianus on behalf of one of Sabinianius's slaves, but Pliny sends his letter to Sabinianus and awaits his response before sending back the slave (Pliny, *Ep.* 9.21). Paul, however, breaks this protocol by sending Onesimus back directly with his first letter, and by doing so, Paul demonstrates his confidence that Philemon will respond in accordance with Paul's appeal, for nothing less than the life of Onesimus is at stake in Philemon's compliance.

Occasion of Colossians

Paul's letter to the Colossians provides the broader context for Paul's appeal to Philemon and it establishes Paul's relationship with the church as a whole. Paul himself has never been to Colossae (Col. 2:1), but it was through the ministry of Paul's coworker, Epaphras, that the church was established, and Paul now rejoices to hear from Epaphras how the gospel is flourishing among them (Col. 1:3–8). Paul naturally feels an apostolic responsibility for these believers, even though he has not met them. They are a young church in need of theological instruction and practical exhortation, and Paul delivers both in this letter.

In the opening prayer, Paul sets forth his overall goal for the Colossians and his purpose in this letter, that they will be filled with spiritual knowledge of God's will so they can walk worthy of the Lord Jesus (Col. 1:9–10). In the rest of the letter, Paul sets forth the spiritual knowledge the Colossians need, including teachings about Christ and his work (e.g., Col 1:15–20) and what believers have received through their union with Christ (e.g., Col. 2:1–15). These teachings lead to the key imperative of the letter, which is that they will "walk" (περιπατέω) or live their lives in a manner fitting for those who belong to the Lord Jesus Christ (Col. 2:6). Their thinking must be reoriented around Christ himself (Col. 3:1), so that they will know how to honor him in every situation, whether facing false teaching (Col. 2:8, 16–23), overcoming sin (Col. 3:5–11), or growing in the virtues that will allow them to have unity together as a body of Christ (Col. 3:12–17) and to bear witness to Christ in the world (Col. 3:18–4:6). Paul's overarching aim in the letter, therefore, is to see these young believers grow in their knowledge about Christ in order that they will honor Christ in every aspect of their lives.

The Intersecting Occasion of Both Letters

We can imagine the dramatic scene Paul orchestrates in Colossae. When these two letters simultaneously arrived in Colossae, the church would have gathered in Philemon's home to hear the letters read. The Colossians would immediately recognize Onesimus and feel the tension between this estranged slave and his master. The letter to the Colossians would be read first, with its instruction about Christ and how believers ought to live in Christ. This letter includes broad implications for slaves and masters, including the elimination of the slave-master distinction in Christ (Col. 3:11) and instructions for how both slaves and masters should serve Jesus as their heavenly Lord (Col. 3:22–4:1). It also describes the reconciliation all believers have received in Christ (Col. 1:20–21) and the need for believers to put aside anger and to forgive one another, that the church might be ruled by peace (Col. 3:8, 13, 15). Surely the entire church had eyes on Onesimus and Philemon when they heard these instructions.

Then the second letter would have been read, this time directly to Philemon, but still in the presence of the entire church, and now the broad instructions of the first letter are applied directly to their personal situation. Paul's appeal for Philemon to welcome Onesimus no longer as a slave, but as a beloved brother in Christ, will require Philemon to adopt the theological thinking and to embody the exhortations of Paul's first letter. He must see that in Christ, the slave-master distinction now means nothing, and he must resolve to set aside his anger, forgive Onesimus's offenses, and pursue peace with him through reconciliation, that they might share unity together in the body of Christ.

The letter to Philemon, in other words, is the particular application of the theology of Colossians. If Philemon can adopt Paul's teaching in Colossians, then he will have the theological framework and perspective he needs to sincerely live out Paul's personal appeal regarding Onesimus. He will walk worthy of the Lord Jesus by receiving Onesimus as his brother in Christ. And if the entire church can adopt Paul's teaching in Colossians, then they will provide the encouragement and accountability both Philemon and Onesimus need to put this into practice, and they will all be transformed together through this experience and be compelled to continue growing to maturity in their walk with Christ.

Preaching Tip

It may be helpful for preaching to introduce the relationship between Colossians and Philemon from the outset, and even to familiarize people with the story of Onesimus and Philemon. This may require preaching a first sermon or two on Paul's letter to Philemon. This way, as you preach through Colossians, you can refer to the situation between Onesimus and Philemon as an example of what Paul is saying. This is especially true when such themes emerge as peace and reconciliation (Col. 1:20–23; 3:15), the unity of all believers in Christ (Col. 3:11), bearing together and forgiving one another (Col. 3:13), and instructions for slaves and masters (Col. 3:22–4:1).

THEOLOGICAL THEMES

Christ

The first and most foundational theme to both Colossians and Philemon is Christ in his person, work, and position. Christ is at the center of everything Paul says in both letters, whether he is in the foreground, as in Colossians, or in the background, as in Philemon. Paul lays Christ as the foundation from the outset with the very important poetic language of Colossians 1:15–20. Here Paul compresses into just a few words some of the most exalted language about Christ in all of the New Testament. He describes the *person* of Christ as the image of the invisible God and the one in whom the fullness of God's nature dwells (Col. 1:15, 19; cf. 2:9). He describes the *work* of Christ first in relation to creation, as Christ is the one by whom, through whom, and for whom all things were created, and he continues to sustain all creation (1:16–17). He then describes the *work* of Christ in relation to redemption, where by his death and resurrection he has accomplished peace and reconciliation for all creation (1:18, 20) and this reconciliation is applied now to all who believe (1:21–22). Therefore, Christ now occupies an exalted *position* of supremacy over all creation (1:15–17) and headship over his body, which is the church (1:18).

These teachings about Christ from Colossians 1:15–20 reappear throughout the letter as Paul further develops the implications of the person, work, and position of Christ for how we ought to live as believers. Indeed, the themes to come are all developments in one way or another of the hymn's teaching about Christ. When Paul describes the union of believers with Christ, he is explaining how the death and resurrection of Christ are applied to believers, so that they become recipients of his redemptive work and receive new life in him (1:18, 20; 2:11–13). When Paul warns against false teaching, it is because Christ alone occupies the position of supremacy, and therefore believers must not depart from Christ by pursuing other gods and traditions (1:15–20; 2:8–10, 14–23). When Paul commands to walk worthy of Christ their Lord, he is drawing out the implications of Jesus being Lord over his body, the church, of which believers have become members (1:18; cf. 1:10; 2:6–7). When Paul addresses particular individuals, including slaves and masters, he is fleshing out the implications of Christ having reconciled all of creation to himself, including even Gentiles and slaves, so that he is Lord over all (Col. 1:20; cf. 1:27; 3:11, 22–4:1). When Paul appeals to believers to work toward reconciliation by bearing together, forgiving one another, and living in peace together, and especially when he appeals for such reconciliation between Onesimus and Philemon, he is asking them to actuate in a small way the broader work of reconciliation Christ has accomplished on the cross (Col. 1:20; cf. 3:13–15; Philem. 10–21). We cannot understand the rest of what Paul writes unless we first appreciate what he says about Christ in Colossians 1:15–20.

Union with Christ

The theological concept of union with Christ describes the nature of our personal relationship with Jesus as believers. We do not find the actual term "union" in either of these letters, but the concept behind the theological theme appears frequently, especially in Paul's repeated description of believers being "in Christ" (e.g., Col. 1:2; 14, 28; 2:6, 10; etc.) and also of Christ being "in you" (Col. 1:27). The language is mysterious and even mystical, as Paul describes the intangible and spiritual nature of our relationship with Jesus. He articulates the nature of our union with Christ most clearly in Colossians 2:10–13. He begins by saying we have been filled in Christ (2:10) and then he goes on to describe the spiritual blessings we have received. He uses circumcision as a metaphor for death to say that we have died a spiritual death in Christ even as Christ died (2:11), and he uses baptism as a metaphor for our "burial with" Christ (συνθάπτω) and our "resurrection with" Christ (συνεγείρω; 2:12), so that God has now made us alive together with Christ (2:13). The imagery depicts believers being so closely joined together with Christ by faith that they now share together in the work of Christ, and his death and resurrection have been applied to them.

Further, our union with Christ continues in the present, so that Paul can say your life is hidden with Christ (3:3), and even more pointedly, Christ *is* your life (3:4). The implication is that we must now live our present lives in a manner worthy of Christ, who is our life (Col. 3:5–17). And in the future, we will also appear with Christ in glory (3:4). When we put these pieces together, we see Paul uniting believers together with the past, present, and future work of Christ, so that we have died with Christ and been raised to new life in Christ, and we now have resurrection life in Christ, so that we must walk worthy of Christ, and we will one day share in the glory of Christ when he returns.

Warnings against False Teaching

In the second chapter of Colossians, Paul sets forth a series of cryptic warnings that may indicate the presence of false teachers in Colossae. He does not want the Colossians to be deceived by "plausible arguments" (πιθανολογία; 2:4) or taken captive by "by the philosophy" (διὰ τῆς φιλοσοφίας; 2:8), which he describes as being according to "elements" (στοιχεῖον) and human tradition rather than according to Christ. Then he becomes more specific, warning first against those who pass judgment on Christians based on food, drink, festivals, new moons, and Sabbaths (2:16), and warning second against those who disqualify Christians and insist they should participate in asceticism and worship of angels (2:18).

Many scholars presume these warnings are directed against a particular religious or philosophical group that was present in Colossae and was actively working to lead the Colossians away from Christ. These scholars have identified several possible first-century groups, including Gnosticism, pagan religions, Hellenistic philosophies, and various strands of Jewish belief and practice.[7] If Paul was indeed warning against such a specific group, we must marvel at how his warnings can successfully be read by today's scholars against virtually every philosophy and religious tradition present in the first century!

In this commentary, we will conclude that Paul's warnings are intentionally generic precisely so that they can be read against any teaching that would lead Christians away from Christ, but at the same time Paul also includes various examples of specific kinds of teachings and beliefs that were surely present in Colossae. Thus, his warnings contain references to Jewish practice (e.g., Sabbath; 2:16) and pagan

7 Several reviews of the vast literature on the false teachers now exist and they provide an initial introduction to the various conclusions scholars have reached (e.g., Francis and Meeks, 1975; Copenhaver, 2018, 1–39).

religions, such as the mysteries of Apollo (e.g., visions seen upon entering; 2:18). These may be the very teachings and practices which these young believers adhered to prior to coming to Christ. Therefore, Paul warns broadly against the false teachings likely to be present in Colossae in order to dissuade Christians in Colossae from being influenced by their friends and family to return to their former practices. His warnings provide the negative counterpart to his positive exhortation for the Colossians to remain in Christ and to walk in him, for in Christ they have everything and lack nothing.

Walking Together in Christ

Paul aims in these letters to exhort the Colossians to walk worthy of Christ together, not least in how they handle the situation between Philemon and Onesimus. He prays for the Colossians to walk worthy of the Lord in all things (Col. 1:9–10) and he commands them to do the same (Col. 2:6; cf. 4:5). This will require their entire life to be reoriented around Christ (Col. 3:1) and they must be completely transformed as they put off the old person with its practices and put on the new person they have become in Christ (Col. 3:9–10). Every believer in Colossae is responsibly to learn how to honor Christ in all that they do (Col. 3:17).

Though every believer is individually responsible for walking in Christ, they are not alone as they walk in Christ. Paul presents the church as the body of which Christ is the head (Col. 1:18) and Paul is a servant (Col. 1:23–25). He now longs to see all believers united together (Col. 2:2) regardless of whatever differences they may have (Col. 3:11), and his exhortations are interpersonal in nature, dealing with how they will treat one another as the body of Christ. They must love and forgive one another, and they must unite peacefully together as one body centered around Christ and his word (Col. 3:12–16). Thus, in Paul's estimation, walking in Christ can only be done together with other believers who are also walking in Christ. For this reason, Paul addresses his second letter not only to Philemon, but also to the entire church (Philem. 2), for even this personal conflict between Onesimus and Philemon is in reality an opportunity for the entire church to learn to walk together as the body of Christ. Paul knows Philemon and Onesimus need the support of the church, and the church needs to learn for from their example. Walking in Christ must be done together.

Slavery

Perhaps the most challenging theme in Colossians and Philemon is slavery, and especially the attitude of Paul toward slavery. Paul does not directly address slavery as an institution in either letter, but he does speak to slaves and masters within the institution of slavery, including Onesimus and Philemon. In our modern world of today, slavery is almost universally regarded as a morally reprehensible institution. We can hardly fathom how a Christian could live without protest within a society where slavery allowed one person to own another person as his possession. Our Western consciences are especially offended because of our acute awareness of the horrors of the African slave trade in the seventeenth through nineteenth centuries. Not only did Paul live within a Roman society where slavery was an active institution all around him, but he left behind such vagueness about slavery in his letters that some self-proclaimed Christians throughout history have used his words to justify owning slaves.

However, though Paul does not speak out directly against the institution of slavery, he does undermine the premise of slavery by rehumanizing dehumanized slaves. He outright rejects any distinction between slaves and free, for all people are the same in Christ (Col. 3:11). He further empowers slaves when he grants to them the ability to fully please their heavenly master, Jesus, by the manner in which they conduct their service to their earthly master, regardless of the nature of their work (Col.

3:22–23). He even promises slaves they will receive an eternal inheritance and justice for whatever injustices they have experienced (Col. 3:24–25). Even as Paul elevates slaves in these ways, he also lowers masters by reminding them they actually have a master over them in heaven, thereby rendering them as slaves of the Lord Jesus as well (Col. 4:1). Thus, slaves and masters are rendered equal in Christ, for both serve Jesus as their master. Slaves participate fully in the life of Christ and of his body, the church. Unlike Aristotle, who says slaves cannot be friends with masters (Aristotle, *Nic. Ethics* 1161b), Paul envisions slaves and masters together as brothers in Christ (Philem. 16).

Paul thereby sows subversive seeds directly into the hearts of Christian slaves and masters. He does not demand emancipation of individual slaves, let alone the abolition of slavery as an institution, but he does call for Christians to have a radically different way of perceiving and interacting with one another as masters and slaves. He then puts these principles into practice with Onesimus and Philemon. He elevates Onesimus when he refuses to label him a "fellow slave" (σύνδουλος) as he does Tychicus (Col. 4:7–9), and he insists Philemon welcome Onesimus as a beloved brother (Philem. 16). Further, Paul's suggestion that Philemon should do even more than he says (Philem. 21) indicates Paul's presumption that the seeds Paul has sown will continue to grow in Philemon's heart as he more deeply embraces the notion that there is no slave or free in Christ.

In a way, Paul actually calls for something even more radical than abolition. Rather than leaning upon Christian masters like Philemon to simply free their slaves and have nothing more to do with them, he instead calls them to bear together with their slaves in a new way in Christ, where they learn to embrace one another as beloved brothers. They must forever set aside any notion that one is more than the other, that slaves are mere property, of a lesser nature even if set free, and must instead learn to walk together as equal slaves of their mutual Lord in heaven. How long, we might wonder, before such a change in perspective leads not only to emancipation but to the ongoing embrace of *former* slaves and *former* masters living together as brothers and sisters in the body of Christ and leaning upon their culture to do the same?

The Long-Term Impact of Subversive Seeds

"When the Gospel taught that God had made all men and women upon earth of one family; that all alike were His sons and His daughters; that, whatever conventional distinctions human society might set up, the supreme King of Heaven refused to acknowledge any; that the slave notwithstanding his liberty was Christ's slave; when the Church carried out this principle by admitting the slave to her highest privileges, inviting him to kneel side by side with his master at the same holy table; when in short the Apostolic precept that 'in Christ Jesus is neither bond nor free' was not only recognised but acted upon, then slavery was doomed. Henceforth it was only a question of time. Here was the idea which must act as a solvent, must disintegrate this venerable institution, however deeply rooted and however widely spread" (Lightfoot, 1981, 325).

Reconciliation

The theme of reconciliation permeates both letters. Paul establishes the foundational theme of reconciliation in Colossians 1:20–22, where Christ has reconciled all creation to God through the cross and this reconciliation has been personally experienced by those who believe in Christ. Though the word "reconcile" (ἀποκαταλλάσσω) only appears in these opening verses (Col. 1:20, 22), the theme carries through the rest of both letters. Paul exhorts the Colossians to do all the things that bring about reconciliation with one another, including setting aside anger and wrath (Col. 3:8), forgiving one another (Col. 3:14), being bound together by love (Col. 3:14), and being ruled by peace as a unified body of Christ (Col. 3:15). He effectively commands reconciliation in principle, as estranged believers must learn to resolve their conflict and to establish a new kind of relationship with one another centered upon Christ.

In his letter to the Colossians, Paul sets forth the general principles of Christian reconciliation; and in his letter to Philemon, Paul appeals for Philemon to put these general principles to work in his particular situation with Onesimus. Though Paul does not use the language of reconciliation, or even of forgiveness, in his letter to Philemon, he still calls for Philemon to do precisely those things. He appeals for Philemon to erase Onesimus's record of sin and debt, even applying them to the account of Paul himself (Philem. 18), and most importantly, he leans upon Philemon to receive Onesimus no longer as a slave but as a beloved brother. This requires not merely reconciliation, insofar as they cannot simply go back to being master and slave in their old way, but they must go forward in a new way, reconciling with one another and establishing a new relationship ruled by the peace of Christ, where they love one another as brothers together in Christ and participate together as full members of the body of Christ in Colossae.

In a roundabout way, the entirety of both letters moves toward this goal of reconciliation between Onesimus and Philemon, so that we might say all of the theological themes of the letter provide the foundation to which reconciliation is the goal. If Philemon and Onesimus can learn to reconcile with one another in this way, and if the church in Colossae also can put this kind of reconciliation to work in their own congregation, then Paul's letters will have been successful—the church will be walking together in a manner worthy of Christ.

OUTLINE

COLOSSIANS

- Greetings and Thanksgiving (1:1–8)
- Paul's Prayer for the Colossian Believers (1:9–14)
- The Hymn about Christ (1:15–23)
- Paul's Universal Ministry (1:24–29)
- Paul's Particular Ministry (2:1–5)
- Filled with the Fullness of Christ (2:6–15)
- Watch Out for False Teaching! (2:16–23)
- Raised with Christ (3:1–4)
- Put Off Your Former Way of Life (3:5–11)
- Put On the Virtues of Christ (3:12–17)
- Following Christ at Home (3:18–4:1)
- Following Christ in the World (4:2–6)
- Closing Instructions and Greetings (4:7–18)

PHILEMON

- Paul's Relationship to Philemon (1–7)
- Paul's Appeal to Philemon (8–16)
- Welcoming Onesimus (17–25)

Colossians 1:1–8

EXEGETICAL IDEA
Paul thanked God for the Colossians because they had heard and received the gospel message from Epaphras and because the gospel was now actively reaching more people and bearing fruit, even as their hope was producing faith toward Christ and love toward the saints.

THEOLOGICAL FOCUS
When people hear and receive the gospel, their lives are transformed as they grow in their faith in Christ, love for one another, and hope for eternity.

PREACHING IDEA
Let's thank God for the good news that changes us.

PREACHING POINTERS
Although Paul had not visited the small town of Colossae, his faithful companion Epaphras preached the good news there, and the first text of Colossians depicts a marvelous real-life picture of the power of the gospel. Greco-Roman culture promoted polytheism and licentiousness, but when some of the people of Colossae heard and understood the gospel, it took root, grew, and bore fruit. No wonder Paul thanked God for the Colossians (v. 3). For these converts, the gospel was more than a stripped-down message of sin and salvation (although it was not *less* than that). It was a full-orbed but shorthand way that Paul used to capture all that God is doing to save his people from sin and redeem this broken world. For Paul, the good news announced how the Colossians had been made blameless in the eyes of God through Jesus; it also produced the fruit of Christlike attitudes and behaviors, as with the Colossians.

The good news has the same power to produce the same results today as well. Too often a "profession of faith" produces little moral change. It has been said that Christianity in North America is a mile wide and an inch deep. The same is also true for many parts of Africa and South America. The "health-and-wealth gospel" produces "converts" who use God as their errand boy and genie. On the other hand, salvation can be framed in a way that implies a burdensome and guilt-producing obligation to please God lest he disown us. That doesn't sound like good news! The first passage in Colossians steers between these shoals, or rather, it rejects both and finds deep water elsewhere—in the good news of the gospel. There we learn how much God loves us and has done for us, and this produces the fruit of faith, hope, and love (vv. 4–6). So, let's thank God for the good news that changes us.

GREETINGS AND THANKSGIVING (1:1–8)

LITERARY STRUCTURE AND THEMES (1:1–8)

These opening verses divide into two sections. First, Paul identifies himself and Timothy as the authors of this letter and the church in Colossae as his audience, and he greets them with grace and peace from God (1:1–2). Second, Paul issues a prayer of thanksgiving in which he reveals the sequence of events that led to his writing the letter (1:3–8). He recalls how the Colossians heard the gospel from Epaphras and how Epaphras has now reported back to Paul regarding the fruit the gospel is bearing among them. Because Epaphras is a coworker of Paul, Paul now feels a close connection to and a responsibility for the church Epaphras has established in Colossae. He therefore writes to them directly and affirms to them the veracity of the gospel message as they have learned it from Epaphras. The major theme of this section arises from Paul's thanksgiving for how the gospel was received by the Colossians and now works among them.

- ***Letter Opening (1:1–2)***
- ***Paul's Thanksgiving for the Colossians (1:3–8)***

EXPOSITION (1:1–8)

In these first eight verses, we learn that Colossians is a letter written by Paul, and we discover the basic history behind its composition. Greco-Roman letters typically opened with an identification of the author and the sender followed by a one-word greeting (χαίρειν). Sometimes these letters also included a prayer to the gods or a wish for good health. Paul follows this basic structure in his letter to the Colossians, but Paul also incorporates his own flourishes along the way, particularly with a lengthy prayer of thanksgiving for the Colossians (1:3–8), the entirety of which is one run-on sentence introduced by the main verb "we give thanks" (εὐχαριστοῦμεν; 1:3). These opening verses establish the basic historical context of the letter, including Paul as the author, the church in Colossae as the recipients, and the history of the church in Colossae.

Ancient Letter-Writing

The following are representative examples of ancient Greek letters. Both were written on papyri and reflect the typical length and simplicity of letters.

Sarapion to his brothers Ptolemaeus and Apollonius greeting [χαίρειν]. *If you are well, (it would be excellent). I myself am well. I have made a contract with the daughter of Hesperus and intend to marry her in the month of Mesore. Please send me half a chous [jug] of oil. I have written to you to let you know. Goodbye. Year 28, Epeiph 21. Come for the wedding-day, Apollonius.* (P.Par. 43; trans. Hunt and Edgar, 1932, 99)

Horus to the most honoured Apion greeting [χαίρειν]. *Regarding Lampon the mousecatcher, I paid him on your account 8 drachmae as earnest money to catch mice in Toka. You will kindly send me this sum. I have also lent 8 drachmae to Dionysius, president of Nemerae, and he has not sent them back; this is to inform you. Goodbye. Pauni 24.* (P.Oxy. 299; trans. Hunt and Edgar, 1932, 108)

Letter Opening (1:1–2)

In his opening salutation, Paul identifies himself as one who writes by the commission and authority of God to the Christians in Colossae, and Paul wishes God's grace and peace upon them.

1:1. Paul opens the letter by identifying himself as an "apostle" (ἀπόστολος). In the New Testament, an apostle is "a man who is sent, and sent with full authority" (TDNT, 1.421). The term can refer generally to a messenger (e.g., Epaphroditus in Phil. 2:25), to devoted servants of Christ (e.g., Barnabas in Acts 14:14, or James in Rom. 16:7), or it can also refer more specifically to the official position of the twelve apostles (Acts 1:26) who had "a special function as God's envoys" (BDAG, s.v. "ἀπόστολος" 2c, p. 122). Paul considers himself an apostle in the latter, more official sense, in which he serves alongside the twelve apostles as one sent to proclaim as an eyewitness the gospel news of Jesus's death and resurrection.

Paul is an apostle "through the will of God" (διὰ θελήματος θεοῦ). He did not designate himself to be an apostle, but he became an apostle in an "abnormal" (1 Cor. 15:8) fashion when he witnessed the resurrected and ascended Jesus on the Damascus Road (Acts 9:1–19). Further, Paul describes himself as an apostle "of Christ Jesus" (Χριστοῦ Ἰησοῦ). As such, Paul both belongs to and serves Christ Jesus.[1] His apostleship exists in an inseparable relationship to Christ.

As an apostle, Paul has been given an office that carries implicit authority over the entire church, including local communities of believers whom he has not yet met, such as the church in Colossae (Col. 2:1). Though Paul knew a few individuals in Colossae (e.g., Philemon and Archippus; Col. 4:17; Philem. 1:1), he lacks a personal relationship with most members of the church, so that they might naturally take offense at a stranger writing to them and even issuing instructions with such boldness. However, Paul anticipates and deflects their potential offense by reminding them at the outset that he writes as an apostle, and his apostleship is not something he sought for himself, but it was given to him "by the will of God" (Col. 1:1). As an apostle, Paul does not presume upon himself the authority to write, but he writes as an apostle out of humble obedience to the God who called him to be an apostle. He does not lord it over the church but he suffers on behalf of the church (Col. 1:23–24). He models the paradox of Christian leadership whereby to lead is to serve, and to be over is to be under. Humility and service are the true expressions of authority in Christ.

The letter comes not only from Paul, but also from "Timothy the brother." Paul will mention his various coworkers throughout the letter (i.e., Col. 4:10–14), but Timothy receives special mention in the letter opening, where in antiquity a letter's sender and receiver are normally mentioned. Paul may be simply honoring Timothy as a coworker of particular distinction, so that he is "the brother" among many brothers. But more likely the mention of Timothy indicates he played an active role in the composition of the letter, perhaps as an amanuensis, or secretary, who was responsible for the actual writing of the letter (Dunn, 1996, 35–39). However, the content of the letter is thoroughly Pauline, regardless of the silent role Timothy may have played in its composition. The letter routinely uses the first person singular to refer specifically to Paul (Col. 1:23), to his particular ministry as an apostle (e.g., 1:23–2:5), and to his present situation (Col. 4:7). Further, Paul signs the letter (Col. 4:18) and sends it through his messengers (Col. 4:7–9). Thus, it is written by Paul.

1:2. Though Paul writes to "the brothers" (τοῖς . . . ἀδελφοῖς), he does not intend to be gender-exclusive here. Indeed, he recognizes women as part of his audience in the letter, including wives (Col. 3:18) and Nympha (Col.

1 Paul uses Χριστοῦ Ἰησοῦ as what Wallace calls a "plenary genitive" that contains both the subjective sense of belonging to Christ Jesus as an apostle and the objective sense of serving Christ Jesus as an apostle (Wallace, 1996, 119–21).

4:15). Paul is using the masculine in an inclusive sense to include *both* men and women; perhaps "sibling" would be an appropriate translation in today's nomenclature. This familial language is a fitting metaphor for the church, where believers are bonded together as a family with God as their Father. Unfortunately, families often encounter internal strife and siblings sometimes feud, but one key distinctive of familial relations is that they remain family even when they quarrel, and they are therefore compelled to forgive and reconcile.

Paul narrows his focus to particular Christian siblings who are "in Colossae" (ἐν Κολοσσαῖς) and "in Christ" (ἐν Χριστῷ). He writes specifically to those siblings who reside within the geographical region of Colossae and he addresses their particular situation (and that of their neighbors in Laodicea; see Col. 4:16). These believers in Colossae are also located spiritually "in Christ." They belong to Christ, and therefore they are bound together with all who belong to Christ (as opposed to those who are outside Christ; see Col. 4:5) regardless of where they live geographically, but especially to those who share their residence in Colossae. They are now bound together as local siblings and therefore they must bear together as a family of Christian siblings in Colossae regardless of whatever situation might threaten to fracture them—even if it be a legitimate grievance between a slave and his master such as with Onesimus and Philemon.

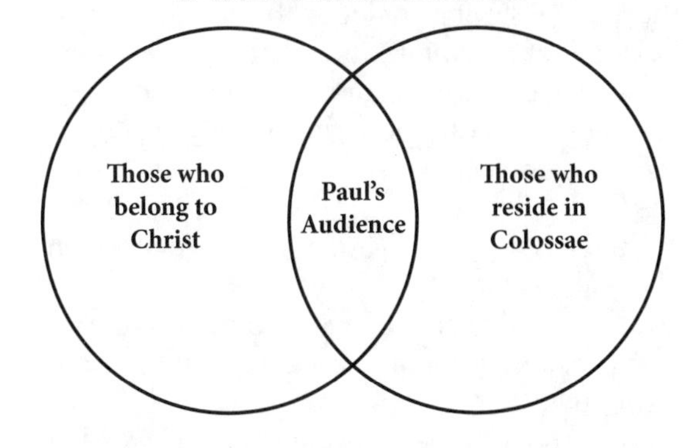

Paul identifies his audience by two characteristics: they are spiritually "in Christ," and they reside "in Colossae."

Paul describes his audience with two adjectives, "holy" (ἁγίοις) and "faithful" (πιστοῖς). As *holy* brothers, the Colossian believers are a people separated by and for God and participating in the moral holiness of God, even as God called the people of Israel to be his "holy nation" (ἔθνος ἅγιον; Exod. 19:6 LXX). Paul thus affirms the moral quality of their lifestyle in Christ. As *faithful* brothers, the Colossian believers share the same quality of service as Paul's own "faithful" coworkers, including Epaphras (Col.1:7), Tychicus (Col. 4:7), and even Onesimus, whom Paul calls specifically a "faithful brother" (Col. 4:9). Paul's commendation ought to have been received not as patronizing flattery, but as genuine approval and implicit exhortation to continue to strive toward the marks of holiness and faithfulness.

Paul then issues his customary blessing of grace (χάρις) and peace (εἰρήνη) toward his audience. Grace plays a central role throughout Paul's theology, even in those letters (such as Colossians) where the word itself rarely appears (see Col. 1:2, 6; 4:6, 18). Nevertheless, Paul opens and closes (see Col. 4:18) this letter with an extension of grace directly to the Colossians. For Paul, grace is not merely a theological concept, but it is the foundation of Christian relationships; Christians only approach one another with a greeting of grace.

Paul also extends to the Colossians the kind of "peace" Jews know as *shalom* (the Greek εἰρήνη being a translation of the Hebrew word "shalom" [שָׁלוֹם]). *Shalom* communicates "completeness" or "soundness" with a particular regard for the health or wholeness of a community (BDB, s.v. "שָׁלוֹם," p. 1022), and when used as a greeting, *shalom* is a formulaic extension of a wish for wellness, health, success, or peace. For the Christian, such peace has been accomplished by Christ (Col. 1:20) and is mandatory for the Christian community (Col. 3:15). Paul extends to them the very peace that ought to rule in their hearts.

Here, as in most of his letters, Paul approaches other Christians with the leading edge of grace and peace, even in the midst of tension and conflict. He thereby sets the pace for how the Christians in Colossae also ought to approach one another, including even Onesimus and Philemon.

Paul's Thanksgiving for the Colossians (1:3–8)

Paul recites his prayer of thanksgiving for the Colossians and traces his connection to the Colossians through Epaphras, who first preached the gospel in Colossae.

1:3. After his opening greetings, Paul begins by saying "we give thanks" (εὐχαριστοῦμεν). The plural "we" may incorporate not only Timothy as his co-sender but also Paul's coworkers (cf. Col. 4:10–14) who join him in thanksgiving and prayer (see Col. 1:9) for the Colossians. Indeed, Epaphras struggles in prayer for the Colossians in an intensely personal way (Col. 4:12). For Paul and his cohort, thanksgiving constituted a regular practice in their prayer gatherings. That they gave thanks for the Colossians "always" (πάντοτε) surely provided encouragement to the Colossian believers.

Though it is perhaps self-evident that Paul's prayer would be directed *to God* (τῷ θεῷ), Paul provides an interesting description of God in relation to Christ—"to God, the Father of our Lord Jesus Christ" (τῷ θεῷ πατρὶ τοῦ κυρίου ἡμῶν 'Ιησοῦ Χριστοῦ). Here Paul highlights several truths about Jesus. First, by describing God as the Father of Jesus Christ, Paul suggests that Jesus is the Son, even as Paul will later describe Jesus as "his [God's] beloved Son" (τοῦ υἱοῦ τῆς ἀγάπης αὐτοῦ; 1:13). Second, though both "Jesus" ('Ιησοῦ) and "Christ" (Χριστοῦ) can be used independently in the New Testament as names for Jesus, the combination "Jesus Christ" ('Ιησοῦ Χριστοῦ) underscores that the historical person of Jesus is the long-awaited Christ (i.e., Messiah) of the Old Testament. Finally, Paul declares Jesus Christ to be "our Lord" (τοῦ κυρίου ἡμῶν). As such, Jesus has full authority over both Paul and the Colossians, who share together the common position of surrender to Jesus Christ as their Lord.

1:4. Paul gives thanks *because* of the account he "has heard" (ἀκούσαντες; causal ptc.) about the faith and the love of the Colossians. Their faith is "in Christ Jesus" (ἐν Χριστῷ 'Ιησοῦ). As such, Christ Jesus may designate the realm within which the life of faith is to be lived (Lohse 1971, 16), or more likely, as Campbell argues persuasively, it may denote Christ Jesus as the object of their faith (e.g., Eph. 1:1; Gal. 3:26; 1 Cor. 15:19; 1 Tim. 3:13; 2 Tim 3:15; Campbell 2012, 112–13). Thus, the Colossians have a faith whereby they trust Christ Jesus. Their love, on the other hand, is "for all the saints" (εἰς πάντας τοὺς ἁγίους). Whereas their faith is directed toward Christ, their love is directed toward other believers. Paul's later instruction to put on love (Col 3:14) suggests that they do love the saints but not yet in an ideal or perfect manner. It is a work in progress.

The Story Behind the Thanksgiving

Paul's thanksgiving includes the following four instances of communication that have preceded his writing of this letter and which provide essential clues for reconstructing the historical circumstances of the letter:

(1) Paul has heard (ἀκούσαντες; 1:4a) of the faith and love of the Colossians.
(2) The Colossians have formerly heard (προηκούσατε; 1:5b) about hope in the word of truth.
(3) The gospel has been bearing fruit and growing among the Colossians from the day they heard (ἠκούσατε; 1:6e) the grace of God in truth.

(4) The Colossians learned (ἐμάθετε; 1:7a) the gospel from Epaphras, who also reported (δηλώσας; 1:8) their faith back to Paul.

1:5. Their faith and love, in turn, arise "because of their hope" (διὰ τὴν ἐλπίδα). Paul uses his well-known triad of faith, hope, and love, but he places them into a relationship whereby hope produces faith and love.[2] This "hope" (τὴν ἐλπίδα) is presently "put away for safekeeping" or "reserved" (BDAG, s.v. "ἀπόκειμαι" 1–2, p. 113) in the heavens for the Colossians. This hope is not merely a sentimental longing or expectation, but it is the very object "for which one hopes" (BDAG, s.v. "ἐλπίς" 3, p. 320). Yet at the present time, the object of their hope remains beyond their reach both spatially (the hope is stored in the heavens) and temporally (the hope will be received in the future). Paul will later point to Christ himself as the glorious hope (Col. 1:27) and he will remind the Colossians of the future day when Christ will appear with them (Col. 3:4) and they will receive their inheritance (Col. 1:12; 3:24). Paul expects that the hope the Colossians have will in turn transform them by producing faith in Christ and love for all the saints. Their eschatology will lead to their sanctification.

This message of hope is precisely what the Colossians "formerly heard" (προηκούσατε) "in the word of the truth, the gospel" (ἐν τῷ λόγῳ τῆς ἀληθείας τοῦ εὐαγγελίου; ESV, NRSV). The "word" (λόγος) refers to a message that Paul describes literally as being "of the truth" (τῆς ἀληθείας). This "truth" may be attributive (thus, "the true message"), but Paul frequently uses this kind of grammatical construction to denote an object (thus, "the message about the truth"). For example, Paul will later speak literally about "the word of Christ" (Ὁ λόγος τοῦ Χριστοῦ) in which Christ is clearly the object of the message (thus, "the message about Christ").[3] Here in Colossians 1:5, therefore, the message is a message "about the truth," or a message that proclaims the truth. Further, Paul says this message (λόγος) is the specific message "of the gospel" (τοῦ εὐαγγελίου). When we put these pieces together, we conclude that the Colossians heard about their hope when they heard "*the* message about *the* truth, which is *the* gospel message." The gospel is not just *a* true message; it is *the* true message.

What Is the Gospel?

In Paul's letters, the "gospel" (εὐαγγέλιον) refers to the proclaimed message of the accomplished work of Christ—especially his death, burial, and resurrection (see 1 Cor. 15:1–8)—and the present implication that all people must now receive this message with faith and repentance. These "gospel" themes appear in Colossians, where Paul mentions the accomplished work of Christ, including his suffering and death on the cross (1:20, 22, 24; 2:14), his burial (2:12), his resurrection (1:18), his ascension (3:1), and his return (3:4). Further, Paul presses beyond these typical gospel categories to speak also of Christ as the creator (1:16) and preexistent sustainer of all things (1:17) in whom dwells the fullness of deity (1:19; 2:9), and his work extends to the cosmos, where he has made peace with all things in heaven and on earth (1:20), and he has set aside the written code (2:14) and defeated the spiritual powers (2:15).

In Colossians, Paul also presents a robust picture of the present implication of the gospel in how it

2 These three are famously used in combination in 1 Corinthians 13:13, where Paul differentiates love as the greatest of the three. He also uses all three in 1 Thessalonians 1:3 and 5:8.

3 Elsewhere Paul speaks of the "word of God" (1 Cor. 14:36), "word of the Lord" (1 Thess. 1:8; 2 Thess. 3:2), "message of reconciliation" (2 Cor. 5:19), and "word of life" (Phil. 2:16), all with an objective sense and all as descriptions of the same gospel message (Lohse, 1971, 19; Lincoln, 1990, 38).

has applied and continues to apply to the Colossian believers. By hearing (1:3–8) and receiving the gospel message, the Colossians have received Christ himself (2:6) and now know personally the mystery of the gospel, which is "Christ in you" (1:27). By union with Christ, the Colossians have been rescued into the kingdom of the Son (1:13); reconciled to God (1:21–22); filled with the fullness of Christ (2:10); united to Christ in his death, burial, and resurrection (2:11–12); given new life in Christ (2:13); forgiven of their trespasses (2:13); raised with Christ (3:1); secured in Christ (3:3); given future hope of appearing with Christ (3:4) and receiving an inheritance (1:12; 3:24); and given a new identity as part of the body of Christ (3:10, 15). No wonder then that Paul appeals to the Colossians to not be taken captive (2:8), judged (2:16), or disqualified (2:18) by ideas contrary to Christ, but rather to continue to walk faithfully in Christ (1:23; 2:6–7) and to be transformed in Christ (3:5–4:6).

In other words, the entire letter of Colossians grows out of the gospel. The letter is all about Christ—who Christ is, what Christ *has done*, and what Christ *does* now among those who receive him; and for those who receive him, the gospel is further about who Christians are in Christ and how Christians ought to live in Christ.

1:6. This gospel was not only formerly heard by the Colossians, but the gospel continues to be present (πάρειμι). Paul does not describe the gospel as present "among you," but as present "to you" (εἰς ὑμᾶς), indicating "motion into a thing or into its immediate vicinity" (BDAG, s.v. "εἰς," p. 288). In other words, Paul emphasizes that the gospel *has come* to them and now has a remaining presence among them (Moo, 2008, 87; Sumney, 2008, 37), even as the gospel is present in "all the world" (ἐν παντὶ τῷ κόσμῳ). The gospel certainly had not at that time literally reached the entire world—though it had tentacles reaching into much of the Roman world—but Paul's hyperbole reminds the Colossians that they are not alone as recipients of the gospel; they are part of a gospel movement that reaches into all creation (cf. Col. 1:27–28).

And the gospel has an active rather than a passive presence. Indeed, the gospel is intrusive, invasive, and infectious. It "bears fruit and grows" (ἐστὶν καρποφορούμενον καὶ αὐξανόμενον) in Colossae. We typically expect plants to first grow and then to bear fruit, but Paul reverses this order and places bearing fruit before growing. Many farmers well know that immature plants begin bearing fruit before they have fully grown to maturity, and mature plants require regular pruning because they never cease to grow even as they enter into their prime fruit-producing years. Growth and bearing fruit, in other words, are simultaneous rather than consecutive activities. Likewise, the gospel bears fruit even as it grows, and believers ought to bear fruit even as they grow toward maturity.

TRANSLATION ANALYSIS: The combination of a present form of εἰμί followed by a present participle (or here two participles, ἐστὶν καρποφορούμενον καὶ αὐξανόμενον) forms a periphrastic participle with a single verbal idea in the present tense (Mounce, 1993, 276–77). Thus, ἐστὶν καρποφορούμενον means "bears fruit" and [ἐστὶν] αὐξανόμενον means "grows." Further, the καί connecting the two participles may indicate a hendiadys whereby the two ideas are so closely conjoined that they are effectively dependent upon each other (BDAG, s.v. "καί" 1aδ, p. 494; Zerwick 1963, §46; Blass and Debrunner, 1961, §442; cf. Sumney, 2008, 38). Thus, bearing fruit and growing are inseparable—each requires the other—and these are precisely the works the gospel is presently doing among the Colossians.

This growth and fruit-bearing may be interpreted either qualitatively or quantitatively. If qualitatively, then Paul is referring to growth in Christian maturity and the fruit of good works (cf. 2 Cor. 9:10; Eph. 4:15; 1 Pet. 2:2). If quantitatively, then Paul is referring to the expansion of the gospel as it reaches more people and the church grows in number (see Acts 6:7; 12:24; 19:20). Both forms of growth are represented in Colossians. Qualitatively, Paul will instruct them to bear the fruit of good works (Col. 1:10) and then give extensive exhortations detailing those good works (Col. 3:5–4:6). Quantitatively, Paul seeks to reach more people, as evidenced by his mission to proclaim the gospel in all creation (Col 1:23) and ultimately to present all people perfect in Christ (Col. 1:28). Paul brings these two forms of growth together in Colossians 4:5 when he exhorts the Colossians to walk in Christ (i.e., qualitative growth) toward those outside of Christ with the presumable goal of bringing them into Christ (i.e., quantitative growth).

Thus, where the gospel is present, there ought to be both qualitative and quantitative growth. Believers in Colossae who were immature yesterday will be mature tomorrow, and the church will continually welcome in new members who only recently received the gospel. Thus, the church in Colossae must be characterized by a perpetual state of change as the gospel reaches more people in their community and they in turn become part of the church. The church should be a dynamic, not static, community of believers.

The gospel has had this dynamic presence in Colossae "from the day you heard" (ἀφ' ἧς ἡμέρας ἠκούσατε). Here Paul points to the particular *day* when they first heard the message and knew "the grace of God" (τὴν χάριν τοῦ θεοῦ). Hearing leads to understanding, and Paul now uses "grace" as a shorthand description of the gospel message. To know God's grace is to know the gospel. And the Colossians knew this grace "in truth" (ἐν ἀληθείᾳ; cf. 1:5). While in Colossians 1:5, Paul described the gospel itself as a message revealing truth, he now speaks to the truthful nature, or integrity, of the gospel presentation the Colossians heard. Paul thus expresses confidence in the veracity of the gospel message as heard by the Colossians. How can Paul validate what they have heard when he has never communicated with them directly?

1:7. Paul's confidence rests firmly upon Epaphras, from whom the Colossians "learned" (ἐμάθετε) the gospel. Such learning is essentially discipleship (the verb μανθάνω is from the same root as "disciple," μαθητής). Epaphras was in the business of teaching and making disciples in accordance with Jesus's Great Commission command to "make disciples" (μαθητεύσατε) in Matthew 28:18–20. Epaphras's instruction began with the one-time proclamation of the gospel on that day when the Colossians first heard it (see Col. 1:6) and presumably continued with a disciplined and organized approach that teaches them to obey all of Jesus's commands (Matt. 28:20). Epaphras was less the Paul-like traveling evangelist who set up a tent for a one-and-done evangelistic meeting and more the local pastor-shepherd who methodically and persistently trained the Colossians in the gospel. Epaphras had invested the time and labor necessary to be confident that the Colossians properly understood the gospel.

Further, Paul affirms Epaphras's ministry on the basis of his personal relationship with Epaphras. By calling Epaphras "our fellow servant" (συνδούλου ἡμῶν), Paul establishes Epaphras as a member of his cohort, and by calling him "beloved" (τοῦ ἀγαπητοῦ), Paul indicates he shares with Epaphras "a very special relationship" (BDAG, s.v. "ἀγαπητός" 1, p. 7). This intimate bond and partnership in the gospel suggests that Paul's relationship with Epaphras preceded Epaphras's time in Colossae. Perhaps Epaphras was even trained by Paul and initially sent to Colossae under the auspices of Paul's mission. If so, then Paul is well-suited to vouch for the integrity of Epaphras's teaching in Colossae.

Yet even as a member of Paul's cohort, Epaphras retains his deepest loyalty to Christ and his homegrown love for Colossae. He is a "minister of Christ" (διάκονος τοῦ Χριστοῦ) who belongs to Christ and serves Christ, but he has a particular calling as a minister "in your behalf" (ὑπὲρ ὑμῶν). Unlike Paul, whose ministry has a global reach (Col. 1:26–28), Epaphras has a very narrowly focused ministry directed specifically toward believers in the region of Colossae. Surely it is no coincidence that Epaphras's ministry targets his hometown (Col. 4:12). Was it Paul's strategy to send his trainees back to their hometowns rather than into new communities, perhaps knowing that some towns (and small towns in particular) were suspicious of outsiders? Or was it Epaphras's love for his hometown that compelled him to take to them the gospel message which he knew they had never before heard? Either way, Epaphras's heart remains in Colossae.

Who Is Epaphras?

Epaphras emerges in Colossians 1:3–8 as a central figure in the Christian history of Colossae, but we learn very little about him from the New Testament. He is mentioned only three times in Paul's letters, and all three times in letters written to Colossae (Col. 1:7; 4:12; Philem. 23).[4] From these references, we may reconstruct what we know of his biography.

(1) Epaphras is a native Colossian (Col. 4:12).
(2) Epaphras received the gospel himself.
(3) Epaphras became a coworker of Paul and was likely trained by Paul.
(4) Epaphras traveled to Colossae, where he taught the gospel faithfully.
(5) Epaphras witnessed the gospel's growth and fruit in Colossae.
(6) Epaphras left Colossae and returned to Paul with a report.
(7) Epaphras continues to labor in prayer for the Colossian believers (Col. 4:12).
(8) Epaphras is imprisoned with Paul (Philem. 23) and unable to return to Colossae.
(9) Epaphras remains Paul's coworker.

Epaphras is a true local church shepherd whose heart is firmly and completely attached to the people in his particular community, even if that community be a humble and unheralded community such as Colossae. Epaphras does not aspire to celebrity status as a pastor; he is not using the Colossians to build a public platform or to promote his brand. Instead, Epaphras has a humble and singular burden for a particular community, and it is through his ministry that the gospel comes to Colossae. Aptly does Paul apply to Epaphras the highest compliment that he is a *faithful* servant (πιστὸς . . . διάκονος).

1:8. Paul's final statement in his thanksgiving states explicitly what should be obvious by now, that Paul's knowledge of the Colossians has come directly from Epaphras, who has "reported" (δηλώσας) to Paul and his cohort. If Epaphras had been dispatched to Colossae by Paul, then it only makes sense that Epaphras would return to Paul with a report.[5] The content of Epaphras's report—of the Colossians' love in the Spirit—brings the entire thanksgiving full circle. Paul began by giving thanks because of the Colossians' faith in Christ and *love* for all

4 His name, Epaphras, is an abbreviated form of the longer Epaphroditus, but the Epaphroditus Paul mentions in Philippians (Phil 2:25; 4:18) seems to be so closely associated with the church in Philippi, and Epaphras with the church in Colossae, that the two are probably different individuals.

5 Pao suggests, "Epaphras *has to* report to Paul concerning the church he had founded," and this requisite report in turn indicates the "implicit role" Paul played in sending Epaphras to Colossae (Pao, 2012, 58, empasis mine). Pao may be correct, but we should note that Paul gives no indication that he mandated this report—he simply states that the report was made.

the saints (Col. 1:4), and it is this same *love* that headlined the report Epaphras brought to Paul. Where such love is present, Paul knows the gospel must also be present and active.

THEOLOGICAL FOCUS

The exegetical idea (Paul thanked God for the Colossians because they had heard and received the gospel message from Epaphras and because the gospel was now actively reaching more people and bearing fruit, even as their hope was producing faith toward Christ and love toward the saints) leads to this theological focus: When people hear and receive the gospel, their lives are transformed as they grow in their faith in Christ, love for one another, and hope for eternity.

This theological focus reveals two important aspects of the gospel message. First, the gospel, by its very nature as a message, must be taught and heard in order to be received. On the one hand, this can be accomplished in a single hearing, as when Paul speaks of "the day" when the Colossians heard and understood the gospel (Col. 1:6). Such proclamations of the gospel are necessarily condensed, focusing on the essential truths about Christ and his work (e.g., his death, burial, and resurrection; 1 Cor. 15:1–8). But on the other hand, such hearing implies an ongoing labor of teaching and instruction, such as the ministry of discipleship that Epaphras had undertaken in Colossae. The gospel may require ongoing teaching before those who hear determine to receive the message and place their faith in Christ. Consider, for example, the months and even years Paul spent in some locations teaching the gospel (e.g., Acts 18:11; 19:10). Believers who seek to proclaim the gospel must make it known, both through condensed proclamation and ongoing instruction, with the goal that those who hear will receive the gospel and place their faith in Christ.

Second, the gospel—when it is heard and received—transforms believers. The gospel's work begins when it is heard and received, and then that work continues as the gospel remains among these believers, who increasingly learn about the gospel and produce the fruit of the gospel, both in terms of good works and of reaching more people with the gospel. Further, the gospel produces hope, faith, and love among believers. More specifically, the gospel offers a secure eternal hope of what awaits believers in heaven, and this hope in turn increases faith in Christ and love for all the saints (Col. 1:4–5). The faith and love that are so central to Christian belief and practice are grounded upon hope as their source, and this hope is in turn found in the gospel. When we put this together, we see that the gospel is not *merely* a message designed for the salvation of unbelievers, but the gospel is *also* a message designed for the sanctification of believers. No wonder then that Paul will spend so much ink and parchment in this letter giving further detail to the gospel and its implications for Christian living.

PREACHING AND TEACHING STRATEGIES

Exegetical and Theological Synthesis

Writing as an apostle of Christ Jesus, Paul, along with his brother Timothy, greets the Colossians and introduces the short epistle with joy and authority (vv. 1–3). Even though Paul had not visited the town, he thanked God and prayed for the church continually (v. 3). He learned about the church in Colossae from his companion Epaphras who had preached the gospel there (v. 7). The Word had taken root and was producing fruit just in Colossae and all over the Mediterranean world (v. 6).

The gospel is the core of this passage. The Word of God took root in in Colossae and produced results. The Colossians heard the announcement of the good news, believed it, found hope in it, and experienced the fruit of changed lives and loving community. Paul received word of how the Colossians became known for their faith, love, and hope (vv. 4–5).

Theologically, Paul showed how the Father, Son, and Spirit are involved in salvation. He thanked the Father (v. 3) because the grace of God (v. 6) promoted faith in the Lord Jesus Christ (v. 3) and love in the Spirit (v. 8).

God oversees all aspects of the spread of the gospel, but humans are involved also as stewards of the message. In the case of Colossians, Epaphras was the steward, a "faithful minister" (v. 7) who served as Paul's partner and emissary. Apparently Epaphras was the first person to have shared the good news about Jesus to the Colossians.

Preaching Idea

Let's thank God for the good news that changes us.

Contemporary Connections

What does it mean?

What does it mean for us to thank God for the good news that changes us? Any time we receive good news, our natural impulse is to say thank you and to respond with actions in keeping with the news. Perhaps a son or daughter is given unexpected leave from a three-year commitment overseas and shows up on your front step. We want to say thank you to the person who granted the leave, and we welcome the son or daughter with joy. A missionary receives support beyond the usual monthly amount so she sends a letter of thanks and makes a wise decision on what to do with the money. In the same way, we say thank you to God for the good news of salvation through Jesus, and we act in ways that please him.

The gospel is the announcement that God is saving his people and redeeming all creation through his Son, Jesus Christ. While a dictionary definition of "gospel" can be of some value in explaining the preaching idea, it might be more effective to use story and analogy to convey a holistic idea of the gospel. The story could be your own, as when your fiancé said yes! Or it might come from a high school student was recently accepted into the air force—the young person is already starting to act like a cadet! The good news is changing her.

The Bible uses many analogies to describe how the good news saves us: such as death to life, blindness to sight, sickness to health, guilty to pardoned, and lost to found. The conversion of John Newton, author of the hymn "Amazing Grace," may work well to expand on the analogies of blindness/sight as well as lost/found. And that story could be coupled with Chris Tomlin's song, "Amazing Grace (My Chains Are Gone)." A contemporary way to flesh out the analogy of lost/found might be a time such as when you lost your child at the mall for a few minutes. You probably panicked, but then you saw the security guard walking toward you holding the child's hand. What joy!

To clarify how good news changes us, it might be helpful to explain what happens spiritually and psychologically when we receive good news. It affects our minds, emotions, and motivations, what the Bible calls the *heart*, the wellspring of life. *Heart* includes emotion but is more than emotion. The heart is the amalgamation of the inner drives that motivate action. The figure of the heart pictures this.

Is it true?

Is it true that we should thank God for the good news that changes us? Jaded by experiences of people who claim to be Christ-followers, yet who show no evidence of this, some listeners may wonder if the good news really does change us. Perhaps they ask, "Why aren't more people changed by the gospel, and why aren't people changed more?" The following approaches may help address that reaction.

Perhaps the local news recently reported how someone won the lottery, and this has already changed how they live—a new house for their aging mother and a new car for their sister. Or perhaps the good news that your daughter

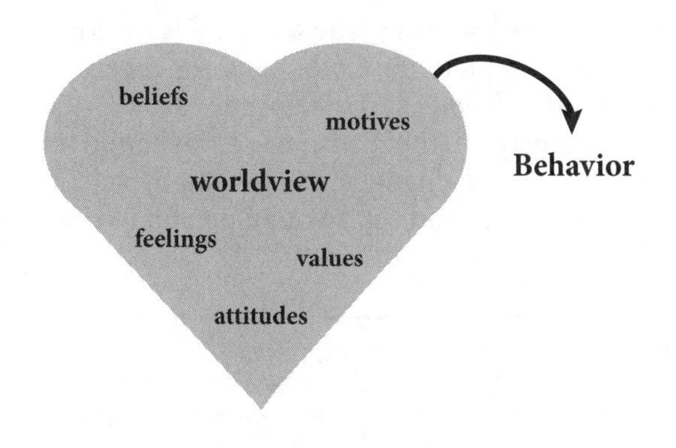

A Biblical View of the Heart

was accepted into Harvard resulted in her reading loads of classic literature to prepare for her first semester.

After establishing the general truth that good news changes people, we might affirm that much of the church does indeed look like the world. When we feel grief over that fact, we mirror God's grief. Statistics on divorce, the percentage of income given to charity, and sexual immorality might be used to "admit" that the church is a mile wide and an inch deep. (For statistics on giving, see emptytomb.com.) To counter the church's poor track record, preachers might also affirm that some people *are* radically transformed by the gospel. Examples from the Bible demonstrate this as in the book of Acts when priests came to faith (6:7), the angry Pharisee Saul was transformed into the selfless apostle Paul (ch. 9), and the jailer in Philippi became a Christ-follower (ch. 16). Following the biblical examples, current examples also show the truth of the preaching idea. Perhaps the leaders of the church could ask someone who has recently come to faith to share his or her first public testimony.

Perhaps the best "proof" for the preaching idea is Christlike action, not just words. When the Lord spoke about the gospel in Luke 4, he talked about how the good news would transform individuals and societies. For example, my (Jeffrey's) home church promotes foster parenting. We partner with government organizations and pray for them. A growing number of church members including single women have taken the life-changing step of becoming foster parents, and the rest of us support them financially and in prayer. My church has experienced the hope that comes from the good news of the gospel, and this causes us to serve others in tangible ways. Chapters 3 and 4 of Colossians will speak about how the gospel affects conduct in the home, community, and among the "outsiders" (4:5).

Finally, returning to the original objection that the gospel does not seem to make much difference, it may be appropriate to suggest why this might be the case: the process of transformation is long and gradual. We cannot see and therefore should not judge interior change based merely on lack of external progress. Furthermore, God wants us to be concerned about our *own* transformation. Holiness is not to be judged by comparing ourselves to each other, but by comparing ourselves to the Son.

Now what?

If good news changes us, what might this look like in concrete action? One action is captured in the first part of the preaching idea—we should thank God. Prayers, songs, and testimonies of thanksgiving would fit naturally into the service when this passage is preached. And thanks should be nonverbal as well as verbal. That is, by serving people in need we offer a sacrifice of praise to God (Heb. 13:15–16). "Nonverbal thanks" is implied in verse 4. The good news created "love for all the saints." Tangible expressions of love might be sharing money, meals, expertise, time, or a listening ear. Perhaps following the sermon, an information table could be set up to let people know about the church's ministries. These might range from GriefShare for those who have lost loved ones (www.griefshare.org), to prayer ministry, to free babysitting and child care.

The preaching idea naturally suggests another response as well: tell people about the good news. We might point to the example of Epaphras. To help people gain confidence and skill in sharing the good news, an Alpha or Christianity Explored course might be offered. This gives people a model for how to communicate with their unchurched friends and also provides a tool to introduce their associates to the gospel in a low-keyed, inviting atmosphere. Training in evangelism is also readily available online. A quick Google search gives resources like the ones in the sidebar, including "How to Share the Gospel in 90 Seconds"!

Resources for How to Share the Gospel

Many organizations offer training videos on how to share the gospel. Try one of these:

- The Billy Graham Evangelistic Association
- The Gospel Coalition
- Dare 2 Share

Creativity in Presentation

In addition to the ideas mentioned above, the following suggestions for creativity may enhance the sermon. These ideas could be incorporated into the outline that follows this section.

Maps, pictures, and timelines can help present background material in an engaging way. For example, a Google search of "timeline of Paul's epistles" gives multiple charts.

The horticulture metaphor in verses 5 and 6 ("growing and bearing fruit") suggests another way that pictures or objects could be used to show how good news changes us. Perhaps a house plant could be displayed. It started as a seed, grew, and had to be transplanted to a larger pot. Or perhaps a picture of an apple orchard that has been attacked by blight could illustrate how growth can be halted.

In order for good news to change the heart, one must truly hear the message. The figure below may be useful to illustrate different levels of hearing or listening. The top level is the kind of listening depicted in Colossians: the receivers heard and *responded* to the gospel.

To illustrate the cause-effect dynamic of how the gospel changes us, we might set up some dominoes and ask a young person to start the chain reaction.

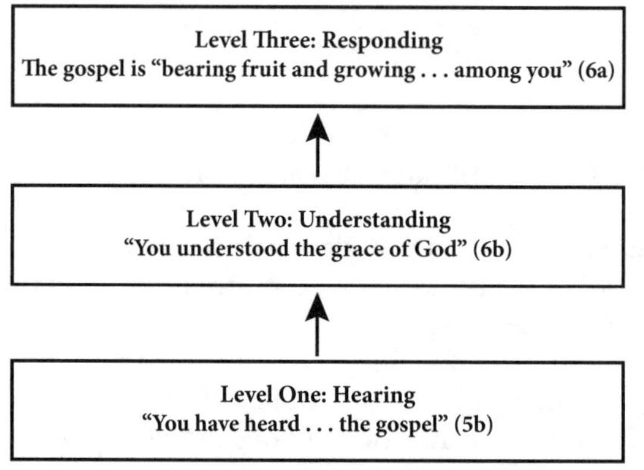

Levels of Listening

The genre of epistle implies a story—people interacting with other people about real issues—so the use of narrative might be a genre-sensitive way to help teach the passage. The first ten minutes of the sermon might use third-person or even first-person narrative. Third-person might sound like this: "Around the year A.D. 40, a very religious but very hateful man named Saul understood the gospel, and the good news changed him. I mean changed him! He no longer persecuted the church, now he protected it. He no longer hated the Gentiles; now he loved them. He dedicated his life to sharing the gospel with them. On one of his journeys, while in the town of Derbe, he met a young man named Timothy. . . ."

A first-person narrative might show slides of the road to Damascus and artwork of Saul's conversion; Google Images offers many paintings and videos. While showing the images, the preacher could offer the following account: "My name is Paul. They used to call me Saul, but that was a long time ago. I took a new name for a new life. Let me tell you what happened to me. I was a Pharisee of the Pharisees—very religious!—a leader of my people and a persecutor of *those* people. You know *those* people, don't you? I'm one of them now [smiling], and it looks like many of you are too. Christians. I persecuted Christians. . . ."

The passage alludes to the founding of the church in Colossae, so this might be a good opportunity to recount the history of your own organization. Pictures, timelines, stories from founding members, etc., can show people what God has done in your part of the world, how the good news changed people.

However we choose to convey our teaching, the thing to focus on is the central idea: Let's thank God for the good news that changes us.

- The good news helps us love (1:3–4).
- The good news gives us hope (1:5).
- The good news spreads (1:6–8).

DISCUSSION QUESTIONS

1. What is the historical context of Colossians? Why is it important?
2. Why did Paul give thanks to God?
3. What is the gospel?
4. How had the gospel come to Colossae?
5. What effect had the gospel had in Colossae?
6. How does the gospel reach new places today?
7. How did the gospel first come to you?
8. What effect has the gospel had in your life?
9. How can you share the gospel with others?

Colossians 1:9–14

EXEGETICAL IDEA
Paul prayed for the Colossians to know God's will in order that they might live worthy of the Lord and fully please him by doing good works, by growing in knowledge, by persevering, and by joyfully thanking the Father, who had delivered them into the kingdom of the Son.

THEOLOGICAL FOCUS
Believers will walk worthy of the Lord and aim to please him in every way when they know his will and the salvation they have received.

PREACHING IDEA
By experiencing God and understanding what he wants, we can live lives of good works that please him.

PREACHING POINTERS
The apostle Paul lifts up a soaring prayer for the believers in Colossae with intercession following thanksgiving (a good pattern for any prayer meeting!). In one long, magnificent sentence that continues through verse 23, Paul and his team pray for the saints living in the small town of the Roman province of southwest Asia Minor, that they would know God's desire—namely, that they would live for God even as they were empowered by God. In this passage, Paul likely has in view concerns that emerge later in the letter, including the pressure the Colossian believers experienced from false teachings and the unresolved situation between Onesimus and Philemon. Here he prays for them in a general sense that they would know God's will and walk in it. The prayer asks for knowledge, strength, and joy.

Those qualities seem to be in short supply today. For instance, consider joy. The "World Happiness Report" found that in 2018, Americans were less happy than they were the year before and ranked nineteenth, behind Australia and Canada. According to *The New Republic*, psychologists reported in 2019 that anxiety was on the rise.

Closely connected to joy is the issue of strength. Christians often feel powerless to overcome bad habits and besetting sins. Depending on willpower alone to break those habits turns into drudgery and leads only to short-term change, but when we are motivated by joy, strength follows. Obedience becomes a delight.

Where are strength and joy to be found? This rich passage tells us: in deep, experiential knowledge of the salvation Jesus Christ provides. By experiencing God and understanding what he wants, we can exhibit lives of good works that please him.

PAUL'S PRAYER FOR THE COLOSSIAN BELIEVERS (1:9–14)

LITERARY STRUCTURE AND THEMES (1:9–14)

In Colossians 1:9, Paul uses one main verbal idea, "we have not ceased praying and asking" (οὐ παυόμεθα . . . προσευχόμενοι καὶ αἰτούμενοι), to introduce a run-on sentence in Greek that technically goes all the way through verse 20. This long sentence contains increasingly subordinate clauses (e.g., participle, relative pronoun, etc.) with changing referents. By the time we reach verse 20, we are left wondering if Paul himself could remember where his sentence began, for what was initially a prayer for the Colossians (1:9) ultimately becomes a poetic summary of the person and work of Christ (1:15–20). In terms of grammar, therefore, the entirety of Colossians 1:9–20 constitutes one exegetical unit. However, because of the substantial amount of significant theological material within these verses, we will divide it into two preaching units.

In this first preaching unit (vv. 9–14), Paul begins with a statement of continual prayer that the Colossians will be filled with spiritual knowledge (1:9) followed by the purpose of this prayer, that the Colossians will walk worthy of the Lord (1:10a). Then he describes the means by which this worthy walk is accomplished, namely, by bearing fruit in every good work, growing in the knowledge of God, being empowered for steadfastness, and giving thanks to the Father (1:10b–12a). Next, Paul turns to the Father, who has qualified the Colossians for an inheritance, rescued them out of darkness, and transferred them into the kingdom of the Son (1:12b–13). Finally, Paul reflects on the Son, in whom we have the ransom and forgiveness of sins (1:14). This transition to the Son sets the stage for the second preaching unit in verses 15–20.

- ***Paul's Prayer: Knowledge That Leads to Worthy Living (1:9–10a)***
- ***The Worthy Life: How to Live It (1:10b–12a)***
- ***The Father's Work: A Rescue Operation (1:12b–13)***
- ***The Son's Work: Ransom (1:14)***

EXPOSITION (1:9–14)

Paul shifts from thanksgiving for the Colossians' Christian faith (1:3–8) to prayer for their growth as Christians (1:9–14). Paul frequently incorporates prayer into the introductory sections of his letters, and those prayers often introduce themes that will be important to the letter. This is sensible, since the concerns that prompt the letter also prompt prayer. Paul's overarching concern for the Colossians is that they will live a life worthy of the Lord Jesus. He is aware of the real-world challenges they face in their own historical context, including both the particular situation between Onesimus and Philemon and also the broader challenges arising from the competing ideologies and practices so prominent in their own community. Indeed, Paul will warn the Colossians about such opposition in 2:8–23. Paul's prayer, therefore, introduces Paul's desire for the Colossians to learn to live a life worthy of the Lord, who has rescued and ransomed them in such a profound way.

Paul's Prayer: Knowledge That Leads to Worthy Living (1:9–10a)

Paul and his coworkers pray that the Colossians

will know God's will so they will be able to live in a way that is worthy of Christ and pleases him in every way.

1:9. Paul begins with the transitional phrase "because of" (Διὰ τοῦτο; BDAG, s.v. "διά" 2a, p. 225), which indicates a "causal relation with the preceding discourse" of Paul's thanksgiving (1:3–8) and the Colossians' reception of the gospel (Runge, 2010, 48). This phrase hinges Paul's prayer (1:9–14) to his thanksgiving (1:3–8) and indicates that Paul's prayer has been prompted by the same circumstances that led to his thanksgiving. Indeed, Paul has continually prayed for the Colossians "from the day we heard" (ἀφ' ἧς ἡμέρας ἠκούσαμεν), a clear reference again to the time when Paul learned from Epaphras about their faith in Christ (1:4, 8), which itself originated in the day when the Colossians heard the gospel message of God's grace (1:6).

Paul says we—referring to himself and Timothy, and likely his entire cohort too—have "not ceased praying and asking" (οὐ παυόμεθα προσευχόμενοι καὶ αἰτούμενοι). Their prayers are petitionary in nature, as they ask God to act in behalf of the Colossians. Paul's prayer meetings thus involve *both* thanksgiving (see 1:3) and supplication (1:9), and they are asking God to fill the Colossians with "the knowledge of his will" (τὴν ἐπίγνωσιν τοῦ θελήματος αὐτοῦ). Those who aim to please God must know his will before they can do his will.

Prayers of Supplication

Wayne Grudem describes prayer as "personal communication with God, corporate or private" (Grudem, 1994, 376). Prayer includes not only worship of God, confession of sin, and thanksgiving, but also supplication, where we make requests for others as well as ourselves (Frame, 2013, 1053). Prayers of supplication presume by their very nature that prayer changes things. Christians often ponder how prayer can change anything when God is already sovereign over everything, but several passages of Scripture suggest that the presence of active praying, or the lack thereof, will determine what God will do (e.g., 2 Chron. 7:4; Luke 11:9–10; James 4:2). Therefore, John Frame concludes that although "prayer doesn't change the eternal plan of God," it nevertheless remains true that "God's eternal plan has determined that many things will be achieved by prayer, and many things will not be achieved without prayer" (Frame, 2013, 1054).

In Scripture, the will of God can be personal and specific, as when God determines the particular course a person ought to take and he expects obedience from that person. For example, Jesus himself obeyed the specific will of the Father for his earthly life (Mark 14:36; John 6:38–40). But God's "will" can also refer more broadly to "God's saving purpose in Christ" (Wright, 1986, 57) and to the general programs and designs of his operations. Paul seems to have in view this latter, broader sense of God's will—for in Paul's estimation, the Colossians will gain full knowledge of God's will in conjunction "with all spiritual wisdom and understanding" (ἐν πάσῃ σοφίᾳ καὶ συνέσει πνευματικῇ).

Wisdom (σοφία) and understanding (σύνεσις) are synonyms, but with perhaps a slight shade of difference, as described by Lightfoot: wisdom refers to "mental excellence in its highest and fullest sense," while understanding "is the critical application of σοφία [wisdom] that understands the bearings of things" (Lightfoot, 1981, 138). Paul will later say that "all the treasures of wisdom and knowledge" are found in Christ (Col. 2:2–3). To know Christ more fully is to more fully have the wisdom of God, and Paul's aim throughout the letter to the Colossians could be summarized as the imparting of such knowledge about Christ. When the Christians in Colossae learn about Christ in the Scriptures, they gain the kind of wisdom that results in knowing God's will for their lives.

1:10a. But even as Paul prays for the Colossians to be filled with knowledge, he is not interested in knowledge for the sake of knowledge. He expects the increase in knowledge to bring about a transformation in lifestyle among the Colossians. Knowing God's will result in "walking" (περιπατῆσαι) in a manner worthy of the Lord himself. "Walking" here is a clear metaphor for the broader concept of one's manner of life. The idea of walking "worthy" (ἀξίως) elicits the image of a scale in which a standard weight is used as a counterbalance for properly measuring an item or substance. In Colossians 1:10, the Lord (who is Jesus Christ in Col. 1:3; 2:6; 3:24) himself is the standard weight against which the Colossians' manner of life ought to be measured, and to be "worthy" is to measure up to that standard.[1] Could there be a weightier counterbalance for the Christian life?

Walking as a Metaphor

The use of "walk" (περιπατέω) as a metaphor for one's manner of life does not appear in classical Greek literature, but it is common in Jewish literature (e.g., Prov. 8:20; Eccl. 11:9; cf. Sumney, 2008, 46–47; Lohse, 1971, 25–26). In the New Testament, this metaphorical use of walking is "decidedly Pauline," and he commonly uses it in his letters (BDAG, s.v. "περιπατέω" 2a, p. 803; see Gal. 5:16, 25; Rom. 6:4; 8:4; 14:15; 1 Cor. 7:14; 2 Cor. 4:2; 5:7; Eph. 2:10; 4:1; 5:2, 15; Phil. 3:17; 1 Thess. 2:12; 4:1).

This worthy life itself has an ultimate goal, namely, "to please (the Lord) in all respects" (εἰς πᾶσαν ἀρεσκείαν; BDAG, s.v. "ἀρεσκεία," p. 129). Paul's ethics, in other words, are Christotelic, oriented around Christ as the goal of Christian living, even as Paul's theology is Christocentric, oriented around Christ as the central theme (e.g., Col 1:15–20). Paul's vision for the Colossians is strikingly bold. He will settle for nothing less than Christian conduct that fully pleases the Lord, and this general principle applies even to the specific situation of Onesimus and Philemon. Such a grand vision demands concrete and manageable steps that will lead the Colossians toward this destination.

The Worthy Life: How to Live It (1:10b–12a)

Paul explains that the worthy life is achieved by bearing fruit, by growing in knowledge of God, by being empowered by God, and by giving thanks.

1:10b. Paul next details four key steps (each identified in the Greek by a participle of means) by which this worthy life is walked toward the goal of pleasing Christ. First, the worthy life is accomplished "by bearing fruit" (καρποφοροῦντες). Previously, Paul said the gospel "bears fruit" (ἐστὶν καρποφορούμενον; 1:6), but then he was ambiguous about whether he meant this quantitatively or qualitatively. Here in verse 10, Paul leaves no such uncertainty. He qualifies "bearing fruit" qualitatively with "in every good work" (ἐν παντὶ ἔργῳ ἀγαθῷ). This is a broad and all-encompassing statement for the virtuous deeds that ought to accompany the Christian life. Paul will further specify the good works he has in mind in his later exhortations (see 3:5–4:6) and especially in 3:17, where he implores the Colossians to do everything in the name of the Lord Jesus, including every word and every deed.

Second, the worthy life is accomplished "by growing" (αὐξανόμενοι; ptc. of means) in the knowledge of God. Paul earlier mentioned knowledge as a precursor to walking worthy (Col. 1:9), and he now mentions knowledge as an ongoing process of growth by which the worthy life is accomplished. This repetition suggests a spiral of knowledge whereby the worthy life requires previous knowledge even as it produces further knowledge that in turn leads to living the worthy life. "Understanding

1 This is much like Paul's injunction in Ephesians 4:1 to "walk worthy of the calling you have received."

will fuel holiness; holiness will deepen understanding (Wright, 1986, 58).

The Relationship Between Knowledge and Works

Many Christians regard knowledge and works as antithetical to one another. In my (Adam's) own experience, I have witnessed theological debates where some are so intent on being *right* that they run roughshod over one another in the church and seem to have lost sight of the fundamental need for love and peace in the church. On the other hand, some Christian communities swing the pendulum to the other side and develop an anti-scholastic spirit in which they consider too much study to be of no value. Indeed, I have been warned more than once that if I keep on studying, I will be of no further use in ministry, the assumption being that too much knowledge inevitably results in diminished faithfulness.

Like many debates, both sides are right in what they affirm and wrong in what they deny. Paul does not place knowledge and works in opposition to one another. Instead, Paul regards knowledge as the essential foundation to Christian works. Indeed, works are the goal and knowledge is the means. Thus, Paul prays that the Colossians will grow in their knowledge of God's will precisely *so that* they will then walk worthy of the Lord, and continuing in the worthy walk will require continually increasing in knowledge. To grow in knowledge without walking worthy is half-cocked Christianity; to attempt the worthy walk without spiritual knowledge is half-baked Christianity. Both knowledge *and* works are essential and codependent for faithful Christian living.

1:11. Third, the worthy life is accomplished "by being empowered" (δυναμούμενοι; ptc. of means). Paul uses the passive voice to indicate that this power is received from another source outside the Colossians, presumably from God. Paul uses three prepositional phrases to further clarify this empowerment. First, they are empowered "with" (instr. ἐν; see Harris, 2010, 29) all power, as God bestows upon the Christian a full measure of the empowerment necessary for walking worthy. Second, they are empowered "in accordance with" (BDAG, s.v. "κατά" 5, p. 513) the might of his glory—a glory sufficient to supply the power the Colossians require for walking worthy. Third, they are empowered "for" (εἰς) the purpose of attaining an abundance (πᾶς) of endurance (ὑπομονή) sufficient for even "an apparently impossible situation" and patience (μακροθυμία) sufficient for even "an apparently impossible person" (Wright, 1986, 60).[2] Paul prayed knowing that God's glory was sufficient to empower the Colossians for faithfully enduring even the most difficult situations and people.

Paul thereby intimates that the worthy Christian walk is not necessarily an easy walk, for it requires divine empowerment. Again, Paul knows the Colossians have challenges facing them, internal challenges of division and offense (namely, Onesimus and Philemon), and external challenges from other teachings and cultural pressures (Col. 2:8, 16–23). Their Christian walk, metaphorically speaking, will be less a leisurely frolic in a lush meadow, lollipop in hand, than it will be a grueling, uphill slog in inclement weather. But these Christians need not despair, for *in accordance with* the strength of God's glory they are empowered *with* all the power they need *for* full endurance and patience in any situation. And this divine provision, quite naturally, inspires joyful thanksgiving.

2 Similarly, "While ὑπομονή is the temper which does not easily succumb under suffering, μακροθυμία is the self-restraint which does not hastily retaliate a wrong. The one is opposed to *cowardice* or *despondency*, the other to *wrath* or *revenge*. . . . While ὑπομονή is closely allied to *hope* (1 Thess. i. 3), μακροθυμία is commonly connected with *mercy* (e.g., Exod xxxiv. 6)" (Lightfoot, 1981, 140).

1:12a. Fourth, the worthy life is accomplished "by giving thanks" (εὐχαριστοῦντες; ptc. of means) to the Father. For Paul, giving thanks is an additional action by which the worthy life is lived, and it is also the attitude that should undergird the entirety of the Christian life. Further, thanksgiving should be given "with joy" (μετὰ χαρᾶς). If the worthy walk is a grueling trial that requires endurance and patience (Col. 1:11), we might be tempted to walk it with an attitude of complaining rather than of joy. But Scripture frequently presents a Christian paradox of simultaneous joy and suffering. Indeed, James tells us to count it all joy when we face trials of various kinds (James 1:2–3), Jesus instructs us to rejoice in the rewards and blessings that accompany persecution (Matt. 5:10–12), and Paul himself sang hymns in prison (Acts 16:25). Regardless of the situation, joyful thanksgiving remains the appropriate attitude for the Christian walking the worthy walk (Col. 3:17).

Paul thus completes the four means by which the worthy walk is accomplished: bearing fruit, growing in knowledge, being empowered, and giving thanks. Though this would be a reasonable place for Paul to make a grammatical break and end his sentence, he instead continues his rambling sentence unabated even as he makes a sharp thematic turn in the following verses. He seems to forget completely his theme of the worthy life as he transitions away from his thanksgiving to the new theme of the Father (to whom thanks is given) and the work the Father has done in rescuing the Colossians and bringing them into a new kingdom.

The Father's Work: A Rescue Operation (1:12b–13)

The Colossians ought to thank God the Father because he has qualified them for the inheritance, rescued them out of darkness, and transferred them into the kingdom of Christ.

1:12b. In verses 12–13, Paul assigns to the Father three works for which he is to be thanked. First, Paul says to give thanks to the Father because he has "qualified" (BDAG, s.v. "ἱκανόω," p. 473) you. Paul's language indicates clearly that the Father did not merely share his inheritance with the Colossians *despite* their lack of qualifications, but he took the steps necessary to *qualify* them and thereby to entitle them to the inheritance they would ultimately receive. This distinction is notable and preachable. It is one thing for a benefactor to write into their will an unqualified heir who would receive a share of the inheritance. Such a person would not normally be regarded as a legal heir but could be designated as a beneficiary nonetheless. It is quite another thing for a benefactor to select an unqualified heir and to bring about a change of legal status such that they become a legally recognized heir. In our contemporary context, it is the difference between leaving an inheritance for a close family friend as opposed to legally adopting that friend as one's own child.

Old Testament Echo: "to share in the inheritance of the saints"

The Greek term Paul uses for "inheritance" (κλῆρος) technically refers to something given by "lot" or as a "portion" (BDAG, s.v. "κλῆρος" 2, p. 548), but when used in the Old Testament it refers to a "portion of land" and especially a portion received as an "inheritance" (κληρονομία; TDNT 3.759; e.g., Num. 26:52; 33:53; Josh. 18:1; cf. Col. 3:24). Further, Paul uses this term (κλῆρος) along with "share" (μερίς) in Colossians 1:12, even as the two are used together in the Old Testament (Deut. 10:9; 12:12) to refer to "the concrete portion of land assigned to Israel, to a tribe, to a family or to an individual" (TDNT, 3.759). Thus, Paul is using Old Testament language regarding the land of Canaan as an inheritance divided into portions and given by the Lord to the people of Israel. In the same way, Christians saints also have an inheritance, but for Christians, their inheritance is not of the earth; rather, the Christian inheritance is a hope stored up in the heavens

(Col. 1:5) that will be received (Col. 3:24) in the future day when Christ appears in glory (Col. 3:4).

Every believer within the Colossian community has been qualified by the Father for their due portion of the inheritance that belongs to all the saints. Even as the promised land was divided among the Israelites, with each tribe and person receiving their due portion, so also Paul describes a Christian inheritance shared among believers. Here there is no difference and no hierarchy between one Christian and the next (Col. 3:11). The Christians in little Colossae are qualified for an inheritance alongside Christians in such places as Jerusalem and Rome, and within the Colossian congregation, Christian slaves share the inheritance equally with their masters (Col. 3:24). Recall yet again the implications for a Christian community consisting of both Philemon and Onesimus!

1:13. Second, Paul says to give thanks to the Father because he "rescued" (ῥύομαι) us out of the authority of darkness. Darkness (σκότος) indicates "moral darkness" (BDAG, s.v. "σκότος" 3, p. 932), and that Paul mentions the "authority" (ἐξουσία) of this darkness suggests the Colossians were formerly ruled over by this moral darkness. This authority, however, was always subservient to Christ, for all authorities were created through Christ (Col. 1:16) and Christ is now the head over all authorities (Col. 2:10), having disarmed them in the cross (Col. 2:15). Nevertheless, if the Colossians were rescued *out* of such a dark authority, then they lived at a former time *under* such authority. During this former time, they lived the kind of life that merits the wrath of God—sexual immorality, impurity, passion, evil desire, covetousness, etc. (Col. 3:5–8). But now God has rescued believers from the *authority* of moral darkness and called them to live a new life pleasing to their new Lord in every way (Col. 1:10). They may still live in the world of depravity, but they are no longer subject to it.

Paul's Conversion (Acts 26:12–18)

In Colossians 1:13, Paul returns to the first person: God rescued *us*. He thus joins himself to the Colossians' former plight under the authority of darkness, and he includes himself in the rescue God has effected. In Acts 26, Paul recounts his conversion story before King Agrippa, and Paul uses similar terminology to what we find in Colossians 1:12–14, including light and darkness, Jesus as Lord, forgiveness of sins, and deliverance:

"In this connection I journeyed to Damascus with the authority and commission of the chief priests. At midday, O king, I saw on the way a light from heaven, brighter than the sun, that shone around me and those who journeyed with me. And when we had all fallen to the ground, I heard a voice saying to me in the Hebrew language, 'Saul, Saul, why are you persecuting me? It is hard for you to kick against the goads.' And I said, 'Who are you, Lord?' And the Lord said, 'I am Jesus whom you are persecuting. But rise and stand upon your feet, for I have appeared to you for this purpose, to appoint you as a servant and witness to the things in which you have seen me and to those in which I will appear to you, delivering you from your people and from the Gentiles—to whom I am sending you to open their eyes, so that they may turn from darkness to light and from the power of Satan to God, that they may receive forgiveness of sins and a place among those who are sanctified by faith in me.'"

A rescue is of minimal benefit if it does not lead to a better location, for "escape involves not just running away, but arriving somewhere" (Schlink, 1997, 180). So third, Paul says to give thanks to the Father because he "transferred" (BDAG, s.v. "μεθίστημι" 1, p. 625) us into the new kingdom (βασιλεία) belonging to his beloved Son. Whatever else we might say to describe this kingdom, it is first and foremost a kingdom where Jesus, the beloved Son, reigns as king.[3] Those who belong to this kingdom, therefore, are those who recognize Jesus as Lord, even as Paul regards Jesus as Lord within this letter (e.g., Col. 1:3; 2:6; 3:22–4:1; 4:7).

Many scholars further identify a subtle distinction in Paul's writings between the "kingdom of Christ" and the "kingdom of God." Generally speaking (with some exceptions, see Vos, 1979, 259–260; and with some overlap, see Eph. 5:5), when Paul speaks of the kingdom of Christ, he tends to focus on the present reality of what has already been accomplished, but when he speaks of the kingdom of God, he tends to focus on the future reality of what is still to be accomplished (Dunn, 1996, 79).[4] In the present kingdom of Christ, Christ exercises "mediatorial sovereignty" that will one day be "merged in the eternal dominion of God" when Christ hands over his kingdom and it becomes the future kingdom of God (Bruce, 1984, 52; see esp. 1 Cor. 15:24). In the present kingdom of Christ, Christ subdues his enemies one by one; in the future kingdom of God, God reigns absolutely and eternally and there is no warfare (Vos, 1979, 260). The present kingdom of Christ embodies righteousness, peace, joy, and power among saints on earth (Rom. 14:17; 1 Cor. 4:20), as well as a "moral and spiritual sovereignty" (Lightfoot, 1981, 142); the future kingdom of God will be a spiritual kingdom to be inherited by the saints who have embodied such righteousness (1 Cor. 6:9; 15:20; Gal. 5:21).

When Paul mentions the "kingdom of Christ" in Colossians 1:13, his emphasis is likewise on the present reality of what the Colossian believers have already received. He depicts the kingdom of Christ as a present reality in which Christ's reign has already begun and Christ's people have already been transferred into it, even if they continue to live in the same physical space on earth. He presents to the Colossians a realized (or inaugurated) eschatology in which their future hope enters into their present reality. The physical world around them may not have changed, but their spiritual reality has certainly changed. They have become saints in the kingdom where the Son is Lord, and Paul now "hopes to make them saints by dwelling on their calling as saints" (Lightfoot 1981, 142). His prayer, in other words, contains the implicit exhortation for the Colossians to walk worthy of their new Lord.

The Son's Work: Ransom (1:14)

In Christ, the Colossians have been ransomed from their bondage to sin.

1:14. Paul next says that in the Son, "we have the ransom" (ἔχομεν τὴν ἀπολύτρωσιν). The word "ransom" (ἀπολύτρωσις) can be translated "release" or "redemption" (ESV, NIV, NASB, KJV) and was at times used for the manumission of slaves or their being bought back by payment of ransom (BDAG, s.v. "ἀπολύτρωσις," p. 117). The basic idea behind the Greek word is "release by payment of a price," and because this idea fits well with Colossians 1:14 (cf. Eph. 1:7),

3 Helpful readings on the kingdom abound. Vos provides a summary of the kingdom in the teaching of Jesus (Vos, 1948, 372–402). Wright lists everywhere the kingdom is mentioned in early Christian literature (Wright, 1997, 663–70). Bird summarizes the kingdom throughout the New Testament and develops his findings into eschatological categories (Bird, 2013, 247–56).

4 A similar distinction between the present and eschatological aspects of the kingdom emerges in the teaching of Jesus. Vos summarizes these differences as follows: the present kingdom comes gradually while the final kingdom comes catastrophically, the present kingdom is internal and invisible while the final kingdom is visible worldwide, and the present kingdom is subject to imperfections while the final kingdom is without imperfection (Vos, 1948, 384).

the term may be better translated "ransom" (see Morris, 1965, 44–47). With this metaphor of ransom, Paul shifts "from the victor who rescues the captive by force of arms" in 1:12–13 "to the philanthropist who releases him by the payment of a ransom" in 1:14 (Lightfoot, 1981, 142). Though Paul does not mention the price of the ransom here, he specifies in Ephesians 1:7 that this ransom was purchased "through his blood" (cf. Col. 1:20).

Further, in Colossians 1:14, this ransom has accomplished "forgiveness of sins" (τὴν ἄφεσιν τῶν ἁμαρτιῶν). Paul now identifies the former bondage as a spiritual bondage to sin. They had been held captive to "the hostile powers of sin" and to "the wages paid by sin, namely death" (Marshall, 2007, 138). But by the ransom payment of the blood of Christ, the Colossians who are "in Christ" (ἐν ᾧ, where Christ is the referent) have been forgiven of their sin and thereby ransomed out of their captivity to sin. For Paul, to be in Christ is to be in union with Christ by faith—it is the spiritual location of those who have heard and received the gospel (Col. 1:5–6), have placed their faith in Christ (Col. 1:4), have been reconciled to God (Col. 1:22), have received new life in Christ (Col. 2:11–13; 3:1–4), and now live a new life in Christ (Col. 3:5–4:6).[5] In short, being in Christ means belonging to Christ, and those who belong to Christ have been forgiven their sins and set free from the tyranny of sin by the blood of Christ, so they now inhabit the kingdom of the Son and serve their heavenly master, Jesus himself.

THEOLOGICAL FOCUS

The exegetical idea (Paul prayed for the Colossians to know God's will in order that they might live worthy of the Lord and fully please him by doing good works, by growing in knowledge, by persevering, and by joyfully thanking the Father, who had delivered them into the kingdom of the Son) leads to this theological focus: Believers will walk worthy of the Lord and aim to please him in every way when they know his will and the salvation they have received.

In Paul's intercessory prayer, he paints a portrait of the Christian life as a journey that is to be walked. Paul's vision is inspiring—invigorating even—as a good vision ought to be. He inspires them to get off the couch, to study the map and learn the trail, and to follow their Lord toward their destination, which is to live lives fully pleasing to him. We can imagine the Colossians responding at this early juncture with a genuine eagerness. "Yes, we will walk worthy of the Lord! We will please him in every way!" This is the romantic ideal, but it must be accomplished in the real world. Like many ambitious hikers hitting the trail today, their romanticized visions of adventure and grandeur were likely soon confronted with the demoralizing reality of uphill slogs where it takes concerted effort just to put one foot in front of the other.

In the real world of Colossae, Paul casts this prayerful vision to a church mired in tension and unresolved conflict, a church gathered with both Onesimus and Philemon present, a church unreconciled. And the path Paul will call them to walk is hardly a lollipop path up Sunshine Mountain! It will be no small thing for Philemon to set aside conventional Roman wisdom in managing Onesimus's rebellion and to instead receive Onesimus, along with the church community, as a full brother and coheir in Christ.

Therefore, Paul prepares them for the reality ahead by praying for them in their journey. He prays for them not because God cannot work in their lives apart from his prayer, but because God has made known that he works through the prayers of his people. More specifically, Paul prays for the Colossians to know God's will, so they will know the terrain and the specific path God calls them to walk in obedience

5 We will further discuss this theme of union with Christ as it emerges throughout the letter, particularly in a sidebar on Colossians 1:27 and in the theological focus of Colossians 2:6–15.

to Christ. He describes the deeds by which they will walk this path, as they put one foot in front of the other, bearing the fruit of good works and growing in knowledge. He points them to God as the source of their strength to persevere. He calls them to maintain a proper attitude of thankfulness in the journey. And, as final motivation, he reminds them of what they have received from God, which is nothing less than inheritance, rescue into his kingdom, ransom, and forgiveness of sins.

In Paul's estimation, therefore, the Colossians will live lives that please the Lord in every way, if and when they fully understand the Lord's will and what they have received from him in their salvation. Paul's prayer sets the broad trajectory for what Paul will seek to accomplish in his letter, especially in the reconciliation of Onesimus and Philemon, and he sets the example for how Christians can and should pray for one another.

PREACHING AND TEACHING STRATEGIES

Exegetical and Theological Synthesis

Following the opening salutation and prayer of thanksgiving (vv. 1–8), Paul and Timothy turn to intercession. From the day that they had heard of the Colossians they had not ceased to pray for them (v. 9a). They ask that the young church would be filled with the knowledge of God's will (v. 9b). Such knowledge was not simply data crammed into the brain; it was experiential and personal. That kind of knowledge would lead to walking in God's will (v. 10), enduring with patience, experiencing joy, and offering thanks (vv. 11–12). The prayer ends with a vision of what God had done for the Colossians. Like a body of former slaves, he had ransomed them and transferred them from Satan's realm into the realm of his beloved Son (vv. 13–14).

Theologically, this passage reveals humanity's need of knowledge of God's will in order to know how to live for him. The mind of the natural person is dark, but the mind of the spiritual person is illumined; yet even so, Paul's prayer implies that for Christ-followers, the work of illumination is ongoing. So, he prayed for God to grant knowledge of his will, so that they would walk, or "live," in a worthy manner. To do that, the Christ-followers of Colossae needed strength to endure and resist the pressure society exerted.

Preaching Idea

By experiencing God and understanding what he wants, we can live lives of good works that please him.

Contemporary Connections

What does it mean?

What does it mean that by experiencing God and understanding what he wants, we can live lives of good works that please him? The first part of the idea explains what "knowing God" means in the passage. This is, first of all, experiential knowledge as when we say, "She knows her neighborhood like the back of her hand." The knowledge is personal. It can even be intimate as when Genesis states that Adam "knew" his wife Eve and she conceived a son. Experiential knowledge of God comes through prayer, meditation, singing, and other acts of worship that touch the affections. Secondly, "knowing God" means that we understand his will—what honors and delights him, his commandments and precepts. This aspect of "knowing" is gained through instruction from parents, mentors, pastors and others.

The short phrase "live lives" paraphrases the biblical term "walk" (v. 10), and it means to live a certain way, as when we say, "Don't walk in the way of fools," or "Her walk with God is rich." After clarifying the meaning of "walking," the metaphor might be leveraged to talk about the power needed for a long "walk" of obedient living. This passage shows that the power comes from God when we know experientially how his strength qualifies us to share the inheritance, rescues, transfers, redeems, and forgives. By the power of God, believers walk the path of discipleship, obeying God in things large and small such as how we treat family members, decisions about money, entertainment choices, and stewardship of our time.

Is it true?

Is it true that by knowing God's will, we can live lives of good works that please him? The preaching idea may seem beyond the reach of some Christ-followers, but what the passage describes is not a stroll up Sunshine Mountain. Rather, the long walk calls for endurance and patience. Discipleship is a matter of putting one foot in front of the other, not sprouting wings and soaring over life's trials, trusting that as we walk God is strengthening us. The use of self-disclosure or a testimony from a long-time Christian in your organization might help to address the question, "Is it true?" For some groups, the stories of Billy Graham, Elisabeth Elliot, or Mother Teresa might illustrate how they have walked in obedience. Other groups may connect better with more contemporary figures such as musician Bono or Jim Caviezel, who played Jesus in Mel Gibson's *The Passion of the Christ* (2004).

Basic Biographies of Christians

- *The Faith of Mike Pence* by Leslie Montgomery (Whitaker House, 2019)
- *Bono* by Michka Assayas (Riverhead Books, 2006)
- Jim Caviezel: do a search for "why Hollywood dropped Jim Caviezel"

Now what?

How can we experience God and understand what he wants in order to live lives of good works that please him. The following disciplines can help:

- Meditation. When the Word of God does not depart from our mouths and minds, it helps us obey and grants success in our endeavors (Josh. 1:8–9). We might encourage listeners to set aside ten minutes three times a week to simply still their rushing minds and imagine what they are reading in the Bible.
- Private worship. David availed himself of this when the enemy burned his town, took captive his wives and children, and his men turned on him. He "strengthened himself in the Lord his God" (1 Sam. 30:6). This can be done by singing, writing in a journal, or listening to praise music.
- Scripture memory, so that we might not sin against God (Ps. 119:11). Every night at dinner the family might read a passage together until they have it memorized.

Living a life that pleases God is often aided with the help of an accountability and prayer partner. If your church or organization offers counseling, life coaching, or spiritual direction, it might be helpful to highlight those ministries.

Creativity in Presentation

To show that pleasing God with a life of good works, a running story could be used throughout the sermon. Perhaps someone in your church recently climbed Mount Hood in Oregon or walked the Way of St. James (Camino de Santiago) in Spain. Perhaps after college you hitchhiked from Amsterdam to Rome. In order to do that, preparation had to be made and a route planned to reach the destination.

A clip from *The Fellowship of the Ring* (directed by Peter Jackson, 2001) also illustrates how strength and provisions are granted for a journey. On the long quest to destroy the One Ring, the nine travelers have become eight because their leader, Gandalf, has fallen in the mines of Moria. The disheartened and exhausted group limps into the forest of Lothlorien. For many days they recuperate in the forest, and then when they set out to continue the quest, the elf-queen Galadriel gives them *provisions*: food, garments, canoes, weapons, rope, and special gifts suited to each person. The best version of this scene for this illustration is in the extended version of the movie.

A clip from another movie about another quest could serve the same purpose: *The Endurance* (directed by George Butler, 2000), the documentary about Ernest Shackleton's epic journey to discover the South Pole. Perhaps use one of the opening scenes where the explorers are carefully thinking through what provisions they will need.

Testimonies of God's strengthening grace would be a natural fit for a sermon from Colossians 1:9–14. Perhaps a young person could talk about how God strengthened her for a short-term mission; a young couple might relate how God used their small group for support when their first child died; or a widower might talk about what it is like to be alone after so many years, yet not alone, for God is with him.

Another way to apply the preaching idea would be to pray the text for your congregation. Paraphrase the words of Paul's prayer, asking that you and your people also would know God experientially, understand what honors him, and then do it.

The key idea to articulate is this: By experiencing God and understanding what he wants, we can live lives of good works that please him.

- Through prayer and the Spirit's work, God fills us with knowledge of his will (1:9).

- God also strengthens us for the journey (1:11–12).

- This knowledge and strength help us walk the path of good works (1:10, 13–14).

DISCUSSION QUESTIONS

1. What did Paul specifically pray for the Colossians?

2. What is the relationship between knowledge and works in Paul's prayer?

3. What are the four key ways a Christian walks worthily?

4. How did Paul use inheritance, rescue, and ransom to describe Christian salvation?

5. Why do you think Paul placed such emphasis on the past work of God in this prayer?

6. Why did Paul pray this particular prayer for the Colossians? What about their situation inspired such a prayer?

7. What is the vision of the Christian life Paul painted in this prayer?

8. How can Paul's vision of the Christian life be established in our lives and churches today?

9. How can you pray Paul's intercessory prayer for your Christian community?

Colossians 1:15–23

EXEGETICAL IDEA

Paul used poetic language to describe the surpassing nature of Christ because of his great work in creation and redemption, and therefore Paul appealed for the Colossian believers to remain faithful to Christ until they are presented blameless with him before God, for there is no one more exalted than Christ.

THEOLOGICAL FOCUS

Believers must remain in the faith they learned in the gospel, for Christ is exalted over all things in creation and redemption, and he has even reconciled believers to God in order to present them perfect before God.

PREACHING IDEA

Christ is above all, he has done it all, and now we have it all—so don't move at all.

PREACHING POINTERS

In a soaring "hymn," the apostle Paul reminds the believers in the little town of Colossae that Jesus is, as theological formulations would later summarize, the exalted second person of the Trinity. That message hit home because in the Greco-Roman world, multiple gods vied for attention. If people had heard about Jesus, he was probably seen as just the newest deity on the block. The Christ-followers in Colossae knew differently, but the pressure of culture was strong, so Paul reminds them who Jesus is: the firstborn from the dead in whom the fullness of God dwells.

Today the situation is similar. People choose religious beliefs from multiple options. One of the options is even "none," which James Emery White claims is the fastest-growing religious demographic (*The Rise of the Nones*, Baker, 2014). A 2020 report from Religion News Service indicates that the "nones" are as numerous as evangelicals or Catholics: 23.1%. Many people are attracted to Jesus (even while they are turned off by organized religion), but they may be creating their own version of the Son of God. Views about Jesus abound: he is a good man, a revolutionary, a sage, and so forth. This passage from Colossians sets the record straight. In the face of religious pluralism, the modern preacher can follow the apostle Paul: lift up Jesus Christ as the eternal Son of God and urge listeners to remain steadfast in their faith because Christ is above all, has done it all, and now we have it all—so we should not move at all.

THE HYMN ABOUT CHRIST (1:15–23)

LITERARY STRUCTURE AND THEMES (1:15–23)

Paul now takes a poetic turn in the letter as he extols the Son with a "hymn" (1:15–20), followed by an application of that hymn to his Colossian audience (1:21–23).[1] The hymn stands apart because of its distinctive poetical features, including brevity, verbless clauses, repetition (both in terms and in structure), and parallelism. It uses short phrases and elevated content to say *more* about Christ with *fewer* words. The hymn itself in some ways seems out of place in the letter as a whole. In the first fourteen verses of the letter, Paul writes in a deeply personal way to the Colossians, using the first and second person voices to forge a personal connection. But in verses 15–20, Paul uses the third person exclusively to speak about the Son. His Colossian audience fades out of view during these verses, only to be abruptly and dramatically brought back into view in verse 21 ("And *you* . . .") as Paul applies the broad reconciliation of Christ specifically to the Colossians (note ἀποκαταλλάσσω in both verses 20 and 22).

The hymn contains two strophes joined together by a bridge (see sidebar). The first strophe of the hymn (1:15–16) presents the role of Christ with regard to creation, while the second strophe of the hymn (1:18b–20) presents the role of Christ with regard to redemption. The bridge transitions between the two strophes by describing Christ as the sustainer of all creation (1:17) and as the head of his redeemed people, the church (1:18a). When we study the hymn, we find ourselves swept up in a rising stream of adoration for the Christ of the hymn.

- ***Christ Is Creator of All Things (1:15–16)***
- ***Christ Is Sustainer of All Things (1:17–18a)***
- ***Christ Is Redeemer of All Things (1:18b–20)***
- ***Christ Has Redeemed You (1:21–23)***

Literary Structure of the Hymn (1:15–20)

N.T. Wright provides the simplest diagram of the best structural analysis of the hymn (Wright, 1990, 101).[2] He divides the hymn into two strophes (A and A′ below) conjoined by a bridge (B and B′ below) as follows:

A "who is" (ὅς ἐστιν; 1:15)
 "because in him" (ὅτι ἐν αὐτῷ; 1:16)
 "through him and for him" (δι' αὐτοῦ καὶ εἰς αὐτὸν; 1:16)

B "and he is" (καὶ αὐτός ἐστιν; 1:17)
B′ "and he is" (καὶ αὐτός ἐστιν; 1:18a)

1 When we use the term "hymn" to describe Colossians 1:15–20, we do not intend to suggest that these verses technically fit an ancient sense of a hymn, nor that these verses should be equated with modern hymnody. Instead, we use "hymn" to describe how in these verses a poetic structure and exalted terminology are being used to offer praise to a divine figure. For a technical discussion, see Fowl, 1990, 31–45.

2 Several scholars agree with Wright (e.g., Aletti, 1993, 89–93; Bruce, 1984, 106; Baugh, 1985, 236; etc.), while others find only two strophes with no abridgement (e.g., Schweizer, 1982, 57; Lohse 1971, 44–45; Lohmeyer, 1953, 51–52; etc.). The differences between various structural analyses bear minimal consequence for interpreting the themes of the hymn.

A′ "who is (ὅς ἐστιν; 1:18b)
"because in him" (ὅτι ἐν αὐτῷ; 1:19)
"through him . . . for him" (δι᾽ αὐτοῦ . . . εἰς αὐτόν; 1:20)

The parallelism between the first (A) and second (A′) strophes is also seen in the repetition of the terms "firstborn" (πρωτότοκος; 1:15, 18), "whether" (εἴτε; 1:16, 20), and "heavens and earth" (ἐν τοῖς οὐρανοῖς καὶ ἐπὶ τῆς γῆς; 1:16, 20).

EXPOSITION (COL. 1:15–23)

The hymn extols Christ with the most exalted statements about Christ that we find in all of the New Testament; indeed, in comparison to all other extant early Christian writings, "there never was a higher Christology than this" (W. Barclay, 1963, 45). It is beautiful verse on a beautiful theme. Paul places the hymn early in the letter to recall for the Colossians what they have already learned about Christ from Epaphras. Remember again the historical context wherein the Colossians are facing difficult challenges regarding false teaching, false practice, and the conflict between Onesimus and Philemon. Paul will address all of these things in the letter, but only within the common understanding that Christ is head of creation and of the church, for it is through Christ that all things have been created and reconciled. These theological truths about Christ will serve as the foundation for the rest of Paul's exhortations in the letter, beginning with his application of the hymn directly to the Colossians (1:21–23).

Christ Is Creator of All Things (1:15–16)

The first strophe of the hymn presents Christ as the image of God and as exalted over all creation, for all things were created through him.

1:15. The first section of the hymn (1:15–16) describes Christ in relation to God and creation. The opening statement declares Christ to be the "image" (εἰκνώ) of the "invisible God" (τοῦ θεοῦ τοῦ ἀοράτου). God is invisible because he is spirit (Gen. 1:2), but though he is invisible he does not remain unseen. Instead, God has revealed himself in various ways throughout history. Creation itself in some ways evidences the existence of its Creator (Ps. 19:1–6), and he also reveals himself through the law he has revealed (Ps. 19:7–11). Further, God sometimes revealed his presence through physical phenomena such as brightness (Exod. 24:10, 17), clouds (Exod. 19:16; 24:16; 34:5), smoke (Exod. 19:18), winds (Exod. 32; 1 Kings 19:12), and thunder (Exod. 19:16; Isa. 6). But on the whole, the making of images of God was expressly forbidden (Exod. 20:4–6), and Paul himself criticizes those who have exchanged the glory of the Creator for an "image" (εἰκών) resembling created things, thereby elevating the image above the Creator himself (Rom. 1:23).

But now Paul declares Christ to be the image of God who in some way manifests the "likeness" or "appearance" of God, being as it were a "living image" of God (BDAG, s.v. "εἰκών" 2, p. 282). This recalls Genesis 1:27, where God created humanity in his own image, blessed them, and tasked them with the God-like duties of filling the earth with life and reigning over the earth. They would carry his reign forward into his creation, perhaps similar to how the images of a ruler were heavily propagated via coins, statues, reliefs, and the like throughout his empire as representations of his authority. In one sense, therefore, we can say that all humans are the "image of the invisible God." But in Colossians 1:15, Paul suggests that Christ is the image of God in a distinctive way—the image *par excellence*, an exceedingly superior and exceptionally unique image.

Christ, in other words, is the image of God in a way in which the rest of humanity is not. Though Scripture does not explicitly describe the image as being lost or marred when humans sinned, the New Testament does imply that the image needs to be restored, and this restoration happens as believers are conformed into the image of Christ (Col. 3:10; cf. Rom. 8:29). Thus, Christ is the exemplary image of God, the standard image to which human image bearers must be conformed. Christ is the faithful representation of God, being nothing less than the very Son of God. To look upon Christ then is to look upon the invisible God. "Whoever has seen me," Jesus says, "has seen the Father" (John 14:9).

The very next statement in the hymn places Christ in relation to creation as the firstborn of all creation. The term "firstborn" (πρωτότοκος) can have a temporal sense with regard to birth order, or it can have a hierarchical sense regarding the "special status associated with a firstborn" (BDAG, s.v. "πρωτότοκος" 1–2, p. 894). From a lexical perspective, the difference between these two meanings is sometimes minimal and even overlapping, especially in many ancient cultures, where the one who proceeds first from the mother's womb holds the position of honor in the family and receives a larger share of the inheritance. In Luke 2:7, Luke uses "firstborn" (πρωτότοκος) with a temporal sense to describe Jesus as the first of his siblings to emerge from Mary's womb.

Here in Colossians 1:15, however, the hymn describes Christ as the firstborn of all creation, and the lexical difference between a temporal and a hierarchical reading takes on immense theological significance regarding the nature of Christ as a created or uncreated being. If "firstborn" is temporal, then Christ would be the first created being to proceed from God and, by implication, Christ is therefore a created being. But if "firstborn" is hierarchical, then Christ holds a position of status over and above all of creation, but he is not necessarily a created being. Thus the one word "firstborn" carves a deep canyon of Christological distinction. If Christ is a created being, then He would necessarily be a lesser being than the God who created him, and we would then be remiss to speak of Christ as *being* God in any Trinitarian sense.

Historically, those who have argued for the temporal view have pointed to the lexical use of the term in which birth order overlaps with the hierarchical status, and they point to the temporal use of the term in Colossians 1:18 to speak of Jesus as the first among many to be raised from the dead. They have then argued by implication that if Jesus precedes creation as a firstborn, then Christ must himself also have been created (see excursus "The Arian Controversy and the Nicene Creed").

Nevertheless, there are good reasons for interpreting "firstborn" (πρωτότοκος) with a hierarchical sense in Colossians 1:15. From a lexical perspective, though the term most frequently refers to birth order and chronology, it does not always do so. For example, Psalm 89 extols the Davidic king with idealizing terminology that may even be described as messianic (e.g., the king is the "anointed" one in Psalm 89:20). In Psalm 89:27, two parallel lines say God will make this king both his "firstborn" (πρωτότοκος; Ps. 88:28 LXX) and "the highest of the kings of the earth." In this case, the second parallel line ("the highest of the kings of the earth") establishes and carries forward the meaning of the first line ("firstborn") with a clearly hierarchical sense. As the firstborn, the king will be "exalted" (ὑψηλός) over all other kings, and birth order is entirely irrelevant, for the kings do not all come from the same mother (cf. Rev. 1:5).

Further, in the immediate context of Colossians 1:15, Jesus is an active agent in the work of creation rather than a passive recipient. The work of creation is done in, through, and even for him. Paul is making the emphatic point that when it comes to the Creator/creation divide, Christ is absolutely Creator over against absolutely "all" (πᾶς) of creation without exception. Thus we may conclude that the hymn presents Jesus as the firstborn in a hierarchical but not necessarily a temporal sense. Some English translations reflect this interpretation with the translation "firstborn over all creation" (e.g., NIV, NLT, HCSB) rather than the ambiguous literal translation "firstborn of all creation" (e.g., ESV, NRSV,

KJV). This interpretation is further affirmed by the fourth-century Nicene Creed.

The Arian Controversy and the Nicene Creed

The ambiguous nature of the term "firstborn" inspired a generation of contentious debate in the fourth century that is now known as the Arian Controversy. On one side, Arius (ca. A.D. 250–336) argued that Christ was a created being, and on the other side, Athanasius (ca. A.D. 293–373) argued for Christ's eternal existence. Our best summary of Arius's teachings now comes to us from an encyclical letter written by Bishop Alexander of Alexandria to condemn Arius and his teachings. The letter describes Arius's position in the following manner:

"God was not always a Father, but there was a time when God was not a Father. The Word of God was not always, but originated from things that were not; for God that is, has made him that was not, of that which was not; wherefore there was a time when He was not; *for the Son is a creature and a work*. Neither is He like in essence to the Father; neither is He the true and natural Word of the Father; neither is He His true Wisdom; but He is one of the things made and created. . . . And the Word is foreign from the essence of the Father, and is alien and separated therefrom" (trans. Schaff and Wace, 1892, 70; emphasis added).

On the other side, Athanasius made a sharp distinction between the idea of being begotten and being made, so that Christians could affirm the idea of Christ as firstborn while denying that he was a created being. The controversy was resolved when the Council of Nicaea produced the Nicene Creed in A.D. 325: "We believe . . . in one Lord Jesus Christ, the Son of God, begotten of the Father, [the only begotten, i.e., of the essence of the Father, God of God, and] Light of Light, very God of very God, *begotten, not made*, being of one substance with the Father; by whom all things were made [in heaven and on earth] . . ." (trans. Schaff, 2006, 3:668–69; emphasis added).[3]

Though we would be remiss to anachronistically read later church debates back into the Colossian text, we would be equally remiss to ignore the interpretive lens church history now offers us. Such a lens can sharpen our vision and provide greater clarity into the text, not least by showing us the ultimate theological outcomes of our interpretive decisions. We do well to consider carefully such statements that have been wrought through many years of intense debate and have now endured fifteen centuries of ceaseless theological discourse.

1:16. In his very next statement, Paul provides further clarity on the relationship between the Son and creation. Christ is the firstborn over all creation precisely "because" (ὅτι)—note the causal relationship—Christ played an active role within the work of creating all things. Paul expounds on Christ's role in verse 16 with a series of prepositional and elaborative phrases.

Paul uses three short prepositional phrases to ascribe to Christ a robust role in creation, leading to what David Pao calls "prepositional Christology" (Pao, 2012, 138). First, all things were created "in him" (ἐν αὐτῷ), suggesting that Christ's person is the sphere *within* which the authority or "creative energy" of creation is contained (Harris, 2010, 40). Second, all things were created "through him" (δι' αὐτοῦ), suggesting Christ is the agent whose hand played an active role in accomplishing creation. Third,

3 The Nicene Creed of A.D. 325 also contained a postscript specifically condemning proponents of Arianism: "And those who say: there was a time when he was not; and: he was not before he was made; and: he was made out of nothing, or out of another substance or thing, or the Son of God is created, or changeable, or alterable—they are condemned by the holy catholic and apostolic church" (trans. Schaff, 2006, 3:669).

and perhaps most shockingly, all things were created "for him" (εἰς αὐτὸν), suggesting that Christ is in some way the goal or *telos* of all creation. The first two prepositions echo the creative role Jewish literature ascribed to Wisdom as the sphere and agent of creation (e.g., Wisdom is the "master workman" of creation in Proverbs 8:30; cf. Ps. 104:24; Prov. 3:19), but there is no Old Testament parallel for the third preposition where Christ is the goal of creation (Bruce, 1984b, 64). This is distinctive to Paul and underscores Paul's overall point in the hymn of magnifying the Son to an absolutely unique position. Creation exists exclusively *for* the Son alone. The Son's exaltation is without parallel.

Further, Paul strengthens the exhaustive and absolute nature of all the things created in, through, and for Christ with a series of elaborative phrases. "All things" (πᾶς) includes first those things located "in the heavens and on the earth" (ἐν τοῖς οὐρανοῖς καὶ ἐπὶ τῆς γῆς). This dual phrase echoes Genesis 1:1, where in the beginning God creates the heavens and the earth, and this statement proves to be a summary statement for the totality of all created things. Everything that is not God the Creator belongs to the realm of creation, described as the heavens and the earth. The next phrase, "visible and invisible" (τὰ ὁρατὰ καὶ τὰ ἀόρατα), parallels the heavens and the earth in reverse order. In Paul's cosmology, the heavens are the realm of the invisible, while the earth is the realm of the visible. This combination of phrases underscores the totality of creation that is subject to the Son, by, through, and for whom it was created.

Seeing the Invisible

Creation consists of *both* physical things that can be seen with the eye *and* invisible things that cannot be seen with the physical eye. Our modern scientific revolution has opened our physical eyes to see many of the wonders contained within the physical creation in our earth. Microscopes allow us to see the most intricate details of physical matter, down to atoms and even the parts of atoms, while telescopes expand our vision to include seemingly infinite solar systems and universes. But this expanded physical vision has led to an increasing worldview of materialism whereby many people deny the existence of the invisible creation associated with the heavens. Christians, too, sometimes struggle to acknowledge an invisible realm where God dwells along with heavenly creatures. Consider, for example, how the heavenly throne room is described in texts such as Ezekiel 1 and Isaiah 6. The description of visible *and invisible* realms in Colossians 1:16 reminds us that the invisible aspects of God's creation are no less real than the visible.

Verse 16 ends with a list of four terms further articulating what is included in the totality of creation. Each of these four terms can describe earthly or spiritual powers, but Paul's other uses of these terms suggest he has spiritual powers especially in view here. "Thrones" (θρόνοι) are the seats occupied by those in power, whether they be earthly kings such as King David (Luke 1:32) or God himself, whose throne is heaven (Acts 7:49). "Dominions" (κυριότητες) reflects the "majestic power" wielded by lords, sometimes by "a special class of angelic powers" (BDAG, s.v. "κυριότης" 2–3, p. 579; cf. Eph. 1:21). "Rulers" (ἀρχαί) are those who bear authority, whether they be earthly rulers (e.g., Titus 3:1) or, especially in Paul, angelic or spiritual powers (e.g., Rom. 8:38; Eph. 3:10; 6:12). "Authorities" (ἐξουσίαι) are those who bear the power to rule and may also refer to earthly authorities (e.g., Luke 12:11; Rom. 13:1–3) but more often in Paul to spiritual, angelic authorities (e.g., Eph. 3:10; 6:12; 1 Pet. 3:22).

The differences between these terms need not be pressed into four distinctive types of spiritual powers, since Paul may be using overlapping or synonymous terms to accomplish his main point, which is to draw together the totality of the angelic powers belonging to the spiritual realm and make them all subject to Christ.[4] When Paul describes Christ as the firstborn over *all* creation, because *all* things were created in, through, and for him, Paul really does mean *all* in the most absolute sense, extending even to the unseen. For Paul, the proverbial saying rings true that "all means all and that's all that all means."

Christ Is Sustainer of All Things (1:17–18a)

The bridge of the hymn presents Christ as the one who is over all things, and the one through whom all things are held together.

1:17. The first phrase of this bridge describes Christ as "before all things" (πρὸ πάντων). This simple statement recalls Christ as the "firstborn," since the preposition "before" (πρό) serves as the prefix "first" in "firstborn" (πρωτότοκος). This repetition also raises the same ambiguity as the term "firstborn" with regard to whether "before" should be read here with the temporal meaning "earlier than" or the hierarchical meaning "precedence in importance or rank" (BDAG, s.v. "πρό" 2–3, p. 864). Does Christ precede all things, or have supremacy above all things? The same arguments apply as we considered in our discussion of Colossians 1:15, so we may simply carry our previous conclusion over to this verse. Christ indeed precedes all created things temporally since he is not a created being, but the emphasis here falls especially upon his privileged position.

Further, in Christ all things "hold together" (συνίστημι). He not only brought all things into existence, but he now sustains all things and gives them their ongoing coherence and unity (BDAG, s.v. "συνίστημι" B3, p. 973; cf. 2 Pet. 3:5). This phrase aptly sits at the center of the bridge, and thereby at the center of the hymn, and it may be understood in light of both what precedes and what follows. Looking back to the first strophe in Colossians 1:15–16, Christ is the sustainer of all creation, giving to creation its ability to continually exist. Looking forward to the second strophe in 1:18b–20, Christ is the sustainer of the church, drawing the church together in unity as the head of the church he has redeemed and empowers the church to endure and to survive all manner of hardship. This phrase, therefore, is the true "pivotal line" of the hymn (Beasley-Murray, 1980, 174). Christ continues to hold together both the cosmos that was created through him and also the church that was created through the redemptive work of his death and resurrection.

1:18a. The final line of the bridge (1:18a) completes the transition from creation to the church and looks forward to the hymn's final strophe (1:18b–20). Christ is now "the head of the body, *which is* the church." As the "head" (κεφαλή), Christ occupies an elevated status of authority with regard to the body. The ongoing ambiguity between the hierarchical verses temporal interpretation no longer applies; the "head" is a clear indicator of hierarchical relationship (BDAG, s.v. "κεφαλή" 2, p. 542). Christ is in the exalted position of supremacy and authority with regard to the body. For the sake of clarity, and lest anyone should think he is referring to the literal, physical body of Christ, Paul clarifies that the body is indeed a metaphorical reference for the "church" (ἐκκλησία; cf. 1:24).

Throughout the letter, Paul will further develop the metaphor of Christ as sustainer and head of the church. The church, like a

4 Walter Wink shows that Scripture often uses these terms to refer to spiritual powers, but because the first century world often blurred the distinction between human powers (i.e., social, cultural, and political powers) and spiritual powers, Paul may have both in view (Wink, 1984, 13–17, 64–66). For example, the goddess Roma was regarded as a spiritual power even as she represented the political power of the Roman empire (see Wright, *Colossians*, 115–118).

body, receives nourishment through its head so the body can grow, and its parts are held together by ligaments, even as even as the members hold fast to Christ as the head (Col. 2:19). Believers must bear with one another (Col. 3:13) and put on love, which binds them together in Christ (Col. 3:13). Thus, Paul can say that the Colossian believers were called to "one body" (Col. 3:15), for there is only one head, Christ, who holds that one body together in unity. With Christ firmly established as the head of the church, the church is in turn better equipped for maintaining unity even when facing the external pressure of false teaching (e.g., Col. 2:16–23) and the internal pressure of offense and dissension (e.g., Philemon and Onesimus). The body metaphor, therefore, provides Paul with numerous opportunities to press specific implications and applications for church life.

Christ Is Redeemer of All Things (1:18b–20)

The second strophe of the hymn presents Christ as the divine one who has redeemed all things through his death and resurrection, so that he is now the head of the church.

1:18b. In this second strophe of the hymn (1:18b–20), Christ is depicted as the redeemer of all things. The second strophe begins with another ambiguous term. Christ is either the "beginning" or "ruler," both of which are appropriate translations for the Greek term (ἀρχή; BDAG, s.v. "ἀρχή," p. 137). In this case, though we cannot eliminate the hierarchical interpretation, we prefer the temporal interpretation because of the special emphasis the context places upon the resurrection of Christ as the first of many future resurrections.

This temporal interpretation carries into the repetition of the term "firstborn" (πρωτότοκος), where Christ is now the "firstborn out of the dead" rather than the "firstborn of all creation" as in 1:15. By his resurrection, Christ is certainly exalted over and against all others who have died and yet remain dead. But from a temporal perspective, Christ's resurrection carries an inherent sense of anticipation. As the *firstborn* from the dead, we naturally expect more to follow in being raised from the dead, much like Christ as the firstfruit of resurrection anticipates a future harvest when the dead will be raised at the return of Christ (1 Cor. 15:23). He is the firstborn temporally, having preceded all others in resurrection, and this in turn provides the grounds for his eternal privilege in the resurrection.

Indeed, Paul connects his preceding resurrection as the precise grounds for his exaltation regarding all who will be raised. Christ was raised as the firstborn "in order that" (ἵνα + sbjv.) he might be in "the first place" (BDAG, s.v. "πρωτεύω," p. 892) among all things. By being raised first, Christ is exalted to the first position, for he alone holds the distinguished honor of being the "first" to be raised from the dead. For all eternity, this honorific title will follow him. He is our trailblazer, the courageous pioneer who has gone from the grave to a place where no man has gone before. He is our Christopher Columbus, our Sir Ernest Shackleton, our Neil Armstrong. He has mapped the resurrection terrain and charted the course from death to life, that we might follow in his footsteps and that he might forever be preeminent among us.

1:19. The following two parallel lines offer the twofold reason why Jesus is worthy to have the eternal preeminence of being the firstborn from the dead. Jesus is the firstborn from the dead (rather than someone else), first, *because* (ὅτι) of his ontological connection to the divine nature of God (1:19), and second, because of the reconciliation he accomplished in the cross (1:20).

First, regarding ontology, Jesus is connected to the divine nature in what the hymn describes cryptically as an indwelling by "the fullness." The term translated "fullness" (πλήρωμα) refers to completeness, or to having the full measure of something (BDAG, s.v. "πλήρωμα" 3b, p. 830; TDNT, 6.303). Paul does not identify the nature of that "something" here in Colossians 1:19, but he does identify it in Colossians 2:9, where all the fullness "of deity" (τῆς θεότητος) dwells in Christ "bodily" (σωματικῶς). The fullness thus refers to the full measure of the divine nature of God himself, and the tautological repetition of "all" and "fullness" underscores the hymn's emphasis on the supremacy of Christ, in whom dwells the absolute full measure of the divine nature. This emphasis surpasses how God previously dwelt among his people through the *shekinah* glory in his holy temple (1 Kings 8:27; Ps. 68:16 [67:17 LXX]). God now dwells not in a place, but in the incarnate body of Christ.

TRANSLATION ANALYSIS: Colossians 1:19 presents translation difficulty. There are two verbal components, the verb "pleased" (εὐδόκησεν) and the infinitive "to dwell" (κατοικῆσαι), but only one noun phrase, "all the fullness" (πᾶν τὸ πλήρωμα), which may function as either the subject or the direct object (the neuter πᾶν having the same form in both the Greek nominative and accusative cases) of either the verb or the infinitive. Confused yet? Some translations take "all the fullness" as the direct object of "pleased" and supply "God" as the implied subject, thus producing the translation, "God was pleased that all the fullness should dwell in him" (e.g., HCSB, NIV, KJV, NASB). Alternatively, if "all the fullness" is personified and taken as the subject of "pleased," then we would translate, "all the fullness was pleased to dwell in him" (e.g., ESV, NRSV). The difference between the two options is mitigated when we take into account Colossians 2:9, where the fullness refers specifically to the divine nature—to God himself! Thus, we may personify the fullness in light of the implied divine nature, leading to the appropriately dynamic translation, "God in all his fullness was pleased to dwell in him" (Harris, 2010, 45; cf. NLT).

The hymn thus maintains a certain distinction between the person of God and the person of Christ while bringing together their shared divine essence. Again, the hymn brings us into a direct encounter with the marvel of Trinitarian theology as expressed by the Athanasian creed, "That we worship one God in trinity, and trinity in unity; Neither confounding the persons; nor dividing the substance" (Schaff, 2006, 3.691; cf. Holcomb, 2014, 66).[5] This, then, is the mystery of Christ, that though Christ is at once both human and divine, he nevertheless remains fully divine in his essence; and though Christ is fully divine in his essence, he nevertheless remains distinctly the Son in his person. Perhaps it is owing to his complex nature that the hymn can make such profound statements with so little explanation, for the mystery of his being defies explanation but demands exclamation.

1:20. The next line in verse 20 continues the explanation introduced by "because" (ὅτι) in 1:19, and provides a second reason explaining why the Son has the honor of being firstborn from the dead: not only *because* God in all his fullness dwells in him (1:19), but now also *because* of the work of the reconciliation accomplished by his blood. The reconciliation itself was accomplished by God, who is the

5 As C. S. Lewis says in his famous introduction to Athanasius's work "On the Incarnation," the Athanasian Creed is "not exactly a creed," and it was most likely not written by Athanasius (Lewis, 2011; originally published 1944). Instead, the creed was probably composed in the early sixth century as a summary of what previous church councils (i.e., Nicaea and Chalcedon) determined regarding the nature of the Trinity (Holcomb, 2014, 63–71).

implied subject of the infinitive "to reconcile" (ἀποκαταλλάσσω). Throughout the hymn, "all things" (τὰ πάντα) refers cosmically to all of creation, including the entire heavens and earth (Col. 1:16). This includes not only humans, but also the material world of inanimate nature and the immaterial world of spiritual beings (Harris, 2010, 46). All things were created by Christ and made subject to him, and yet the need for reconciliation implies that at some point enmity entered the picture. The hymn itself does not articulate when or how this enmity arose, but elsewhere Paul points directly to the sin that entered the world through the trespass of the first Adam in the garden of Eden (Rom. 5:12–14) and the subsequent curse upon the earth that subjected all creation to decay (Rom. 8:20–22; cf. Gen. 3:17–19).

> *WORD STUDY:* The Greek word for "reconciled" (ἀποκαταλλάσσω) appears only three times in the New Testament (Col. 1:20, 22; Eph. 2:16) and it does not appear in extrabiblical literature prior to Paul's usage (TDNT, 1.258). It may, therefore, be a term coined by Paul by attaching a prefix (ἀπό) to the common term "reconcile" (καταλλάσσω), perhaps for the purpose of intensifying the reconciliation Paul is describing (Porter, 1992, 140–41). This accords with the expansive scope of reconciliation Paul envisions in Colossians 1:20, where all things are reconciled by Christ. The utterly unique nature of this reconciliation may be the reason why Paul employed such a unique and intensified word to describe it.

Though the hymn does not describe the implicit enmity that required reconciliation, it does specify the means by which reconciliation was achieved. The reconciliation was accomplished "*by* peace-making" (εἰρηνοποιέω; ptc. of means) that was accomplished through the "blood of the cross." What irony!—that Christ would make peace by means of the violent bloodshed of crucifixion. Let us not forget that the cross in the first century was the barbaric tool employed by the Romans for the subjugation of their enemies, including Jews and Christians. And yet Christ turns such hostility against itself. By surrendering himself to violence, he defeats violence and achieves peace. Enmity turns to peace when the Son of God endures the enmity of the cross.

The hymn further describes this reconciliation in immediate and cosmic terms. The scope of the reconciliation is entirely universal here, extending to all of creation, "whether on the earth or in the heavens" (cf. 1:16). There is nothing untouched by his reconciliation. And the hymn also suggests that this reconciliation has already been accomplished. Jesus has, after all, already shed his blood on the cross. Taken by itself, therefore, the hymn would suggest that all of creation should already be reconciled to God. Yet we rightly wonder how this can be when we still observe so much enmity toward God in our world, both as active hostility or persecution toward God's people and passive neglect of God by countless peoples. Indeed, Paul himself suggests that creation continues to groan in its bondage even after the cross, and God's people continue to long for their final adoption (Rom. 8:20–22). And in the very next verses (Col. 1:21–23), Paul will describe this reconciliation as if it was only actually applied to the Colossian believers when they heard and received the gospel from Epaphras (Col. 1:3–8). Thus, the reconciliation the hymn describes aligns more closely to the future eschatological reality of the new heavens and new earth, when all things will have been made new and there is no more sin, or curse, or death, or any of the effects of sin (Rev. 21:1–5).

The hymn presents to us another instance of realized or inaugurated eschatology in which Paul speaks of our future hope as something that has already been accomplished and is already being effected in the present time (cf. Col. 1:13). Throughout Colossians, Paul stretches the future cosmic reconciliation into the present in light of the past (the cross). He says that Jesus has already triumphed over the rulers and authorities (Col. 2:15) and believers have already been seated with Christ (Col. 3:1–3). Yet at the same time, the idea of the incompleteness of Jesus's work permeates Colossians. Believers still await the day they will be revealed with Christ in glory (Col. 3:4); in the meantime, the gospel message must continue to be preached and to reach new people (Col. 1:6, 23; 4:2–6), believers must continue in their faith (1:23) and grow in maturity (Col. 1:9–11; 2:6–7; 3:5–4:1), and Paul will continue to labor on behalf of the church (Col. 1:24–2:5), even personally embodying "what is lacking" in Christ's afflictions (Col. 1:24).

How can Paul both affirm the present, universal reality of reconciliation, and yet speak of so much left to be accomplished? We might say the reconciliation has been fully accomplished, but it is not yet fully effected. The cross is in the past, the blood of Christ has been shed, and the means of reconciliation has been fully accomplished. But the full and cosmic realization of this reconciliation is our eschatological hope to be fully effected in the new heavens and earth. In the present time, there remains a "ministry of reconciliation" whereby God makes his plea through the gospel to "be reconciled to God" (2 Cor. 5:18–20). The reconciliation is only presently effected insofar as people receive the gospel message and put their faith in Christ. Paul unveils the personal and present application of reconciliation in the following section of Colossians 1:21–23.

Christ Has Redeemed You (1:21–23)

Paul applies the hymn directly to the Colossians, who were enemies of God, but now they have been reconciled by Christ, and therefore they must remain in the faith that they might one day be presented holy before God.

1:21. If the cosmic reconciliation has been fully accomplished but not cosmically effected, then verse 21 focuses our attention on where this reconciliation is being effected in the present time, namely, among believers. Paul begins verse 21 with a dramatic shift from the third person to the second person to bring his Colossian audience back into the picture. The focus now shifts from a cosmic focus to a personal focus, from considering the heavens and the earth to considering "you."

> *TRANSLATION ANALYSIS:* The first two words of Colossians 1:21 ("and you") merit special attention because of the extreme dislocation of the pronoun "you" (ὑμᾶς). In the Greek text, "you" appears in the accusative form (ὑμᾶς), indicating that it functions as a direct object in the sentence. However, the next transitory verb (i.e., a verb that takes a direct object) is "reconcile" (ἀποκατηλλάγητε) in 1:22. Thus, "you" (ὑμᾶς) has been separated from its verb by the entire clause of 1:21 ("who once were alienated and hostile in mind, doing evil deeds"). This is known as "left dislocation," since "you" has been dislocated to the left of its accompanying verb. Such dislocations can function rhetorically as what the ancient rhetorician Longinus calls a "vivid second person," an "abrupt introduction of direct speech" that uses a "direct personal address" to "put the hearer in the presence of the action itself" (Longinus, *On the Sublime*, 26–27). After the hymn's exclusive use of the third person to describe the Son, the sudden appearance of the dislocated second person "you" in verse 21 serves as a "vivid second person," placing the Colossians directly and personally within the cosmic action of the reconciling work of Christ in verse 20.

Paul describes their personal reconciliation in terms of a contrast that has been effected between their former condition and their present condition. "Formerly" (ποτέ), the Colossians were at enmity, "alienated" (ἀπαλλοτριόω) from God and were nothing short of "enemies" (ἐχθρός) of God in their minds as evidenced by their evil deeds. Here Paul explicitly describes the enmity that required reconciliation, an enmity that the hymn assumed but did not define. Now Paul defines this enmity in personal rather than cosmic terms. Paul characterizes the Colossians' pre-Christian condition as one of estrangement and hostility toward God, but notably Paul does not mention here God's hostility toward them. The enmity is distinctly one-sided. Yet surely when the Colossians were in their former, pre-reconciled condition, they did not consciously think of themselves as God's enemies. They may have formerly participated in various pagan religions known to the Roman Empire, or they may have been Jewish, but in either case, they probably did not consider themselves to be God's enemies. Indeed, prior to Epaphras presenting the gospel to them, the Colossians had probably heard very little about Christ. Yet for Paul, such ignorance is not an excuse (see Rom. 1:18–23; 2:14–16); instead, ignorance is an insult. Because they did not know Christ, they were *ipso facto* enemies of God.

Unwitting Enemies of God

Even the apostle Paul, in his former life of persecuting Christians, fancied himself to be operating in obedience to God, not in enmity. Thus, when Saul (the pre-Christian Paul) headed toward Damascus on a mission to arrest any followers of Christ he might find, he did so with the permission and authorization of the high priest in Jerusalem (Acts 9:1–2). He operated with intentional submission to his religious leaders and, therefore, ostensibly with obedience to God. After he becomes an apostle, Paul reflects back on his life before Christ and he characterizes himself as "being zealous for God" and living "according to the strict manner of the law of our fathers" (Acts 22:3) even as he "persecuted this Way [i.e., Christians] to the death" (Acts 22:4). And still later, Paul says he "was convinced that I ought to do many things in opposing the name of Jesus of Nazareth," including imprisoning them and voting for their deaths and persecuting them with "raging fury" (Acts 26:9–11). Thus, Paul develops a new perspective on his own past, that even when he thought he was obeying God, he was in fact an enemy of God (cf. Gal. 1:13–14).

1:22. But that was then, and this is now! Paul announces the present reality with the resounding declaration, "but now" (νυνὶ δέ). A deep shift has taken place in the present time, a contrast has been invoked, so that what once was, no longer continues to be. The hostility toward God was in the past, a former way of life. The transformation from that past to a new present occurred when "he reconciled" (ἀποκατήλλαξεν) you. We find in 1:21 both the same term for reconciliation (ἀποκαταλλάσσω) and the same means for accomplishing reconciliation as we found in the hymn's final statement of 1:20. In the hymn, the reconciliation was accomplished by means of the blood of the cross, and in 1:21, the reconciliation has been accomplished "through the death," pointing to the particular death of Jesus on the cross. This death was a literal death experienced by Jesus, not in the metaphorical body of the church (as in 1:18) but in the physical "body of his flesh" (ἐν τῷ σώματι τῆς σαρκὸς αὐτοῦ). Thus Paul applies the cosmic reconciliation envisioned in 1:20 directly and personally to the Colossians in the present moment.[6]

6 Lightfoot understands this application of the reconciliation more broadly in terms of the Gentiles and their relationship to God through the gospel, rather than more personally applied specifically to the Colossian believers (Lightfoot, 1981, 161). Indeed, the term "alienation" (ἀπαλλοτριόω) refers in its limited New Testament usage to Gentile alienation (Eph. 2:12; 4:18; see Foster, 2016, 202–203). However, the immediately following exhortation to remain firm in the faith (1:22) and the specific narrative told in 1:3–8 suggest Paul has in mind the Colossian believers who received the gospel from Epaphras.

On Reconciliation with God

With regard to reconciliation in 2 Corinthians 5:17–21, Seyoon Kim writes: "Paul never says that God is reconciled (or, that God reconciles himself) to human beings, but always that God reconciles human beings to himself or that human beings are reconciled to God. It is not, in fact, God who must be reconciled to human beings but human beings who need to be reconciled to God. Nor is it by people's repentance, prayers or other good works that reconciliation between God and human beings is accomplished, but rather by God's grace alone" (Kim, 1997, 103; cited by Volf, 2000, 10).

This personal application brings important clarity to the broad sweep envisioned by the hymn's cosmic reconciliation. The hymn alone suggests a universalism in which the reconciliation was automatically accomplished and applied to all of creation (including all people) at the moment of the cross. Yet Paul's description of the Colossians' experience of reconciliation suggests that they were not reconciled until many years after the cross when they received the gospel from Epaphras and placed their faith in Christ Jesus (Col. 1:3–8). They were not, therefore, reconciled automatically at the moment of the cross. The hymn's broad statement in 1:20 should not be taken as evidence of a universalism whereby all mankind have been reconciled regardless of their faith or faithfulness regarding Christ. On the contrary, Paul suggests that even the Colossians themselves still await the full realization of their reconciliation, which will only be received in their eschatological presentation before God, when there will also be a judgment consisting of both reward and punishment (see Col. 3:24–25).

Indeed, God has reconciled the Colossians for a specific future purpose, "to present" (παραστῆσαι; inf. of purpose) them holy, blameless, and irreproachable before God. The language of presentation here recalls both the Mosaic system of sacrifices and the future judgment of Christ. The Old Testament rituals, as described in the Levitical law, centered around the holiness of God and the need for God's people to be holy because God is holy (i.e., Lev. 11:44–45; 19:2; 20:7, 26; 21:8). The remedy for unholiness included the bringing or "presenting" (ἵστημι; e.g., Lev. 16:7, 10 LXX) an animal as a substitutionary sacrifice. The animal would be holy and blameless (Lev. 1:3, 10; 3:1, 6; 4:3, 23; etc.) while the worshipper was unholy and guilty. When God reconciles the Colossians, his goal is to present them to himself in the moral condition previously known only to the animal sacrifices. They will themselves be holy and blameless before him because of the blood of Christ in the cross.

Paul's language of presentation also invokes a legal setting in which the Colossians will be presented before God's judgment seat (i.e., 1 Cor. 8:8; 2 Cor. 4:14). They will there be found to be not only holy and blameless, but also "irreproachable" (ἀνεγκλήτους) and without guilt before him. This eschatological goal also has present implications. The Colossians are already holy as saints (ἅγιος; Col. 1:2, 4, 12; 3:12); and Paul famously instructs the Roman Christians to present themselves as living sacrifices, holy and pleasing to God (Rom. 12:1). Church leaders are to exemplify these traits in the present time, even being irreproachable (1 Tim. 3:10; Titus 1:6–7). God has a definite eschatological purpose of completing the work of making his people holy and blameless before him, but that work is also being undertaken in the present, that God's people might be becoming before God what they will one day be before God.

1:23. Paul next issues an indirect warning and command by way of a conditional statement (see sidebar "Translation Analysis: A Conditional Clause in 1:23"). The final accomplishment of God's eschatological purpose is itself conditional upon the Colossians' enduring faithfulness in the present time. Paul will further describe the transformation of character and the moral conduct that must characterize their faithfulness (namely, in 3:5–4:6), but at this point in the letter he simply describes their faithfulness as staying fixed upon Christ. They must "remain" (ἐπιμένω) where they are. So long as they don't move away from Christ, they will realize their presentation before God.

TRANSLATION ANALYSIS: The Greek construct Paul uses in Colossians 1:23 (εἴ + an indicative verb) indicates a first-class conditional clause. In some contexts, first-class conditions assume the truthfulness of the condition for the sake of argument, prompting some scholars to translate first-class conditions with "since" rather than "if." If we interpret Colossians 1:23 in this fashion (thus, "*since* you remain in the faith"), we find a strong support here for a doctrine of perseverance. However, the translation "since" goes beyond what the grammar supports by obscuring the conditional nature of the statement, overstating what may be implied by the first-class construction, and proving problematic in many contexts (Wallace, 1996, 690–94). In fact, the grammatical construction itself does not indicate the truthfulness of the condition; such an interpretation can be applied only by context (Zerwick, 1963, §§ 303–7). Thus, the translation "if" retains the true conditional nature of Paul's statement and in turn reveals the rhetorical meaning lying just beneath the surface.[7] Paul's deeper message is an appeal for the Colossians to enact the condition and to remain in the faith in order that they might experience the consequence of being presented before God as holy and blameless (1:22). *If* the consequence of remaining in the faith is eschatological presentation before God as holy and blameless, then the application is obvious to all: remain in the faith!

They must remain "in the faith" (τῇ πίστει). Paul does not emphasize the individual and subjective nature of *your* faith or belief in Christ; rather, he emphasizes the external and objective sense of *the* faith as the content of the gospel presented to them by Epaphras. The faith is a place to be inhabited or, as Paul next describes, a foundation *upon* which to remain. Thus Paul uses architectural imagery to describe how they remain. They remain *by* being firmly "established" (τεθεμελιωμένοι; per. ptc. of means), "firm" (ἑδραῖοι; adjective), and "not shifting" (μετακινούμενοι; pres. ptc. of means) away from their foundation, which is "the hope of the gospel." Surely we can all appreciate a building that rests firmly and securely upon its foundation without moving. Surely the Colossians could appreciate such a building, living as they did in an area prone to earthquakes! In the gospel, they have been established upon a firm foundation. So long as they continue upon that foundation and don't move away from it, they will surely realize the eschatological purpose for which they were reconciled, their presentation before God as holy, blameless, and irreproachable.

Perseverance of the Saints in Colossians

What implications, if any, does Colossians 1:22 have for broader discussions of eternal security (or lack thereof) for believers? If Paul's conditional statement is to have its proper effect as warning and command, then it must be taken as a real indication that believers could indeed fail to reach the eschatological goal of their faith. They can move away from the gospel and abandon their faith in such a way that God will not present them holy and blameless before him. However, when we reach Colossians 2:10–13, we encounter Paul's language of union with Christ whereby believers have died with Christ and been raised to new life in Christ. If believers move away from their

7 Wallace gives an example of a pragmatic meaning lying just below the surface of a conditional sentence. When a mother says to her child, "If you put your hand in the fire, you'll get burned," she is really saying, "Don't put your hand in the fire!" (Wallace, 1996, 693).

faith and lose their salvation, then this saving work must also effectively be undone—believers must be *un*-united from Christ and move from new life back to the old state of being dead in sin. But Scripture describes union with Christ as a one-way street. We read of believers moving from death to life but never from life to death, of being united to Christ but never of being torn asunder from him. So Colossians leaves us in the same tension we find throughout Scripture. Eschatological salvation is both guaranteed (see Eph. 1:14) and conditional (Col. 1:22–23). We may not solve the theological debate, but we can resolve to continue in the faith, for so long as we continue in the faith, our salvation is indeed guaranteed.

The second part of verse 23 brings the entire section (1:15–23) to a conclusion and transitions to the next section about Paul's ministry (1:24–3:5). The very gospel that the Colossians have been established upon is the same gospel that is being preached in all creation under heaven, of which Paul himself has become a servant. Paul echoes the hymn's emphasis on the totality of creation, and he also recalls the hyperbole he used in the thanksgiving to describe the presence and growth of the gospel worldwide (1:6). At the time Paul penned this letter, the gospel was not literally being preached everywhere in creation, though arguably there may have been gospel believers in most major regions of the Roman Empire. Paul's statement was not designed to provide an empirical census of the spread of Christianity; rather, his statement points toward his own apostolic ministry of taking the gospel to all nations because the good news of the gospel is for all nations (1:26). This is the nature of Paul's own ministry for the gospel, to which Paul, a "minister" (διάκονος) himself of the gospel, next turns (1:24–29).

THEOLOGICAL FOCUS

The exegetical idea (Paul used poetic language to describe the surpassing nature of Christ because of his great work in creation and redemption, and therefore Paul appealed for the Colossian believers to remain faithful to Christ until they are presented blameless with him before God, for there is no one more exalted than Christ) leads to this theological focus: Believers must remain in the faith they learned in the gospel, for Christ is exalted over all things in creation and redemption, and he has even reconciled believers to God in order to present them perfect before God.

Few, if any, other texts in the New Testament compress so much theology into so few words. In just six short verses (1:15–20), the Christ-hymn presents us with some of the New Testament's most exalted statements about the person, position, and work of Christ, and how his work applies personally to Christians.

The hymn says regarding the *person* of Christ that he is the image of God and that all the fullness of God dwells in him. He simultaneously reveals the divine being and he is the divine being. The hymn also presents his exalted *position* in relation to creation and redemption. He precedes and is exalted over all creation, he is the head of the body (the church), and by his resurrection he is preeminent over all who will be raised from the dead. The hymn connects his exaltation closely to his *work* in creating and redeeming all things. All creation was created in him (as the sphere), through him (as the agent), and for him (as the goal). By his death he reconciled all things and his resurrection led to his exaltation. When we put all this together, we can affirm that he indeed is exalted over all things in creation and redemption and he holds it all together. Who can compare to Christ? He is truly unparalleled. He is exalted far beyond our imagination.

Yet at just the moment the hymn elevates Christ into a transcendent place beyond our grasp, Paul draws him back within reach, reminding us that the surpassing work of this exalted Christ has been applied directly and personally to us by faith. When Paul applies the hymn to the Colossians in verses 21–23, he tells the story of their experience with Christ in the past, present, and future. They (in the past) were enemies of God, but now (in the present) they have been reconciled by Christ and they must therefore remain in the faith, that they might (in the future) be presented holy before God. This is the story of every Christian who hears and receives the hope of the gospel. We have been swept up into the triumphant work of Christ in his death and resurrection, we have been reconciled to God by the death of Christ, and we have the future hope of resurrection and righteousness in the judgment.

Though the practical implication for believers is in many ways self-evident, Paul makes it explicit: believers must remain in the faith they have received (1:23). Indeed, to depart from Christ would be eternally disastrous, for there is no other being capable of reconciling believers to God and presenting them holy before him. This point was perhaps best summarized by an old, expiring farmer who articulated his Christian hope from his deathbed with these words: "The way I see it, it's like this: if a man doesn't have Christ, what has he got?" Apart from Christ, we have nothing, but Paul draws out the implications for those who have everything in Christ. His logic is simple: Christ is above it all and Christ has done it all and in Christ you have it all; therefore, don't move at all.

PREACHING AND TEACHING STRATEGIES

Exegetical and Theological Synthesis

Writing what may be the most concentrated theology of the New Testament, Paul uses a poetic creedal statement, perhaps a hymn of the early church, to describe the nature and roles of Jesus. He is "the image of the invisible God" (v. 15) and "in him all the fullness of God was pleased to dwell" (v. 19); these phrases speak about the deity and incarnation of Christ. Paul also describes him as the "firstborn of all creation" (v. 15), meaning that he was supreme overall. Furthermore, Paul depicts him as creator and sustainer of all things in heaven and earth (vv. 16–17), the "head of the church," "the beginning," and "the firstborn from the dead" (v. 18). Here the term "firstborn" refers to time: Jesus was the first one to be raised, and his resurrection was a down payment that anyone in union with him will also be raised.

The "hymn" also describes Jesus's work. He reconciled all things in heaven and earth by the blood of the cross (v. 20). This universal cosmic reconciliation is an example of inaugurated eschatology with the future depicted as something already accomplished that was in the process of coming to full fruition. Paul does not dwell on cosmic reconciliation but moves quickly to apply it to Colossians. The enmity between them and God was erased. Jesus could now present them as holy, blameless, and above reproach before God (v. 22).

Although this passage emphasizes the supreme glory of Jesus Christ and the efficacious work he performed at the cross, humans have a part to play also. The Colossians were to "continue in the faith" and not shift from the hope of the gospel that they heard from Epaphras and of which Paul had been made a minister (v. 23).

Preaching Idea

Christ is above all, he has done it all, and now we have it all—so don't move at all.

Contemporary Connections

What does it mean?

What does the first phrase of the preaching idea mean: "Christ is above all"? The passage answers that in many ways—the image of the invisible God, the firstborn of all creation, the head of the church, and so forth. As later theological formulations would put it, he is the second person of the Trinity. The Nicene Creed (written around A.D. 325) states that he is "true God from true God, begotten not made." To explain that Jesus is the "foundation" (v. 23), a construction worker could be invited to share about the importance of foundations. Or perhaps a personal trainer could describe "core strength," the body's "foundation" that aids posture and flexibility. Other terms in the Christ-hymn also convey that Christ is above all. One of those is "firstborn" (vv. 15 and 18). This may create confusion because it sounds as if Jesus was created or came into existence after the Father. But the term refers to hierarchy rather than time sequence. "Firstborn" is another way of saying that Christ is above all.

What does the second phrase of the preaching idea mean: "he has done it all"? This summarizes the work of reconciliation accomplished by Jesus's death (vv. 20–22). Through the blood of the cross God made peace between himself and the Colossians, and indeed between himself and all of creation. The reconciliation this passage describes is an example of inaugurated eschatology: it is fully accomplished—nothing needs to be or can be to be added to it—but it is not yet fully effected. An analogy of D-Day may help. When the landing at Normandy was successful, victory in Europe was assured. The United States had entered the war and the Axis powers were declining, but the long push to Berlin still lay ahead and the date of final victory was not yet known. In terms of the Colossians, even though Jesus had died decades before Epaphras visited them, they were still alienated from God. They needed a messenger to preach the gospel to them, and they needed to believe the gospel. This is why Paul says that we currently have the ministry of reconciliation (2 Cor. 5:18) even though Jesus accomplished reconciliation.

How about the third phrase: "and now we have it all"? This means that believers are no longer alienated and hostile in mind toward God (v. 21). Jesus has made peace with God. Cross-references could be used to flesh out the spiritual benefits that come because of union with Christ—we are chosen, adopted, blessed, redeemed, and forgiven (Eph. 1:3–7); and we are assured of victory and eternal life (1 John 5:4, 11; Rom. 8:11). In addition to "vertical" reconciliation with God, Jesus's death also inaugurates "horizontal" peace between people. This is the theological basis for the instructions that come later in the book and in Philemon: masters and slaves who are in Christ should be reconciled to each other.

What does the final phrase mean—so don't move at all? This summarizes verse 23. Reconciliation is personally appropriated only if we "continue in the faith, stable and steadfast." Jude says something similar: "Building yourselves up in your most holy faith and praying in the Holy Spirit, keep yourselves in the love of God" (vv. 20–22).

The four phrases are the points of an outline at the end of this section.

Possible Outline

Because this passage is so theologically dense, it may be difficult to handle in one sermon. Perhaps the four phrases could become the Preaching Ideas for a four-part series:

- Christ (vv. 15–20)
- Us
  - Past: We Were Alienated (v. 21).
  - Present: We Are Reconciled If We Continue in the Faith (v. 22a, 23).
  - Future: He Will Present Us Without Blemish (v. 22b).

Is it true?

Is it true that humans need to be reconciled? The need for horizontal reconciliation can be easily demonstrated with current examples of wars, racial tensions, political divisions, and generational differences. The need for vertical reconciliation might be harder to swallow for some people. The text's assertion that outside of Christ people are hostile toward God may sound severe. Postmodern standards of right and wrong tend to be situational, personal, or tribal—we let ourselves down, or we let each other down—but verse 21 emphasizes that outside of Christ we are in state of rebellion against God. One way to demonstrate this could be by quoting Jesus: "Whoever does not believe is condemned already" (John 3:18). Another way could be analogy: if an actor in a play repeatedly disregards the director's instructions, this would create a rift in their relationship because when we obstinately reject the director's instructions, we simultaneously reject the director. The Creativity in Communication section below offers a few stanzas of a poem that illustrate hard-heartedness that results in alienation from God.

In this text, even ignorance of Christ does not excuse us or heal the alienation. As the book of Romans teaches, general revelation provides enough knowledge about God, so that we are without excuse. The illustration in the following sidebar "Ignorance as Insult" may help.

Ignorance as Insult

On one occasion, I (Adam) was conversing with a gentleman from Scotland when the subject of American baseball arose. When I mentioned the Yankees, the other fellow responded with casual indifference and sincere ignorance: "Who are the Yankees?" As every baseball fan knows, the Yankees are a polarizing team—you either cheer for or against them, you either love them or you hate them—and I do *not* cheer for them. But from my Scottish friend, I discovered an entirely new level of insult: he had not even heard of them! What could be a greater slight to the Yankees than to simply not know they even exist?

Now what?

In light of the fact that Jesus has done it all for us, what response should we make? The last phrase of the preaching idea answers: don't move at all. But how? In *Mere Christianity*, C. S. Lewis (1952a, 124) gives this concrete advice: "One must train the habit of Faith [by making] sure that . . . some of its main doctrines shall be deliberately held before your mind for some time every day. That is why daily prayers and religious reading and church-going are necessary parts of the Christian life. We have to be continually reminded of what we believe. Neither this belief nor any other will automatically remain alive in the mind. It must be fed."

Training "the habit of Faith" might include:

- Listening regularly to the Word, perhaps using dailyradiobible.com. On this daily podcast, Hunter Barnes reads the Bible aloud, and by listening for fifteen minutes a day, you can hear the Old Testament once and the New Testament twice in one year.
- Reading Christian books. The quality of books varies greatly, but perhaps a list of recommendations could be made available. The list might include classics that fit well with Colossians 1:15–23 such as *Knowing God* and *Keep in Step with the Spirit* by J. I. Packer, and *Loving God* by Charles Colson.
- Singing and listening to music that magnifies Father, Son, and Spirit. Music penetrates the heart and helps ideas lodge. As Plato said, poets and singers have more influence in a state than lawmakers "because rhythm and harmony find their way into the inward places of the soul" (*The Republic*, bk. 3).
- Courses. Many seminaries and organizations offer inexpensive or free online courses in theology, church history, Bible study, etc.

Courses to Help Ground Us in the Faith

- "Discovery Series" from Our Daily Bread Ministries.
- Seminary courses in partnership with the Gospel Coalition.
- Free courses from Dallas Theological Seminary.

Creativity in Communication

Because the Christ-hymn was probably an early creedal statement, the use of a creed, perhaps in the conclusion of the sermon, might be appropriate. The congregation could recite the Nicene or Apostles' Creed to remember that they are part of the universal church and that our faith is firm, the same faith of Paul, the Colossians, and the early church. If reciting an ancient creed is foreign to your organization, perhaps an original confession could be written and read. The sidebar has one that I (Jeffrey) wrote.

A Confession of Faith

We believe in God the Father:
Creator, Sustainer, Lawgiver, Redeemer, and Judge. He is over all, and through all, and in all.
We believe in Jesus Christ, his only begotten Son:
He is the resurrection and the life.
Whoever believes in him has eternal life.
We believe in the Holy Spirit:
Sent from the Father, he baptizes, fills, seals, guides, and graces the Church.
Father, Son, and Spirit:
from everlasting to everlasting,
Amen.

To illustrate how reconciliation is both "vertical" and "horizontal," a cross might be displayed. The long vertical beam pictures how God came down in order to make us holy, blameless, and above reproach before him (v. 22). The horizontal beam represents the distance between people as with the Jews and Gentiles in the first century. Paul argues in Ephesians that Jesus came to "reconcile us both to God in one body through the cross, thereby killing the hostility" (Eph. 2:16).

To foster horizontal reconciliation, some ministers swap pulpits. This can be powerful especially if the churches are different culturally such as African-Caribbean and Euro-American, or denominationally such as those from Holiness and Reformed traditions. Similarly, churches might band together in cooperative efforts for evangelism, homeless ministry, or foster care. A yearly highlight in Jeffrey's church is "Night to Shine" with the Tim Tebow Foundation. Local churches as well as local colleges cooperate to host a prom for disabled people.

The following facts and demonstration could help portray Jesus as creator (v. 16): the Sun is 93 million miles away. The North Star is 400 trillion miles away. The star Betelgeuse is 880 quadrillion miles away (that's 880 followed by fifteen zeroes). Holding a tennis ball to represent the sun (2.7 inches in diameter), and the edge of a dime to proportionally represent the size of the earth (0.0247 inches), step off twenty-four feet to demonstrate the distance between the Sun and the Earth. The auditorium where you are speaking will be far too small to demonstrate the longer distances, so continue with a verbal analogy to explain the distance to Alpha Centauri, Statistics like this can be found with an internet search on "size of the universe."

To illustrate verse 17, "In him all things hold together," perhaps a youngster could be invited to display an elaborate Lego model. The "creator" knew the design, put everything in place, and locked it together. Before-and-after pictures could be projected—thousands of pieces, then an elaborate and cohesive whole.

To demonstrate our need for horizontal reconciliation, a video clip of political rancor could be shown. If the video is of a foreign culture, the point could be made without appearing to take a side in American politics.

And to help convey the irony of the passage (by surrendering to violence, Jesus defeated violence), story or analogy of a great reversal might help vivify the *greatest* reversal. For example, if your congregation appreciates illustrations from sports, the greatest comeback in Super Bowl history—New England's stunning victory in 2017—can show a remarkable turnaround. Similarly, reversals appear regularly in literature. Aristotle called this technique "peripeteia" (*Poetics*, 1452a), and examples include the story of Cinderella, *The Prince and the Pauper* by Mark Twain, and the movie *Pursuit of Happyness* (directed by Gabriele Muccino, 2006). The last example is the true story of Chris Gardner, who was homeless for almost a year before he found success as an investor.

Published in 1888, William Henley's poem "Invictus" (meaning "unconquerable") depicts a hard heart that needs to be reconciled to God.

> Out of the night that covers me
> Black as the pit from pole to pole,
> I thank whatever gods may be
> For my unconquerable soul. . . .
>
> It matters not how strait the gate,
> How charged with punishments the scroll,
> I am the master of my fate:
> I am the captain of my soul. (vv. 1, 4)

The irony of the cross was scandalous in the first century. As Paul said in 1 Corinthians 1:23, it was a stumbling block to the Jews and foolishness to the Greeks. To help convey the repugnance of the cross to first-century minds, a quotation from *The Passion of the Christ* (Mel Gibson, 2004) could be used. One of the criminals crucified next to Jesus scoffs, "Why do you embrace your cross, you fool?" Likewise, ancient graffiti from around the year A.D. 200 depicts a man with a donkey's head on a cross. Underneath are scrawled words: "Alexamenos worships his god."

Michael Card develops the theme of the scandalous cross in the cover song "Scandalon" (1985) as does Phil Mehrens in "Sovereign Lord" (2008).

Vector traced from "Ancient Rome in the Light of Recent Discoveries" (1898) by Rodolfo. Public domain.

Be sure to stress the main point and the main *person* of the text. It's all about Jesus and how we draw our spiritual life from him. That's why we stay true to him and his gospel. Christ is above all, he has done it all, and now we have it all—so don't move at all.

- Christ is above all (1:15–19).
- Christ has done it all (1:20).
- Now we have it all (1:21–22).
- So don't move at all (1:23).

DISCUSSION QUESTIONS

1. What does "the image of the invisible God" mean? (Note: this question—what does *x* mean—could be used for any of the phrases describing Christ.)

2. What are some implications for us from the description of Jesus as "head of the body" (v. 18)?

3. Share your own story of being "alienated and hostile in mind" but now being reconciled to God.

4. Do you have a similar story of being alienated to a person or group? How were you reconciled?

5. Verse 23 challenges us to continue in the faith. What tempts you to drift from the "hope of the gospel"?

Colossians 1:24–29

EXEGETICAL IDEA

As an apostle, Paul was entrusted by God with an obligation to proclaim the mystery of Christ to all people, including the Gentiles, that all people might be united to Christ and brought to maturity in Christ. Toward this end, Paul labored exhaustively and suffered extensively.

THEOLOGICAL FOCUS

In Christ, God's mysterious plan has been made known, so that all people are invited into saving union with Christ, exhorted to grow to maturity in Christ, and called to embrace the mission of making Christ known to all people.

PREACHING IDEA

The mystery of Christ concealed is now revealed.

PREACHING POINTERS

With a touch of autobiography Paul returns to the theme of his own ministry as an apostle—how he suffered and labored to present everyone mature in Christ. Yet even as he speaks of his afflictions, there is also joy and confidence because the suffering came in his role as a minister of the mystery that was hidden for ages. That mystery is summarized as the "gospel," or "good news," the whole magnificent story about the person and work of Jesus—his divinity, incarnation, sacrificial death, resurrection, intercession, and imminent return. By making peace through the cross, Jesus broke down the wall to include Gentiles as part of his covenant people, so that his righteousness and honored standing before God became theirs also. Thus, the Gentiles experienced the "hope of glory" (v. 27). That is the good news, and ministers like Paul made it known.

The same good news operates today as well. And God still uses spokespeople like Paul to steward the message. Yet some followers of Christ find it difficult to manage their stewardship. We tend to be reticent in sharing the good news, the hope of glory. Perhaps we find it easier to talk about current events or personal ailments. This is understandable in our pluralistic culture, where certainty can be seen as close-minded and sharing might be seen as proselytizing. This passage challenges and encourages us to work hard in evangelism with the inspiration and courage God provides to make the good news known, because the mystery that was once concealed is now revealed.

PAUL'S UNIVERSAL MINISTRY (1:24–29)

LITERARY STRUCTURE AND THEMES (1:24–29)

In Colossians 1:24, Paul indicates a transition in his letter with the word "now" (νῦν). He shifts away from his reflections on Christ (1:15–23), and now develops the theme with which he concluded that previous section, which is his role as a minister of the gospel (Col. 1:23). In the Greek text, this entire section (1:24–29) is another long, run-on sentence as Paul employs a series of relative pronouns to connect his phrases together, but most English translations break this sentence into smaller sentences to make the paragraph readable.

This passage leads us into some deeply rewarding theological reflections about Christ and the gospel. At the same time, this text also includes some of the most challenging exegetical problems in the entire book. It is not immediately clear what Paul means when he says his own sufferings somehow fill up what is lacking in the afflictions of Christ (1:24), and when Paul describes his labor to make known the mystery of Christ (1:26), he uses such mysterious language that we might wonder whether he has really made the mystery known at all! But in the end, the rich theological truth of "Christ in you" (1:27) compels Paul to exhaust himself with endless labor in order to see all people brought to full maturity in Christ (1:28–29), and in this, Paul serves as our example.

- ***Paul's Sufferings (1:24–25)***
- ***The Mystery (1:26–27)***
- ***Paul's Proclamation (1:28–29)***

EXPOSITION (1:24–29)

In these verses, Paul establishes his credibility in writing a letter to the church in Colossae. He writes to believers with whom he does not have a personal relationship, and though the Colossians have surely heard of Paul the apostle, Paul himself does not presume they will understand the nature of his ministry or why he would write to them. Therefore, Paul here establishes his own credibility as an apostle, identifies himself with Christ, assures the Colossians that they have the fullness of every truth about Christ, and establishes the auspices under which he writes them a letter. It is because Paul has been stewarded by God with an obligation to make known the mystery about Christ that Paul suffers and labors to proclaim Christ to all people, and this "all people" includes even the Colossians whom he has never met. Thus, Paul describes his universal ministry in 1:24–29 to establish the context for his particular ministry to the Colossians in 2:1–5, and he thereby aims to compel the Colossians to listen to what he says in his letter.

Paul's Sufferings (1:24–25)

Paul rejoices because he sees how his sufferings accomplish the mission God has given to him of making Christ known.

1:24. Paul begins his description of his ministry with a discussion of his own sufferings, and this paragraph presents a number of vexing interpretive problems revolving around the precise nature of how Paul's own sufferings could somehow accomplish what is lacking in Christ's afflictions. Careful exegesis of this difficult passage requires us to walk diligently through the various lexical, grammatical, and theological details that will lead us to a prudent interpretation. We will conclude that Christ in his suffering has fully and finally accomplished all that is necessary for our redemption, so that there is nothing lacking in the quality or sufficiency of his atoning work. But his work requires his followers to take up the subsequent mission of making Christ known to all people, and it is with regard to this ongoing mission that Paul sees his own sufferings contributing to what is yet required with regard to Christ's afflictions.

Paul begins by saying literally, "I now rejoice in the sufferings in your behalf" (Νῦν χαίρω ἐν τοῖς παθήμασιν ὑπὲρ ὑμῶν). The term "now" (νῦν) may be temporal and reflect an emphasis upon Paul's imprisonment at the time of his writing the letter, but more likely Paul uses "now" as a literary transition within the letter. He is "now" shifting topics away from the Christological abstractions of 1:15–20 to the more personal focus on his own ministry (1:24–29) and its application to the Colossians (2:1–5).

Technically speaking, Paul does not claim these sufferings as his own, but he refers to them in a disembodied sense as "the sufferings" (τοῖς παθήμασιν); however, he goes on to say later in this same verse that these sufferings occur "in my flesh" (ἐν τῇ σαρκί), so we are justified in understanding these as Paul's personal sufferings, or "my sufferings" (e.g., KJV, ESV, NIV, NRSV). Paul's sufferings include, but are not limited to, his present chains and imprisonment (see Col. 4:18; cf. 2 Cor. 11:23–33). Suffering is ubiquitous to the Christian experience in the New Testament—and suffering is even promised to us as Christians! (2 Tim. 3:12)—and we are commanded to endure suffering with the abnormal attitude of rejoicing (Rom. 5:3–5; James 1:2–4; 1 Peter 4:12–13). We will all suffer, but will we all rejoice? Rejoicing in suffering arises from a deep assurance of God's providence, whereby we rest in the confidence that our suffering is not in vain. If God is both sovereign and good, and if his plans are never sadistic or arbitrary, then we must view our sufferings as fruitful and productive contributions to the accomplishment of God's will in all things.

Indeed, Paul's own rejoicing correlates directly with his perception of what his sufferings are actually accomplishing. Paul speaks in 1:24 of filling up (ἀνταναπληρόω) what is lacking (ὑστέρημα) regarding the afflictions (θλῖψις) of Christ. What does Paul mean by this? Already in this letter Paul has affirmed the absolute completeness of the reconciliation Christ accomplished by his blood on the cross, so that the work of Christ alone is sufficient to reconcile believers to God (Col. 1:20–23; 2:10–15). So Paul is certainly not suggesting that the atoning sufferings of Christ were in some way insufficient. Instead, the word Paul uses for "afflictions" (θλῖψις) is never used in the New Testament with reference to Christ's sufferings on the cross, but it is used most often to refer to persecution faced by believers (Moo, 2008, 151; Wilson, 2005, 171). Therefore, Paul surely is not saying the atoning sufferings of Christ are lacking in and of themselves. Instead, Paul is identifying something that is lacking in association with the afflictions of Christ, or in reference to his sufferings.

Some scholars locate these lacking afflictions within the eschatological tribulations, sometimes referred to as "Messianic woes," that Christians can expect to experience leading up to the day of Christ (Bauckham, 1975; Wright, 1986, 87–88; Bird, 2009, 65). Perhaps even early Christians followed a Jewish idea that their afflictions were contributing to a required quota of sufferings that had to be accomplished before the end could come (4 Esd. 4:36; Rev. 6:11). In such a context, Paul would see his sufferings as his personal contribution toward "filling up" (ἀνταναπληρόω; ESV, NIV) or "completing" (NRSV, HCSB) the required measure of these afflictions and thereby quickening the arrival of the eschatological end.

This view has much to commend it, and it may indeed reveal an important aspect of Paul's thinking at this point. However, when we take into consideration the context of 1:24–2:5, we find that Paul is introducing a discussion in 1:24 that has minimal eschatological overtones, if any at all. Indeed, Paul focuses not on the *future* eschaton in this passage but on his *present* ministry as a steward of the gospel. As we move forward into his discussion of this stewardship in verse 25, we will find increasing light cast back upon what he means here in verse 24, as it becomes increasingly clear that his duty to make Christ known plays a fundamental role in the filling up of what is lacking in the afflictions of Christ.

1:25. In the very next verse, Paul describes his ministry in terms of a "stewardship" (οἰκονομία) he has received from God. As a steward, Paul has been entrusted with an office or a position of management similar to the stewardship entrusted to household managers in his day. Paul's stewardship requires him to administrate a particular task in 1:25, namely "to make the word of God fully known." In the following verses, Paul unpacks how he goes about this task. He equates "the word of God" (τὸν λόγον τοῦ θεοῦ) with the mystery that has been entrusted to him, and the mystery is Christ himself (Col. 1:26–27), so the word of God refers essentially to the gospel "delivered as it was by word of mouth" (Dunn, 1996, 118). Paul makes this word of God known by proclaiming Christ and by teaching and admonishing all people (Col. 1:28–29). In this way, the word of God is fulfilled (Col. 1:25), when it achieves its purpose and is made known to the nations.

Stewardship in the Ancient World

When Paul speaks of the "stewardship" (οἰκονομία) he has received from God, he invokes a concept well-known to the ancient world. The term could refer to managers of personal estates or households, and it could also refer to vicegerents appointed by kings or emperors to exercise power on their behalf. Josephus recalls the Genesis story of Joseph being entrusted by Pharaoh with the "stewardship" (οἰκονομία) of grain dispensation in ancient Egypt (Josephus, Ant. 2.89), while Xenophon (ca. 400 BC) describes a good "estate manager" (οἰκονομία) as a person who, when put in charge of another man's estate, manages it as well as his own (Xenophon, *Oec*. 1.1).

We must further remind ourselves that for Paul, the proclamation of the gospel was intrinsically linked to suffering for the gospel. Indeed, Paul labors to proclaim the gospel "in your behalf" (ὑπὲρ ὑμῶν; 2:1) in the precise same way he suffers "in your behalf" (ὑπὲρ ὑμῶν; 1:24). For Paul, suffering and proclaiming are not two separate activities, but are one and the same. Or to be more accurate, Paul suffers both as a consequence of his proclamation (e.g., Col. 4:3) and as a means for advancing his proclamation (e.g., Phil. 1:12–18).

We may now return to verse 24 and put together the interpretive pieces of what Paul means by "filling up what lacks in Christ's afflictions." Christ has fully and completely accomplished the suffering necessary for atonement, but his afflictions still need the accompanying work of proclamation, and until the gospel has been proclaimed to all people in all nations, a deficiency remains. Paul has been stewarded by God with the responsibility of making this gospel known. When Paul suffers, he suffers as a steward of the gospel, and his suffering further makes Christ known and thus contributes to what yet remains unfinished regarding the proclamation of Christ and his atoning afflictions. This bigger picture takes us to the heart of Paul's simultaneous reaction of joy even when suffering, for he rejoices not masochistically in the suffering itself, but he rejoices in what his suffering accomplishes, for it is only by his suffering that Paul can fully discharge his ministry of proclamation.

The Mystery (1:26–27)

In his ministry, Paul makes known the mystery that God has now revealed, and the mystery is Christ and the reconciling work of Christ among the Gentiles.

1:26. Paul now picks up where he left off in verse 25 by reflecting further on the purpose of his stewardship, the fulfillment of the "word" (λόγος; 1:25) of God. Paul now explains that this fulfilled word in some way constitutes "the mystery" (τὸ μυστήριον) that was once concealed but has now been revealed. This mystery concerns nothing less than the person of Christ himself (Col. 2:2; 4:3), who is present both specifically "in you" (ἐν ὑμῖν) and generally "among the Gentiles" (ἐν τοῖς ἔθνεσιν; 1:27). We may be tempted to more narrowly define the precise content of the mystery as *either* the person of Christ *or* the inclusion of the Gentiles within the gospel. However, in Paul's thinking, the two are inseparable aspects of the one mystery. When Christ was revealed, he accomplished a salvation universal in scope and of such magnificent scale (e.g., Eph. 2:1–10) that the wall dividing Jews and Gentiles must necessarily come down (e.g., Eph. 2:11–22). Thus, Paul can say the mystery is both Christ (Eph. 3:4) *and* Gentile inclusion (Eph. 3:6).

Paul places this mystery within a time frame of past and present. In the *past*, God concealed the mystery from the "ages" (αἰών) and "generations" (γενεά) of people throughout history. The discerning Israelite reader would have anticipated from their Scriptures that such a Christ would come, one who would descend from David and occupy his throne (Isa. 9:6–7), who would suffer for sins (Isa. 52:13–53:12), and who would initiate a new covenant (Jer. 31:31–34).[1] But the full and clear reality of Christ was not known to the people of Israel in the past because God had not yet revealed Christ. Thus, Christ remained a mystery not to God, who foreordained Christ, but to his people, until such time as God revealed Christ. The mystery of Christ was formerly concealed.

But "now" (νῦν), in the *present* moment, God has revealed this secret and made it known. The secret was revealed in a universal sense in the incarnational appearing of Jesus (2 Tim. 1:10), and the secret is revealed in a personal sense whenever the gospel is preached and others hear and turn to Christ in faith (Rom. 16:25; Titus 1:3; cf. Eph. 3:4–5). Thus, though the mystery has already been revealed in the first coming of Jesus, God nevertheless has an ongoing desire for the mystery to continue being revealed through the preaching of Jesus Christ (Rom. 16:25).

It is in the latter, personal sense that the mystery was made known not just "to his saints" (τοῖς ἁγίοις αὐτοῦ) generically, but specifically to the saints in Colossae to whom Paul addresses his letter (1:2). The mystery has been revealed to them as well, not in a mystical, supernatural, or magical sort of way, but rather in a very natural, coherent, and logical sort of way, as Epaphras presented to them the gospel of Jesus Christ. In this sense, the mystery of Christ continues to be revealed wherever Christ is preached, and the further that gospel goes into Gentile communities far from God, the more the fullness of the mystery of Gentile inclusion is itself revealed. No wonder, then, that Paul exerts all of his energy toward the end of proclaiming Christ to all people (1:28–29)!

1:27. Paul next leads us into the mind of God by setting forth God's purpose in making this mystery known. Paul no longer gives an objective description of the work of God, but he now probes deeper into the mind and divine counsel of God's desire. God did not merely "choose" (ESV, NIV, NRSV) but he "wanted" (HCSB,

1 For a comprehensive approach to the various ways the Hebrew Scriptures look ahead to Christ, see Greidanus, 1999.

NET) or "willed" (cf. BDAG, s.v. "θέλω" 2, p. 447) to make a particular aspect of this mystery known to the saints, namely the "abundance" (πλοῦτος) of the "glory" (δόξα) of this mystery. Paul's language here parallels his language in Eph 1:3–11 where he suggests that the spiritual blessings we have received in Christ serve to magnify the praise of God's glory (Eph. 1:6, 12, 14). When God revealed Christ, he revealed the full abundance of his glory. There is nothing more glorious than Christ as he has been revealed to the nations and as he dwells within us. The mystery truly is abundantly glorious.

In the second half of verse 27, Paul describes this glory in light of three features of the mystery: Gentile inclusion, union with Christ, and hope. First, Paul uses the phrase "among the Gentiles" (ἐν τοῖς ἔθνεσιν). This phrase may modify "this mystery" to suggest that the mystery itself belongs to the Gentiles or it may modify "the saints" to include the Gentiles among those to whom God wanted to make the mystery known. Either way, the point is essentially the same: the gospel is for the Gentiles too! Or, to say it circularly, the mystery is for the Gentiles because the mystery includes the gospel being for the Gentiles. The Hebrew Scriptures anticipated this inclusion of the Gentiles in various ways, including the promise to Abraham (Gen. 12:3) and various provisions for welcoming foreigners into the people of Israel (e.g., Lev. 19:33–34; Deut. 10:18–19), including Rahab and Ruth. The prophets anticipated a day when all nations would worship the God of Israel (e.g., Isa. 2:2; 66:18–20), and the begrudging prophet Jonah was sent to preach God's mercy to the Ninevite Gentiles.

The gospel truly is for all people (see Col. 3:11) and therefore Paul directs his missionary efforts toward all people (1:28), including even Gentile believers in the remote village of Colossae! God does not reveal the mystery exclusively to the saints, but he makes it widely known to the nations; and he does not share the mystery as a secret that must be closely guarded by those who receive it, but he reveals the secret precisely with the intent of making it widely known. Indeed, if we have received the mystery, we are not to protect it as a secret, but we are to proclaim it publicly.

Mystery Religions and the Mystery of Christ

In the first-century Roman world, so-called mystery religions (i.e., the cults of Isis, Osiris, Cybele, Attis, Mithras, etc.) prided themselves in their secret knowledge. Only devout members of the religion gained access to the mysteries through secret initiation rites, and they were then required to maintain "a strict silence" regarding their rituals and practices (Lohse and Steely, 1976, 233, 238). This is why contemporary historians refer to them as mystery religions, because so little is now known about what their religion actually entailed. But not so with Christ! The "mystery" of Christ has been publicly revealed and it is openly and fully proclaimed to all who would hear Paul's message. All that Paul knows he openly makes known. There are no further secrets being withheld from the Colossians, but they have full access to all there is to know about Christ. Likewise today, the church does not cloister itself around secrets, but the church throws open its doors and makes the message about Christ fully known through the proclamation of the gospel.

Second, Paul uses the phrase "Christ in you" (Χριστὸς ἐν ὑμῖν) to detail the precise content of the mystery. The phrase may be translated "Christ among you" which would profitably indicate the plural nature of "you" in the Greek text and it would point again to the mystery's reach into the nations (Lohse, 1971, 76). However, such a translation would essentially constitute a restatement of the previous "among the Gentiles" and would add little to Paul's description of the nature of the mystery. But when the phrase is translated "Christ in you," then we find that Paul makes a significant contribution here to our understanding of the mystery in Colossians.

Paul reverses the typical "you in Christ" language of Colossians (Col. 1:2, 4, 16, 17, 19; 2:6–7, 9–10) and uses the less common "Christ in you" (e.g., Rom. 8:10; 2 Cor. 13:5; Gal. 2:20; Eph. 3:17) to indicate the indwelling of Christ among his people. This language refers to our union with Christ vis-à-vis the indwelling of the Spirit of Christ within us as believers. Such union is personal and individual insofar as each believer has individually been united to Christ in his death and resurrection by their individual faith (Col. 2:11–13). However, we must be careful not to hyper-individualize Paul's meaning here, but we must remember that Paul uses the second person *plural*: Christ "in you *all*" (ἐν ὑμῖν). Believers are not only united to Christ but are also united to one another, for the community of believers together constitute the one body of which Christ is the head, and Christ dwells collectively within the communion of his saints.

Union with Christ

It is with great irony that Paul attempts to clarify what he means by this mystery with the phrase "Christ in you," for few theological notions are as esoteric and mysterious as that of union with Christ. Constantine Campbell thoroughly surveys Paul's language of union with Christ and he concludes that this complex theme can best be described as a compilation of four themes: *union* as a description of the mutual indwelling of Christ and believers, *participation* as a description of believers partaking in the narrative of Christ's death and resurrection, *identification* as a description of believers' location in the realm of Christ and allegiance to his lordship, and *incorporation* as a description of believers' membership in the body of Christ (Campbell, 2012, 413). The mystery may be unveiled in the sense that the secret of Christ has been revealed to us, and we may even be partakers in the mystery, so that Christ dwells *in us*, but the secret still remains mysterious in the sense that we cannot fully comprehend the abundant riches of the mystery that we now know.

Third and finally, Paul describes this mystery as "the hope of glory" (ἡ ἐλπὶς τῆς δόξης), a phrase which can be translated descriptively as "the glorious hope." Such hope has been a subtle theme in Colossians already (see Col. 1:5, 23) and it grows out of the gospel and it has eschatological implications (Col. 1:22, 27). Even as we look forward to our presentation before God, and even as Paul labors to present believers mature at that time, we hold to the gospel with a confidence of hope, for we have already received Christ and his work within us is certain to carry us to the realization of our hope, when we will be revealed with Christ in glory (Col. 3:4). Our glorious hope, therefore, is "the certainty that we will experience final glory" (Moo, 2008, 159).

Paul's Proclamation (1:28–29)

Paul describes his mission in universal terms as he labors to proclaim Christ to all people and to bring all people to maturity in Christ.

1:28. Paul now shifts toward his particular ministry with regard to the mystery of Christ and the role he plays in making Christ known. Paul says, "whom we proclaim" (ὃν ἡμεῖς καταγγέλλομεν), where the "we" refers to Paul and his missionary cohort and the "whom" refers to Christ. The ease with which Paul shifts from speaking in the singular of his own suffering in verse 24 to now using the plural to speak of our proclamation shows how inseparable his own ministry is from that of his cohort. He is part of a team that works together to proclaim Christ. The word Paul uses, "proclaim" (καταγγέλλω), implies a public announcement or proclamation "with implication of broad dissemination" (BDAG, s.v. "καταγγέλλω" p. 515), and the present tense of the verb suggests this proclamation is an ongoing activity presently in progress. Even his current chains can't keep Paul from making Christ known, and thus we should not be surprised that Paul has recently become a spiritual father to Onesimus (Philem. 10).

Paul further explains *how* and *why* he undertakes this proclamation. Regarding *how*, Paul proclaims Christ by "warning" (νουθετέω) and "teaching" (διδάσκω). "Warning" suggests a negative form of instruction with the sense of correcting wrong thinking and behavior, while "teaching" suggests a positive form of instruction with the sense of supplying right thinking and behavior. Thus, Paul replaces wrong ideas about Christ with correct ideas, and he replaces wrong living before Christ with proper living. Regarding *why*, Paul proclaims Christ in order that he might present all men "perfect" (τέλειος; NLT, KJV) or "mature" (ESV, NIV, NRSV) in Christ. In his ministry, Paul takes the long view, looking all the way to the eschaton when believers will be presented before God as holy (see 1:22), and as an apostle, Paul carries the responsibility before God to develop the requisite maturity among believers.

Perfection: Is It a Reasonable Goal?

Modern conventional wisdom tells us that when we set goals for ourselves, we should make sure they are realistic and achievable lest we grow discouraged and give up on our goals altogether. Such conventional wisdom is lost on Paul, who sets for himself the seemingly impossible goal of presenting all people perfect in Christ. The word "perfect" (τέλειος) may refer to literal and absolute perfection in the sense of having no flaws (i.e., Matt. 5:48; James 1:4), or it may refer to maturity, as when a child grows to their full stature as an adult (i.e., Eph. 4:13). For the Christian, such maturity includes no less than standing firm and fully assured in the faith (Col. 4:12), having a clear and coherent form of thinking and ethics (1 Cor. 14:20; Phil. 3:15; Heb. 5:14), knowing fully about Christ and becoming like him in character (Eph. 4:13), and controlling the tongue (James 3:2). Paul might say a Christian is perfectly mature when they walk worthy of the Lord Jesus in every aspect of life (Col. 1:10; 2:6). That we might never fully attain such a lofty goal in this life, or that we should seem so far from it, should remind us again of our dependence upon Christ to empower us for the task (Col. 1:11; cf. 2:29) even as we relentlessly persevere toward such perfection as our goal for both ourselves and everyone else.

Finally, in 1:28, we must note again the extraordinary emphasis Paul places on the universal scope of his mission. Three times Paul repeats the phrase "all people" (πάντα ἄνθρωπον). He happily undertakes his labor of ministry toward every person who comes his way without discrimination. Not only does this mean that Paul will publicly proclaim Christ to a diverse crowd, but it also means that Paul will personally interact with any individual regardless of their background or identity. He is not above talking to any person, and thereby he lives out his own mantra that Christ transcends the walls that normally divide humans, including those constructed on ethnic, social, economic, and linguistic grounds (Col. 3:11).

Thus Paul, the Roman citizen, can establish a sincere and loving relationship with an ignoble runaway slave, Onesimus, and he can also write to the wealthy master, Philemon, with whom Paul also shares a meaningful relationship. Onesimus and Philemon represent two opposite ends of the socioeconomic spectrum, yet Paul befriends them both and desires to see them both mature in Christ. When Paul says all people, he really means *all* people. Even as Christ died to bring reconciliation to *all* people (Col. 1:20), so also Paul proclaims Christ to *all* people. Even as Christ excludes no one, so also Paul excludes no one. Without exception.

1:29. Having set forth in 1:28 his goal in ministry, Paul describes his efforts to accomplish this proclamation in 1:29. He now speaks personally, for himself, in the singular to describe how he himself labors and struggles for the gospel. He borrows the term "labor" (κοπιῶ) from the world of occupation, so that even as a farmer labors in his work (2 Tim. 2:6), or a fisherman labors all night (Luke 5:5), so also Paul labors for the accomplishment of his mission. He borrows the term "contending" (ἀγωνιζόμενος) from the world of athletics, so that even as an athlete contends to win the prize (1 Cor. 9:25), or a runner contends to win the race (2 Tim. 4:7), so also Paul contends in the proclamation of Christ. Put together, Paul fully exerts all of his energy, to the point of utter exhaustion, as he contends for the sake of the gospel.

Further, Paul exerts all of his energy "in accordance with his working" (κατὰ τὴν ἐνέργειαν αὐτοῦ). But whose work is this, and how is it being done? Clearly Paul has in view divine empowerment (cf. 1:11; Bird, 2009, 69), but we may more specifically designate from the context that Paul likely has Christ in view (see 1:28, where Christ was just named). Paul may be doing the work of proclaiming Christ to all men, but he does not do so alone. He exerts his labor in conjunction with the present work of Christ, and Paul describes the present work of Christ in a very personal way as Christ working "in me" (ἐν ἐμοὶ). This points again to our union with Christ (see 1:27), but now with a particular focus on the empowering work of Christ accomplished through the mediation of the indwelling Spirit (e.g., 1 Cor. 12:11). This work inside Paul is "powerful" (ἐν δυνάμει), therefore, even as the Spirit empowers Paul for the proclamation of Christ. Thus Paul undertakes his labor with an energy that comes from *within* him even though it does not come *from* him, for he is empowered from the inside through the work of Christ.

Divine or Human Agency?

Paul's statement in 1:29 leads us directly into a tension within Pauline studies that many scholars describe in terms of agency. The critical question is, who does the work—God or humans? Sometimes Paul can speak of various aspects of our Christian life as being the direct work of God, but other times he attributes those very same aspects to human effort. Likewise, here in 1:29 Paul blurs together his own energy with the empowering energy he receives from God. The two are inseparably linked, so that neither Paul nor God accomplish Paul's mission unilaterally, but the mission is only accomplished when both symbiotically labor together. More specifically, the mission is accomplished when Paul labors with all of his own energy that he has in turn received from God, and such labor is especially accomplished through prayer (Col. 4:12; cf. 1:9).

THEOLOGICAL FOCUS

The exegetical idea (As an apostle, Paul was entrusted by God with an obligation to proclaim the mystery of Christ to all people, including the Gentiles, that all people might be united to Christ and brought to maturity in Christ, and toward this end Paul labored exhaustively and suffered extensively) leads to this theological focus: In Christ, God's mysterious plan has been made known, so that all people are invited into saving union with Christ, exhorted to grow to maturity in Christ, and called to embrace the mission of making Christ known to all people.

Paul sees himself occupying a unique historical moment with profound implications for life and ministry, for the mystery of Christ has now been revealed to all people, including even the Gentiles. This revelation has turned the pages of history from the *past* ages of mystery to the *present* age of Christ, who is himself the mystery. Now the full riches of Christ have been made known, and it is good news for all people, including even the Gentiles, for all people can now be united with Christ and receive the full blessings of such a union (see Col. 2:11–15).

The revelation of the mystery of Christ has direct personal implications for Paul, who has been given a unique stewardship from God to serve as an apostle to the Gentiles. His entire life now revolves around his responsibility to make known the message from God about

Christ, that the Gentiles might also receive the salvation that comes by faith and union with Christ. Toward this end, and toward the goal of seeing all people grow to maturity in Christ, Paul now expends all of his energy in a ministry of proclamation and teaching, and he even embraces suffering as a necessary and fruitful means of fulfilling this goal.

Paul's mission, then, sweeps up even the Colossians into its expansive breadth. When they heard and received the gospel from Epaphras, they were not only brought into the mystery of union with Christ, but they were also brought under the stewardship of Paul, who is an apostle even to them. They are included in the "all people" for whom Paul labors as an apostle. This validates Paul's letter that he now writes to them with the very same goal of teaching and correcting the Colossians in the faith. They have an explicit responsibility to receive ministry from Paul that they might grow to maturity, and they have an implicit obligation to become like Paul in his mission. They will not necessarily become apostles sharing Paul's precise obligation of itinerant proclamation, but they will have the duty of proclaiming Christ in their own community in Colossae (see Col. 4:2–6).

These implications carry forward to the church today. We share in Paul's historical moment, albeit two thousand years later, for we also live in the present age when Christ has been made known and we have been united to Christ. Therefore, like the Colossians, we need to grow to maturity in Christ by being warned and taught by faithful servants, including the teachers, pastors, and leaders God has given to the church (Eph. 4:11–16). We must carefully receive and learn from their instruction, with discernment (see Acts 17:11), as it is centered upon God's word. We must also take up these same responsibilities for the sake of others, so that we, like Paul, labor and even suffer for the sake of Christ and his church with the goal that all people will know Christ and grow to maturity in Christ. In all things, we seek to make known the demystified mystery of "Christ in you, the hope of glory."

PREACHING AND TEACHING STRATEGIES

Exegetical and Theological Synthesis

Following the description of Jesus and the reconciliation he accomplished at the cross (vv. 15–23), Paul expresses his joy at being a minister of that good news. He describes his calling as a "stewardship from God . . . to make the word of God fully known" (v. 25). God's plan for reconciliation was formerly a "mystery" that was hidden from previous generations, but then it was made known through messengers like Paul. In the past, the truth about Jesus was veiled, so God took the initiative to make the mystery plain. Jesus himself is the mystery as revealed through his incarnation, teaching, perfect life, signs, resurrection, and ascension. One astounding part of the mystery Paul expounds is that Gentiles are included and can experience union with Christ. That is what Paul proclaimed, toiling with God's energy (v. 29) to present everyone mature in Christ (v. 28). For the Colossian church, maturity came through the ministry of proclaiming, warning, and teaching.

Preaching Idea

The mystery of Christ concealed is now revealed.

Contemporary Connections

What does it mean?

What does it mean that the mystery of Christ concealed is now revealed? Perhaps a contrast could be made between the modern concept of mystery and the biblical concept:

A third column could be added to the chart above: ancient "mystery religions." The sidebar on verse 27 illustrates those religions, especially the fact that their adherents hoarded knowledge. Not so with the mystery of the gospel, which is to be proclaimed.

Modern Mystery: "Who-done-it?"	Biblical Mystery: "Christ-did-it"
A puzzle to be solved	A truth that was revealed
Solved by sleuths	Revealed by God
Clarity comes at the end of the story.	Clarity comes after ages with the coming of Christ.
Once solved, the case is closed.	Once revealed, the truth must be proclaimed.

Further explanation of the "mystery" could be provided with the cross-references: the gospel is associated with (1) the inclusion of the Gentiles in the body of Christ (e.g., Rahab, Ruth, and the Ninevites), (2) union with Christ, and (3) hope.

God has revealed the mystery by sending his Son and making that message known to the Gentiles. In Paul's day, the fact that Gentiles were part of God's plan met incredulity and even resistance (Acts 15), but Colossians makes it clear that God has reconciled Jews and Gentiles into one body. Reconciliation has been accomplished between other groups also as taught in Galatians 3:28, "There is neither slave nor free, there is no male and female, for you are all one in Christ Jesus." By extension, this truth applies to differences of race socioeconomic standing, nationality, age, and culture.

A Difficult Concept

A river of ink has been expended on the confusing verse, "I am filling up in my flesh what is lacking in Christ's afflictions" (v. 24), and the exposition has offered a clear interpretation: Paul was saying that his apostolic ministry of announcing Christ could not be divorced from suffering because his work as a missionary brought trials. Thus, his sufferings helped bring to completion Christ's sacrificial death. Jesus provided a one-time sacrifice for all of humanity; and then Paul's apostolic ministry informed and persuaded people about that sacrifice. Thus, Paul's sufferings helped bring Christ's work to the Gentiles.

Is it true?

Is it true that the mystery of Christ concealed is now revealed? The Old Testament contains much information about the Messiah and his plan to give salvation to Gentiles, but the information was scattered and often needed to be inferred. For example, from the Old Testament we knew that Messiah would come from the tribe of Judah and be born in the town of Bethlehem; and we knew that the nations would be included in the roll call of Zion (Ps. 87); but the details of how this would be accomplished were a mystery. The prevailing expectation was that Messiah would come as a military deliverer. Only when Jesus came to earth and his story was recorded in the Gospels did theological thinkers like Paul understand more fully how Messiah is God himself and that his death and resurrection make salvation possible for all of humanity—Gentiles in particular. Hebrews 1:1–2 contrasts God's communication through the prophets of the past and then his incarnational communication through Jesus. The incarnational communication was far superior to the hints and intimations from the prophets. The mystery gradually became clear to the disciples in the book of Mark. At first they called Jesus "teacher" (even when he was transfigured in chapter 9), but years later Peter came to understand more fully the mystery of Christ: "we have the prophetic word more fully confirmed" (2 Pet. 1:19). Jesus himself showed that what was written about him in the writings and prophets was concealed to the eyes of the disciples on the road to Emmaus, but then he pulled back the curtain that prevented them from understanding (Luke 24:27).

One of the ideas that supports the main idea is that God uses suffering in the revelation of that mystery. That is Paul's assertion in verse 24, yet it might be met with questions. God uses suffering in the revelation of that mystery. To support this biblical truth, we might offer an example of how suffering led to good, such as the "pain" of a diet that led to successful weight loss. Second, we could extend the argument to more poignant cases as when the loss of a job opened doors never dreamed of. Biblical examples include Joseph's sufferings that led to the rescue of his family (Gen. 45:7–11; 50:20), and Naomi/Ruth's sufferings that made possible the line of David and Christ. If Naomi had not suffered in Moab, and if Ruth had not accompanied her to Bethlehem, thus exposing herself to privation, Ruth would not have borne a son with Boaz. Third, we could point out that history's most astounding instance of good-from-evil—the trial and suffering of Jesus—led to his great work of redemption. By his stripes, we are healed. Fourth and finally, we might point to historical case studies where suffering led to the expansion of the gospel as was true when Jim Elliot and his team were martyred in South America. They called their missionary enterprise, "Operation Auca." Similarly, the film, *Molokai: The Story of Father Damien* (directed by Paul Cox, 1999) shows the true story of a priest from Belgium who went to Molokai, one of the Hawaiian Islands. Formerly the island was used as a colony for quarantined lepers, but Father Damien (1840–1889) reasoned that those abandoned people needed God's love too. He eventually contracted leprosy. There was no way to separate his ministry from suffering. In fact, it was part of his ministry as he showed love in the most concrete way possible. Google Images and Wikipedia have the last picture taken of him.

Now what?

If God has revealed the mystery of Christ, what difference should it make? We should tell people! That is what Paul did with both toil and joy. An evangelistic ministry such as Alpha or Christianity Explored could be promoted in conjunction with this sermon, or perhaps a training program for evangelism. Proactive training is a key to church growth. For example, the website of the North American Mission Board states: "Top evangelistic churches train their members to share their faith and to initiate gospel conversations." Many free resources for training are available with a Google search of "evangelism training." Another way to equip people to share the good news is by modeling it in sermons. We might weave in the ABCs of the gospel—*Admit* that we are sinners, *Believe* that Christ died for our sins, and *Call* on him to be saved. Another way to encourage the congregation to participate in God's revelation of Christ might be with stories or interviews with the evangelists in your group. Proclaiming Christ calls for "toil" and "struggle," but they might be encouraged to hear that ministry is not only "toil"—it also gives joy (v. 24).

Creativity in Presentation

The passage uses many metaphors and any of them could be expanded into stories or demonstrated with visual aids. The primary metaphor is picked up in the preaching idea, "mystery." This could be expanded with a story from modern literature such as Agatha's Christie's novels. In 2017, Christie's *Murder on the Orient Express* (directed by Kenneth Branagh) was made into a film, and a clip might work well here. The chart above could be used to compare modern mysteries with biblical mystery. A young person might be invited to share about playing the board game Clue.

The metaphor of concealing and revealing might be illustrated with a story of a surprise birthday party where you were kept in the dark until everyone shouted, "Surprise!" Likewise, a visual aid of an object covered with a veil could be revealed by removing the veil. A visual of the seal of Harvard University also illustrates the theme of concealing and revealing. The seal has three books along with a shield and the word *Veritas* (Truth). Since the 1830s the three books have been open, pictured as they might look while held in your hand. But older versions of the seal show two books open but one closed, as if it were laid face down on a desk. Why was the seal changed? Some people speculate that in a previous generation it was believed that some knowledge can be known through research and study (the open books), but some knowledge cannot be discovered by human reason (the closed book). It must be revealed. As the university drifted from its Christian moorings, the seal was altered to represent a more humanistic stance. For pictures and a discussion of the seal, search Corydon Ireland's *Harvard Gazette* article, "Seal of Approval," on Harvard University's website.

The metaphor of maturity/perfection could be illustrated with a story of a child growing to maturity, the *telos* of our parenting. A visual aid could show a seed growing into a plant. The metaphor of stewardship might suggest a story of a caretaker on an estate, or a visual aid of keys to the neighbor's house for whom you are housesitting.

To illustrate how God chose the unlikely Gentiles for his "team," the true story of Michael Oher could be used. Michael is the main character in the movie *The Blind Side* (directed by John Lee Hancock, 2009). He became a professional football player with the Baltimore Ravens, but he began with a troubled home. Michael's father frequently was in prison and eventually was murdered. His mother was addicted to crack cocaine, and Michael was in foster care by age seven. After attending eleven schools in his first nine years as a student, the Tuohy family took him in and eventually adopted him. After being educated by a tutor, he went to Briarcrest Christian School, where these words are placed at the entrance: "With God, all things are possible." Adoption and transformation came through the power of God and the love of the Tuohy family.

The point to emphasize is this: The mystery about how Jesus would come to form a new people was hidden for generations but now is being proclaimed by faithful stewards of God. The mystery of Christ concealed is now revealed.

- The mystery was concealed (1:26a).
- The mystery has been revealed (1:26b–27).
- So, tell people (1:24–25, 28–29)!

DISCUSSION QUESTIONS

1. What does "mystery" mean in this passage? How do we use the term today, and how does our usage compare to the biblical idea?

2. When was the last time you shared the gospel? How did it go?

3. Have you ever suffered for sharing the gospel? Tell about it. Why do people resist and resent evangelism?

4. What is your response to Paul's statement that he "rejoices" in his sufferings for the Colossians? Is rejoicing possible for you? Why or why not?

5. What might "laboring" for evangelism look like for you? Do you know someone who is laboring?

Colossians 2:1–5

EXEGETICAL IDEA

Paul described how he worked specifically for the Colossians: that they would be able to stand against deception because they were a tight-knit church community, and because they stood firm in the full treasures of knowledge in Christ.

THEOLOGICAL FOCUS

To avoid being deceived and led astray in our faith, God's people need strong relationships with other believers and good teaching about Christ.

PREACHING IDEA

When we're knit together in love and knowledge, deception won't unravel us.

PREACHING POINTERS

Paul was laboring to protect the little church in Colossae from false teachers. He called this a "great struggle" (v. 1). The problem of false teachers and teaching is described on many pages of the New Testament such as Galatians where some people were propounding a combination of grace and legalism; and 1, 2, 3 John, which battled the "antichrists." Heresies continued to plague the early church, and the problem has not abated since then. The message of the false teachers will be discussed later in Colossians (2:16–23), but in this text Paul rings the warning bell about their "plausible arguments" (v. 4).

Today false teachers continue to offer plausible arguments through print media, blogs, podcasts, and television. The teachers might say that Jesus is just a man or that God is an impersonal "force." A brilliant scientist like Richard Dawkins uses interviews, articles, and books to sound his shrill message of atheism. In *The God Delusion* (2006) he says: "The God of the Old Testament is arguably the most unpleasant character in all fiction: jealous and proud of it; a petty, unjust, unforgiving control-freak; a vindictive, bloodthirsty ethnic cleanser; a misogynistic, homophobic, racist, infanticidal, genocidal, filicidal, pestilential, megalomaniacal, sadomasochistic, capriciously malevolent bully." A white witch named Starhawk calls nature "the Goddess." In *The Spiral Dance* (1979) she opines, "The Mysteries are teachings that cannot be grasped by the intellect alone, but only by the deep mind made accessible in trance. They may be conveyed by an object . . . by a key phrase, or symbol. . . . Only within the framework of the ritual does it take on its illuminating power."

PAUL'S PARTICULAR MINISTRY (2:1–5)

LITERARY STRUCTURE AND THEMES (2:1–5)

This section begins with the word "for" (γάρ), which indicates a literary transition as Paul now explains the purpose for the previous section of his letter. He has told the Colossians about his broad mission as an apostle (1:24–29), so that he can now explain how they fit within his broader mission, for he also labors on their behalf even though he has not met them. Here Paul finally uses (nearly) proper sentence length rather than the unwieldy run-on sentences of 1:9–20 and 1:24–29. He begins with one long sentence describing his particular struggle in behalf of the Colossians (2:1–3), then he mentions the purpose behind his words (2:4) and he affirms his presence with them (2:5). The central theme of this section is Paul's warning regarding false teaching and how believers can stand firm without being deceived, namely by being integrated into a community of believers and by having a fullness of knowledge about Christ.

- ***Woven Together in Unity (2:1–3)***
- ***Evading Deception (2:4)***
- ***Standing Firm (2:5)***

EXPOSITION (2:1–5)

Paul now moves from his universal mission in behalf of all people (1:24–29) to his particular mission in behalf of the Colossians (2:1–5). Paul writes here to specific people within a specific historical context. The town of Colossae and its neighboring towns, including Laodicea, were home to a wide diversity of religious movements and ideologies, each of which purported to have a proper way of explaining the world and how to live within it. Paul will give specific warnings regarding various false teachings arising from Judaism and paganism in 2:8–23, but here, Paul delivers a broad warning against any kind of argument that might deceive the Colossians by presenting error in a fine-sounding way (2:4). They should regard any teaching as false that does not measure up to Christ, in whom are found all the riches of true wisdom and knowledge. Paul strengthens them to stand firm against such false teaching by placing them within a network of relationships including Christ, Paul, one another in the church, and neighboring churches.

Woven Together in Unity (2:1–3)

Paul desires for the Colossians to be encouraged in their hearts by being united together in love and into the fullness of wisdom in Christ.

2:1. Paul uses the conjunction "for" (γάρ) to denote a particular kind of literary transition. Having presented his apostolic suffering and universal ministry in 1:24–29, he now presents not only the implication of his universal ministry in relation to the Colossians, but he also denotes the very reason for which he expounded on his universal ministry in the first place (BDAG, s.v. "γάρ" 1, p. 189). Paul's "desire" in discussing his own ministry within this letter is that the Colossians can in turn come to know "how great" (ἡλίκος) Paul's struggle is for them. Paul has already described this struggle in 1:24–29—note the repetition of "struggle" as a participle in 1:29 (ἀγωνιζόμενος) and a noun in 2:1 (ἀγῶνα)—but now Paul envelops the Colossians within the universal fold of believers for whom he struggles. Even though Paul has not met the Colossians personally, he nevertheless incorporates them within his apostolic mission, along with all other believers Paul has not met. Paul's universal labor for all people (1:29) is not mere abstraction for Paul, but it is deeply personal and rooted directly in particular church communities in particular places. Thus, Paul mentions the Colossian and Laodiceans by name, and he includes broadly all others who have not met him personally. Paul struggles directly in their behalf.

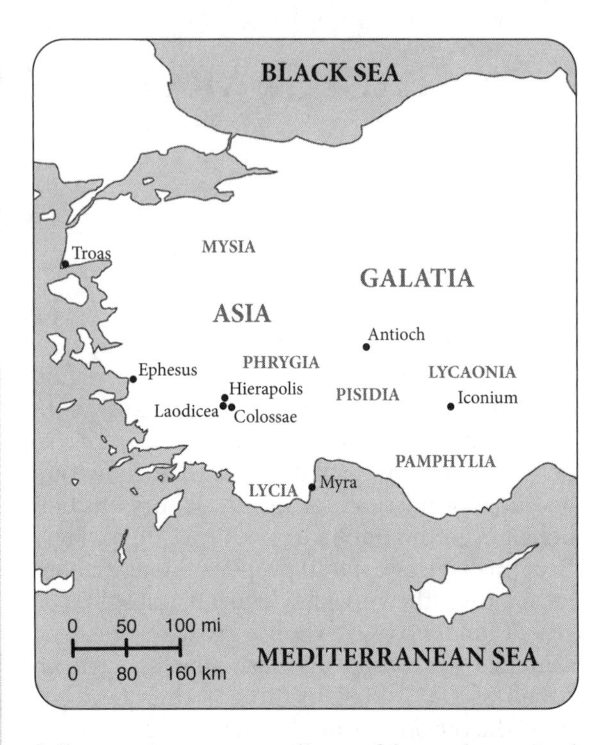

The Lycus Valley

In 2:2, Paul mentions not only his direct audience of the Colossian believers, but he also mentions "those who live in Laodicea" (τῶν ἐν Λαοδικείᾳ). Both the Colossians and the Laodiceans fit into the larger category of all the believers whom Paul has not met personally. Though Paul addresses the letter specifically to the Colossians (2:2), he mentions neighboring cities on three occasions in the letter (2:2; 4:13, 16). In the final occurrence, Paul instructs the Colossians to share this letter with the church in Laodicea. Paul seems to anticipate interaction between the church communities in these neighboring cities, and he even envisions this letter facilitating such interaction. The Colossians do not hold a privileged position with Paul or within the Christian movement, but neither are they underprivileged or marginalized; instead, they hold a common position that is shared throughout the Christian movement, even among their immediate neighbors.

Paul wants the Colossians to see themselves in relation to his mission in the same way he sees them, namely as fitting squarely within his mission rather than as outsiders looking in from a distance. The fact that Paul has not been able to travel personally to Colossae must not preclude the Colossians from personally identifying with Paul and the mission he represents, namely the mystery of Christ. They too possess the fullness of Christ and his mystery (2:3) even if they do not have face-to-face history with the apostle himself. To have received the gospel, and to know Christ and to be in Christ, *is* the full experience, regardless of how the gospel has come to you, or the identity of the particular messenger. Those who have heard the gospel from Paul himself have gained nothing more than those who have heard the gospel from a "lesser" servant such as Epaphras. To have Christ is to have Christ. Period.

2:2. And yet, though the Colossians have Christ, Paul nevertheless wants them to know the full measure of his labor in their behalf. What difference does it make whether or not the Colossians know the weight of Paul's struggle for them? Paul's goal is not mere boasting or grandstanding, but he shares his own burdens for the sake of the Colossians, that their hearts might be encouraged (παρακαλέω). This encouragement suggests a comforting of their hearts whereby the Colossians will have an inner peace that enables them to rest contentedly in the sufficiency of all that they have in Christ. We learn from Paul's other letters the various ways Paul struggles to achieve this encouragement, summarized by Harris as Paul's toil to further the gospel (Phil. 1:12, 30), the burden of his pastoral concern for the churches (2 Cor. 11:28), his struggle against opponents (1 Cor. 15:21; 16:9), and, perhaps especially in Colossians, prayer (Col. 4:12; Harris, 2010, 71). Of these, prayer is a particular struggle we can all undertake in behalf of others from a great distance, and Paul has already described his unceasing intercessory prayer for the Colossians (Col. 1:9).

Through these labors, Paul intends for their hearts to be encouraged. More specifically, Paul describes the means by which this encouragement will take place. They will be encouraged "*by* being knit together" (συμβιβασθέντες; ptc. of means).[1] The thread that knits them together is love—they are knit together "by love" (ἐν ἀγάπῃ). Similarly, in 3:14, love is the perfect bond. The Colossians already possess this love for one another and for all the saints (1:4, 8), and this love in turn weaves its way through the tapestry of their community, binding them to one another and strengthening their unity.

A Note on Denominationalism

When we think of church unity, we naturally think of the unity of a local church body. Paul certainly has such unity in view, but we must also remember that in 2:1 Paul brings the Laodiceans into view, as well as all other Christians he has not met, and in 2:2 Paul switches to the third person ("in order that *their* hearts might be encouraged"). To some degree, therefore, Paul also aspires to see local church communities knit to one another in loving unity. In the same way that no person is an island but must remain knit together within a local church community, we may conclude that no local church is an island but must remain knit together within a larger body of multiple local churches. To press Paul's metaphor of knitting, if each believer is a thread, and each local church is a patch of cloth, then only when churches network together can a beautiful and functional patchwork quilt be threaded together. Every local church ought also to seek out ways of belonging to a broader network of churches. Paul's mission supplied such a network to the Colossian church, and in our world today, many local churches find this ecclesial togetherness in the loving unity of a denomination.

The strength of their unity will only be revealed by the testing of hardships that seek to tear them apart. We know the integrity of our clothing only when it becomes snagged; likewise, the strength of the Colossian unity will be revealed only when the fabric of their community becomes snagged and their love is tested. The case of Onesimus and Philemon presents a dramatic snag that potentially pulls the church in opposite directions, as some Christians will be prone to sympathize with one party over the other. Sides will be taken and various positions will emerge, animosity and judgment will pull from both sides, slaves will rally to their man and masters will do the same. No wonder, then, that Paul will make his appeal to Philemon on the basis of love (Philem. 9), for love is the very thread that knits the community together and will sustain that unity in the midst of violent rending.

Such loving unity in turn leads to two parallel goals that Paul presents in the end of verse 2, each of which is introduced by the word "for" (εἰς), indicating purpose (Campbell 2013, 28–29). First, Paul uses superlative terms to describe all the riches of fullness of knowledge he wants the Colossians to possess. The term Paul uses for "fullness" (πληροφορία) may simply indicate completeness in contrast to emptiness (NIV), or

1 The aorist tense of the participle συμβιβασθέντες suggests their being knit together will precede their being encouraged; and if we interpret συμβιβασθέντες as a participle of means, then Paul is saying they will be encouraged *by* being knit together. Thus, Dunn says this passage refers to "an encouragement which facilitates and is facilitated by their experience of being 'held together in love'" (Dunn, 1996, 130).

it may suggest assurance or confidence as well (ESV, HCSB, NRSV, KJV). Either interpretation is appropriate, but the fullness appears to be a contrast to the emptiness of logic that Paul will warn against in verse 4. He wants the Colossians to have a fullness of knowledge about Christ so they will not be vulnerable to empty logic.

Similarly, Paul's second and parallel goal focuses more specifically on the Colossians' knowledge of God's mystery. He has already described this mystery at length (see 1:26–27), so now Paul simply identifies the mystery as being the person of Christ himself (τοῦ μυστηρίου τοῦ θεοῦ, Χριστοῦ; see sidebar). Christ is the mystery now revealed, which he aims for the Colossians to know. When we put these two parallel goals together, we see that for Paul, to know Christ *is* to have all the riches of full understanding.

TRANSLATION ANALYSIS: The genitive string τοῦ μυστηρίου τοῦ θεοῦ, Χριστοῦ merits special mention because of the difficulty of unraveling the relationship of the genitives and because of the potentially enormous Christological implications. The key question is whether Χριστοῦ is in apposition to τοῦ θεοῦ (thus, "the mystery of God, *who is* Christ") or to τοῦ μυστηρίου (thus, "the mystery of God, *which is* Christ). It is most likely that Χριστοῦ should be understood in apposition to τοῦ μυστηρίου because (1) this would be consistent with 1:27, where Christ is clearly appositional to the mystery, and (2) taking Christ in apposition to God himself would create a statement of Christ's deity that would be unusually direct and explicit for Paul, and even for the entire New Testament.

2:3. The notion that we can have fullness of understanding and knowledge in Christ is all the more remarkable when we consider the magnitude of knowledge to be found in Christ. In verse 3, *all* the treasures of wisdom and knowledge are hidden in Christ. Paul again uses the superlative "all" (πᾶς; cf. 1:15–20, 28) to indicate that nothing is lacking regarding the wisdom found in Christ. This both assures us of the sufficiency of Christ and compels us not to seek treasure elsewhere.

Paul uses the metaphor of "treasures" (οἱ θησαυροὶ) to describe this wisdom. The book of Proverbs also describes wisdom as a treasure that ought to be eagerly pursued (Prov. 2:4; 8:11), and Jewish tradition extols the superior nature of wisdom (Prov. 8:22–31; Sir. 24:1–23; Bar. 3:15–4:1; 2 Bar. 44:14; 54:13; cf. Bird, 2009, 69). Paul now says that all these treasures of wisdom have been gathered in one place, namely, Christ. The person who seeks after wisdom like a treasure will find that wisdom when he or she finds Christ. If X marks the spot of the treasure on a pirate's treasure map, then Christ marks the spot of the treasure on the biblical treasure map. Our pursuit of wisdom must take us to Christ. Thus, though Paul says here that the treasure is "hidden" (ἀπόκρυφος), its location is not a secret. It is hidden not to protect it from us (as in Josephus *Ant.* 12.250) but to secure it for us that it might be found by us (as in Mark 4:22; Luke 8:17). Christ is the repository and he invites all to come and draw upon his knowledge and wisdom. It is there for the taking.

In the same way that our pursuit of this treasure must lead us to Christ, we who have laid hold of that treasure must in turn not leave Christ. There is nothing to be gained by wandering from Christ as if there are further spiritual treasures to be pursued elsewhere. All wisdom is found in Christ (2:2), and Paul aims for the Colossians to have all the wisdom found in Christ (2:3). If we are dissatisfied with our spiritual experience, or if we feel a lack of knowledge about God and his ways, the solution is not to look for supplemental experiences or teachings outside of Christ, but the solution is to look all the more closely to Christ himself. We need to grow in knowledge (1:9–10) and draw more deeply from the treasures of wisdom found in Christ, not least by learning from teachings of such servants as Paul and

Epaphras (1:29). The problem is never that Christ is deficient; the problem can only be that we need to grow in our knowledge of Christ.

If we summarize Paul's argument in 2:1–3, we find circular logic trending upward, like a spiral. The Colossians have been brought together in Christ and by their common faith in Christ, and they are now being knit together in Christ as the body of Christ. And yet it is only as they are knit together in Christ, and to the measure that they attain a unity in love, that they then come to have a full measure of understanding of the very mystery that brought them together in the first place.

To put it directly, we can only fully know Christ within the experience of membership in the body of Christ. Or, to put it crudely, apart from the body of Christ, we cannot know Christ himself. Here, then, is an answer to those who would suggest we can be Christian and not be part of the church. How can we enter into the *fullness* of assurance, and of knowledge of Christ, if we have not entered into the *unity* of the body that comes by being knit together in love? Indeed, if we may press the case, the very tensions in the church that cause many Christians to leave the church and stay home are the exact tensions that invite us to grow in the love that knits us together, and this growth in uniting love would in turn lead to strengthened hearts and greater assurance and knowledge in Christ. In other words, the tensions that cause some to flee the church are the very tensions that would promote their growth in Christ. Without the *together* there can be no *tension*, and without the *tension*, there will be no further *knitting*, and without the *knitting*, our hearts cannot be *encouraged*, and without the *encouragement*, we cannot know the fullness of *assurance* and *riches* in Christ. The *together* is the key!

Evading Deception (2:4)

Paul writes these things in his letter to prevent the Colossians from being deceived by other fine-sounding arguments.

2:4. In verse 4, we encounter a rather startling statement from Paul regarding the possibility of opposition and deception. Thus far in the letter, we have enjoyed Paul's eloquent speeches about Christ and the mysteries to be found in him, and we have also ventured deeply into Paul's mission, both in his purpose and his intense passion, but the letter has not yet given any indication of something amiss in Colossae. But now Paul expresses his purpose ("in order that"; ἵνα) in writing these things by referring to unnamed persons who might deceive the Colossians and lead them into error.

Paul's mention of this threat is made all the more ominous because he does not name his opponents. He speaks very simply and very broadly of allowing "no one" (μηδείς) to deceive them. However, though Paul does not identify a particular person or organization at this point in the letter (but note the further details in 2:16–23), he does identify their method. They deceive with fine-sounding arguments. To "deceive" can be translated "reckon fraudulently" (BDAG, s.v. "παραλογίζομαι" 2, p. 768), and in this context it refers to tricking the Colossians into believing something false, much as a disguise might deceive someone (see Dio Chrystostom, *Troj.* 11.108) or lead them astray (Epictetus, *Diatr.* 2.20.7). And this deceit accomplishes its work with the tool of "fine-sounding arguments" (πιθανολογία; see word study) that may seem logical enough but are actually built upon false premises. This term takes us back into the world of ancient rhetoric, where arguments were carefully crafted to maximize their persuasive power, and hearers were called upon to exercise discretion in determining which arguments were most compelling and truthful. Only close inspection can expose the fatal flaws of an argumentation that sounds plausible.

> *WORD STUDY:* "Plausible Arguments" The Greek term πιθανολογία is variously translated in Colossians 2:4 as "plausible arguments" (ESV,

NRSV), "persuasive arguments" (HCSB), "well-crafted arguments" (NLT), "fine-sounding arguments" (NIV), and "enticing words" (KJV). The word occurs only here in the New Testament, but it appears within the literature of Greek rhetoric to describe an argument that sounds plausible but is not necessarily compelling. For example, in Plato's *Theaetetus*, Socrates contrasts πιθανολογία with ἀπόδειξις (which refers to pointing away to something else as a demonstration or "proof" [BDAG, s.v. "ἀπόδειξις," p. 109]), to criticize Theaetetus: "but you do not advance any cogent proof [ἀπόδειξις] whatsoever; you base your statements on probability [πιθανολογία]" (Plato, *Theaet.* 162e; trans. Fowler, 1921). Further, Plato's Socrates places this in relation to mathematics: "If Theodorus, or any other geometrician, should base his geometry on probability [πιθανολογία], he would be of no account at all" (ibid.). Thus, πιθανολογία refers to an argument that may have the appearance of validity, as probabilities do, but it lacks the certainty or proof required for fields such as mathematics. Such an argument may be persuasive, fine-sounding, and even plausible, but it falls short of the compelling certainty of a proof. Such arguments may not be as sound as they first appear!

In response to such opposition so broadly conceived, Paul engages in a verbal duel of persuasive words. Paul deploys his own words by which he speaks (λέγω), albeit in the written form of a letter, for this very purpose. He says "these things" (τοῦτο) with the intention of safeguarding the Colossians against such potential deception. These things may refer broadly to the entire letter Paul pens to the Colossians, but it also refers more specifically to the particular things Paul has just said. In the immediately preceding context of 2:2–3, Paul has drawn together two themes from his letter, the first being the fullness of wisdom to be found in Christ, and the second being the importance of being knit together with other believers within the church.

These two themes, Paul now suggests, provide for the Colossians a twofold defense against deception. The first defense is a social defense in which Paul knits the Colossians into a web of relationships. If we look back over 1:24–2:5, we find that Paul has developed the relationships between the Colossians and God, Christ, Paul himself, and the church. By describing how all of these persons relate to one another, and especially to the Colossians (who are at the center of the diagram), Paul draws the Colossians further and further into the web of relationships and he thereby strengthens the social ties that hold them together in the faith and weakens the influence of a person who would seek to draw them away from Christ with false teaching. Again we see that the togetherness of the church body is absolutely essential to every individual believer.

The second defense is an ideological defense as Paul develops the theological ideas that will ground the Colossians in the "*true word* of the gospel" (1:5). We ought to take note of Paul's approach in the letter. He views the Colossians as potentially vulnerable to the persuasive, yet false, arguments of other rhetors, and Paul responds in like fashion, taking on the role of a rhetor himself and seeking to persuade the Colossians to adhere solely to Christ. Paul does not employ his authority over the Colossians as an apostle to command adherence from them, nor does he resort to *ad hominem* attacks against potential opponents or exhort the Colossians to cease all communication with such persons. Instead, Paul approaches the Colossians with respect for their intellectual ability to reason carefully and to weigh competing arguments and to embrace truth and to reject deceit. Paul goes toe-to-toe with any competing ideology on its own level, in a duel of words and arguments, with the confidence that Christ, when properly and fully considered, will prevail. Indeed, any argument contrary to Christ, when placed alongside Christ, is reduced to "sounding fine" at best. One of the most essential tools for strengthening

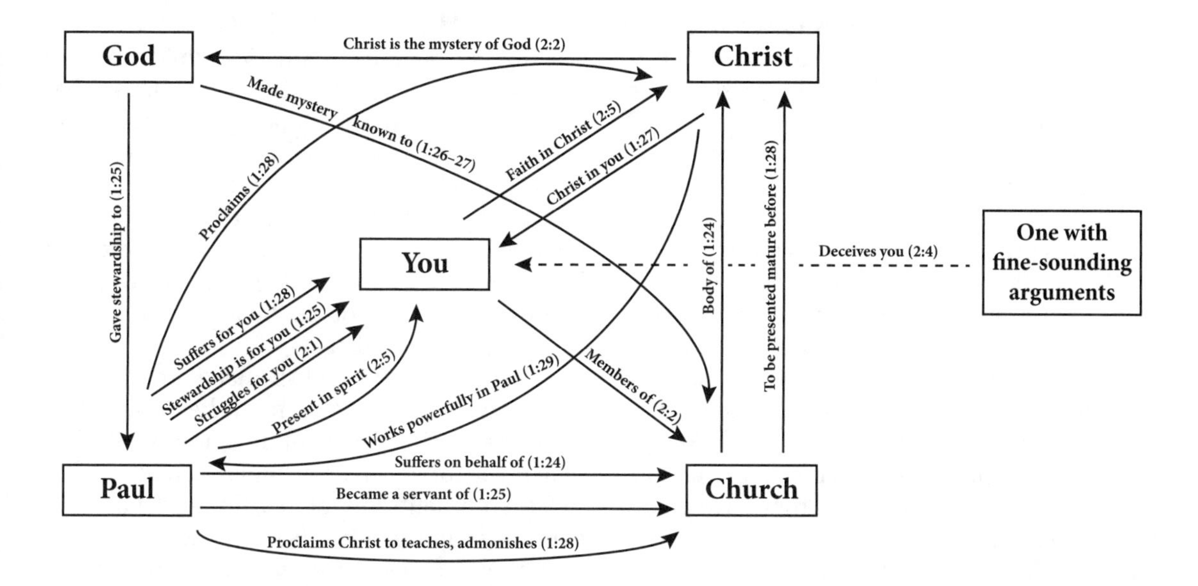

believers in their faith is the spoken word about Christ, delivered with wisdom, precision, and persuasion.

Standing Firm (2:5)

Paul assures the Colossians that he is present with them in the Spirit, and he rejoices to see that they are orderly and steadfast as they stand together in unity.

2:5. Paul knows his warning in 2:4 may have startled the Colossians and even left them nervous and unsettled, so Paul now comforts them with the assurance of his presence and his confidence in their present condition. Paul first states the obvious: he is "absent" (ἄπειμι) from them physically, in the "flesh" (σάρξ). This is why Paul must write the letter in the first place, because he himself is not able to come to Colossae. Naturally, as Paul raises an alarm in 2:4, he would prefer to be present with them, and surely the Colossians would prefer to have Paul nearby to identify and deflect any opposition on their behalf. But Paul assures them that he is in fact with them in a less obvious way, "in the spirit" or "in the Spirit" (τῷ πνεύματι).

This spiritual presence may refer to an unseen and intangible sense of connection directly between one person and another in the "spirit" such that Paul feels so closely bonded to the Colossians that he senses his presence with them when he is not with them. However, if the Colossians do not share in this feeling—which would seem likely, given that they have never even met Paul (2:1)—then such a connection would offer little comfort to the Colossians. It seems more likely that Paul refers here to their connection "in the *Holy* Spirit" who indwells all believers, including Paul and the Colossians. Even as the Spirit is with Paul, so also the Spirit is with the Colossians, so that by the Spirit, Paul and the Colossians are bonded together. In the same way, therefore, that Jesus comforted his disciples with promises of the Holy Spirit, even as they faced Jesus's own physical absence from them (John 14:16–17, 25–26; 16:4–7), so also Paul now comforts the Colossians with the reminder that the same Spirit connects believers closely together even when they are geographically far apart.

By the Spirit, and through the report he has received, Paul has developed an overall affirmative attitude toward the Colossians in their present situation. Paul rejoices to see that their faith in Christ is both "orderly" (τάξις) and "steadfast" (στερέωμα).[2] The adjective "orderly" refers to a "state of good order" (BDAG, s.v. "τάξις" 2, p. 989) and could be used as a military metaphor to refer to a unit that was arranged in sequence, with each soldier positioned according to rank, and it was prepared to function with maximum efficiency. The Colossians are a church with a good organizational chart, where people have been brought together and are working together cohesively as they follow Christ. Paul characterizes their faith as also having a condition of "firmness" or "steadfastness" (BDAG, s.v. "στερέωμα" 2, p. 943), as they rest upon the solid foundation of Christ, in whom they have placed their faith. Even as a building is only as strong as its foundation, so also faith is only as strong as its object. The Colossian believers can be confident that with Christ as the object of their faith, their foundation is steadfast.

These two adjectives remind us again of Paul's twofold defense against deception in 2:2–4, the first sociological (being knit together) and the second ideological (knowledge of Christ). Paul now affirms the Colossians sociologically for being well-ordered as a body of believers, having come together with a sense of unity rather than division, and Paul affirms the Colossians ideologically for the steadfastness of their faith in Christ whereby they are prepared to stand against opposing ideas and deceit. In this way, Paul concludes this section (2:1–5) with positive encouragement and reassurance. He may have sounded an alarm with his warning in 2:4, and he may have sufficient reason for concern, but Paul has confidence that these believers in Colossae will stand together with strength, for they have been knit together in Christ and together they share the full riches of knowledge in Christ.

THEOLOGICAL FOCUS

The exegetical idea (Paul described how he worked specifically for the Colossians, that they would be able to stand against deception because they were a tight-knit church community and because they stood firm in the full treasures of knowledge in Christ) leads to this theological focus: To avoid being deceived and led astray in our faith, God's people need strong relationships with other believers and good teaching about Christ.

In these verses, Paul speaks out of his concern that the Colossians might be deceived by someone voicing fine-sounding arguments, but Paul does not yet give particular details of what those arguments might be. Some details will come later in the letter (see Col. 2:16–23), but even then Paul lacks the specificity and intense polemic he is known to employ when he faces specific false teaching opposing the gospel (e.g., Gal. 1:6–9), including calling out names (e.g., Gal. 2:11–14) and even calling names (e.g., Phil. 3:2). Nevertheless, in Colossians, the possibility of any kind of deception in Colossae is real enough that Paul writes this letter as a preventative measure hoping to preempt such deception before it gains a foothold.

In Colossians 2:1–5, Paul models how believers can be equipped for repelling any flawed argument that would lead them away from Christ. He uses the two-pronged approach of ecclesiology and Christology. First, regarding ecclesiology, Paul seeks to strengthen Christians in their relationships with one another, both as individual Christians within their local church and also as a local church with other churches. Likewise, we must create an environment where believers are growing together in love for one another and where local churches are growing together in love for one another.

2 The two participles "rejoicing" (χαίρων) and "seeing" (βλέπων) may be interpreted as a hendiadys whereby two verbal terms combine to communicate one verbal idea, in this case "rejoicing to see" (Harris, 2010, 79). This helps makes sense of what would otherwise be an illogical order of words, for Paul puts rejoicing before seeing, when normally we see and then we rejoice in light of what we see.

When we have close relationships with one another as Christians, being knit together in love, we watch over one another and protect one another from being deceived. And when we, as a local church, have loving relationships with other churches, we stand together in Christ against fine-sounding arguments. The togetherness of ecclesial unity secures the church against deception. The together is key!

Second, regarding Christology, Paul strengthens the Colossians by reminding them of the fullness of riches found in Christ. In Paul's mind, the more they know about Christ, the less likely they are to be deceived and led away from Christ. Like an art appraiser who knows authentic artwork so well she can identify any counterfeit, so also we ought to know our theology of Christ and his work so well that we can identify any counterfeit ideology, even when it sounds plausible. The church that lacks good teaching is bound to be deceived, but sound theology vaccinates the church against the disease of false teaching. Faithful teaching about Christ is essential in the church, for the more educated Christians are in their theology, and especially in their Christology, the more equipped they are to stand against deceit.

Ecclesiology and Christology, being knit together and growing in knowledge of Christ—both are indispensable for standing against false teaching. The church must be passionate about both, balancing and holding the two together, not emphasizing one to the forsaking of the other, in order that the church might be orderly and steadfast.

PREACHING AND TEACHING STRATEGIES

Exegetical and Theological Synthesis

Having lifted up Christ in chapter 1, the apostle Paul now expounds what motivated the previous material: the possibility that the Colossians could be deceived by fine-sounding arguments (v. 4). He worked hard to protect the Colossians and Laodiceans even though he had never met them face-to-face (v. 1). Instead of being deluded, he wants them to know the riches of full understanding of Christ (v. 2) in whom are treasures of wisdom and knowledge (v. 3). Paul rejoices that the recipients were in good order, standing firm in their faith (v. 5).

To address the possibility of sheep straying, beguiled by smooth-talking teachers with their plausible arguments, Paul presents two solutions: community and knowledge. Loving community is spiritual armor against the deceptions of Satan who would divide the church and pick off weak Christians like wolves targeting a straggling elk, so God provides the Colossians with loving relationships and sound teaching through the divine institution called *church*.

Preaching Idea

When we're knit together in love and knowledge, deception won't unravel us.

Contemporary Connections

What does it mean?

What does it mean to be knit together in love and knowledge? It means that the community of Christ-followers loves and cares for each other. They practice the "one another" commands found in the New Testament such as "pray for one another," "encourage one another," and "admonish one another." Gene Getz unpacks those commands in *Building Up One Another* (1976). Being "knit together in love" can be explained with biblical examples such as David and Jonathan, and Ruth and Naomi. Personal stories can serve the same purpose. Perhaps when you were in college you had a friend that changed your life. And even fiction such as *The Fellowship of the Ring* by J. R. R. Tolkien can illustrate being knit together. A diverse group of four hobbits, two men, an elf, a dwarf, and a wizard love and care for each other. They band together in the quest to resist the evil being named Sauron.

The use of historical context may also help explain the Preaching Idea as slave owner Philemon had to deal with his runaway slave and *brother* Onesimus. How could they be knit together in love? After explaining the context of the book a transition to the contemporary context could be made where we are divided by race, politics, convictions, and so forth.

What does the last part of the preaching idea mean—"we won't be unraveled"? This refers to verse 4: being deluded by fine-sounding arguments. Faith can be unraveled, or as Hebrews 2:1 says, people can "drift away." The opposite of unraveling is in verse 5: being in good order and firm in the faith.

Is it true?

Is it true that being knit together in love and knowledge protects the church from deception? The possibility of deception will be developed more thoroughly later in Colossians, but here it might be introduced with quotations like the ones from Richard Dawkins and Starhawk in Preaching Pointers. Scores of such quotations are available at Goodreads.com. Apologists such William Lane Craig (2008, 79–81) can provide knowledge that helps the church from unraveling. For example, Craig demonstrates the inconsistency in one "ism" that can unravel the church—atheism. He notes that although the atheist Richard Dawkins solemnly claims, "There is at bottom no design, no purpose, no evil, no good, nothing but pointless indifference," Dawkins constantly makes moral pronouncements. The British scientist calls compassion and generosity "noble emotions," and he vigorously condemns actions such as the harassment of homosexuals, religious indoctrination of children, and the Incan practice of human sacrifice. He even offers his own version of the Ten Commandments, all the while apparently oblivious to the contradiction this moral stance creates with his ethical subjectivism.

The knowledge the preaching idea refers to deals with Christ. The whole book of Colossians repeatedly lifts up the uniqueness of Christ. In a day of relativism and pluralism, belief in the exclusiveness of Christ can be difficult. To counter doubts about Christ, preachers and teachers might affirm common grace. That is, other religions, philosophies, and scientific discoveries have indeed captured some truth. For example, Islam teaches that God is personal, not simply a "force" as in the Star Wars movies. Science has also discovered facts such as radio waves and black holes. These are "true truth" (to borrow Francis Schaeffer's term). But contradictions also exist between God's revelation about Christ and other truth claims about him. For example, the Qur'an is ambiguous about Jesus's death and categorically opposed to his divinity. Surah 3:55, 5:17, and 19:33 speak of Jesus's death, but Surah 4:157 says, "They did not kill him, nor did they crucify him, but they thought they did." Surah 4:171 states, "People of the Book, do not transgress the bounds of your religion. Speak nothing but the truth about God. The Messiah, Jesus the son of Mary, was no more than God's apostle and His Word. . . . So believe in God and his apostles and do not say: 'Three.'"

After pointing out conflicts between Christianity and other religions and philosophies, we might review Colossians 1 to confirm that he is the Redeemer (1:14), the image of the invisible God (1:15), Creator (1:16), the head of the church (1:18), resurrected (1:18), and Savior (1:21–22). Instruction about Jesus can help the church from unraveling and drifting into false teaching.

Now what?

What might it look like to be knit together in love? Perhaps the church has a "benevolence fund" that is used to help people with special financial needs. A special offering could be taken for that fund. At one church where I (Jeffrey) served, we had a list of things we were willing to give away such as a pair of ice skates, a lawnmower, or the use of a time-share condominium for a week. Expertise and labor can also be shared—cooking lessons, help in cleaning out the shed, or accounting in tax season.

Some groups find that a foot-washing ceremony knits them together. Communion can do that too. Some churches serve the bread and wine at a rail in the front of the church. People walk forward together and kneel shoulder to shoulder.

Another element in the preaching idea—knowledge—keeps the church from unraveling. Knowledge can be offered with supplemental teaching on theology and apologetics and the listeners can be encouraged to engage with those materials. In the Preaching and Teaching Strategies for Colossians 1:15–23, a sidebar listed tools such as books and websites for continuing education. Also, one-on-one discipleship might also be used to impart knowledge to new believers. A small group might memorize Scripture together or read Timothy Keller's *The Reason for God* (2009). Websites of organizations like Cru and Navigators provide other practical resources. To help older Christians continue in the faith, we might offer training for new leaders in the church. The writings of Alexander Strauch can help raise up new elders for the church and his website (Biblical Eldership Resources at biblicaleldership.com) also has training videos.

Creativity in Presentation

The metaphor of knitting could be woven (pun intended) throughout the sermon. For example, the introduction could begin with an illustration of a beginner trying to knit and finding out that it takes skill and the right instruments. A helper might knit while you speak. An interview with a skilled knitter could illustrate the preaching idea.

Perhaps we could play "Spot the Lie" with children to illustrate how false ideas are subtle. Show a soda commercial and ask if drinking sugary soft drinks really helps us stay young and trim like the actors frolicking at the waterfall. Or show a new electronic device and ask if it will really guarantee that we will never be bored.

To help the congregation be "knit together in love," the service might be arranged to include an opportunity to express thanks and encouragement. At the end of the sermon perhaps words of appreciation could be spoken either spontaneously or prearranged.

Illustration: Ants cling together to form a raft to cross a river. When they are "knit" together, the raft floats, and the colony survives. In the same way, the church stands when united, but when divided it falls.

A diagram might help picture the logic of Paul's argument as summarized in the Exposition: Without the *together* there can be no *tension*, and without the *tension*, there will be no further *knitting*, and without the *knitting*, our hearts cannot be *encouraged*, and without the *encouragement*, we cannot know the *assurance* of *riches* in Christ.

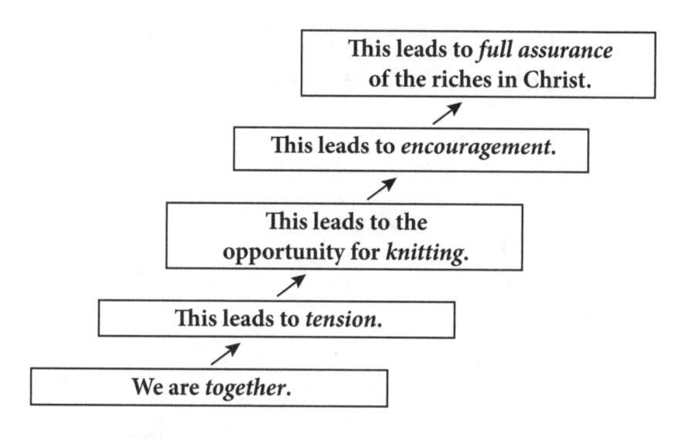

"Together" is the Key

Throughout the sermon, we will want to focus on how God's wants his people to be united in love and not torn apart by deceptive teachings. When we're knit together in love and knowledge, deception won't unravel us.

- When we are knit together in love, we will not be deceived (2:1–2a).
- When we know Christ, we will not be deceived (1:2b–5).

DISCUSSION QUESTIONS

1. What drives this passage? That is, what danger lies underneath our need for community and knowledge?

2. Can you think of some current examples of "fine-sounding arguments"?

3. Does your experience in the church match the description "knit together in love"? Give an instance or two.

4. If knowledge gained from things such as Bible study and listening to sermons is not an end in itself, what *is* the end? How does gaining knowledge help accomplish that goal?

5. What is the "mystery of God"?

6. Is your faith in Christ firm? What helps (or hinders) that foundation?

Colossians 2:6–15

EXEGETICAL IDEA

Paul appealed to the Colossians to live faithfully with Christ as their Lord, resisting all teachings and powers contrary to Christ, for by faith they have been united to Christ in his death and resurrection, so that they shared in the full blessings of Christ.

THEOLOGICAL FOCUS

When believers understand the fullness of blessings they have received by union with Christ, they will hold fast to Christ and not be captured by false teachings or defeated spiritual powers.

PREACHING IDEA

Jesus is better than religion, so don't let religion take you captive.

PREACHING POINTERS

Paul was concerned about the false teachings that circulated in the Greco-Roman world. Some of those philosophies made their way into the church in Colossae, or at least threatened to infiltrate it. The church in Colossae was surrounded by a culture that worshipped many gods. In the ancient world shrines dotted the landscape, and feasts and festivals punctuated the yearly calendar. The philosophies of the day offered their own take on values, personhood, the afterlife, community, knowledge, and theology, and the teachings tempted the Colossians to stray from Christ.

Today in the West, the worship of idols is not as overt as it was in the first century with shrines and temples, although neo-paganism seems to be on the rise. James Emery White (2019) summarizes the present situation: "Most Americans mix traditional faith with beliefs in psychics, reincarnation and spiritual energy that they say can be found in physical objects such as mountains, trees and crystals." In addition to the mainstreaming of such ideas, the more traditional "isms" of nationalism, materialism, and agnosticism are magnets that try to draw the hearts of Christ-followers. The rise in both neo-pagan and secular philosophies prompted Pope Francis in 2019 to state starkly that "we are not in Christianity anymore."[1] The United States and Canada should now be considered mission fields. Whether the philosophies are religious or secular, this text from Paul to the Colossians warns, "Don't be led astray!" Jesus is better than religion, so we are on our guard to not let it capture us.

1 Francis X. Rocca, "Pope Francis, in Christmas Message, Says Church Must Adapt to Post-Christian West," *The Wall Street Journal*, December 21, 2019.

FILLED WITH THE FULLNESS OF CHRIST (2:6–15)

LITERARY STRUCTURE AND THEMES (2:6–15)

Paul uses the transitional term "therefore" (οὖν) to indicate a major transition in the letter from exposition to exhortation. He has been primarily descriptive in his comments up to this point, as he has described how the Colossians received the gospel, the work of Christ, and his (Paul's) own ministry. Now, Paul will deliver the first imperative in the letter, when he commands the Colossians to "walk" (περιπατεῖτε) in Christ (2:6). He then follows this with a second imperative in the form of a warning, telling them to "watch out" (βλέπετε) for false teachers who would take them captive (2:8). He will not give another imperative in this section—the third imperative finally arrives in 2:16—but he instead engages in another theological treatise, this time centered upon the fullness believers have received via union with Christ and the absolute victory of Christ over all the powers that oppose believers.

- ***Walking in Christ (2:6–7)***
- ***Watching Out for False Teachers (2:8–10)***
- ***The Personal Benefits of Being in Christ (2:11–13)***
- ***The Victory of Christ over the Written Code and the Powers (2:14–15)***

EXPOSITION (2:6–15)

In this section, Paul exhorts the Colossian believers to walk in Christ, which will require them also to watch out for false teaching. In their own historical context in Colossae, there circulated many different religious and philosophical ideologies, including the worship of local Phrygian gods, Roman gods (and the worship of the Roman emperor), and Egyptian gods, as well as Judaism and Greek philosophy. Paul does not here define a specific false teaching he has in view, but he does warn broadly against any form of belief that does not accord with Christ. He warns specifically against "the philosophy" (τῆς φιλοσοφίας), which likely refers to any kind of systematized worldview. He also points toward "the traditions of men" (τὴν παράδοσιν τῶν ἀνθρώπων), which likely refers to Jewish belief and practices, and also against "the elements of the world" (τὰ στοιχεῖα τοῦ κόσμου), which likely refers to the pantheon of gods. All such teachings fall short of Christ, who has won the victory over all competing powers in his cross. Therefore, believers who have been united with Christ—including the Colossians—must walk faithfully in Christ by rejecting any religious teaching or philosophical system that does not measure up to Christ.

Walking in Christ (2:6–7)

Paul begins his exhortations in the letter by describing how believers ought to live in a manner fitting to the Christ and Lord whom they have received.

2:6. This new section begins with the conjunction typically translated "therefore" (οὖν), but here it suggests continuation (BDAG, s.v. "οὖν" 2, p. 736) and a shift to the "next major topic (Runge, 2010, 43), so it could perhaps be translated "now." Paul shifts from describing the work of Christ for the Colossians to "now" instructing the Colossians regarding how they ought to live in Christ. Paul delivers the first imperative of the entire letter when he tells the Colossians to "walk" (περιπατέω) in Christ, a command that embodies the entirety of how we live. Earlier in the letter, Paul prayed for the Colossians that they would be filled with knowledge of God's will in order that they might "walk worthy" of the Lord (Col. 1:9–10). Now, Paul turns his prayer into a command: since the Colossians belong to Christ, they must live like it.

Paul further explains how this life can be lived in verses 6–7. In the first half of verse 6, Paul makes a point of comparison between receiving and living: "as" (ὡς) the Colossians received Christ Jesus the Lord, so must they walk in him. They received Christ through the teaching ministry of Epaphras whereby they heard the truth of the gospel and placed their faith in Christ Jesus (1:3–8). Paul is clear here that at that time, the Colossians not only received the gospel message about Christ Jesus, but they also received the person of Christ Jesus himself.[2]

And "the Christ Jesus" (τὸν Χριστὸν Ἰησοῦν) Paul now emphasizes is also "the Lord" or "Master" (τὸν κύριον). It is surely no coincidence that Paul applies the title "Lord" to Jesus for the first time in the letter in conjunction with his first imperative in the letter, for when the Colossians received Christ, they also received a new master whose commands they must now obey. To refer to Jesus as a master in this way would certainly have resonated deeply for a church in which both slaves and masters were present, namely Onesimus and Philemon, and Paul will later in the letter draw out further implications for how having Jesus as master ought to transform how both masters and slaves treat one another in Christ (see 3:22–4:1).

2:7. Paul uses four adverbial participles in this verse to explain how the Colossians are to walk in Christ. First, they are to walk "having become rooted" (ἐρριζωμένοι, perf. ptc.; see BDAG, s.v. "ῥιζόω," p. 906). Like a tree, the Colossians have put down roots and are therefore now rooted. If we take his metaphors literally, they are contradictory: How can a person walk if they are rooted to one place like a tree? Here is the irony: the Colossians walk in Christ by staying right where they are—or more specifically, they are to live their lives in Christ without moving from the gospel about Christ into which they have sunk their roots.

Second, they walk in Christ "by being built in him" (ἐποικοδομούμενοι ἐν αὐτῷ, pres. ptc.). Paul envisions the laborious process of erecting a building one stone at a time. Perhaps Paul is referring to the personal, spiritual building up of Christian faith and virtue within individual believers, but Paul's other uses of the term suggest Paul is referring to the community of Christians (i.e., the church), which is built as more members are added to their number and as they develop increased fidelity to Christ as their Lord (see 1 Cor. 3:10–14; Eph. 2:20). Thus, they are built *together* in Christ as a church, and the church needs every member in the same way a building needs every stone.

Third, they walk in Christ by "being established" or "being strengthened" (βεβαιούμενοι; pres. pass. ptc.; BDAG, s.v. "βεβαιόω" 2, 173) with regard to "the faith" (τῇ πίστει). Paul does not speak of the strength of *their* faith, but of their strength with regard to *the* faith. The faith here is not the subjective aspect of their own belief, but it is the objective gospel message they have been taught by Epaphras (Col. 1:5–7). Thus Paul says it is the faith "even as you were taught" (καθὼς ἐδιδάχθητε). This is this gospel message that compelled them to receive Christ Jesus as their Lord in the first place (Col. 2:6). They grow stronger by learning

2 The word "received" (παραλαμβάνω) can at times carry the technical sense of receiving a tradition that is being transmitted from one person to the next, or from one generation to the next. Paul sees himself as the recipient and transmitter of such traditional material (e.g., 1 Cor. 11:23; 15:1, 3; Gal. 1:9, 12; 1 Thess. 4:1–2), but only here in Colossians does Paul use Christ himself as the personal object being received rather than teaching about Christ (Moo, 2008, 177; cf. Wright, 1986, 98; Lightfoot, 1981, 176; Bruce, 1984, 93).

the gospel more fully, by understanding its implications more deeply, and by embracing the gospel more firmly. In other New Testament texts, God himself strengthens the hearts of Christians that they might be blameless, resisting false teachers, and enduring until the final day of Christ's return (see 1 Cor. 1:8; 2 Cor. 1:21; Heb. 13:9). Here Paul points to instruction in the gospel as the means by which God strengthens his church.

Fourth, Paul describes the attitude with which they must walk in Christ, which is an attitude "abounding with thanksgiving" (περισσεύοντες ἐν εὐχαριστίᾳ; pres. ptc.). Thanksgiving recurs as a theme throughout the letter (see Col. 1:12; 3:15, 17; 4:2), and no wonder, if Paul intends for it to abound among believers. Can a Christian ever be too thankful for what we have received in Christ? Whether we are enduring stress or peace, whether we are suffering or prospering, whether we are reaching people for Christ or enduring opposition, regardless of our circumstance, we remember always the fundamental truth of the gospel and the overwhelming blessings we have received in Christ. Being thankful is essential to walking in obedience to Jesus Christ our Lord.

Watching Out for False Teachers (2:8–10)

Paul warns the Colossians against those who would lead them away from Christ and the fullness they have received in Christ.

2:8. Paul turns from exhortation to warning, as he both recalls the generic warning he gave previously in 2:4 and prepares for the detailed warnings he will give in 2:16–23. Here Paul tells them to "watch" or "beware" (BDAG, s.v. "βλέπω" 5, p. 179) lest someone might take them captive (συλαγωγέω). The image of being captured and hauled away is quite vivid, especially in the ancient world. The Romans, like other ancient empires, took captives as they expanded their empire by military conquest, and many of those captives in turn became slaves within the Roman Empire. Even in a rural place such as Colossae, slaves may have come into their position when someone took captive either themselves or their ancestors.

But Paul warns of a different kind of captivity, an intellectual or spiritual captivity accomplished through the ensnaring power of false teaching. Paul's concern in 2:8 is less with the identity of such false teachers than with the means by which they would capture the Colossians. He speaks generically of "someone" (τις) who would capture them not with sword or spear, but through the philosophy and empty deceit. Philosophy (φιλοσοφία) refers generally to a system of thought, whether that be a formal philosophical school, a religious system, or any other pattern of thinking. While the term was certainly used by Greek philosophical schools, it was also used with reference to "methodical attempts to understand the world around man" (Aristotle, *Metaph.* 1, 3), to Judaism and Jewish sects (Josephus, *Ag. Ap.* 2.47; *Ant.* 18.9.23), and to academic argumentation in general (Josephus, *J.W.* 3.161; cf. Dunn, 1996, 147; Lightfoot, 1981, 179; TDNT 9.183–84). Paul does not identify a particular philosophy by name, though he does call it "the philosophy" (τῆς φιλοσοφίας) and he describes it as "empty deceit" (κενῆς ἀπάτης). In Paul's estimation, this philosophy is of a particular kind, being "devoid of intellectual, moral, or spiritual value" (Moo 2008, 186), and it stands in stark contrast to the fullness found in Christ (Col. 2:9–10).

Paul further clarifies the nature of such a philosophy with three parallel prepositional phrases, each introduced by the preposition "according to" (κατά). First, the philosophy accords with "the tradition of men" (τὴν παράδοσιν τῶν ἀνθρώπων). The word "tradition" refers to a handed-down teaching or a body of knowledge passed from one person to another, and even from one generation to another (BDAG, s.v. "παράδοσις" 2, p. 763; TDNT 2.172–73). Such traditions may be a positive thing, as when the gospel itself is so transmitted (e.g., 1 Cor. 15:1), but in Colossians 2:8 Paul speaks of a transmission derived from mankind as its source rather than being derived from Christ. Most religions and schools of philosophical thought had such bodies of knowledge transmitted from one person to another. Jesus, however, uses this phrase "traditions of men" to denounce the traditional teachings and practices of the Pharisees (e.g., Mark 7:8; cf. Matt. 15:2–9). Likewise, Paul may very well envision Jewish customs as the particular referent of such traditions.

Second, such a philosophy accords with "the *stoicheia* of the world" (τὰ στοιχεῖα τοῦ κόσμου). The Greek word *stoicheion* (στοιχεῖον) resists simple translation because of its wide range of meaning (see sidebar), but Paul's frequent references to the spiritual powers and authorities through his polemic (esp. Col. 2:10, 15; cf. 1:16) suggests he may have in view the gods and angels venerated by humans that are *merely* of this world and not truly worthy of worship in relation to the exalted Christ. Examples of such divine beings abounded in the ancient world, where cities such as Colossae typically contained shrines and temples to plurality of deities, and regular feasts and festivals were held in honor of various gods. Even in such a small town as Colossae, many gods were likely venerated, including local gods associated with the region of Colossae as well as Artemis of Ephesus, Isis of Egypt, the emperor of Rome, and the God of the Jews. In some way, Paul perhaps sweeps all of these together (with the exception of the Jewish God!) into his one term *stoicheia*, for they are all lesser gods with illegitimate claims to deity.

WORD STUDY: The Greek word stoicheion (στοιχεῖον) can have three different meanings, all of which are attested in the New Testament: first, the natural elements of the physical world (e.g., 2 Peter 3:10, 12; cf. Plato *Theaet.* 201e); second, basic or elementary teachings as opposed to complex teachings (e.g., Heb 5:12; cf. Xenophon, *Memor.* 2.1.1); third, spiritual beings such as gods, angels, or demons (e.g., Gal. 4:8–9). The first or third options are most likely in Colossians 2:8 and 20, but the context offers few clues to help us select one over the other with any degree of certainty. We must remember that the ancient worldview did not make a sharp distinction between the material world and spiritual beings, so the first and third options may not be so far apart as we might suppose. In the end, Paul's emphasis in Colossians on spiritual beings as "rulers and authorities" (e.g., Col. 1:16, 18; 2:15) makes spiritual beings the most likely meaning of *stoicheion*.

The third and final prepositional phrase also carries the most weight as Paul warns against any philosophical system that does not accord with Christ himself (οὐ κατὰ Χριστόν). Here is the bottom line for Paul: if a teaching does not fit with the gospel teaching about Christ, then it must be seen as a threat capable of enslaving a believer. Paul warns broadly against any kind of teaching that would lead believers away from Christ, whether that teaching arises from the realm of Jewish traditions or from those who worship other gods altogether. The Colossians must watch out for any such "someone" whose teaching runs contrary to Christ, for they have the power to take captives with their teachings.

2:9. Paul now offers a twofold reason for why the Colossians should take care lest they be led away from Christ, first because all the fullness of the divine nature dwells in Christ (2:9) and second because they have been filled in Christ (2:10). Paul's statement in 2:9 about all the fullness dwelling in Christ clarifies the ambiguities of the hymn's similar statement in 1:19. Paul now explains clearly what the *nature* of this fullness is and the *manner* in which it dwells in Christ. Regarding *nature*, the fullness is of "deity" or the "divine nature" (BDAG, s.v. "θεότης," p. 452). The idea here is not so much that Christ possesses the divine nature, as if deity is something that can be obtained and lost, but the idea is that Christ is identified by the divine nature.[3] Deity is the essence of who he is, it is the "quality of being divine" (Lohse 1971, 100). And Christ is not just one among many such deities, but Paul uses the article here for emphasis: "*the* divine nature resides in Christ." By this statement, Paul underscores a monotheistic God whose deity belongs even to Christ in such an exclusive way that all other deities are thereby repudiated. If the one divine nature resides in Christ, then it does not reside in the spiritual powers or authorities.[4]

Regarding *manner*, Paul says the divine nature dwells in Christ "bodily" (σωματικῶς). In Colossians, the word "body" (σῶμα) refers to a human body (1:22; 2:11, 23), to the church as the body of Christ (1:18, 24; 2:19; 3:15), or to that which is real as opposed to that which is a shadow (2:17). Here in 2:9, Paul focuses on the nature of Christ himself, and especially his incarnation whereby he had a physical body suitable for death on the cross (1:20, 22; 2:14) and for resurrection. Indeed, his death and resurrection will be at the center of Paul's argument moving forward (2:11–15). Further, Paul uses the present tense here—the divine nature *dwells* in Christ bodily—to indicate that Jesus's bodily nature continues even after Jesus's resurrection and ascension (Sumney, 2008, 133; Schweizer, 1982, 138). Jesus was raised bodily and he now sits at God's right hand bodily (3:1), even as the one divine nature dwells within him. He is both God and he sits next to God, he is both divine in nature and human flesh as well. These antithetical realities are simultaneously true in Christ, and they remind us of the mysterious, baffling, and glorious mystery of our God, who is far beyond our comprehension.

2:10. Paul next gives the second part of his twofold explanation for the warning in 2:8. Not only does all the fullness dwell in Christ (2:9), but now also "you are filled" in Christ (ἐστὲ . . . πεπληρωμένοι; see sidebar). Paul does not designate what precisely believers have been filled with, but he instead uses an absolute statement of being filled as if they have been filled with *everything*, so that nothing is lacking. He will summarize some of the blessings the Colossians have received in Christ in 2:11–15, but his thinking parallels Ephesians 1:3, where believers have received *every* spiritual blessing. Paul's logic seems to be that since they have been filled with everything in Christ, they therefore lack nothing in Christ, and they therefore have nothing to gain by departing from Christ in pursuit of an alternative philosophy. No philosophy or teaching can offer to Christians anything they have not already received in Christ.

> *TRANSLATION ISSUE:* The combination of a present εἰμί verb and a perfect participle together constitutes a perfect periphrastic construction with a "single finite verb tense" (Wallace, 1996, 647–48). Thus, ἐστὲ . . . πεπληρωμένοι may be translated literally with the perfect sense as "you have been filled," but in the context of 2:10, the perfective likely has an intensive force emphasizing the present result of the past action, and may thus be translated "you are filled." Paul's point is not only that the Colossians were at one time filled in Christ but that this fullness is their present and ongoing condition.

In the end of 2:10, Paul reminds the Colossians that Christ is the head over all rulers and authorities. The "head" (κεφαλή) implies

3 Thompson says, "'Divinity' or 'divine nature' is not, strictly speaking, something that God 'possesses' so much as something that simply defines the one God. When Paul writes that the 'fullness of deity' dwells in Christ, he means that the very fullness of the one true God is to be found in Christ" (Thompson, 2005, 55).

4 Paul thus shows that "all other lords become idols when contrasted with Christ" and that "all the advantages of monotheism . . . accrue to Christianity" (Wright, 1986, 103).

authority over such beings. Christ rules not only over those who have willfully surrendered themselves to his reign, namely his church (1:18), but also over the spiritual beings that oppose him, not least because Christ has conquered and subdued them (2:15). Paul thus reminds the Colossians of the absolute supremacy of Christ over all of heaven and earth, including even the spiritual powers (cf. 1:16).

Who or What Are the Rulers and Authorities?
Three times in Colossians, Paul refers to the "rulers and authorities" (ἀρχαί and ἐξουσίαι), saying they were created in Christ (Col 1:16), Christ is their head (Col 2:10), and Christ has triumphed over them (Col 2:15). These rulers and authorities may be human powers, namely political rulers, or they may be spiritual powers. Walter Wink observes that outside of Scripture, the terms most often refer to human structures of power, but in Scripture they frequently point to spiritual powers (Wink, 1984, 13–17, 64–66). As with the earlier Greek word *stoicheion* (2:8), the distinction between human powers and spiritual powers may not have been so far apart in the ancient worldview as they are today. In parallel texts in Ephesians (e.g., 1:21; 3:10; 6:12), the powers are clearly identified as spiritual powers in the heavens, so it is best to understand them as spiritual powers in Colossians as well, though political powers cannot be conclusively excluded.

When we put together Paul's explanation in 2:9–10 with his warning in 2:8, his overall point becomes clear. Christ is indeed the absolutely supreme and exalted divine being described in 1:15–20, and those who know Christ by faith have indeed received absolutely everything he offers to all who believe. Christ lacks nothing and we lack nothing in Christ. Why, then, would we allow ourselves to be taken captive away from Christ? Anyone who presents a philosophy—a way of thinking, or a religious idea, or a foreign deity—that is not based firmly and exclusively upon Christ is offering a substandard product, a counterfeit, smoke and mirrors. They are pied pipers sounding an enticing tune that will lead only to captivity and doom. Watch out!

The Personal Benefits of Being in Christ (2:11–13)

Paul elaborates on what believers have received when they were filled in Christ (2:10), for they have been united with Christ in his death, burial, and resurrection such that believers have now been raised to new life in Christ.

2:11. Paul develops further what the Colossians have received in Christ now with the language of circumcision. The Colossians "have been circumcised" (περιετμήθητε) in Christ. The practice of circumcision comes directly from the Old Testament, where God commanded Abraham to circumcise his household as a sign of the covenant God made with him and his descendants (Gen. 17). From that time forward, circumcision served as a key marker of the people of God. All Hebrew males who belonged to the people of God were known by the physical and visible sign of their circumcision.

But Paul now speaks of another kind of circumcision, one "not made by (human) hand" (BDAG, s.v. "ἀχειροποίητος," p. 159–160). The circumcision the Colossians have received was not a literal circumcision in which physical flesh was cut away from the body. Instead, Paul speaks here of removing "the body of flesh" (τοῦ σώματος τῆς σαρκός), which is a figurative reference to the putting off of the sinful nature (cf. Rom. 2:28–29; Phil. 3:3). This spiritual circumcision reaches back to the Old Testament prophets who spoke of a circumcision of the heart (Jer. 4:4; Ezek. 44:7; cf. Deut. 10:16; 20:6). For the Colossians, this circumcision was accomplished when they came to be "in Christ," namely when they received the gospel by faith (Col. 1:3–8). Thus, their own circumcision was accomplished by means of another circumcision external to themselves, the circumcision belonging to Christ (ἐν τῇ περιτομῇ τοῦ Χριστοῦ). Paul seems to be speaking euphemistically of Christ's own death, when his "body of flesh" died on the cross (Col. 1:22). In other words, when the Colossians put their faith in Christ, they were united to Christ in his circumcision, or his death, so that even as Christ's flesh was cut off on the cross in a literal and physical death, so too the Colossians flesh has been cut off in a spiritual death whereby the sinful nature was removed. This reference to the death of Christ leads naturally into the next verse (2:12), where Paul will speak of the burial and resurrection of Christ.

Death in Colossians

Paul uses the terminology of death in an inconsistent way in Colossians. He speaks of the physical death of Christ on the cross (1:20, 22; 2:11). He speaks of believers who were already dead in their transgressions and sins (2:13). Believers have also died with Christ by virtue of being united with Christ in his death (2:11, 20). Therefore, believers must put to death the worldly attributes that remain among them (3:5). Paul's overall meaning arises like a phoenix from within Paul's morbid language: because believers have died with Christ and now have new resurrection life in Christ, they must no longer live in the sinful ways of their former mortal lives.

We might wonder why Paul uses the indirect language of circumcision to speak of dying with Christ when we know he is capable of making such statements directly (e.g., "you died with Christ" [Col. 2:20], or "I have been crucified with Christ" [Gal. 2:20]). Paul uses the language of spiritual circumcision here perhaps as a reflection of those so-called Judaizers who would advocate that Christ-followers ought to adhere to the Old Testament requirement of circumcision. Such Judaizers were a regular opponent of Paul (e.g., Phil. 3:2–3) and were perhaps present in Colossae as well. However, we must also remember that circumcision functioned in the Old Testament as a sign of entrance into the people of God. Paul's point in 2:11 is that the Colossians have already received this "sign" of circumcision by faith in Christ—no physical act of circumcision necessary. Indeed, the physical rite that now marks the people of God in Christ is baptism, as Paul details in the very next verse.

2:12. Paul connects the baptism the Colossians have received to their union with Christ in both his burial and his resurrection. He says they have been "buried with" (συνταφέντες) Christ in baptism and "raised with" (συνταφέντες) Christ. His mention of "baptism" (βαπτισμός) invites the Colossians to recall their earliest moments of faith, when they first received the gospel from Epaphras (1:7) and were presumably baptized by him. New believers receive baptism as a simple act of obedience to the command of our Lord Jesus Christ (e.g., Matt. 28:18–20), but by virtue of being new believers, those being baptized typically have a rather unsophisticated understanding of the conversion and baptism they are experiencing. Likewise, the Colossians have been baptized but they likely do not know the full theological richness associated with their baptism, at least as Paul describes it here.

Therefore, Paul describes what the Colossians have already received through faith and baptism, though they did not fully understand or realize it at the time. In baptism, the physical action of going under the water and rising up from the water symbolizes the burial and resurrection of Christ, who went down into the grave and was then raised up from the grave. To be united to Christ, by faith, necessarily implies the spiritual experience of dying with Christ and being raised to new life in Christ, which is in turn symbolized by the act of baptism. In the next verse (2:13), Paul will clarify that the new life for believers is spiritual in nature, for they were dead in their sins but now, having been forgiven of those sins, they have new life with Christ.

Unraveling a Genitive String: διὰ τῆς πίστεως τῆς ἐνεργείας τοῦ θεοῦ

In this string of genitives, the first genitive, τῆς πίστεως ("the faith"), is the object of the preposition διά ("by, through"). This prepositional phrase indicates the means by which the Colossians have been raised, and we make this clear by inserting the implied second person pronoun leading to the translation, "by *your* faith." The second genitive, τῆς ἐνεργείας ("the work"), is most likely an objective genitive, since πίστις ("faith") is often followed by an objective genitive (Lightfoot, 1981, 185) and would thus be rendered "faith *in* the work." The final genitive, τοῦ θεοῦ ("the God"), is subjective and denotes to whom the previous genitive, τῆς ἐνεργείας ("the work"), belongs, and would thus be rendered "the work *done by* God." Put together, the phrase is best translated "by *your* faith *in* the work *done by* God," or as Harris expresses more dynamically, "through your faith in the effective power exercised by God" (Harris, 2010, 94).

Baptism, therefore, offers a vivid image of the believer's union with Christ in death and resurrection. But lest the Colossians should think they have gained such new life simply because of their participation in the act of baptism, as if baptism itself accomplishes their salvation, Paul reminds them again that everything they have received in Christ has come "through faith" (διὰ τῆς πίστεως). Indeed, their faith is placed in the work of God who raised Christ from the dead, the God who has power over death, and the God who has also raised them with Christ.[5] The baptism itself does not bring new life, but the God who raised Jesus from the dead brings new life in Christ for those who have faith in him. Faith is the instrument of our saving union with Christ and baptism is the symbol.

Finally, let us not overlook the community implications of this text. By invoking the imagery of baptism, Paul draws upon the visible experience the entire community of believers holds in common.[6] They are witnesses of one another's baptism, and their baptism identifies not only their participation in Christ by faith but also their membership in the community. Even as they share together the common experience of baptism, so also they share together in the fullness of what they have received in Christ, even as they died, were buried, and were raised to new life in Christ. These common experiences, physical and spiritual, unite the church community together.

2:13. Paul continues his discussion of the believer's personal experience of death and resurrection in Christ, but now Paul focuses on the past and present conditions rather than the experience of conversion itself. He uses the transition "and you" (καὶ ὑμᾶς) to point attention directly toward the personal experience of his audience, the Colossians.

In the past, prior to their faith in Christ, the Colossians were "dead" (νεκρός) in two regards: first, in their "transgressions" (παράπτωμα), and second, in "the uncircumcision of flesh" (τῇ ἀκροβυστίᾳ τῆς σαρκός). It stands to reason that prior to their circumcision in Christ (2:11) they were uncircumcised in their flesh. Of course, many of the Colossians were likely physically uncircumcised insofar as they were Gentiles, but Paul here is more focused on circumcision as a symbol of spiritual alienation from God and from the people of God, so that they were also effectively dead in their transgressions. Of

5 Paul's descriptive statement about the God "who raised him [Christ] from the dead" (τοῦ θεοῦ τοῦ ἐγείραντος αὐτὸν ἐκ νεκρῶν) may be a reference to a "confessional formula" already known to the church, perhaps like the Christ-hymn of 1:15–20 (Dunn, 1996, 162).

6 Thus, Meeks suggests that Colossians, like Ephesians, appeals "to the liminal unity of baptism as the foundation of the church's unity" (Meeks, 1983, 167).

course, they were not dead in a physical sense in which their lungs had stopped breathing or their hearts had stopped beating; rather, they were dead in a spiritual sense in which they were immersed in their transgressions and therefore deserving objects of the wrath of God (Col. 3:6–7; cf. Eph. 2:1–3). So long as they were encumbered by their transgressions, they were functionally uncircumcised and spiritually dead before God. Their transgressions were the albatross dragging them into the pit of death, the terminal disease bringing death from the inside, so that they were dead even as they lived. They were zombies, the so-called living dead.

However, their morbid condition is now a thing of the past, for by their union with Christ, God has "made them alive with" (συνεζωοποίησεν) Christ. God raised Christ to new life physically from the dead, and in a similar way, God has raised the Colossian believers to the new life that comes by the forgiveness of transgressions. Where sins are forgiven, the curse of death is lifted and new life is granted. Remember again that this new life comes by faith and forgiveness (Col. 2:12; cf. Rom. 4:9–12), not by physical circumcision, for circumcision in and of itself counts for nothing in Christ (1 Cor. 7:19; Gal. 5:6; 6:15). All who have received this new life in Christ share together fully in Christ without differentiation, regardless of their status in any other capacity, as circumcised or uncircumcised, and even slave or free (Col. 3:11). Not surprisingly, therefore, Paul finishes the verse by switching from the second person to the first person, stating that God has forgiven *us* (ἡμῖν) all the trespasses. Even Paul himself is no different than the Colossians, for he too shares in the new life in Christ only by virtue of his participation in the very same forgiveness the Colossians have received.

Putting It Together

If we rearrange Paul's statements in 2:11–13 into chronological order, we find the follow summary of the believer's experience in Christ:

Past condition: We were dead in transgressions and the uncircumcision of our flesh
- We were circumcised (i.e., died) with Christ
- We were buried with Christ in baptism
- We were raised with Christ by faith

Present condition: We have been made alive with Christ by the forgiveness of our sins.

The Victory of Christ over the Written Code and the Powers (2:14–15)

In his cross, Christ removed our guilt before the law and he defeated the spiritual powers that opposed us.

2:14. Paul continues his description of the fullness believers receive in Christ (cf. 2:10), but now he shifts away from the directly personal implications to the broadly cosmic implications. Paul first describes how Christ has solved the problem of the law and our guilt in 2:14, then he describes the victory of Christ over the powers and authorities in 2:15. When we reflect on these accomplishments of Christ, we begin to appreciate that the full scope of what Christ has accomplished extends far beyond me and my personal salvation. Gathercole describes two sides of the atonement, one being the personal problem of sin and guilt, and the other being the apocalyptic problem of enslavement to oppressive and hostile forces. Many Pauline texts address one or the other side of the atonement, but Gathercole points to Colossians 2:13–15 as a key text that "seamlessly combines the two" (Gathercole, 2015, 47).

Paul says in 2:14 that Christ has removed the written code that stood against us. This enigmatic statement raises three key questions for interpretation: what is the written code, in what sense was it against us, and how has it been removed? The term "written code" (χειρόγραφον) itself is a rare term used only here in the New Testament. Generally speaking, it refers to "an autograph of any kind" (Lightfoot, 1981, 187). It is a "handwritten document" and may more specifically describe a "certificate of indebtedness" or a "record of debts" (BDAG, s.v. "χειρόγραφον," p. 1083), leading to translations such as "handwriting" (KJV), "record" (NRSV), "record of debt" (ESV), or more expressively, "charge of our legal indebtedness" (NIV). Based on the semantics of the term, some scholars suggest Paul is referring to a debt that believers had before God, as if apart from Christ our relationship with God is akin to the relationship between a debtor and creditor (Lohse, 1971, 108). However, in 2:14, Paul says this written code stands against us "by its dogmas" (τοῖς δόγμασιν), and he uses this same phrase for the dogmas in Ephesians 2:15 with clear reference to the Mosaic law (νόμος) that has been nullified by the cross of Christ, so that the hostility between Jews and Gentiles has been removed. The written code, therefore, refers primarily to the Mosaic law with its dogmas rather than to a record of debt.

However, if the written code refers to the Mosaic law, then we must consider how it is that this law stood against humanity prior to Christ. Paul uses two phrases to say the code was "against us" (καθ' ἡμῶν; BDAG, s.v. "κατά" 2bβ, p. 511) and "opposed to us" (ὑπεναντίον ἡμῖν). Both of these phrases imply hostility or opposition, even accusation, and the second phrase (ὑπεναντίον ἡμῖν) especially implies the active aggression of an adversary. Taken together, these two phrases serve as "an interpretative device to highlight hostility" (MacDonald, 2000, 103). We must note that this hostility stands over against *us* and not *God* himself. The law of Moses does not oppose God's purposes—indeed, God revealed it and it reflects his holiness!—but the law does oppose humanity, for it exposes our lawlessness and establishes our guilt, and thereby it effectively accuses and condemns us. In other words, the law stands against us because of our sin rather than because of any deficiency inherent to the law itself. It is the Mosaic law's "writ of accusation" against us (Harris, 2010, 96).

The Law as Adversary

In his stand-up routine, comedian Jim Gaffigan jokes that Bibles are placed in hotel rooms as a record of all the immoral things that have been done in that very room. He quips, "The ten commandments are based on what's already happened in your hotel room. That's why there's a Bible in there—for reference!" (Gaffigan, 2012). Of course, his comedy contains an element of truth, not only about immoral conduct in hotel rooms, but also about the nature of the Bible, for the law's dogmas both prescribe proper human behavior *and* record by their antithesis the actual improper deeds we have committed. The law thus becomes a record of our lawbreaking that can be used against us in God's court of law. It is because of our transgressions and guilt that the law stands against us.

But now, Paul describes three ways in which the opposition of the law has been resolved in Christ. First, Christ "erased" or "removed" the written code (BDAG, s.v. "ἐξαλείφω," p. 344). The term is sometimes used for the "blotting out" of our sins when we repent (e.g., Ps. 51:1, 9 [LXX 50:3, 11]; Acts 3:19). Paul's statement here implies permanent and absolute erasure such that the very record itself disappears. Second, Paul says the written code has literally "been removed from our midst" (αὐτὸ ἦρκεν ἐκ τοῦ μέσου), or periphrastically, "set aside" (ESV, NRSV), such that it no longer applies to those who are in Christ. Third, Paul says this written code has been "nailed to the cross" (προσηλώσας αὐτὸ τῷ σταυρῷ). When Christ was nailed to the cross (i.e., Col. 1:20), so too, figuratively speaking, was this written code.

When we take these three statements together, we have one of Paul's strongest statements about the relationship of Christ to the law. Indeed, we might well use words like "abrogate" or "annul" to describe what Christ has done to the law. However, we must remember again that Paul's primary aim here is to describe what has happened to the law insofar as the law opposed mankind as a record of our transgressions.[7] When our transgressions were forgiven because of our faith and Christ's work in the cross (2:13), the law's ability to prosecute our transgressions was taken away. The law itself was not necessarily annulled, but its charges against us were vacated and its accusations voided. So far have our transgressions been removed that no record of them exists and even the dogmas of the Mosaic law are forever incapable of rendering us guilty before God, for we belong to the Christ of the cross.[8]

2:15. But the victory of Christ in the cross goes further—much further—than merely assuring the removal of our guilt before the law. Indeed, the cross has cosmic implications, for in the cross, Christ achieved a victory over the rulers and authorities themselves. Verse 15 is fraught with grammatical and interpretive challenges, but the overall point again emerges unscathed. The main verb in verse 15 tells us that Christ has "exposed" or "disgraced" (BDAG, s.v. "δειγματίζω," p. 214) the powers "in public" (ἐν παρρησίᾳ). This disgrace comes as the result of Christ "disarming" (ἀπεκδυσάμενος; see sidebar) these same powers, and he disgraces them when he "leads in a triumphal procession" over them (BDAG, s.v. "θριαμβεύω" 1b, p. 459).

TRANSLATION ANALYSIS: The Greek word ἀπεκδυσάμενος is a middle participle meaning "take off, strip off" in the middle voice or "disarm" in the active voice (BDAG, *s.v.* "ἀπεκδύομαι," p. 100). If the direct implications of the middle voice are retained, then ἀπεκδυσάμενος suggests Christ has in some way divested himself of the powers. Thus Lightfoot famously concludes, "The powers of evil, which had clung like a Nessus robe about His humanity, were torn off and cast aside forever" (Lightfoot, 1981, 190). However, it is not clear in what sense the powers "clung" to Christ, nor how divesting them could lead to his victory. On the other hand, if the middle voice is understood with an active meaning, as is grammatically possible, and if God is understood as the subject, then the clause may indicate that God has disarmed the rulers and authorities. Thus, Moo concludes, "God in Christ has 'stripped' the rulers and authorities of their power" (see discussion in Moo, 2008, 213–14). While most modern commentators agree with Moo's view because it best fits the context, the Greek fathers favored Lightfoot's position because it retains the straightforward rendering of the middle voice. We favor the active sense of "disarm," because it best suits the contextual idea of a military victory.

With these phrases, Paul invokes military imagery to describe what takes place after a victory has been achieved. The Romans in particular enjoyed an extravagant celebration to welcome home their victorious general and his armies. The glorious victory of the Roman general stood in stark contrast to the pitiful spectacle of his captives, who were exposed to public shame as they were paraded as trophies through the streets of Rome. Thus, when Paul says that Christ has led the powers in a triumphal procession, he implies that the powers were once in rebellion, but their rebellion is no more, for "in it" (ἐν αὐτῷ), that is, in the cross (2:14), Christ has stripped them of their armaments and taken them captive.

A Triumphal Procession

The Greek writer Plutarch (ca. A.D. 45–120) describes one such victory procession in extensive detail, when in 167 B.C. the Roman emperor Aemilius Paulus defeated the Macedonian king,

7 "What is envisaged is not the actual destruction of the bond (*pace* Lightfoot, 176, 187), but the cancellation of its validity by the death of Christ" (Harris, 2010, 98).

8 Wright helpfully reminds us also that Paul's language here "re-emphasizes the uselessness of looking to Judaism for a richer or more complete membership in the people of God" (Wright, 1986, 114).

Perseus (Plutarch, *Aem.* 32–34). The festivities included three parades on consecutive days to carry all the plunder into Rome, including the cultural treasures of Macedonia (e.g., statues, paintings, etc.), the captured armaments of the Macedonian army, silver (requiring three thousand men to carry it), and gold. On the final day, 120 bulls were led to the slaughter, followed by the captured king, Perseus, and his children, whom Plutarch describes as being so pitiable that even the Roman crowd shed tears for them. Then came four hundred gold wreaths given to the emperor Aemilius as his prize and, "mounted on a chariot of magnificent adornment, came Aemilius himself, a man worthy to be looked upon even without such marks of power, wearing a purple robe interwoven with gold, and holding forth in his right hand a spray of laurel" (Plutarch, *Aem.* 34; trans. Perrin 1918). Behind Aemilius marched the victorious army of Rome, to the cheers of the people.

Such a victory parade only occurred when the battle was completely done, when the enemy was completely defeated, and when the victor was prepared to return home. So also, the victory of Christ over the powers is complete. The powers have been disarmed and shamed; they are powerless. Paul's emphasis on this resounding victory brings us full circle to his warning in 2:8, where Paul cautions the Colossians lest they should be taken captive. Why be taken captive by powers that have no power because they have themselves been taken captive by Christ? And this victory foreshadows his further warning in 2:18–19, where Paul will warn the Colossians against participating in the worship of other gods.

The Oxymoron of Cross and Triumph

We must remember again the irony of the victory achieved by Christ in the cross. The cross was an execution device utilized by the Romans to inflict maximum suffering and humiliation upon its victims, and crucifixions were often performed near the most crowded roads where the visible suffering would invoke fear in the rest of the population (see Quintilian, *Decl.* 274). It was considered such a cruel form of punishment that it was only used upon noncitizens and especially upon slaves. When Jerusalem was sieged by the Romans in A.D. 70, Josephus records that the Romans would execute those Jews caught trying to escape the city by crucifying them near the city walls, so all in the city would hear their cries and be compelled to surrender (Josephus, *J.W.* 5.446–51). And when slaves revolted *en masse* under Spartacus, they were subsequently crucified *en masse* by Rome. The Roman Senate also established a law that if a slave killed their master, all the slaves in the entire household would be crucified as a consequence (Tacitus, *Ann.* 13.32.1; cf. Elliott and Reasoner, 2010, 102–3). This law undoubtedly was intended to deter rebellion among foreigners and slaves through outright intimidation. The cross was clearly an instrument and symbol of the suffering of slaves and other powerless victims of Rome.

If we take this view of the cross into Colossae, we may envision how Philemon and Onesimus would have had two very different perceptions of the cross. For masters such as Philemon, the cross was an instrument that served his purposes and furthered his ends by enabling him to control his household by deterring insubordination and even protecting him from the potential violence of a slave revolt. As a citizen of Rome, Philemon had the assurance that he would himself never face crucifixion, no matter how horrific his crimes.[9] It was simply not a possibility for him, and he had no personal fear of the cross. But for slaves such as Onesimus,

9 In one of his letters, Cicero scolds Verres for beating a criminal and "hurrying to the cross" without regard for that criminal's repeated cries, "I am a Roman citizen." In Cicero's opinion, such a claim to citizenship ought to

the cross was an instrument of oppression that symbolized their suffering and plight as slaves. Its possibility hung always over Onesimus's head as an ominous threat, for even should he never merit such a torturous punishment, he might yet be crucified should the slaves around him act out in rebellion.

But in the Christian gospel, the cross belongs to Christ. Among the myriad accomplishments of Christ in the cross, we often neglect this important element, that in the cross Christ identified himself most closely with the lowest in society. He truly did take upon himself not only the form of a slave but also the death of a slave (Phil. 2:7–8). This brings into clearer focus the scandal of the cross whereby Christ's heroic victory emerges from within the oppression experienced by slaves. Heroes, and especially divine heroes, ought to come from above, from positions of power and authority, much like Philemon, not from below, from experiences of oppression and submission, much like Onesimus. The cross both defrauds Philemon of his assumptions of power and brings unexpected hope to Onesimus, for the means of oppression toward slaves such as Onesimus has become in Christ the means of victory over all the powers and authorities.

THEOLOGICAL FOCUS

The exegetical idea (Paul appealed to the Colossians to live faithfully with Christ as their Lord, resisting all teachings and powers contrary to Christ, for by faith they have been united to Christ in his death and resurrection, so that they shared in the full blessings of Christ) leads to this theological focus: When believers understand the fullness of blessings they have received by union with Christ, they will hold fast to Christ and not be captured by false teachings or defeated spiritual powers.

The key theological theme of these verses is the union of believers with Christ, and this theme provides the explanation for Paul's exhortations to walk in Christ and to watch out for false teaching. In theological terms, "union with Christ" refers to the mystical relationship between human beings and the divine Christ, that in a mysterious and inexplicable way believers experience an ontological transformation whereby our very state of existence is transformed by virtue of being transferred into the realm of Christ, so that we can now be said to have new life in Christ. Or, to say it plainly, when we by faith receive Christ as our Lord, we become so closely conjoined to Christ that all of his accomplishments and blessings extend to us, and our life and our living lie in him.[10] He belongs to us and we belong to him; we are in Christ and Christ is in us. In modern colloquial terms, we have a personal relationship with Jesus.

In Colossians 2:6–15, Paul provides a robust summary of the essential tenets of our union with Christ. The *means* of our union is the work of Christ in his death, burial, and resurrection, and our faith in the God who raised him from the dead (2:11–13). The *symbol* of our union is baptism in its depiction of being buried with Christ and being raised to new life with him (2:12). The *blessings* of our union include the fullness of all Christ has to offer, including our forgiveness of sins and new life in Christ (2:10, 13). The *assurance* of our union is the victory of Christ over our adversaries, especially the law that declares our guilt and the powers that oppose us (2:14–15).

---

be fully investigated *before* the punishment, and if the claim is true, then the criminal deserves at least a "respite from death," if not an escape (Cicero, *Verr.* 2.5.61, 64; cited by Elliott and Reasoner, 2010, 104).

10 Wayne Grudem defines union with Christ in the following way: "Union with Christ is a phrase used to summarize several different relationships between believers and Christ, through which Christians receive every benefit of salvation. These relationships include the fact that we are in Christ, Christ is in us, we are like Christ, and we are with Christ" (Grudem, 1994, 841).

The *exhortation* of our union is that we must live our lives in a new way that honors Christ as our Lord (2:6–7). The *admonition* of our union is the stern warning to resist any kind of teaching that does not conform to Christ (2:8).

Our union with Christ is central to the salvation we have received in Christ and the life we now live in Christ. From this, we may develop the practical implication that the key to growing in our Christian walk is to look first and foremost not to what we can do for him but to what he has done for us and who we have now become in him. We flourish as Christians when we understand and live out the reality of what we have already received and become in Christ. We become who we are in Christ that we might be who we have become. We therefore ought to beware lest we be taken captive and led away from Christ by false teaching, and we should instead walk faithfully in union with Christ Jesus our Lord.

PREACHING AND TEACHING STRATEGIES

Preaching Idea

Jesus is better than religion, so don't let religion take you captive.

Exegetical and Theological Synthesis

In the beginning of this passage, the apostle Paul begins to transition to exhortation after having set forth the magnificent Christology in chapter 1 and the first verses of chapter 2; but his heart and mind were so full of his favorite subject—Christ—that he stays with that theme. After brief exhortations to walk in Christ and not let anyone take them captive by philosophy, deceit, or human traditions (vv. 6–8), Paul quickly returns to the glories of Jesus and the salvation he brought the Colossians. For Paul, Christ was the only one who could save, so straying from him was tantamount to being taken captive, a potent metaphor for people living under Roman rule. In triumphal processions, Rome displayed their captives and plunder. To not be taken captive, the apostle Paul urges the Colossians to walk in Christ by being rooted, built up, and established in the faith (v. 7). A particular doctrine addressed in this passage was probably a Jewish teaching on circumcision (vv. 11–12), but when Christ imparts his life to sinners and they are buried with him in baptism, circumcision is unnecessary. The Mosaic code no longer testifies against them and spiritual circumcision occurs (v. 13). Christ's death on the cross was cosmic in scope as he disarmed the rulers and authorities, triumphing over them (vv. 14–15).

Theology bursts from the passage and includes the incarnation, evil powers, and sanctification, but the heart of the text is Christology and soteriology through union with Christ. Paul urges listeners to be on their guard lest they be taken captive by any power or philosophy that demotes Christ. He took captive those powers and triumphed over them.

Contemporary Connections

What does it mean?

What does the preaching idea mean by saying that Jesus is better than religion, so we should not let it take us captive? The metaphor of "taking captive" is military imagery of a triumphal procession. Examples from the first century can illustrate those processions as can examples and pictures from modern history and literature. On one occasion, I (Jeffrey) was teaching in Indonesia during their Independence Day (August 17). I watched elaborate and colorful processions as they paraded through the heart of the capital. No captives were displayed, but there were plenty of missiles, vehicles, and troops from all the branches of the military. In ancient Rome, along with military tour de force they also displayed the conquered people who were destined to become slaves.

But how did Paul use the metaphor? He was saying that by the cross and resurrection Jesus triumphed over human traditions, philosophies, and spiritual authorities. Jesus provided all that is necessary for justification with God and thus nullified systems of rule-keeping that promise salvation but only end up condemning us. As the Exposition states for Colossians 2:14, "The dogmas of the Mosaic law are forever incapable of rendering us guilty before God." Jesus canceled the debt we owed God for our sin. Since the debt is paid, we do not need moralistic rules to be right with God, something that Paul will address in more detail in the next pericope.

What moralistic ideas circulate today? Conservative churches may imply that people are justified by keeping man-made rules about dress, entertainment, alcohol, and politics. Liberal churches have their own shibboleths such as politically correct speech and the "correct" stance toward government programs. None of these save. Only the cross and resurrection have the power to cancel the debt of sin and only when we are in Christ by faith is his right standing before God transferred to believers.

Is it true?

Is it true that Christ-followers are in danger of being taken captive by various ideas and practices? Paul might answer, "Yes! That is why I wrote this passage." Verse 8 says, "See to it that no one takes you captive." Traveling teachers, both secular and religious, were common in the first century, perhaps even visiting the little town of Colossae. Other books of the New Testament speak often about such teachers as in 1, 2, and 3 John. Jude says that teachers had crept into the body and were perverting the grace of God and causing divisions (vv. 4, 19). Paul warned the Galatians about turning to a different gospel even if an angel from heaven should preach it (Gal. 1:6–9). In the second century, the church father Irenaeus (115–202?) said, "Error . . . is never set forth in its naked deformity, lest, being thus exposed, it should at once be detected. But it is craftily decked out in an attractive dress . . . to make it appear to the inexperienced . . . more true than truth itself" (*Against Heresies*, 1.2).

Moving to contemporary experience that supports the preaching idea, the sermon might point out that astrology is far from dead in the West. According to a 2017 Pew Research Center poll, almost 30 percent of Americans believe in astrology. *The New York Times* titled a piece, "How Astrology Took Over the Internet" (January 1, 2018), and the paper heralded astrology's return. One report found that Americans spend $2.2 billion annually on "mystical services" (including palmistry and tarot reading). The astrology app Co–Star is backed by $6 million and has been downloaded six million times.)

Further support for the preaching idea might simply be found in the fact that many people drift from the faith. Examples are all around us, but these should be used with discretion. Some of the people who drifted were captured by other religions or cults, and some simply became disillusioned with Christianity. Sometimes the drift occurs because of intellectual doubts, and sometimes because of emotional trauma. The story of Charles Darwin illustrates both (see sidebar).

The Slow Drift of Charles Darwin

The great scientist Charles Darwin was brought up in a conventionally Christian home in Victorian England and accepted the veracity of the Bible and the church's creeds. For a time he considered going into the ministry as a gentlemanly profession. While traveling the world as a naturalist aboard the *HMS Beagle*, Darwin became convinced that species developed by chance over vast epochs of time. That belief eventually led him to reject the Genesis account of creation, and eventually he rejected the whole Old Testament. Then he rejected the Gospels because of their accounts of miracles and the discrepancies in what claimed to be eyewitness accounts. Then a severe personal storm caused him to drift further—the death of his dear daughter, Annie, when she was only ten years old. Although the great scientist never became an outright atheist, his belief in God slowly evolved into something like the deist's "first cause." In Darwin's own words, "I gradually came to disbelieve in Christianity as a divine revelation. . . . I was very unwilling to give up my belief . . . but I found it more and more difficult . . . to invent evidence which would suffice to convince me. Thus disbelief crept over me at a very slow rate, but was at last complete. The rate was so slow that I felt no distress" (Darwin, 1911, 1:278).

Now what?

If Jesus is better than religion and has taken false teachings and powers captive, how should listeners respond? They should avoid being taken captive themselves (v. 8). But how? We might answer that question with three suggestions. First, we can learn to identify "philosophy and empty deceit" (v. 8). Second, we must reject the deceit. Third, we should then replace it with the truth.

The first step, identify lies, may be most difficult because false ideas often come packaged in art. We tend to listen to music and watch movies with shields lowered. For example, in "Mercy" (single on album *Rockferry*, 2008) Welsh pop singer Duffy asks for mercy from someone who has her under a "spell." She says that she can be free only if her lover releases her, so the message underneath the message is that romantic relationships have ultimate power to bind or free us. The *Star Wars* series of movies has popularized New Age ideas about a semiconscious, spiritual "Force" that infuses inanimate objects such as rocks and water. In *The Empire Strikes Back* (1980) Yoda states, "My ally is the Force, and a powerful ally it is. Life creates it, makes it grow. Its energy surrounds us and binds us. Luminous beings are we, not this crude matter. You must feel the Force around you; here, between you, me, the tree, the rock, everywhere, yes. Even between the land and the ship." Luke Skywalker passes on the same teaching to Rey in *The Force Awakens* (2015).

More pressing than the likelihood of being tripped up by New Age beliefs is unbiblical syncretism that blends religion and nationalism. The view that America is a chosen nation goes back to John Winthrop, who stated in a speech given in 1630 aboard the *Arbella* not long before reaching New England that the Puritans would be a "city on a hill"—a shining example of a Christian nation under God's special favor. Some Christians believe that even today and in their minds nationalism is part and parcel of the Christian faith.

Identifying and rejecting the world's deceptions is only half of the battle in not being taken captive. We also need something positive to embrace. Humans cannot continually say no to something unless something more attractive captivates our hearts and causes us to say yes. The "yes" this passage (and the whole book of Colossians) offers is Christ. The universal search for security and significance leads to Christ. As the Lord Jesus said to the Samaritan woman in John 4, "Whoever drinks of the water that I will give him will never be thirsty again" (v. 14). The citizens of Zion say truly, "All my springs are in you" (Ps. 87:7). Listing and explaining the many attributes of Christ in this passage may help listeners grasp his supremacy:

- He is the head of all authority (v. 10).
- He was resurrected (v. 12).
- He canceled the condemnation of the Mosaic code (v. 14).
- He triumphed over the rulers and authorities (v. 15).
- We are filled by him (v. 10), spiritually circumcised by him (v. 11), buried and raised with him in baptism (v. 12), made alive with him, and forgiven (v. 13).

Action steps that help people say yes to the Lord could be suggested: spiritual friendships where we pray for and encourage one another; the use of music as part of one's devotional practices; and meditation on Scripture about the glory of God.

How to Meditate on Scripture

1. Emphasize different words in the text.
2. Rewrite the text in your own words.
3. Think of an illustration of the text—what picture explains it?
4. Ask how the text points to something about Jesus.
5. Ask what question is answered or what problem is solved by the text.
6. Pray through the text.
7. Memorize the text.
8. Create an artistic expression of the text.
9. Ask the Philippians 4:8 questions of the text:
   - What is *true* about this, or what truth does it exemplify?
   - What is *honorable* about this?
   - What is *just* or right about this?
   - What is *pure* about this, or how does it exemplify purity?
   - What is *lovely* about this?
   - What is *commendable* about this?
   - What is *excellent* about this (that is, excels others of this kind)?
   - What is *praiseworthy* about this?[11]

Creativity in Presentation

To learn to identify false ideas, perhaps a participatory exercise could be arranged: display modern proverbs such as, "You only go around once," and "Your body is your own." Then play commercials that show the ideas in action and give listeners time to discuss which proverb best captures the commercial. The 1970s commercial made Schlitz beer famous with the slogan: "Go for the gusto" because "life's too short to go for less." That idea could be held up to the light of Scripture for analysis. A similar sentiment is taught in the movie *Dead Poets Society* (directed by Peter Weir, 1989) when Mr. Keating (played by Robin Williams) exhorts prep school young men to "*carpe diem*" (seize the day) because as mortals we are only "food for worms." Listeners could engage with one another or the preacher to examine that idea.

Although nations no longer lead captives in triumphal processions, pictures of grand military parades from Nazi Germany, the Soviet Union, or modern North Korea can convey the preaching idea. Illustrations of being taken captive into slavery could also serve that purpose. Historical stories such as Booker T. Washington (*Up from Slavery*, 1901), Solomon Northup (*Twelve Years a Slave*, 1853—made into a movie in 2013, directed by Steve McQueen), and *Amistad* (directed by Steven Spielberg, 1997) show captivity and release.

The Arch of Titus—Leading Captives

The first-century Arch of Titus was erected in Rome in A.D. 82 to commemorate Roman emperor Titus's victories, including his victory over the Jewish people in the year A.D. 70. The arch's engravings depict the triumphal procession as Titus entered Rome with the spoils of war taken from the Jewish people and the temple in Jerusalem, which Titus had destroyed. The spoils include a menorah.

To be "dead in trespasses" (v. 13) speaks about the human propensity to do wrong. William Golding's novel *Lord of the Flies* (1954) illustrates this. British schoolboys are stranded on an island after their plane crashes. There are no adults. They live in a paradisiacal setting. At first the well-educated, genteel boys attempt to rule themselves with a democratic system, but they soon devolve. They form tribes and survival of the fittest becomes the law of the land. Two film versions were made of the novel: 1963 (directed by Peter Brook) and 1990 (directed by Harry Hook).

Search the Internet for the short film "Falling Plates,"which is an artistically produced video (four minutes) that depicts the

11 Adapted from Donald Whitney, *Spiritual Disciplines for the Christian Life* (Colorado Springs: NavPress, 2014).

The treasure of Jerusalem, relief under the Arch of Titus, Rome, Italy. Public domain.

same truth—humans fail and sin in many ways—but it goes further than *Lord of the Flies* by also providing the solution. That solution is Jesus who came to redeem and reconcile.

The figure in the next column is a visual diagram of what it means to be dead in trespasses. Religion cannot solve these problems. Sin is first of all offense against God. This creates enmity between God and humans, and then it ripples out to alienate humans from themselves, from other people, groups of people (including collectives as large as nations), and even from nature.

To illustrate how we can resist being taken captive, we might contrast the stories of Odysseus (*The Odyssey*) and Orpheus (*The Argonautica*). Both of them sailed by the island of the Sirens who lured sailors to steer toward the island in order to shipwreck them on the rocks. Odysseus dealt with the problem by plugging his sailors' ears with

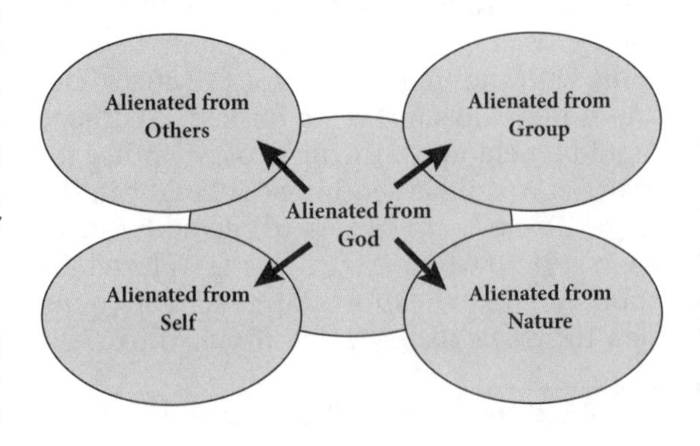

beeswax and having himself roped to the mast. A better way to resist the Siren song (and more comfortable!) was conceived by Orpheus. He drew his lyre and played louder and more beautifully than the Sirens were able to sing. He drowned them out. Christ sings a more beautiful song than the philosophies and powers. When we experience the fullness of union with Christ, we find it much easier to resist capture by false teaching.

Our creative methods and illustrations are tools to help us proclaim the main idea of the text: legalistic rules and man-made religions are inferior to Jesus, and they can do nothing to save and sanctify us. Jesus is better than religion, so don't let religion take you captive.

- The "powers" want to take us captive (2:8).
- But Christ has defeated the "powers" (2:9–15).
- So, don't let the powers take you captive (2:6–8).

DISCUSSION QUESTIONS

1. What or who are the "authorities"?
2. How has Christ triumphed over the authorities?
3. How does "all the fullness" dwell in Christ?
4. Discuss how stories and images may be the most potent forms for conveying "philosophy." Give an example of a TV commercial that uses "empty deceit" to promise more than it can deliver.
5. What are the blessings with which we have been filled in Christ?
6. What do you do when tempted to find satisfaction outside of Christ?
7. How does our union with Christ equip us to remain faithful to Christ?

Colossians 2:16–23

EXEGETICAL IDEA
Paul warned the Colossian believers against submitting themselves to teachings and practices that were unable to save them from the sinful flesh, whether Jewish laws that were outdated in light of Christ or pagan religions that were the vain fruit of human imagination.

THEOLOGICAL FOCUS
Believers must be on their guard against false teachings and religious practices that purport to offer something better than Christ when in reality they are empty, vain, and useless for conquering the flesh.

PREACHING IDEA
Shadows can't save us, but the Son can.

PREACHING POINTERS
In Paul's day, the Jewish and pagan teachers counseled, "Touch not, taste not, handle not—that's the way to conquer sinful desires!" But the apostle said: "Wrong!" Neither Jewish regulations nor the rituals of pagan worship could curb sinful desires and change the heart. Furthermore, the teachers in Paul's day were judging the members of the Colossian church for failing to follow Jewish and pagan rules, and Paul responded: "Don't let them do it!" Returning to the old practices, whether Jewish or polytheistic, is tantamount to abandoning Christ, and doing so would disqualify the Christ-followers in Colossae from receiving their reward.

Asceticism and legalism are alive today too: crawl up the towering flight of stairs on your knees, and you will earn God's favor; fast until your bones protrude, and you will get God's attention; deny yourself sex with your spouse because that's what the cult leader says to do, and then you will be free from carnal desire. This passage addresses people who have been saved from heavy-handed, false religions. Ironically, some Christians are tempted to return to those old ways. Legalism goads them: do more, do better, and then God will give you grace. But religious rules are just a shadow of the deeper reality that is Christ. He has already defeated the flesh, so we must cling to him alone. Making an idol out of anything—even spiritual practices like fasting, prayer, and self-denial—leads to shame and withdrawal when we fail, or pride and scoffing when we succeed. Legalistic rules and man-made religious ideas are just a shadow, and shadows can't save us, but the Son can.

WATCH OUT FOR FALSE TEACHING! (2:16–23)

LITERARY STRUCTURE AND THEMES (2:16–23)

In Colossians 2:16–23, Paul engages in outright polemic against false teaching. He previously warned broadly regarding "someone" (τις) who might take believers captive through philosophy and empty rhetoric (Col. 2:8). Now, Paul reintroduces this "someone" (τις; 2:16; similarly, "no one" [μηδείς] in 2:18) and he defines more specifically the kinds of teachings that might capture believers. He issues two parallel warnings, first warning the Colossians to "let no one judge you" (κρινέτω; 2:16), and second warning them to "let no one disqualify you" (καταβραβευέτω; 2:18). Both of these warnings are followed by a brief explanation introduced by the relative pronoun "which is" (ἅ; 2:17, 18–19). The final verses, 2:20–23, provide a transition within the letter. The content of these verses looks back to Paul's warnings and offers the final, devastating critique that these false teachings offer no solution to the problem of the flesh.

- ***Warning against Jewish Traditions (2:16–17)***
- ***Warning against Pagan Religions (2:18–19)***
- ***Summary of Warnings and Final Critique (2:20–23)***

EXPOSITION (2:16–23)

This section includes clear historical parallels to opponents who lived within the historical context of Paul's Colossian audience, but Paul's cryptic language makes it notoriously difficult to identify these opponents with precision today. The simplest and most straightforward way to interpret and exposit this section is to interpret each of the three sections in light of their particular historical background. The first warning speaks especially to Jewish traditions (2:16–17), the second warning speaks especially to pagan religions (2:18–19), and the final section (2:20–23) summarizes all of Paul's warnings and issues a final critique that applies to both Jewish traditions and pagan religions apart from Christ (see sidebar). Further, the explanations Paul attaches to each of these warnings effectively ground the warnings in Christ, who is the full reality (2:17), who is the head of the body (2:19), and in whom believers have died to the world (2:20). Paul's main point, in other words, is not only to warn against opponents, but also to appeal to believers that they must hold fast to Christ and not allow themselves to be judged or disqualified by these or any other opponents.

Literary and Historical Analysis

In Colossians 2:16–23, Paul weaves together two threads of polemic targeting Jewish regulations on the one hand and pagan worship on the other. These two threads also appear in 2:8 and 2:14–15, and we can trace these two threads in the figure on the next page.

Warning against Jewish Traditions (2:16–17)

Paul warns the Colossians against those who would judge them on the basis of Jewish laws and customs that belong to a former age where they were foreshadows of Christ.

Watch Out for False Teaching! (2:16–23)

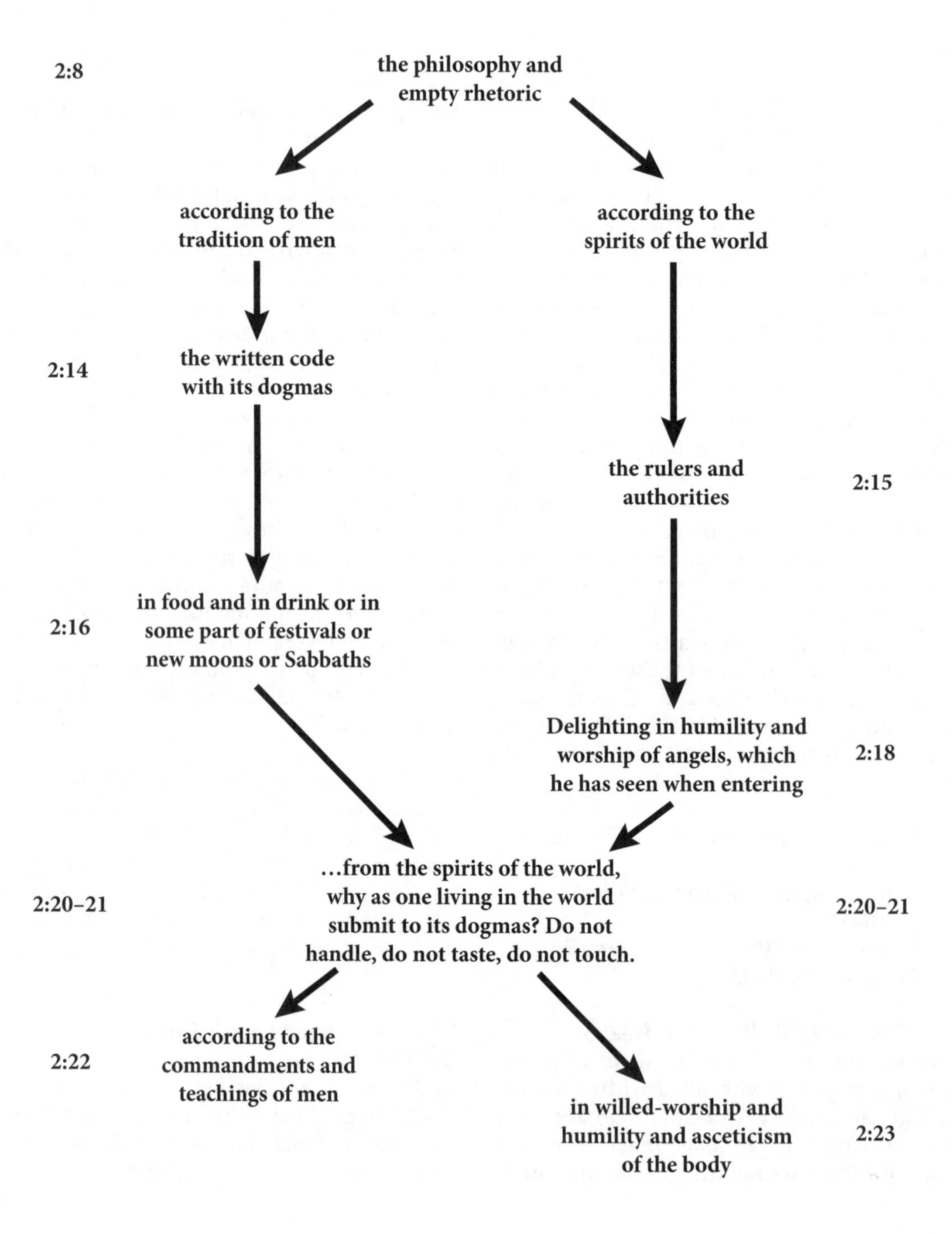

2:16. Paul's first warning comes in the form of a third person imperative, which could literally be translated as, "Therefore, someone must not judge you" (μὴ οὖν τις ὑμᾶς κρινέτω). In Greek, the third person imperative issues a command regarding a person who is not actually the direct audience to whom the command is spoken. Even though the command is for *them* the implications are actually for *you*, to whom the command is spoken. Thus, Paul expects the Colossians to understand the implications for themselves of this command spoken with regard to those who are doing the judging, namely, that they should "let no one pass judgment on you" (ESV; cf. HCSB, NIV, KJV, NRSV).

Third Person Imperatives

If a child tells his parents about a particular bully at school, that parent might respond with a third person imperative, expressed in English as, "He shall not bully you." By speaking this command to the victim rather than to the actual bully, the bullying behavior is condemned and the victim is encouraged to take appropriate steps to see that behavior ended. In other words, the child actually hears their parents say, "Bullying is wrong and you should not have to be affected by it. Let's find a way to make it stop."

The term "judge" (κρίνω) is neutral with regard to the outcome of the judgment. It may refer to the positive judgment of vindication or to the negative judgment of condemnation. But the context of Paul's warning here and the parallel imperative in 2:18 ("let no one disqualify you") indicate that Paul speaks here of a negative and discrediting kind of judgment. Such persons would criticize Christians for their faith in Christ, as if their religious experience in Christ is somehow deficient or incomplete. In Paul's estimation, such judgments are inherently invalid because they do not properly grasp the true nature of Christ and his work, and therefore these self-appointed judges "must always be avoided" by Christians within the church (Harris, 2010, 104).

Paul lists five criteria these judges use as a basis for their invalid judgments, and this list moves from the vague to the particular. The first two criteria—food and drink—are so generic they could apply to virtually any philosophical or religious group in history, and the final three criteria—feasts, new moons, and Sabbaths—are increasingly Jewish in nature. The final criteria, Sabbaths, is so distinctively Jewish that it suggests Paul has Jewish regulations in mind throughout 2:16.

The list of criteria begins with "food" (βρῶσις) and "drink" (πόσις), but Paul does not indicate whether the issue is one of partaking or of abstaining from such food and drink. The Old Testament law contains numerous regulations regarding food. Some laws prohibit certain foods, such as blood (Lev. 17:10–16) and unclean animals (Lev. 11:1–47). On certain occasions, the law commands particular foods to be eaten, especially in the observance of specified feasts, including the Feasts of Firstfruits, Weeks, Trumpets and Booths (Lev. 23:9–25; 33–44). At times, the prescriptive and proscriptive laws merge together, as in the instructions for the Passover Feast, which call for a slaughtered lamb to be eaten after seven days of eating bread but excluding leaven (Exod. 12:1–28, 43–5; Lev. 23:4–8). Few laws pertain to drink, as mentioned by Paul, but the Nazirite vows provide a notable exception (Num. 6:1–4), and Paul himself may have taken such a vow (Acts 18:18).

Dietary Regulations in the First-Century World

Jews were not the only first-century group with regulations pertaining to food and drink. Many religious groups, including both philosophical groups (e.g., Stoicism, Epicureanism, etc.) and pagan religions had various regulations, some calling for abstention and others for participation in meals and libations. One could almost say that first-century religious observance of any kind was inseparable from food and drink rituals. In the city of Hierapolis (six miles from Colossae), archaeologists have uncovered a *scaenae frons*—the engravings that decorated the front of the theater—depicting a festal procession leading to the theater, where a bull was sacrificed and a feast undertaken, all in honor of the goddess Artemis (see discussion in Copenhaver, 2018, 190–91; Mellink, 1987, 29; D'Andria, 2001, 108). Indeed, feasts were often associated with pagan sacrifices, and they were so ubiquitous that Clement of Alexandria (ca. A.D. 150–215) remarks, "Sacrifices were devised by men, I do think, as a pretext for meat meals" (Clement of Alexandria, *Strom.* 7.6.89; trans. Butterworth). Christians would have faced pressure to observe ritualistic dietary practices from many different directions.

Paul next mentions a "feast" (ἑορτή), whether in "part" (μέρος) or a whole, and in the first-century world, people loved a good feast every bit as much as we do today! Indeed, pagan religions followed calendars prescribing various feasts, and cities actually competed against one another to hold the most extravagant feasts in honor of the gods. Wealthy residents would sponsor such feasts to demonstrate their generosity and to seek favor with the emperor and the gods (Macro, 1980, 682–83; cf. Jones, 1963, 7). These feasts were closely associated with pagan worship, and many Christians therefore abstained from eating the food because it had first been sacrificed to idols (e.g., 1 Cor. 8:1–13).

But the Jewish calendar of feasts presented an even more vexing problem for these Christians. Should they participate in the feasts such as Passover, Tabernacles, and Pentecost? These feasts are, after all, prescribed in the Old Testament Scriptures! Jewish communities scheduled additional religious rituals and festivals according to the monthly cycles of the "new moon" (νεομηνία) as mentioned here by Paul (Thornton, 1989, 97–100; VanderKam, 1998, 111–12). Natural pressure surely fell upon the Colossian Christians to participate in these annual and monthly Jewish feasts even in Colossae.

The final criteria Paul mentions in 2:16 is "Sabbaths" (σαββάτων), a term virtually synonymous with the Jewish Scriptures and practice. Rarely, if ever, was the term used or the practice observed by a non-Jewish group in the ancient world. The mention of Sabbaths here confirms that throughout Paul's list in 2:16, he has Jewish regulations in view. Indeed, the final three terms—feasts, new moons, and Sabbaths—appear together as a summary of Jewish practices in Jewish literature including the Septuagint (e.g., 1 Chron. 23:31; 2 Chron. 2:3; 31:3; Ezek. 45:17), Josephus (e.g., *Ant.* 11.77; 3.237–238; *J.W.* 229–230) and Philo (*Spec. Laws* 2.41).Early Christian literature also summarizes Jewish practice with these terms (e.g., Justin, *Dial.* 8.4; Diogn. 4.1–6).

On the whole, therefore, Paul's warning in 2:16 envisions Jewish adherents who are exercising judgment upon Christians based on their observance of food, drink, and calendrical rituals. By this judgment, the Colossian believers themselves are under pressure to follow such regulations, and they are being treated with scorn and derision for their disregard of these practices. We must remember again that those who exercise this kind of judgment have a certain logic on their side. If Christians regard the Jewish Scriptures also to be Christian Scriptures, why shouldn't they observe the very practices set forth in those Scriptures? Paul answers this very question with a shorthand answer in the next verse.

2:17. Paul now gathers together all five criteria with a plural relative pronoun (ἅ) and he subjects these criteria to a singular critique introduced by the singular verb "is" (ἐστιν). All such regulations share a common deficiency in that they are a "shadow" (σκιά) as opposed to the "reality" (σῶμα), which is Christ. This kind of contrast between shadow and reality was well known to the ancient world, but typically the shadow was set in contrast to "substance" (εἰκών). Paul employs unusual—but acceptable—language for his contrast when he uses the term that literally means "body" (σῶμα; KJV) but may also indicate "reality" (NIV, NLT) or "substance" (ESV, NRSV, HCSB). Indeed, Paul uses this word in Colossians to refer to the physical body of Jesus (1:22) and to the church as the body of Christ (1:18, 24; cf. 2:19; 3:15). His play on words here may be an intentional way of pointing us to the body of Christ, both physical and ecclesial, as the substance or reality in opposition to shadows. In other words, the regulations are a shadow, but Christ in his person and church are the reality.

Paul takes great care to define the temporal sense in which these regulations served in their own time as shadows looking forward to "things to come" (τῶν μελλόντων). We might call them "foreshadows" since they precede and look ahead to that which they shadow. For Paul, in other words, the deficiency of these Jewish regulations is temporal in nature. They were given by God for a season in history, during which time they were binding upon God's people, but they were never intended to be the final revelation from God. Now that Christ has come in the body, these regulations are exposed as *mere* shadows. For those who live in the present time and who have received the reality of Christ, these regulations lose their authority even as shadows disappear under the full blaze of the noonday sun. Those who have Christ and belong to Christ in the present moment have no obligation to observe the regulations of a bygone era, and therefore they should not submit themselves to those who still live and judge by such antiquated criteria. Those who have the Jesus of today should not be judged according to the regulations of yesterday.

The Apocalyptic Paul and the Turning of the Ages

Paul's explanation in Colossians 2:17 reflects his underlying "apocalyptic imagination" in which he sees in Christ a turning of the ages (Blackwell, Goodrich, and Maston, 2016). Scholars define this apocalyptic mindset in light of certain ancient Jewish texts that feature, among other themes, the idea that history can be divided into two ages and that a day is coming when God will turn the pages of history from one age to the next (e.g., Ezek., Dan., *4 Ezra*, *2 Bar.*). In Paul's estimation, Christ marks the dividing point between the ages anticipated by these texts, so that in Christ, the ages have been turned from what *was* to what *is*, from *then* to *now*.

At the same time, "Paul's conception is necessarily more nuanced" than Jewish apocalyptic thought in that for Paul, though the Messiah has now accomplished redemption and the Spirit is poured out, the final establishment of God's kingdom, including the eradication of sin and the general resurrection, have not yet been completed (Moo, 1996, 26). Thus, the new era has begun, but the old era has not completely been replaced, so the two eras overlap and presently coexist. This demonstrates that "Paul is not concerned about purely chronological differences but about the difference in *character* between the two ages," so that the age of flesh, law, and sin has been replaced by the age of faith, promise, and salvation (Silva, 1988, 186; cited by Moo, 1996, 26). Therefore, for Paul, the pages of history turned from one era to another when Christ died on the cross, but only those who are in Christ experience the present benefits of participation in this new era while those who are not in Christ remain in the old age.

This turning of the ages necessarily carries numerous implications, including important implications for the Jewish law and customs.

Paul does not argue in 2:17 that the law was inherently deficient, nor that these Jewish regulations were erroneous or even incomplete; rather, Paul contends that the law belonged to the former age and must now be reassessed in light of what God has accomplished in Christ.[1] In the former age, these Jewish regulations served an essential purpose among God's people even as they anticipated events that were still to come, but now that the fulfillment has arrived, Paul looks back upon these regulations as former shadows that are no longer binding in the same way upon those who belong to Christ in the present age. Therefore, though some Old Testament laws are directly applied to Christians in the new age (e.g., Matt. 22:34–40), and though Christians may choose to observe additional regulations for various reasons of conscience—as even Paul does in Acts 21:17–26, and as Paul allows others to do in Romans 14—these additional regulations must not be imposed as binding upon all Christians, nor may judgment be passed based upon them. Such baseless judgments do not belong in the present age of Christ.

Warning against Pagan Religions (2:18–19)

Paul warns the Colossians against those who would disqualify the Colossians' worship experience in Christ because of their lack of participation in other worship experiences such as the cult of Apollo, and Paul explains the futility of worshipping pagan gods and the foolishness of not holding fast to Christ as their head.

2:18. In its grammatical structure, Paul's second warning in 2:18 parallels his first warning in 2:16. Paul again uses a third person imperative but now explicitly rejects not only the judgment (as in 2:16) but also the verdict of that judgment. The Colossians should allow no one to "condemn" or "disqualify" them and thereby condemn or rob them of the prize that is due them (BDAG, s.v. "καταβραβεύω," p. 515; Lohse, 1971, 117; Yinger, 2003). The term recalls a context of athletic games where the victor receives the prize, but should the victor be disqualified, they would be stripped of that prize. For believers, the prize of our faith is eschatological in nature as we anticipate the coming appearing of Christ, when we will share in his glory (3:4) and be presented blameless before him (1:22). However, receiving the prize is in some measure dependent upon our continuing in the faith (1:23) such that should we abandon our participation in Christ, our prize is in no way assured to us (see the earlier comments regarding perseverance in 1:23). In this way, therefore, those who seek to lead believers away from faithfulness to Christ in fact seek to disqualify believers from receiving their prize. Believers must resist such external pressures with all diligence, for the stakes could not be higher.

Here in 2:18, Paul warns against a specific kind of disqualification that comes from those who participate in pagan religions and apply pressure to believers to do the same. Such a person "delights in" (NIV) or is "taking pleasure in" (BDAG, s.v. "θέλω" 3b, p. 448) or "insisting on" (ESV, HCSB) humility and angel worship, both of which can be traced to pagan worship in the first century. "Humility" (ταπεινοφροσύνη) typically refers to a positive virtue in the New Testament (e.g., Eph.. 4:2; Phil. 2:3; 1 Pet. 5:5), and indeed Paul will commend the Colossians to put on humility as a Christlike attribute mentioned in Colossians 3:12. However, in the hands of these disqualifiers, humility takes on a negative character opposed to Christ. Thus, some translations indicate this negative form of humility by rendering it "asceticism" (ESV, HCSB) or "false humility" (NIV) in this context. Within the context of pagan religions, and especially

1 Paul's view of the law continues to be debated among scholars and countless books have been written on the topic, but Thielman provides a good place to begin reading (Thielman, 1995).

the mystery religions, practices of humility, including fasting and self-denial, played a central role for all involved. Participants in such cultic activity often fasted in preparation, and the oracles and priests practiced fasting and sexual abstention as part of the ritual.

Their humility pairs with their "worship of angels." Paul uses a word here for worship that often denotes the cultic rituals associated with temple worship (BDAG, s.v. "θρησκεία," p. 459), and such worship is here offered to angels. In pagan religion, angels are spiritual beings that serve the gods and bear their messages, not unlike how angels in Christian Scripture serve the one true God. Angels are subservient to the gods such that even in the hyper-polytheistic ancient world, where gods multiplied *ad nauseum*, we are hard-pressed to find examples of a cultic system devoted directly to angels rather than to the gods. In other words, even pagans did not worship angels. Paul's reference to the worship of angels, therefore, must be carefully interpreted in light of his next phrase, that this worship was "seen when entering" (ἑόρακεν ἐμβατεύων).

The word "entering" (ἐμβατεύω) was closely associated with mystery religions in the ancient world, so much so, that some modern-day scholars think it may have been a technical term for initiation into one of these pagan cults (Dibelius, 1975). For example, when worshippers arrived at the door of the temple of the god Apollo in the nearby city of Claros, they underwent a system of ritual (including fasting and sexual abstinence) to prepare them for their entrance into the temple. Upon "entering" (ἐμβατεύω), they were led into an underground chamber where the cultic worship of Apollo was conducted and where oracles delivered messages they received from Apollo in their visions. Those who "entered" into such a place certainly saw an elaborate system of worship centered upon the gods.

Entrance (ἐμβατεύω) and the Oracle of Apollo at Claros

Many cities from all around Asia Minor sent official delegations to Claros to consult with Apollo's oracle, and the record of their visit was sometimes memorialized in inscriptions. Four inscriptions uncovered at the temple in Claros use the word "entering" (ἐμβατεύω) to describe delegations being led underground to consult the oracle, including a delegation from Laodicea (Arnold, 1995, 110–13). Another inscription (ca. A.D. 165–170) discovered in Hierapolis records the message a delegation from Hierapolis had received from the same oracle in Claros regarding a devastating disease (Ritti and Arthur, 2006, 94–99). The oracle instructed the citizens of Hierapolis to offer sacrifices and feasts to the gods and to erect sacred images of Apollo at the city gates of Hierapolis so Apollo could fend off the disease with his bow. The prominent placement of the inscription in Hierapolis suggests the oracle of Apollo was widely known and highly regarded at that time in the Lycus Valley.

Paul uses all of the proper language to identify such pagan worship, including practices of humility (ταπεινοφροσύνη), cultic worship (θρησκεία), and the entrance itself (ἐμβατεύω). But Paul disrupts the normal language of mystery religion with one word: angels. He shocks us by describing the worship that takes place in these temples as worship being delivered to angels rather than to gods. The participants of such worship certainly viewed their worship as being delivered to a god, and in the case of Apollo, to the *supreme* god. But Paul will not dignify such worship as being devoted to a genuine god; instead, Paul slights the gods and diminishes their rank by referring to them as *mere* angels. The gods—Apollo, Artemis, Hekate, Isis, Osiris, and the like—belong to the realm of the elemental spirits (στοιχεῖα), the powers and authorities that have been created through Christ (1:16) and subdued by Christ (2:15). These gods are not higher powers—they are lower powers.

Paul and the Art of the Not-So-Subtle Slight

When Paul speaks of pagan gods and their worship, he sometimes refuses to use the language of those who worship such gods. Though such worshippers might use divine and exalted language to speak of their gods, Paul rejects their language and instead describes their gods as *he* sees them. For example, in 1 Corinthians 10:20–21, Paul refers to the food served in pagan temples as having been offered not to gods but to demons, and in 1 Thessalonians 1:2–7, Paul pejoratively characterizes the pantheon of ancient deities as idols (cf. Hurtado, 2017, 40–41). Adherents to these gods would surely take offense at hearing their gods labeled as demons or idols. In the same way, in Colossians 2:18 Paul pejoratively describes pagan worship as being offered not actually to gods but rather to angels.

In Paul's estimation, though those who enter into such worship may have a sincere experience, and though they may even genuinely encounter spiritual beings, they are not actually worshipping a god—and certainly not a god so highly exalted as Christ himself. Therefore, Paul says such experiences are "to no avail" (BDAG, s.v. "εἰκῇ" 2, p. 281). They bear no result, and how could they, when such a lesser power is supplicated? Instead, the pleasure such participants experience and describe is really only the result of their own minds that have been overinflated (φυσιόω) by their flesh, which is itself corrupted by sin and in need of redemption (Col. 1:21–22).

In other words, their "religion" is a failure. Religions in general purport to offer us a way to worship a higher being external to ourselves, turning us away from ourselves and toward the spiritual realm of the divine. But these participants in 2:18 have had the precise opposite experience, in Paul's estimation. Their worship has collapsed inwardly, so that their experience arises from the overinflated imaginings of their own corrupted minds. This is the ultimate self-absorption, a religion that connects us to ourselves rather than to God and that entrenches us in our own delusions and self-deceptions. It is vanity at every level, it is failed worship, and it is ultimately conducted in vain, regardless of the positive and appealing descriptions offered so confidently by its adherents.

2:19. What relation, then, does such pagan worship have to Christ himself? None, and that is precisely the problem. Paul continues his critique by now suggesting that those who hold to such worship of angels do not in fact "hold fast" (κρατέω) to "the head" (τὴν κεφαλήν), who is Christ (1:18). Paul does not indicate whether or not they ever held to Christ in the first place, but they certainly do not hold to Christ now. In Paul's estimation, the very fact that they participate in pagan worship indicates they do not hold to Christ. The two are mutually exclusive: the one who holds to pagan religion necessarily does not hold to Christ, and the one who holds to Christ necessarily does not hold to pagan religions. To hold to one is to let go of the other. Paul's evaluation here thus contains strong traces of irony, for those who would purport to disqualify the Colossians for their lack of participation in pagan worship have in fact become disqualified themselves by their very participation in that pagan worship. Paul disqualifies the would-be disqualifiers, placing them under the very judgment they foist upon believers. Because they do not hold to Christ, *they* are disqualified and their disqualifying judgments of believers have no credibility.

Further, it is from Christ as the head that the "entire body" (πᾶν τὸ σῶμα) grows with the growth that comes from God (αὔξει τὴν αὔξησιν τοῦ θεοῦ). This growth, as in Colossians 1:6, can be both quantitative and qualitative, pointing toward the continual adding of new members and the maturing of the body in

Christ. Clearly Paul views the body as dynamic rather than static, with everything that we need for the ongoing changes and transformations being provided by Christ himself. He "supplies" (ἐπιχορηγέω) the body with all that we need for sustained life in him, and he "unites" (συμβιβάζω) the body and holds us all together. In the church, we are interconnected, as if we are held together by joints and ligaments (διὰ τῶν ἁφῶν καὶ συνδέσμων), and as we together hold to Christ as our head, he unites us and resources us, so that we grow in Christ and have the full measure of religious experience.

There is nothing, therefore, that we could want to experience in our worship that we do not already have access to in Christ. There is no higher power out there, no experience more delightful, no worship more meaningful, no ritual more effective, no membership more fulfilling than what we have in Christ. So when someone describes their religious experience and it seems otherworldly and superior, let us take care that we see it for what it really is—the vain worship of lesser beings that is being exaggerated by the minds of those who do not know Christ.

Summary of Warnings and Final Critique (2:20–23)

Paul summarizes his entire polemic and exposes the utter futility of all dogmas and religious practices that are opposed to Christ, for they are actually worthless for solving humanity's ultimate spiritual problem of sin and the flesh.

2:20. Paul now begins a transition from polemic to positive exhortation. The parallel grammatical structure of 2:20 ("if you died with Christ") and 3:1 ("if you were raised with Christ") indicate the two parts of this transition. In 2:20–23, Paul looks backward and summarizes his polemic to this point, while in 3:1–4 he looks forward and introduces the exhortations to follow. When we closely read 2:20–23, we find terms and themes recalling Paul's warnings in 2:8, 14–15, and 16–19. Some of these verbal parallels and thematic repetition can literally be lost in translation, but when they are recovered and closely considered, they reveal that Paul uses 2:20–23 to summarize his entire polemic and to offer his strongest critique. Here Paul emphasizes the utter futility of adhering to religious practices apart from Christ, whether they be outdated Jewish practices or idolatrous pagan practices.

Paul begins with a direct question based on a condition: "*If* you died with Christ . . . *why* still submit to dogmas?" Paul bases his argument here on the established theology of believers' union with Christ in his death and resurrection (2:11–12). Now Paul adds a further implication—when they died with Christ, they simultaneously were transferred into a new sphere of existence. Their death moved them "away from" (ἀπό) the "spirits of the world" (τῶν στοιχείων τοῦ κόσμου; cf. 2:8). Paul speaks here not of a physical relocation but of a change of domain such that believers no longer live under the authority of the spirits, and they thereby no longer carry out their existence within the realm of the world.

Life in the World (κόσμος)

Paul uses the location of our lives as a metaphor for the sphere of authority under which we live our lives, and he contrasts life in the world with life in Christ. In one sense, believers who live under the authority of Christ continue to live in the world, perhaps even in precisely the same geographical location within the world. But at the same time, Paul can say that they no longer live in the world, for Paul regards the world to be contrasted with Christ such that the two are mutually exclusive. A person's life belongs to one or the other, to the world or to Christ. Further, all people live in the world prior to converting to Christ, at which time they die out of the world and are raised to new life in Christ. Therefore, all who are apart from Christ are part of the world, including all of Paul's adversaries in his polemic, be they attached to pagan religion or Jewish practice.

Because believers no longer live in the world, Paul asks a penetrating question: Why "submit to its regulations" (δογματίζω) as if you do still live in the world? Previously, Paul associated dogma (δόγμα) with the Jewish law (see 2:14), but he seems to be speaking more broadly now of any regulations that are not according to Christ. Paul's question may be based either in reality or in the hypothetical. He may be admonishing the Colossians for their present and ongoing error, in the sense of "why *continue* submitting to its regulations?" (taking δογματίζεσθε as a continuous present) or he may be warning against a hypothetical or unrealized threat, in the sense "why *would you* submit to its regulations?" Either way, Paul's point is resoundingly clear: those who no longer live under the domain of the world should not obligate themselves to obey the world's principles.

2:21. Paul gives the following three examples of the dogmas he has in mind, but he mixes in a little hyperbole for effect: "Do not handle" (Μὴ ἅψῃ), "nor taste" (μηδὲ γεύσῃ), "nor touch" (μηδὲ θίγῃς). These three prohibitions recall the food and drink regulations of 2:16 and the humility (which likely included fasting) in 2:18. These kinds of regulations, we have seen, were part of various religious practices among both Jewish and pagan worshippers. Here, however, Paul cites extraordinarily restrictive prohibitions—don't even touch or taste—and Paul does not specify whether he has a particular food or drink, or perhaps even sexual conduct, in view. His commands are far broader and less defined than any actual religious restrictions in the first century. It appears, therefore, that Paul is making an *argumentum ad absurdum* ("argument to absurdity") in which he exaggerates their prohibitions to the absurd extreme to demonstrate the ineffectiveness of such prohibitions.[2] Indeed, such prohibitions, even when followed to the extreme, prove themselves to be impotent and ineffective for the accomplishment of their intended ends, and this failure is precisely Paul's point in 2:22–23.

2:22. Paul now critiques the dogmas, and he includes a specific echo of his statements about Jewish regulations in 2:16–17. He contends that such dogmas lead their adherents in a decidedly negative direction, for prohibitions are "destined" (NIV; cf. BDAG, s.v. "εἰς" 4d, p. 290) for "corruption" or "destruction" (BDAG, s.v. "φθορά" 1, pp. 1054–1055). Indeed, it is by their very use (τῇ ἀποχρήσει; instrumental dative) that this destruction draws near, as if submitting to these dogmas (and letting go of Christ) hastens self-destruction. It is no small thing to become detached from Christ, who reconciles us to God (1:20–21), forgives our sins, and raises us to new life (2:12–13). Apart from Christ, we experience the slow destruction of daily attrition that comes with not receiving his nourishment (2:19) and we are at risk of the eternal destruction that comes if we enter judgment having shifted away from our hope in the gospel (1:22–23). Paul could hardly have found more damning language for the consequences of capitulating to these dogmas—they will destroy us!

In the final phrase of 2:22, Paul narrows his focus specifically to those dogmas that are according to the "commands" (ἔνταλμα) and "teachings of men" (διδασκαλίας τῶν ἀνθρώπων). This last phrase echoes Paul's language in 2:8, where he spoke of Jewish practices as "according to the traditions of men" (κατὰ τὴν παράδοσιν τῶν ἀνθρώπων).

2 Lightfoot suggests Paul's prohibitions are quoting "the false teachers in their own words," and he points to uncited rabbinical passages and to the "rigorous asceticism" of the Essenes as examples (Lightfoot, 1981, 202–3). However, Paul's language goes so far beyond historical parallels that he is more likely speaking "sarcastically" (MacDonald, 2000, 116) or with exaggeration.

Paul now replaces "traditions" with "teachings," but in so doing, he creates a deliberate echo of Isaiah 29:13, where the prophet Isaiah criticizes Israel for drawing near to the Lord with their lips while their hearts are far from him, so that their fear of the Lord is *merely* a "commandment and teaching taught by men" (ἐντάλματα ἀνθρώπων καὶ διδασκαλίας; Isa. 29:13, LXX; cf. Beetham, 2008, 251–88). Similarly, when Jesus criticizes the Pharisees and scribes for their hypocrisy regarding dietary laws, he uses this same language from Isaiah (Matt. 15:9; Mark 7:7). Thus, when Paul refers to the commandments and teachings of men in Colossians 2:22, he is thinking especially of those regulations that arise from within the Mosaic law but that served in a former age as shadows looking ahead to Christ (see 2:16–17). Therefore, those who hold to these regulations still today and do not hold to Christ will reap the destructive consequences.

2:23. Paul finishes his polemic with a second evaluation parallel to that in 2:22, but now Paul shifts his focus again to pagan religion. This verse contains yet another round of complicated grammar that is not easily untangled. The verse makes the best sense if we divide it into two contrasting statements, as in "on the one hand . . . but" (a μέν . . . δέ construction in Greek in which the δέ has been elided; see Lightfoot, 1981, 203–4). The first statement begins with a relative pronoun (ἅτινά) referring again to the dogmas of 2:21. These dogmas "have" (ἐστιν . . . ἔχοντα; periphrastic part; cf. Wallace, 1996, 648) only an appearance of wisdom. We may not typically understand Paul's Greek term here (λόγος) as "appearance," but such a reading is lexically possible (BDAG, s.v. "λόγος" 1aβ, p. 599) and makes the best sense in this context, since Paul will create a contrast in the second half of 2:23 suggesting that they have no actual wisdom. Most translations therefore use "appearance" (e.g., ESV, NIV, NRSV), or even "shew" (KJV).

In other words, these dogmas, when viewed from a certain perspective, do indeed *appear* to have wisdom, especially in their rules directing worship (ἐθελοθρησκία), their call for "humility" (ταπεινοφροσύνη), and their attempt to control the body through the harsh restrictions of ascetism (ἀφειδίᾳ σώματος). Paul's language here echoes very clearly his polemic in 2:18, where he criticized pagan religions for their "worship" (θρησκεία) of angels conducted with "humility" (ταπεινοφροσύνη). Now, in 2:23, Paul acknowledges the attraction such pagan worship holds, since they offer a form of worship and discipline that seems to contain a certain amount of wisdom. But appearances can be deceiving, and close approximations can be deceiving indeed. The appearance of wisdom associated with pagan dogmas pales in contrast to the true and abundant wisdom found in Christ, in whom are "all the treasures of wisdom" (2:3).

Further, Paul ends 2:23 by exposing the ultimate futility of these regulations to accomplish the most important goal. They have no "value" (BDAG, s.v. "τιμή" 1, p. 1005), Paul says, when it comes to opposing or standing "against" (BDAG, s.v. "πρός" 3d, p. 874; cf. Col. 3:13) the indulgence or "satisfaction" (BDAG, s.v. "πλησμονή," p. 830) of the flesh (σάρξ). For Paul, the ultimate human problem is the problem of the flesh, by which Paul means the sinful nature with its corruption and desires. When we are united to Christ by faith, the problem of the flesh is fully resolved and removed completely from us (2:11). But pagan religions with their dogmas are completely incapable of solving this problem. They cannot hold their ground against the flesh or restrict its sinful desires and consequences, no matter how severe the dogmas and asceticism become. The victory we have gained in Christ over the flesh truly belongs to Christ alone; no other religion, tradition, or set of dogmas can compete.

Indeed, Christ takes us across the finish line, while other religions leave their adherents at the starting line. They only *appear* to offer a solution. Again Paul's point resounds: why would anyone exchange fullness for emptiness, treasures for appearances, real solutions for empty promises?

THEOLOGICAL FOCUS

The exegetical idea (Paul warned the Colossian believers against submitting themselves to teachings and practices that were unable to save them from the sinful flesh, whether Jewish laws that were outdated in light of Christ or pagan religions that were the vain fruit of human imagination) leads to this theological focus: Believers must be on their guard against false teachings and religious practices that purport to offer something better than Christ when in reality they are empty, vain, and useless for conquering the flesh.

Paul's warnings in these verses are passionate and defensive, as he appeals to the Colossian believers to be on guard against the winds of judgment arising from Jewish regulations and the tectonic shifts of disqualification arising from pagan religious practices. Though Paul's precise opponents in the first century may no longer be active in our twenty-first-century world, the same kinds of teachings and patterns of practices exist today, and they can still exert negative impact upon believers.

The false teaching of legalism resurfaces regularly in various forms, seeking to impose additional rules and regulations upon believers and judging those who do not comply. Such forms of legalism suggest that we must solve the problem of our flesh through self-discipline, as if the work of Christ in his death and in our union with him was not sufficient for putting off our flesh (Col. 2:12–13). Paul does not have in view here the kinds of spiritual disciplines that lead to sanctification in Christ, the likes of which he himself will endorse in 3:15–17; rather, Paul has in view legalistic disciplines that are devoid of Christ and lead to destruction. Paul reminds us that all legalistic approaches to regulations are insufficient for those who belong to Christ, even when such regulations arise from the Old Testament law, for Christ is the full reality of what the law could only foreshadow.

Likewise, false claims about spiritual worship abound today, even if Apollo and other pagan gods are no longer worshipped. Paul establishes a rubric for worship in Colossians 2:19 whereby any worship that is not connected directly to Christ is in fact vain, even if the worshippers are sincere in their intent and genuine in their claim. Indeed, their sincerity is only a sign of how far they have deceived themselves. Spiritual "experiences" are not to be measured by the internal feelings or the external claims of the worshipper but by their adherence to Christ who is the head of the body. Only through Christ is the body held together and nourished, so that apart from Christ, no true nourishment can be found. This rubric applies to organized religions that deny the full person and work of Christ and it applies to the individualized and internalized vague sense of spirituality that is so in vogue today. These (and many more) errant ideas circulate around us in various forms.

Believers, therefore, must be on their guard lest they should be judged and disqualified by such errors, and for believers to be on their guard, they must be warned even as Paul warns the church in Colossae. Too often, church leaders err on the one hand by exercising a form of tolerance that refuses to explicitly identify errors, or on the other hand by exercising an obsession with polemical teaching such that they become more known for what they oppose than for what (and whom) they affirm. Paul, however, warns against false teaching with specificity and urgency, clearly identifying the kinds of teachings and practices he has in mind and exposing their error in light of Christ, for whom Paul stands. At the same time, Paul also affords his opponents a measured anonymity whereby he does not call them out by name;

instead, he holds the door open to them that they might also be brought to Christ.

Paul's warnings balance passion with restraint, clarity with anonymity, and criticism with grace, all with the goal of equipping believers to remain faithful to Christ in the face of false teaching. The church requires nothing less today.

PREACHING AND TEACHING STRATEGIES

Exegetical and Theological Synthesis

In the previous passage Paul began a topic that continues here: the dangers of human traditions that demote Christ. In verse 8 he warned the Colossians to not be taken captive, and in this pericope (2:16–23) he expounds the warning with a different metaphor: shadow. The legalistic traditions were just a "shadow of the things to come, but the substance belongs to Christ" (v. 17). Legalism promoted by teachers in the Lycus Valley took the form of asceticism: "do not handle, do not taste, do not touch" (v. 21). Specifically, troublesome teachers were instructing the Colossians to follow rules about food, drink, and festivals, but Paul says, "Let no one pass judgment on you" if you disregard their rules (v. 16). The teachers even counseled the Colossians to worship angels. The result of following their false teaching would be disqualification (v. 18); that is, Christ would not give his followers a reward when he returns. The reward was not guaranteed, so believers were to be on guard against self-made, ascetic religion that had no value in stopping sinful indulgences (v. 23). Some of the believers in Colossae were tempted to return to the old rules of Judaism created before Christ inaugurated the new covenant. Others were tempted to return to the old rituals of paganism. So, Paul reminds the Christ-followers to hold fast to the head of the body, Jesus, even when the world passed judgment on them. The old rituals were simply a shadow. Like a shadow, they served a helpful role in projecting an outline of reality, but they were not the actual solid truth about Christ and his work of redemption. The old ways, whether pagan mysticism or Jewish asceticism could not help the church grow. Only Jesus, the head, can do that.

Preaching Idea

Shadows can't save us, but the Son can.

Contemporary Connections

What does it mean?

What does it mean that shadows can't save us, but the Son can? Borrowing the metaphor from verse 17, the "shadow" is the old rituals of Judaism and paganism (vv. 17–18, 20–23). To explain this concept, consider starting with a literal shadow. A lamp or flashlight could illuminate an object such as an apple and cast a shadow on a screen or wall. It could be pointed out that the shadow is partly accurate as it displays the outline of the object, but the shadow has no substance. Perhaps a young person could be brought forward to demonstrate that we can't grasp, weigh, or eat a shadow! When we have needs, a shadow can do nothing to save us.

After demonstrating a literal shadow, we might provide exegetical background to explain Paul's figurative meaning: the Colossians seem to have been troubled by teachers from both Jewish and pagan backgrounds, or perhaps the teachers mixed both backgrounds. Their ascetic teaching pertained to dietary laws, mortification of the flesh, and observation of festivals; and their mystical teaching pertained to the worship of angels and special knowledge.

After that, we might bridge to the contemporary world with examples of the rules offered by world religions. Islam has its five pillars, Buddhism its eightfold path, and even modern religions like the New Age Movement teach that enlightenment can be achieved with right techniques.

Rules and Techniques of Religions

The Five Pillars of Islam

- Shahadah (profession of faith: "There is no God but Allah and Muhamad is his prophet")
- Salat (prayer—five times a day with ritualized procedures)
- Zakat (almsgiving)
- Sawm (fasting, especially during the season of Ramadan)
- Hajj (pilgrimage to Mecca)

The Eightfold Path of Buddhism

- Right View (belief in the Buddha's teachings, especially karma and rebirth)
- Right Resolve (giving up home to live as a mendicant)
- Right Speech (abstaining from lying, divisive speech, abusive speech, and idle chatter)
- Right Conduct (no killing, stealing, sex, or material desires)
- Right Livelihood (begging)
- Right Effort (preventing unwholesome mental states; restraint of the senses)
- Right Mindfulness (being aware of current physical and mental states)
- Right Meditation (to achieve a new, peaceful consciousness)

A Sample of New Age Techniques

- Channeling
- Use of objects such as crystals to achieve "higher consciousness"
- Eclectic and selective teachings from past civilizations such as the Egyptians and Celts, and modern science such as Darwinism and the Gaia hypothesis

Finally, we might suggest that Christians are not immune to asceticism and mysticism. Some preachers and teachers promise that the right set of prayers and words can bring health and wealth. Extreme forms of prayer, fasting, meditation, and service may flirt with the things Paul had in mind in this passage. Self-made religion promises more than it can deliver because it cannot justify us with God and bring shalom. Those are already provided by Christ who died and rose again.

Is it true?

Is it true that the shadow of legalistic rules and man-made religious ideas can't save us? That pill might be hard to swallow for people who assume that we must do something to cause God to extend forgiveness. Ironically, the truth of grace may be hardest for folks reared in the church. A twofold approach might be used to show the truth that the shadow of legalism doesn't help us grow closer to God.

First, we might agree that Scripture *does* promote self-discipline. Our Lord fasted for forty days and went often to quiet places to pray. The book of Colossians itself states, "Put to death therefore what is earthly in you: sexual immorality, impurity, passion, evil desire, and covetousness" (3:5). James 4:8 is similar: "Draw near to God, and he will draw near to you. Cleanse your hands, you sinners, and purify your hearts, you double-minded. Be wretched and mourn and weep. . . . Humble yourselves before the Lord, and he will exalt you." Authors from a past age used the word "mortification" to describe spiritual disciplines that help followers of Christ put to death their sinful impulses.

Willow Creek Community Church used social scientific methods to study the effects of spiritual disciplines on one's relationship with God and discussed their findings in *Follow Me* (Hawkins and Parkinson, 2008). The researchers asked what personal spiritual practices catalyze spiritual growth. Answers included prayer, solitude, confession, and tithing, but the strongest catalyst was "reflection on Scripture." It was the top factor that helped people in all stages of spiritual maturity to grow. In fact, the researchers called it the "vanilla factor" (pp. 53, 116) because vanilla ice cream is more than twice as popular as number two (chocolate). Thus, they discovered that reflecting on Scripture is by far the most helpful spiritual discipline in producing growth.

So, to uphold the preaching idea, we might begin by affirming the value of spiritual disciplines. Then we might build on that by contrasting two approaches to the spiritual life. The first is captured in the biblical passages above and the second in the empty rituals of Colossians 2:16–23, or as the preaching idea states, legalistic rules and man-made religious ideas that are just a shadow. The two approaches are radically different in purpose and motive, even if some of their practices (such as fasting) are similar. The Jewish and pagan teachers in Colossae were instructing and shaming the believers toward legalism *in order to earn favor with God.* But God's favor has already been extended. It does need to be and cannot be earned. God is a river of grace overflowing its banks. Through Christ and the work of the Spirit, the Father has "qualified," "delivered," "redeemed," and "reconciled" believers (Col. 1:13–14, 21). Thus, the purpose of proper spiritual disciplines is not to manipulate God, catch his wandering attention, or soften his habitual scowl. The purpose is to use the means of grace such as prayer, fasting, confession, and reflection on Scripture to be progressively sanctified. Spiritual disciplines help us experience our union with Christ. The motive for mortification is not fear of punishment or pride in moral achievement but gratitude and determination to imitate Jesus who is our example. This contrast is crucial in expounding the book of Colossians and crucial for the entire Christian life. We work *from* our salvation, not *for* it.

Now what?

How can a Christ-follower avoid the shadow of legalistic rules and man-made religious ideas that can't save us? Perhaps practical instruction on proper spiritual disciplines could be offered. That instruction could be done from the pulpit, and it might also be combined with discussion, classes, and mentoring. For example, a class might read and discuss Richard Foster's classic, *Celebration of Discipline* (1998), or Ken Shigematsu's *Survival Guide for the Soul* (2018). I (Jeffrey) have incorporated two of Shigematsu's suggestions into my own devotional life: silence and gratitude. Before I open the Bible, I spend three minutes in silence, calming my racing mind and asking God to speak. After reading the Bible and journaling briefly, I list three things I am thankful for. With this spiritual discipline I remind myself that good things come from God and are not the result of my own "luck" or merit. Research shows that thankful people experience a 25 percent increase in alertness and energy, and they also sleep better. Search TED Talks on this topic for speeches like the one from Dan Gilbert, "The Surprising Science of Happiness."

Spiritual Disciplines from
Celebration of Discipline **by Richard Foster**

- Meditation
- Prayer
- Fasting
- Study
- Simplicity
- Solitude
- Submission
- Service
- Confession
- Worship
- Guidance
- Celebration

From *Survival Guide for the Soul*
by Ken Shigematsu

- Meditation
- Silence
- Gratitude
- Simple Abundance
- Servanthood
- Friendship
- Vocation

A troublesome issue that can impact our spiritual disciplines is media saturation. When we become addicted to noise, activity, interruptions, and fragmented attention, spiritual practices can be laborious. A small group might profit from reading and discussing Quentin Schultze's *Habits of the High-Tech Heart* (2002).

In this passage, spiritual growth is a group activity, not just the pursuit of an individual. Verse 19 states that the whole body grows with a growth that is from God. This corporate approach to spiritual growth might be especially appealing to Generation Z (born in the mid- to late 1990s). That demographic group is lonely. Using the "UCLA Loneliness Scale," a twenty-item questionnaire designed to gauge loneliness ranging from 20 on the low end to 80 on the high end, the global insurance company Cigna polled 20,000 Americans age 18 and older. The survey asked how often they agreed with prompts such as, "There is no one I can turn to," and "I feel part of a group of friends." Seniors (age 72 and older) scored lowest, meaning they are the least lonely. Generation Z, at least those age 18–22, was the loneliest by far, and ubiquitous connection via social media doesn't seem to help. According to Jagdish Khubchandani, a health science professor at Ball State University, social media can provide a false sense of relief: "I have students who tell me they have 500 'friends,' "but when they're in need, there's no one." Why would an insurer like Cigna conduct this study? Loneliness doesn't just make us sad, it makes us sick. Loneliness actually has the same effect on mortality as smoking fifteen cigarettes a day.[3]

Creativity in Presentation

Consider recruiting a young person to help with your sermon: a week before preaching, the boy or girl should get permission to experiment with two houseplants, one placed in darkness and one in sunlight. After the week-long experiment, before and after pictures could show how the plants fared, or the plants could be displayed on stage. The purpose is to illustrate that we cannot grow in darkness, or the "shadow" of legalism.

A testimony from someone saved from severe fundamentalism, whether it be the fundamentalism of Hinduism, Islam, Roman Catholicism, or even dour and demanding Protestantism, might help illustrate the inability of legalism to reconcile us to God and produce shalom.

The tragic death of John F. Kennedy Jr. (1961–99) could be used to illustrate verse 23: false teaching can have "the appearance of wisdom." JFK Jr., along with his wife, Carolyn Bessette, and her sister Lauren Bessette, died on July 16, 1999. Kennedy was piloting a small plane near Martha's Vineyard, Massachusetts. They took off in the early evening, navigating over water after dark. It is likely that the pilot became disoriented because of haze over the horizon and was not able to distinguish sky from water. This phenomenon is called "spatial disorientation." The plane spiraled out of control, nose-diving into the water. Kennedy probably had too little experience flying by instruments at night. Pilots must learn to trust the instruments more than their own sense of direction. Their sense seems right to them—it has the appearance of wisdom—but it can lead to death.

---

3 Sources (summarized in "Church and Culture" 14/36):

- "Cigna's U.S. Loneliness Index: Survey of 20,000 Americans Examining Behaviors Driving Loneliness in the United States," Cigna, May 1, 2018.
- Jayne O'Donnell & Shari Rudavsky, "Young Americans Are the Loneliest, Surprising Study from Cigna Shows," *USA Today*, May 1, 2018.
- Jamie Ducharme, "Young Americans Are the Loneliest, According to a New Study," *TIME*, May 1, 2018.

Verse 19 depicts the church as a body where all parts are nourished and knit together. Two illustrations might convey this. The first is knitting. Perhaps a skilled knitter from the congregation could display some handiwork, and an interview could be conducted about various knitting techniques and problems that commonly arise. The second illustration compares the church to an orchestra, but an orchestra of broken instruments.

Symphony for a Broken Orchestra (Barone, 2017).

Dec. 4, 2017—Four hundred musicians gathered in the 23rd Street Armory of Philadelphia to perform "Symphony for a Broken Orchestra" by David Lang. The orchestra included amateurs, professionals, and even members of the storied Philadelphia Orchestra. The youngest performer was a nine-year-old cellist; the oldest, an eighty-two-year-old oboist. It might have been the most diverse orchestra in America.

The four hundred brought broken instruments: a trumpet held together with blue painter's tape, a violin with no A string, a bow that had lost most of its hair, a cello carried in multiple pieces. You see, the government had cut funding for music programs in public schools, and many school instruments fell into disrepair. But Lang made something beautiful of them.

As the musical piece opened many of the instruments were silent, but gradually they found their voices—while a trumpet might not be capable of a sound, the keys could tap a rhythm; the scraping of a bow over the silhouette of a violin body could add an unusual element. At one point, a cellist made noise by turning a stringless peg. As the forty-minute symphony progressed, the instruments roared to life. Some musicians struggled, like a clarinetist who could get out only short spurts of sound and a French horn player who kept losing his mouthpiece. But together, the orchestra produced rich harmony. The music was playful and joyous. As the performance wound down each section bowed out one by one, until all that remained was the humble squeal of a broken clarinet.

In the church, each broken instrument adds its own voice. The best that some can do is simply tap or squeak, but with each other the orchestra produces a joyful song of praise under the hand of the Director.

The main point is this: the laws of religions are a thin copy of Jesus. Shadows can't save us, but the Son can.

- Empty ceremonies are only a shadow (2:17a).
- Christ is the substance (2:17b).
- So, reject the shadow and cling to Christ (2:16, 18–23).

DISCUSSION QUESTIONS

1. Describe the setting Paul was addressing. Who were the teachers and what were they teaching?

2. Which verses summarize what the Jewish teachers were promoting? Which verses summarize the teachings of the pagans?

3. Why does verse 23 say that those rituals have the "appearance of wisdom"?

4. Contrast genuine spiritual disciplines such as prayer and fasting with the kinds of rituals Paul was talking about.

5. Do you practice spiritual disciplines? Why or why not?

6. Name a discipline you would like to pursue. What would it take for you to begin and maintain it?

Colossians 3:1–4

EXEGETICAL IDEA
Paul exhorted the Colossians to seek to live in light of heaven, where Jesus reigns as Lord, and in light of their identity in Christ—for they have died and been raised with Christ in the past, their lives now belong to Christ in the present, and they will in the future be revealed with Christ in glory.

THEOLOGICAL FOCUS
Believers must reorient their present lives on earth around the heavenly reality that Jesus lives as the exalted Lord in heaven and that they have a new identity in Christ and will one day share in his eternal glory.

PREACHING IDEA
Live on earth by thinking of Christ in heaven.

PREACHING POINTERS
Having lifted up Christ and put down the false teachers in the previous sections of Colossians, Paul now turns toward application to daily life. But before becoming intensely practical, Paul has a few more words to say about the mind: fix it on "things that are above, not on things that are on earth" (v. 2). The mind was valued highly in Greco-Roman culture. When he was in Athens, he debated in the marketplace every day and then gave an extended address on the Areopagus (Acts 17:17, 19–31); in Ephesus, not far from Colossae, he reasoned daily for two years in the lecture hall of Tyrannus (Acts 19:9), presumably a venue for the TED Talks of the day.

The mind matters today just as it did then. How we think, and what we think about, have an enormous influence on how we live. Like "garbage in, garbage out," poor thoughts in, poor actions out. This cause-effect dynamic may be reflected in the dramatic increase in the suicides in rural areas of the United States. The Center for Disease Control recorded 1.4 million total attempts and 47,173 suicides in 2017. The highest rates were in Montana, Alaska, Wyoming, New Mexico, Idaho, and Utah. Poverty, isolation, and the easy availability of guns were key factors, but according to one researcher, the men's mentality was also a factor. As quoted in Stephen Rodrick's *Rolling Stone* article "All-American Despair," Dr. Craig Bryan of the University of Utah, who studies military and rural suicide, put it this way: "There's been an increase in the 'every-man-for-himself mentality.'"

Positive thinking is also beneficial: heavenly thoughts in, God-honoring actions out. In this text, the Lord commands us to "set our minds on things above" and to "seek the things above." We live on earth by thinking of Christ in heaven.

RAISED WITH CHRIST (3:1–4)

LITERARY STRUCTURE AND THEMES (3:1–4)

Colossians 3:1–4 is the second half of a major transition begun in 2:20. Paul begins Colossians 3:1 with a conditional statement ("*if* you have been raised with Christ") that is parallel with his conditional statement in Colossians 2:20 both in grammar and theme ("if you died with Christ"). This completes Paul's transition away from warnings in 2:16–23 to moral exhortation in 3:5–4:6. He formerly warned the Colossians against continuing in false practices that belong to the world, since as Christians, they have died out of the world. Now, beginning in 3:1, Paul will appeal to the Colossians to live out their new lives in Christ by orienting their lives around Christ. As he makes this appeal, Paul summarizes the Colossians' experience in Christ in terms of the past, the present, and the future. In their past experience, the Colossians have died and been raised with Christ (aorist verbs; 3:1, 3). In their present reality, the Colossians have been and now remain hidden (perfect verb; 3:3) with Christ in God. Finally, in the future, they will one day be revealed (future verb; 3:4) with Christ in glory. This first section of exhortation (3:1–4) lays the foundation for all that will follow by focusing on how the Colossians should think.

- ***Seek the Things Above (3:1–2)***
- ***Hidden with Christ (3:3)***
- ***Appearing with Christ in Glory (3:4)***

EXPOSITION (3:1–4)

In this opening paragraph of moral exhortation, Paul begins making practical application for how the believers in Colossae must live in Christ. Paul knows of their historical background though Epaphras, who recently brought the gospel to them and now has reported to Paul about their faith in Christ (Col. 1:3–8). Paul now coaches these new believers in how they ought to think. He has already told them to stop thinking according to the structures of the world, with its various philosophies and religious ideas against which Paul warned in previous verses (Col. 2:8, 16–23). These were the very patterns of thinking the Colossians embraced prior to coming to Christ. Paul knows that if they are going to successfully stop thinking in their old ways, they must be given a new way to think. Old mentalities cannot be eliminated unless they are replaced. Therefore, Paul instructs them to adopt a new framework of thinking oriented around heavenly realities, for Christ lives in heaven and their lives now belong to Christ.

Seek the Things Above (3:1–2)

Paul appeals to the Colossians to reorient their lives around heavenly things, where Christ is, for believers have been raised with Christ.

3:1. Paul begins his exhortations to the Colossians for how they should now live in Christ with a conditional statement: "*if* you have been raised with Christ." As in 2:20, the structure of the conditional statement in 3:1 (εἰ followed by an indicative verb) indicates that Paul presumes the statement to be true for the sake of argument (see Wallace, 1996, 689–90). Thus, it may be translated *since* (e.g., NIV, NLT), though many English translations prefer to retain the translation *if*, "since this rendering forces the reader or listener to assent to the proposition" (Moo, 2008, 245; e.g., KJV, ESV, NRSV). Paul expects his readers to agree with his premise here, namely that they have been raised with Christ.

Paul can expect his readers to know this because he has already used the verb "raise with" (συνεγείρω) in 2:12, where he reminded the Colossians of their baptism and its representation of the spiritual burial and resurrection they have experienced in union with Christ. Therefore, when Paul speaks of being "raised with" Christ in 3:1, he is first and foremost referring back to the new spiritual life believers have as the result of their union with Christ in his resurrection. However, in his following instructions (3:1–3), we will see that Paul seems to expand the idea of being "raised with" Christ to also include the ascension of Christ, so that believers were in some way united with Christ in his being taken up into heaven and sitting down at the right hand of God.

The Importance of Baptism

When Paul structures his conditional statement in 3:1 with the presumption that his audience will agree with his premise, he is not only making a logical inference based on his earlier teaching in the letter regarding union with Christ, but he is also assuming that his readers themselves have actually experienced the baptism that signifies union with Christ (Col. 2:12). This speaks to the importance of baptism still today. Often we become so zealous to proclaim salvation by faith *alone*—not by works!—that we inadvertently diminish the essential nature of baptism. As a result, we end up with congregations where many of our people are purportedly following Christ and yet they have not been baptized. As a result, we lose the opportunity to use baptism as Paul does in Colossians—as a heuristic tool whereby we call upon our congregations to recall their own baptisms and then to reflect upon the implications of having died and been raised with Christ. This teaching method only works if every believer has a personal baptism experience to recall.

Thus, on the basis of having been raised with Christ, Paul instructs the Colossians to seek the things above. To "seek" (ζητέω) means more than simply aiming for a goal; it means also "to devote serious effort to realize one's desire or objective" (BDAG, s.v. "ζητέω" 3, p. 428). It is both having a goal and doing what is required to achieve that goal. Some goals in life may be simple and relatively easy to grasp. We might, for example, seek a cup of coffee in the morning, or seek to be at an event on time. But other goals require large commitment and sustained effort. We might seek to pay off a large debt that will require reordering our spending for several years, or we might seek to raise our kids in a particular way, knowing that it will take decades of sacrifice. In these instances, seeking a goal requires nothing less than reorienting our entire life around the pursuit of that goal. This is the kind of determined seeking that Paul commands here.

Such seeking aims for "things above" (τὰ ἄνω). This spatial reference to a place that is "at a position above another position" (BDAG, s.v. "ἄνω" 1, p. 92) refers in cosmological terms to the heavenly realm that is above the earth. Thus, Peter in Acts 2:19 speaks redundantly of the "heavens above," and Paul in Colossians 3:2 will place the "things above" in contrast to the things on earth. But here Paul is less interested in *where* the things above are and more interested in *who* dwells there. This is the place where Christ himself presently *is* (ἐστιν)—it is where Christ "sits at God's right hand" (ἐν δεξιᾷ τοῦ θεοῦ καθήμενος) This reminds us that Jesus not only died and was resurrected from the dead, but he then also ascended into the clouds and sat down at the right hand of God (Luke 24:51; Acts 1:9; 2:33–36).

Paul borrows the language of "sitting at God's right hand" directly from Psalm 110:1, which is itself one of the most frequently cited Old Testament texts in the New Testament. Theologians refer to Christ's posture of sitting as his *session*, and his session has various implications. In Hebrews, Christ sits down as an indication that he no longer needs to stand and offer sacrifices, now that he has completed one sacrifice sufficient for all time (Heb. 10:12–14). In Acts 2:33–36, Peter cites Psalm 110:1 to explain that when Jesus sat down at God's right hand, he was being exalted and established as Lord, and he received authorization to pour out the Holy Spirit. As Christ now sits at God's right hand in his session, he continues to work by interceding for his people (Rom. 8:34), reigning (1 Cor. 15:52), and awaiting the coming day of his return and final victory.

When Paul speaks of Christ sitting at God's right hand in Colossians 3:1, he has in mind especially the present reign of Christ in contrast to the powers (στοιχεῖα) who reign on earth (Col. 2:20). Indeed, when Christ ascended, he was exalted to a position above all other powers and authorities (see Eph. 1:20–23). Therefore, when Paul explains the "things above" in terms of Christ sitting at God's right hand, he is defining the things above as that domain where Christ reigns as Lord. So when Paul commands the Colossians to seek the things above, he is essentially commanding them to seek to participate in the present reign of the resurrected and exalted Christ.[1] As we surrender and orient our lives around Jesus as our exalted and reigning Lord, we are effectively seeking the things above.

3:2. Paul repeats and clarifies his command from 3:1 to "seek the things above" by giving a parallel command to "think about things above" (τὰ ἄνω φρονεῖτε). The "things above" (τὰ ἄνω) remain the same, but now Paul uses the verb "think" (φρονέω). To think can mean simply to have a thought run through our minds, but it also implies in contexts such as this that we would give "careful consideration to something" (BDAG, s.v. "φρονέω" 2, p. 1065–1066). It is often translated "set your minds on" (ESV, NIV, NSRV) or "set your affection on" (KJV). This requires intentional and sustained engagement of our minds, where we seek to fill our minds with the reality of Jesus reigning in heaven as Lord and we determine that our lives must be reoriented according to his will. Thinking and seeking go hand-in-hand, for our lives go where our minds lead. Remember again Paul's opening prayer for the Colossians, where he prayed for them to be filled with knowledge of the will of God, *so that* they could then live in a way that pleases him (Col. 1:9–10). A similar principle is at work here. Through the rest of chapter 3, Paul will instruct the Colossians in how to live in light of things above, but it begins with what fills their mind. Thus Lightfoot says, "You must not only *seek* heaven; you must also *think* heaven" (Lightfoot, 1981, 209).

Moreover, to think heaven means to stop thinking earth. Think upon the things above, Paul says, "not the things on earth" (μὴ τὰ ἐπὶ τῆς γῆς). The "earth" (γῆ) is the realm opposite of heaven. It is the things below. And even though the earth is included in the totality of creation that was created through Christ (Col. 1:16) and reconciled by his blood (Col. 1:20), the earth nevertheless still awaits the day when all things will once and for all be made subject to Christ (1 Cor. 15:24–28). In the present time, the earth refers to the same domain as the "world" (κόσμος; Col. 2:20) and it represents the realm where Christ is not recognized as Lord. It is the realm where the powers and authorities continue to operate, albeit as disarmed powers (Col. 2:15).

This creates a tension for the Colossians, as they must carry out their existence on earth, but their thinking must be shaped by heavenly realities rather than by earth. In a similar passage, Paul describes what life looks like for those who set their minds on earthly things: they "walk as enemies of the cross of Christ. Their end is destruction, their god is

1 Similarly, Wright says, "The command to aspire to the things of heaven is a command to meditate and dwell upon Christ's sort of life, and on the fact that he is now enthroned as the Lord of the world" (Wright, 1986, 132).

their belly, and they glory in their shame, with minds set on earthly things" (Phil. 3:18–19). Such a lifestyle represents precisely the opposite of the kind of life Paul will call for in Colossians 3:5–4:6. The difference between these two lifestyles begins in the mind. We must think heavenly thoughts, and especially fill our minds with the truth that Jesus dwells and reigns in heaven at the right hand of God.

Can You Be Too Heavenly Minded?

Sometimes Christians denigrate one another by saying, "Oh, he's too heavenly minded to be of any earthly good." Often this criticism is applied to those Christians who are so devoted to spiritual disciplines (e.g., prayer, meditation, Scripture reading, etc.) that they neglect the world around them (e.g., loving their neighbor, showing kindness, etc.). But in Paul's estimation, being truly heavenly minded should result in being of more earthly good, not less. He will describe how seeking things above ought to transform how we live on earth primarily in terms of our relationships with the people around us (Col. 3:5–17), as we continue to live in our earthly roles as husbands, wives, children, employees, employers and so forth (Col. 3:18–4:1). And our transformed conduct should result in increased credibility with outsiders who do not know Christ (Col. 4:2–6). Thus, a proper heavenly fixation should turn our eyes toward the world around us and make us of increasing earthly good. In fact, if we are lacking in earthly good, then we must not be properly heavenly minded. We cannot possibly be too heavenly minded to be of any earthly good.

Hidden with Christ (3:3)

Paul reorients the Colossians' identity in light of the new life they have in Christ.

3:3. Paul drives home his point once again that the Colossians have died and been raised to new life in union with Christ and that this provides the underlying reason (note the explanatory conjunction γάρ, "for") why they should seek and think heaven in the previous verses. In Colossians 3:3, Paul uses just one word in Greek to say "you died" (ἀπεθάνετε). The abruptness of the statement is shocking—how can Paul declare to living persons that in fact they have died? Paul expects his readers to understand by now that he is referring to the spiritual death believers have died in union with Christ (Col. 2:20; cf. 2:11). The use of such a crude, shorthand reference (or *synecdoche*)—"you died!"—emphasizes the reality of the death believers have in fact died in Christ. They must have a new way of thinking and seeking because their old life has died. They died in Christ. We died in Christ. *You* died in Christ. Time to acknowledge it and begin thinking and living like it!

But this death was of a peculiar nature, for by dying the Colossians did not cease to live. Instead, their physical life actually continued uninterrupted even as they underwent a spiritual death and resurrection. Thus, Paul can say to them, "you died," and then immediately speak of "your life" (ἡ ζωὴ ὑμῶν) as something they currently possess. Again, Paul presumes his readers will recall that this new life is spiritual in nature and that they have received it by being united with Christ in his resurrection and being raised to new life with him (Col. 2:12–13; 3:1). Just as the death of Christ ultimately gave way to resurrection life, so also the death of a believer does not mean the end of life, but it means transference into a new and fuller kind of life. Death is the means by which believers now live and flourish.

Paul now describes the location of this new life, which is "hidden" (κρύπτω) with Christ in God. As in Colossians 2:3, something may be hidden to keep it a secret or to keep it secure. On the one hand, believers' lives are secure in Christ, for they can never be lost and their future is guaranteed, so long as they continue to hold fast to him (Col. 1:22–23). True as this security may be, it seems more likely that Paul here intends to convey the sense of a secret, as if the Colossians' identity and new life are united with Christ (σὺν τῷ Χριστῷ) within the realm of God (ἐν τῷ θεῷ) in heaven above, but at the same time veiled to the world. Their identity will only finally be revealed in the future day of Christ's return (see 3:4); until that day, they remain concealed, hidden with Christ in God.[2]

Thus, Paul's metaphorical language of death indicates "a radical change of identity" (MacDonald, 2000, 128). Believers have undergone a total transformation and have an entirely new identity in Christ, having gone from being spiritually dead to being spiritually alive with him. They have come to realize the heavenly reality of the Christ who lives and reigns, and their lives have been united with him and hidden in him. This must now transform their thinking and reorient the entirety of their lives. But at the same time that their lives have been dramatically transformed, as they go from death to life, they also continue to live on earth behind a veil, so to speak, as their identity on earth remains unchanged and the world around them remains completely unaware of what is taking place within them. They continue to inhabit their same social spaces and identities, continuing in their households as husbands and wives, slaves and free, and so forth. This gives them a kind of dual identity, a heavenly and earthly identity, as their minds are being taken over by heaven even as they continue living on earth.[3] They must live heaven on earth, and though the earth does not recognize the heaven within them, their heavenly identity must begin to reshape how they live out their earthly identity.

Thinking Heaven Transforms How We Live on Earth

This double identity of living heaven on earth will become increasingly apparent throughout the rest of Paul's exhortations, but we can anticipate even now how this might play out. Think of the implications here for Philemon and Onesimus. Both master and slave have come to Christ and have died and been raised with Christ, and both of their lives are now hidden with Christ in God. As they now think upon and seek after things above, they must undergo the transformation of character Paul sets forth in Colossians 3:15–17, including the new realization that in Christ, there is no slave and free, but Christ is everything (Col. 3:11). Philemon and Onesimus are equal partakers of the new life in Christ, and there is no distinction between them. This is their heavenly reality that must now infuse their minds and reorient their lives.

But at the same time, they continue to live on earth, where the world in their day continues to operate a system of slavery, and where Philemon continues to carry the status of a master and Onesimus continues to carry the status of a slave. The earth does not recognize heaven's transformation, so Philemon does not lead a movement of prohibition from the top down, nor does Onesimus lead a rebellion for freedom from the bottom up. Instead, both return to their respective roles within the household and continue to live within their earthly identities. Though in modern times, we may find this acquiescence to slavery offensive, and though we might wish that Paul and the church

2 Lightfoot summarizes well Paul's argument here: "The Apostle's argument is this: When you sank under the baptismal water, you disappeared for ever to the world. You rose again, it is true, but you rose only to God. The world henceforth knows nothing of your new life, and (as a consequence) your new life must know nothing of the world" (Lightfoot, 1981, 209).

3 MacDonald speaks similarly of a "double consciousness" with particular reference to slaves, who must consider themselves free in the spiritual realm even as they continue to live as slaves in the earthly realm (MacDonald, 2000, 166; cf. D'Angelo, 1993, 320).

would have called for an immediate transformation of earth in this regard, we must set aside such sensitivities and recognize what Paul does in fact accomplish.

He here sows the seeds for a kind of revolution of earth that will be truly transformative. It will not merely change unjust institutions and social structures of discrimination while leaving hearts unchanged, but he works to change hearts and to transform people from the inside out, beginning with their minds and their hearts. And where hearts are changed, institutions and structures are sure to follow. Does Paul really leave Philemon and Onesimus in an unchanged status on earth? How could Philemon and Onesimus think heaven and not be changed in how they live on earth?

At the very least, Onesimus must become a new kind of slave in his own thinking. He cannot simply declare himself to be free, but he can control what *kind* of slave he will be. Thus Paul appeals for him to be transformed in his thinking, to perceive of himself as a slave of his master in heaven, the Lord Jesus, who sits at God's right hand (Col. 3:22–25). As such, Onesimus must work to please Jesus. And Philemon must become a new kind of master in his thinking. He must become a fair and just master accountable to his own master in heaven, the Lord Jesus (Col. 4:1).

And as both Philemon and Onesimus think heaven more deeply and seek heaven more completely, how long will it be before the truth of their equality in Christ, both in terms of spiritual life and status in Christ, comes to have a direct impact on their earthly life? How long before Philemon and Onesimus find a way to operate the heavenly reality on earth through radical emancipation and restoration? Indeed, earth may not recognize heaven, but heaven *will* transform earth as God's people think and seek things above.

Appearing with Christ in Glory (3:4)

Paul reminds the Colossians of their future hope, that though their identity in Christ may be veiled to the world now, it will one day be revealed when they share in the glory of Christ's return.

3:4. The final verse of this section points to the future in the most explicit eschatological statement in all of Colossians. What is hidden (v. 3) will one day be revealed (v. 4). Paul begins with a clear statement about the second advent of Christ, "when Christ will appear" (ὅταν ὁ Χριστὸς φανερωθῇ). Christ has already appeared once, in his first advent, when the mystery of Christ was revealed to all the saints (Col. 1:26). But now Paul looks ahead to the second appearing of Christ, when he will fulfill his promise to return in the same way he left, but now with glory (Acts 1:9–11; cf. Matt. 24:30; Titus 2:13; 1 Pet. 1:20). That Christ will one day be revealed implies that Christ himself remains hidden in some sense at the present time. Not only is the identity of Christ unknown to many in the world—in a similar manner to the hidden nature of our identity in Christ (Col. 3:3)—but Christ is also *physically* hidden from the world, now that he has ascended into heaven and sits at God's right hand. Thus, he hides from sight and the world does not see him, but only for a season. The day is coming when he will appear and every eye will see him.

On Hiding

A favorite joke in our (Adam's) household of boys: Why don't you ever see elephants hiding in trees? Because they're really good at it.

In the meantime, however, Christ not only continues to live in heaven but believers also have life in him. Christ *is* your life, Paul now says. This is an "advance on the previous statement," where Paul said your life is hidden *with* Christ; now Paul "declares that the life *is* Christ" (Lightfoot, 1981, 210). Paul has in mind here not only that the Colossians have their existence in Christ, as does all of creation (1 Cor. 8:6; Col. 1:16), but again, that by their death and resurrection with Christ, their lives have now taken on a new nature, so that "to live *is* Christ" (Phil. 1:21; cf. Gal. 2:20). Their new life in Christ is inseparable from Christ in every way, and Christ has become "the source, center, and goal" of their lives (Harris, 2010, 123).

It is because the believer's life is bound up in the life of Christ that the appearing of Christ is also the appearing of believers. When Christ "will appear" (φανερωθῇ), Paul says in 3:4, then you also "will be made to appear" (φανερωθήσεσθε). Here Paul uses the same Greek word (φανερόω) to speak of both events, but he uses the passive form for believers to indicate their appearing is caused by someone else. Thus, many translations choose to say believers "will be revealed" (e.g., NRSV, HCSB) in order to reflect this passive sense, though others say believers "will appear" (as in ESV, NIV; cf. KJV) in order to retain the repetition of terminology with Christ's appearing. Either way, Paul's central point remains the same, that when Christ will *appear*, seemingly having control over the timing and mechanism of his appearing (though Christ himself yields such control to the Father; e.g., Matt. 24:36), Christians will *be revealed*, having no apparent control over the timing or mechanism of their appearing. We must simply wait upon Christ, enduring our hiddenness in the present time and knowing with confidence that because Christ is our life, his appearing will necessarily reveal us as well.

In that day, believers will be revealed "in glory" (ἐν δόξῃ). Jesus himself promised that he will return with such glory that every tribe and person on earth will see him, even as he sends forth his angels to gather together his people, both the living and the dead who will be raised (Matt. 24:27–30; cf. Rev. 1:7). When Paul says that believers will be revealed with Christ in glory, he means not only that they will appear with Christ in the midst of his glory, but also that they will share together in his glory. Elsewhere, Paul says that believers will be changed in that day, as mortality clothes itself in immortality (1 Cor. 15:51–54). This will be the final stage of God's saving work, when those whom he has called and justified he also glorifies (Rom. 8:30). John says that when Christ appears, "we shall be like him, for we shall see him as he is" (1 John 3:2), and this certainly applies to the glory of Christ—we shall be like him in his glory.

Here, then, is hope for lowly Christians who live in ignominy in a world that refuses to acknowledge their magnificent identity in Christ. Again, we must think especially of the marginalized and the downcast, for whom Onesimus is representative—a slave who has gained new life and full status in Christ, but whose heavenly identity contrasts sharply with the shackles that still constrain him on earth. Yet his present, earthly status is only temporary, and one day his heavenly status will be revealed, and he will share fully in the glory of Christ for all the world to see.

THEOLOGICAL FOCUS

The exegetical idea (Paul exhorted the Colossians to seek to live in light of heaven, where Jesus reigns as Lord, and in light of their identity in Christ—for they have died and been raised with Christ in the past, their lives now belong to Christ in the present, and they will in the future be revealed with Christ in glory) leads to this theological focus: Believers must reorient their present lives on earth around the heavenly reality that Jesus lives as the exalted Lord in heaven, and that they have a new identity in Christ and will one day share in his eternal glory.

In these verses, Paul introduces and lays the foundation for his upcoming exhortations in 3:1–4:6 by drawing upon his theological exposition in chapters 1–2. He here presents the past, present, and future experience of believers, based directly upon the past, present, and future work of Christ. Regarding the past, Paul looks back again to the death, resurrection, and ascension of Christ, and by faith and baptism believers also have died with Christ and been raised to new life with Christ. In the present, Paul looks to Christ's present life in the heavens above, where Christ sits at the right hand of God. The lives of believers also are hidden with Christ above, and Christ *is* their life even now, so that believers have life in Christ. And regarding the future, Paul looks ahead to when Christ will one day appear in glory, and in that day, believers will be revealed with him in glory. Thus, believers share in the past, present, and future work of Christ. We could say that we have been co-crucified, co-buried, co-resurrected, and co-ascended with Christ, so that we now co-live with Christ, and we will one day be co-revealed and co-glorified with Christ.

In Colossians 3:1, Paul appeals for how we should live *now*, on the basis of the past, present, and future work of Christ. We should center our thinking upon the things above and seek after them, so that our entire life now becomes reoriented around the heavenly reality that Jesus is the exalted Lord and around our heavenly identity of life in him. Though our identity and status on earth may remain unaltered, we must be dramatically transformed by this heavenly reality of life in Christ. As we learn to think of ourselves and of our world in heavenly perspective, it will transform how we live. In his ensuing exhortations of 3:5–4:6, Paul will give detail to just how radical this internal transformation is, even as we remain in our same earthly positions. But as the foundation of all his specific instructions we find this underlying instruction that we must learn to think heaven and seek heaven even as we live on earth.

To this end, C. S. Lewis critiques Christians, saying our desires are too weak because the object of our desires is too banal. He says, "It would seem that Our Lord finds our desires not too strong, but too weak. We are half-hearted creatures, fooling about with drink and sex and ambition when infinite joy is offered us, like an ignorant child who wants to go on making mud pies in a slum because he cannot imagine what is meant by the offer of a holiday at the sea. We are far too easily pleased" (Lewis, 1949, 2). If only we would grasp the heavenly glory we will one day share with Christ, and if only we would appreciate the new life we have received in Christ, and if only we would embrace our heavenly identity with Christ—if only we would make things above the object of our desires!—then surely our heavenly desires would be inflamed and we would reorient our lives on earth around the pursuit of things above. Let us, then, fill our minds with heaven that we may learn how to live heaven on earth.

UNION WITH CHRIST REVISITED (COL. 2:11–13, 20–3:4)		
Past	Jesus died	We have died with Christ
	Jesus was buried	We were buried with Christ
	Jesus was resurrected	We have been raised with Christ
	Jesus ascended	
Present	Jesus lives at God's right hand	Our lives are hidden with Christ, who is our life
Future	Jesus will appear in glory	We will be revealed with Christ in glory

PREACHING AND TEACHING STRATEGIES

Exegetical and Theological Synthesis

In this passage, the apostle Paul hinges between the theology in the first half of the book and the application in the second half. The door between the two sections swings on the doctrine of union with Christ. The Colossians were "hidden with Christ in God" (v. 3). That is, they were included spiritually in Jesus's death and resurrection, and his coming in glory meant that they too would appear with him in glory (v. 4). The fact of their identification with Christ meant that they should "seek the things that are above" (v. 1) and set the mind "on things above, not on things of the earth" (v. 2). Verse 1 begins with the word "if," but the conditional phrase means "since," or "because." *Because* the Christ-followers of Colossae had died and risen with Christ, they were to set their minds above.

The doctrine of union with Christ saturates this passage (indeed, it saturates the whole book). As stated in the Exposition: believers have been "co-crucified, co-buried, co-resurrected, and co-ascended with Christ, so that we now co-live with Christ, and we will one day be co-revealed and co-glorified with Christ." The theology of union with Christ forms the basis of the numerous exhortations that follow in chapters 3 and 4. In fact, exhortation begins even here: "seek the things that are above" (v. 1). In the rest of the book, Paul will specify ways to do so.

Preaching Idea

Live on earth by thinking of Christ in heaven.

Contemporary Connections

What does it mean?

What does it mean to live on earth by thinking of Christ in heaven? The idea suggests that the way we think, and what we think about, affects our behavior. Athletes know that. The golfer visualizes himself making the perfect shot before beginning his backstroke. The skier in the starting gate sees herself entering each gate at the perfect angle, shifting her weight this way and that.

"Thinking of Christ in heaven" means remembering that we are included in his death, resurrection, and return. This helps us "live on earth." The rest of the letter will specify what that looks like in practical terms: forgiving one another, being humble, giving thanks, submitting, loving, praying, and so forth.

The preaching idea is grounded in the theology of the passage—union with Christ. "Hidden with Christ" (v. 3) likely means "concealed." The world does not recognize the splendor of the believer's inner life that is made possible by the grace of God and the resulting concord with him.

We look like everyone else, and indeed we *are* like everyone else as our bodies age and our life circumstances sometimes spiral down. Christians are subject to the same difficulties many people face such as a hostile work environment or a wayward child. The single person, even if a Christian, may be lonely; the married couple, even if bona fide disciples of Jesus, may not be able to conceive a child. But as Paul says in 2 Corinthians 4:6, "We have this treasure in jars of clay." This means that Christ dwells in our limping bodies and perplexing circumstances, but through the power of the Holy Spirit, Christians do not give in to despair. We can have hope even in a broken world, and when Christ appears, our union with him will be manifest. A visual aid in the Creativity section below can help clarify the doctrine of union with Christ.

Is it true?

Does thinking of Christ in heaven really have an effect on daily life? Matthew 12:34–35 tells us that how we think in our hearts affects the words that come from our mouths: "Out of the abundance of the heart the mouth speaks. The good person out of his good treasure brings forth good, and the evil person out of his evil treasure brings forth evil." Matthew 15:19 is similar: "Out of the heart come . . . murder, adultery . . . [and] theft." Proverbs 17:22 states that "a joyful heart is good medicine," implying that our thinking habits affect our bodily status.

Neuroscience confirms this with the discovery of "neuroplasticity." Previous theories of the mind held that the brain and personality were fixed early in youth, but now scientists have concluded that the brain continues to change even in adulthood. It is "plastic." By training our minds to "think heaven," we can make actual changes in worldview, emotion, and behavior. A search in a standard tool like Wikipedia can provide a quick education in neuroplasticity.

Long before the discovery of neuroplasticity, playwright George Bernard Shaw wrote about it in *Pygmalion.* (This play is the basis of *My Fair Lady* by Lerner and Lowe.) Eliza Doolittle is a Cockney flower girl in the slums of London, but she is transformed into an elegant lady by the coaching of Professor Henry Higgins, a hard-bitten and condescending man. The twist in the play is that the professor's coaching is not the primary factor of transformation. Rather, it is the kindness of Higgins's associate, Colonel Pickering, who always treats Eliza like a lady. He thinks of her that way, and she begins to think of herself that way, and then she became that way. Just so, God declares followers of Christ to be dead, alive, and glorified; by faith we see ourselves that way, and this helps us live that way. A plot summary of *Pygmalion* can be found in SparkNotes.

Now what?

What concrete practices might help listeners to live on earth by thinking of Christ in heaven? We might supply a list of suggestions: reflecting on Scripture, memorizing Scripture, journaling our prayers, small group conversation where iron sharpens iron (Prov. 27:17), and worship. Many people find that music helps theology penetrate the affections. Perhaps you might like to explain the time-tested pattern of prayer: ACTS (Adoration, Confession, Thanksgiving, and Supplication).

Applying the preaching idea might be done with the sobering lyrics of Peggy Lee's evocative song from 1969, "Is That All There Is?" In the song there is no heaven, so it is impossible to think about heaven. This earth is "all there is," and the lyrics describe out the implications of that belief. While life contains some pleasures such as a child's first visit to the circus and a girl's first love, everything terminates in disappointment, and the chorus hauntingly answers the song's question,

> If that's all there is my friends, then let's keep dancing
> Let's break out the booze and have a ball
> If that's all there is

What might the second part of the preaching idea look like—"live on earth"? It looks like any God-honoring activity, as grand as giving up one's career to become a missionary, or as mundane as allowing another driver to enter the line of traffic in front of you. The missionary thinks of Christ in heaven by remembering that he came from heaven to reconcile humanity to God, and we carry on the ministry of reconciliation (2 Cor. 5:18). The motorist thinks of Christ in heaven by not looking out for his or her own interests but by looking to the interests of others (Phil. 2:4). "Living on earth by thinking of Christ in heaven" might lead to efforts toward racial reconciliation because heaven will be a multi-language, multi-tribe mosaic (Rev. 7:9) as reflected in the multicultural composition of the church in Antioch (Acts 13:1).

Creativity in Presentation

The power of thought to influence action can be illustrated in many ways. Hypnotism is an extreme form of mind control that affects behavior. Less extreme and controversial might be "visualization"—the technique golfers and skiers use. To break a cement block, karate masters teach their students to think through the block, visualizing the stroke of their hand as ending on the other side of the seemingly impenetrable surface. This could even be staged with a live demonstration if you have someone capable of breaking a block!

Learning to focus on spiritual truths such as the believer's death and resurrection with Christ could be illustrated with a "Magic Eye" image, also called an "autostereogram," according to Wikipedia. A two-dimensional, computer-generated pattern of colors has an image embedded into the pattern, perhaps a shark or the Statue of Liberty. The image is present but not readily seen with a casual glance. We must train our eyes to see it by focusing at different depths, and when done correctly, a 3D image emerges. A similar illustration might be done with the popular app called "Hidden City" developed by G5 Entertainment. Objects are hidden in plain view but must be visually disentangled from a busy scene such as an antique shop or Victorian parlor.

Another way to talk about thinking of Christ in heaven is to compare it to tuning in to a radio or internet music station. With a smart phone listeners might tune in music streaming service such as Pandora. The wifi signal that links to Pandora is present even when we cannot sense it. To access the music we need the right equipment. Just so, using spiritual disciplines we "tune in" to the invisible yet real realities of union with Christ.

In the film *Avatar* (directed by James Cameron, 2009), the lead character is a wheelchair-bound paraplegic Marine (played by Sam Worthington), but in the land of the Na'vi people he has an incredible avatar body. The more he lives in that body, the more he wants to leave behind his frail earthly body and all things of that world. In the same way, the more we experience new life in Christ, the more we want to leave behind the old ways of lust, pride, and power (1 John 2:16).

To illustrate how our lives are "hidden with Christ in God" (v. 3), consider inviting a child to the stage to find something hidden, perhaps a tennis ball or piece of candy, that has been placed inside something else, perhaps a piano bench. Similarly, union with Christ can be illustrated with a flower. The flower does not have the power to raise itself, but when it is placed inside a book and someone lifts the book, the flower also rises. If we want to rise in resurrection we must be "in Christ" whom God raised from the dead.

The third verse of the hymn, "Before the Throne of God Above," celebrates union with Christ and uses the language of Colossians 3:3.[4] The congregation could sing this song, or could view one of the music videos that are available with a quick internet search. One of the memorable lines is:

> My life is hid with Christ on high,
> With Christ my Savior and my God.

However we choose to present our teaching, we can demonstrate how to fix our minds on our union with Christ, and this will help us live obediently. We live on earth by thinking of Christ in heaven.

- We died with Christ (3:3).
- We rose with Christ (3:1a).
- We will appear with Christ in glory (3:4).
- So, seek the things that are above (3:1b–2).

4 "Before the Throne of God Above," written by Charitie Lees (née Smith) Bancroft and Vikki Cook; music by Vikki Cook of Sovereign Grace Worship.

DISCUSSION QUESTIONS

1. What does “think heaven” mean? Name some concrete ways to do this.

2. What does “live on earth” mean? Give some examples from the activities you will do tomorrow.

3. Do you feel like you have died with Christ and been raised with him? Why or why not?

4. When Christ appears, he will come in glory. What does that mean, and how will we also appear in glory?

5. How does the fact that Christ is “seated at the right hand of God,” assure us? What does being seated symbolize?

Colossians 3:5–11

EXEGETICAL IDEA

Paul exhorted the Colossians to stop living in their former way of life apart from Christ, by putting to death the practices of that former life and embracing their identity as new persons being transformed into the image of Christ, as members together in the body of Christ.

THEOLOGICAL FOCUS

Believers must be transformed into the image of Christ by putting off their old habits of sin, and by living out of the new nature and identity they have received in Christ and in the body of Christ.

PREACHING IDEA

Now that we are spiritually alive in Christ, let's put to death the old ways.

PREACHING POINTERS

In the previous passages of Colossians, Paul focused on pagan beliefs, and in this passage he focuses on pagan lifestyle. The church in the village of Colossae was an island in a sea of paganism. The Colossians should no longer display the old habits of paganism because they were now alive in Christ. That spiritual reality was to be demonstrated in daily living: no sins of passion such as sexual immorality; no sins of anger such as slander; and no sins regarding material wealth such as greed. The Colossians knew well the old ways because they used to drift in the stream of their culture, but then they became new in Christ. Impurity, malice, and greed must be put to death and put off like a dirty garment

The lists of sins Paul gave the Colossians could have been gleaned from today's talk radio, evening news, advertisements, schools, and workplaces. Little has changed in two thousand years. Politicians slander each other with vituperative malice; sitcoms parade obscene talk with a wink and a titter; and websites make sexual impurity just a click away. The Pew Research Center found that in 2019, more Americans cohabited than were married: 59% and 50%. (In 2002 the figures were 54% and 60%.) Sixty-nine percent of Americans say that it is okay to cohabit even if they don't plan to marry, and 78% of respondents under the age of thirty say it's okay. (These statistics can be found at Pew Research.) With sins like polyamory and virtual sex with robots on the rise, this passage has much to say today.

Christ-followers have been made new, so they must act like it by putting to death impurity, greed, and anger, along with factions. All of that belongs to the old way, but we are now spiritually alive in Christ, so let's put to death the old ways.

PUT OFF YOUR FORMER WAY OF LIFE (3:5–11)

LITERARY STRUCTURE AND THEMES (3:5–11)

In the previous section (3:1–4), Paul gave the Colossians broad instructions regarding how they reorient their thinking and their lives around things above. Now, Paul enters into detailed moral exhortation, as he picks up again the theme of having died and been raised with Christ. As those who have died with Christ, the Colossians must now "mortify" (νεκρώσατε; 3:5) the behaviors and attitudes associated with their former way of life in the world, particularly sexual immorality, evil desires, and greed. Paul also introduces the metaphor of changing clothes, as they must "put off" (ἀποτίθημι; 2:8) additional vices, and in 3:12 Paul will issue a parallel command to "put on" (ἐνδύσασθε) the virtues appropriate for the people of God. The vices they must put off include anger, filthy language, and lying (2:8–9). These commands for moral transformation are based upon the spiritual transformation the Colossians have already experienced in Christ, whereby they have taken off the old person and put on the new, so that they now have a new social identity together based in Christ (3:9–11). This section (3:5–11) tells us what the church is *not* to be in preparation for the next section (3:12–17), where Paul will give instructions for what the church *is* to be.

- ***Mortify the Things of the Earth (3:5–7)***
- ***Put Off Anger and Sinful Speech (3:8–9a)***
- ***The New Humanity (3:9b–11)***

EXPOSITION (3:5–11)

In these moral exhortations, Paul gives two lists of vices that must be put to death and put off. The first list of vices in 3:5 focuses on themes of sexual immorality and evil desires, while the second list in 3:8 focuses on anger and evil speech. These vices were very real and personal to the Colossians, for these were characteristic of how they lived prior to their faith in Christ (3:7). For example, in a historical situation such as that between Onesimus and Philemon, their former way of life would have called for them to manage their conflict with greed, anger, hateful speech, and lying. Such vices inevitably result in division, pulling people apart in conflict, even in the body of Christ. But Paul envisions something radically different for the body of Christ in Colossae. They must become unlike the world around them as they put these vices to death and are transformed into new people according to the image of Christ. And when believers undertake such a transformation together as a corporate body of Christ, then they become a radically new kind of people, where old systems of status and identity are superseded by Christ himself, and where diverse believers can set aside their differences and find unity together in Christ (3:11).

Mortify the Things of the Earth (3:5–7)

Paul commands the Colossians to put to death various vices that belong to their former way of life on earth, including sexual immorality and evil desires, for such things merit the wrath of God.

3:5. Paul's first command is to put to death certain deeds that belong to the earth. In previous paragraphs, Paul has preceded the verb with a conjunction (e.g., 2:6, 16, 20; 3:1); now, however, Paul places emphasis on the command by placing the conjunction "then" (οὖν) after the imperative "put to death" (νεκρώσατε). He intends to startle his readers with the abrupt morbidity of his macabre command. This startling effect is better achieved by the English translation "mortify" (KJV) than the explanatory translation "put to death" (ESV, NIV, NRSV). Perhaps we could even say "kill" or "execute"!

The command itself has the straightforward meaning of taking the necessary action to transform a living thing into a dead thing. In a literal sense, to "put to death" can mean taking someone's physical life, or the term can also be used metaphorically for someone who is impotent and powerless, or "as good as dead" (BDAG, s.v. "νεκρόω," p. 668; e.g., Rom 4:19; Heb 11:12). In 1656, John Owen published a series of sermons that have now become a classic work, *The Mortification of Sin*. He says to mortify someone or something "is to take away the principle of all his strength, vigour and power, so that he cannot act, or exert, or put forth any proper actings of his own" (Owen 2006, 22). Therefore, to mortify a vice, as Paul commands here, is to take from that vice its power or ability to exert influence over ourselves, so that we no longer succumb to its directives.

Believers are to take such executionary action against "the members *which are* things on the earth" (τὰ μέλη τὰ ἐπὶ τῆς γῆς). In the preceding context, the earth refers to the lower domain where Christ is not regarded as Lord, in contrast to the heavens above where Christ sits and reigns at God's right hand (3:1–2). The earth (γῆ) is tantamount to the world (κόσμος) insofar as it stands for the domain where the powers (στοιχεῖα) dwell and reign (2:8, 20). For believers, the earth is their *former* domain; it is what they died *from* (3:2) and that to which they no longer belong, now that their lives have been raised with Christ above (3:3). Paul now calls for believers to stand opposed to their former way of life and to even discharge a certain hostility and violence toward it.

The Practice of Resurrection Requires the Practice of Death

Eugene Peterson says, "Resurrection does not have to do exclusively with what happens after we are buried or cremated. It does have to do with that, but first of all it has to do with the way we live right now. But as Karl Barth, quoting Nietzsche, pithily reminds us: 'Only where graves are is there resurrection.' We practice our death by giving up our will to live on our own terms. Only in that relinquishment or renunciation are we able to practice resurrection" (Peterson, 2011, 290).

More specifically, Paul provides a list of five vices that are themselves such members of the earth. These vices each have their distinctive meanings yet at the same time share some semantic overlap and common themes. In general, the list focuses on sexual immorality and it begins with deeds and moves toward desires. The first vice refers generally to "unlawful sexual intercourse" (BDAG, s.v. "πορνεία" 1, p. 854), where unlawful refers to any sexual intercourse other than that between a husband and wife, and especially perhaps the intercourse of prostitution. It therefore is translated as "fornication" (KJV, NRSV) or more generally as "sexual immorality" (NIV, ESV, HCSB).[1] Thus, in 1 Corinthians 5:1, sexual immorality describes the specific instance of a man having relations with his father's wife,

1 The Greek word for "sexual immorality" (πορνεία) occurs frequently and prominently in vice lists (Mark 7:21; Gal. 5:19; Eph. 5:3; Rev. 9:21). Throughout the New Testament, it stands as a trademark of the works of the flesh (e.g., John 8:41). In Acts 15, sexual immorality is affirmed as an Old Testament prohibition that applies to Gentiles, and it may therefore serve as a summary term for the sexual ethics of the Old Testament, particularly Leviticus 17–18 (Gagnon, 2002, 435).

while in 1 Corinthians 6:18, Paul exhorts the Colossians to flee from all sexual immorality, specifically relations with prostitutes (1 Cor. 6:15–16). Whatever form sexual immorality might take, Paul prescribes sexual relations within marriage as the proper alternative to sexual immorality (1 Cor. 7:2–5).

Second in his list, Paul forbids "impurity" (ἀκαθαρσία). The term can refer literally to that which is dirty, but when used metaphorically, it refers to moral corruption or impurity (BDAG, s.v. "ἀκαθαρσία," p. 34). It is often used in relation to cultic practices to designate those who are ritually impure and therefore unfit for worship in God's presence. Such impurity is the opposite of holiness (1 Thess. 4:7) and is the "moral impurity which excludes man from fellowship with God" (TDNT 3.428). The term frequently appears alongside "sexual immorality" in vice lists (e.g., 2 Cor. 12:21; Gal. 5:19; Eph. 5:3), as here, and therefore Paul seems to be calling for the mortification of any kind of sexual impurity that makes the people of God unfit for serving the holy God.

Third, Paul calls for the mortification of "passion" (πάθος). In the New Testament, this word always occurs within contexts of deviant sexual behavior, so that it refers to the strong desire for illicit sexual conduct (Rom. 1:26; 1 Thess. 4:5). Therefore, the translation "lust" (HCSB, NIV) is preferred over "passion" (ESV, NRSV) or "inordinate affection" (KJV) in order to bring out the sexual implications of the term. It is "erotic passion" (TDNT 5.928) perhaps arising even to "uncontrolled sexual urges" (Wright, 1986, 134).

Fourth, the Colossians are to put to death "evil desire" (ἐπιθυμίαν κακήν). The desire itself is innocuous and amoral, being inherently neither good nor bad, though it typically was used in a negative sense in Paul's day (Gagnon, 2002, 232). Indeed, Paul himself desired to be with Christ (Phil. 1:23) and with the Thessalonians (1 Thess. 2:17; 3:2). However, Paul here adds the adjective "evil" (κακός) to indicate the *kind* of desire he prohibits. Desire becomes bad when it desires that which is bad—we could say that a desire is only as good or evil as that which it desires. Thus, Paul forbids those evil desires that are contrary to our proper desire, which is to be a desire for things above, where Christ is Lord (Col. 3:1).

Finally, Paul concludes his list of vices with a particular evil desire, "greed" (πλεονεξία). Greed is "the state of desiring to have more than one's due" (BDAG, s.v. "πλεονεξία," p. 824). We often associate greed with an undue desire for an abundance of possessions (e.g., Luke 12:15), but it could also be used with other objects. For example, the law of Moses commands against coveting your neighbor's house, wife, servants, ox, donkey, and anything else belonging to him (Exod. 20:17). Further, Dunn suggests the word could be used in the first century to speak of sexual greed, "when the sexual appetite is unrestrained in a man" (Dunn, 1996, 215). Whatever its object, greed is problematic because the desire becomes the driving force of a person's life, to continually acquire more and more and never to be satisfied. It becomes incompatible with life in Christ and the seeking of things above, and therefore, Paul calls greed what it is—idolatry (εἰδωλολατρία).

The direct connection Paul makes between greed and idolatry serves to expose greed for what it actually is. The object of our greed takes the place of God in our lives, becoming that which we worship and serve in place of God. In the Old Testament, idolatry was specifically about the making of idols that would be worshipped as God (Exod. 20:4–5; Deut. 5:8–9). For example, the people of Israel committed blatant idolatry when they fashioned a golden calf, bowed down to it, and claimed it to be the god who had brought them out of Egypt (Exod. 32). Such worship was clearly displaced, being directed to a physical idol made by human hands rather than to the invisible God who made humans by his hands. Idolatry worships creation rather than the Creator. Anything, therefore, that becomes the object of our affections and worship other than our Creator has become an idol for us, whether it be something physical, such as money, possessions, or icons, or something abstract, such as career, fame, or romance.

Paul's language, therefore, has great effect. Many of us may be complacent about greed in our lives even as we condemn idolatry in the strongest of terms. But what if greed *is* idolatry? What if *my* greed is idolatry? Then surely I must put it to death. Let us, then, not miss the impact of presenting sin such as greed for what it truly is, an idol that demands for itself the worship that belongs to God alone.

Tim Keller on Idolatry

In his book *Center Church*, Tim Keller contends that many people today more readily grasp the idea of sin when it is described in terms of idolatry. In other words, rather than teaching sin as a violation of God's law—which it is—Keller presents sin as "building your life's meaning on anything—even a very good thing—more than on God." He draws upon Augustine's *Confessions* to discuss sin "as a disorder of love" that "always leads to misery and breakdown." We lie in order to bolster our love for our own reputation, or we steal to satisfy our love for money, or we take performance-enhancing drugs to indulge our love for our bodies. This helps people to see that we are all worshippers of something, but our worship is often displaced. Keller concludes, "Depicting sin as an act of misplaced love, not just a violation of law, is more compelling to many people in our culture today" (Keller, 2012, 127–28). For Keller, therefore, not only is greed idolatry, but all sin is idolatry.

3:6. Paul now raises the stakes by pointing out the consequences associated with these vices. It is because of these things, Paul says, that the wrath of God comes upon the sons of disobedience. God's "wrath" (ὀργή) is not a popular topic of conversation in the church today. We would much rather meditate upon his love and define God as such. Surely God is love, as the apostle John so directly states (1 John 4:8), but the counterpart of his love is his wrath. The wrath of God "means that he intensely hates all sin" (Grudem, 1994, 206), and John Frame places God's hatred of evil alongside his love of goodness: "God cannot love goodness without hating evil. The two are opposite sides of the same coin, positive and negative ways of describing the same virtue" (Frame, 2013, 272). God's wrath is always directed toward that which is evil, and God's wrath is different from the wrath of man in that God is in a position whereby his "wrath actually executes punishments" (Frame, 2013, 273). Therefore, Paul can describe God's wrath (ὀργή) here as a just and righteous virtue of God, even while two verses later he can instruct God's people to put wrath away from them (ὀργή; 3:8).

Paul uses the present tense to say the wrath of God "comes" (ἔρχεται). This may be understood as a gnomic present stating a timeless fact, or this may be understood as a progressive present indicating an ongoing activity. In either case, Paul does not defer God's wrath into the future, but he draws it into the present. We know that God's wrath is an eschatological certainty that will be associated with the coming of Christ in glory (Col. 3:4). He will not only deliver and glorify his saints in that day (Rev. 19:1–10), but he will also trample the wicked in the "winepress of the fury of the wrath of God" (Rev. 19:15; cf. 19:11–21). Paul's use of the present tense here emphasizes the immanence of God's wrath, which will so surely come that it is effectively already here. Indeed, God's wrath is already "being revealed" (Rom. 1:18) in some form or measure even now, as he gives humanity over to rebellion and issues forth natural—and perhaps unnatural, or supernatural—consequences for sin (Rom. 1:18–32).

This wrath comes specifically "upon the sons of disobedience" (ἐπὶ τοὺς υἱοὺς τῆς ἀπειθείας). In Scripture, such disobedience is displayed toward God and carries with it the "connotation of disbelief" in God (BDAG, s.v. "ἀπείθεια," p. 99). For example, the author of Hebrews describes the Israelites' disobedience in their failure to enter the Promised Land as a lack of faith (Heb. 4:4–6). To be a son of disobedience is to live a life characterized by disobedience and disbelief toward God and even to be under the influence of spiritual powers of evil (Eph. 2:2–3). Upon them the wrath of God comes, Paul says here (cf. Eph. 5:6), but lest we should become proud to think *they* merit the wrath of God while *we* do not, Paul next reminds us that we all formerly lived as sons of disobedience and deserved God's wrath.

John Steinbeck's *The Pearl*

John Steinbeck's *The Pearl,* originally published in 1945, illustrates the destructive consequences of greed. When Kino discovers a very rare pearl of extraordinary value that will make him wealthy far beyond his impoverished peers, he takes bold measures to secure his treasure for the benefit of himself and his family. (Spoiler alert!) However, rather than blessing his family, the pearl begins to exact an increasing cost, taking them from their village and home, exposing them to danger, and testing their sanity, until it finally takes the life of Kino's son. In many ways, Kino experiences a small measure of God's wrath, as the pearl leads to destruction rather than flourishing, to death rather than life. He surely would return to the life he knew before acquiring the pearl, if only he could turn back time. Instead, he does the best he can do. Kino hurls the pearl back into the sea, effectively mortifying it. The final line of the story says, "And the music of the pearl drifted to a whisper and disappeared" (Steinbeck, 1974, 118). His story warns that greed will destroy us if we do not destroy it first.

3:7. Paul reminds the Colossians of their own background before Christ, that they formerly lived in the ways of these sons of disobedience. The "former" (ποτέ) time points back to their life before Christ, when they were unreconciled enemies of God (1:21–22) and were dead in their sins (2:13). Paul uses his typical word "walk" (περιπατέω; cf. 1:10; 2:6; 4:5) to refer to their way of life at that time, so that walking among the sons of disobedience means they were also engaging in their conduct. By implication, when Paul commands the Colossians to put these vices to death, he is speaking of the very vices by which they have lived. They have been engaging in the sexual immorality and evil desires that they now must mortify.

And not only did they walk in this way in their former life, but they also "lived among them" (ἐζῆτε ἐν τούτοις). This phrase recalls the abstract language Paul used in 2:20 to describe those who live under the domain of the world and are subject to its dogmas. But here in 3:7, Paul suggests something more tangible and personal. The Colossians lived among the sons of disobedience as friends, neighbors, and even family, but even more, as allies in the vices Paul has listed. They were brothers and sisters together as sons of disobedience.

But this *was* their *former* way of life. They now have new life in and with Christ (2:12–13; 3:3), and in this new life Christ has called them out of the domain of the world even as he has left them to live in the world. Thus, they continue to live alongside the sons of disobedience even as they no longer belong to them. The Colossian believers have gone from being insiders with the sons of disobedience to being outsiders. Or, more properly, they have become insiders with Christ, so that the sons of disobedience are now the outsiders (4:5). They will both leave behind and live among these sons of disobedience, leaving behind their way of life but living out their new life for the sons of disobedience to see.

Put Off Anger and Sinful Speech (3:8–9a)

Paul gives another vice list in which he instructs the Colossians to put off various forms of anger and evil speech, including lying to one another.

3:8. In contrast (δέ) to the former way of life, Paul "now" (νυνί) exhorts the Colossians to put off even more of the vices of the old way of life. Paul shifts from sins of sexual immorality and desire to sins of anger and evil speech. Wright observes that many churches will denounce one of these vice lists over the other. They may not tolerate an ounce of sexual immorality, yet they are full of gossip, malice, and so forth; or they may be so focused on maintaining harmony in the body that they tolerate grievous sexual immorality (Wright, 1986, 133). But Paul will have none of either. All vices must go.

Paul changes the imperative he uses from "mortify" in verse 5 to "put off" (ἀποτίθημι). This "putting off" pairs nicely with his command in verse 12 to "put on" the virtues belonging to Christ. Such language could easily be used for changing clothes. Indeed, some scholars see an association with baptism here, when converts may have removed their clothes prior to baptism and put on a new set of clothes after baptism, perhaps even being baptized *au naturel* (Meeks, 1983, 151; cf. MacDonald, 2000, 136). Even as they changed their clothes in baptism, so also they must change their lifestyle in following Christ. And the first step in a changed lifestyle is removing from yourself "all the things" (τὰ πάντα; cf. Col. 1:16–17, 20) included in the following list of five vices, all of which deal in one way or another with interpersonal relationships.

First, they must put off "anger" (ὀργή), which is a "state of relatively strong displeasure," with particular focus on the "emotional aspect" of anger (BDAG, s.v. "ὀργή" 1, p. 720). This is the anger of one person toward another, when we hold animosity in our hearts toward others. Anger represents the very opposite of the peace of Christ that ought to rule in our hearts (Col. 3:15). Believers must learn to release anger back to God, to whom alone belongs the right to such anger (Rom. 12:19). Thus, Paul can in the same breath tell believers to put off anger (ὀργή; 3:8) even as he describes God's pouring out of his wrath (ὀργή; 3:6), and Paul apparently sees no conflict between the two statements. In the case of anger, what is appropriate for God is not appropriate for his people. Anger belongs to God alone.

Second, Paul tells them to put off "wrath" (θυμός), a very close synonym of anger (ὀργή). The combination of these two terms typically serves to strengthen the thought (BDAG, s.v. "θυμός" 2, p. 461), and together they might be translated "fury of wrath" (e.g., Rev. 16:19; 19:15). Lightfoot discerns a sliver of difference between the terms, so that "the one [anger, ὀργή] denotes a more or less settled feeling of hatred, the other [wrath, θυμός] a tumultuous outburst of passion" (Lightfoot, 1981, 214). Anger and wrath together, in other words, refer to both the internal passion of the heart and the external expressions that accompany it, and one is not better than the other. The Christian who harbors anger silently as bitterness in their heart is no better than the Christian who explodes in uncontrolled rage. Both forms of anger—*all* forms of anger—must be put off.

Can Anger Be Righteous?

Often Christians justify their anger as being "righteous" in light of Ephesians 4:26—"be angry and do not sin"—to suggest that anger is acceptable so long as we do not sin in our anger. However, a closer look at anger in the New Testament reveals far less justification for anger, if indeed there is any justification at all. Scripture only actually says that Jesus was angry in one instance prior to healing a man in the synagogue (Mark 3:5). We often *presume* Jesus to have been angry in other instances, such as when he criticized the Pharisees or cleansed the temple, but the text does not explicitly describe him as such. In fact, in Mark's account of the temple cleansing, Jesus looks around the temple in the evening and then returns the following day to cleanse it (Mark 11:11, 15–17). This was hardly an explosion of unrestrained anger upon first provocation; indeed, it seems almost premeditated. Perhaps as Christians we should expend less effort justifying our anger in light of Ephesians 4:26 and more effort expunging our anger in light of Ephesians 4:31, "Let *all* bitterness and wrath and anger and clamor and slander be put away from you, along with *all* malice" (ESV; emphasis added). Consider also James 1:19–20: "Everyone should be . . . slow to become angry, for *man's anger does not produce the righteousness that God requires*" (ESV; emphasis added). When it comes to anger and righteousness, the former does not lead to the latter, and perhaps, therefore, we should be far more cautious about harboring our anger under the stratagem of righteousness.

Third, they must put off "malice" (κακία), which can refer generally to wickedness or more specifically to "a mean-spirited or vicious attitude or disposition" (BDAG, s.v. "κακία" 2, p. 500). In this context, where Paul has just listed anger and wrath, he seems to have in view mean-spiritedness, or malice. It is the spite that determines to do harm to others.

Fourth, "slander," or literally "blasphemy" (βλασφημία), must go. We most often associate blasphemy with defamatory speech toward God, but given the interpersonal nature of this list, Paul more likely has in view abusive language toward others. These are words intended to do harm to others by opposing them and speaking evil about them and to them, thereby damaging their reputation and injuring their spirit (see Acts 13:45; 18:6; Titus 3:2).

Fifth, they must put off "obscene speech *that comes* out of their mouths" (αἰσχρολογίαν ἐκ τοῦ στόματος ὑμῶν). The term Paul uses for "obscene speech" (αἰσχρολογία) appears only here in the New Testament and is variously translated as "obscene talk" (ESV), "filthy language" (HSCB, NIV), "abusive language" (NRSV), or "filthy communication" (KJV). What precisely constitutes obscenity appears to be culturally defined, as every culture and language regards particular words and phrases to be scurrilous whenever they are spoken, regardless of the context or situation. Such language is the opposite of the dignified speech of gentlemen and ladies. The Colossians in the first century would have had to determine what constituted obscene speech in their world just as we must determine the same within our own language and culture today. For English-speaking Christians, this surely forbids the use of certain four-letter words and other vulgar terms that even our children know to be unbecoming, as well as dirty jokes and off-color remarks. Christians must not have potty mouths.

When we put all of these vices together again, we can see the cumulative effect of Paul's list in 3:8. All of these vices are characteristic of strife and broken relationships, and they run directly contrary to the virtues Paul will command in 3:12–17. These are the opposite of kindness, meekness, love, and peace. Here again, we might remember the fractured relationship between Onesimus and Philemon. Both likely feel wronged by the other, and therefore both could attempt to validate their anger toward the other and to justify slandering the other. But Paul will have none of it in the church. Both of them need a transformation of the heart, and it begins with putting off anger, malice, and slander, that they might in turn put on the compassion, humility, and love required if they are to forgive one another and have peace restored not only in their relationship but in the entire church.

3:9a. In the first words of verse 9, Paul gives another command: "Do not lie to one another." To lie is to "tell a falsehood" (BDAG, s.v. "ψεύδομαι" 1, p. 1096). It is the opposite of truth. God by his very nature is true, so that it is impossible for him to lie (Heb. 6:18). Lying has its source in Satan himself, who is the father of lies (John 8:44). Thus, the Colossians, having now received the truth of the gospel (Col. 1:5–6), must live in truth rather than falsehood. This commitment to the truth manifests itself first and foremost in a commitment to be truthful with one another in our daily interactions. Honesty and forthrightness must replace lying in all of its various forms.

The New Humanity (3:9b–11)

Paul gives the reason behind his preceding instructions to mortify and remove vices, for the Colossians have become a new kind of people who are being transformed into the image of Christ, so that Christ is now all that matters among them.

3:9b. Paul follows his command to not lie to one another with an explanation that reaches back to all the vices he has commanded should be put off. He uses two parallel statements, both introduced by participles (both aorist), to recall what the Colossians have already experienced: they "have taken off" (ἀπεκδυσάμενοι; 3:9) the old person and they "have put on" (ἐνδυσάμενοι; 3:10) the new person. Here again, Paul reminds the Colossians of the transformation they experienced when they first received the gospel from Epaphras and put their faith in Christ (Col. 1:3–8), and thereby they died and were raised to new life in union with Christ (2:11–13). As in the previous verse (3:8), Paul may be envisioning the baptism the Colossians underwent (2:12) and perhaps also the changing of clothes that would have accompanied the inevitable sogginess of baptism (e.g., MacDonald, 2000, 137). We have no way of knowing with certainty that Paul intended a connection to baptism, but regardless the imagery stands well enough on its own—even as a person takes off one set of clothes and puts on another, so also the believers have taken off one person and put on another.

Paul's mention of a "person" (ἄνθρωπος) that has been taken off echoes other Pauline letters where Paul speaks of the inner person or the soul in contrast to the outer person or the body (2 Cor. 4:16), or the old person that has been crucified and brought to death (Rom. 6:6). In such cases, the person is specific to the internal nature of individual persons and is suitably translated "self" (so ESV, HCSB, NIV, NRSV). Therefore, here in 3:9, the "old" (παλαιός) self recalls Paul's earlier reference to our individual and internal human nature that was formerly dead in sin but has now given way to new life in Christ (2:13), and Paul calls it "old" precisely because it is now in the past for the Colossians. It is the person they once were but no longer are.

Paul's point here in 3:9 comes with the final phrase. When the old person was taken off, it was removed "with its actions" (σὺν ταῖς πράξεσιν αὐτοῦ). Its actions and behaviors were discarded along with the old self, or at least they should have been. That person has become the former self of the Colossians, and now the conduct of that former self must also become the former conduct of the Colossians. They must take off the conduct that belongs to the old person they have taken off, and they cannot take off the one and not the other. This provides the reason for Paul's exhortation to remove the vices of verses 6 and 9. They belong to a former person, and therefore they must become the former behavior of the Colossians.

3:10. Paul now gives the second part of his explanation in parallel with the first. Even as the Colossians have taken off the old self (3:9), so also they have now put on the new (3:10). These are two sides of the same coin, or two outworkings of the one act of salvation. It is not possible to put off the old and *not* put on the new. This new person refers again to the new life these believers have received in union with Christ, when they were raised with Christ by faith and made alive together with him (Col. 2:12–13). They have become a new person defined entirely by Christ. This has been the former working of Christ in their life—a one-time work they experienced at the moment of salvation which theologians call regeneration.

Regeneration

The theological concept of regeneration may be defined as "a secret act of God in which he imparts new spiritual life to us" (Grudem, 1994, 699). Regeneration "assumes the deadness of the human condition and the singular power of God to effect an instantaneous spiritual vivification in a person," and the work of regeneration is effected by the Holy Spirit (Bird, 2013, 533–34). Ezekiel spoke of regeneration when he envisioned God giving new hearts and spirits to his people (Ezek. 36:26–27), and in John's gospel, Jesus speaks of the necessity of being "born again" by the Spirit (John 3:3–8). This work is no less real for being mysterious and spiritual in nature. The end result, Paul says, is that a person has become a new creation entirely, for the old has passed away and the new has come (2 Cor. 5:17).

Paul, however, does not dwell upon this past regeneration for nostalgia's sake; rather; Paul is interested in the past for the sake of the present, where the work continues as the new person is continually "being renewed" (τὸν ἀνακαινούμενον). The present tense points to an ongoing work while the passive voice suggests it is the work of someone other than the Colossians. Strictly speaking, Paul does not command the Colossians here to renew themselves, as he does in Romans 12:2 and Ephesians 4:23, but he speaks here of renewal as the work enacted upon them by an external person. In cases such as this, where Paul uses the passive voice without identifying the active agent by name, we may legitimately presume he has a divine actor in view. Thus, these are sometimes called "divine passives," where Paul uses the passive voice with the assumption that we will recognize God as the acting agent. God does the work of renewal upon the Colossians, who in turn receive it.

This renewal, Paul says, takes place first and foremost in the sphere of their knowledge. This "knowledge" (ἐπίγνωσις) recalls Paul's circular prayer in Colossians 1:9–10, where he prayed that the Colossians would be filled with knowledge of God's will so they could live in a way that pleases God even as they continue to grow in the knowledge of God. Further, the content of this knowledge centers on Christ himself, who is the mystery of God (Col. 2:2). To grow in knowledge, or to be renewed in knowledge, is to increase in knowledge of Christ.

But for Paul, knowledge never exists for knowledge's sake alone; it always goes hand-in-hand with transformation of behavior. Thus, this renewal is not only in knowledge but also in conduct, as the new person is being transformed according to the image (εἰκών) of the one who created (κτίζω) him. Paul's language here borrows directly from the hymn of 1:15–20, where Christ was declared to be the "image" (εἰκών; 1:15) of God, who is the firstborn of all creation (κτίσις; 1:15) and the one through whom all things were created (κτίζω; 1:16). Paul now focuses on one particular aspect of God's creative work, namely the creative work of regeneration whereby God grants new life to believers in Christ. The goal of this renewing work is to produce people who reflect fully the image of Christ, being like him in character and conduct. This has been God's predestined plan for believers from the very beginning (Rom. 8:29), and it will be an ongoing work in the believer in the present time (2 Cor. 3:18) until it is finally completed at the final resurrection, when Christ returns in glory (1 Cor. 15:49).

God is the agent who does this work of renewal in every believer. God *is* renewing his people into the image of Christ, and thus Paul establishes the grounds for his exhortations. If this is the work God *is* doing, namely, a transformative work of renewal into the image of Christ, and if God has done the work of regeneration, so that the old person has been taken off and a new person has been put on, then naturally the Colossians must apply themselves to participating firsthand in this work of renewal by mortifying and putting off those practices that belong exclusively to the former person whom they no longer are. Paul exhorts the Colossians to actively participate in the renewing work of God by putting off the vices of their former self in order that they might thereby be renewed by God into the image of Christ.

This gives the hope of new beginnings. Who we formerly were is no indicator of who we now are in Christ, much less of who we are becoming in Christ and who we will one day be. We must take care lest we judge others based on their former conduct without allowing that the person they are today may be much more Christlike than who they were yesterday.

Here again, we can see Paul laying the foundation for his appeal to Philemon to reconcile with Onesimus. Paul works on the assumption that both Philemon and Onesimus are believers in Christ, and therefore Philemon is experiencing renewal as a new person in Christ, and Onesimus also is experiencing renewal as a new person in Christ, so that both are growing in knowledge and being conformed to the image of Christ. Therefore, the Onesimus of today who returns to Colossae is no longer the Onesimus of yesterday who left Colossae, and the Philemon of today who receives Onesimus back to Colossae is no longer the Philemon of yesterday who saw him leave. Thus, not only must they themselves no longer be the person of yesterday, but they must also recognize that the other is also no longer the person of yesterday. This allows them the opportunity to put away the relationship of yesterday, and to establish a new relationship today as new persons being renewed. Here then is the grounds for reconciliation within the body of Christ, as new people build new relationships in accordance with the renewing work of God within them.

The Problem with Bitterness in the Church

When as Christians we refuse to forgive those who have sinned against us, and instead reserve for ourselves the right to continue in our anger and to hold their sin against them, we are resisting the work of God on two fronts. On the one hand, we are resisting his work of renewal in our own lives, where he calls us to put off anger and to instead forgive (3:8, 13); and on the other hand, we are resisting his work of renewal in the other person's life, where God is renewing them, so that they are putting off the sinful habits of their past—including their sins against us—and are being transformed into the image of Christ. Our bitterness precludes us from recognizing and fully enjoying God's renewing work both in ourselves and in the other, and it is therefore a denial of faith in the God who is making all things new.

3:11. Paul's final words in this broader section of exhortation are simultaneously a contradiction and a confirmation of his previous statements about the transformation of the old person to the new person. The contradiction is at once apparent. He has spoken of taking off and putting on the old and new person, respectively, where the *person* is singular and individual in nature. But in verse 11, Paul uses the word "where" (ὅπου) with reference to "the new *person*" (τὸν νέον) of verse 10, and he uses corporate language to describe what we find within this new person. The new person is a place *where* social categories no longer apply, such as Greek and Jew, circumcised and uncircumcised, Barbarian, Scythian, slave, and free. But how can various and diverse people be included in the "new person" if indeed the new person is a singular individual? Perhaps Paul intended for the "person" (ἄνθρωπος) of 3:9–10 to refer not to an individual person but to a corporate humanity (as in Eph. 2:15–16), and indeed some work backward from 3:11 to interpret Paul's language throughout 3:9–10 as such (e.g., Moo, 2008, 267; Wright, 1986, 138).

However, the contradiction between the individual and the corporate is better understood as a disruption that alerts us to a marvelous continuation in Paul's thinking. For Paul, the *personal* transformation is inseparable from the *corporate* community of God's people. The new *person* (ἄνθρωπος) belongs to the *body* (σῶμα) of Christ, which is the church

(Col. 1:18, 24), so that to put on the new person is to become a member of the people of Christ. Thus, the new person is a new member in the body of Christ, and when Paul speaks of one he implicates also the other. The individual person belongs to the corporate body and the corporate body is composed of individual persons.

Therefore, when an individual believer puts on the new person of 3:10, he or she *de facto* becomes a member in the new body of Christ. And thus this new person, together with other members of the body, is "where" (ὅπου) old categories of social identification are no longer present. Here Paul explicitly rejects four categories of social identity, each expressed as a binary pair.

First, Paul rejects the distinction between "Greek" (Ἕλλην; not "Gentile" as in NIV) and "Jew" (Ἰουδαῖος). The Greeks prided themselves in their superior culture, while the Jews prided themselves in their superior religion—so that both looked down upon and despised the other. "No iron curtain of the present day presents a more forbidding barrier than did the middle wall of partition which separated Jew from Gentile" (Bruce, 1984, 149).

Second, Paul rejects a similar distinction between circumcised (περιτομή) and uncircumcised (ἀκροβυστία). Circumcision was held up as a badge of pride among the Jews, though it was mocked as needless mutilation by the uncircumcised, including the Greeks. For Paul to reject circumcision was itself a scandal, since circumcision was commanded by God as the sign of his covenant with Abraham whereby the Jewish people were established as his chosen people (Gen. 17). Circumcision was what identified the people of God and uncircumcision identified those who were outside his people. By rejecting this fundamental distinction, Paul effectively reincorporates the people of God with a new admission standard based entirely upon Christ.

Third, Paul rejects categories of identification such as barbarian and Scythian. "Barbarian" (βάρβαρος) refers generally to foreigners, and specifically to those who speak a foreign language (BDAG, s.v. "βάρβαρος," p. 166). Greek speakers used "barbarian" as a derogatory name for those who did not speak Greek, perhaps because the unknown sounds of a foreign language sounded to them like *bar-bar*. In modern times, we exercise a similar dismissiveness when we mock someone's speech as being *blah-blah-blah*. To be called a Barbarian, therefore, carried an "implied nuance of cultural inferiority" (Moo, 2008, 271).

Scythians are not so much the opposite of Barbarians as they are a "notorious example of" Barbarians (Harris, 2010, 134). They lived in the area of the Black Sea and were at the outermost edge of the Roman Empire (Maier, 2013, 90). They were "frequently viewed as the epitome of unrefinement or savagery" and were frequently satirized as uncouth brutes (BDAG, s.v. "Σκύθης," p. 932). Such lowly, foreign, uncultured, and barbaric people as the Barbarians and Scythians were not welcomed into the privileged social clubs of Greco-Roman culture, but Paul welcomes them into the body of Christ as full members, for in Christ, linguistic and cultural value systems have been leveled and disregarded, and the new person in Christ pays no mind to such differences.

Fourth and finally, and perhaps most shockingly, Paul rejects the distinction between slave (δοῦλος) and free (ἐλεύθερος). All persons in the Roman world belonged to one category or the other, being either legally enslaved to another person or legally free. Though Paul frequently rejects this social distinction in the church (e.g., 1 Cor. 12:13; Gal. 3:28; Eph. 6:8), and though the modern world has mostly made slavery illegal, we must remember again that slavery was simply the way the world worked in the first century. In that world, people could no more easily imagine a world without slavery than we can imagine a world without employment. The roles and language of employees and employers are inherent to the fabric of modern society, being woven into social structures and economic functions, so that we derive not only our livelihood, but also our identity, based on how we answer the simple question, "What do you do?" When we consider how difficult it is for us to imagine a place where the roles of employee and employer are eliminated and rendered meaningless, then we can appreciate just how radical a statement Paul makes when he says slave and free do not exist within the corporate body of new persons in Christ.

The Diversity of the Early Church

Paul's list of social categories that do not apply within the church reveals the diverse nature of the church itself, for presumably the church in Colossae included Greeks, Jews, circumcised, uncircumcised, Barbarians, Scythians, slave, and free. Larry Hurtado has researched the diversity of people who were part of the church in its earliest history. Hurtado quotes the Roman official Pliny, who claimed the Christians who were denounced before him included "many of all ages and every rank, and also both sexes" (Pliny, *Ep.* 10.96.9; Hurtado, 2016, 34). Similarly Celsus, who was refuted in Origen's *Contra Celsum*, "accuses Christians of welcoming the worst kind of people into their fellowship, in contrast with other religious and philosophical groups of the time that had proper standards for admission" (Hurtado, 2016, 72). Thus, Hurtado states about the early church what Paul implies in 3:11: "This suggests a movement of an interesting social diversity" (Hurtado, 2016, 34).

In contrast (ἀλλά) to these various ethnic, cultural, social, and economic forms of identification, Paul employs one simple trait that alone differentiates those who belong to the body from those who are outside: Christ. Paul is both emphatic and vague when he says Christ is "all and in all" (πάντα καὶ ἐν πᾶσιν). As in English, the Greek word "all" (πᾶς) can refer to impersonal things ("everything") or to persons ("everyone"), depending on the context. Recall Colossians 2:9–10, where Paul said first that all the fullness of deity dwells within Christ (2:9), and second that you have been filled in Christ (2:10), so that the fullness of Christ is the precursor to our fullness in Christ. Similarly, Paul's statement in 3:11 is best seen as reflecting first the nature of Christ himself and second the believer's experience in Christ, leading to the translation, "Christ is everything and is in everyone." In the body, Christ is all that matters, and all who are in the body have been filled with Christ, so that all persons in the body have absolute and equal standing, with no one being above or better than another. Therefore, any ethnic, cultural, or social distinctions that exist within the body have been superseded by Christ himself.

Scout's Analysis

In Harper Lee's *To Kill a Mockingbird*, Scout says, "I think there's just one kind of folks. Folks" (Lee, 1960, 230).

The profound statement of Colossians 3:11 sends shockwaves of implication reverberating outward in every direction. Consider, for example, how this empowers individuals. Most of the distinctives he lists in 3:11 were received by fate upon birth. A person does not choose their ethnicity or nationality, or the language they will speak, or to be a slave. These categories are inherently rigid by nature and people were almost entirely powerless to change their status. But Paul empowers believers in an extraordinary way by wrestling identity out of the hand of fate and placing it within their grasp. When they chose to receive the gospel and trust in Christ, they also chose to become a new person in Christ with a new identity in the body of Christ. The gospel, in other words, empowers every person, regardless of the status fate has handed them, with the opportunity to take hold of Christ and to receive a new identity in his body. Here slaves are empowered to grasp freedom, here Barbarians are empowered to find dignity, here free persons are empowered to lay down their freedom and Greeks are empowered to set aside their pride, and all together are empowered to embrace their new identity in Christ. The body of Christ, then, holds open the door for all to enter through Christ, but it requires everyone to check their status at the door, to adopt a new identity in Christ, and to unite together as one body in Christ even in the midst of extraordinary diversity.

For the church in Colossae, Paul's vision in 3:11 has very practical implications. They are going to have to actually put this into practice with one another, including Onesimus and Philemon. Paul's statement here, with its wholesale rejection of slave-free distinctions, is ultimately a call for *this* slave and *this* master to reorient their relationship with one another, no longer as slaves, but as new persons who have been brought together in the body of Christ. Paul will have much more to say about this in the rest of Colossians and in his letter to Philemon, but he lays the foundation here: Onesimus and Philemon have a new relationship defined entirely by Christ, for in the body, Christ is everything and Christ is in everyone, and where Christ is everything, nothing will remain the same.

THEOLOGICAL FOCUS

The exegetical idea (Paul exhorted the Colossians to stop living in their former way of life apart from Christ by putting to death the practices of that former life and embracing their identity as new persons being transformed into the image of Christ, as members together in the body of Christ) leads to this theological focus: Believers must be transformed into the image of Christ by putting off their old habits of sin and by living out of the new nature and identity they have received in Christ and in the body of Christ.

Paul's transition in this section from education to exhortation reminds us that believers have a responsibility to continue being transformed into the image of Christ. Believers have become new persons in Christ, but for Paul, God's past work of regeneration in our lives must also lead to his ongoing work of sanctification. Those who have been born again into new life (2:13) and into a new identity in Christ (3:9–10) must now undergo the ongoing work of being transformed into the image of Christ, both in knowledge and conduct. For Paul, regeneration and sanctification are inseparable; the former *must* lead to the latter. Those who have been made new must be made new.

This text may cause some confusion regarding who is responsible for doing the work of sanctification. On the one hand, Paul commands believers to do this work, as if we are responsible to put to death these vices in and of ourselves; but on the other hand, Paul uses the passive voice to describe sanctification as an ongoing work of "being renewed" (3:10), as if God acts upon us to do this work in our lives. Jerry Bridges holds together the tension of this twofold responsibility with the phrase "dependent discipline," by which he means that we discipline ourselves in dependence upon the Holy Spirit who transforms us (Bridges, 2004, 83–91). Similarly, John Owen points to Romans 8:13, where we are called to mortify the deeds of the body "through the Holy Spirit," and he suggests, "The principal efficient *cause* of the performance of this duty is the Spirit" (Owen, [1656] 2006, 20). God does not regenerate us and then abandon us to sanctify ourselves, but God works in us by his Spirit, and he empowers us for accomplishing the task to which he has called us.

Nevertheless, believers have a somber responsibility to mortify sin. We find sin constantly at work in our lives, as our former ways of thinking and living apart from Christ continue to linger and to unduly influence us. And the stakes are high. If we fail to mortify sin, then we are giving refuge in our own souls to the vices that bring about God's wrath (Col. 3:6)! Thus Owen reminds us to "be killing sin or it will be killing you," for "if sin be subtle, watchful, strong and always at work in the business of killing our souls, and we be slothful, negligent, foolish, in proceeding to the ruin thereof, can we expect a comfortable event? There is not a day but sin foils or is foiled, prevails or is prevailed on; and it will be so, whilst we live in this world" (Owen, [1656] 2006, 26, 29). When believers are actively mortifying sin, and when they are together being renewed into the image of Christ, then the body of Christ becomes the kind of body Paul envisions in verse 11, where Christ is everything and differences fade as believers are united together in Christ.

PREACHING AND TEACHING STRATEGIES

Exegetical and Theological Synthesis

Paul reminded the readers of the theological foundation for new life in Christ (3:1–4), and in this passage he turns from instruction to application with a focus on "mortifying" (3:5) and "putting off" (3:8) the old nature. Each of those commands is followed with a list of vices. The first list (3:5) focuses on sexual immorality and evil desires. Those sins bring the wrath of God (v. 6). The second list (3:8) focuses on anger and evil speech. Mortification was possible for the believers in Colossae because they had been regenerated—a dual action of putting off the old sinful ways and putting on new habits congruent with being renewed in the image of God (vv. 9–10). Furthermore, Paul says that the new person also has a new status as a member of the body of Christ. The old system of status based on race and social standing has been replaced with identity in Christ who is "all and in all" (v. 11).

Preaching Idea

Now that we are spiritually alive in Christ, let's put to death the old ways.

Contemporary Connections

What does it mean?

What does it mean to be spiritually alive in Christ and to put to death the old ways? The preaching idea refers to two actions—God's and ours. God regenerates us when we come to him in faith and humility, and then we respond by putting to death the old ways. The preaching idea might be explained with analogy: a seed has within it all the life necessary to develop into a mature plant, but the seed must be nurtured with good soil, light, water, and space for the roots to expand. We might also discuss what happens when a seed is choked by weeds or receives no water. After using the analogy we might explain what it means to put to death the old ways. In this passage, it means putting off the sins in the three lists. The first list deals with illicit sexual passion, the second with anger, and the third with prejudices that divide people. Contemporary examples could clarify the lists as well.

Sexual Sins in the Bible and Today

- Abraham didn't believe God's promise of a child, so in his impatience, he committed adultery and fathered a child with Hagar his handmaid. This was "socially acceptable" in Abraham's day, but it was still wrong (Gen. 16).
- The men of Sodom attempted to rape the male visitors who came to the city (Gen. 19).
- Lot's daughters had sex with their father to make sure his line of descendants didn't die out (Gen. 19).
- Wandering Israel—Abraham's promised nation—gave themselves to sexual impropriety, even deviancy, as the prohibitions in Leviticus 18 make clear.
- David, a man after God's own heart, saw beautiful Bathsheba bathing on the roof of a house. She became the object of his desire, and he used his authority to satiate his lust and murder her husband (2 Sam. 11).
- In the New Testament, Paul tells the Corinthian church that they should be ashamed of themselves because of their sexual immorality (1 Cor. 5:2). They not only tolerated but also celebrated this sin and their progressive views (see also Rom. 1:32).

Reflecting on the sad depiction in the Bible of sexual sins, Alex Duke sees parallels in today's world: sex outside of marriage isn't new, but due to certain technological advances—birth control, condoms, legal and "safe" and cheap abortions—consequence-free sex basically is. The desire to look at naked women and to act on it isn't new (David), but pocket-sized devices that offer buffets of easy-to-find, all-you-can-ogle naked women are. Celebrated sexual sin isn't new (Rom. 1; 1 Cor. 5), but homosexual sex that's incentivized under the auspices of the state and called "marriage" is. Men who predatorily prey on women aren't new; neither are men who pride themselves on their inability to commit. But thanks to popular dating apps such as Tinder and all the rest, the market has been flooded with sexual opportunity.[2]

One of the sins believers are to put off is covetousness, which is idolatry (v. 5). Describing greed as a "disordered love" might help explain Paul's phrase. Coveting arises from the mistaken belief that things, not God, bring fulfillment. In an age when advertisements stir desires with metronymic regularity, this sin may be ubiquitous, but acquisition often leaves us unfulfilled. The sidebar provides support for this claim.

Bigger Homes, Happier Lives?

In 1973, when the Census Bureau started tracking home sizes, the median size of a newly built house was just over 1,500 square feet; that figure reached nearly 2,500 square feet in 2015. This rise, combined with a drop in the average number of people per household, has translated to a lot more room for homeowners and their families. By one estimate, each newly built house had an average of 507 square feet per resident in 1973, and nearly twice that—971 square feet—four decades later.

But Americans aren't getting any happier with their bigger homes. Clément Bellet studies this phenomenon at a European business school, and he writes, "Despite a major upscaling of single-family houses since 1980 house satisfaction has remained steady in American suburbs." This may be because the dynamics of comparison, judgment, and self-justification are at play. Bellet continues: "The problem is that the satisfaction [with having a larger house] often doesn't last if even bigger homes pop up nearby. If I bought a house to feel like I'm 'the king of my neighborhood,' but a new king arises, it makes me feel very bad about my house. It is an unfulfilling cycle of one-upmanship."[3]

Is it true?

Is it true that believers have been made spiritually alive in Christ, and should now put to death the old ways? Perhaps people feel spiritually stuck, not alive. Yet the Bible holds out hope with many examples of individuals who put to death the old ways in the power of God: Saul the angry Pharisee became Paul the compassionate apostle; the man in Corinth who was sleeping with his stepmother repented and was welcomed back into the church (2 Cor. 2:5–11); after listing the sins of sexual immorality, idolatry, adultery, same-sex relations, stealing, and greed, Paul says, "And such were some of you. But you were washed, you were sanctified, you were justified in the name of the Lord Jesus Christ and by the power of the Spirit of God" (1 Cor. 6:11). Testimonies along the line of "here's what I'm learning about following Christ," and "how God is delivering me," can provide contemporary cases of transformation to go along with the biblical ones. Ultimately, the preaching idea

2 Alex Duke, "How Sex Became King," *The Gospel Coalition*, January 8, 2020, https://www.thegospelcoalition.org/article/sex-became-king.

3 Joe Pinsker, "Are McMansions Making People Any Happier?" *The Atlantic*, June 11, 2019.

is true because transformation is not dependent entirely on human will. If that were the case, then there would be little warrant for hope, but God is at work in believers to will and to do his good pleasure (Phil. 2:13). Our hope for transformation is grounded in God, not ourselves.

Verse 6 may prompt a question in the minds of listeners: "Why does sexual impurity bring the wrath of God?"

Why Does Sexual Impurity Bring the Wrath of God?

Using pornography as a case study can help explain why God is angered by sexual sins that are ubiquitous in many cultures.

- Porn harms children. When children are depicted in porn, it warps their sense of self, adults, and sex. It uses those who are powerless—children—for selfish and pecuniary ends. Ninety-three percent of boys and sixty-two percent of girls under age 18 have viewed porn, and many of the same twisted attitudes on the screen accrue to them.[4]
- Porn dishonors women. They become objects rather than persons.
- Porn diminishes marriage. The covenant relationship of marriage is the God-given place for sex. Porn makes sex individualistic, not a one-flesh relationship with husband and wife; and self-gratification decreases the drive to get married.
- Porn rewires the brain. It is linked to social anxiety, depression, low motivation, erectile dysfunction, concentration problems, and negative self-perceptions of one's physical appearance and sexual functioning. Porn is associated with increases in loneliness, divorce, and acceptance of sexual assault and harassment.[5]

Now what?

How can those who follow Jesus respond to the fact that they are now spiritually alive in Christ and so should put to death the old ways? We might borrow a phrase from Jerry Bridges: "dependent discipline." We depend on God to change us, and that humble attitude of dependence leads us to use disciplines such as prayer, self-examination, confession, worship, fasting, meditation, and study. These are means of grace that God uses for transformation. They can be difficult to practice in a busy, fast-paced world, but centuries of "evidence" indicate that they are tools God uses to sanctify his children. Perhaps we can suggest modest first steps: spend five minutes a day in solitude and silence, set an alarm on your watch to remind yourself to pray, or meditate on Scripture by listening to an audio Bible. Another means of grace is spiritual friendships. When iron sharpens iron through listening, conversation, advice, rebuke, and encouragement, rusty old metal can take on a fine edge and gleam.

Many books discuss how to form spiritually enlivening habits. These could be the basis of a small group study. Here are three:

- Richard Foster, *Celebration of Discipline: The Path to Spiritual Growth* (San Francisco: HarperCollins, 1978)
- John Ortberg, *The Life You've Always Wanted: Spiritual Disciplines for Ordinary People* (Grand Rapids: Zondervan, 1997)
- Ken Shigematsu, *Survival Guide for the Soul: How to Flourish Spiritually in a World That Pressures Us to Achieve* (Grand Rapids: Zondervan, 2018)

4 Chiara Sabina, Janis Wolak, and David Finkelhor, "The Nature and Dynamics of Internet Pornography Exposure for Youth," CyberPsychology & Behavior 11, no. 6 (December 1, 2008): 691–93, https://doi.org/10.1089/cpb.2007.0179.

5 Joe Carter, "4 Reasons Christians Should Support Banning Pornography," The Gospel Coalition, December 14, 2019, https://www.thegospelcoalition.org/article/4-reasons-christians-ban-porn/?mc_cid=379d2493d8&mc_eid=1076878034.

One of the cultural forces that deafens us to the truth that we are spiritually alive is the constant and ubiquitous noise provided by media. Constant distraction keeps us from being transformed. To become a "tech-wise" family, we might share some wisdom from Andy Crouch, author of *The Tech-Wise Family: Everyday Steps for Putting Technology in Its Place* (2017). These bits of advice are gleaned from an audio interview with the author that can be found at The Gospel Coalition in the podcast titled, "Andy Crouch on How to Become a Tech-Wise Family" (listen or see transcript):

- Leave your cell phone far from your bedroom. Make the beginning and ending of your day a time to reconnect with God and remind yourself of his presence. Set aside the frenetic search for entertainment and information.
- As you "put off" media overload, "put on" fun replacements such as games, bike rides, cooking, and singing together.
- Explain your family's standards to other families, so that when your children visit their friends' homes, the host families understand what your children are allowed to do. Explaining your standards may also help enlist the other parents' support.
- Model. Let your children see how you handle boredom and do not give into instant gratification. Let them see you working, not just consuming.
- Enjoy Sabbath, a God-ordained day where we set aside the things we count on for provision.
- Realize that handing a glowing rectangle to a bored children is actually a solution for the parents' problem, not the children's. The children need to learn how to handle boredom in patient and creative ways.

One way God wants us to display our new life in Christ relates to unity. God is forming his people into one body regardless of race, language, and cultural differences (v. 11), yet many believers have few friends outside of their own race. We mirror American culture in this regard. A study by the Public Religion Research Institute discovered that if a white American has one hundred friends, ninety-one are white, and they have one friend from each of these groups: black, Latino, Asian, mixed race, other race, and three of unknown race. Blacks don't fare much better. Of one hundred friends, eighty-three are black, eight are white, two are Latino, none are Asian, three are mixed race, one of other race, and four are unknown (Ingraham, 2014). To put to death the old ways and to live out spiritual life in Christ, believers might be encouraged to pray that God would give them friends outside of their race and then to seek opportunities to build those friendships.

Members of Christ's body deserve equal honor—"no Greek and Jew . . . barbarian, Scythian, slave, free" (v. 11)—but we are often tempted to show favoritism, so we must be made new. I (Jeffrey) saw this actualized in a church service that I attended as a visitor—The Falls Church, Virginia. This is the church where Vice President Mike Pence was a member, and when he attended church there was always a hullabaloo of metal detectors, and a cavalcade, of secret service. When the VP entered the room, hundreds of people would turn around, whip out their phones, and take pictures. On the particular day I visited, Vice President Pence as *not* present, so Pastor John Yates took the opportunity to gently correct his people. Yates said: "My friends, we have come to worship God. This isn't the time to play paparazzi. Please put your phones away and focus on God, and allow our brother [the VP] to do the same."

Creativity in Presentation

To flesh out the concept of dependent discipline, we might offer models. The use of self-disclosure can present your own model, or the testimony of a church member might embody principles of sanctification and inspire hope. Testimony might follow the sermon, or might be placed in the church newsletter or blog. It can also take place in group discussion. This opens the door for spontaneous testimonies and advice on how God transforms us.

Mortification of the old nature is a painful and joyful process. C. S. Lewis's *Voyage of the Dawn Treader* (1952b, 90–91) captures both experiences. Eustace, a sour and spoiled boy, is transformed into a dragon. A gold band he had worn on his arm as a boy now cuts into his large dragon leg. As he weeps over his ugly and painful condition, Aslan appears and offers to transform him, but doing so will not be easy or pleasant, for the scaly dragon skin must come off. Eustace recounts the experience: "The very first tear he made was so deep that I thought it had gone right into my heart. And when he began pulling the skin off, it hurt worse than anything I've ever felt. . . . Well, he peeled the beastly stuff right off . . . and there I was as smooth and as soft as a peeled switch and smaller than I had been. Then he caught hold of me . . . and threw me into the water. It smarted like anything but only for a moment. After that it became pretty delicious and . . . I started swimming and splashing. . . . I'd been turned into a boy again."

A scene from *The Passion of the Christ* (directed by Mel Gibson, 2004) uses symbols to convey how Jesus mortified temptation. He is praying in the garden in great distress with face to the ground. Satan appears in the form of a woman with a man's voice and tempts Jesus. A serpent glides out from under Satan's robe and touches Christ's hand. Satan smiles, sure of victory, but Jesus rises and crushes the head of the serpent.

One way to display the unity of Christ's body where there is no favoritism might be by honoring and preserving one another's traditions. That's what a small team of audio engineers did with early recordings of black gospel music. The songs on scuffed vinyl were transferred to a digital archive at Baylor University. Innumerable records, particularly from the "Golden Age" of the mid-1940s to the mid-70s, were at risk of being lost. In 2005, Robert Darden, a journalism professor at Baylor, wrote in *The New York Times* that "it would be more than a cultural disaster to forever lose this music. It would be a sin." One of the rare songs that Darden helped recover was "Old Ship of Zion," recorded in the early 1970s by the Mighty Wonders. Darden recalls the first time he heard it: "Our engineer played it for me in the studio, and we both broke into tears. I just want to make sure that every gospel song, the music that all American music comes from, is saved"[6]

A scene from Harper Lee's novel *To Kill a Mockingbird* (1960) could illustrate the need for racial reconciliation. The central plot involves a kind black man, Tom Robinson, who is accused of raping a poor white girl who attempted unsuccessfully to seduce him. Atticus Finch eloquently defends Tom in court; nevertheless, he is sentenced to be hanged. Through her character Atticus Finch, Harper Lee rebukes the South, which embraced racism while trying to remain a decent society, an impossible task. The film version (directed by Robert Mulligan, 1962) contains a powerful scene of Finch's closing speech in the trial.

In the church, God has unified not only people of different races, but also of different economic levels. The novel *Same Kind of Different as Me* (Hall and Moore, 2006) tells the stories of an unlikely friendship between coauthors Ron Hall, a wealthy art dealer, and

6 Santi Elijah Holley, "How a Newspaper Article Saved Thousands of Black Gospel Records from Obscurity," AtlasObscura.com [Sept. 24, 2019].

Denver Moore, a homeless man, and a gutsy woman named Debbie Hall who brought them together. The two men became friends through the gospel and helped each other help others (see also the film version, directed by Michael Carney, 2017).

Perhaps a demonstration could be arranged with a young person or other volunteer to convey the "put off, put on" metaphor: as you discuss the sins in the lists, they could take off an item of clothing such as a scarf, jacket, and vest, and drop them into a clothes basket. The next sermon (3:12–17) could use the same demonstration in reverse by putting on new articles of clothing.

The big idea to reiterate is that God has made us alive in Christ, and thus we have the power to obey his command to mortify (kill!) the old ways of disobedience. Now that we are spiritually alive in Christ, let's put to death the old ways.

- Now that we are alive in Christ (this point is taken from the context—the previous four verses). . . .
- Put to death and put away old pattern of living (3:5–9).
- Put on the new pattern of living (3:10–11).

DISCUSSION QUESTIONS

1. What are the five sins in the first list that we are supposed to kill? And what are the five in the second list we are supposed to put off?
2. If we have been made new, why do we have to be commanded to be made new? Similarly, if we have already died with Christ, why do we have to put to death the things that are dead?
3. What do the words "regeneration" and "sanctification" mean? What is their relationship?
4. Are you experiencing spiritual growth? Describe it. What is helping you?
5. Name someone you admire who has a tamed tongue, someone who does not lash out or sulk in anger. What can you learn by that person's example?

Colossians 3:12–17

EXEGETICAL IDEA

Paul exhorted the Colossians to put on the virtues of Christ, especially love, that they might have peace and unity together as the body of Christ, where the word of Christ dwells richly among them and they bring honor to the name of the Lord Jesus in all that they do.

THEOLOGICAL FOCUS

Believers must put on the virtues of Christ that will allow them to live in peaceful unity with one another as the body of Christ, to grow together through the word of Christ, and to honor the Lord Jesus in all things.

PREACHING IDEA

Only Jesus can dress you for church.

PREACHING POINTERS

When Paul spoke to the church in the little town of Colossae, he addressed a surprisingly diverse group of people: Jew and Gentile, slave and free, barbarian, and Scythian. Christ had called and regenerated people from many backgrounds and strata of society. That diversity testified to the power of Christ's call. The door to his kingdom is narrow, but all who desire to enter may do so. But this inclusivity was not only inspiring; it was also challenging, because diversity easily brings disunity. That was the challenge this first-century church faced, and percolating beneath the surface of Colossians is a particularly divisive issue—Philemon and his slave, Onesimus. How could master and runaway slave, brothers in Christ, demonstrate the unity of their spiritual standing?

Today we also face the issue of divisiveness. Racial, economic, cultural, and political diversity must not be allowed to divide Christ's body. One member of the church tunes in to a conservative news station and another to a progressive station. One member works at manual labor and another works in the world of ideas. Still another speaks with an accent and sometimes feels left out. Cultural differences and personal preferences, not to mention the daily irritations of living in community, must not trump the fact that we are one in Christ. How is this ideal to be actualized? By putting on love and the qualities that flesh out love: kindness, humility, meekness, patience, forgiveness, and thankfulness. Now that we've put off the dirty clothes associated with life before believing in Jesus, it's time to dress in those beautiful garments. Let's let Jesus dress us for church.

PUT ON THE VIRTUES OF CHRIST (3:12–17)

LITERARY STRUCTURE AND THEMES (3:12–17)

Here Paul's exhortations reach full stride as Paul gives the positive counterpart to the negative commands he has already given. Previously, Paul instructed the Colossians to put to death and "put off" (ἀποτίθημι; 2:8) various vices associated with the old person (3:5–11). Now, Paul commands them to "put on" (ἐνδύσασθε; 3:12) a list of virtues appropriate for the new person they have already put on in Christ (see 3:10), including compassion, humility, love, and the like. He then gives several additional instructions related to how they must live together as the body of Christ, including forgiving and bearing with one another, and keeping the peace of Christ and his word central in their gatherings. These virtues will enable them to have unity with one another as the church, and these characteristics will eventually lead into how Christians should relate to those outside the church, including fellow members of their households (3:18–4:1) and all those who do not belong to Christ (4:2–6).

- ***Put On Virtues (3:12–13)***
- ***Put On Love (3:14)***
- ***Be Ruled by Peace (3:15)***
- ***Be Indwelt by the Word of Christ (3:16)***
- ***Do Everything in the Name of the Lord Jesus (3:17)***

EXPOSITION (3:12–17)

These verses are a rich passage of pastoral exhortation to a congregation. In the historical context of Colossae, there were countless social gatherings, whether informal gatherings between friends and neighbors, or formal gatherings of institutions and religious groups. Paul here instructs the believers in Colossae to have a social gathering completely unlike any other social gathering in their town, for they gather as the elect people of God (3:12). Therefore, they must not only honor Christ with the entirety of their lives, including every word and deed (3:17), but they must be devoted to one another as the body of Christ, being bound together by love (3:14). They must learn to forgive one another and to bear together through any conflict or hardship, so that peace and unity are the trademark of their body, and their gatherings must be filled with singing and teaching centered upon Christ. This will require the Colossian believers to dress themselves with the virtues appropriate for the new people they have become in Christ (3:12). If and when the Colossians become this kind of body together, then they will bring honor to the name of the Lord Jesus, and they will be a gathering of people unlike any other social gathering in their community.

Put On Virtues (3:12–13)

Paul commands the Colossians to put on the virtues of Christ even as they strive to bear with one another and to forgive offenses between each other in the body of Christ.

3:12. Paul first commands the Colossians to put on five virtues. The imperative "put on" (ἐνδύσασθε) serves as the antithesis of his previous command to "take off" (ἀπόθεσθε) in Colossians 3:8, and it continues to flow out of the previous exchange of identity in Christ in 3:9–10. Paul continues his metaphor of changing clothes, now instructing the Colossians to put on, or to "clothe themselves" with virtues as a garment. Paul, in a sense, now offers fashion advice to the Colossians. But his advice does not arise merely from personal taste, which can vary from one person to the next; rather, Paul presents these virtues as the only fitting and fashionable style for the body of Christ, to which the Colossians now belong.

A Chiastic Structure

Paul uses a chiastic structure in his repetition of verbs about putting off and putting on.

A Put off vices (3:8)
  B Having put off the old person (3:9)
  B′ Having put on the new person (3:10)
A′ Put on virtues (3:12)

Before listing the virtues specifically, Paul uses three terms as a brief summary and reminder of who they are in Christ. First, Paul says they are those who have been "chosen" (ἐκλεκτοί) by God, or "the elect of God" (KJV), implying that their faith in Christ and membership in the body were in some way foreordained by God himself (cf. Eph. 1:3). Second, they are "holy" or "saints" (ἅγιοι; cf. Col. 1:2), having been set apart to God and called to become like God in his holiness (see Lev. 11:44; 1 Peter 1:16). Third, they are "beloved" (ἠγαπημένοι), having become recipients of God's love in Christ. Taken together, these three terms recall God's relationship with the people of Israel, whom God chose and called to be holy, and upon whom God placed his love and affection (e.g., Exod. 19:4–6; Deut. 7:6–11). In the New Testament, similar language is used of the church, the body of Christ, as the people of God (e.g., 1 Peter 2:9; cf. 1 Thess. 1:4; 2 Thess. 2:13).

Each of these terms—election, holiness, and love—plays a foundational role in the exhortations to follow. As saints who have been made holy, they must live their lives in a holy way, becoming like Christ in his forgiveness (3:13) and putting on the virtues (3:12) that will make them holy as God is holy. As those who have been chosen by God as members of his people, the Colossian believers must bear with one another, recognizing that God has chosen *them* as well as *me* to be in this body (3:13). As those who are beloved, they must put on love toward one another, even as they are each loved by God (3:14). In short, they must wear attire that fits who they have become.

Paul next lists five specific virtues to put on. First, they must put on "compassion" (σπλάγχνα οἰκτιρμοῦ), or what could literally be translated "bowels of mercy" (KJV). In the ancient world, the "inward parts" (BDAG, s.v. "σπλάγχνον" 1, p. 938) often referred to the emotional center of a person, more like how we would speak of the heart today. "Mercy" (οἰκτιρμός) refers to sympathy felt and kindness expressed toward those in need. The combination of bowels and mercy may be translated simply as "compassion" (NIV, NRSV), or more expressively as "compassionate hearts" (ESV), "heartfelt compassion" (HCSB), or "tenderhearted mercy" (NLT). Believers are to be characterized by an inner disposition of mercy that displays itself in acts of kindness, even as God himself is merciful (e.g., Luke 1:78; 6:36). We must be like the Samaritan man who felt and showed mercy to a stranger beaten and left for dead (Luke 10:30–37, esp. v. 33).

Second, Paul instructs the Colossians to put on "kindness," which is "the quality of being helpful or beneficial" (BDAG, s.v. "χρηστότης" 2, p. 1090). Such kindness belongs to God himself, who demonstrates the full riches of his grace through the kindness he shows us in Christ (Eph. 2:7; Titus 3:4), and it ought to be a fruit produced by the Spirit in the believer's life (Gal. 5:22). It refers to the "Christian temper of mind" in how we relate to others (Lightfoot, 1981, 221), as we think of others in the same way God thinks of them, in accordance with his grace. This kindness becomes a way of life, as we learn to be gracious in all our dealings; it is the "art of being a dear" (Wright, 1986, 142; citing [without reference] Lord Hailsham).

Third, Paul commands "humility" (ταπεινοφροσύνη), which is the opposite of selfish ambition and means counting others as better than ourselves (Phil. 2:3). Christ in his incarnation serves as the premier example of genuine humility, as he humbled himself all the way to the point of death, putting the needs of the world ahead of his own comfort and security (Phil. 2:5–11). Likewise, believers are to have a proper disposition toward oneself before God, exercising sober judgment and not thinking of oneself more highly than is merited (Rom. 12:3).

Humility can be elusive, for just the moment we think we grasp it, it slips from our hand in a moment of pride. Thus, Paul can both reject one form of humility (see Col. 2:18, 23) even as he calls for another (Col. 3:12). The humility he rejects is a false humility concerned with outward demonstrations of humility (e.g., ascetic practices) that accomplish nothing more than an inflation of pride (see comments on 2:18–23). Any expression of humility that only serves to elevate self is no humility at all! Instead, Paul calls for genuine humility, the kind of humility that benefits others rather than self, the humility that functions in conjunction with the virtues of mercy and kindness, of bearing together and forgiving others, and ultimately, of love.

Fourth, and similar to humility, they must put on "gentleness" (HCSB, NIV, NLT) or "meekness" (ESV, NRSV, KJV). The Greek word refers to "the quality of not being overly impressed by a sense of one's self-importance" (BDAG, s.v. "πραΰτης," 861), a quality better expressed as meekness rather than gentleness. Meekness also is a virtue belonging to Christ himself (Matt. 11:2; 21:5) and it is another fruit of the Spirit (Gal. 5:23). It also appears in the Beatitudes as an essential characteristic of the kingdom (Matt. 5:5).

We find a helpful picture of meekness in Psalm 37:11, where the LXX uses this same Greek term (πραΰτης). The psalmist describes "the meek" in a parallel verse as "those who wait for the Lord" (Ps. 37:9), and he then contrasts those who wait for the Lord with evildoers whose evil arises from anger and fretting (Ps. 37:7–8). Thus, from Psalm 37, we learn that meekness arises from a deep trust in God and it results in refraining from anger. The underlying issue is one of trust. When we trust in ourselves, we must defend ourselves at all costs, and thus we are prone to fretting and anger. But when we trust in God and learn to wait patiently for him, then we no longer fret and we relinquish our right to self-defense and the anger that goes with it. Meekness, therefore, is the consequent virtue of our trust in God and it is the counterpart virtue to the anger we are called to put off in Colossians 3:8. To put on meekness is to put off anger.

Meekness and Anger

In his *Nicomachean Ethics*, Aristotle defines meekness as the middle point between irascibility and spiritlessness. Irascibility refers to unrestrained anger, where we get angry at the wrong people at the wrong time and too violently. Spiritlessness refers to the opposite extreme, where we never show emotion or passion of any kind. Meekness is the virtue that resides perfectly in the middle ground, so that the meek person "feels anger on the right grounds and against the right persons, and also in the right manner and at the right moment and for the right length of time" (Aristotle, *Nic. Eth.* 2.1108a). Similarly, the Puritan Jeremiah Burroughs described meekness in terms of the object of anger (meekness is angry at only those things for which it can give an account to God), time of anger (meekness is not sudden, unseasonable, or lasting in its anger), measure of anger (meekness is no more angry than is necessary), ground of anger (meekness is not grounded in pride, lusts, weakness, etc.), effects of anger (meekness's expressions of anger do not lead into sin), and end of anger (meekness is not angry for its own sake, but for the good of others and the glory of God) (Burroughs, [1659] 1988, 71–73).

Practical Helps toward Meekness

Jeremiah Burroughs offers sixteen practical helps toward meekness, summarized as follows (Burroughs, [1659] 1988, 82–89):

1. Learn to set a high price upon quietness of spirit. Our experience tells us that when our spirits are quiet we have the sweetest time with God and in our lives. As we learn to value this quietness, we will learn to value meekness.
2. Learn to often covenant with God. Start each day by covenanting with God to not give way to passion and anger throughout that day, or until noon. If you can overcome your anger for a short time and realize how sweet it is, you will be more inclined to let it go again for another short time, and soon you will have let it go for a long time.
3. Learn to be humiliated for your past. If you are not humiliated for your past failures and your lack of meekness, you cannot be changed.
4. "Take heed of the first beginning of passion." It is easier to quench anger at the beginning than when it has gained full-steam. Think of putting out a fire, or giving an antidote to poison, or treating a fever. All are better dealt with at the first stages than when they have had full effect. Proverbs 17:14 says, "Starting a quarrel is like breaching a dam; so drop the matter before a dispute breaks out."
5. Realize beforehand that you will encounter things in life contrary to your will. Realize in your own mind even now that you will not be getting your way in life and that things will go wrong, and then you will not be surprised when things do go against your will and you will not have a need to be angry.
6. Consider your own weakness. Let him who is without sin throw the first stone. Whatever it is in someone else that angers you, realize your own ability to do the same thing and thereby provoke someone else to anger. Treat others' shortcomings in the way you want to be treated.
7. Labor to keep your peace with God. Peace on the inside makes it easier to be peaceful in the midst of a storm on the outside.
8. Convince yourself that there can be nothing done in anger that is not better done out of it. Remember James 1:20: "For anger does not bring about the righteous life that God desires." What do you need to do in anger that you cannot better do without anger? When in this life will you get ahead by being angry? When you discipline your children? When you respond to criticism? When you try to fix a wrong? Meekness is always the better way.
9. Learn to replace anger with mourning over sin. When you feel anger rising, labor to turn your passion in another direction. Is someone sinning against you? Rather than defending yourself, mourn over the sin of the other person and their spiritual poverty. Is there no sin to be mourned against, then what, exactly, is the reason for your anger? Mourning over sin would put an end to much anger.
10. Do not multiply words. If offended, give a short, gentle, non-provoking answer and turn away. Jesus says in the Sermon on the Mount, "Love your enemies and pray for those who persecute you" (Matt 5:44). Walk away and pray for them rather than multiplying words.
11. Don't take upon yourself business that God has not called you to. Has God called you to be angry? Has he called you to right a wrong? Has he called you to fix the situation or the person? If not, then let it go and don't make it your business.
12. Don't have too much curiosity. If you go looking for reasons to be angry, you will find them.
13. Beware that the temptation may be from the devil. The devil would love to have us angry,

for he knows that stirred passions move us toward sin.

14. Set the example of God, of Jesus Christ, and of His saints before you. Remember especially the meekness of Jesus, the Lamb that was slain. Looking upon His example will affect your temptation to anger.
15. Take heed of the next temptation. Be aware that anger will knock at your door and resolve now to be meek.
16. Remember to acknowledge your vileness before God. You cannot be angry about the sins of others when you are thinking about your own offenses against God and His grace to you.

Fifth and finally in this list, Paul commands "patience" (μακροθυμία). God himself demonstrates patience when he restrains his wrath and grants time for repentance and salvation (e.g., Rom. 2:4; 9:22; 1 Peter 3:20). For believers, patience is yet another fruit of the Spirit (Gal. 5:22) and it refers to the steadfastness with which believers must endure sufferings and hardship, trusting that their reward will come from God in the proper time. We must be patient in the same way as the prophets (James 5:8–10) and Abraham (Heb. 6:15), who faithfully persevered in trusting God even as his promises remained unfulfilled for many years and their suffering multiplied. Likewise, believers must wait with patience upon the Lord, trusting that he will appear in his time and make all things right (e.g., Col. 3:4). Until that day, we must endure whatever offenses may come our way without losing hope, even should those offenses come from one another within the body of Christ. Indeed, in the church, patience expresses itself as "the willingness to put up with the exasperating conduct of others" (Thompson, 2005, 83).

When we step back and look at these five virtues as a whole, we find a common thread woven through them all, a theme of selflessness for the sake of the other within the body of Christ. And this selflessness develops from the inside out, beginning deep in our bowels, affecting our emotions and our thinking, so that our inner self is characterized by mercy, kindness, humility meekness, and patience. These virtues must fill the hearts of individual Christians, and they must become the characteristic virtues of the body of Christ gathered together. Only where these virtues are present can a body such as the Colossian church hope to practice what Paul will call for in the very next verse.

3:13. Here Paul gives two participles to describe specifically how the virtues of 3:12 must lead to specific actions by the Colossians toward one another in the body of Christ, namely bearing with one another and forgiving one another. First, Paul says they must "bear with one another" (ἀνεχόμενοι ἀλλήλων). Here is perhaps one of the most raw and brutally honest statements in Scripture about the true nature of life together in the church. Even as Paul waxes eloquent about the virtues with which believers are clothed (3:12) and the rich diversity of members of the church (3:11), such idealism and visionary portraits of the church only thinly veil the true reality, where members sometimes must exert extraordinary effort simply to "endure" or to "put up with" (BDAG, s.v. "ἀνέχω" 1, p. 78) one another when the overwhelming temptation is to walk away.

Surely in a local body of Christ where both Onesimus and Philemon are members, and where the personal offenses run deep, where society calls for slaves to not associate with masters in such a familiar way, and where the path forward toward unity in Christ requires more virtue than seems humanly possible—surely in such a context, the Colossians would have heard Paul's call to simply bear with one another as an overwhelming, daunting, and even impossible task. Yet Paul will not allow the church to even consider the possibility of dividing into two separate bodies of Christ in Colossae. These believers *must* bear with one another. The rudimentary principle undergirding church life together is the basic commitment that we who are Christians here in this place will work this out *together*, regardless of the nature or severity of the present conflict that threatens to divide us. And when we are committed to bearing together through whatever challenges come our way, then we have an environment for extraordinary Christian growth, because bearing together will certainly require that we put on all of the virtues Paul extols, including patience, kindness, love, and forgiveness.

Easy Leavism in the Church

Christian leaders often decry a problematic culture of "easy believism" in the church, where we simplify Christianity into an "easy" form in which believing in Jesus need not entail commitment to following him and obeying his commands. Perhaps equally problematic—and perhaps even more prevalent—is a culture of "easy leavism" in the church, where we simplify the church into an "easy" form in which going to church need not entail commitment to the church or to one another in the body. The church, then, becomes mere religious theater centered around worship performances, and members become mere consumers of religious experiences and, should they feel uncomfortable, underserved, insulted, or offended, they immediately exercise their right to go shopping for a better performance in another church! The sad irony is that many Christians decide to leave a church at just the moment when they are about to experience extraordinary spiritual growth. If we resolve to "bear with one another" in those times when we most desire to walk away, we will find that staying requires us to show more patience with others, and kindness, and compassion, and even to forgive and be forgiven. In other words, a culture of easy leavism actually leaves Christians in their immaturity, while a commitment to bearing together creates a culture where maturity is incubated and Christians flourish.

If bearing together is not hard enough, Paul goes one massive step farther with a parallel participle, "forgiving each other" (χαριζόμενοι ἑαυτοῖς). Forgiveness means we choose not to treat others according to their offenses. It does not mean we forget that the offense happened, or that we trivialize the offense as if it was no big deal, or that we minimize the need for repentance from the offender, or that we blindly ignore the consequences of the offense, including the consequences of broken relationship and trust. But forgiveness does mean that we set aside our right to demand justice and our desire for retribution, we entrust vengeance to the Lord, who knows of the offense, and we commit ourselves to loving those who have offended us, not least by praying for them and seeking to bless them (see Matt. 5:44).

Paul drives home the importance of forgiveness by inserting a generic hypothetical scenario in which "someone" (τις) has "some kind" (τινα) of complaint.[1] The indefinite pronouns intentionally leave the particular situation undefined, but the Greek term Paul uses for the complaint itself implies having "cause for" that complaint (BDAG, s.v. "μομφή," p. 657), so that the complaint arises from a legitimate grievance and not a mere disagreement. In such a situation, Paul sets forth the standard that believers must forgive "just as" (καθώς) the Lord forgave each one of them. Paul calls upon the Colossians to recall the grace they have received through Christ, including the forgiveness of all of their sins (Col. 2:13), and this

1 The construction here of ἐάν plus the subjunctive (ἔχῃ) is a third-class condition in which the protasis is "uncertain of fulfillment, but still likely" (Wallace, 1996, 689, 696). Thus, it is not certain that one person will have a complaint against another, but it is quite probable, and when such a complaint does arise, then the forgiveness described in the apodosis must be applied.

forgiveness they have received must become the model for how they handle complaints against one another within the body.

Martin Luther on Forgiveness

Martin Luther comments on Matthew 6:12, 14–15, as follows: "For it cannot be otherwise than that many offenses will daily occur amongst us in all callings and kinds of business, when we are saying and doing towards one another what one does not like to hear or endure, and give occasion to wrath and contention. For we still have our flesh and blood, that acts after its own fashion, and easily lets slip an evil word, or an angry sign or deed, by which love is wounded, in such a way that there must be much forgiveness among Christians; as we also incessantly need forgiveness from God, and must always cling to the prayer: Forgive us, as we forgive; unless we are such ungodly people, that we always more readily see a mote in our neighbor's eye than the beam in our own, and throw our sins behind us. For, if we should look at ourselves daily from morning till evening, we should find so many cleaving to us that we should forget other people, and be glad that we could engage in prayer" (Luther, [1532] 1892, 268–69).

Further, Paul lends this standard of forgiveness a strong sense of authority by referring to Jesus simply as "the Lord" (ὁ κύριος). Jesus is the Lord of the body and of each individual member of the body (cf. Col 1:18). If the Lord has forgiven you who holds the complaint, and if the Lord has forgiven the one who caused the grievance, then how can you who have been forgiven justify *not* forgiving those whom *your* Lord has forgiven? This certainly applies even to Onesimus and Philemon and whatever complaints have led to the fracture in their relationship, regardless of the severity or legitimacy of those complaints. They must not become so proud that they feel they should not need to forgive the other, nor should they play the victim, as if they do not also need to be forgiven by the other. Instead, they should become the standard bearers ushering in a revolutionary culture of forgiveness among the Colossian believers.

Put On Love (3:14)

Paul commands the Colossians to put on love as the supreme virtue that binds the body together in unity.

3:14. When it comes to virtues, Paul saves the best for last. He does not include an actual imperative in verse 14 because he sees his comments here as a continuation of the virtues he commands be "put on" in verse 12. "Over all these" (ἐπὶ πᾶσιν δὲ τούτοις) virtues, Paul instructs them to put on "love" (τὴν ἀγάπην). Paul echoes the teaching of Jesus, who identified love for God and for neighbor as the most important commands of the Old Testament and the commands upon which all the other commands depend (Matt. 22:36–40; Deut. 6:5; Lev. 19:18; cf. Rom. 13:10; Gal. 5:14). Further, in 1 Corinthians 13, Paul defines love as being the very kinds of virtues he has commanded in Colossians 3:12, so that love *is* patient and kind, and love keeps no record of wrongs. Therefore, love is the supreme and all-encompassing virtue that brings together and activates all the other virtues.

Further, Paul describes love literally as "the bond of perfection" (KJV; σύνδεσμος τῆς τελειότητος), but Paul does not state explicitly what precisely love binds together or in what way it is perfect. Some translations give the impression that love binds together all of the other virtues in a perfect way, as in the following translation: "which binds them all together in perfect unity" (NIV; cf. ESV, NRSV). However, in this context, Paul more likely envisions love binding together believers in the church, for Paul has just spoken of bearing together in the previous verse, and in the next verse he will emphasize that there is one (and only one!) body. Indeed, all of these instructions in 3:12–17 work together for the unity of the body. Therefore, love is the ligament that holds one believer to another within the body (σύνδεσμος; Col. 2:19).

If love is the outer garment that binds believers together in the church, then love might best be compared to the jersey worn by an athlete on top of their undergarments and pads. The jersey identifies each athlete as a member of a team of athletes, all of whom wear the same jersey. The jersey unites the team as a team, with each member being a part. Likewise, love is the outer layer that is visible to the rest of the world. It defines Christians as members of the body of Christ and it unites Christians together as a team. Love should be our first impression and our lasting impression, that with which we introduce ourselves to the world and that by which we are known in the world. Love gives cohesion to the body and unites the body in a perfect way. "Love knows nothing of schisms, love leads no rebellions, love does everything in harmony" (*1 Clem* 49:5; trans. Holmes, 2007).

The Challenge to Love

"It's a great challenge to love in the church. All of us know that it's easier to love our neighbors in the abstract, those who are far away, than to love people with whom we must intimately work and pray within the Christian community" (Hauerwas and Willimon, 2015, 76).

Be Ruled by Peace (3:15)

The Colossians must make peace the authoritative rule among them, so that they may be united as a body.

3:15. Paul makes a natural transition from love to peace, for where love is the bonding agent, peace is the prevailing characteristic. By definition, peace is simply the absence of hostility between two parties, though Paul may also have in view the more holistic idea of the Hebrew *shalom* wherein peace entails overall good welfare and state of being (BDAG, s.v. "εἰρήνη" 2a, p. 287; cf. comments on Col. 1:2). More specifically, Paul speaks of the "peace of Christ" (ἡ εἰρήνη τοῦ Χριστοῦ), an unusual phrase used only here in the New Testament. The phrase recalls the hymn's depiction of the cosmic reconciliation accomplished by Christ when he made peace by the shedding of his blood on the cross (Col. 1:19) and the personal application of this peacemaking work to the Colossians themselves, so that their former enmity with God has now been reconciled (1:21–22). Through Christ, they have received peace with God and now Paul commands them to be ruled by peace.

Paul commands the Colossians to let peace "rule" (βραβευέτω), suggesting that they must take active responsibility to implement peace as their rule. The imperative of peace is expressed elsewhere in various forms, including "do whatever leads to peace" (Rom. 14:19) and "strive for peace with everyone" (Heb. 12:14). Peace does not happen upon a passive church; rather, it is achieved by the active church that labors toward peace. At the same time, peace is a fruit of the Holy Spirit (Gal. 5:22), and even here in Colossians 3:15, peace is "of Christ." This suggests that peace may be "something the Colossians have not to accomplish but to let happen" (Dunn, 1996, 234), or a "grace to be received" (Sumney, 2008, 220) rather than a duty to be accomplished. Nevertheless, the third person imperative communicates actual "volitional force" (Wallace, 1996, 485–86), so that Paul places upon the Colossians the duty to make peace the rule in their body even as they receive peace from Christ through the Holy Spirit.

More specifically, Paul instructs the Colossians to let the peace of Christ "rule in your hearts" (ἐν ταῖς καρδίαις ὑμῶν). The heart may refer metaphorically to the inner person, where thoughts, emotions, and convictions reside, or it may be a synecdoche for "the whole person" (Harris, 2010, 143). The latter is preferable here, since Paul gives no indication that peace should be anything less than comprehensive to life. Further, Paul lays this obligation of peace upon every member of the Colossian church, so that each must personally adopt this rule of peace in the totality of their lives, and thereby this peace ought to be a genuine and sincere attribute of the community as whole. Paul does not envision here the mere appearance of peace, where believers maintain peace as a veneer in the form of smiles and handshakes while harboring bitterness and hostility just beneath the surface. Instead, Paul calls for the body to be ruled by the very same peace they have received in Christ, namely a peace that has sincerely forgiven offenses and has produced genuine reconciliation and restored relationships with one another.

LITERARY ANALYSIS: In Colossians 3:15–16, Paul uses two third-person imperatives to command the Colossians to let peace "rule" (βραβευέτω) in their hearts and to let the word of Christ "dwell" (ἐνοικείτω) richly among them. This parallels very closely the two imperatival warnings he previously issued in the letter, instructing the Colossians not to allow themselves to be "judged" (κρινέτω; 2:16) or "disqualified" (καταβραβευέτω; 2:18). Paul's instructions in 3:15–16 stand in contrast to his warnings in 2:16, 18, and perhaps even provide an antidote. The judging and disqualifying of members of the church stands opposed to the peace that ought to rule in the body and the word of Christ that ought to dwell among the body, and where peace and the word have their proper place, those who would judge or disqualify find no quarter.

Such peace is mandatory, Paul suggests, because of the very nature of the calling that the Colossians have received. They have not only received peace with God through Christ, but they have also been called "into peace" (εἰς ἥν, in which the feminine relative pronoun refers back to "peace," εἰρήνη), so that peace must now typify how they live. Further, they were called "as one body" (ἐν ἑνὶ σώματι). Here Paul repeats his theme of the church as the body of Christ, where Christ is the head, but now Paul emphasizes the singular nature of that body as being *one* body (cf. Eph. 4:4–6). In some ways, Paul is stating the obvious, for even as a healthy human being has only one body attached to their head, so also Christ as the head has only one body attached to him. Remember again that in Christ, all other social and ethnic divisions break down (Col. 3:11). By stating such an obvious truth, Paul underscores just how prone Christians are to obscure or downplay the singular nature of the body, especially when peace no longer rules the body.

When the body experiences conflict, the members of the body face essentially two choices: first, they can bear with one another and work toward forgiveness and reconciliation, so that the unity of the body is preserved, or second, the factions on either side of the conflict can separate from one another and seek to establish their own bodies with members sympathetic to their side of the issue. In Colossae, the conflict between Onesimus and Philemon has likely evoked competing sympathies within the body, as some naturally sympathize with the plight of Onesimus and others with the plight of Philemon. Rather than reconciling, they could seek to split the body and organize their followers into two bodies, respectively.

Peace in a Small Town

In a small town such as Colossae, we can presume that additional grievances surely existed between various believers. These believers would have known one another personally for many years, and even many generations, long before they heard the gospel and were brought together as the church. Some multigenerational feuds may have existed between families, so that the current generation could not recall the reason for the feud but nevertheless embraced the hatred that came with it. Others surely had memories of being teased and bullied by one another as children, or being cheated by one another as business associates, or being annoyed by one another as neighbors. There were also unspoken rules about those folks in town who should be avoided at all costs, those whose inflated egos ought to be stroked, and those whose poor character must be dutifully overlooked. As with small towns today, Colossae likely had a quaint charm that only thinly masked the underlying histories of conflict impeding the unity of the body.

But Paul will not entertain such an option. They were called into peace as *one* body, and therefore, peace and unity are *both* mandatory and conflict must not be allowed to compromise either the peace or the oneness of the body. For one member or the other to leave the body would compromise the body's unity, and for those members to continue to harbor hostility within the body would compromise the body's peace. Their only option for maintaining both the peace *and* the unity of the body is to do the hard work of reconciliation accomplished as they exercise the virtues Paul has exhorted, including meekness, kindness, patience, forgiveness, and, above all, love. Peace must rule so the body may be unified, and the indivisible nature of the body necessitates that it be ruled by peace. What a high calling indeed!

Paul concludes verse 15 with a brief command to "be thankful" (εὐχάριστοι γίνεσθε). Thankfulness is a recurring theme throughout the letter (Col. 1:3, 12; 2:7; 3:16–17; 4:2) and especially in the final verses of this section, where thankfulness appears three times in three verses (3:15–17). But here, Paul interjects yet another reminder for thanksgiving, perhaps as an indication that the way of life he envisions within the body ought to be typified with a grateful attitude. As believers wrestle with the difficult challenges of life together in the body, including the overwhelming difficulty of bearing together, forgiving one another, and being ruled by peace, it is essential they maintain a sense of gratitude for what they have received in Christ, including membership in the body and including all the other members of the body. If I can give thanks to God for them and see them as a gift of God to me, perhaps I can find the strength to love, forgive, and bear with them another day.

Be Indwelt by the Word of Christ (3:16)

The word of Christ must be central to the Colossian church as it comes forth in their speaking and in their singing.

3:16. Not only must the Colossians let peace rule in their hearts, but now Paul commands that they must also let the word of Christ dwell richly among them. The "word" (λόγος) recalls Paul's opening thanksgiving where he referred to the message the Colossians received from Epaphras as "the message about the truth, which is the gospel" (ἐν τῷ λόγῳ τῆς ἀληθείας τοῦ εὐαγγελίου; 1:5). Now, Paul refers to the "word of Christ" (Ὁ λόγος τοῦ Χριστοῦ), by which he means the message about Christ and his work (see comments on 1:5; cf. 1:25). Therefore, the "word of Christ" here in Colossians 3:16 refers to the message about Christ, namely the gospel message that recalls the fullness of what Christ has accomplished for believers. This message has permeated Paul's letter to the Colossians to this point, especially as Paul has extolled the riches of what Christ has accomplished (e.g., 1:15–20) and the blessings the Colossians have received by union with Christ (e.g., 2:10–15).

This message must now "dwell" (ἐνοικέω) among the Colossians (ἐν ὑμῖν), and it must do so "richly" or "abundantly" (BDAG, s.v. "πλουσίως," p. 831). Paul envisions a church community where each member is well-versed in the fundamental message about Christ and where the message about Christ continues to be the central message that organizes the church in all her gatherings and ministries. Maintaining the centrality of this message must be done "with all wisdom" (ἐν πάσῃ σοφίᾳ), and Paul surely is circling around again to the treasures of wisdom that are found within Christ

(Col. 2:3). Paul sets forth the ongoing work of the body, where Christians who have received the gospel about Christ and who know the treasures of wisdom found in Christ must continue to grow in wisdom and increasingly infuse the gospel into their life together as a body. The gospel, in other words, must be as fresh and invigorating today as it was the day it was first received, and it must be treated as relevant—and even essential—not only for "getting saved" but also for the ongoing life of Christians together.

Paul next sets forth how the word comes to dwell richly among believers, namely through teaching and admonishing each other. "Teaching" (διδάσκοντες) means to "provide instruction" (BDAG, s.v. "διδάσκω" 2, p. 241), or to bring forward information for the expanding of knowledge, while "admonishing" (νουθετοῦντες) implies the confrontation of wrong thinking or conduct, so that inadequate ideas are replaced with right understanding and a proper course is established. Most importantly, Paul draws these two ideas of teaching and admonishing directly from his own apostolic ministry, in which he proclaims Christ by teaching and admonishing all people with the goal of presenting them mature in Christ (Col. 1:28). He now instructs the Colossians to engage in the same work of teaching and admonishing but with a narrower scope. Where his apostolic ministry lays upon him the global burden of "all people" (πάντα ἄνθρωπον; 1:28), the Colossian congregation has the narrower obligation of teaching and admonishing "each other" (ἑαυτούς; 3:16). They are to function as mini-apostles toward one another in the church, doing the work Paul would do if he was personally present among them.

Paul next speaks to the musical component of the church. He mentions "singing" (ᾄδοντες) in the same grammatical form as teaching and admonishing (all three verbs are present participles), indicating that singing functions as another means by which the word of Christ dwells among the Colossians. More specifically, Paul uses three terms for musical compositions that have little discernable difference between them. A "psalm" (ψαλμός) can generally include any "song of praise" (BDAG, s.v. "ψαλμός," p. 1096), but in the New Testament, it often refers specifically to psalms contained within the canonical book of Psalms (Luke 20:42; 24:44; Acts 1:20; 13:33), or sometimes to undefined Christian psalms (1 Cor. 14:26; Eph. 5:19). Similarly, a "hymn" (ὕμνος) refers to "a song with religious content" or, again, a "song of praise" (BDAG, s.v. "ὕμνος," p. 1027), and hymns and psalms often are mentioned together (e.g., Eph. 5:19; Josephus, *Ant.* 7.305). Finally, a "song" (ᾠδή) need not be religious in nature, but it is only used in contexts of worship in the New Testament (Eph. 5:19; Rev. 5:9; 14:3; 15:3). By using all three terms together, Paul does not discriminate between styles or forms of music that the church might sing.

At the same time, Paul does include clear parameters to the content and attitude of the music he promotes for the church. These songs must first be "spiritual" (πνευματικός) in nature. By this, Paul may mean either that these songs should have been composed under the inspiration of the Spirit, or that they must be able to be sung by the Spirit (Dunn, 1996, 239; Sumney, 2008, 225). In either case, the songs should complement and even contain the gospel message the church teaches and admonishes, so that theology intersects with liturgy, and preaching welds together with praise.[2] Next, these songs should be sung "with thanksgiving" (ἐν χάριτι). Believers should offer these songs in response to what God has done for them, as they give thanks. Further,

2 Bird says the combination of teaching and singing indicates that "teaching is meant to take on a worshipful character while musical praise is to take on a didactic role in order to comprehensively impart the word" (Bird 2009, 109).

singing should be done "with your hearts" (ἐν ταῖς καρδίαις ὑμῶν), where also peace rules (3:15). Paul does not mean that singing should be done internally and silently. In fact, quite the opposite, Paul means that singing should be done with all of one's being, with sincerity that reaches all the way to the inner core of emotion and will. To sing with your heart means bold and unashamed singing, regardless of the quality of the tune.

The Intersection of Theology and Liturgy

James K. A. Smith identifies three ways in which the church's singing leads to spiritual formation (Smith, 2009, 170–73). First, "singing is a full-bodied action that activates the whole person" by requiring church members to be active participants rather than passive observers in worship. Second, singing activates the imagination and enters the memory of worshippers, so that when a congregation sings theological songs, they are knit together by "an embodied theology." Third, these songs serve a catechetical role in teaching us the "compacted theology" found within their lyrics. Taken as a whole, corporate singing in the church has value not only as a vehicle for praises to be offered to God, but also as a didactic tool for inscribing the word of God deep within the minds and memories of church members. The content and form of liturgy, therefore, ought to serve a church's vision of theology and instruction, and theological instruction in turn ought to come to expression in a church's liturgy.

Finally, whereas teaching and admonishing were directed toward one another, the church must sing these psalms, hymns, and songs directly "to God" (τῷ θεῷ). This reverses the normal interaction between the performers and the audience in a theater setting, where a crowd gathers to form a respectful audience while those on stage perform for the audience. Here, Paul envisions the church community gathering to focus attention on God, who sits enthroned on the stage, as it were, but it is the church that performs while God is the audience. The church sings *to God* with thanksgiving to him. This singing resembles the standing ovation at the end of the performance, where the audience has received the full work of God through Christ in their behalf, and now has been instructed and admonished again regarding the message of Christ, and in response to the "performance" of Christ on their behalf, they now rise as one, in standing ovation, offering applause and thanksgiving to God as they sing together the message of what Christ has done.

Do Everything in the Name of the Lord Jesus (3:17)

Paul concludes these virtues with an all-encompassing command that the Colossians must do everything in a way that honors the name of the Lord Jesus.

3:17. In his final exhortation of this section, Paul shifts dramatically from worship (3:16) to instruction regarding the totality of life (3:17). His comprehensive command here will set the stage for the household code of 3:18–4:1. Paul uses a convoluted phrase to say "whatever" (πᾶν ὅ τι; BDAG, s.v. "πᾶς" 1b, p. 782), and he adds an awkward conditional phrase "if you might do" (ἐὰν ποιῆτε) that indicates "uncertainty of fulfillment" (Wallace, 1996, 689, 696). This use of the conditional marker (ἐάν) alongside the relative pronoun (ὅ) "serves to heighten the indefiniteness" of the phrase (Harris, 2010, 148). All of these elements of indefiniteness work together to express a wide-reaching comprehensiveness, meaning something like, "and regarding absolutely everything you might ever do." Further, to be sure this totality cannot be missed, Paul includes the parallel prepositional phrases "in word" (ἐν λόγῳ) or "in deed" (ἐν ἔργῳ), the combination of which "is a common way of referring to the totality of one's interaction with the world" (Moo, 1996, 291; e.g., Rom. 15:18; 2 Thess. 2:17; 1 Cor. 10:31).

Paul brings this totality of life together as "all things" (πάντα) and now gives his exhortation: all these things must be done "in *the* name of *the* Lord Jesus" (ἐν ὀνόματι κυρίου Ἰησοῦ). In the New Testament, name and power are "parallel concepts" (TDNT 5.277) insofar as many healings are done in Jesus's name, meaning under his authority and by his power (e.g., Luke 10:1 Acts 3:6). But here, Paul is more concerned with the manner in which life is conducted rather than the source of the power behind it. Therefore, Paul calls upon the Colossians to conduct themselves with regard for the name of the Lord Jesus, acknowledging that Jesus is Lord over all of life, and that all things should be done for his honor. As they bring all of their speaking and doing under his lordship, they honor his name and bear witness to their world that Jesus is indeed Lord. Believers, in other words, bear the name of the Lord Jesus and must conduct themselves accordingly in every situation, at times by obeying the explicit commands that apply directly to a particular situation, while at other times relying upon their knowledge of the will of God that gives them wisdom to know how to walk worthy of the Lord and please him in every way (Col. 1:9–10).

F. F. Bruce on the Comprehensiveness of Colossians 3:17

The Christian "when confronted by a moral issue, may not find any explicit word of Christ relating to its particular details. But the question may be asked: 'What is the Christian thing to do here? . . . Can I do it (that is to say) "in the name of the Lord Jesus"—whose reputation is at stake in the conduct of his known followers? And can I thank God the Father through him for the opportunity of doing this thing?' Even then, the right course of action may not be unambiguously clear, but such questions, honestly faced, will commonly provide surer ethical guidance than special regulations may do. It is often easy to get around special regulations; it is less easy to get around so comprehensive a statement of Christian duty as this verse supplies" (Bruce, 1984, 160).

Finally, Paul adds for good measure another reminder toward thankfulness, making this the third mention of thankfulness in as many verses. Believers must do all things in the name of the Lord Jesus with an attitude of "being thankful" (εὐχαριστοῦντες). More specifically, this thankfulness is directed to "God *the* Father" (τῷ θεῷ πατρὶ) "through him" (δι᾽ αὐτοῦ), namely Jesus. The reference to God as Father underscores the relation of the Colossian believers to God, whereby through Jesus they have become children of God and heirs of the inheritance belonging to the saints (Col 1:12; cf. Sumney, 2008, 229). This inheritance includes all the blessings they have received by union with Christ, including union with Christ in his death and resurrection, which are works of God (Col 2:12).

Therefore, even as Paul calls upon the Colossians to surrender their entire lives to Jesus as Lord, they must do so in light of what they have received through Jesus as their Lord. And because the Father is the ultimate source behind all that believers have received through Jesus, all thanks ought to be directed back to the Father through Jesus Christ. For believers, therefore, the seemingly contradictory tasks of sacrifice and thanksgiving come together in Jesus Christ as we both submit our lives to his lordship and at the same time give thanks to the Father.

THEOLOGICAL FOCUS

The exegetical idea (Paul exhorted the Colossians to put on the virtues of Christ, especially love, that they might have peace and unity together as the body of Christ, where the word of Christ dwells richly among them and they bring honor to the name of the Lord Jesus in all that they do) leads to this theological focus: Believers must put on the virtues of Christ that will allow them to live in peaceful unity with one another as the body of Christ, to grow together through the word of Christ, and to honor the Lord Jesus in all things.

In Colossians 3:12–17, Paul sets forth a number of exhortations intended to guide how believers must live together in unity as the body of Christ. The body of Christ has been a theme throughout Colossians, reaching all the way back to the hymn, where Christ is extolled as the head of his body, which is the church (Col 1:18; cf. 1:24; 2:19). Paul does not state it explicitly, but he presumes throughout the letter that every believer in Christ in Colossae is a member of the body of Christ. Christ and his body are a package deal. To be united with Christ is to be called into his body, and a person cannot have one without the other.

The body, Paul has said, includes a great diversity of people brought together in Christ (3:9–11). But even in the modern world, with all of our advances in civil rights and race relations and equality, it remains easier to celebrate a community of diverse people as an ideal from a safe distance than it is to actually live in real and active partnership with diverse people. How much more in the world of Colossae, where social class was rigidly stratified, and impassable boundaries existed between such statuses as master and slave. Surely it would have been much easier to divide into multiple churches in Colossae, where believers could gather around common ethnicities, or economic status, or interests, with a community of people like unto myself. In other words, we want a church that is united around *me*, as if *I* am the head of the body rather than Christ.

But Paul insists that if Christ is the head of the body, then the body must be defined by the one who reconciles all peoples to himself by faith (1:20–22), so that his *one* body includes all kinds of people, including people unlike me, and including even my enemies. Perhaps the most shocking thing about Paul's teaching is that he really means what he says—that he really expects the Colossians to become the one body of Christ in Colossae. Paul is not lost in romanticized ideals detached from the reality of human nature and the inevitability of conflict. In fact, quite the opposite, Paul sets forth this expectation even as he sends Onesimus back to the Colossian church to stand face-to-face with the unresolved tension of his conflict with Philemon and perhaps others. Paul fully understands the headwinds blowing against church unity, yet he nevertheless calls upon the Colossians to turn directly into the wind, with every believer pulling at the oars, devoting themselves to the attributes and activities Paul sets forth in 3:12–17, until they reach their calling to be one body of Christ in Colossae.

Thus, Paul commands every believer in Colossae, including even Onesimus and Philemon, to put on the attributes of compassion, kindness, humility, meekness and patience. Every believer must learn to bear with one another in every situation and to forgive all debts against one another. The body must be bound together by the love of believers for one another, and ruled by peace as believers reconcile with one another. And when believers gather together as the body, the gospel message about Christ must be central, as believers teach, admonish, and sing together, so that all the members of the body might work together to honor the name of Lord Jesus in everything they do. And what could bring more honor to the name of the Lord Jesus than for the diverse amalgamation of people he has called into his body to actually conduct themselves as the one body of Christ?

PREACHING AND TEACHING STRATEGIES

Exegetical and Theological Synthesis

In the previous passage, the Colossians were to "put off" and "put to death" the old ways of anger, wrath, malice, and so forth. In this passage, Paul continues with the metaphor of clothing, as the Colossians should "put on" the opposite virtues of compassion, kindness, humility, meekness, patience, and above all, love, which binds everything together in perfect harmony (v. 14). This whole section is permeated with Paul's concept of the body of Christ and how the virtues were to guide members to bear with and forgive one another (v. 13), as well as teach and admonish one another with psalms, hymns, and spiritual psalms (v. 16) The four imperatives ("put on," v. 12; "let it rule," v. 15; "be thankful," v. 15; and "let it dwell," v. 16) exhorted the believers in Colossae to pursue a new way of living commensurate with their new identity in Christ and members of one body.

But that was more easily said than done because potential divisiveness came along with diversity. As previous passages indicate, the church in Colossae was made up of Jews and Gentiles, slaves and free, not to mention "barbarians" and "Scythians." And a particularly divisive issue simmered—Philemon and the runaway slave Onesimus. How were a master who had been wronged according to Roman law and a slave who had been wronged through the dehumanizing institution of slavery to demonstrate their unity in Christ? Paul roots his answer in the theology that Christ is the head of the body. All members of the body draw life, direction, and identity from the head. Believers' union with Christ is stronger than sociological, ethnic, and personal divisions. Believers in the Colossian church were "chosen, holy, and beloved" (v. 12), so they had the power to put on love.

Preaching Idea

Only Jesus can dress you for church.

Contemporary Connections

What does it mean?

What does it mean that only Jesus can dress us for church? Examples of each item in the list of virtues might be offered, time permitting, such as a story of kindness from a husband to his wife, or the patience of two siblings with each other. I know one husband and wife who have made it a practice to hold hands when they are arguing. This helps them express love and reminds them of their unity even in conflict.

The preaching idea can be explained in relation to some of the troubling issues that divide the church today such as race and politics. I have good friends on both sides of the political spectrum, and in separate conversations each has lamented to me: "I just don't see how [the other friend] can be a Christian and vote for [the demonized candidate]." So, divisions are deep within the body, but this passage says that something is deeper—the unity that individual members have in Christ. The way to actualize our spiritual unity is by letting Jesus dress us in the virtues of kindness and humility.

Part of the believer's clothing to be put on is singing of psalms, hymns, and spiritual songs (v. 16). Brief explanations of each term could be provided and then followed with musical demonstrations of each. Modern examples could provide parallels to the ancient kinds of music used in the church.

Is it true?

Is it true that only Jesus can dress us for church? Some people may feel that because they are forgiven, they can live any way they please, but this passage (and the whole Bible!) says something different. True, we are saved by faith alone, but it is the kind of faith that is never alone. It includes good works. True faith is not simply "head knowledge" devoid of obedience. Someone who merely says "Lord, Lord" will not enter the kingdom of heaven but only the one who does the will of God (Matt. 7:21). The man or woman who says they love God but hates a brother or sister is a liar (1 John 4:20). Just as God forgives and bears with us, so we should forgive and bear with each other (Col. 3:13).

The example of Christ shows the truth of the preaching idea and has the power to move hearts to imitate him. Jesus wore all of the "clothing" in this passage such as:

- Kindness: To the woman caught in adultery he said, "I do not condemn you. Go and sin no more" (John 8:11).
- Humility: He washed the disciples' feet, including the feet of Judas who would betray him (John 13).
- Meekness: "When he was reviled, he did not revile in return" (1 Peter 2:23).
- Patience: "Consider him who endured from sinners such hostility against himself, so that you may not grow weary or fainthearted" (Heb. 12:3).
- Forgiveness: On the cross Jesus prayed, "Father forgive them" (Luke 23:34).

If listeners have questions about forgiveness, These words from the Exposition are helpful:

> Forgiveness means we choose not to treat others according to their offenses. It does not mean we forget that the offense happened, or that we trivialize the offense as if it was no big deal, or that we minimize the need for repentance from the offender, or that we blindly ignore the consequences of the offense, including the consequences of broken relationship and trust. But forgiveness does mean that we set aside our right to demand justice and our desire for retribution.

Verse 16 commands: "let the word of Christ dwell in you richly." Statistics from a 2019 report from the Barna Research Group show the need to obey:

- 48 percent of American adults are "Bible disengaged." (They "interact with the Bible infrequently, if at all. It has minimal impact on their lives.")
- 5 percent are "Bible centered" (They "interact with the Bible frequently. It is transforming their relationship and shaping their choices.") (Barna, 2019).

Now what?

How might we allow Jesus to dress us for church? One way is through unity. We might point out that the church should not be divided by the things that often divide society like politics and ethnicity. God identifies our essence as beloved in Christ (v. 12) and members of one body (v. 15), not according to secondary matters. Perhaps an example could be shared of two people who are dissimilar—different age groups, ethnicities, or cultural background. They might have joined the same small group and gotten to know each other in a deep and spiritually rich way. Another way to build unity is by serving together. People of different backgrounds might find common ground by traveling together on a missions trip or building a house with Habitat for Humanity. Differences are put into perspective when we join hands to serve God and the unfortunate. Some pastors have bridged the gulf between ethnically dissimilar churches by swapping pulpits. This shows the congregations that the pastors trust and respect each other, and it exposes them to different preaching styles. A secondary issue that has been known to divide churches is "worship wars"—preferences in style of music or degree of formality.

Worship Wars

Perhaps a very eclectic service could be arranged. The service might include elements like a high-church processional, Korean-style prayer where everyone prays aloud at the same time, and an African collection where people walk or dance their way to the front of the church to give their offering. A sermon from this passage might offer an opportunity to teach on the theology of worship. Verse 16 suggests principles including the following:

- The word of Christ should permeate worship services. Songs should be theological and biblically sound.

- Flexibility and variety in the content of our songs is the norm (psalms, hymns, and spiritual songs).
- A heart attitude of thankfulness should motivate and permeate singing.
- We sing to one another, not only to God. Thus, the music of a worship service should not be a performance for spectators but an aide to congregational involvement.

Interpersonal relations in the body should be marked by selflessness and harmony. The advice from Jeremiah Burroughs in the sidebar above gives sixteen concrete ways to pursue that goal.

In the sidebar below, Jen Wilkin gives some practical advice for helping teenagers engage with the Bible to let the word dwell richly in them.

How to Help Teens "Let the Word of Christ Dwell Richly"

- Read and discuss the passage with the teen.
- Use a Bible that has room for taking notes.
- Write (or make a drawing of) the main idea of the passage.
- Find one attribute of God that the passage is teaching. (Search The Gospel Coalition for a list of attributes that can help your teen practice reading the Bible with a Godward focus.)
- Write two things you observe in the margin.
- Write two questions you have about what you've read.
- For an engaging overview of a book and helpful background, watch the animated videos from The Bible Project (thebibleproject.com).
- Set a schedule for one appointment a week—just 30 minutes.[3]

Creativity in Presentation

The preaching idea lends itself to the use of props—articles of clothing to be put on. To review the previous passage, "Put off the old self" (v. 9), the preacher might hold up dirty articles of clothing and throw them in a hamper, naming each vice in the list. Then the preacher could put on clean articles, explaining each virtue in turn: compassion, kindness, and so forth. "Love" might be an overcoat or belt that "binds everything together in perfect harmony" (v. 14).

The passage suggests another approach to creative communication: singing together. Many possibilities exist here. For example, the congregation could be divided into halves. Each side could sing a line from a song, and the other half could answer with the next line. Likewise, the metaphor of "harmony" in verse 14 could be leveraged. A music director might coach the congregation to sing melody *and* harmony. Advanced congregations might try four parts!

To illustrate verse 13, "Bearing with one another . . . and forgiving each other," a description of the Academy Award–winning movie *Babette's Feast* (directed by Gabriel Axel, 1987) could be recounted. Babette was a prominent chef in Paris, but she was forced to flee to a village of Jutland (Denmark) because of a political uprising related to the Franco-Prussian War. The weather in Jutland is gray and dreary, and the religion is just as dour. The people of the village church constantly bicker and malign each other. Two spinster sisters, Martine and Philippa (named after Martin Luther and Philip Melanchthon by their father who was the pastor of the church), hire Babette as a servant. After fourteen years as their cook, she wins the lottery back in Paris and is informed

3 Jen Wilkin, "How To Help Your Teen Study the Bible," The Gospel Coalition, January 15, 2019, https://www.thegospelcoalition.org/article/teach-teenager-study-bible.

of her windfall. She leaves to collect her small fortune and then returns and spends the entire bankroll on a sumptuous feast for the community and prepares the whole meal by her own hands. As they eat, the church members thaw, ask for forgiveness, and begin to let the peace of Christ rule. Babette's feast of extravagant grace wooed them out of selfishness into love. At the end of the feast, one of the characters gives a toast, saying that today "mercy and truth have met together, and righteousness and bliss shall kiss one another."

To learn to forgive people who have hurt us, we might want to start with easy cases and then move on to hard ones. That was C. S. Lewis's advice. The chapter entitled "Forgiveness" in *Mere Christianity* was written shortly after World War II and first spoken on the radio *during* the years of that war. After the broadcast, many people wrote to him and wondered if God's command to forgive applied to the Germans. Lewis responded:

> Every one [sic] says forgiveness is a lovely idea, until they have something to forgive, as we had during the war. And then, to mention the subject at all is to be greeted with howls of anger. . . . "That sort of talk makes them sick," they say. And half of you already want to ask me, "I wonder how you'd feel about forgiving the Gestapo if you were a Pole or a Jew?"
>
> So do I. I wonder very much. . . . [But] I am not trying to tell you in this book what I could do—I can do precious little—I am trying to tell you what Christianity is. I did not invent it. And there, right in the middle of it, I find "Forgive us our sins as we forgive those who sin against us." . . . What are we to do? . . .
>
> When you start mathematics you do not begin with the calculus; you begin with simple addition. In the same way, if we really want (but all depends on really wanting) to learn how to forgive, perhaps we had better start with something easier than the Gestapo. One might start with forgiving one's husband or wife, or parents or children, [or fellow members of the church] . . . for something they have done or said in the last week. That will probably keep us busy for the moment. (Lewis, 1952a, 104–5).

The witty American poet Emily Dickenson (1830–86) could add her voice to your sermon, commenting on humility:

> I'm Nobody! Who are you?
> Are you - Nobody - too?
> Then there's a pair of us!
> Don't tell! they'd advertise - you know!
>
> How dreary -to be - Somebody!
> How public - like a Frog -
> To tell one's name - the livelong June -
> To an admiring Bog![4]

To foster unity nurtured by humility, consider calling a "sacred assembly" (sometimes called a "solemn assembly.") These gatherings include public reading of Scripture, prayer, repentance, confession, and reconciliation. Such an event should not be entered into lightly, but if the leadership of the organization is behind it, and if sufficient planning and preparation is put into it, the assembly could be a beautiful time of experiencing the reconciliation God accomplished. Instructions and advice are available at on the internet by searching on "sacred assembly."

The illustration in the sidebar could be used to make the point that Christians lay down their rights and bear with one another (v. 13).

---

4 Quoted in *The Poems of Emily Dickinson: Reading Edition*, ed. R. W. Franklin (Cambridge: Harvard University Press / The Belknap Press, 1999), 116–17.

Samoan Rugby Players Cover Tattoos

While participating in the 2019 Rugby World Cup, the manager of Samoa's men's team asked his players to cover their tattoos with special sleeves. He did this to participate in an emphasis issued by the World Rugby organization to promote cultural awareness. Manager Va'elua Aloi Alesana said, "We have to respect the culture of the land we are in wherever we go. We have our own culture as well, but we are not in Samoa now."

In Pacific Island culture tattoos are revered, but in Japan they can connote Japanese crime syndicates. Captain Jack Lam observed: "Tattoos are "quite normal in our culture. But we are respectful and mindful to what the Japanese way is."[5]

Verse 15 says, "Be thankful." In this verse it is a command, not an effect that occurs when we achieve the good life. As the sidebar recounts, Laurie Santos teaches along those lines in the most popular course ever catalogued in the 316-year history of Yale University.

Happiness and the Good Life

In the fall of 2017, Professor Laurie Santos offered "PSYCH 157: Psychology and the Good Life." Nearly one-fourth of Yale undergraduates registered for it. Santos "tries to teach students how to lead a happier, more satisfying life." And apparently that instruction is needed. A 2013 report by the Yale College Council found that "more than half of undergraduates sought mental health care from the university" while they were enrolled.

The Yale undergrads may have been surprised to hear that high grades, a prestigious internship, or a lucrative job does not increase happiness at all. Professor Santos says, "Scientists didn't realize this in the same way ten or so years ago. . . . Our intuitions about what will make us happy, like winning the lottery and getting a good grade, are totally wrong."

Verses 16 features thankfulness, not happiness, but maybe when we discipline ourselves to look for grace and express our thanks to God and each other, happiness tags along.[6]

Ultimately, the emphasis of the sermon should be on the beautiful virtues God commands us to wear. The virtues help us live together in harmony. That is how we can allow Jesus to dress us for church.

- Put on the virtues of love that lead to unity (3:12–15).
- Keep the unity by letting the word of Christ dwell in you richly (3:16–17).

5 "Rugby: Tattooed Samoans Don Skin Suits to Avoid Offending Japanese Hosts," Reuters, September 17, 2019, sec. Oddly Enough, https://www.reuters.com/article/us-rugby-union-worldcup-wsm-idUSKBN1W216S.

6 David Shimer, "Yale's Most Popular Class Ever: Happiness," *The New York Times*, January 26, 2018.

DISCUSSION QUESTIONS

1. Name a time when you needed to put off dirty clothes and put on clean ones. Maybe you were working on the car or were hiking through the mud, but you had to dress quickly for a wedding.

2. Review the vices we are to "put off" (vv. 5, 8–9) and the virtues we are to "put on" (vv. 12–17).

3. Does one of the virtues stand out to you as something you need to put on? Explain.

4. What steps can you take to put on that virtue? Ask your discussion group for practical action steps to put on that virtue.

5. Do you ever think of congregational singing as means of teaching and admonishing one another (v. 16)? What implications for our singing arise from that command?

Colossians 3:18–4:1

EXEGETICAL IDEA

Paul instructed the Colossians regarding how they ought to live out their new life of Christ within their former household roles in a transformed manner, so that they will please the Lord Jesus in whatever they do as wives and husbands, children and fathers, and slaves and masters.

THEOLOGICAL FOCUS

Believers must learn to serve Jesus as Lord within every aspect of their lives in the world, including their household roles and other circumstances that they are powerless to change, for the Lord Jesus is more concerned with their internal transformation than he is with their external situation.

PREACHING IDEA

In the Christian household, we have different roles but the same Lord.

PREACHING POINTERS

Although Paul was not married and lived as an itinerant missionary, he wrote often about home life. In this passage, he takes up that theme and draws out the practical implications of being "in Christ" in the home. Households in Colossae, including Christian households, followed traditional Greco-Roman codes that specified how husbands and wives, fathers and children, and masters and slaves were to treat each other. This passage is similar to those household codes, so in one sense, Christianity in Colossae was traditional and conservative, but Paul also introduces a progressive, even revolutionary, approach to family life. Wives, children, and slaves are elevated, while husbands, fathers, and masters are tempered. Paul treats all members of the household as responsible moral agents.

In a day when the concept of family is being redefined, Colossians 3:18–4:1 takes Christ-followers back to their roots and shows them what it looks like to be in Christ under one roof. Our spirituality rises no higher than the way we treat our families. As the old Firestone tire commercial says, this is "where the rubber meets the road." In this passage theology is put into practice in the most mundane and constant of our environments, the home. Christianity is neither exclusively traditional nor exclusively radical. The Christian home transcends those categories because all members of the household dethrone self and enthrone Christ. The theology of the first three chapters walks into our homes and arranges things in surprising ways because in the Christian household, we have different roles but the same Lord.

FOLLOWING CHRIST AT HOME (3:18–4:1)

LITERARY STRUCTURE AND THEMES (3:18–4:1)

In Colossians 3:18–4:1, Paul gives instructions for how the Colossians believers are to live out the radical nature of who they are in Christ within the context of their sociocultural station in life. Paul sets forth these instructions for Christians according to the particular role they occupy within their household. These household roles were organized around their relationship to the head of the household, who was simultaneously husband, father, and master, while other household members were simply wife, child, or slave. Paul organizes the household code by giving instructions in pairs according to these household roles, first to wives and husbands, second to children and fathers, and third to slaves and masters.

- ***Instructions to Wives and Husbands (3:18–19)***
- ***Instructions to Children and Parents (3:20–21)***
- ***Instructions to Slaves and Masters (3:22–4:1)***

EXPOSITION (3:18–4:1)

Here we find what is commonly called the "household code" of Colossians. Similar household codes appear in other ancient literature, so that the household code (or *Haustafel*, in German) has become a distinctive literary category.[1] As with these other household codes, Paul concerns himself with how individuals should conduct themselves within their household in accordance with their role in the household. However, unlike other household codes, Paul's predominant concern is with how believers should honor Jesus as Lord in how they undertake their household roles. With his code, Paul sets forth a radical vision for how Christians who have taken on a new identity in Christ should live out that new identity in the workaday world. It is one thing to say social distinctions such as slave and free do not apply when the church gathers on Sunday (Col. 3:11), but what happens on Monday morning? Paul calls upon the Colossian Christians to continue in their household duties, but in a radically transformed way, as a form of service to their heavenly Lord Jesus. In this way, they can fully please the Lord regardless of their circumstance, and over time this inward change will influence their world for Christ.

Instructions to Wives and Husbands (3:18–19)

Paul instructs wives to submit to their husbands and husbands to love their wives.

3:18. First, Paul addresses "wives" (Αἱ γυναῖκες) within the household. This is a break from traditional household codes such as Aristotle's insofar as Paul prioritizes the marriage relationship over the parental and master relationships, and Paul further elevates wives by addressing them before their husbands. Paul's original audience, therefore, would have heard Paul's opening household instruction in a different way than modern, Western audiences. They

1 Other household codes appear in Greco-Roman writings (Aristotle, *Pol.* 1:5; Dionysius of Halicarnassus, *Ant. Rom.* 2:24–27; Seneca, *Ep.* 94:1), Jewish writings (Josephus, *Ag. Ap.* 2.190–219; Philo, *Hypoth.* 7:1–9), and early Christian writings (*Did.* 4:9–11; *Barn.* 19:5–7; *1 Clem.* 1:3–2:1; 21:3–9; Bird, 2009, 113; cf. Sumney, 2008, 230–38).

would have been shocked to hear Paul mention wives first while we are shocked to hear Paul instruct wives to submit to their husbands. Whether Paul is elevating or subjugating wives is often a matter of perspective.

The Role of Wives in Aristotle's *Politics*

In his *Politics*, Aristotle divides the household into the same three primary relationships as does Paul, but in a notably different order. Aristotle says that "the primary and smallest parts of the household are master and slave, husband and wife, father and children" (Aristotle, *Pol.* 2.1; trans. Rackham, 1932). In contrast to Aristotle, Paul elevates marriage as the first and primary relationship in the household, rather than the master-slave relationship, and he privileges wives by mentioning them before their husbands. Paul orders the household in a countercultural way where wives appear first among all household members, even if they are instructed to submit.

Paul's instruction to wives to "submit" (ὑποτάσσω) themselves "to *their* husbands" (τοῖς ἀνδράσιν) involves "recognition of an ordered structure" (BDAG, s.v. "ὑποτάσσω" 1bβ, p. 1042), namely a hierarchy in which one person occupies a position of authority or dominance over another. The word is used for wives submitting to husbands (Eph. 5:22; Titus 2:5; 1 Peter 3:1), slaves submitting to masters (Titus 2:9; 1 Peter 2:18), and citizens submitting to governing authorities (Rom. 13:1; 1 Peter 2:13). Further, the Son submits to the Father (1 Cor. 15:28), the church submits to Christ (Eph. 5:24), and we all must submit ourselves to God (James 4:7) and to one another (Eph. 5:21). Quite frankly, God has ordered his creation with a hierarchy that requires multiple layers of submission from all of his creatures. Neither wives in particular, nor women in general, are unique in this regard.

Nevertheless, Paul instructs wives to submit to their husbands "as is fitting in the Lord" (ὡς ἀνῆκεν ἐν κυρίῳ). This is the appropriate attitude for wives to appropriate, not because of the particular cultural moment in which Paul lived, or because Paul was acquiescing to the patriarchal attitudes of his day, but because this is the appropriate hierarchical structure for those who belong to Jesus as their Lord. Paul does not, however, explain precisely *why* this submission is fitting in the Lord. For Paul this submission to some degree reflects the ordered nature and hierarchical structure of creation (1 Cor. 11:3; 1 Tim. 2:11–15; see Bruce, 1984, 164; Bird, 2009, 114–55), but Paul also acknowledges equality and mutuality in marriage (1 Cor. 7:2–4).[2] Paul leaves it to wives to finally determine what submission ought to look like in their marriages, but the preceding command of Colossians 3:17 surely applies: that wives should submit to their husbands in such a way that their conduct brings honor to the name of the Lord Jesus.

We must remind ourselves that Paul's injunction upon wives to submit to their husbands does require actual submission, and we ought not to shy away from his instruction because it is so unpopular today. At the same time, we must carefully nuance this submission lest it be misconstrued by modern audiences. We must note first that Paul is careful to differentiate wives from slaves, both by privileging their role within the household and by taking care not to use the language of obedience as he does with children and slaves, who must "obey" (ὑπακούω; Col. 3:20, 22) their father and master. Further, and most importantly, Paul places the responsibility for

2 Hurtado also observes that when Paul instructs the believing husband to live peacefully with his unbelieving wife (1 Cor. 7:12), he demonstrates an underlying presumption that wives have the right to personal choice regarding their religious beliefs and husbands ought not to compel wives to follow their own religious conversion (Hurtado, 2016, 85). This provides another example of how the command for wives to submit does not entitle husbands to rule over their wives.

wives' submission solely upon the wives themselves; he does *not* instruct husbands to rule over their wives or to compel wives to submit or even to encourage their wives toward submission. The submission of wives is in no way the duty of the husband. Submission must be offered freely by wives, not extracted violently or otherwise by husbands.

3:19. Paul's command to husbands, therefore, does not treat husbands as master over their wives. Most household codes gave detailed instructions to husbands regarding how they manage their wives as they would slaves and property within their household. For example, Xenophon instructs husbands to see their wives as essential partners in the proper management of the household, but Xenophon also puts the burden upon husbands to instruct their wives in how to fulfill their duties, as if wives need to be trained by their husbands (Xenophon, *Oec.* 7.5–43). And Aristotle says the husband ought to rule over his wife, albeit in a manner different from how he rules over slaves, for he rules over his wife and children as free persons rather than as slaves, and over his children he exercises monarchical rule, while over his wife he exercises republican rule (Aristotle, *Pol.* 1.5.2).

Paul, however, does not instruct husbands in how to rule, manage, or educate their wives; instead, Paul strikes "a somewhat revolutionary note of reciprocity" when he commands husbands to love their wives (Moo, 2008, 303). Indeed, to "love" (ἀγαπάω) means "to have a warm regard for and interest in another" (BDAG, s.v. "ἀγαπάω" 1, p. 5), and love also expresses itself in acts of service. The one who loves does good toward others at the expense of self. Thus, Jesus teaches that love and doing good go hand-in-hand (Luke 6:27, 35), and John teaches that we can know that we are witnessing love when we witness a person willingly and sacrificially giving of themselves for the benefit of someone else, and Jesus himself is the premier example of such self-sacrificing love (1 John 3:16).

Paul has a similar view of how husbands ought to love their wives. In Ephesians 5:22–33, Paul gives household instructions that are very similar to his household code in Colossians. But in Ephesians, Paul expands on his instruction to husbands to love their wives. He repeats the command three times (Eph. 5:25, 28, 33), and he points to Christ as the example for how husbands must love their wives. In the same way Christ loved the church, so also husbands should love their wives, and Christ loved the church by giving himself up for the sake of the church, that the church might be sanctified (Eph. 5:25–26). Husbands too must love their wives as their own flesh, nourishing their wives and cherishing them, and giving up themselves for the benefit of their wives, that their wives might flourish in fullness of life.

Xenophon on the Value of Wives to Their Husbands

Xenophon (ca. 430 to 354 B.C.), a friend of Socrates, purports to record in *Oeconomicus* a discussion Socrates had regarding estate management in which he discusses the crucial role wives play in the success of the household. According to Xenophon, in a successful household, wives manage expenditures and the internal affairs of the household while husbands manage the external affairs and bring in income (Xenophon, *Oec.* 3.12, 14–16; 7.17–31). However, husbands who do not trust and empower their wives in these ways end up bringing ruin upon their household (Xenophon, *Oec.* 3.10). A good wife, however, is like a queen bee who sends out workers, tends to the combs in the hive, and rears the little bees (Xenophon, *Oec.* 7.33–37; 9.15), and she ultimately gains honor for herself and her husband. Thus, a husband can say to his young wife, "But the pleasantest experience of all is to prove yourself better than I am, to make me your servant; and, so far from having cause to fear that as you grow older you may be less honoured in the household, to feel confident that with advancing years, the better partner you prove to me and the better housewife to our children, the greater will be the honour paid to you in our home" (Xenophon, *Oec.* 7.42–43; trans. Marchant).

The command to love wives is followed by its antithesis, "and do not be embittered against them" (μὴ πικραίνεσθε πρὸς αὐτάς). To "be embittered" (πικραίνω) evokes the image of food that has spoiled and is no longer fit for eating (e.g., Josephus, *Ant.* 3.30), but Paul refers here to an embittering of the heart, where the affections of love have decayed and given way to the bedfellows of bitterness, wrath, and anger. An embittered husband harbors hostility toward his wife, and he speaks bitter words that curse rather than bless his wife (Rom. 3:14), and by his actions, he seeks to cut her down rather than build her up. In bitterness, a husband establishes himself over his wife and looks down upon her, so that she withers before him. It is the very opposite of the sacrificial love that brings about flourishing.

If, by loving their wives, husbands are humbling themselves in order to see their wives elevated, then we must confess that love is strikingly similar to submission. Paul's instructions to wives and husbands are much closer to one another than it first appears. Paul does not envision a hierarchy of spouses within a marriage in which one spouse occupies a higher position than the other. Nor does Paul even envision a level playing field, in which both spouses seek to occupy the same plane as the other. Rather, Paul envisions Christian households where both husband and wife position themselves below the other in the lower position of humble service. Husbands are lower than their wives and wives are lower than their husbands, if such a thing were actually possible. Wives submit, surrendering themselves for the sake of their husbands. And husbands love, sacrificing themselves for the sake of their wives.

Instructions to Children and Parents (3:20–21)

Paul instructs children to obey their parents and fathers to not provoke their children.

3:20. The second relationship addressed in this household code belongs to children and their parents. Paul addresses "children" (τὰ τέκνα) first, and the significance of this address must not be lost. Ancient household codes do not speak directly to children; rather, they address only how parents must raise children. By addressing children, Paul elevates children both in the church and in the household. He presumes children are present when the church gathers in Colossae, and he presumes children ought to be addressed as responsible individuals within the church regardless of their youth (Dunn, 1996, 250). And he further expects that children can and should learn to live in obedience to Christ in much the same way adults should do the same. Thus, Paul dignifies children as legitimate members of the body of Christ.

Paul gives to children the simple yet all-encompassing command to obey their parents in everything. They "obey" (ὑπακούω) by subjecting themselves to their parents and following their parents' instructions. "Parents" (γυναῖκας) refers not only to fathers but also to mothers, and it occurs in the New Testament only in the plural (BDAG, s.v. "γονεύς," p. 205), sometimes with clear reference to the father and mother as the parents of a particular child (e.g., Luke 2:27, 41, 43; John 9:2, 18–22). Father and mother, therefore, have equal and full authority over their children, and children are obligated to obey both father and mother. Paul will not yield more authority to one parent over the other, and he certainly will not elevate children above their parents. And just to avoid any ambiguity, Paul emphasizes the broad scope of his command—children must obey their parents "in everything" (κατὰ πάντα). Sorry kids, no exceptions here!

This command to children comes with an explanation. Children must obey, "for" (γάρ) their obedience is "pleasing" (εὐάρεστος) in the Lord. Some translations suggest their obedience "pleases the Lord" (ESV, NIV, HCSB, NLT), but technically Paul says their obedience is pleasing "*in* the Lord" (ἐν κυρίῳ). Paul's language of "in the Lord" recalls his previous language in the letter of union with Christ (see the "in Christ" emphasis in the Theological Focus section on Col. 2:6–15), so that Paul views these children who are present within the Colossian church to also belong to Christ and to be under his authority as Lord. Therefore, they must obey their parents because they too belong to the Lord and have an obligation to please him, and obedience to their parents is the means by which they please him. Children, in other words, have one duty above all else in the Lord, and this is to obey their parents (cf. Exod. 20:12; Deut. 5:16; Eph. 6:1–3).

3:21. Parents, therefore, have a sacred trust, being in authority over children who have a universal command to obey them in all things. Paul now speaks directly to the nature of the trust with particular regard to fathers (οἱ πατέρες). Here Paul does not give a command to fathers about what to do, but he gives only a command about what *not* to do—fathers must not "provoke" (ESV, NRSV, KJV), "exasperate" (HCSB), "aggravate" (NLT), or "embitter" (NIV) their children. Fathers provoke when they challenge their children in a way that causes them to react (BDAG, s.v. "ἐρεθίζω," p. 391), and in this case the reaction is a negative reaction, where fathers irritate and arouse evil behavior from their children. Thus, the reason why fathers must not provoke is "in order that" (ἵνα) their children might not become "discouraged" or "dispirited" (BDAG, s.v. "ἀθυμέω," p. 25). A father's provocations lead to a spirit of defeat and despondency in their children, where their children realize they are incapable of satisfying their father's exacting demands despite their best efforts to obey.[3]

In other words, fathers must exercise their authority over their children in such a way that children can successfully fulfill their duty to obey their fathers. How can children obey their fathers if their fathers are provoking them to disobey? Instead of provoking, fathers ought to create a home environment where they can raise their children in the instruction and obedience of the Lord (Eph. 6:4), that they might flourish in their Christian faith. Fathers ought to diligently teach their children God's commands and the history of God's redemptive activity (e.g., Deut. 6:6–9, 20–25), and to instruct their children in wisdom and to warn against the path of sinners, that they might learn the fear of the Lord (e.g., Prov. 2–7). Children, like all other disciples, have many pressures weighing against them as they seek to follow Christ in the world; they need their fathers to be *for* them rather than *against* them.

Instructions to Slaves and Masters (3:22–4:1)

Paul instructs slaves to obey their masters and masters to be just with their slaves.

3:22. As the third and final household relationship, Paul addresses slaves and masters, and again he begins by addressing the one who has the lower status. Paul instructs "slaves" (Οἱ δοῦλοι) to obey their masters with the same word he used to tell children to obey their parents (ὑπακούω), and like children, slaves must obey "in everything" (κατὰ πάντα; 3:20). As modern Western readers, we are immediately

3 Lightfoot says irritation (ἐρεθίζω) "is the first consequence of being too exacting with children, and irritation leads to moroseness," where children "lose heart" (ἀθυμέω) and "go about their task in a listless, moody, sullen frame of mind" (Lightfoot, 1981, 227).

disappointed in Paul because of this command. How could Paul subject Christian slaves to further suffering under the institution of slavery rather than calling for their manumission and the abolition of slavery altogether? Why would Paul endorse rather than subvert slavery? However, as mentioned earlier (see comments on 3:11), when we read Paul's command carefully, we find his instructions to be more subversive than we might initially suppose.

Already latent in Paul's opening instruction to slaves, we find subversive layers to his instruction. On the one hand, by addressing slaves at such length and in such personal terms, Paul not only dignifies slaves, as he did by addressing children, but he also humanizes slaves. Aristotle objectified a slave as "living property" (*Pol.* 1.2.4–5; trans. Rackham 1932) and said, "the slave is a living tool and the tool a lifeless slave" (*Eth. nic.* 8.11; trans. Rackham 1934). Slaves, in other words, had only utilitarian value according to their productivity—they had no value as persons or as humans—and naturally, therefore, Greco-Roman household codes typically do not address slaves directly. But Paul speaks to slaves as persons and as members of the Christian community in Colossae. They are persons worthy of address, intellectual beings capable of hearing and understanding, genuine humans who can know Christ and who are capable of serving Jesus as Lord.

Aristotle's Definition of a Slave

"Hence whereas the master is merely the slave's master and does not belong to the slave, the slave is not merely the slave of the master but wholly belongs to the master. These considerations therefore make clear the nature of the slave and his essential quality: one who is a human being belonging by nature not to himself but to another is by nature a slave, and a person is a human being belonging to another if being a man he is an article of property, and an article of property is an instrument for action separable from its owner" (Aristotle, *Pol.* 1.2.6–7; trans. Rackham 1932).

On the other hand, Paul also diminishes the authority of slave owners by referring to them as "masters according to the flesh" (τοῖς κατὰ σάρκα κυρίοις). By this designation, Paul intends to differentiate them from Christ, whom Paul has already addressed as Master or Lord throughout the letter (κύριος; e.g., 2:6; 3:17, 18, 20) and whom Paul refers to repeatedly as Lord in 3:22–24 (note the unusual phrase "the Lord Christ" in 3:24). Slaves have an absolute master who rules over them, which is Christ, and the earthly master to whom they belong as a slave, therefore, is a secondary and subsidiary master, a master *merely* by the flesh. Nevertheless, slaves who are no longer slaves in Christ (3:11) remain slaves in the flesh and must continue to serve their masters in all things.

Further, slaves must be transformed in how they conduct themselves as slaves, effectively using their new life in Christ not to subvert their masters, but rather to serve their masters in a sincere and efficient way. Paul instructs slaves not to obey their masters literally "with eye-service" (ἐν ὀφθαλμοδουλίᾳ; KJV; cf. ESV), by which Paul means service performed "only while being watched" (NRSV; cf. HCSB, NIV). Nor should slaves obey their masters "as people-pleasers" (ὡς ἀνθρωπάρεσκοι; ESV), which apparently refers to an attitude that does only the minimum amount of labor necessary to keep their master happy and may even exercise deceit toward this end (Ps. Sol. 4:7–8, 19).

Slaves and Sincerity

In his *De re rustica* (*On Agriculture*), the Roman author Columella (first century A.D.) warns landowners against allowing slaves to manage distant estates where they receive little supervision, for slaves will not care for the property as well as free tenant farmers will. If slaves really did work as poorly when unsupervised as Columella thinks, then Paul's instruction for slaves to work as diligently when unsupervised as when supervised is truly revolutionary.

"On far-off estates, to which visits by the owner are not easy, it is in the long run preferable to keep the land under free tenant farmers than under slave overseers. This is true of all types of land, but particularly of grain-producing land, which a tenant farmer can injure only minimally (as he might injure vineyards or orchards). Slaves, however, damage grain land very seriously. They rent out the oxen; they do not feed them or the other animals well; they don't plow the land with the necessary energy; they record the sowing of far more seed than they have actually sown; as for the seed which they have sown, they don't look after it in the way necessary for it to grow correctly; and when they bring the harvest to the threshing floor, day after day while they are threshing, they lessen the total amount by outright dishonesty or by carelessness. They themselves even steal it, and they certainly don't guard against theft by others. And they don't even record the amount of stored grain honestly in their account books. The result is that both overseer and slaves commit crimes, and the land quite often gets a bad reputation. Therefore, as I have said before, if the owners cannot be present, I think that a farm of this type should be leased out" (Columella, *Rust.* 1.7.6–7; cited by Shelton, 1998, 156).

Instead, Paul enters into an extensive description of how slaves ought to obey their masters. They must obey "with sincerity of heart" (ἐν ἁπλότητι καρδίας; ESV, NIV), where sincerity refers to the integrity that arises from a person who exhibits the same character in all situations. Sincerity may therefore be understood as "singleness" (KJV) or "simplicity" (BDAG, s.v. "ἁπλότης" 1, p. 104), as opposed to the duplicity of a person whose character changes in various situations. Further, Paul instructs slaves to be sincere in their hearts—and the heart, we have seen in 3:15–16, is a synecdoche for "the whole person" (Harris, 2010, 143). Slaves must obey their masters through and through, so that their entire being, including their thoughts, attitudes, words, and deeds, are all singularly focused on doing what their masters command them to do.

Such sincere obedience should be conducted with a fear of the Lord. The participle "fearing" (φοβούμενοι) may describe the manner in which sincere obedience is conducted (ptc. of manner), or it may describe the cause of sincere obedience (causal ptc.; so Moo, 2008, 311). Both aspects are surely at work here, as Paul describes the fear that should motivate slaves toward obedience and thereby should cause their obedience to be characterized by sincerity. For many slaves, fear was a daily reality, since many Roman masters sought to rule their slaves with fear. Masters feared that their slaves might revolt against them, so masters would inspire fear among slaves by treating them harshly with torture, beatings, and psychological stress, including the separation of families. But Paul points Christian slaves to an even higher fear that is ascribed not to human masters but to "the master" (τὸν κύριον), who is the Lord Christ (3:24).

3:23. Paul continues to describe how slaves should obey their masters by addressing the attitude with which they undertake their duties. He uses a conditional clause to speak generally of "whatever you might do" (ὃ ἐὰν ποιῆτε), and thereby Paul implicitly acknowledges that slaves have limited control over what they actually do. They are not the masters of their own time or toil, but they are completely at the mercy of their master, whom Paul has just obligated them to obey in all things. Thus, slaves do whatever their master tells them to do. One slave, for example, was contracted out to labor as a weaver during the day, but her owner also retained the right to have her bake bread for him during the night (*P. Wisc.* 16.5; cited by Shelton, 1998, 165–66). Such a slave rarely had discretionary time during her day or night when she could sleep, let alone determine for herself what she would do. Her rental contract allotted her just eight days off work over the course of an entire year!

But Paul is less concerned with *what* she does as a slave than with *how* she does it, for though the slave may have no control over her time and what labors she will or will not perform, she still has full control over her heart and the attitude with which she will perform her labors. Thus, Paul instructs slaves to "work" (ἐργάζεσθε), literally, "from the soul" (ἐκ ψυχῆς). Translations have rendered this in various ways, including "heartily" (KJV, ESV), "enthusiastically" (HCSB), "willingly" (NLT), or, more loosely, "with all your heart" (NIV) and "put yourselves into it" (NRSV). The underlying idea echoes the sincerity of heart in the preceding verse, as slaves should work with the totality of their being, from the inside out, so that they hold nothing back in their labor. They are to invest themselves into their work, so that what they offer is not merely outward, perfunctory service, or the bare minimum required to skate by, but they instead take deep pride in their work, caring deeply about the quality of their production and service, and laboring with passion and conviction.

Do Slaves Serve Two Masters?

Paul seemingly puts slaves in an impossible position of serving two masters, for he simultaneously commands slaves to serve their earthly masters with genuine sincerity and to serve their heavenly master with absolute fear and loyalty. How can slaves serve two masters, a task which Jesus himself declared to be impossible (Matt. 6:24)? Slaves accomplish this by first serving the Lord Jesus above all, and then in their service to the Lord Jesus, they take seriously his command to obey their masters on earth with integrity and sincerity. Slaves, in other words, do not choose between obeying the Lord Jesus or their earthly master; rather, they obey the Lord Jesus *by* obeying their earthly master. When slaves do their work hard at their jobs with sincerity and integrity, they serve and honor Jesus as their Lord.

But at the same time, Paul again speaks to the motive underlying their labor. Even as they were to be motivated by their fear of the Lord in 3:22, so also now they must work "as for the Lord and not for men" (ὡς τῷ κυρίῳ καὶ οὐκ ἀνθρώποις). This speaks again to the orientation of their hearts rather than the deeds of their hands themselves. Slaves must conduct the duties prescribed to them by men, but they do so out of fidelity to the Lord. Even if their master is a despicable tyrant who in no way deserves the best a Christian slave has to offer, that Christian slave must nevertheless offer their best, not for the sake of their master, but for the sake of the Lord, who himself deserves the best we have to offer.

3:24. Just in case Christian slaves need further motivation to obey their masters in the way Paul describes, he now reminds them of the glorious future that awaits them. They should work for the Lord as Paul described in verse 23 because they know that from the Lord they will receive their reward, which is an inheritance. This should be a fundamental truth that underpins the conduct of slaves, for the transformation of their behavior arises from a transformation in their thinking. In this case, their work ethic as slaves arises from what they should already "know" (εἰδότες; the perfect participle is causal here) about the future promised to them. They "will receive" (ἀπολήμψεσθε) from the Lord what is due to them in exchange for their work, or the "reward" (BDAG, s.v. "ἀνταπόδοσις," p. 87). Christian slaves serve a Master who is watching their labor and who pays them accordingly. They earn wages, so to speak, and their wages come in the form of the "inheritance" (κληρονομία).

The inheritance Paul has in mind here belongs to all the saints (Col. 1:12), and it will be received when Christ returns and gathers his saints into his glory (Col. 3:4). This inheritance truly belongs to *all* the saints, slaves included, even if they have no hope of an inheritance on earth. This knowledge ought to motivate them to undertake their work as slaves with the utmost diligence and care, for every task is being observed and their labor has value to their heavenly master, and he will reward them with the inheritance.

Slaves and Inheritance

In the first century, rewards and inheritance were closely connected to a slaves' hope for freedom. There were two primary ways for slaves to gain their freedom (Shelton, 1998, 186–91). First, slaves could sometimes earn wages, or rewards, through tips, extra labor, or even raising their own cattle on a farm. They could save enough money to purchase their own freedom, and sometimes it only took a few years to accumulate the sum. Second, a benevolent master might declare his slaves free in his will. In this way, a master could retain full use of his slaves for his entire life, and yet also reward his slaves with freedom for the latter part of theirs. This hope of freedom provided incentive for slaves to work hard for their master. In some rare cases, where slaves were deeply loyal and developed personal relationships with their masters, they might also become heirs to their master's property (Dill, 1956, 116–19). It was not uncommon for Roman slaves to gain their freedom in these ways, and some even became citizens of Rome.[4]

And just to clarify any confusion, Paul concludes verse 24 with an outright statement declaring what he has suggested along the way regarding *who* their master is. He has already used "lord" or "master" (κύριος) three times with reference to Christ in 3:22–24, but now he states explicitly that he means "the Lord, *who is* Christ" (τῷ κυρίῳ Χριστῷ) as the one whom they serve. The verbal form of "serve" (δουλεύετε) may be either indicative ("you serve") or imperative ("you shall serve"). If taken imperatively, the force of the command captures the context's emphasis on how slave's should conduct themselves, as demonstrated in Wright's paraphrase, "so work for the true Master—Christ!" (Wright, 1986, 150).

If taken indicatively, the emphasis shifts slightly to the identity of slaves in relation to their master by answering the question once and for all regarding whom slaves actually serve. This sense of identity surfaces even more clearly when we remember the connection between the verb here, "serve" (δουλεύω), and the opening noun by which Paul addressed slaves as such (δοῦλος). They are not merely to serve Christ as their Lord, but they are to view their own identity as slaves in terms of Christ as their master, so that their very slavery is absorbed into his lordship, and their service as slaves becomes service to Christ as Lord. Thus, we might paraphrase Paul's emphasis in this way: "you are slaves of the Lord, who is Christ." This approach more fully captures the dramatic shift in perception Paul calls for among Christian slaves. Where once their life was reduced to simply "me and my human master," now Paul expands their vision to also include the Master who is Christ himself. And this new vision of "me and *the* heavenly Master" is so profound and all-encompassing that the human master seems to fade from view entirely, so that now what I must do for my human master pales into insignificance relative to who I am in Christ and what I will receive from Christ as my inheritance. In this

4 Dionysius of Halicarnassus actually complains that slaves are too frequently being manumitted and allowed to be Roman citizens, so that slaves began resorting to theft and other crimes in order to earn enough wealth to purchase their freedom and citizenship. Dionysius suggests that laws should be amended such that owners would have to justify their decision to manumit slaves, and slaves should be scrutinized to determine whether they are worthy of citizenship (Dionysius of Halicarnassus, *Ant. Rom.* 4.24.4–8).

knowledge a slave finds motivation to obey their human master with sincerity and hard work, for they are serving their human master only as a means to a glorious end, which is serving their heavenly Master.

3:25. A note of final emphasis and rationale comes in the form of a warning that further argues for why (γὰρ) slaves should work sincerely as to the Lord, and the warning contains two complementary principles of justice: retribution and impartiality. First, regarding retribution, Paul suggests a person's wrong deeds will boomerang back upon them. He uses the same word twice to refer both to the "the one who does wrong" (ὁ ἀδικῶν) and "the wrong which they have done" (ὃ ἠδίκησεν), but the great irony is that the one who does wrong will receive that wrong themselves. In fact, the word "receive" (κομίζω) may also have a sense of getting back what is owed to them (BDAG, s.v. "κομίζω" 2, p. 557), or we might say colloquially, it is "getting what you deserve." Wrongdoers do wrong with the expectation that their wrong will inflict others to the benefit of themselves, but here Paul sets forth a retribution principle whereby wrongdoers actually harm themselves by their wrongdoing, because they will receive back a measure of wrong commensurate with the wrong they have done.

Uncle Tom's Cabin

We must remember that retributive justice means both that the wrongdoer will be punished and that the one wronged will be restored. Thus, in Harriet Beecher Stowe's 1852 novel *Uncle Tom's Cabin*, one slave reasons with another that they should trust in God because in the day of judgment, he will make things right for those who have been wronged. "'If this world were all, George,' said Simeon, 'thee might, indeed, ask, where is the Lord? But it is often those who have least of all in this life whom he chooseth for the kingdom. Put thy trust in him, and, no matter what befalls thee here, he will make all right hereafter'" (Stowe, [1852] 2005, 190).

We could read this warning as merely a pithy proverb regarding natural consequences, for a wrongdoing slave will surely be discovered and duly punished by his or her master. This would create an ongoing cycle of wrongdoing, whereby slaves do wrong to masters, and masters then respond by doing wrong to slaves, and slaves double down on doing wrong, and on the cycle goes. But more likely Paul is referring to divine retribution, whereby wrongdoing slaves can expect to receive a due measure of consequence from the Lord. This is the opposite side of the future inheritance Paul just mentioned in 3:24. Though Paul does not come right out and say wrongdoing slaves will lose their inheritance, he certainly implies the inheritance may be at risk. The warning recalls his earlier warning in 1:22–23 that our eschatological hope is in some manner contingent upon continued fidelity to the faith we have received. Slaves who continue wronging their masters are actually living in persistent disobedience to their Lord Jesus, and if they are not walking in a manner worthy of him (1:10; 2:6), might it be because they do not belong to him and are thereby exposed to the danger of receiving God's judgment rather than his inheritance?

The second half of the warning refers to a second principle of justice, that of fairness wherein there is no partiality. "Partiality" (προσωπολημψία; ESV, NRSV) or "favoritism" (NIV, HCSB) refers to differentiating between people and offering preferential treatment on false or illegitimate grounds. James provides a vivid example of partiality when he describes how a church community might treat a rich person better than a poor person, based entirely upon the appearance of their clothing (James 2:1–4). Most all of us have an instinctive sense that such partial treatment is inherently unjust, including children who take offense if their parents show preferential treatment to their siblings. In the church, James explains that the terrible irony of showing partiality is that it runs contrary to the judgment of God who often favors those whom we spurn, even as God has chosen the economically poor to be spiritually rich (James 2:5).

When Paul states simply that there is no partiality, he surely does not intend to describe the state of our world, as if partiality does not exist; rather, he is describing the nature of God, as in a similar passage in Ephesians 6:9, where there is no partiality "with the Lord Jesus" (cf. Rom. 2:11). In other words, no one should expect to receive special treatment from the Lord, whether slaves by virtue of their miserable estate or masters by virtue of their privileged status. This heightens Paul's warning to the wrongdoer, for if the Lord will judge without partiality, then all should take care not to write an exemption for themselves by excusing their own wrongdoing and expecting favorable treatment. Such an attitude presumes upon the grace of God by ignorantly assuming that God's grace will always increase to cover ongoing sin, when in fact Paul would argue on the basis of our union with Christ that those who have died with Christ have died to sin and therefore dare not continue in it (Rom. 6:1–3). Thus, the principles of justice and retribution require that wrongdoers take warning, for they will receive justice in the form of impartial retribution from the Lord.

4:1. Lest we should think Paul is coming down too hard upon slaves only, and thereby showing partiality against them, Paul next applies these principles of justice directly to masters as well. Paul speaks directly to "masters" (οἱ κύριοι) with regard to how they treat their slaves, and he says masters must "grant" (BDAG, s.v. "παρέχω" 3b, pp. 776–77) or "supply" (HCSB) their slaves with two things related to justice, that which is just and that which is fair. First, they must grant "that which is just" (KJV) or "right" (HCSB, NIV), which some translations render as treating slaves "justly" (ESV, NRSV). The word Paul uses for "justice" (δίκαιος) refers to "that which is obligatory in view of certain requirements of justice" (BDAG, s.v. "δίκαιος" 2, p. 247). It shares the same root as "righteousness" (δικαιοσύνη), a term that carries significant theological weight in Paul's writings in association with God's character and the work of redemption (e.g., Rom. 1:16–17; 3:21–26; 4:5–6; etc.). The standard of justice according to which masters must supply that which is just to their slaves is nothing less than the righteous character of God himself.

Roman Laws Restricting Masters

At various points in Roman history, laws were established to place limits on a master's ability to punish his slaves. These laws reveal two sides of how society viewed slaves at that time. On the one hand, the content of these laws demonstrates the kinds of excessive abuse apparently being perpetrated by masters, but the successful enforcement of these laws also suggests a certain level of public resistance to such abuse. Shelton provides the following two examples of such laws (Shelton, 1998, 184–85):

A law established during the reign of Claudius (A.D. 41–54): "Certain slave-owners abandoned their sick and worn-out slaves on the island of Aesculapius [Greco-Roman god of healing] since they were loathe to provide them with medical care. Claudius ordered all slaves so abandoned to be granted their freedom. And if they recovered, they were not to be returned to the control of their master. He also decreed that anyone who chose to kill a slave rather than abandon him should be arrested on a charge of murder" (Suetonius, *Claud.* 25.2).

A law established during the reign of Hadrian (A.D. 117–138): "Hadrian forbade masters to kill their slaves; capital charges against slaves were to be handled through official courts and execution, if necessary, carried out by those courts. He forbade a master to sell a male or female slave to a pimp or to a gladiator trainer without first showing good cause. . . . He forbade private prisons. . . . If a slave-owner was murdered in his own home, not all his slaves were to be tortured for evidence but only those who were close enough to have had some knowledge of the case" (*Scriptores Historiae Augustae* [Aelius Spartianus, *The Life of Hadrian*] 18.7–11).

Second, masters must supply that which is "fair" (HCSB, NIV), or treat them "fairly" (ESV, NRSV). This "fairness" (ἰσότης) means applying equitable treatment to all slaves, in the same way the Lord himself shows no favoritism (Col. 3:25). The term even implies equality, such as when Paul appeals for the wealthy Corinthians to give to the poor in Jerusalem, so that there will be equality (2 Cor. 8:13–14). But if masters are to grant equality to slaves, the question surfaces: equal to whom? At minimum, Paul intends for masters to treat all their slaves equally, so that some slaves do not receive preferential treatment above the others. But Paul also seems to imply that masters should regard their slaves as equal to themselves as persons before God and, where both master and slave are Christians, as members of the body of Christ (cf. Col. 3:11).

Indeed, Paul explains that the justice and fairness masters must give to their slaves arises from their "knowing" (εἰδότες; causal participle) that they share with their slaves the same Master in heaven. Even as slaves know that they will receive an inheritance from the Lord (Col. 3:24), so also masters must know that "you also have a Lord in heaven" (καὶ ὑμεῖς ἔχετε κύριον ἐν οὐρανῷ). If a master has a Master, then the master is himself a slave in his own right. So much for the master's pride and posturing over slaves; now the master must demonstrate the same humble attitude of servitude that he requires from his slaves. And when it comes to humbling oneself before the Master, these masters have much to learn from their slaves, who are well-practiced in the art of rendering service.

The Lord Christ, therefore, is the ultimate equalizer of persons, including slaves and masters, Onesimus and Philemon. Slaves and masters together share in the promise of inheritance and reward, and slaves and masters together share in the warning of retribution without partiality. Neither can expect preferential treatment from the Lord Christ. Masters have no claim to privilege and slaves have no claim to victimhood; all are responsible to conduct themselves in a manner appropriate before the Lord Christ in heaven. For Onesimus and Philemon, who both belong to Christ and who have a duty to forgive and to reconcile with one another (Col. 3:13), they must now begin the hard work of discerning how to conduct themselves in Philemon's household as a slave and master who both serve the one Master in heaven. When Sunday turns to Monday, and when the gathered church disperses into their respective household roles and duties, the true test begins. The household becomes the crucible for discipleship, the place where the rubber meets the road, where the Christian ideal of justice and equality must be implemented.

THEOLOGICAL FOCUS

The exegetical idea (Paul instructed the Colossians regarding how they ought to live out their new life of Christ within their former household roles in a transformed manner, so that they will please the Lord Jesus in whatever they do as wives and husbands, children and fathers, and slaves and masters) leads to this theological focus: Believers must learn to serve Jesus as Lord within every aspect of their lives in the world, including their household roles and other circumstances that they are powerless to change, for the Lord Jesus is more concerned with their internal transformation than he is with their external situation.

In the household code, Paul applies everything he has said so far in the letter about the gospel of Christ and new life in Christ to the everyday life of the average Christian in Colossae. Paul says three things about how the gospel affects life in the household: first, nothing will change; second, everything will change; and third, the world will be changed.

First, nothing will change. Though Paul previously cast aside social distinctions among believers in the body of Christ (Col. 3:11), he now calls for those same believers to return to their previous social stations and to continue the humdrum rhythms of household life as if nothing has changed. Christian wives are still wives, Christian husbands are still husbands, Christian children are still children, and perhaps most shockingly, Christians slaves and masters are still slaves and masters. Of course, where believers can change their circumstances to better follow Christ, they ought to do so (e.g., slaves in 1 Cor. 7:21), but the household code makes clear that no such change in circumstance is necessary.

Nothing Changes?

The same can and should be said about Christianity today. C. S. Lewis observes, "Before I became a Christian I do not think I fully realized that one's life, after conversion, would inevitably consist in doing most of the same things one had been doing before: one hopes, in a new spirit, but still the same thing" (Lewis, 1949, 46).

Second, everything will change. Paul calls for a transformation of the heart, so that believers will now undertake their household roles in a new way, as a service to their heavenly Lord, who is Christ. Paul empowers all believers to accomplish the goal of fully pleasing the Lord in how they live (see Col. 1:10) within any circumstance, simply by being transformed in how they conduct themselves within their circumstance. Children are empowered to fully please the Lord when they obey their parents, and slaves are empowered to fully please the Lord in how they serve their masters. This means we should seek less to change our circumstances and more to be changed in our inner disposition, as we seek to obey and honor the Lord Jesus within our current circumstance, whether we are single or married, children or adults, employed or unemployed, upwardly mobile or entrenched in poverty. If we belong to Christ, then everything about us must change, even if our situation does not change.

Third, the world will be changed. The household code lays the seeds for the transformation of the entire world, albeit one believer and one household at a time. This global transformation will begin with Philemon's household in Colossae, where it will have particular impact on the master-slave relationship of Philemon and Onesimus, who must now view one another as equal brothers in Christ (Col. 3:11). Onesimus must become a new kind of slave, serving the Lord Jesus by working with sincerity and integrity, and Philemon must become a new kind of master, serving the Lord Jesus by managing with justice and fairness. Then, a similar transformation will take place in neighboring households, as the gospel grows and reaches more people in Colossae (Col. 1:6), so that society as a whole will feel the impact. How long could slavery continue to exist in a town full of Christian households employing Paul's vision of slaves and masters? The household code undermines the entire institution of slavery and sets the course for widescale emancipation and abolition.[5]

Thus, the household code is both surprisingly benign and shockingly transformative. Paul's vision is for believers to focus on faithfully serving Christ in the ordinary rhythms of daily life in such a transformed way that the entire world will ultimately be changed. If you want to

5 We could make the case that Paul's strategy of doing nothing but being personally transformed is precisely the best way to effect broad social change, including even the emancipation of slaves. Had Paul called publicly for immediate emancipation, he surely would have brought upon himself and the church the violent retribution Rome reserved for those who threatened social order. But by setting forth his plan for transformation in a subtle way, by sowing

change the world for Christ, the most important thing you can do is go home and learn to honor Christ in your closest relationships, as a husband or wife, parent or child, employer or employee. Where believers are transformed in such mundane ways, the world will inevitably be impacted.

PREACHING AND TEACHING STRATEGIES

Exegetical and Theological Synthesis

Adopting the form of the household code from Greco-Roman culture, the apostle Paul affirmed elements of the code even while subtly subverting other elements. In Christ, wives were given dignity and choice, children were seen as responsible moral agents and members of the church, as were slaves. In Christ, the authority of the husband-father-master was not to be despotic, and the slave owner was reminded that he or she had a Master in heaven who sees all and will reward or withhold reward. Furthermore, the mother, not just the father, was given authority to rear her children in the nurture and admonition of the Lord. Each member of the household had his or her role to play, but in the Christian home Paul showed how each role came under the direction of Christ. All members were to reflect the fact that Jesus is Lord of all by treating the others with submission and love because Christ is the ultimate head of the house.

Preaching Idea

In the Christian household, we have different roles but the same Lord.

Contemporary Connections

What does it mean?

What does it mean that in the Christian household we have different roles but the same Lord? Our roles might be similar to what we see in any particular culture, just as the Colossian homes retained the basic form of Greco-Roman household codes. But God also subverts the roles by placing all members of the Christian household under the lordship of Christ. As stated in the Theological Focus, this passage is "surprisingly benign and shockingly transformative." Under the rule of Christ, authority is exercised in love and humility. Conversely, under Christ submission and obedience are not dirty words. Submission to human authorities (a duty of all Christians, not only wives even though wives are specifically mentioned here) is motivated by submission to God.

Examples of fulfilling our roles under the Lord could be given for each group: children go to school, play afternoon sports or take music lessons, and do homework; and when doing these activities they should consciously serve Christ. Parents work, make dinner, talk about money, and arrange holiday celebrations; and they do those roles as for the Lord (v. 23). In the Christian home, children do not (or should not!) lie to their parents, steal from each other, or make an idol of their grades or athletic and other achievements. In the Christian home, parents do not (or should not!) avoid their children by using drugs or the internet, avoid each other in icy silence, or judge their neighbors. In the Christian household, we each have a role to play, and ultimately all serve the Lord.

Is it true?

Is it true that in the Christian household, we have different roles but the same Lord? The various roles could be demonstrated with biblical narratives such as Sarah who submitted to her husband Abraham (1 Peter 3:1–6),

---

the seeds in the hearts of believers, Paul allowed the church to live within mainstream society but in an invisible way, not attracting unwanted attention from Rome even as they affirmed Jesus as Lord and renounced the values of Rome (cf. MacDonald, 2000, 161–69).

Boaz who honored his soon-to-be wife Ruth (Ruth 2–4), and Isaac who obeyed his father Abraham on Mount Moriah (Gen. 22). But most of the biblical stories of families show relations that were broken, self-centered, harsh, or deceptive. That is true of Jacob with his four wives and twelve sons who tried to outmaneuver each other (Gen. 29–30), Eli who did not bring up his sons in the fear of the Lord (1 Sam. 2), and David's wife Michal who mocked him (2 Sam. 6). Most families do not live up to the picture of Colossians 3.

Yet, columnist Mark Regnerus observes in his *New York Times* article "'Family Values' Benefit Children" that the "intact nuclear family may seem like an endangered species, but it remains the hope and dream of the vast majority of young Americans. They want to marry. Most hope for children. And they aspire to fidelity. (No one aims for 'monogamish')." He says, "You don't have to like the suburbs or minivans or soccer or even monogamy to comprehend that the biological nuclear family's stability and repertoire is tops over the long run."

In Paul's day, readers of Colossians might have balked at the way God elevates the roles of wives, children, and slaves. In our day, readers may be more likely to balk at the supposed lowering of wives and the apparent condoning of slavery.

"Wives should submit, and slaves should obey."

How might this passage be preached unapologetically and yet sensitively? Let's take wives first. We might point out:

- Submission is a duty of all Christians (Eph. 5:21), not just wives, and Christ himself submitted to the Father.
- The word for "submit" is different than the word for "obey" which is applied to children and slaves.
- The command to submit is directed to *wives*, not women in general. This passage is a household code, not a marketplace code. Furthermore, husbands are not addressed in the command to wives. Husbands are not to demand, coerce, or force submission. Wives are given the dignity of choice and responsibility.
- The husband is commanded to love his wife. The parallel passage in Ephesians states this three times (5:25, 28, 33). When the husband honors, blesses, and sacrifices for his wife, submission is a delight more than a duty. Wives may ask if they must submit if their husbands do not love them, or if their husbands coerce submission.

This is a tough question and the answer demands wisdom. This brief passage does not address all of the circumstances wives face in this fallen world such as abuse. God was not addressing that scenario in this passage, and we should support abused wives and help them seek shelter.

Now let's address the issue of slavery, specifically, the fact that this passage does not declare emancipation. In the United States the history of slavery is bound inseparably to racial prejudice and discrimination. Today slavery is universally condemned, yet the strongest "anti-slavery statement" in the New Testament may be the tepid verse, "Were you a slave when called? Do not be concerned about it. But if you can gain your freedom, avail yourself of the opportunity" (1 Cor. 7:21).

If listeners respond negatively to verse 22 where slaves are commanded to obey, two lines of reasoning might be used:

- Slavery in the New Testament was not racially motivated. Slaves were often prisoners of war and race was not the primary factor that determined who was enslaved.

  Understanding that fact may not solve the problem of slavery in the New Testament, but it may help listeners consider the issue with less emotion.

- The New Testament, including this passage and the book of Philemon, sows the seeds of abolition. In time the seeds would sprout, stretch out branches, and bear fruit. In time, Christians such as William Wilberforce were major players in the abolition of slavery. In Colossians Christ has obliterated hierarchies of value between men and women, Jews and Gentiles, and slaves and free. As has been mentioned above, this passage elevates slaves as full-fledged members of the church. They are treated as responsible moral agents, not mere property.

  The subversive nature of this passage would not have been lost on first-century readers. Books like Colossians and Philemon moved the church onto the path of abolition. This passage may seem like a modest step on that path, but the theology of union with Christ and equality of value was a snowball that became an avalanche.

Now what?

What difference should it make that in the Christian household, we have different roles but the same Lord? One real-world application might relate to communication. For example, simply listening with undivided attention can be a great way to display love and submission. Spouses can use this simple tool, as can parents and children.

A "Ladder" of Listening Skills

Look at the person.
Ask Questions.
Don't interrupt (to change the subject).
Don't necessarily offer advice.
Express understanding and empathy.
Restate.

Another tool of life-giving communication is praise. John Gottman is a researcher on marriage and parenting. In his book *Why Marriages Succeed or Fail*, he reports his discovery that in strong, long-lasting relationships, positive comments and behaviors outweigh negative twenty to one (Gottman, 1995).

Teaching from this passage may give preachers an opportunity to speak in behalf of wives who feel vulnerable or are abused. Perhaps support could be offered them in the form of counseling, small groups, a marriage retreat, and suggestions of where to turn if in danger. A particular issue that causes many wives to feel unloved and dishonored is pornography. Software such as Covenant Eyes (covenanteyes.com) could be suggested, and small groups might offer accountability by discussing *Every Man's Battle* (Arterburn and Stoeker, with Yorkey, 2009) and *Every Woman's Battle* (Ethridge, 2009).

Male preachers may want to tread lightly as they speak about the command to wives to submit, leaving application in the hands of those who are addressed—wives. Likewise, female preachers may want to tread lightly as they expound the command to husbands, "Love your wives." Perhaps application could be suggested indirectly by recounting some ways your father showed love for your mother.

The sidebar suggests ways that parents violate the command to not provoke their children so as to avoid such behaviors.

Ten Ways Parents Provoke Their Children

Erik Raymond shares these ways parents provoke and discourage their children.

1. Bullying: Parents are generally bigger, stronger, and more intelligent than their kids. Bullying can take place verbally as well as physically.
2. Showing favoritism: If parents favor one child over another discouragement is inevitable (think about Jacob and Esau).
3. Unclear standards: Kids need to know and understand the standards they are being held to. If not, then they'll be confused, surprised, and discouraged.
4. Unexplained discipline: Discipline requires instruction.
5. Inconsistency: Parents need to be consistent with their kids. If something is wrong on Tuesday, it should be wrong on Thursday. Inconsistency sends mixed messages, and, when punished, they lose trust.
6. Excessive or unreasonable discipline: Just as there are levels of rebellion, there should be corresponding levels of discipline.
7. Discipline out of anger: Parents who are out of control and losing their temper will hurt their children and discourage them. Think of how twisted it is to inflict harm in the name of love. Be careful, parents. (Sometimes *we* may need a time out.)
8. Humiliation: If parents humiliate their kids in public, in front of their siblings, or even one-on-one, they will most certainly exasperate them.
9. Never admit you are wrong: Kids live with their parents. They see when they mess up. If the parent never admits they are wrong, especially when the offense is toward the child, then they will soon see through all of the Bible talk.
10. Overprotection and smothering: Well-meaning overprotection can cause discouragement and resentment. Remember, kids are people who need to grow. Their wills should be shepherded, but they can't be controlled absolutely. (Raymond, 2020).

Adults may wonder what obeying parents looks like for them. Perhaps suggestions like the following could be gleaned from people who have aging parents: seek the advice of the aging parents; give one's time through visits, Facebook, FaceTime, and phone calls; and keep them apprised of the extended family. Meeting the financial needs of aging parents could also be mentioned as a way to thank them and honor the Lord.

Can the verses addressed to slaves and masters be contextualized to address employees and bosses? We believe they can. First, it might be wise to point out differences in social setting between the first century and the twenty-first. For example, unlike slavery, employment is voluntary, remunerated, and governed by a contract. Slaves had few "benefits" or laws to protect them. Having pointed out differences, application might be made by reasoning from the greater to the lesser. If slaves were commanded to obey not with eye-service, *how much more* should employees work willingly and with integrity for their employers? Christian employees serve Christ. That is our motive and reward. The same line of reasoning might be applied to bosses. If masters were commanded to treat their slaves justly and fairly, *how much more* should employers do so? All of us have a Master in heaven. Employers might be exhorted to treat subordinates the way they want to be treated themselves: fair wages, respect, and open to suggestions.

How might workers do their jobs with a consciousness that they are serving the Lord (Col. 3:23)? The sidebar gives some suggestions.

How to Practice the Presence of God at Work

1. *Midday kneeling prayer.*
   Align your soul and body in the middle of a busy day.

2. *Avoid distractions as your spiritual act of worship.*
   Justin Whitmel Earley states, "Your smartphone, Gmail, text chains, and social alerts aren't just reducing your productivity—they're reducing your capacity for sustained attention and fracturing your presence. It is impossible to fully love a human being without sustained attention or presence."
3. *Look at people's eyes.*
4. *Use the power of words.*
   Especially use the power of speaking the truth in love.
5. *Let Sabbath pace your work.*
   Earley states, "Living at a baseline pace of frenetic urgency is fundamentally incompatible with the command to 'be still and know that I am God'" (Ps. 46:10). (Earley, 2020).

Creativity in Presentation

An interview of a church member or a whole family might be arranged. This could convey the fact that all families have joys and struggles, but when Christ is Lord of the house we also experience security and support. A similar interview with an employee or employer could show how he or she is bringing Christ into the workplace. Likewise, a Q and A session after the sermon could provide an opportunity for listeners to dialogue on how to apply this passage to their circumstances (Keller, 2016).

Perhaps two stations could be arranged on the platform—one for discussing what we have in common with traditional households, and the other for discussing how Christ subverts traditional culture. Each station could use a visual symbol. A black-and-white photo of a family taken in the 1950s might represent the traditional family, and a color photo might represent a modern, progressive family. Between the two stations might be a cross to show that in Christ we are neither purely traditional nor entirely progressive. The gospel creates a third way where our homes are microcosms of the kingdom of God. Slides of a turn-of-the-century house and a modern house might be displayed behind each station; or an artist from the congregation might draw or paint the houses and place the artwork on easels.

"Can't Live Without 'Em" is a sketch that also points out how Christianity is countercultural. In a sweeping depiction of childhood, high school, and marriage, this short drama shows humorously how things like clothing and appearance are the bases of being accepted or rejected. Those values are compared to Jesus's countercultural teaching in the Sermon on the Mount. Search the Internet for this sketch.

When addressing the children of the congregation, we might follow Paul's lead in treating them as responsible moral agents with their own relationship to God. Perhaps a pre-sermon interview or group discussion with children or teens could give them voice to articulate their frustrations, temptations, and hopes. In this way, children can be encouraged to own the faith, declaring how they are trying to respond to the truth that Christ is Lord of the house.

Statistic: This could be used to support the institution of marriage. Married adults have a higher level of relationship satisfaction than those cohabiting. On a Pew Research survey, 58% of married people answered: "Things are going well" (with their spouse or partner), compared to 41% of those cohabiting (Graf, 2019).

Quotation: This could be used when you talk about provoking our children. When Julian Lennon was five years old, his father, John Lennon, abandoned him. At thirty-five years of age, he said: "I felt he was a hypocrite. Dad could talk about peace and love out loud to the world, but he could never show it to the people who supposedly meant the most to him: his wife and son. How can you talk about peace and love and have a family in bits and pieces—no communication, adultery, divorce? You can't do it, not if you're being true and honest with yourself" (*Servant*, Summer 1998, 9).

This passage covers so much ground in so little space (nine verses) that it could be made into a miniseries.

When preaching on the Christian home from this passage, the sermon should stress that every member of the family honors and submits to the others because we honor and submit to Christ. We are serving him in our various ways. In the Christian household, we have different roles but the same Lord.

- Wives and husbands: submit and love (3:18–19).
- Children and fathers: obey and do not provoke (3:20–21).
- Employees and employers: submit and treat them fairly (3:22–4:1a).
- Because all of us are "in the Lord."

DISCUSSION QUESTIONS

1. Name the commands given to wives, husbands, children, parents, slaves, and masters.
2. How is the command to "submit" different than "obey"?
3. Parents, share some ideas for how we can "not provoke" our children.
4. Are the commands to slaves and masters applicable for today's work relations? How so?
5. How does being "in Christ" create a "third way" for the household? Why are we both traditional and progressive, yet ultimately neither?

Colossians 4:2–6

EXEGETICAL IDEA

Paul instructed the Colossians to make the gospel known by praying for him in his global mission of proclaiming the gospel in new places, and by embracing their local mission in Colossae of answering knowledgably about the gospel when asked about their transformed speech and conduct.

THEOLOGICAL FOCUS

All Christians bear the responsibility to make the gospel known, not only by persistently praying for preachers and missionaries but also by faithfully honoring Christ in how they live, by speaking graciously in every situation, and by answering the inevitable questions that arise about their faith.

PREACHING IDEA

To spread the good news, pray for the preachers and salt your own speech.

PREACHING POINTERS

Writing from jail, Paul asks the Colossians to pray that a door would be opened, so that he could return to his work as an apostle, declaring the mystery of Christ. He also asks them to pray that he would make that message clear. Working in conjunction with the public ministry of preaching was the interpersonal witness of church members. Paul exhorts them to walk in wisdom toward "outsiders," use gracious speech, and then be ready to explain why they lived differently than the people of the Greco-Roman world. In this passage, Paul puts evangelism on center stage.

The same emphasis is needed today. Few churches in North America are growing from conversions, but partnership between public proclamation and interpersonal witness is a timeless combination, as effective in our day as in the first century. Thom Rainer observes that excellent preaching is crucial to what he calls "breakout churches," congregations that are growing because of conversions. He states that preaching is the "number one correlated factor related to the evangelistic growth of the church. . . . It is hard to overstate how important the centrality of preaching was in these breakout churches" (Rainer, n.d.). I suspect that behind the clear, passionate, and relevant expository preaching that Rainer discovered in these churches there is also a host of members who have formed relationships with "outsiders," to use Paul's term (v. 5). They witness by their words and lifestyle and invite their friends to church to hear the Word of God. Public proclamation and interpersonal witness is a winning combination, so to spread the good news we pray for the preachers and partner with them by salting our own speech.

FOLLOWING CHRIST IN THE WORLD (4:2–6)

LITERARY STRUCTURE AND THEMES (4:2–6)

In Colossians 4:2–6, Paul concludes his exhortations regarding how the Christians in Colossae ought to live in Christ by assigning to them a crucial role within the evangelistic mission of the gospel. His previous instructions focused on personal character and the internal life of the church (3:5–17) as well as household duties (3:18–4:1). Now, Paul gives three imperatives that shift their focus outward, away from their own navels and "toward those outside" (πρὸς τοὺς ἔξω) the church. The first imperative commands the Colossians to "devote" (προσκαρτερεῖτε) themselves to prayer, praying especially that Paul's message would find an open door for the gospel (4:2–4). The second imperative commands the Colossians to "walk" (περιπατεῖτε) in wisdom by considering especially how their conduct might influence unbelievers toward or away from Christ (4:5). The final imperative is an implied stative verb (e.g., ἔστω) commanding that the Colossians' speech must be infused with grace, so that they are equipped for answering questions people might ask about the gospel (4:6).

- ***Persevere in Prayer (4:2–4)***
- ***Be Wise toward Unbelievers (4:5)***
- ***Watch Your Mouths (4:6)***

EXPOSITION (4:2–6)

In this passage, Paul presents his vision for how the church in Colossae ought to conduct itself with relationship to the world. Previously in the letter, Paul has told the Colossians that they died "away from" (ἀπό) the elements of the world (Col. 2:20) and that they "formerly" (ποτέ) lived among the those who do evil (Col. 3:7). The Colossian believers could have understood these statements to imply that they should separate themselves from the world, as did some religious groups in their historical context. For example, some members of a Jewish sect called the Essenes may have practiced a communal and monastic life in a desert community known as Qumran. They emphasized piety and devotion to their faith, and they may have hidden the Hebrew manuscripts we now call the Dead Sea Scrolls. But Paul's vision for the relationship of the church to the world differs considerably. The Colossians will participate in the mission of reaching the world by praying for Paul in his duty (δεῖ; 4:5) to proclaim the gospel and by discharging their own duty (δεῖ; 4:6) to have a gospel answer ready for those who will inquire of them when they see their faithful conduct and hear their gracious speech.

Persevere in Prayer (4:2–4)

Paul instructs the Colossians to persevere in prayer and to pray especially for Paul's ministry to be effective.

4:2. This section begins with a simple command for the Colossian church to develop a consistent and faithful life of prayer. "Be devoted" (προσκαρτερεῖτε), Paul says, to prayer. Such devotion means to "be busily engaged in" prayer (BDAG, s.v. "προσκαρτερέω" 2a, p. 881), as if prayer is always close at hand, a companion standing nearby and calling for attention, so that prayer becomes a recurring habit and a pattern of life. In Romans 13:6, Paul uses this same word (προσκαρτερέω) to describe the devotion government authorities demonstrate in ensuring everyone pays their taxes. Think of the enthusiastic perseverance of a politician seeking to maximize tax revenues—Christians must demonstrate a similar devotion to prayer! Indeed, the first Christians devoted themselves especially to prayer and the teaching of the Word, along with the breaking of bread and fellowship together, gathering together frequently for this very purpose (Acts 1:14; 2:42, 46; 6:4). Similarly, Paul says he has not ceased in his prayers for the Colossians (Col. 1:9), and Epaphras always labors for the Colossians in prayer (Col. 4:12).

Paul combines prayer with mental acuity when he says the Colossians must "be watchful" (γρηγοροῦντες; ESV, NIV) or "keep alert" (NRSV; cf. HCSB) in their praying. Such alertness means having a sharp mind and keen mental awareness, and it is the very opposite of falling asleep or even dying (1 Thess. 5:6–10; Rev. 3:2–3), where our minds are disengaged and unaware of our surroundings, and we have lost sight of our calling in Christ. In Scripture, Christians are to keep watch for the return of Christ, that they might be properly prepared (e.g., Matt. 24:42–43; 25:13; Rev. 16:15), and they must keep watch for false teaching (Acts 20:31) and the works of the devil (1 Peter 5:8), that they might take proper precautions against them. This same kind of attentive watchfulness, Paul says, should characterize how the Colossians pray.

The combination of prayer and watchfulness finds its greatest example in Jesus in Gethsemane just before his arrest (Matt. 26:36–46), where Jesus's attitude in prayer stands in stark contrast to that of his disciples. Jesus is acutely aware of the significance of the trial to come, and he is very sorrowful as he instructs his disciples to "watch with me" (Matt. 26:38). Jesus then falls on his face in prayer before the Father, praying for the cup of suffering to pass from him, but also surrendering himself to the Father's will. The disciples, however, are sleeping rather than keeping watch, so Jesus rebukes them and instructs them to "watch and pray that you may not enter into temptation" (Matt. 26:41). They sleep because they recognize neither the trial that is coming upon them nor the salvation that God is accomplishing in their midst. Sleeping is the opposite of keeping watch, but keeping watch is more than simply being awake. Jesus demonstrates that keeping watch means being alert to the present moment, to both its temptations and to its significance, to the trials and to the Father's will. Jesus's prayer, therefore, arises directly from his awareness of what is taking place around him, and his prayer is fervent in accordance with his desire to fully surrender his will to the Father in that moment.

Thus, to pray by keeping watch requires close attentiveness to the present realities of life in this world, so that the Colossians must learn to pray to God from the midst of their present circumstances, whatever they may be. Prayer is not an escape from the world, as if we must forget ourselves in our praying, or exchange the stark reality of life for esoteric abstractions about God. Instead, prayer should arise from within the context of life itself as we attend to our circumstances and present our lives before God as they actually are, including our sorrow and weakness in the face of trials and temptations. At the same time, prayer also heightens our alertness to God's presence and his will that he is accomplishing within our present world, so that we keep watch for his work and renew our surrender to his will within the present moment. Watchful prayer, in other words, arises from a brutal honesty regarding the harsh reality of life, and watchful prayer develops an alertness to the personal presence of God, who is with *us* within the present reality of *our* lives.

Paul also adds a final word regarding the proper attitude with which the Colossians must pray—they must pray "with thanksgiving" (ἐν εὐχαριστίᾳ). We have already noted that thanksgiving surfaces regularly as a theme in Colossians (cf. Col. 1:12; 3:15–17), and for good reason, when we remember all the work of Christ as described throughout the letter. Thanksgiving also pairs nicely with watchful praying, for as we watch and pray, we recognize God's presence with us and his work among us, and we respond to him with thanksgiving. If watchfulness is the demeanor of our praying, then thanksgiving ought to be our attitude.

4:3. Paul continues his instructions regarding prayer by adding himself to the Colossians' prayer list. They must not only pray with watchfulness regarding their own situation, but "at the same time" (BDAG, s.v. "ἅμα" 1, p. 49) they should also pray "concerning us" (περὶ ἡμῶν). This is intercessory prayer, where the Colossians must look beyond themselves and their own circumstances and pray also for other Christians in the light of *their* circumstances. The "us" whom Paul mentions here recalls his coauthor, Timothy (Col. 1:1), and likely also includes his team of coworkers, some of whom he will mention by name in his closing greetings (Col. 4:10–14). These are the same folks who also have been praying for the Colossians, when Paul says "we" have not stopped praying for you (Col. 1:9). Intercessory prayer thus becomes reciprocal prayer, as we pray for you even as you pray for us.

More specifically, Paul urges the Colossians to pray with regard to Paul's ministry in order that (ἵνα) God might open a door for the "word" (λόγος), which is the message of the gospel (Col. 1:5). This picture of a door being opened inspires a number of possible interpretations. It may be a metaphorical door by which the word enters into hearts and minds (Wright, 1986, 152; cf. Rev 3:20), or a metaphorical door of opportunity for Paul to proclaim the gospel with effective results (e.g., 1 Cor. 16:9; 2 Cor. 2:12), or a literal door opening to allow Paul out of prison (Harris 2010, 167), or a literal door opening to allow his message to enter into various house churches (MacDonald, 2000, 171). The immediate context suggests Paul has in view his release from prison that will in turn afford him more opportunities for gospel proclamation.

In the very next statement, Paul connects the open door to his ability "to speak the mystery, which is Christ" (λαλῆσαι τὸ μυστήριον τοῦ Χριστοῦ; cf. Col. 1:27)—in other words, the gospel.[1] This is less about how the message is received and more about Paul's ability to freely speak the message. It is not without coincidence that Paul first mentions his bonds at this point in the letter, explaining that he is presently "bound" (δέω) because of the mystery of Christ. Paul does not desire release for his own comfort, since he rejoices in his sufferings (Col. 1:24), but he does here express his desire to be released for the sake of the gospel, as it would allow him to continue more freely with his apostolic mission of universal proclamation (Col. 1:23, 28–29). Therefore, he enjoins the Colossians to pray together with him that the door would be opened that would release him from prison and allow him to resume his travels and proclamation.

4:4. Paul gives a second aspect to how the Colossians ought to pray concerning him and his coworkers. Even as in the previous verse they were to pray in order that (ἵνα) God might open a door for Paul the mystery of Christ to be proclaimed, now they are to pray in order that (ἵνα) Paul himself will make "it" (αὐτό, referring to the mystery of Christ) known. Paul's concern here goes beyond a mere desire for clarity in his speaking, as expressed by some translations (e.g., the ESV's "that I may make it clear;" cf. NASB, NLT, NIV, NRSV). Instead, Paul is recalling his earlier language about God revealing (φανερόω) the mystery of Christ that

1 Wright explains that the "mystery of Christ" summarizes earlier passages in Colossians and refers to "the secret plan of God for the salvation of the whole world as this has now been made known in and through Jesus Christ. It is the mystery which consists in Christ—not merely in him as an individual, but in the wide implications of who he is and what he has achieved" (Wright, 1986, 152).

had formerly been hidden (Col. 1:26–27; see Wright, 1986, 152–53). As a servant entrusted with the stewardship of this mystery (Col. 1:25), Paul aligns his personal duty with the work of God, so that he too must make known the mystery of Christ. Thus, he implores the Colossians to pray toward this end, that he would himself "reveal" (φανερόω) the mystery of Christ (thus HCSB, "that I may reveal it").

Further, the mystery will be revealed by Paul in accordance with his speaking. He strives to reveal the mystery "as" (ὡς; a comparative particle), or in accordance with, his duty to speak. When Paul says "it is necessary" (δεῖ) for him to speak, he describes a personal obligation that has placed him under compulsion (BDAG, s.v. "δεῖ" 1a, p. 214). This is his apostolic duty wrapped up in the stewardship he has received, that he now is compelled to speak in such a way that the mystery of Christ is revealed. His ministry agenda entails proclaiming Christ and laboring to see all people know Christ and grow to maturity in him (1:28–29). This proclamation is nothing short of a duty for Paul. He is not free to decide for himself whether or not he will speak of Christ; he is obligated to speak, and he carries the responsibility of making sure the words he speaks truly do reveal the mystery of Christ.

By asking the Colossians to pray for him toward this end, Paul reveals his own humility and his realization of his limited ability to make Christ known. In Colossians 1:29, he recognized God as the source of empowerment for his ministry, and he confesses this same dependence when he requests prayer. In and of himself, Paul will not be able to formulate the words that will effectively reveal Christ. He is dependent upon God, and God's work is interconnected with the prayers of his people. And if the prayers of the Colossians are an essential element of Paul's ministry, then the Colossians themselves are essential partners of Paul and of his ministry. Not all are called to public proclamation, but all are called to pray, and those who pray are just as vital to the mission as are those who preach.

Thus Paul invites the Colossian believers into his ministry and makes them an essential part of it. They need not leave Colossae to partner directly with Paul, but they can aid his mission simply by praying, right where they are. Here again, Paul empowers those who are powerless, now with the power of prayer. Even a slave, who has no control over his time, no ability to change his circumstance, and no means for establishing a platform for public proclamation, can pray for Paul and his ministry. And by praying, that slave plays as essential a role in Paul's proclamation as does Paul himself. Prayer is another equalizer, and it is a spiritual resource that can never be snatched away from us no matter how oppressed we may be. No wonder, then, that we often turn to prayer in those times when we feel we have the least control over our circumstances, for prayer is the one thing we can always still do.

Prayer and Missions

Paul's instructions to the Colossians to pray for him and his coworkers implies an underlying understanding of the role teamwork plays in the propagation of the gospel. In addition to his coworkers, Paul also depends upon a broad network of Christians who pray for his ministry. He does not place upon the Colossians a duty to proclaim the gospel in the same way he does, but he does place upon them a responsibility to pray for him as he proclaims the gospel. We could apply the same principle today and differentiate the various gifts and responsibilities God apportions within the church. Perhaps only some are gifted for public proclamation and obligated to speak in the same way Paul charged his coworkers to preach and to evangelize (cf. Eph. 4:11; 2 Tim. 4:2, 5). Today those who carry such an obligation are often known as preachers, evangelists, pastors, or missionaries. But all Christians, even those who do not bear these particular gifts and duties, must commit themselves to praying for those who are obligated to speak the gospel, that Christ might be revealed to more people through their message. Not all are called to preach, but all are called to pray.

Be Wise toward Unbelievers (4:5)

Paul instructs the Colossians to be wise in how they conduct themselves around those who do not know Christ, that they too might come to Christ.

4:5. Here Paul issues his final imperative in the main body of the letter. He will use additional imperatives in his closing instructions related primarily to greetings and reminders (Col. 4:16–18), but his final command to the Colossians in his exhortations is that they must "walk with wisdom" (ἐν σοφίᾳ περιπατεῖτε). The command to "walk" (περιπατέω) is a fitting final command, since this was also the first command Paul gave (2:6) and it was the goal of Paul's opening prayer (1:10). Here as in the earlier references, walking serves as a metaphor for the totality of a person's manner of life. The Colossians are to walk "in wisdom" (ἐν σοφίᾳ). In general, wisdom refers to a proper understanding of how God calls us to conduct ourselves in the world, but in Colossians, all the treasures of wisdom are found in Christ (2:3), so that to walk in wisdom is tantamount to walking in Christ (2:6) and walking worthy of Christ (1:10). Thus, Paul is here repeating his call for the Colossians to conduct their entire life in accordance with the wisdom and ways of Christ, the specifics of which he set forth in the exhortations of Colossians 3:5–17.

But now, Paul directs their walking specifically "toward those outside" (πρὸς τοὺς ἔξω). The preposition "toward" (πρός) here serves as a "marker of movement or orientation toward someone," and more specifically in this context, it is the orientation "of relationship" (BDAG, s.v. "πρός" 3dβ, p. 874) toward "those who are outside" (τοὺς ἔξω), but Paul does not here define of whom or what they are outside.[2] In 1 Corinthians 5:12, Paul uses this same term to refer clearly to those who are outside the church as opposed to those who belong to the church. But in Colossians, Paul has repeatedly described union with Christ through the preposition "in" (ἐν)—you are in Christ (Col. 1:28; 2:6, 10–13) and Christ is in you (Col. 1:27). Therefore, within the context of Colossians, to be "outside" (ἔξω) is the opposite of being "in" (ἐν) Christ. Outsiders are regarded as such primarily because they do not belong to Christ and secondarily because they do not belong to the body of Christ. Paul thereby draws a clear boundary between two groups of people, those who are in Christ and those who are outside Christ.

Wilson's *Patterns of Sectarianism*

Bryan Wilson surveys the nature of sectarianism among religious groups in the twentieth century and identifies four patterns of sectarianism: (1) the conversionist sect focuses on evangelism and bringing in new members; (2) the adventist, or revolutionist, sect anticipates the overturning of the present world order and therefore distances itself from the world; (3) the introversionist, or pietist, sect withdraws from the world and focuses attention inwardly on the community, so that the demands of group solidarity overshadow evangelism; and (4) the gnostic sect focuses on a charismatic leader and special teaching to advance itself within the world (Wilson, 1967, 27–29). Each of these types of sect must deal with the tension of incorporating new members from the world while at the same time maintaining its unique identity in contrast to the world by isolating and insulating itself from the world. Wilson observes that sects focused on evangelism (e.g., the conversionist sect) struggle the most to maintain their group identity, since they tend to focus

2 When the adverb "outside" (ἔξω) appears with the article, as it does here, it is substantive and thereby means "those who are outside" (BDAG, s.v. "ὁ" 2f, p. 688; cf. Harris, 2010, 169).

less on isolation from the world and more on evangelizing the world.[3] The apostle Paul envisions the church as a conversionist sect focused on evangelism through direct and sustained engagement with "outsiders." He rebuffs isolation and even insulation from the world, and he seems to presume that Christ has a strong enough unifying force that the church can maintain its unique identity as a defined community in Christ even as it is dispersed into its local community to live among outsiders.

If, upon hearing this rhetoric of outsiders and insiders, the Colossians were to conclude that they should become an exclusive club intent on keeping the outsiders outside, they would have sorely missed Paul's point, for Paul does not intend his exclusive language to be exclusionary. Instead, Paul's entire point here is about how believers ought to conduct themselves toward outsiders as those who are not *yet* insiders. The implied purpose underlying Paul's instructions is that those who are outside ought to be drawn inside, in the same way these Colossian believers were themselves outsiders who only recently were brought in when they heard and received the gospel from Epaphras. The boundary between insiders and outsiders is clearly defined but it is also porous, and the goal is to continue to bring more people inside. Toward this end, Paul calls upon the Colossians to allow their new lifestyle of wisdom in Christ to bear upon not only their relationships within the body, but also their relationships outside the body. In their interactions with unbelievers, they must put off immorality, anger, wrath, greed, and uncouth speech (3:5–11), and they must put on patience, kindness, humility, mercy, love, and the like (3:12–17).

As they live in this way of wisdom among outsiders, they will be "redeeming the time" (τὸν καιρὸν ἐξαγοραζόμενοι; KJV). The word "redeem" (ἐξαγοράζω) arises from a commercial context, where it means to "buy" or to "buy up" something, but it can also refer more generally to "gain something" or, as in most English translations, to "make the most of" (BDAG, s.v. "ἐξαγοράζω" 2, p. 343; cf. NIV, NRSV, HCSB). The "time" (καιρός) of which they are to make the most can have eschatological overtones in which the present season exists only temporarily and will one day give way to a future season of glory ushered in by the imminent return of Christ (e.g., Rom. 8:18; 13:11; 1 Cor. 4:5; 7:29; 1 Tim. 4:1). In this sense, Paul exhorts the Colossians to make the most of the present season, since the opportunities of today may not exist tomorrow, if Christ has appeared in glory. But at the same time, Paul's exhortations also carry the much simpler application that believers are to be sensitive to the opportunities afforded to them throughout their day rather than allowing time to idly pass by them. In other words, as the Colossian believers interact with other unbelievers in their hometown, "every opportunity is to be snapped up . . . like a bargain" (Wright, 1986, 153).

But how, precisely, will they maximize every opportunity? Not primarily by their words about Christ but by their lifestyle in Christ. Paul calls upon the Colossians to attend themselves first and foremost to their walk. They must ensure that their conduct honors Christ in every situation, so that they have developed the proper habits for how to behave in every interaction with unbelievers. This will include their speech, as Paul sets forth in the very next verse, but it also applies to

3 Wilson says, "The principal tension between the demand for separateness and other sect values arises in the injunction, accepted by many sects, to go out and preach the gospel. Evangelism means exposure to the world and the risk of alienation of the evangelising agents. It means also the willingness to accept into the sect new members." Therefore, each sect must find the "position of optimal tension" as it seeks to maintain its values in separation from the world even as it evangelizes the world (Wilson, 1967, 37–39).

their conduct more broadly construed. Those characteristics that accompany their new life in Christ must be applied also to their interactions with those outside the body of Christ. In their business dealings, they must put off greed and lying (3:5, 9). Christian employers must make the most of every opportunity to show compassion, kindness, patience, and fairness to their "outsider" employees (3:12; 4:1). When a Christian is wronged by an outsider, she must maximize the opportunity to show mercy and to forgive (3:13) rather than to react with anger (3:8). Christians should also overlook the social boundaries established by the world and be the first to treat as equals those who are different from themselves in terms of ethnicity, background, language, or economic status (3:11). Christian husbands should demonstrate love for their wives among unbelievers, even when their wife is not present, and should maintain the highest standards of sexual purity (3:5). The list of practical applications is seemingly endless, but the overall point stands clearly enough: Christians should operate with integrity rather than hypocrisy, so that their new life in Christ effects every aspect of their lives in every context, being lived out with wisdom even among outsiders.

On Living the Gospel

Eugene Peterson, in his epilogue to the second edition of *A Long Obedience in the Same Direction*, describes his core convictions as a pastor, one of which "was that everything in the gospel is livable and that my pastoral task was to get it lived. It was not enough that I announce the gospel, explain it or whip up enthusiasm for it. I wanted it lived—lived in detail, lived on the streets and on the job, lived in the bedrooms and kitchens, lived through cancer and divorce, lived with children and in marriage. Along the way I found that this also meant living it myself, which turned out to be a far more formidable assignment" (Peterson, 2000, 201–2). Likewise, Paul's exhortation to the Colossians that they should live out the gospel evidences his underlying conviction that the gospel is livable and therefore must be lived.

Watch Your Mouths (4:6)

Paul instructs the Colossians to speak with grace and to be prepared to answer inquiries about their faith in Christ.

4:6. Paul continues his preceding discussion about how believers ought to interact with outsiders with a special focus upon speech. Words matter, not merely in what we say, but especially in how we say it. Thus, Paul addresses first the manner of speech and secondly the content of speech. Regarding manner, he tells the Colossians that their "speech" (λόγος) must "always" (πάντοτε) be characterized by grace (ἐν χάριτι).[4] This grace can refer to an overall gracious quality of speech, whereby speech has "a winning quality or attractiveness that invites a favorable reaction" (BDAG, s.v. "χάρις" 1, p. 1079). The precise characteristics of speech that constitute this attractive quality can vary from one culture to another, but it certainly implies at the very least the kind of kindness and compassion prescribed in Colossians 3:12 as opposed to the anger, malice, and obscenities proscribed in Colossians 3:8. Further, for Paul, grace (χάρις) is a key attribute of God himself, and his grace is associated directly with the gospel, for the gospel is the message of God's grace revealed through the work of Christ in his incarnation and death and resurrection (Col. 1:6; cf. Rom. 5:15, 17; Gal. 1:6; Eph. 2:5–8; Titus 2:11). Therefore, Paul may also have in mind that speech should always be characterized by the specific grace of God as made known in the gospel message.

4 The clause itself (ὁ λόγος ὑμῶν πάντοτε ἐν χάριτι) does not have a verb, but Paul implies a stative verb with imperatival force, such as "let it be" (ἔστω).

Paul adds a metaphor for this quality of speech: "being seasoned with salt" (ἅλατι ἠρτυμένος). Here is a transcultural palate pleaser! Salt was not only useful as a fertilizer in the ancient world, but then as now, salt was used widely by many cultures as a seasoning for a wide variety of dishes. Most all people appreciate salt as a seasoning, within proper moderation. Likewise, Paul says speech should be appropriately seasoned with grace, so that it is palatable to the one who hears it. We must be fluent in the language of grace, exercising graciousness in all of our interactions and speaking freely and properly of God's grace, whether in subtle and passing comments, or in direct and extended conversations. Even as a dash of salt can transform an otherwise bland dish into something delectable, so also a dash of grace can make an otherwise wearisome conversation into something fresh and delightful, even appetizing and desirable. Indeed, in an age of social indifference and rudeness, where kind and meaningful conversation can be hard to find, a gracious word spoken with wisdom can be as endearing as it is uncommon.

The sum result of this life among outsiders, with its wise conduct and gracious speech, is the specific opportunity that comes when these outsiders question believers regarding their life of faith. Paul instructs the Colossians to know how they ought to answer each one who asks them such questions. The infinitive "to know" (εἰδέναι) may be telic (indicating purpose) or ecblatic (indicating result), so that this knowledge is either the intended purpose or the natural consequence of the gracious speech in the first half of the verse (Wallace, 1996, 590–94; Harris, 2010, 171). The overall sense seems to be that Christians must learn to infuse grace into their conversation even as they also learn how to respond to the specific questions of outsiders, and the former leads into the latter, both by creating the opportunities and by guiding the Christian in how to speak. In other words, our gracious speech leads to outsiders asking questions about our faith in Christ, and we use gracious speech in how we respond.

Christians, therefore, must know how to articulate their faith in personalized situations. The "how" (πῶς) refers to the "means or manner" in which something is done (BDAG, s.v. "πῶς," p. 901), and particularly here the manner with which the Colossians must undertake their duty to answer each one. Here Paul repeats the word "it is necessary" (δεῖ), which describes a personal obligation that places a person under compulsion (BDAG, s.v. "δεῖ" 1a, p. 214). Two verses earlier Paul referred to his own obligation to speak and to make known the mystery of Christ (Col. 4:4), but now he uses the same term to describe the obligation of the believers in Colossae. It is necessary for "you" (ὑμᾶς), Paul says, "to answer each one" (ἑνὶ ἑκάστῳ ἀποκρίνεσθαι). Paul's language of "each one" (ἑνὶ ἑκάστῳ) emphasizes the personal nature of these interactions, as if the Colossians must engage people "one by one" (e.g., Matt. 26:22; Luke 4:40; 16:5; 1 Cor. 12:18), and this approach contrasts directly with Paul's own mission to proclaim Christ widely to "every person" (πάντα ἄνθρωπον; Col. 1:28). Paul does not obligate the Colossians to initiate opportunities for gospel proclamation with broad audiences, but he does obligate them to respond properly when individual persons raise specific questions (cf. 1 Peter 3:15).

The Answer Invites the Question

In *The Gospel in a Pluralist Society*, Lesslie Newbigin addresses how the right answer of the gospel prompts people to ask the right questions: "In discussions about the contemporary mission of the Church it is often said that the Church ought to address itself to the real questions which people are asking. That is to misunderstand the mission of Jesus and the mission of the Church. The world's questions are not the questions which lead to life. What really needs to be said is that where the Church is faithful to its Lord, there the powers of the kingdom are present and people begin to ask the question to which the gospel is the answer. And that, I suppose, is why the letters of St. Paul contain so many exhortations to faithfulness but no exhortations to be active in mission" (Newbigin, 1989, 119).

Thus, Paul sets forth his agenda for ongoing evangelism in Colossae, and it centers upon a transformed life that will be noticed and commented upon by outsiders. Indeed, in a small town such as Colossae, simple lifestyle changes are readily noticeable to all. A person could remain in their same household and career, and continue in their same rhythms of life, but if they simply undergo a transformation of speech in which uncouth words are replaced by grace, and if they learn to apply the wisdom of Christ to how they live, the transformation will be quickly noticeable to all. In many small towns, such a transformed person would become the talk of town! These Christians do not need to pursue evangelistic opportunities in the form of cold-calling or street preaching; instead, they need only to focus on walking faithfully in Christ and being prepared for the inevitable questions certain to come their way. In this way, the gospel will continue to be made known in Colossae, not by the public proclamation of a gifted apostle, but by the faithful living of a community of Christians devoted to following Christ and to graciously making Christ known in their community, one person at a time.

THEOLOGICAL FOCUS

The exegetical idea (Paul instructed the Colossians to make the gospel known by praying for him in his global mission of proclaiming the gospel in new places and by embracing their local mission in Colossae of answering knowledgably about the gospel when asked about their transformed speech and conduct) leads to this theological focus: All Christians bear the responsibility to make the gospel known, not only by persistently praying for preachers and missionaries, but also by faithfully honoring Christ in how they live, by speaking graciously in every situation, and by answering the inevitable questions that arise about their faith.

In Colossians 4:2–6, Paul presents his vision for the role the local church plays within the mission of the gospel. He presumes here that the gospel is a message that must be made known to all people, even as the Colossians have themselves heard and received the gospel (1:4–6), and even as Paul labors to preach the gospel and to all creation, so that the word of God is fully known by all people (1:23, 25, 28). But though the mission of advancing the gospel belongs to all Christians, Paul here identifies two distinct aspects of that mission, for only some are obligated like Paul (δεῖ; 4:4) to proclaim the gospel, but the entire church is obligated (δεῖ; 4:6) to answer those who ask about the gospel. Paul thereby differentiates proclaiming the gospel from replying with regard to the gospel, so that the former is proactive, formal, and public, while the latter is reactive, informal, and personal. Those who proclaim the gospel seek to establish new relationships with strangers or with a public audience in order to share the gospel broadly, while those who answer questions make themselves available to those with whom they already have relationships (e.g., friends, family, neighbors, coworkers, etc.) in order to answer whatever questions might arise about the gospel.

On the one hand, therefore, Paul relieves the Colossians of the obligation to proclaim the gospel—he distinctly does *not* instruct them to become like him in his mission—but on the other hand, Paul does lay upon the church-at-large three duties that are essential for the effectiveness of the mission. First, all Christians must persistently and attentively pray for those who proclaim the gospel, that God would open the doors and enable the gospel to reach new people in new places through them. Second, all Christians must attend to their own walk in Christ, ensuring that their conduct and especially their speech properly reflects Christ their

Lord to the outsiders in their own circles of relationships. Third and finally, all Christians must know how to speak about the gospel with boldness and clarity when called upon to do so.

Paul thereby sets forth the manner with which a local church seeks to evangelize the world, beginning with their own community. Paul does not commission the local church for short-term, itinerant, tent-revival ministry; rather, he envisions a long-term, homegrown, grassroots approach to reaching our neighbors for Christ. And this is not a second-rate calling behind the "higher calling" of the missionaries and preachers, who strategize and follow the open doors to other communities; in reality, this is an even more difficult calling that requires continuing to follow Christ faithfully in a community *until* the door opens. It is much easier to proclaim the gospel from a stage to strangers; it is much harder to live among neighbors who watch your every move and determine whether or not your life bears out the truth of the gospel. But how great is the rejoicing when the door finally opens, and a neighbor becomes inquisitive and a Christian is prepared to answer graciously and clearly, and the gospel reaches one more outsider right here inside our hometown community.

PREACHING AND TEACHING STRATEGIES

Exegetical and Theological Synthesis

Transitioning from the long section of exhortations in chapter 3, the apostle Paul begins to wrap up the letter to the Colossians with a personal word and final exhortation. Mentioning his imprisonment for the first time, he asks the Colossians to pray steadfastly that the door would be opened for him to resume his evangelistic ministry of preaching the "mystery of Christ" (v. 3) and that he would make that message clear (v. 4). Following immediately on these thoughts related to evangelistic preaching, Paul offers exhortations related to interpersonal witness: walk in wisdom toward outsiders, and let your speech be seasoned with salt (vv. 5–6). These commands summarize what Paul presented in chapter 3—avoid sexual immorality, put away sins of the tongue such as slander and obscenity, forgive one another, dwell together in unity, and so forth. When outsiders see that kind of behavior, Paul implies that they will take notice, and that is when the Christ-followers of Colossae must be ready to explain the transforming power of Christ and his gospel (v. 6).

Preaching Idea

To spread the good news, pray for the preachers and salt your own speech.

Contemporary Connections

What does it mean?

The preaching idea refers to evangelism, and the first way to do this is to "pray for the preachers." We often do well in praying for things like the pastor's family and personal integrity, but in the context of 4:2–6, the preaching idea means that we should pray for the public ministry of evangelism. And what should we pray? That doors will be opened and that the preaching will be clear. Suggestions are given below on how we can devote ourselves to prayer for preachers' evangelistic work.

The second part of the preaching idea—"salt your own speech"—turns to the responsibility laypeople have in evangelism. They are to walk in wisdom toward outsiders and let their speech be gracious. With the quick strokes of a watercolorist, Paul sums up the long list of commands given in 3:5–17. That is what it means to walk in wisdom. A quick review of those exhortations might be offered here. Examples can include truthful speech at work, instead of gossip; giving up one's preferences in a staff meeting; and apologizing for a missed deadline or late submission. When the text joins "walking" (behavior) with "speech," it touches on the importance of personal credibility in persuasion. Augustine, the church father who was also a rhetorician, put it this way: "The life of the speaker has greater weight in determining whether he is obediently heard than any grandness of eloquence" (*On Christian Doctrine*, Book 4, chapter 26).

Who are the "outsiders" Paul refers to in verse 5? These people are not "in Christ." Thus Paul maintains an important distinction, as Jesus did, between those who are on the road that leads to destruction and those who are on the road that leads to life (Matt. 7:13–14). Yet even with that distinction in place, the boundary between insiders and outsiders should not lead to pride or standoffishness. The goal is not to separate from "outsiders," but to bring more people inside by sharing the message of grace and hope.

Is it true?

Is it true that to spread the good news we should pray for preachers' evangelistic ministries? We see this modeled in Scripture, as when the Lord Jesus sent out seventy-two workers and said, "The harvest in plentiful, but the labors are few. Therefore, pray earnestly to the Lord of the harvest to send out laborers" (Luke 10:2). In Romans, Paul says, "Strive together with me in your prayers," so that he would be delivered from prison and enabled to continue his church planting ministry (Rom. 15:30). Not all are called to public proclamation of the gospel, but all are called to pray for that ministry.

What about the second part of the preaching idea? Is it really necessary to salt our speech and walk wisely toward the outsiders? The Lord does not obligate every person to engage in public preaching, but he does expect every believer to respond wisely when questioned interpersonally. In an age of public rudeness, self-promotion, and harsh attacks, gracious speech will stand out like diamonds on black velvet. And when that kind of speech is framed by wise and godly behavior, the verbal and nonverbal elements work in harmony like apples of gold in a setting of silver (Prov. 25:11). Philippians 2:14–15 suggests that Christ-followers can witness simply by not complaining and arguing. We can shine in this crooked age. Gracious words seasoned with salt may lead non-churched people at our workplace, school, sports team, or in blogs to ask about our behavior, and then we will want to be ready to answer that God has been gracious to us and that is why we don't complain.

In a classic study, social scientist Albert Mehrabian studied the juxtaposition of behavior and speech and verified what we know from common experience: when nonverbal action contradicts spoken words, listeners are much more likely to trust the nonverbal element (Mehrabian, 1968). So, we need both—walking in wisdom and gracious words.

Be Ready to Give an Answer

A personal illustration might be used to support how we can walk in wisdom and salt our own speech with gracious words when questioned. My (Jeffrey's) wife ordered and paid for a case (twelve boxes) of a special pancake mix from Trader Joe's. But when the case came in, it actually contained twenty-four boxes, twice as many as she paid for. She didn't realize that it had twenty-four until she arrived home, so she returned the extra boxes. The clerk was astounded: "Why are you doing this? You could have kept the boxes and never paid for them and no one would have known!" My wife had recently taught on how each person is made in the image of God, so the response came easily to her lips: "Well, I believe that each person is made in God's image; so I want to treat each person fairly and kindly, the same way I want to act towards God." The clerk got tears in his eyes and said, "That's beautiful." Then he gave her some flowers from the store to say thank you!

Now what?

What action steps might we take to spread the good news by praying for the preachers and salting our own speech? Prayer for evangelism can be promoted in the church's monthly newsletter or a weekly email. Individuals might pray for evangelistic enterprises every day at noon, every Wednesday at 7:00, or when the family says grace before dinner. When this passage is taught in church, perhaps a layperson might pray for the pastoral staff, that their evangelistic ministries would be fruitful. The words of the passage could provide a template for what to pray: first pray with thanksgiving, then pray for open doors, and then pray for clarity. Some churches have a prayer team that prays for the preacher while the sermon is underway.

"Watchful" prayer (v. 2) implies awareness and mental acuity. I have friends who pray for their missionary daughter who is living among a tribal people in Africa. My friends have created a hand-drawn map of her village to pray knowledgably. On the map are huts with the names of people who live there, the river where the women collect water, and the places where the elders gather. My friends pray their way around the map. As in the Exposition, this kind of prayer "requires close attentiveness to the present realities of life in this world."

A particular reality that this passage touches is persecution that often accompanies evangelism. Paul refers to his imprisonment in verse 3. So one way to "pray for the preachers" is by interceding for the persecuted church. Perhaps the church's own missionaries are facing persecution and can be upheld in prayer. Websites of advocacy organizations or ministries like Help the Persecuted (htp.org) and The Voice of the Martyrs (persecution.com) provide knowledge of concrete needs that can be met through prayer and aid.

Verse 2 also says that we should pray with thanksgiving. Intercession might be mixed with thanks by remembering that God is already at work among the outsiders and is already empowering the evangelists. We might also thank God that through prayer *we* can participate in the life-changing, kingdom-building activity of evangelism.

The preaching idea implies teamwork—public proclamation from a preacher and interpersonal witness from laypeople. This might provide an opportunity to suggest how various spiritual gifts can be used not only for the "insiders," but also to reach "outsiders." A person with the gift of hospitality or administration might organize an Alpha course; another person with the gift of encouragement might serve as a hospital chaplain and set up chapel services where his or her pastor can present the gospel.

Creativity in Presentation

A handful of metaphors are embedded in the preaching idea and passage, and these might be leveraged for creative communication. When Paul asks the Colossians to pray that a door may be opened, perhaps a door, or picture of a door, could be set up on stage. When the door is closed, the preacher might discuss things that hinder the work of the evangelist such as persecution, hard-hearted or distracted listeners, or the church's poor witness through negative words and actions. Then the door could be opened to accompany a discussion of how to overcome those problems.

Salt could be used also. Perhaps a saltshaker could be displayed as the second part of the preaching idea is taught, or for even more creativity, a "taste test" could be performed. A volunteer, perhaps a young person, could be invited to the stage to taste bland food and then deliciously spiced food. They might be interviewed to see which food they prefer and why.

As we teach about praying for the preachers, we might point out that the word for "devote yourselves" (to prayer) is the same word used in Romans 13:6 to describe the diligence the government uses in collecting taxes, and that could lead to an illustration, especially if you are approaching tax season: the government knows who owes taxes and how much, employs legions of workers to assure that taxes are paid, and sets deadlines and procedures for collecting what is owed.

The concept of "redeeming the time" (v. 5) might be illustrated with another prop and exercise. Using a timer or alarm clock, listeners might be instructed to learn as many new names of people in the congregation as they can in sixty seconds. After the buzzer sounds, the preacher or worship leader could ask the winner what techniques helped him or her make the most of the opportunity. This could then lead into a discussion on how we can make the best use of time by walking in wisdom and using gracious speech.

The stories of brothers Christopher and Peter Hitchens could be used to illustrate "outsiders" and "insiders." Christopher is an outspoken atheist, and Peter is a Christian. After Peter regained his faith, he wrote *The Rage against God: How Atheism Led Me to Faith* (2010). Earlier, older brother Christopher wrote *God Is Not Great: How Religion Poisons Everything* (2007). It should be noted that Christopher's primary argument is against organized religion (more than theism), primarily the Abrahamic religions—Judaism, Christianity, and Islam.For a summary of *The Rage against God*, do an internet search for that title and you will find summary videos. The same is true for *God Is Not Great*.

The point to stress deals with evangelism. Ministers play their part as do laypeople. So, to spread the good news we should pray for the preachers and salt our own speech.

- Introduction: How can we spread the good news?
- Pray for the preachers (4:2–4).
- Salt our own speech (4:5–6).

DISCUSSION QUESTIONS

1. Where was Paul when he wrote this passage (v. 3)? Does that make any difference to your understanding of the passage?
2. What are we to pray for steadfastly (vv. 3–4)? Name some ways we can do this.
3. What does it mean to walk in wisdom toward the outsiders (v. 5)? Name some ways we can do this.
4. How are nonverbal communication (actions) linked with verbal communication (words)? Give an example.
5. Which do you find most challenging: praying for preachers in their evangelistic work, walking in wisdom, or letting your speech be gracious, seasoned with salt?
6. How can you partner with the evangelists with your own gifts?

Colossians 4:7–18

EXEGETICAL IDEA
Paul closed his letter with a series of greetings and instructions that connected the Colossian church with the broader body of Christ, for the purpose of mutual encouragement and regional partnership together in the global mission of proclaiming the gospel and strengthening believers in Christ.

THEOLOGICAL FOCUS
When local churches partner together and strive to encourage one another and work together for the gospel, they are mutually strengthened and together they accomplish the mission of living and proclaiming the gospel.

PREACHING IDEA
To spread the good news, work locally and partner globally.

PREACHING POINTERS
Paul wraps up his epistle with the standard form of first-century letters. He sends greetings from his team, makes a few "announcements," and gives a few directives. That was the conventional way to conclude, but Paul uses the convention to drive home some of the key themes of Colossians one more time. Those themes are the advance of the gospel and the nature of the church. With references to house churches such as the one that met at Nympha's (v. 15) and the citywide church in towns like Laodicea (vv. 15–16), we see that the church was a regional body. Paul and his team had a vision to reach the whole district.

Today that vision is needed as well. The legacy of the Protestant Reformation is separation more than unification. According to the authoritative *World Christian Encyclopedia,* there are more than thirty-three thousand denominations, so Jesus's prayer rings urgently today: "that they may all be one" (John 17:21). A vision of unity and partnership between churches is the heart beneath Colossians 4:7–18 and perhaps by preaching on this final section, it can become the heart of our churches too. Evangelism is best done when churches partner with each other. To spread the good news, the church should work locally and partner globally.

CLOSING INSTRUCTIONS AND GREETINGS (4:7–18)

LITERARY STRUCTURE AND THEMES (4:7–18)

This final unit serves as the closing to the letter. Such greetings are in line with the literary conventions of Paul's day and with Paul's own habits in his letter-writing (e.g., Rom. 16:1–23; 1 Cor. 16:10–20; 2 Tim. 4:19–21; Titus 3:12–15; Philem. 23–24). In a letter the length of Colossians, such a closing would typically include exchanging pleasantries and tying up loose ends, such as when Paul introduces the letter carriers (4:7–9). Paul's greetings here also recall various themes he has addressed throughout the letter. For example, he points to the diversity of his own cohort, even as the body of Christ is diverse (4:11; cf. 3:11), and the contents of Epaphras's prayer align with Paul's stated goal in the letter, namely that believers will grow to maturity and live according to the will of God (4:12; cf. 1:9–10, 28–29). These greetings, together with Paul's final instructions, aim to network the Colossians together with Christians and churches in other communities so they will come to share in the mutual encouragement and partnership that comes with membership in the universal body of Christ.

- ***Instructions Regarding Letter-Carriers (4:7–9)***
- ***Greetings from Paul's Teammates (4:10–14)***
- ***Final Instructions (4:15–18)***

EXPOSITION (4:7–18)

In his closing words, Paul develops a who's-who list of his associates and connections. He names eleven individual people, including Tychicus, Onesimus, Aristarchus, Mark, Barnabas, Jesus (called Justus), Epaphras, Luke, Demas, Nympha, and Archippus. Though it may be tempting to read over this list of names, a careful exposition of the text reveals that each of these historical figures have a personal story of following Christ and working with Paul. Their stories serve as an encouragement to the Colossians, who will discover that they are not alone in their walk with Christ, and they are not the first Christians to face difficult challenges in their faith, such as the challenge of reconciling Philemon and Onesimus. Paul also mentions the church of the Laodiceans and the church that meets in the home of Nympha. Paul intends not only for believers in Colossae to have personal relationships with believers outside their church, but he also intends for the church in Colossae to be partnered together with other churches in their region. The Colossian church, in other words, must be networked together with other churches in order to encourage one another and work together in the mission of proclaiming Christ.

Instructions Regarding Letter-Carriers (4:7–9)

Paul introduces the two carriers of this letter with great care and distinction such that he affirms Tychicus as a reputable colaborer with Paul, and he commends Onesimus as a brother who belongs to the community of believers in Colossae.

4:7. In the letter, Paul has focused his attention on instructions for the benefit of the Colossians within their environment, but he has said relatively little about his own situation. He spoke generally about his role as an apostle (1:24–29) and his desire for churches such as that in Colossae (2:1–5), but he has provided only minimal insight into his own circumstances. Indeed, he will only finally give a hint about his imprisonment in his closing statements (4:18). We might expect a personal letter to contain more personal information and updates, but Paul excludes personal updates because he trusts Tychicus to personally "make known" (γνωρίζω) the full scope of the things that have been occurring in Paul's own life (τὰ κατ' ἐμὲ πάντα), whether we call those things his "state" (KJV), "activities" (ESV), or "news" (HCSB, NIV, NRSV).

Paul establishes Tychicus as a trustworthy emissary with three descriptive phrases. First, Tychicus is "the beloved brother" (ὁ ἀγαπητὸς ἀδελφὸς). Paul frequently used this familial term to describe the relationships between Christians. He earlier described Timothy as a brother (1:1) and the Colossians as faithful brothers (1:2), and the Christians in Laodicea are brothers as well (4:15). Paul's apparent indiscriminate use of the term suggests that for Paul, to be a "brother" simply means to belong to Christ; it does not necessarily describe the familiarity and intimacy of a particular relationship between believers. Tychicus, however, receives higher accolades as a "beloved" brother—he has become a particularly endeared brother to Paul.

Who Is Tychicus?

Tychicus appears in Colossians 4:7 as a letter-carrier and coworker of Paul, but we receive minimal additional information about him. We can piece together a biography of sorts from a few scattered mentions of Tychicus in the New Testament. We learn that he was initially from the province of Asia (Acts 20:4), a broader region that encompassed modern-day Turkey. Thus, when Paul commissioned him to carry letters to Ephesus (Eph. 6:21) as well as Colossae, Tychicus was traveling familiar territory. Paul considered sending Tychicus to Titus in Crete (Titus 3:12) and did send him to Timothy in Ephesus (2 Tim. 4:12). Based simply on how many times Tychicus is mentioned in conjunction with Paul's ministry, he likely ranked alongside Silvanus as one of Paul's "closest associates" behind Timothy and Titus (Dunn, 1996, 272).

Second, Paul describes Tychicus as a "faithful minister" (πιστὸς διάκονος). The word "minister" (διάκονος) refers to a person who "discharges a specific ministry" (Lohse, 1971, 171). Paul used this very same term to describe his own ministry as one who has been entrusted with proclaiming the gospel of Christ (Col. 1:23, 25), and he commended Epaphras as a "faithful minister" (Col. 1:7). Thus, Paul places Tychicus within the company of Paul the apostle and Epaphras, whom the Colossians know personally, and Paul thereby establishes Tychicus's credibility in discharging the very ministry Paul has assigned to him, namely to carry the letter to the Colossians and to deliver to them a personal report about Paul's circumstances.

Third and finally, and also most interestingly, Paul describes Tychicus as a "fellow-slave" (BDAG, s.v. "σύνδουλος" 1, p. 966), for Tychicus serves the same Master or Lord (ἐν κυρίῳ). Again, Paul used this language to speak of Epaphras as well (Col. 1:7; cf. 4:12), and for Tychicus to be a "fellow" slave implies Paul also views himself as a slave, as indeed Paul states explicitly elsewhere (e.g., Titus 1:1; Phil. 1:1). Paul clearly has no trouble describing himself or his coworkers as slaves, but in this instance with Tychicus, Paul seems to be especially intentional in describing Tychicus as such. In a very similar parallel, Paul also entrusts the letter to the Ephesians to Tychicus as the letter-carrier, and there Paul also describes Tychicus as a beloved brother and faithful minister, but *not* a fellow-slave. Most likely Paul includes "fellow-slave" in Colossians 4:7 because of the person and situation he will mention in 4:9, namely Onesimus, whom Paul carefully avoids describing as a slave. Thus, Paul seems to be quite particular in humbling Tychicus as a slave—along with himself and Epaphras—so that Tychicus occupies a station no higher than Onesimus, even as he will elevate Onesimus to a status parallel to their own, as a faithful and beloved brother (4:9).

4:8. Paul now further articulates the purpose for which Tychicus has been sent with the letter. That Paul "sent" (ἔπεμψα) Tychicus reflects both Paul's position of leadership and Tychicus's role as a faithful minister serving alongside Paul. Paul sends and Tychicus goes. At the same time, Paul hand-selected Tychicus and sent him "to you" (πρὸς ὑμᾶς) for a very specific purpose (indicated by εἰς αὐτὸ τοῦτο). Paul presumably could have used virtually anyone to carry and deliver the letter, if the delivery of the letter was his only aim, but Paul expects more from his letter-carrier. In this instance, Paul assigns to Tychicus a purpose that involves two interconnected parts: he will share an update regarding Paul's ministry, and he will encourage the hearts of the Colossians.

Letter-Carriers

In Paul's day, most private letters were sent with a personal letter carrier rather than through the Roman postal service, which was not available for private use. These letter carriers could serve various functions in addition to simply handing off the letter, including vouching for the letter's authenticity, carrying additional items (e.g., gifts), providing additional details, and personally relaying confidential messages (Richards, 2008, 641). In addition, letter carriers might elaborate on the letter's message and clarify confusion. Paul may have expected Tychicus to perform several of these duties as the carrier of his letter to the Colossians.

First, Paul sends Tychicus "in order that . . . you might know our circumstances" (ἵνα γνῶτε τὰ περὶ ἡμῶν). This effectively repeats what Paul just said in verse 7 about Tychicus sharing Paul's personal circumstances (the things concerning *me*); now Paul broadens this report to include *our* circumstances. It seems Paul's focus here is not so much on his own situation, namely his imprisonment, as it is on the state of the broader mission, including his teammates, though the mission has certainly been impacted by his imprisonment. Paul includes a similar kind of report in Philippians 1:12–18, where Paul rejoices to see how the gospel is proclaimed as a result of his imprisonment, both through his own testimony among the prison staff, by the increased boldness of his partners who are not imprisoned, and even through rival preachers who see an opportunity to increase their own ministries with Paul imprisoned. For these reasons, Paul rejoices to see that his imprisonment is for Christ and serves to advance the gospel.

Such a report would help Tychicus accomplish the second part of why Paul has sent him, in order that "your hearts might be encouraged" (παρακαλέσῃ τὰς καρδίας ὑμῶν). This encouragement (παρακαλέω) refers to encouragement or even exhortation designed not merely to make a person feel better about themselves but to give the courage necessary for accomplishing a task, in this case the task of following Christ faithfully. Paul himself labors for the Colossians to be encouraged by their unity together in love and their growing in knowledge of Christ (Col. 2:2). Tychicus, therefore, will further contribute toward the encouragement of the Colossians' hearts. He will stand in for the absent Paul and he will embody Paul's struggle to see the Colossians encouraged, and he will do so by working toward their unity and growth in Christ. And toward this end, Tychicus will guide the church through the situation with Onesimus and the particular exhortations of Paul in this regard (note παρακαλέω in Philem. 9–10), even as Onesimus presently stands alongside Tychicus as the next to be introduced by Paul in the letter.

4:9. Onesimus, however, needs no introduction, being from Colossae, but he does need commendation. Paul exercises extraordinary pastoral care and political sensitivity—and perhaps even shrewdness—in how he describes Onesimus. To all the world, Onesimus is a runaway slave, but to Paul, Onesimus is a faithful and beloved brother, and the church must exchange the former characterization for the latter. The significance of Paul's language is found in the similarities and dissimilarities with how he introduced Tychicus in 4:7. Like Tychicus, Onesimus is a "beloved brother" (ἀγαπητὸς ἀδελφός) and he is "faithful" (πιστός), and these are the very same terms Paul used to describe Timothy and the Colossian believers (1:1–2). However, Paul does not call Onesimus a "minister" (διάκονος), perhaps indicating that Onesimus has "no explicit responsibility" within Paul's ministry (Dunn, 1996, 273). Most pointedly, Paul applies the language of slavery to Tychicus, calling him a "fellow slave" (σύνδουλος), but he eliminates this language altogether for Onesimus, even though Onesimus *is* a slave. Paul surely is making a powerful and personal application of the elimination of categories such as slave and free within the body of Christ (cf. Col. 3:11), and this lays the groundwork for his direct appeal to Philemon to receive Onesimus no longer as a slave (δοῦλος), but as more than a slave, as a beloved brother (ἀδελφὸν ἀγαπητόν; Philem. 16).

Further, Paul says about Onesimus that he is "of you all" (ἐξ ὑμῶν), which here refers to his place of origin (BDAG, s.v. "ἐκ" 2, p. 296). Onesimus, like Epaphras (4:12), is a native of Colossae and therefore has a kinship with them. He is "one of your own number" (Harris, 2010, 174). By this, Paul may be implying not only that Onesimus belongs to the community of Colossae but more specifically that he belongs to the community of the saints in Colossae. As a brother, he belongs to Christ and to this body as much as any other believer, and as a native Colossian, he belongs to Colossae as much as any other Colossian does. Therefore, Onesimus has as much a claim to membership in the Colossian church as does any other believer. He is not beneath them or outside them, but he is part of them and must be received as such. Of course, Paul writes this being fully aware of the personal conflict between Onesimus and Philemon that complicates his reception into the church, but Paul fully expects that as the body of Christ, they will be able to forgive one another, reconcile, and be ruled by the peace of Christ in accordance with Paul's previous instructions (e.g., Col. 3:12–15).

Paul concludes his brief comments about Onesimus here with a final phrase that has a subtle effect of further elevating Onesimus. He repeats the essence of his opening line in this section but with one particularly significant change. He began in 4:7 by stating that Tychicus would make known everything pertaining to Paul's own situation; now, in 4:9, Paul switches from the singular "he will make known" (γνωρίσει) to the plural "they will make known" (γνωρίσουσιν), thereby incorporating Onesimus in the delivery of the report. Even now, Onesimus will not function as a background figure, as a lowly slave consigned to silence, as a token diversity prop used to enhance the church's claim to be diverse even as it marginalizes him. Instead, Onesimus will stand on the platform alongside Tychicus and share the microphone as an equal voice with essential things to say on behalf of the apostle Paul, for Onesimus, too, is a faithful and beloved brother of equal value and standing.

This requires a dramatic transformation of mind and heart to sweep through the entire church, for if they are going to learn to listen to a slave, they must first find the grace and mercy to reconcile their past offenses, and they must second develop the Christian worldview Paul has promoted throughout Colossians, which will allow them to humbly listen to the very slaves whom their culture more broadly treats as lowly and unworthy of such a microphone. Onesimus must find the courage to speak up and the church must find the humility to pipe down, and both are essential for the health of the church. Paul entrusts to Onesimus a role alongside Tychicus in delivering the very report that will strengthen the hearts of the church. The church, then, stands to lose this strengthening—and to thereby be weakened—should the church marginalize and silence Onesimus. For hearts to be fully strengthened in the church, every person must have proper dignity and every voice must be respectfully heard.

Greetings from Paul's Teammates (4:10–14)

Paul sends greetings from six of his teammates by name, and every name represents a person, and every person has a story, and every story exemplifies and reinforces various themes about Christ and the church that have already appeared in the letter.

4:10. Paul begins his list of greetings with Aristarchus. He "greets" (ἀσπάζομαι) the Colossians, meaning he engages "in hospitable recognition of another" (BDAG, s.v. "ἀσπάζομαι" 1, p. 144). In other words, Aristarchus extends to the Colossians, through Paul's letter, the same exchange of customary pleasantries he would give if he were personally present with them. By receiving his greeting, the Colossians should feel recognized and valued by Aristarchus, since they are important enough to him that he calls them to mind and takes the initiative to reach out to them through Paul.

Throughout these greetings, Paul will offer brief commentary on most of his teammates. For Aristarchus, Paul describes him simply as "my fellow prisoner" (ὁ συναιχμάλωτός μου). The underlying term here typically refers to a "captive" (BDAG, s.v. "αἰχμάλωτος," p. 32) with reference to a person who has literally become a prisoner of war or who has metaphorically come under the control of forces such as sin (e.g., Rom. 7:23). Aristarchus may, therefore, share with Paul in his metaphorical captivity to Christ, whereby Paul has been pressed into the service of Christ as a slave and apostle. However, it is more likely that Paul is speaking to Aristarchus's presence with Paul in the midst of his literal imprisonment, which is itself a form of captivity. Aristarchus has previously stood with Paul in turbulent situations, including being dragged into the theater in Ephesus by a riotous—not righteous!—mob and yet continuing on with Paul thereafter (Acts 19:29; 20:4). He would later travel with Paul to Rome and perhaps endure the shipwreck along with him (Acts 27:2). Therefore, it would be in accordance with Aristarchus's demonstrated character for him to share in Paul's present captivity as a fellow prisoner, either because Aristarchus has also been arrested and imprisoned, or because Aristarchus has willfully determined to continue to serve closely alongside Paul even during his imprisonment.

A second greeting comes from Mark, who is the "cousin" (BDAG, s.v. "ἀνεψιός," p. 78; ESV, HCSB, NIV, NRSV)—not "sister's son" (KJV)—of Barnabas. That this Mark is one and the same with the John Mark in the book of Acts is a "virtual certainty," especially in light of his close relationship with Barnabas throughout Acts (Bruce, 1985, 73).[1] If so, then Mark's personal story makes sense of Paul's parenthetical reminder to the Colossians here. Paul presumes the Colossians have already "received commands" (ἐλάβετε ἐντολάς) about what they should do if Mark arrives in Colossae, but Paul repeats the essential command here: if he comes to you, welcome him. When Paul says "if he comes to you" (ἐὰν ἔλθῃ πρὸς ὑμᾶς), he uses a third class conditional clause (ἐάν + subjunctive) that "generally expresses a higher

1 "Like many Jews of the period, including Paul himself, Mark had two names—a Jewish name, John (*Yohanan* in Hebrew), and a Gentile name, Mark (the very common Roman name *Marcus*)" (Bruce, 1985, 74).

degree of probability of fulfillment" (Harris, 2010, 177). This expectation of fulfillment can lead to the possible translation of "when" rather than "if" and would thereby indicate that Paul does not view Mark's visit as a hypothetical scenario that may or may not materialize; rather, Paul expects that Mark will visit Colossae in due time and he thereby wants to prepare the Colossians for how they ought to receive him.

But why should Paul have to remind the Colossians that they should "welcome" (δέχομαι) him with proper hospitality, and why was such instruction necessary in the first place, if Mark is a member of Paul's team alongside Epaphras? This exceptional command reveals a legitimate concern that the Colossians might *not* receive him, and this in turn points to the story of Mark's failure, which was apparently widely known even among the Colossians. John Mark grew up in Jerusalem and his mother was a follower of Christ known personally by the apostles (Acts 12:12). For a time, Mark traveled with Paul and Barnabas and worked alongside them (Acts 12:25–13:12), but eventually he left them and traveled back to Jerusalem (Acts 13:13). This eventually led to a dispute between Paul and Barnabas, when Barnabas wanted to take John Mark with them in a later journey, but Paul did not want to take along someone who had previously abandoned them and their work. Barnabas would not travel without John Mark, and Paul would not travel with him, so the only resolution was for Paul and Barnabas to separate from each other, so that Paul and Silas became companions, and Barnabas and John Mark were companions (Acts 15:36–40).

Mark's story does not appear again in Acts, but Paul's instructions here in Colossians suggest a reconciliation has taken place between Paul and Mark. Mark is among Paul's teammates sending greetings to the churches under Paul's care, and Paul is at the very least aware of Mark's movements, if not directing them. Thus, Paul now has confidence that Mark's arrival in Colossae will be beneficial rather than harmful. At the end of his life, Paul will actually desire to have Mark with him, for by that time, Mark has become very useful to Pauland his ministry (2 Tim. 4:11).

Mark as Exemplar of Reconciliation

Perhaps—if we may engage in some speculation—Paul has a particular reason for instructing the Colossians to welcome Mark. Perhaps Mark has a story to tell of failure and of restoration. Paul does not presume to tell Mark's story for him in the letter, but he will allow Mark to tell his own story of how he and Paul reconciled with one another. It surely required the kind of humility and compassion Paul has commanded, along with forgiveness and love leading to peace and thankfulness (Col. 3:12–16). And thereby these two persons, Paul and Mark, having been once locked in deep conflict and bitter dissension, eventually found the grace and maturity they needed to reconcile their differences and to partner together for the sake of Christ and the church. Perhaps their story would serve as a model for Onesimus and Philemon, that the day would come when they too would have a story to tell—a story not only of offense and separation, but a story also of forgiveness and reconciliation. Indeed, these kinds of stories ought to continue being written over and over in the lives of Christians and in the history of the church, so that even today we are able to welcome as ministers among us those who once were failures.

4:11. In addition to Aristarchus and Mark, Paul adds a third person with minimal commentary: "Jesus who is called Justus." This Jesus (Ἰησοῦς) may have been called Justus (Ἰοῦστος) because this was his surname, so that his full name is "Jesus Justus" (Bruce, 1985, 76, 86; cf. BDAG, s.v. "Ἰοῦστος," p. 480), or Justus may have been a nickname by which he came to be known, so that he is "Jesus (the one we call Justus)" (NLT). In either case, he may have been commonly called Justus either because the name Jesus was "common among Jews" in this time period (BDAG, s.v. "Ἰησοῦς," p. 471) and so required differentiation from others with the same name, or because of a desire by the Pauline team to avoid using the name of the Lord Jesus in such a common way.

Paul then shifts to the plural (οἱ ὄντες) to group together these first three teammates—Aristarchus, Mark, and Jesus Justus—and to say three things about them. First, these three are all "of circumcision" (ἐκ περιτομῆς). Most translations express this awkward phrase as "of the circumcision" (ESV, HCSB, NRSV, KJV) to indicate a group of people who have been circumcised, and thus some translations offer the more interpretive "Jews" (NIV) or "Jewish believers" (NLT). This is in keeping with Paul's usage of the term to refer to Judeans in general as those who have been circumcised as opposed to the non-Judeans who are uncircumcised (BDAG, s.v. "περιτομή" 2a, p. 807; Rom. 3:30; 4:9; Eph. 2:11; cf. Acts 10:45; 11:2). At times, Paul uses the term to designate a particular party of Jews who sought to enforce circumcision upon all believers, including Gentiles (e.g., Gal. 2:12), but here Paul is simply referring to their Jewish national identity (Moo, 2008, 342). These three teammates come from Jewish backgrounds, as indicated by their circumcision.

Second, Paul says these three alone are presently his coworkers for the kingdom of God. Surely he does not mean that "these alone" (οὗτοι μόνοι) are literally his only coworkers, since he will mention three more in these greetings (Col. 4:12–14), not least of whom is Epaphras. Rather, Paul seems to mean that these are his only teammates from the circumcision—all the rest are not Jewish. As his "coworkers" (συνεργοί), these three work alongside Paul, sharing in both his vision and his labors. Paul describes this mission in shorthand here as working "for the kingdom of God" (εἰς τὴν βασιλείαν τοῦ θεοῦ), a phrase that appears only here in the writings of Paul but that on all other occasions in the New Testament refers to entrance into the kingdom of God (e.g., Matt. 19:24; 21:31; Mark 9:47; 10:23–25; Luke 18:24–25; John 3:5; Acts 3:5; 14:22). This recalls Paul's labors in Colossians 1:24–29 to proclaim the mystery of Christ to all of creation and to present all people mature in Christ. He aims to see all people brought into the kingdom and made complete within the kingdom, but this ambitious goal is much bigger than what any one man can accomplish. Paul needs teammates, and he has three Jewish coworkers laboring alongside him.

The Exclusivity of Christ

The way in which Paul speaks of his circumcised coworkers serving alongside him for the kingdom of God carries with it a subtle demonstration of the exclusivity of Christ with regard even to Judaism. Paul's describes them as being "of the circumcision" (ἐκ περιτομῆς), using the preposition "out of" (ἐκ), which can imply movement or even "separation" away from their Jewish background (BDAG, s.v. "ἐκ" 1, p. 295). Then, just a few words later, Paul uses the opposite preposition "into" (εἰς), implying "motion toward a place" (BDAG, s.v. "εἰς" 1a, p. 288), to describe their service "for" the kingdom of God. He uses the same combination of prepositions in Colossians 1:13 to describe how Christians have been rescued "out of" (ἐκ) the authority of darkness and "into" (εἰς) the kingdom of his beloved son. This language in Colossians 4:11 suggests that these Jewish coworkers have come out of their circumcision (i.e., their Jewish background) into the kingdom of God, and this would in turn mean that Paul does not view them as having been part of the kingdom of God prior to coming to their faith in Christ. Thus for Paul, there is only one way into the kingdom of God, by faith in Jesus Christ, and all who do not know Christ remain outside the kingdom of God, including even circumcised Jews.

Third, Paul remarks on the encouragement these three have provided specifically to

Paul himself. Paul speaks personally regarding their work "to me" (μοι), that they have become "a source of encouragement" (BDAG, s.v. "παρηγορία," p. 777). This unique term for encouragement is used elsewhere in medical contexts, as for example when Philo says a legitimate doctor will be careful to provide comfort to a dangerously ill patient rather than provoking despondency, even if this means not being forthcoming about the nature of the illness (Philo, *Deus* 65). It can also refer to "benevolent comfort" (e.g., 4 Macc 5:12) and appears with such a meaning in a number of funerary inscriptions (Lohse, 1971, 173). Thus, "the idea of consolation, comfort, is on the whole predominant in the word" (Lightfoot, 1981, 239). As Paul suffers under the weight of his imprisonment and unknown fate, and as he carries the burden of suffering and laboring for the church, he has found comfort in the presence and comradery of three people: Aristarchus, Mark, and Jesus Justus.

4:12. But these three are not the only ones present with Paul, for he also has greetings from three further individuals, Epaphras, Luke, and Demas. Of these three, Epaphras receives relatively extensive commentary from Paul (4:12–13), while Luke and Demas receive only brief mention (4:14). Epaphras has already appeared earlier in the letter as the link between Paul and the Colossians, for Epaphras has taken the gospel to Colossae and then traveled back to Paul with a report about the newly established Colossian church (Col. 1:7–8). In Colossians 1:7, Paul described Epaphras with language very similar to what he has now been using for his other coworkers in Colossians 4:7–11, for Epaphras is "our beloved fellow servant" (τοῦ ἀγαπητοῦ συνδούλου ἡμῶν). Now Paul further describes Epaphras's background and his present labor as a servant of Christ, with a particular emphasis on the sincere labor Epaphras continues to undertake on behalf of the Colossians, even while he is separated from them.

Paul begins his description of Epaphras with a reminder that Epaphras is "one of you" (ὁ ἐξ ὑμῶν). Like Onesimus (4:9), Epaphras too is a native of Colossae, and as a believer, Epaphras belongs to the body of Christ, so that he belongs to both Colossae and to the church, and therefore belongs to the Colossian church. But here Paul's focus is on Epaphras's current ministry as a "slave of Christ" (δοῦλος Χριστοῦ). We have come to expect Paul to describe his coworkers with the language of slavery (e.g., Col. 1:7; 4:7), and Paul uses precisely the same phrase "slaves of Christ" to describe himself and Timothy (Rom. 1:1; Phil. 1:1). Epaphras has a particular duty as a slave, and it is an ongoing labor undertaken on behalf of the Colossians. Paul uses the same term for Epaphras's "labor" (ἀγωνίζομαι) here as he used to describe his own labor in 1:29, and the term describes an active fight or struggle in which immense energy is expended. He is "struggling" (ESV), "contending" (HCSB), "wrestling" (NIV, NRSV), or "labouring" (KJV).

Epaphras can "always" (πάντοτε) be laboring in this way for the Colossians (ὑπὲρ ὑμῶν) even though he is not present with them because of the boundless power of prayer. He labors "in *his* prayers" (ἐν ταῖς προσευχαῖς), and his praying transcends the geographical distance between them. When he prays to the God who is with him and hears his prayers, he is also praying to the God who is with the Colossians and works among them, so that he prays with the conviction that his prayers really are effective and productive for the Colossians. Prayer is powerful to accomplish its end, not because of the nature of the one who prays but because of the transcendent nature of the One to whom prayers are offered. It is because Epaphras believes prayer to be powerful in this way that he devotes himself to always laboring in it. Epaphras thereby prays in the same way Jesus prayed in Gethsemane, where prayer (προσεύχομαι) and labor (ἀγωνία) joined forces to create deeply earnest prayer (Luke 22:44).

More specifically, Epaphras prays "that" (ἵνα) the Colossians might stand mature and fully assured in all the will of God, a statement that recalls multiple themes from the letter of Colossians. To "stand" (ἵστημι) means "to stand firm so as to remain stable" or "to hold one's ground" (BDAG, s.v. "ἵστημι" 4, p. 482), and for believers it means to remain fixed upon the gospel even in the face of temptation and spiritual conflict (e.g., 1 Cor. 15:1; Eph. 6:11–14). Paul has used similar language to implore the Colossians to be stable, steadfast, unmoving from the gospel, rooted, and established (Col. 1:23; 2:7). Further, Epaphras prays for the Colossians to stand "mature" or "perfect" (τέλειος), the very same word Paul used to describe the broad goal of his mission, that he might present all people "perfect" in Christ (1:28). Epaphras also prays that they might be "fully assured" in all the will of God (πληροφορέω; ESV, NIV, NRSV, HCSB), even as Paul prayed for the Colossians to be filled with knowledge of the will of God (1:9) and aimed for the Colossians to have "full assurance" (πληροφορία) of understanding (2:2). Epaphras, therefore, prays for the Colossians to become in reality what Paul has envisioned them to become throughout the letter. Epaphras shares in the mission of Paul and he has converted the aims of Paul's mission into fervent intercessory prayer on behalf of the Colossians.

4:13. Paul now "bears witness" (μαρτυρέω) regarding just how sincerely and laboriously Epaphras carries out this work of prayer. To bear witness means to attest to the veracity of something based on personal knowledge (BDAG, s.v. "μαρτυρέω" 1, p. 617), and it could often refer to the witness given in legal settings. The use of the term here places emphasis on the veracity of Paul's statement, as Paul affirms that he has firsthand knowledge and therefore is willing to stake his own credibility upon his statement. In this context, Paul has personally witnessed the labors of Epaphras and his statement should therefore be received as incontrovertible evidence that Epaphras has not forgotten the Colossians or moved on to a bigger and better ministry assignment; rather, Epaphras continues to labor for the Colossians even as he is physically absent from them. They remain the primary occupation of his heart.

Literally, Paul bears witness that Epaphras has "labor" (πόνος), which refers to "work that involves much exertion or trouble," or even "pain" (BDAG, s.v. "πόνος" 1–2, p. 852), and Epaphras has "much" (πολύς) of this labor not only for the Colossians, but also for those in the neighboring towns of Laodicea and Hierapolis. The labors of Epaphras for these churches in the Lycus Valley recall the labors Paul endures on behalf of all the churches. In Colossians 1:24, Paul spoke generically about his sufferings for the church, and in 2 Corinthians 11:23–19, Paul details the nature of his sufferings. He provides an extensive list of the physical abuse and persecution he has endured, including flogging, beatings, stonings, hunger, thirst, and even being shipwrecked. But in addition to these things, Paul also mentions his daily burden he carries for all the churches, as he shares in their weakness and burdens. In the same way, Epaphras carries a burden of "much labor" for the churches under his care, and he cannot help but feel the weight of this burden, even while he is apart from them.

This is the unquantifiable burden the pastor carries for his flock. Epaphras carries a localized version of Paul's universal concern for the church, so that Epaphras continues to labor specifically for the churches in the Lycus Valley. Epaphras has not abandoned the Colossians or been reassigned to another mission field; to the contrary, Epaphras's ongoing pastoral concern for the Colossians is evident in his active labor for them in his prayers. Epaphras truly is a "man after Paul's own heart" (Bruce, 1985, 83), for Epaphras prays as Paul prays and he labors as Paul labors because he wants for the churches in the Lycus Valley what Paul wants for all the churches.

Epaphras as Local Church Pastor

Epaphras provides a first-century role model for twenty-first-century pastors who are called to be the spiritual shepherds of local congregations. For Epaphras, ministry is not a job or a paycheck, nor is ministry a platform for personal promotion, but ministry is a spiritual duty in which he shoulders the burden of his flock. Epaphras knows his congregation intimately; he knows their burdens, their weaknesses, their temptations and sins, their vulnerabilities. He knows, for example, how the conflict between Onesimus and Philemon has strained the church, and he knows all of the risks of sending Onesimus back to reconcile. He can predict with great accuracy how various members of the church will respond—who will remain silent, who will seethe with resentment, who will speak up first with critical words, and who will respond immediately with kindness. He knows his people, and he carries within himself deep concern for his people, so he longs to be with his people, and so long as he is absent from his people, he pray intensely for his people.

Epaphras, in other words, is not just a preacher with a message; he is a pastor with a flock. Too often do pastors today sit around pondering how to build a large ministry like the apostle Paul, and too rarely do pastors sit around pondering how to shepherd a local church like the pastor Epaphras. We want to be apostles rather than pastors, visionaries rather than servants, leaders with large influence rather than shepherds of modest flocks. But in Epaphras, we see the profound difference between preaching to a crowd and pastoring a flock. Even as sheep need shepherds, so also churches need pastors—pastors who embrace the call to shepherd their flock, not least by carrying their burdens and laboring in prayer.

4:14. The last two associates of Paul to send their greetings are Luke and Demas. About Luke, Paul says simply that he is the beloved doctor. This makes Luke the only coworker of Paul's to be described according to his profession. As "the doctor" (ὁ ἰατρός), Luke had become highly educated through the study of medicine, and he had devoted his work to helping the sick. However, he had at some point become a companion of Paul, perhaps even serving as Paul's own physician in his advancing years and during his imprisonments. The church historian Eusebius (ca. A.D. 260–339) reports that this same Luke was the author of both the gospel of Luke and the book of Acts, and if so, then Luke is the only known Gentile author of any biblical writing (Eusebius, *Hist. Eccl.* 3.4.6). Further, if Luke wrote Acts, then we know that he traveled extensively with Paul, at least during the "we" passages, when the book of Acts is written in the first person (Acts 16:10–16; 20:5–21:18; 27:1–28:16). Over the course of time, Luke developed an intimate relationship with Paul, becoming "beloved" (ὁ ἀγαπητός) in the same way as Epaphras, Tychicus, and Onesimus (1:7; 4:7, 9). At the end of Paul's life, only Luke remains with him (2 Tim. 4:11), indicating not only Luke's loyalty to Paul and his willingness to suffer but also his likely role as Paul's secretary during that time.

An Early Description of Luke

In the middle of the fourth century, the so-called *Anti-Marcionite Prologues* were written. These prologues introduce the gospels of Mark, Luke, and John, and it is possible that at least part of the prologue to Luke's gospel was written much earlier—perhaps as early as the second half of the second century. This prologue to Luke includes a description of the person of Luke as follows: "Luke is a Syrian of Antioch, a Syrian by race, a physician by profession. He had become a disciple of the apostles and later followed Paul until his (Paul's) martyrdom, having served the Lord continuously, unmarried, without children, filled with the Holy Spirit he died at the age of eighty-four years in Boeotia" (Koester, 1990, 243, 335).

Last—and perhaps least—Demas sends greetings. Demas receives no accolades or commentary from Paul here, though in the greetings recorded in Philemon, Demas is grouped together with other of Paul's coworkers as "my fellow workers" (οἱ συνεργοί μου; Philem. 24). The time would come soon enough when Demas's love of the world would cause him to abandon Paul (2 Tim. 4:11). Perhaps his love of the world was already surfacing at the time when Paul wrote Colossians, so that Paul's instinctive sense of problems to come precluded him from giving overt positive commendation to Demas at this point in his ministry. Demas, therefore, stands in contrast to Mark among Paul's associates, for while Mark was on a path toward reconciliation and partnership together with Paul, Demas was on a path toward division and desertion. Perhaps Demas, like Mark, would one day return from his wandering, renounce his love of the world, and devote himself again to following and serving Christ within the auspices of Paul's mission, but we have no evidence of the final outcome of his journey.

Final Instructions (4:15–18)

Paul concludes his letter with a series of final instructions that call upon the Colossians to take an active role in partnering together with other churches and Christians for the sake of the gospel.

4:15. Here Paul continues with his theme of greetings, but now in a different format. He has modeled how greetings are passed along from one Christian to another, from his teammates to the Colossians, and now he calls upon the Colossians to join in the fun. He gives to them the instruction to "greet" (ἀσπάσασθε) neighboring Christians. Many English translations interpret this as an instruction to pass along a greeting from Paul, leading to the translation "give my greetings" (e.g., ESV, HCSB, NIV, NRSV). While it may be plausible that Paul intends for them to greet other Christians on his behalf, the literal instruction simply directs the Colossians to greet them, and it stands to reason that Paul would instruct them to reach out to neighboring Christians with greetings of their own as a way of facilitating a relationship between regional churches. Indeed, Epaphras himself links these churches together (Col. 4:13), and Paul has expressed a desire for the Colossians to be better knit together with other Christians (see comments on 2:1–2). Thus, Paul calls upon the Colossians to establish relationships of goodwill and partnership with neighboring Christians by reaching out to them with greetings.

Paul further defines three persons or groups of people the Colossians should greet. First, they are to greet "the brothers in Laodicea" (τοὺς ἐν Λαοδικείᾳ ἀδελφοὺς). Laodicea was one of the nearest towns to Colossae, so naturally Paul intends for the Colossians to begin networking with the church next door. Second, they are to greet Nympha, a person about whom we know little more than what we learn from the third and final greeting, which Paul directs to "the church according to her [Nympha's] house" (τὴν κατ᾽ οἶκον αὐτῆς ἐκκλησίαν). This directly implies that Nympha hosted gatherings for the church in her home and perhaps also provided leadership, in much the same way Philemon hosted and led a church community in Colossae (Philem. 2).

Nympha's Gender

The name "Nympha" raises a question of gender, for the accusative form Paul uses may be accented as Νύμφαν and thus derive from the feminine Νύμφα, or it may be accented as Νυμφᾶν and thus derive from the masculine Νυμφᾶς (Metzger, 1994, 560). Textual variants accent the name both ways, so that Nympha may be the name of a woman or a man. The issue is further complicated by an additional textual variant regarding the ensuing pronoun, with some manuscripts referring to the church in "her" (αὐτῆς) house while other manuscripts refer to the church in "his" (αὐτοῦ) house. The manuscripts perhaps lean slightly toward the feminine reading (so Metzger 1994, 560), and the internal criterion whereby the harder reading is more likely to be original leads to a preference for the feminine, since scribes were more likely to alter the text toward a masculine name rather than toward a feminine name, whether intentionally or unintentionally. Thus, most English translations favor the feminine reading, "Nympha and the church in her house" (NRSV; cf. ESV, NIV, NASB), over the masculine reading, "Nymphas and the church which is in his house" (KJV). Nympha thereby emerges as a female hostess and leader in the earliest church, standing parallel to Philemon in Paul's characterization of her role (cf. Philem. 2).

Thus, in this simple instruction for greeting, we gain insight into the structure of the church in the first century. That Paul must identify a particular church in Laodicea according to Nympha indicates the presence there of additional churches that met in the homes of others. There were, then, multiple churches in Laodicea, each meeting in separate homes, in a time when a large home could host a gathering of about thirty to fifty people (Thompson, 2005, 107). But in the very next verse, Paul will speak of just one church in Laodicea that presumably consists of all these believers together. The multiple house churches together comprise the one church in Laodicea, and perhaps they all gathered together at times as one church. And Paul then appeals for partnership between the church in Laodicea and the church in Colossae, for all churches together comprise the one body of Christ, which is the one church (Col. 3:15; cf. 1:18, 24). Home churches together constitute one citywide church, and citywide churches together constitute the one universal church, which is the body of Christ.

4:16. The partnership between Colossae and Laodicea will be further strengthened through the sharing of apostolic letters with one another. Paul describes what the Colossians should do once they have finished reading this letter. The word Paul uses for "read" (ἀναγινώσκω) normally implies being read aloud, sometimes even in a public setting (BDAG, s.v. "ἀναγινώσκω" b, p. 60). When one person reads, therefore, it is often presumed that many people hear (e.g., 1 Thess. 5:27; Rev. 1:3; Josephus, *Ant.* 4.209). For example, in the first century, the Scriptures were read publicly in the synagogues every Sabbath (Luke 4:16; Acts 13:27; 15:21). Such public readings were necessary both because of the prohibitive cost of printing personal copies of writings and because of the low rates of literacy. Paul does not envision his letter being passed around to individual Christians, each of whom will read it privately. Instead, Paul envisions a gathering of the church in which his letter will be read aloud for all to hear and to discuss together, so that the church community works together to understand and to apply his letter.

Literacy Rates in the First Century

Estimates of literacy rates in the first century vary widely, due primarily to the fact that it is much easier for literate people to leave behind evidence of their literacy than it is for illiterate people to leave behind evidence of their illiteracy. Nevertheless, Gamble's estimate that on average, perhaps only 10 to 15 percent of Greco-Roman society was literate, and certainly less than 50 percent, serves as an important correction on our modern, Western assumption that most, if not all, people could read with some literacy (Gamble, 1995, 2–10; cf. Walton and Sandy, 2013, 111–20). By publicly reading Scripture, even illiterate Christians were nevertheless able to become conversant with biblical texts and letters such as Paul writes to the Colossians. Thus, a letter such as Colossians would have been read aloud in the assembly of the church, and perhaps read successively in multiple household assemblies (Meeks, 1983, 143).

Upon finishing this work of reading and hearing the letter, they are to "do" (ποιήσατε) whatever is necessary, so that two things will happen. First, they are to ensure that this letter which Paul has written to them in Colossae will also be read (ἵνα . . . ἀναγνωσθῇ) in the same way to the church in Laodicea. Paul does not outline the particular steps the Colossians should take to make this happen; instead, he simply delegates the responsibility to the Colossians and trusts them to create a plan and to implement it, so that the Laodiceans hear this letter. Second, Paul refers to an additional letter from Laodicea (τὴν ἐκ Λαοδικείας) and instructs the Colossians to ensure that this letter will also be read in Colossae (ἵνα . . . ἀναγνῶτε). This was apparently a letter written by Paul to the Laodiceans, but it has been lost to history.[2]

This exchanging of letters further establishes the collaboration between the two churches and also reveals the universal nature of Paul's teachings and the similarity between various churches. In other words, Paul knows the nature of various churches to be so alike, and the issues they face to be so similar, that the letters he writes to one church could easily be applied to another. These two churches, therefore, have an opportunity to work together to understand Paul's letters and to apply them to their own contexts, so that both churches will benefit by their partnership together.

4:17. As Paul draws ever closer to the end of his letter, he includes a very odd instruction, both because it seems completely detached from the rest of the letter and because it pertains to the relaying of a command to a particular person heretofore unmentioned in the letter. Paul commands the church to "speak" (εἴπατε) to a man named Archippus, and they are in turn to command Archippus to "see the ministry" (Βλέπε τὴν διακονίαν). The word "see" (βλέπω) here means to "direct one's attention to something" (BDAG, s.v. "βλέπω" 6, p. 179), and it may be translated "see to it" (NIV), or "take heed" (KJV), or "pay attention" (HCSB). In the same way that Paul told the Colossians to watch out (βλέπω) lest they should be taken captive (Col. 2:8), so also Archippus must devote his attention to this particular ministry.

Paul does not here identify the precise nature of Archippus's ministry, but both Archippus and the Colossians presumably know what Paul has in mind. The term Paul uses for "ministry" (διακονία) may refer generally to any act of service (e.g., 1 Cor. 12:5), but Paul regularly uses the word with reference to his own ministry of proclaiming the gospel (e.g., 2 Cor. 4:1; 5:18). Further, Paul calls himself a "minister" (διάκονος) of the gospel and of the church (Col. 1:23, 25; cf. Eph 3:7), and he labels his coworkers also as ministers, including Epaphras (Col. 1:7) and Tychicus (Col. 4:7). It stands to reason, therefore, that the ministry Archippus has "received from the Lord" (παρέλαβες ἐν κυρίῳ; cf. Acts 20:24) must be parallel to the ministry Paul himself received from the Lord and undertook together with his coworkers, namely laboring to proclaim the gospel and to shepherd the church toward maturity in Christ. Indeed, Archippus may have received this particular ministry within the auspices of Paul's mission and as a coworker of Paul.

But why should Paul have obligated the entire church to deliver this instruction to Archippus, thereby bringing Archippus's personal ministry work and struggles to the attention of the church at large? Paul states his purpose: "in

2 At least one ancient letter claimed to be Paul's letter to the Laodiceans, but it was rejected as a forgery by the early church. About this letter, the Muratorian Fragment (ca. A.D. 150–200) says, "There is said to be another letter in Paul's name to the Laodiceans, and another to the Alexandrines, [both] forged in accordance with Marcion's heresy, and many others which cannot be received into the catholic church, since it is not fitting that poison should be mixed with honey" (Bruce 1988, 160).

order that he might accomplish it" (ἵνα αὐτὴν πληροῖς). For Paul here, the end determines the means, so that he relays his exhortation to Archippus in the way most likely to result in Archippus getting the job done. Seen negatively, this amounts to a shrewd manipulative ploy by Paul to use the church in Colossae to squeeze compliance out of Archippus. But seen positively, Paul here calls upon the body of Christ to bear with Archippus and to extend the patient and merciful encouragement Archippus needs to live in obedience to the Lord Jesus. Archippus is much more likely to fulfill his ministry with an entire church standing behind him and alongside of him than if he stood alone, or with only the apostle Paul encouraging him from a distant prison cell.

Archippus, therefore, prepares the way for Paul's letter to Philemon, where Paul will put immense pressure upon Philemon to reconcile with Onesimus by having the letter read in the audience of the entire church. Philemon might easily feel unduly bullied by the apostle Paul were he the only one to receive such treatment, but before Philemon there is Archippus, and Archippus will set the example for how personal spiritual struggles are also the responsibility of the church and for how the church encourages individual members toward obedience and faithfulness to the Lord.

4:18. Paul concludes the letter with three brief statements. First, Paul gives a final "greeting" (ἀσπασμός) to the Colossians, this time from himself personally. This greeting is written "in my hand, *that is*, Paul's" (τῇ ἐμῇ χειρὶ Παύλου). The rest of the letter was apparently penned by Paul's secretary, known as an amanuensis in the ancient world. Paul used such a scribe for the penning of Romans (Rom. 16:22), and it is possible that Timothy helped compose this letter in a similar way (Col. 1:1). The entire letter remains a composition of Paul himself, for Paul names himself within the letter (e.g., Col. 1:23) and speaks in the first person throughout (e.g., Col. 1:24–2:5), and Paul attests to its authenticity by writing the final greeting himself, thereby effectively adding his signature to the letter.

Second, Paul implores the Colossians to "remember my chains" (μνημονεύετέ μου τῶν δεσμῶν). Paul offers no further commentary here regarding his imprisonment, but he has already indicated that Tychicus and Onesimus will be able to update the church on his situation (Col. 4:7–9). He here appeals to them to simply remember his suffering, but for Paul, remembering leads to prayer and prayer entails remembering (e.g., Eph. 1:16; Phil. 1:3; 1 Thess. 1:2; 2 Tim. 1:3; Philem. 4), so that by commanding the Colossians to remember his chains, Paul implicitly exhorts them also to pray for him.

Third and finally, Paul concludes the letter with a final wish of grace for the Colossians. His letter closes in the same way it began, but now Paul is more specific, speaking not of grace generically (χάρις; Col. 1:2) but specifically of *the* grace (ἡ χάρις). This is the grace of God revealed in the message of the gospel, even as Paul equated hearing the truth of the gospel with hearing and knowing the grace of God in truth (Col. 1:5–6). In other words, Paul wishes grace upon the Colossians not merely as a sentimental concept of goodwill but as the specific and objective grace of God made manifest in Christ. So when Paul wishes for this grace to be "with you" (μεθ' ὑμῶν)—with the Colossians—he wishes for the gospel of Christ to remain active among them, even as they hold fast to Christ and learn to walk faithfully in him.

THEOLOGICAL FOCUS

The exegetical idea (Paul closed his letter with a series of greetings and instructions that connected the Colossian church with the broader body of Christ for the purpose of mutual encouragement and regional partnership together in the global mission of proclaiming the gospel and strengthening believers in Christ) leads to this theological focus: When local churches partner together and strive to encourage one another and work together for the gospel, they are mutually strengthened and together they accomplish the mission of living and proclaiming the gospel.

At a recent gathering of pastoral leaders, one pastor lamented that the Bible does not provide a theology for how churches should network together. This particular pastor would do well to carefully read Colossians 4:7–18, for here we find a biblical foundation for just such a theology of interaction and partnership between local churches for the sake of the gospel. The Colossians could not possibly have read these verses and concluded that they were alone as a church and isolated from other groups of believers. Paul lays the groundwork for the believers in Colossae to be woven into the global body of Christ, and they will not only belong to this body, but they will also be active participants in the mutual exchange of encouragement, prayer, and admonition between believers and local churches in different communities. Others will strengthen them through this network and they will strengthen others. The body of Christ thereby becomes a global network of regional partnerships working together for the sake of Christ.

Consider all the ways Paul connects the Colossian church to other Christians and churches. He sends Tychicus to them, and Tychicus (together with Onesimus) will inform the Colossians about Paul's situation and will encourage their hearts. Paul also sends greetings from six of his coworkers, and in so doing he suggests his team is not so unlike the Colossians as they might think, since his team is comprised of both Jews and Gentiles. He instructs the Colossians to be prepared to welcome Mark, who will be coming to them presumably at Paul's behest and as part of Paul's ministry. He informs the Colossians about the ongoing labor of Epaphras, who prays earnestly for them even while he is away. Paul has made sure the Colossians are known to his cohort and are receiving proper encouragement, instruction, and prayer.

At the same time, Paul instructs the Colossians to build local relationships with other believers and churches in their region. They must in turn greet the churches and leaders (e.g., Nympha) in Laodicea, and they must work together with the Laodiceans to facilitate the exchanging of letters, so that both churches can be further instructed and edified. The Colossians will also be responsible to admonish and encourage Archippus toward the fulfillment of his ministry duties, and they must remember—and by extension, pray—for Paul in the midst of his sufferings. In these ways, the Colossians will be active participants in this global network, themselves encouraging other churches and supporting the ministry taking place around them.

No church is too small and no community is too insignificant for partnership in the universal church that is the body of Christ. Paul sees the value and necessity of churches that are grounded in their local community and at the same time are aware and active in regional and global ministry. When local churches network together, and when believers in one community find ways to support believers in another community, then the body of Christ takes on the synergistic character of a team where everyone contributes, everyone gains more than they give, and everyone wins. Lessons are learned. Labors are shared. Hearts are encouraged. Ministries are completed. Prayers are offered all around. And through this network of partnerships, a team is born that will continue to accomplish Paul's ambitious mission, the twofold mission of Colossians 1:23 and 1:28 to proclaim the gospel in all creation and to present all people mature in Christ.

PREACHING AND TEACHING STRATEGIES

Exegetical and Theological Synthesis

In the final section of this relatively brief but exceedingly rich letter, Paul offers news, greetings, and instructions to the regional church in the

Lychus Valley (Colossae, Laodicea, and Hierapolis). With a "who's-who roll call," Paul names eleven people (Tychicus, Onesimus, Aristarchus, Mark, Barnabas, Jesus [called Justus], Epaphras, Luke, Demas, Nympha, and Archippus). First-century epistles typically closed this way, but Paul used the greetings and final notes for more than convention. He augments theological themes in Colossians related to ecclesiology and the gospel. The roll call illustrates how Paul and his companions labored to preach the gospel to the whole world (1:23) with a view toward presenting every person mature in Christ (1:28). The roll call implies that those lofty goals were to be accomplished with teamwork, so Paul greeted, encouraged, prayed for, honored, and admonished the team. The roll call also implies that a single local church such as the group that met in Nympha's house was just one part of a larger body—*the* church in Colossae composed of multiple house churches, and *the* church in that geographical area. Indeed, the church was spreading throughout the world (1:18, 24). The fact that Paul concludes with an emphasis on gospel teamwork and the universal nature of the church implies that the recipients needed a final reminder, so the apostle taught even as he signed off. A theology of church cooperation in gospel ministry runs like a subterranean river under this pedestrian "roll call."

Preaching Idea

To spread the good news, work locally and partner globally.

Contemporary Connections

What does it mean?

What does it mean that to spread the good news, the church should work locally and partner globally? The preaching idea attempts to capture the subtle but striking depiction of the church in this passage and throughout the letter. First, by sending Epaphras and Onesimus to Colossae to share news (vv. 7–9), Paul shows us that the church is grounded in real people and real circumstances in a certain locale. Paul was in prison, but the gospel was still advancing, and that is news worth hearing. Similar stories of how the gospel is advancing in our towns and cities can show what the principle looks like today.

The next phrase of the preaching idea—partner globally or through regional partnerships—summarizes the section of greetings (vv. 10–15) where we see that any single church is part of a network of churches, and these churches should partner together. It also implies a regional partnership as Paul instructed the Colossians to have the letter read to the Laodiceans (and vice versa) and to exhort Archippus, one of their leaders. Perhaps a map could be used to describe the region of Colossae, Laodicea, and Hierapolis. A contemporary example of partnership could be the North Shore Gospel Partnership, a group of churches on Cape Ann (north of Boston) that have banded together for the advance of the gospel.

In today's global village, our "region" could even be considered the whole planet. This might be illustrated with the Lausanne Movement where denominations from around the world band together for world evangelization.

Is it true?

Can the church spread the good news by working locally and partnering globally? Your church's ministries that bless the local area could be mentioned—perhaps the church's food bank, give-and-take shop, or after-school children's program. Overviews of those ministries could be offered from the leaders, or perhaps featured on pre-service announcement slides.

The second phrase—partner globally—could also be demonstrated with examples of the church's cooperative efforts. If a church lacks such partnerships, then the second phrase could become a rallying cry for more cooperation.

Jesus's "high priestly prayer" supports the truth that the church should be unified with neighboring churches. The section below gives suggestions for how to upgrade partnership.

God commands us to partner with him in spreading good news and working to build his kingdom. Nadia Murad and Denis Mukwege have caught that vision. Nadia is an ISIS victim and Denis is a Congolese physician nicknamed "Doctor Miracle" for his pioneering work as a surgeon who has treated thousands of victims of sexual violence. In 2018, Nadia and Denis shared the Nobel Peace Prize. Dr. Mukwege urged fellow believers: "As long as our faith is defined by theory and not connected with practical realities, we shall not be able to fulfil the mission entrusted to us by Christ. If we are Christ's, we have no choice but to be alongside the weak, the wounded, the refugees and women suffering discrimination" (McLaughlin, 2019, 207).

Now what?

How might a church spread the good news by working locally and partnering globally? One way to work together locally is by implementing the "one another" commands of the New Testament. Gene Getz has identified thirteen one another commands (Getz, 1976), and all of them are implied in this passage. When a local assembly performs these activities, it helps them present an attractive picture of the good news. The commands can also be implemented between churches.

"One Another" Commands in the New Testament

- Build up one another.
- Members of one another.
- Be devoted to one another.
- Honor one another.
- Be of the same mind with one another.
- Accept one another.
- Admonish one another.
- Greet one another.
- Serve one another.
- Carry one another's burdens.
- Bear with one another.
- Submit to one another.
- Encourage one another.

Prayer might be organized to help the church spread good news, as seen in the example of Epaphras who worked hard at prayer (v. 12). We might establish prayer meetings for local and regional needs; make prayer requests known in the church's newsletter; pray for the "missionary of the week" during Sunday services; or pray for local, state, and national governments (1 Tim. 2:1–4).

To partner regionally and globally, here are ideas gleaned from the North Shore Gospel Partnership: have pastors make brief videos of greeting to be shared with all of the churches in the consortium; after the video is played, pray for that pastor and church; organize interchurch prayer meetings at places like local libraries and community centers; swap pulpits; band together in an evangelistic outreach; clean up a park together or do other community service; raise a special offering for a regional need such as illiteracy or seniors in financial straits; and sponsor lectures or trainings for your region.

Creativity in Presentation

To contrast a narrow focus with a global focus, perhaps a demonstration could be arranged. A volunteer, perhaps a young person, might be asked to view a large, magnificent photo or painting through a narrow aperture such as the cardboard tube inside a roll of wrapping paper. The volunteer should not be allowed to move his or her head to view the whole scene but must try to get a sense of the picture from the narrow focus. Then the tube can be removed so the volunteer can see the whole picture.

Behind every name in the "roll call" is a story, so perhaps stories of the history of your church. These might be presented as a short drama performed live or on video. Current members have their own stories too, and these could be shared during the church service, in written form or verbally in small groups. The sidebar gives an illustration of honoring unsung heroes, which is what Paul does in his roll call.

Honoring Unsung Heroes

At Princeton University, an artist set his eye on honoring unsung heroes. Mario Moore painted a series of ten portraits of the workers who help keep the campus working smoothly in areas such as maintenance, facilities, dining, grounds, and security. Usually this kind of honor is reserved for top-level donors, former presidents, or founding charter holders. But in an interview with CNN, Moore said he wanted to depict the workers "in a position of power." University spokesman Ben Chang said, "Mario's portraits capture beautifully the character and contributions of valued members of our campus community and bolster our broader efforts to . . . reflect the University's values and diversity."[3]

To enhance teamwork in the local fellowship, perhaps every attender could wear a name tag, and a few minutes in the service might be set aside for everyone to greet three people. One pastor asked his people to wear name tags on a Sunday when he served communion. As the congregation came forward to receive the bread and wine, he greeted each person by name.

Paul's instruction to have the letters read aloud (v. 16) might present the opportunity for a special Scripture reading. Perhaps the whole book could be presented orally by a gifted reader, or a "speaking choir" might read sections. While a reading is presented, visual aids could be displayed such as a telescopic photo of the cosmos: "By him all things were created" (1:16); or a map could be displayed when the text refers to Colossae, Laodicea, and Hierapolis. For other ideas on how to read Scripture creatively, see *Devote Yourself to the Public Reading of Scripture* (Arthurs, 2012).

In short, the sermon should emphasize the gospel and how it expands. To spread the good news, the church should work locally and partner globally.

- We can spread the good news by working locally (4:7–9).
- We can spread the good news by partnering globally (4:10–17).

3 Monica Haider, "Princeton University Is Hanging a Series of Portraits That Honor Its Blue-Collar Campus Workers," CNN, Jan. 6, 2020.

DISCUSSION QUESTIONS

1. Behind every name in this "roll call" is a story. Share some things you learned about the individuals in the list.

2. Name some ways our church/organization is "locally grounded." Name some ideas how we might do more of this.

3. Have you been a part of a cooperative venture between churches? Describe how you partnered regionally.

4. Why do you think Paul said so little about Demas?

5. How do you react to the designation that Christ-followers are "slaves" of the Lord?

Philemon 1–7

EXEGETICAL IDEA

Paul addressed his letter to Philemon and the church in Colossae, and rather than malign Philemon's character because of his conflict with Onesimus, he gave thanks to God for Philemon's genuine Christian faith and love that had benefited many Christians, including even Paul himself.

THEOLOGICAL FOCUS

Believers must discipline themselves to give thanks to God for one another and acknowledge the positive work of Christ in one another's lives, including and especially in the context of conflict that must be addressed.

PREACHING IDEA

When there's a conflict, what you share is better than what you win.

PREACHING POINTERS

Paul opened this letter, the most personal one he wrote, by greeting and blessing Philemon, a well-to-do patron of a house church. That kind of opening was typical in ancient letters, yet in the introduction of this letter to Philemon, Paul goes far beyond convention. The introduction cultivates the soil for the seeds to be planted later—a command and appeal to receive back the runaway slave, Onesimus. Paul cultivates the soil by emphasizing his interpersonal relationship with Philemon, full of genuine affection and sincere admiration. But cultivation was more than a rhetorical device designed to put Philemon in a receptive state of mind, because Paul meant every word.

Thus, Paul sets a good model for us today when dealing with conflict. At a tense board meeting or when the family can't get along or when the congregation is divided, before planting seeds of exhortation, cultivate the soil with prayer, thanks, and encouragement. Before trying to persuade someone, begin by affirming them. Unfortunately, today persuasion is often carried on with rancor. Accusations, overstatement, sarcasm, and one-sided arguments may win applause from those who already agree with our position, but those tactics do nothing to persuade skeptics or heal divisions. A better way, the one modeled by Philemon 1–7, is to begin with humility, prayer, thanks, and praise. Conflict is unavoidable in the world and in the church, so to bind together what has come loose. Let us first remember the tie that binds. When there's a conflict, what you share is better than what you win.

PAUL'S RELATIONSHIP TO PHILEMON (1–7)

LITERARY STUCTURE AND THEMES (1–7)

In this opening section of his letter to Philemon, Paul generally follows his customary pattern of identifying the letter's authors and recipients (Philem. 1–2), extending a greeting of grace and peace (Philem. 3), and articulating a prayer of thanksgiving for his audience (Philem. 4–7). All of these themes appear in various forms in Paul's other letters, not least his letter to the Colossians (Col. 1:1–8; cf. 1 Cor. 1:1–9; Phil. 1:1–8; 1 Thess. 1:1–10; etc.). However, this opening section of the letter to Philemon stands apart because of its intensely personal nature as Paul writes to one individual, Philemon, with whom Paul shares a meaningful relationship as a brother (Philem. 7). The positive tone of this letter opening prepares the way for the dramatic appeal Paul will make on behalf of Onesimus.

- ***The Letter Opening (1–3)***
- ***Paul Prays for Philemon (4–6)***
- ***Paul Affirms Philemon (7)***

EXPOSITION (1–7)

The warmth of Paul's opening greeting to Philemon sets the stage for the somber appeal Paul will make on behalf of Onesimus. This letter has perhaps the most vivid historical context of all Paul's writings, for the letter centers upon the unresolved conflict between Onesimus and Philemon. We know from the letter to the Colossians that Paul has already sent Onesimus back to Philemon (Col. 4:9), and we know from the letter to Philemon that Paul intended for this letter to be read in the context of the gathered church (Philem. 2), and therefore we conclude that Paul envisioned Philemon hearing this letter in the presence of his church family and of Onesimus himself, with whom Philemon has not yet reconciled. Paul will make his appeal soon enough, but first, in this opening section of the letter, Paul gives thanks for Philemon and affirms Philemon for the sincerity of his faith and the encouragement he has given to other saints, including even Paul himself. Paul begins by giving thanks to God for Philemon, and thereby he models what should be the attitude of all Christians toward one another, where thankfulness for the other precedes any necessary hard conversations.

The Letter Opening (1–3)

The letter opening introduces Paul and Timothy as the authors; it addresses Philemon and his Christian cohort as the audience; and it expresses a blessing of grace and peace.

1. As per his custom, and in accordance with the letter-writing customs of his day, Paul opens this letter by identifying himself as the author. Strangely, however, Paul also begins by identifying himself as a "prisoner of Christ Jesus" (δέσμιος Χριστοῦ Ἰησοῦ). Though he does on occasion make similar mention of his imprisonment in his other letters (e.g., Eph. 3:1; 4:1; 2 Tim. 1:8), this is the only time he begins with such a self-identification. He thereby postures himself in a strikingly humble manner, setting aside whatever honor and authority belong to him as an apostle—and he typically opens his letters by identifying as an apostle (e.g., Rom. 1:1; 1 Cor. 1:1; 1 Cor. 1:1; Gal. 1:1; Col. 1:1; etc.)—in favor of his humble and incarcerated status as a prisoner. We can only speculate as to why Paul identifies himself in this way, but it seems to be consistent with what will come later in the letter, when he will set aside his right to command Philemon and will instead appeal to him (Philem. 8–9). Further, Paul's imprisonment highlights upfront the contrary position of the Roman culture and specifically the Roman legal system toward Christ and the gospel. Following Christ has placed Paul at odds with the legal system, and by implication, for Philemon to follow the legal system in how he manages Onesimus will place him at odds with Christ and the gospel.[1]

Paul also names his frequent coauthor, Timothy, who receives the simple description "the brother" (ὁ ἀδελφὸς). This recites precisely the way in which Paul introduced Timothy in the opening verse of Colossians, and it reflects the endearment with which Paul sometimes describes his coworkers (e.g. 1 Cor. 1:1; 2 Cor. 1:1; Eph. 6:21; Col. 4:7, 9). As in Colossians 1:1 (see comments there), the mention of Timothy likely indicates the role Timothy plays as a secretary or amanuensis who helps compose the letter, but the entire letter is written in the first person singular from the perspective of Paul, so that it is Paul speaking through the letter, and he is properly referred to as its author.

Paul next identifies the intended recipients of his letter. He begins with Philemon, whom he characterizes with two adjectives, first as "the beloved" (τῷ ἀγαπητῷ) and second as "our fellow worker" (συνεργῷ ἡμῶν). These are adjectives Paul uses for those closest to him. Those beloved to Paul include Epaenetus (Rom. 16:5), Ampliatus (Rom. 16:8), Stachys (Rom. 16:9), Persis (Rom. 16:12), Timothy (1 Cor. 4:17; 2 Tim. 1:2), Tychicus (Eph. 6:21; Col. 4:7), Epaphras (Col. 1:7), Onesimus (Col. 4:9), and Luke (Col. 4:14). Those who are coworkers of Paul include Mark, Aristarchus, Demas, and Luke (Philem. 24; cf. Col. 4:10–11), as well as Prisca and Aquila (Rom. 16:3), Urbanus (Rom. 16:9), Timothy (Rom. 16:21; 1 Thess. 3:2), Titus (2 Cor. 8:23), Epaphroditus (Phil. 2:25), and Clement (Phil. 4:3). Thus, by calling Philemon beloved and our fellow worker, Paul incorporates Philemon within the elite company of his cohort who are dear to him and work alongside him. In short, Paul honors Philemon.

2. But the letter is not to Philemon alone, for Paul addresses additional recipients. He next mentions Apphia, who is a "sister" in Christ (τῇ ἀδελφῇ), but about this woman we receive no further information. Her mention by name sets her apart from the other members of the church in Colossae that meets in Philemon's house, and this may suggest that she was also a member of Philemon's own household, perhaps as a relative of Philemon (e.g., mother, sister, etc.), or more specifically, as the wife of Philemon (BDAG, s.v. "Ἀπφία," p. 126). Lightfoot determines it to be a "safe inference" that Apphia is Philemon's wife, and thus he comments about her, "Equally with her husband she had been aggrieved by the misconduct of their slave Onesimus, and equally with him she might interest herself in the penitent's future well-being" (Lightfoot, 1981, 308). This would certainly explain why Paul names her personally among the letter's recipients.

Next Paul mentions Archippus, who is no doubt the same Archippus who needed to be implored to complete the ministry duty assigned to him at the end of Colossians (Col. 4:17). Now, in the beginning of the letter to Philemon, Paul addresses this same Archippus as the "fellow soldier" (συστρατιώτης). This is an unusual Pauline term drawn from a military context, and only Epaphroditus receives the same description elsewhere in Paul's letters (Phil. 2:25). Such a description may point narrowly to the particular challenges Archippus

1 In addition, Witherington suggests Paul's up-front declaration of his imprisonment is an "effective tactic" for generating sympathy for himself, while Moule calls this "skillful diplomacy" designed "to enforce his appeal for what must seem a trifling sacrifice in comparison with imprisonment" (Witherington III, 2007, 53; Moule 1962, 140).

faces in his own ministry duty, perhaps even a metaphorical or spiritual battle that must be fought, or it may point more broadly to the labors and struggles of Paul's cohort, and perhaps of all Christians, as they strive to faithfully serve Christ in the midst of the very same opposition that has landed Paul in prison. Thus, Paul can exhort all Christians to dress themselves for the same kind of spiritual battle in which he himself engages (Eph. 6:10–17; cf. 2 Cor. 10:1–6). Either way, Paul sees Archippus as a spiritual soldier battling alongside Paul.

Finally, Paul addresses the letter "to the church according to your house" (τῇ κατ' οἶκόν σου ἐκκλησίᾳ). The structure here mirrors Colossians 4:15, where Paul identified a church in Laodicea according to the particular home in which the church met, which in that case belonged to Nympha. When Paul speaks here of the church that meets in your house, the second person pronoun "your" (σου) refers not to the most recent antecedent, who would be Archippus, but "to the addressee named first as the principal recipient of the letter," who is Philemon (Harris, 2010, 208). This church is identified by Philemon's home as the place where they gather. We thereby learn about Philemon that he is a person of relatively substantial economic means, since he owns a home suitable for hosting such a gathering. At the same time, his willingness to host reflects his own Christian maturity, for he is generous with his home, willing to identify himself publicly with the Christian movement, and in all likelihood serving in a role of leadership within the church.

Paul's address here to the entire church stands in stark contrast to most of the rest of the letter, where he will use the singular second person to speak directly to Philemon (Philem. 4–22a). Further, the matter at hand seems to be deeply personal and, in some ways, even private for Philemon and Onesimus. We would presume their conflict to be in no way the business of the entire church, but Paul makes it the business of the church by addressing the letter not only to Philemon, but also to the entire congregation. He makes this a public letter to be read to Philemon within the hearing of his church family who are gathered in his own home.

On one level, this seems to be a shameless manipulative ploy by Paul, for he backs Philemon into a corner where should Philemon choose to ignore Paul's appeal, or even hesitate in honoring Paul's appeal, he will immediately lose honor within his own church family, who are surely watching with eager anticipation for how he will respond. But, if we are more charitable toward Paul, then we can see how Paul intends to make this personal issue into an issue for the entire church, so that the resources of the entire congregation can be leveraged toward the fulfilment of Paul's appeal. It will take the collective wisdom of the congregation, and the love and grace of each Christian together, to walk with Philemon toward embracing and enacting the radical nature of Paul's appeal. Discipleship is never an individual endeavor—it always requires the community working together for the obedience of each member—and thus Philemon's personal situation becomes an opportunity for spiritual growth throughout the entire congregation.

3. Paul offers a blessing for "grace" (χάρις) to be given to "you" (note the plural ὑμῖν here, referring to the entire church), along with "peace" (εἰρήνη) from God our Father and the Lord Jesus Christ. Paul customarily opens his letters with such a blessing, so that we might dismiss it as mere routine, but grace and peace are especially pertinent to the matter at hand, for Philemon must show grace to Onesimus in order to restore peace within the church and Philemon's household. Though grace and peace do not appear again within the letter, save for a closing mention of grace in the benediction (Philem. 25), the theological principles they represent undergird the entirety of Paul's instructions to Philemon. Philemon will need an extraordinary measure of grace if he is to welcome Onesimus in the manner Paul prescribes, and Paul desires peace as the necessary outcome for this situation, both peace between Philemon and Onesimus personally and also peace throughout the entire church community, so that the peace of Christ truly reigns in all of their hearts and produces unity among them (cf. Col. 3:15).

Paul Prays for Philemon (4–6)

Paul articulates his prayer for Philemon, including his thanksgiving for Philemon's genuine faith and his prayer for Philemon's continual growth in Christ.

4. Paul retains his customary pattern of beginning the letter with an expression of thanksgiving and prayer for his recipient(s). On this occasion, his prayer is intensely personal, as Paul uses the first person singular "I pray" (εὐχαριστῶ) and directs his prayer "to my God" (τῷ θεῷ μου). This personalized way of defining a relationship with God, so that God is *my* God, echoes Jesus's prayer from the cross, "My God, my God, why have you forsaken me?" (Mark 15:34), which is itself a reflection of the type of prayer found in the Psalms (e.g., Ps. 22:1; 25:1; etc.; cf. Moo, 2008, 385). This form of prayer, seen occasionally elsewhere in Paul (e.g., Rom. 1:8; 1 Cor. 1:4; Phil. 1:3), provides for us a small window into how Paul perceives his own relationship with God. For Paul, God is not far away, impersonal, and detached from the affairs of life, but rather God is close at hand, relational, and deeply interested, so that Paul can give thanks to him with confidence that he is *my* God.

Paul's Prayer Pattern

Paul's thanksgiving and pray for Philemon are similar to but shorter than his thanksgiving and prayer for the Colossians. However, in Philemon, Paul's prayer is more personal, for he prays in the first person singular ("I") rather than the plural ("we").

Philemon 4–5	Colossians 1:3–4
[4]When I remember you in my prayers, I always thank my God [5]because I hear of your love for all the saints and your faith toward the Lord Jesus.	[3]In our prayers for you we always thank God, the Father of our Lord Jesus Christ, [4]for we have heard of your faith in Christ Jesus and of the love that you have for all the saints.

Such thanksgiving is a constant practice of Paul's, as he "always" (πάντοτε) gives thanks for Philemon "in my prayers" (ἐπὶ τῶν προσευχῶν μου), indicating that in Paul's estimation, Philemon has the kind of Christian character that always merits thanksgiving. Paul gives thanks "by making" (ποιούμενος; part. of means) what can be translated as either "remembrance" or "mention" (BDAG, s.v. "μνεία," p. 654) of Philemon. Some English versions translate the term (μνεία) as "when I remember you" (ESV; cf. NIV, NRSV), suggesting that Paul's prayers for Philemon arise spontaneously whenever Philemon comes to mind, while others translate it "when I mention you" (HCSB; cf. KJV's "making mention of thee"), suggesting that Paul's prayers are organized, so that Paul disciplines himself to regularly mention Philemon in prayer. In either case, Paul's point stands, which is that he is constantly finding himself giving thanks for Philemon as he prays.

This thanksgiving establishes Paul's demeanor toward Philemon and his overall assessment of Philemon's character. Paul has high esteem for Philemon and deems Philemon to be worthy of constant thanksgiving, and this in turn establishes how Paul will approach Philemon in this letter. Though Paul will address the complicated problem of Onesimus, and though Paul will lean upon Philemon to undertake a path of reconciliation that Philemon might not have otherwise taken, Paul nevertheless regards Philemon as a sincere believer worthy of thanksgiving, and he approaches Philemon as such. His statement of thanksgiving here is not empty flattery intended to warm Philemon before assailing him with his shortcomings; rather, Paul is sincerely thankful for Philemon and he views whatever shortcomings Philemon might have as secondary to his overall faith and good standing as a Christian.

5. Paul gives thanks "because he has heard" (ἀκούω; causal part.) about Philemon's love and faith. The Greek word order here has created some variation in translations, for Paul gives two nouns, "love" (ἀγάπη) and "faith" (πίστις), followed by their two objects, "toward the Lord Jesus" (πρὸς τὸν κύριον Ἰησοῦν) and "for all the saints" (εἰς πάντας τοὺς ἁγίους). Some translations strictly adhere to this word order (e.g., HCSB's "because I hear of your love and faith toward the Lord Jesus and for all the saints"; cf. ESV, KJV), but the suggestion that faith (πίστις) could be directed toward the saints as well as to the Lord Jesus is otherwise unknown to Paul. It is better to interpret Paul's phrase here in light of the parallel text in Colossians 1:4, which clearly differentiates the objects of faith and love as follows: "we have heard of your faith in Christ Jesus and of the love that you have for all the saints" (NRSV, ESV). Thus, Paul's commendation of Philemon is best viewed as a chiasm that would be translated, "because I hear of your love for all the saints and your faith toward the Lord Jesus" (NRSV; cf. NIV, NLT).

Chiasm

In a chiastic structure, a sequence of themes is presented and then repeated in reverse order. In verse 5, the chiastic structure works as follows:

A Your love
    B your faith
    B′ toward the Lord Jesus
A′ for all the saints

Thus, the report Paul has heard about Philemon first speaks to "the love" (τὴν ἀγάπην) that Philemon has "for all the saints" (εἰς πάντας τοὺς ἁγίους), where "saints" refers broadly to all the members of the body of Christ (e.g., Col. 1:2). Philemon's love goes beyond mere sentimentality to tangible acts of love that have brought joy and comfort to Paul and refreshment to other Christians (Philem. 7), not least through his hospitality in hosting the church (Philem. 2) and potentially Paul himself (Philem. 22), as well as his partnership in Paul's ministry (Philem. 17). Second, the report regarding Philemon highlights "the faith" (τὴν πίστιν) of Philemon "toward the Lord Jesus" (πρὸς τὸν κύριον Ἰησοῦν). This "faith" (πίστις) may mean either "trust" or "faithfulness" (BDAG, s.v. "πίστις" 1a, 2, p. 818)—or even "allegiance" (Bates, 2017)—and it may therefore refer to either Philemon's sincere trust in the Lord Jesus or his faithfulness in following and serving the Lord Jesus. The two are interconnected, since faithfulness arises out of sincere faith, but the commendation here may refer to the tangible expressions of faith that parallel his tangible expressions of love, and thus Paul may especially have Philemon's faithfulness in view.

But who or what was the source of Paul's information about Philemon's love and faith? Paul may have heard these things from Epaphras, who brought a report to Paul about the Colossian church more broadly (Col. 1:8) and still remains with Paul (Philem. 23). Or alternatively, we could speculate that Paul has gleaned this report from Onesimus himself, since we know that Onesimus has recently traveled from Philemon to Paul. If, and to whatever degree, this report has come from Onesimus, it speaks to the character of Onesimus, that he is able to speak highly of his master's love and faith, even while he is at odds with him and perhaps even experiencing the worst of his master's anger. This also speaks highly of Philemon's character, that even in the midst of this present conflict, his love and faith remain known and reportable.

The Complexity of Philemon

Philemon is a complicated fellow. Our modern antipathy to slavery could easily lead us to simplify Philemon's character and to cast him as entirely evil, for surely only a thoroughly wicked person could bring themselves to own another person as a slave. Further, Philemon has possibly mistreated Onesimus, or at the very least left Onesimus feeling as if he has no choice but to run away from Philemon's household. Paul, however, sees complexity in Philemon's nature. On the one hand, Paul will directly instruct Philemon in how he must welcome Onesimus in a new way (Philem. 16–17), suggesting Paul lacks confidence that Philemon would otherwise take this proper course of Christian action. But on the other hand, Paul gives genuine thanks for Philemon on the basis of his demonstrated Christian character, namely his faith in Christ and his love for the saints (Philem. 5). Both are true of Philemon at the same time. He is a genuine believer with demonstrated Christian faithfulness, and he has fallen short to some measure in how he has treated Onesimus. Therefore, Paul can simultaneously affirm and correct Philemon, and it is on the basis of Philemon's Christian character that Paul will send Onesimus back to Philemon without first verifying how Philemon intends to receive him, for Paul has confidence that Philemon will yet again prove faithful to Christ by his love for the saints, this time the saint Onesimus.

6. Paul's next statement is flooded with lexical and grammatical challenges that make it a notoriously difficult verse to translate and interpret. The verse begins with a conjunction (ὅπως) that in this case replaces the infinitive that would often follow a verb of asking (BDAG, s.v. "ὅπως" 2b, p. 718). It can therefore be translated "that" and it looks back to Paul's prayers in verse 4 and gives the content of his prayers for Philemon. Thus, the single word "that" (ὅπως) is often translated in light of Paul's prayers as "*I pray* that" (e.g., NIV, ESV, NRSV, HCSB).

TRANSLATION ANALYSIS: Modern English translations vary widely in how they translate Philemon 6.
ESV: "and I pray that the sharing of your faith may become effective for the full knowledge of every good thing that is in us for the sake of Christ."
HCSB: "I pray that your participation in the faith may become effective through knowing every good thing that is in us for the glory of Christ."
NIV: "I pray that your partnership with us in the faith may be effective in deepening your understanding of every good thing we share for the sake of Christ."
NRSV: "I pray that the sharing of your faith may become effective when you perceive all the good that we may do for Christ."
KJV: "that the communication of thy faith may become effectual by the acknowledging of every good thing which is in you in Christ Jesus."

The content of Paul's prayer in verse 6 focuses on the *koinōnia* (κοινωνία) of Philemon's faith. This Greek word *koinōnia* abounds with layers of rich meaning that cannot be fully encapsulated in a single English word. The basic idea is of a "close association involving mutual interests and sharing," so that it can be translated "association, communion, fellowship" or "participation, sharing" (BDAG, s.v. "κοινωνία" 1, 4, p. 552–53). Wright properly surmises that these English words fall short because they lack the central idea of mutuality. Thus, *koinōnia* is not "fellowship," which often refers merely to enjoying one another's company, nor is it "sharing," which is limited to giving and receiving, nor is it even "interchange," which can be mechanical. Instead, the key idea of *koinōnia* is the "mutual participation" that arises from or is proper to Philemon's faith ("your faith"; τῆς πίστεώς σου), and this mutual participation signifies that "in Christ, Christians not only belong to one another but actually become mutually identified" (Wright, 1986, 175–76).[2] Paul's prayer, therefore, draws attention again to the corporate nature of Philemon's faith, where his identity in Christ is inseparable from his identity as a member of the body of Christ, the very church that meets in his house. He shares in mutual participation with Christ along with the rest of the people of Christ.

It is the *koinōnia*, or mutual participation, which Paul prays might become "effective" (ἐνεργής). Here is the one place where most English translations agree, in rendering the term "effective," and it means to have the capability or even power to accomplish an intended purpose (e.g., 1 Cor. 16:9). More specifically, Paul prays for the *koinōnia* to become effective "in knowledge" (ἐν ἐπιγνώσει). The preposition "in" (ἐν) can actually have a variety of meanings depending on its context, and here it has been translated in virtually every conceivable way, as expressing purpose ("for"; ESV), agency ("through"; HCSB; also "by"; KJV), location or sphere ("in"; NIV), and temporal correlation ("when"; NRSV). Our interpretation here must be guided by the context, and it hinges upon whether Paul presumes this knowledge to be the prerequisite for *koinōnia* becoming effective or the consequence of *koinōnia* being effective. In other words, must knowledge come first as the sphere ("in"), agent ("through, by"), or correlative ("when") for *koinōnia* to become effective, or does Paul intend for *koinōnia* to become effective first and to then bring about knowledge ("for")? The latter option ("for") prevails when we consider the knowledge Paul here describes.

The word "knowledge" (ἐπίγνωσις) often refers not only to mental awareness that someone or something exists but to knowing that person or thing through a personal experience or relationship with them; it refers to "both understanding and experience" (Harris, 2010, 217). Here, the object of this knowledge is "every good thing" (παντὸς ἀγαθοῦ) that is present "among us" (ἐν ἡμῖν), that is, among the community of believers, and "in Christ" (εἰς Χριστόν), that is, by union with Christ.[3] This entire phrase drips with optimism and idealism, as Paul aspires for believers to personally experience the full measure of all the good things Christ has in store for us. But these good things can only be realized through the community of believers, since they are "among us" (ἐν ἡμῖν), and therefore experiencing these good things requires *koinōnia*. Thus, Paul prays for *koinōnia* to become effective for Philemon with the goal or purpose that he will then realize the ideal by personally knowing or experiencing every good thing in Christ.

When we put all of these pieces together, we can paraphrase verse 6 as follows: Paul prays for Philemon that his mutual participation with

---

2 Dunn describes Paul's idea of *koinōnia* as "the subjective experience of a faith shared in common," and similarly, Moo says about *koinōnia*, "When people believe in Christ, they become identified with one another in an intimate association and incur both the benefits and responsibilities of that communion" (Dunn, 1996, 318–19; Moo, 2008, 392).

3 Paul's language of "every good thing" (παντὸς ἀγαθοῦ) recalls Colossians, where the word "every" (πᾶς) was used frequently to refer to the supremacy and sufficiency of Christ (e.g., Col. 1:15–20). Further, Paul used the language of union with Christ to describe how believers have been filled in Christ, namely by having died with Christ and been raised to new life with Christ (Col. 2:10–13). Believers lack nothing by their union with the supreme Christ, and thereby they have received every spiritual blessing in him (Eph. 1:3).

other believers through their shared faith in Christ will become fully effective, in order that they might then experience the full measure of all the good things that belong to the community of believers through their union with Christ.

The implications of this prayer reverberate throughout the letter as Paul appeals to Philemon that he would reconcile with Onesimus and welcome Onesimus as a brother in Christ (Philem. 16–17). This reconciliation serves as a tangible way in which the *koinōnia* of faith must be fully effective, as Philemon and Onesimus must come together in mutual participation in their faith in Christ. And this reconciliation will have direct benefits for Philemon, and indeed for the entire church community, for through it they will experience the full measure of the good things Christ has on offer for them, which would here include such things as grace, mercy, forgiveness, and reconciliation, and even the blessing of each other as brothers in Christ. In other words, should Philemon *not* reconcile with Onesimus, then *koinōnia* would not be fully effective and Philemon—as well as Onesimus and the entire church in his house—would not have a full experience of Christ's goodness, namely his mercy that leads to reconciliation. No wonder Paul prays for their *koinōnia* to be effective, and likewise we ought to pursue the same in the church today.

Paul Affirms Philemon (7)

Paul personally attests to how Philemon's character and conduct have positively impacted him, as he has received great joy and encouragement because of Philemon's efforts to strengthen other believers.

7. Here Paul continues to adulate Philemon's character, which has itself provided the grounds (γάρ) for Paul's thanksgiving. This sentence begins with the word "joy" (χαρά), which has been placed at the beginning of the sentence for the sake of emphasis. This joy belongs to Paul in abounding measure, so that he has "much joy" (χαρὰν . . . πολλήν). And in addition to this joy, Paul also has "encouragement" (παράκλησις). Paul is providing personal attestation to the genuine but overflowing sentiment of his own heart, whereby he has experienced abounding joy and an uplifted spirit.

He has received this joy and encouragement "by your love" (ἐπὶ τῇ ἀγάπῃ σου), by which he means Philemon's love. He has already mentioned the love Philemon has for all the saints (Philem. 5), but here Paul explains that he is encouraged specifically "because" (ὅτι) of the positive impact Philemon's love has had upon the saints. He "has refreshed" (ἀναπέπαυται) the saints, a term that refers to giving someone rest from their toil (BDAG, s.v. "ἀναπαύω" 1, p. 69).[4] In a military context, it could be used to describe the rest an army would take in the midst of a march (Wright, 1986, 178). Philemon has provided such refreshment to the "inward parts" or "entrails" (BDAG, s.v. "σπλάγχνον" 1, p. 938) of the saints. The inner guts of a person was a metaphorical way of referring to the emotional center of a person, in much the same way we might today speak of the heart. Here it "refers to the whole person (by synecdoche) as having experienced refreshment at the deepest emotional level" (Harris, 2010, 219). Paul is commending Philemon, for it is "through you" (διὰ σοῦ)—through Philemon—that the saints themselves have been truly and internally refreshed.

This compliment speaks to the core of Philemon's character. Paul recognizes the influence of Philemon with regard not only to the church in his own house, as he referred to his local community of saints in verse 2, but with regard to all the saints

4 The perfect "has refreshed" (ἀναπέπαυται) may refer to a one-time act (Lohse, 1971, 195) or it may reflect the ongoing impact of his ministry (Moo, 2008, 396). Most likely, the perfect "indicates some past ministry of Philemon which had enduring results" (Dunn, 1996, 321; cf. 2 Cor. 7:13).

more broadly (as in verse 5).[5] Paul does not here detail the specific acts of love which Philemon has done for these saints, but in some way, perhaps through Philemon's presence, or his generosity, or some other form of loving favor, he has had a positive impact on Christians beyond Colossae. He has a reputation for acting in such a way that causes other believers to grow in their faith and the church to be strengthened. In this way, Philemon also has given great joy and encouragement to Paul, not necessarily because Philemon has acted directly in Paul's behalf, but because Philemon has loved and refreshed those whom Paul loves and desires to see refreshed, namely the saints. There is no greater joy for a minister such as Paul than to see the Christians under his charge genuinely refreshed in their spirits.

This verse, therefore, overflows with a circle of genuine emotion. Philemon loves the saints, and thereby the saints have been refreshed in their inner being, and thereby Paul has received great joy and encouragement, and therefore Paul now gives thanks for Philemon. Paul attributes this circle of sentiment and blessing to Philemon's love, where it all began. This circle explains why Paul can himself refer to Philemon in the end of this verse with a term of endearment, as "brother" (ἀδελφέ). And this circle provides the foundation for Paul's appeal in the letter, where Paul will lean upon Philemon to again act with love toward a particular saint, Onesimus, so that Paul's own heart will be refreshed (Philem. 20).

THEOLOGICAL FOCUS

The exegetical idea (Paul addressed his letter to Philemon and the church in Colossae, and rather than malign Philemon's character because of his conflict with Onesimus, he gave thanks to God for Philemon's genuine Christian faith and love that had benefited many Christians, including even Paul himself) leads to this theological focus: Believers must discipline themselves to give thanks to God for one another and acknowledge the positive work of Christ in one another's lives, including and especially in the context of conflict that must be addressed.

Paul's introductory verses in this letter give no indication of the letter's actual purpose. Here we find no mention of Onesimus and no hint of conflict that needs to be resolved, and this is surely intentional on the part of Paul. He begins with Christian greetings and sincere thanksgiving for Philemon, including honest appreciation for Philemon's Christian character up to this point. Paul sets an example for us in how we should engage our Christian brothers and sisters when we experience conflict with them. Paul easily could have believed the worst about Philemon, could have assigned to Philemon the worst of all possible motives, and could have reinterpreted Philemon's entire character according to this conflict with Onesimus. Yet Paul begins the letter by staunchly refusing to do any such thing. Instead, he begins with thanksgiving, and by placing this thanksgiving early in a letter intended to be read in the midst of the entire church, with even Onesimus present, Paul guides the church to also acknowledge Philemon's reputation and to give thanks for his outstanding faith in Christ and love for the saints.

Such thanksgiving is precisely what Paul demonstrates in his letter to Philemon. First and foremost, Paul gives thanks for who

5 Dunn observes that Paul does not address the Christians in Colossae as "saints" (ἅγιοι), suggesting his reference to saints here refers to Christians beyond Colossae. Perhaps Philemon's partnership in ministry with Paul has led Philemon to travel and to serve in other regions, so that the impact of his love has been felt far beyond the church that now meets in his home (Dunn, 1996, 320–21).

Philemon actually is as his brother in Christ rather than complaining and accusing him for not being the person Paul envisions he ought to be. This orients Paul's entire letter around the grace of God toward Philemon rather than around Paul's disappointment with Philemon. This thanksgiving will also guide the manner in which Paul will address Philemon's conduct later in this letter. Thanksgiving tempers Paul's demeanor, his attitude, and his reaction, so that Paul does not approach Philemon in a spirit of disappointment and disillusionment, let alone anger, as if Philemon's character is severely and fatally flawed. Instead, Paul approaches Philemon with thanksgiving as a brother in Christ, who sincerely trusts Christ and loves the church, who stands together with Paul under the grace of God, and who is worthy of affirmation even as he needs gentle correction in this particular situation.

Thanksgiving, therefore, is foundational and essential to the health of Christian community, as evidenced by Paul's repeated appeal to the Colossians to be thankful (Col. 1:12; 2:7; 3:15, 16, 17). Dietrich Bonhoeffer suggests believers should give thanks daily for the community in which God has placed them, so that believers ought to enter into the community "not as demanders but as thankful recipients" (Bonhoeffer, 1954, 28). Our brothers and sisters in Christ are gifts to us from God, and we ought to receive God's gifts with thankfulness. Especially when we are faced with weakness and sin in our brothers and sisters in Christ, we must discipline ourselves to always give thanks for them, lest we should become complainers and accusers rather than thankful participants together (*koinōnia*!) with them in the grace of God.

Dietrich Bonhoeffer on Giving Thanks for One Another

In his *Life Together*, Dietrich Bonhoeffer sets forth the importance of giving thanks for our brothers and sisters in the community of Christ (Bonhoeffer, 1954, 26–30). He warns against the temptation to enter into the community with idealistic visions of what the community ought to be, for the community will inevitably fall short of such visions and leave the visionary thinker disappointed, disillusioned, and complaining against God and men. This shortfall affects pastors and leaders as much as church members, who may take upon themselves the role of the accuser of their congregation before God and men, if they become disillusioned complainers.

Instead of complaining and accusing one another, Bonhoeffer suggests we should give thanks for one another as gifts that God has given to us by his grace. We should give thanks for the reality of what God has actually given us in one another rather than becoming disillusioned because of our unmet ideals regarding the kind of people we think God should have given to us. When we exercise such thanksgiving, then it also infuses how we approach sin in one another's lives, for now the reality of our brother's sin is itself evidence that we all live under the forgiveness of God together, and it is a reminder of God's grace to us all. So we must be grateful for our brothers not only in their strength but also in their weakness, because their weakness serves as testimony of God's grace and forgiveness.

"Because God has already laid the only foundation of our fellowship, because God has bound us together in one body with other Christians in Jesus Christ, long before we entered into common life with them, we enter into that common life not as demanders but as thankful recipients. We thank God for what He has done for us. We thank God for giving us brethren who live by His call, by His forgiveness and His promise. We do not complain of what God does not give us; we rather thank God for what He does give us daily. And is not what has been given us enough: brothers, who will go on living with us through sin and need under the blessing of His grace? Is the divine gift of Christian fellowship anything less than this, any day, even the most difficult and distressing day? Even when sin and misunderstanding burden the communal life, is not the sinning brother still a brother, with whom I, too, stand under the Word of Christ? Will not his sin be a constant occasion for me to give thanks that both of us may live in the forgiving love of God in Jesus Christ? Thus, the very hour of disillusionment with my brother becomes incomparably salutary, because it so thoroughly teaches me that neither of us can ever live by our own words and deeds, but only by that one Word and Deed which really binds us together—the forgiveness of sins in Jesus Christ. When the morning mists of dreams vanish, then dawns the bright day of Christian fellowship" (Bonhoeffer, 1954, 28–29).

PREACHING AND TEACHING STRATEGIES

Exegetical and Theological Synthesis

Using the conventional form of a first-century epistle, yet also transforming that form for pastoral concerns, Paul greets Philemon, Apphia (probably Philemon's wife), Archippus (Paul's "fellow-soldier," v. 1), and the whole church that met in Philemon's house (v. 2). Philemon was probably well-to-do and had a house large enough to serve as a gathering place for worship. He generously used his wealth and status to refresh the hearts of the saints (v. 7). Paul himself was filled with joy and thanked God in prayer for Philemon, the "beloved brother" (vv. 1, 7) because Philemon did so much to promote the fellowship—*koinōnia*—of the saints.

The term *koinōnia* is too rich to be captured with just one English word. "Fellowship," "participation," and "association" are in the semantic cluster. As the Exposition points out, it means a "close association involving mutual interests and sharing." The "mutual interest" Paul had with Philemon was serving Christ and his people. Paul served as an apostle (although he designated himself only as a "prisoner for Christ Jesus," v. 1), and Philemon served in his role as the host and probable leader of a house church.

It is notable that in the "introduction," Paul says nothing about the purpose of his letter (requesting that Philemon receive back Onesimus, his runaway slave, recently converted). Instead, Paul uses the introductory greeting and blessing to set the table for the difficult conversation to follow. Paul prays for Philemon, expresses kinship with him, praises his love and faith, and states how he had derived joy and comfort from him. Thus, the apostle Paul cultivated the soil of their interpersonal relationship before planting seeds of exhortation.

Preaching Idea

When there's a conflict, what you share is better than what you win.

Contemporary Connections

What does it mean?

What does it mean that in conflict, what we share is better than what we win? The preaching idea captures the situation behind the book of Philemon—interpersonal conflict between a first-century slave owner and a first-century runaway slave. Both of them followed Christ, yet Philemon probably felt betrayed by the lawbreaker, and Onesimus probably felt exploited or even abused by the slave owner. Their feelings probably affected the house church also, and this is why Paul addressed Philemon *and* the "church in your house" (v. 1). The theology of Colossians is put to the test in a severe "case study" that shows us why Christ-followers should forgive: both slaves and masters have a Master in heaven (Col. 3:22–4:1); and as the Lord has forgiven you, so you also must forgive (Col. 3:12–13).

The preaching idea is also grounded in the spiritual unity that members of the church share. This is the basis of *koinōnia.* According to Colossians, members of the church are "in Christ," and that truth trumps all divisions based on things like race, language, age, gender, ethnicity, and social standing. Even slaves and masters have an equal footing in the kingdom, so they should treat each other with deference. Cultural factors play into the preaching idea—house churches of the first-century, wealth and class, and slavery in the Roman world. All of these factors easily led to conflict, but when in conflict, Christ-followers should not exacerbate the problem by criticizing each other. Instead they should focus on their unity in Christ.

Is it true?

Is it true that in conflict, what we share in Christ is better than what we win? Thanking God for each other and avoiding criticism can help retie the strings of relationships that have come loose. A simple analogy of a loose shoe string might pique interest and create receptivity: the flopping shoe string could be secured with a double knot or even duct tape. Then after the analogy, examples from current events might support the preaching idea, showing how focusing on what we share rather than on winning an argument is to be preferred. Perhaps a family was brought together after the death of a loved one. The brevity of life showed them what really matters, the hope of heaven, and helped them put aside their squabble. A dramatic example of forgiveness was embodied in a 2019 tragedy. Botham Jean, the older brother of Brant Jean, was mistakenly shot and killed by off-duty police officer Amber Guyger, but in court Brant said, "I forgive you," and he alluded to the forgiveness all can receive through Christ. For Brant Jean's stirring speech in court, many links are available.

The German philosopher Arthur Schopenhauer (1788–1860) wrote a parable that supports the preaching idea by illustrating the conundrum humans face (*Parerga und Paralipomena*, vol. 2, ch. 31, §396). We are like a group of porcupines on a bitterly cold night. The only way to live is by huddling together for warmth, but as soon as we do that, we prick each other with our quills. When we move apart to avoid pain, we soon discover that isolation is not the solution. Schopenhauer's parable summarizes the problem, but the church has the solution: we must all face one direction—toward the Lord—and thank him for the benefits we share because of Jesus. Though we still possess quills, our quirks and idiosyncrasies—not to mention our brokenness and selfishness—we can avoid harming each other by focusing on the thing we have in common, the most important thing in the world, Jesus Christ. Every follower of Christ has been forgiven, and so he or she should likewise forgive others. Every follower of Christ has the same Father in heaven, so we should treat each other with honor, deference, and affection as members of one family. This is Paul's reasoning in Ephesians 4:1–6:

> I . . . urge you to walk in a manner worthy of the calling to which you have been called, with all humility and gentleness, with patience, bearing with one another in love, eager to maintain the unity of the Spirit in the bond of peace. There is one body and one Spirit—just as you were called to the one hope that belongs to your call—one Lord, one faith, one baptism, one God and Father of all, who is over all and through all and in all.

Now what?

How might we act on the idea that when in conflict, what we share is better than what we win? We can follow Paul's example of dealing with conflict in a constructive way. Before addressing conflict, and before delivering an admonition, we might begin with humility. Paul does not pull rank and open his letter by calling himself an *apostle*. Instead, he designates himself simply as "a prisoner of the Lord" (v. 1). Then he expresses tender regard for Philemon who is his "beloved fellow worker" and "brother" (vv.

1, 7). In prayer, Paul thanks God for Philemon's love and faith (vv. 4–5). Furthermore, Paul has derived joy and encouragement from Philemon because the hearts of the saints have been refreshed through his good works (v. 7). That's the way to address conflict in the church! Begin with humility, prayer, thanks, and honor.

Contemporary examples could show how to implement this approach. When parents need to correct their child, they might begin by affirming their love and expressing sincere praise. When an employer needs to admonish an employee, it should be done with humility. When a pastor needs to exhort the congregation, 2 Timothy 2:24–25 points the way: "The Lord's servant must not be quarrelsome but kind to everyone, able to teach, patiently enduring evil, correcting his opponents with gentleness."

One of the reasons we can approach conflict with a gentle spirit is because each of us, like Philemon, is a "complicated fellow" (to use Adam's phrase in the Exposition). Philemon was truly a generous sponsor of the house church, but apparently he was also unforgiving toward his slave. He refreshed the hearts of the saints, but apparently he also struck fear or resentment into Onesimus's heart. As the bumper sticker says, "Be patient with me. God is not finished with me yet." That sentiment is captured in the quotation above from Bonhoeffer. Instead of being disillusioned with each other, we should give thanks for each other.

Another way to emphasize what we share is to follow Paul's lead with public praise. The personal letter to Philemon was addressed to and read in front of the whole house church, but before they heard Paul command and appeal to Philemon (v. 8), they first heard him honor their leader. One way to express public praise today might be with a banquet honoring volunteers. Some churches do this yearly. Or at staff meetings, the supervisor might publicly praise employees for their accomplishments. Even simple politeness is like warmth to wax, making it pliable. Dale Carnegie's classic *How to Win Friends and Influence People* provides concrete suggestions on how to correct people with humility. The book was first published in 1936, but many of its principles are timeless and could have been lifted from the opening section of Philemon.

Dale Carnegie's Advice for "How to Change People without Giving Offense or Arousing Resentment"

- Begin with praise and honest appreciation.
- Call attention to people's mistakes indirectly.
- Talk about your own mistakes before criticizing the other person.
- Let the person save face.
- Praise the slightest improvement and praise every improvement. Be hearty in your approbation and lavish in your praise.
- Give the other person a fine reputation to live up to.
- Make the other person happy about doing the thing you suggest.[6]

Creativity in Presentation

Henry is a nine-minute virtual reality film (directed by Ramiro Lopez Dau, 2015) based on the porcupine image suggested by Schopenhauer. Narrated by Elijah Wood, it is the story of a cute hedgehog (voiced by Jen Tullock) whose spikey coat threatens to make his birthday party a lonely affair. The film shows how Henry and his friends learned to live together without hurting each other.

The intensely personal nature of the letter to Philemon might be captured with a creative sermon form—the first-person narrative, sometimes called a dramatic monologue (Arthurs, 1997, 30–35). This is a type of sermon

6 Carnegie, *How to Win Friends and Influence People* (New York: Pocket Books, 1932), 186–217.

that expounds the preaching idea and the details of the passage from the perspective of one of the characters in the story. The narrator could be Philemon, Paul, Onesimus, or a member of the house church who heard the letter. If Philemon is the narrator, the message might start like this: "I received a letter yesterday from my friend, Paul. Poor fellow. He's in jail . . . again! He wrote to me, actually he wrote to everyone in my church, in order to talk about something I'd like to tell you about. You see. . . ."

Similar to the first-person sermon, another genre-sensitive form for the sermon might be writing a letter. Paul might dictate the letter to Timothy, pausing to explain his reasoning and responding to Timothy's questions. Or, instead of adopting the persona of Paul, the preacher himself or herself might write to the actual congregation. The issue to be addressed will not be a runaway slave, but perhaps another conflict is on people's minds.

In some teaching venues, perhaps a youth group or college ministry, the concept of "refreshing the saints" might be illustrated with a participatory exercise. Perhaps a volunteer could undertake a grueling exercise like "planking." As the preacher comments on the passage, he or she might ask the volunteer from time to time how they are feeling. Once the volunteer begins to tire and shake, another volunteer could help the first one hold the pose. How refreshing! This could illustrate how the church is a body and family, and every part supports the other parts. As we read in the Exposition, "Discipleship is never an individual endeavor—it always requires the community working together for the obedience of each member."

Visual aids might be used to explain the geographical and cultural background of the letter. Many maps are available at Google Images by searching for "Philemon" or "Colossae." A simple diagram can picture the reciprocal process of love, refreshment, joy, and thanks:

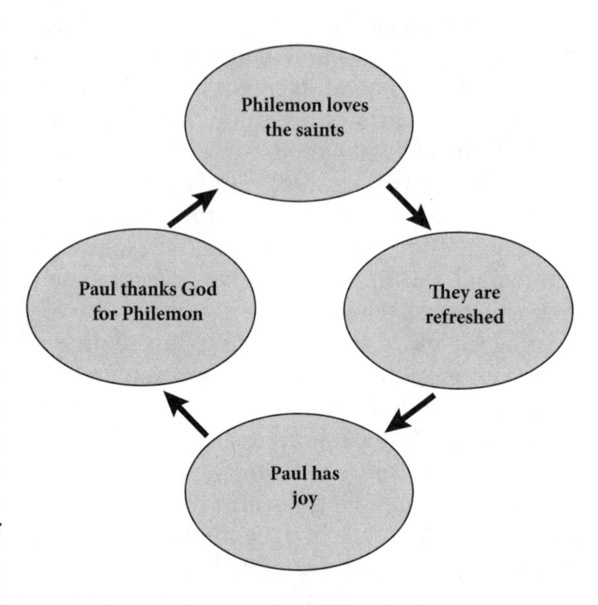

Whatever illustrations you weave into the sermon, be sure to emphasize the implications of this personal letter and the conflict between Philemon and Onesimus. When there's a conflict, what you share is better than what you win.

- In conflict, we share a relationship with God, so thank God for one another (4).
- In conflict, we share a relationship with God, so love one another (5).
- In conflict, we share a relationship with God, so refresh one another (6–7).

DISCUSSION QUESTIONS

1. Why do you think Paul avoided calling himself an "apostle," and instead called himself "a prisoner for Christ Jesus" (v. 1)?

2. Who was Philemon? What do we know about him? In what ways was he a "complicated fellow" (like all of us)?

3. Have you ever been refreshed by someone when your spirit was low? Tell about it.

4. When you admonish someone, do you begin with sincere thanks? Why or why not?

5. Have you ever been challenged by someone who sincerely loved you? If you don't mind, share the story. Or what about the opposite—someone who didn't like you challenged you. How did you receive that?

6. Name some of the things that bind Christians together. How can these overshadow lesser things that divide us?

Philemon 8–16

EXEGETICAL IDEA

Paul appealed on the basis of love for Philemon to do the proper thing toward Onesimus, for God had perhaps superintended the entire situation so that Philemon would embrace Onesimus no longer *merely* as a slave, but as *more than* a slave, as a beloved brother.

THEOLOGICAL FOCUS

Believers must recognize the work of Christ in one another's lives and thereby come to no longer view one another in worldly terms, *merely* as objects to be utilized or rejected for personal gain, but must learn to embrace one another as *more than* such objects, as beloved brothers and sisters in Christ.

PREACHING IDEA

Before believing, we were "merely"—but now we are "more than."

PREACHING POINTERS

Tension pulses under the surface of Paul's seemingly simple letter—the tension of a runaway slave and his offended master. Roman law was clear that Onesimus should be returned to his master, but the situation was more complex than that, because God had arranged things so that Onesimus came under the ministry of Paul and was converted. Onesimus and Philemon now had a new relationship in Christ. The one who was "useless" in Philemon's estimation had become a disciple and was now "useful." Paul wants to make him part of his church planting team, helping the old apostle especially while he is still in jail, so he writes to Philemon to receive his new brother in the Lord. The church that met in Philemon's house probably leaned in to hear Paul address his friend. How would the old veteran address Philemon, his fellow-soldier? Would he command him or shame him? Would he abandon Onesimus, his spiritual child? No. All three of the men were brothers, so Paul appealed to Philemon, not commanded him. Onesimus is no longer what he was, "merely" a slave; he is now "much more" and should be treated as such.

The same reasoning is needed today. We see a propensity to dehumanize people by reducing them to hits on social media. A better propensity is based on the theological sociology modeled in Philemon. Everyone (including slaves!) is made in the image of God, and all followers of Christ have one Father. In the church, we are not "merely" objects or statistics, we are "more than" that; we are fellow workers in God's vineyard (v. 1), fellow soldiers in the fight (v. 2), brothers and sisters (vv. 7, 16), spiritual children (v. 10), formerly perceived as useless, but now useful in the Lord's work (v. 11). Before believing, we were "merely"—but now we are "more than."

PAUL'S APPEAL TO PHILEMON (8–16)

LITERARY STRUCTURE AND THEMES (8–16)

Paul uses the term "therefore" (διό) to indicate that this upcoming portion of his letter will build directly upon the thanksgiving he has already given for Philemon in the previous section (Philem. 4–7). In this section (Philem. 8–16), Paul twice says he "appeals" (παρακαλέω; Philem. 8, 9) to Philemon, but he shrouds the precise content of his appeal in hints and subtleties until finally, in verse 16, he drops the bombshell that Philemon ought to welcome Onesimus "no longer as a slave, but as more than a slave, as a beloved brother" (Philem. 16). Though Paul softens his appeal by refusing to issue a command (Philem. 8) and instead deferring to Philemon's consent on the matter (Philem. 14), he nevertheless seeks to make his appeal as compelling as it is serious. He tells the backstory of Onesimus's faith in Christ (Philem. 10), he describes his own affection for Onesimus (Philem. 12), he affirms Onesimus's usefulness for the gospel (Philem. 11, 13), and he opines regarding God's sovereign reason for Onesimus's departure (Philem. 15). He hopes in this way to persuade Philemon not only to take the proper course of action, but also to adopt a proper attitude in his heart toward Onesimus.

- ***The Basis for His Appeal (8–9)***
- ***Onesimus's Conversion (10–11)***
- ***Paul Trusts Philemon to Do the Right Thing with Onesimus (12–14)***
- ***The Divine Purpose behind This Conflict (15–16)***

EXPOSITION (8–16)

Paul's appeal to Philemon arises directly from the historical context of this letter. One of Philemon's slaves, named Onesimus, has become estranged from Philemon and in this letter, Paul appeals for them to be reconciled. History has yielded other examples of estranged slaves being reconciled to their masters, but in all such cases, the master was simply reinstating the kind of relationship they had as master and slave prior to their estrangement. Paul, however, goes much farther by appealing for Philemon to establish a new kind of relationship with Onesimus, no longer as master and slave, but now as brothers in Christ. Such a relationship will require Philemon to set aside the dehumanization of slavery and to instead regard Onesimus as a person. Even more, Philemon must build a new relationship with Onesimus structured entirely around their shared identity in Christ, for both belong to Christ and therefore both are brothers in Christ. Onesimus is no longer a slave in Christ (cf. Col. 3:11) but a brother, and Philemon must welcome him as a brother, even if he is his slave.

Paul appealed on the basis of love for Philemon to do the proper thing toward Onesimus, for God had perhaps superintended the entire situation, so that Philemon would embrace Onesimus no longer *merely* as a slave, but as *more than* a slave, as a beloved brother.

The Basis for His Appeal (8–9)

Paul explains that though he could issue a direct command to Philemon based on his apostolic authority, he will instead appeal to Philemon on the basis of love.

8. This section begins with a transitional term (διό) that implies some kind of logical inference and it has been variously translated "accordingly" (ESV), "for this reason" (HCSB,

NRSV), "therefore" (NIV), and "wherefore" (KJV). This indicates that Paul intends for what he will say next to build upon and to develop what he has already said. His prayer for Philemon in verses 4–7 has laid the groundwork for the appeal that Paul will now make. But before Paul enters into his actual appeal in verse 9, Paul first raises and rejects the possibility of using a more authoritarian approach in addressing this issue with Onesimus.

Paul says he has great confidence in Christ to command Philemon regarding the proper thing to do. His "confidence" or "boldness" (BDAG, s.v. "παρρησία" 3, p. 781) implies fearlessness on the part of Paul, so that he has no reservations about his ability or authority to issue commands. And by saying he has such boldness "in Christ" (ἐν Χριστῷ), Paul suggests that such an approach would be appropriate even in the eyes of Christ, whom Paul serves. Therefore, Paul considers himself to have full authorization "to command" (ἐπιτάσσειν) Philemon in this letter. Paul could survey the situation with Onesimus and make his own determination regarding what would be the "proper" or "fitting" (BDAG, s.v. "ἀνήκω" 2, p. 79) course of action for Philemon to undertake, and Paul could simply command Philemon to do it.

However, Paul's statement here that he has this boldness must be interpreted in light of what he says next in verse 9, that he would rather appeal to Philemon instead of commanding Philemon. Thus, when Paul uses the participle "having" (ἔχων) with regard to his boldness to command, he uses it in a concessive manner with the meaning, "*though* having" such boldness. Paul is fully aware of his authority to issue commands to other Christians, and he boldly utilizes this authority in many of his letters. Even now, he still has this same authority whereby he could issue simple and direct commands specifying precisely what Philemon ought to do, but Paul deliberately chooses not to approach Philemon in this manner, and Paul wants Philemon to know this from the outset. Paul will not decide for Philemon what Philemon must do; instead, Paul will defer his authority and will instead appeal to Philemon on the basis of love.

9. The next sentence, therefore, begins by emphasizing the reason behind the kind of appeal Paul will actually make. It is "because of love," or "for the sake of love" (διὰ τὴν ἀγάπην) that Paul has rejected an authoritarian approach in favor of a persuasive approach. Paul may have in view here love as a general Christian virtue, since all Christians are called to love one another even as God is love (e.g., 1 John 4:10–12). Indeed, love is the greatest command (Matt. 22:34–40) and the supreme virtue to be put on above all other virtues (Col. 3:14). But Paul may also be thinking more specifically of Philemon's own love for all the saints, which Paul has already extolled in his prayer (Philem. 5, 7) and which Paul now appeals for Philemon to demonstrate yet again in this particular situation, where the fitting course of action will be the loving course of action.

"Rather" than or "instead" of (μᾶλλον) issuing a command, Paul will appeal to Philemon. The word he uses for this "appeal" (παρακαλέω) can mean a number of different things depending on the context. Literally, the two parts of the word mean "alongside" (παρά) and "call" (καλέω), meaning literally to come alongside someone to call upon them or to "call to one's side (BDAG, s.v. "παρακαλέω" 1, p. 764). In this context, Paul means by the term something like "appeal to" or "exhort" or "implore" as opposed to "comfort" or "encourage" (BDAG, s.v. "παρακαλέω" 2–4, p. 765), though we should note the mutuality of the exchange in which Paul has received encouragement from Philemon (παρακαλέω; Philem. 7) and now gives an appeal (παρακαλέω) to him.

At this point, Paul deliberately is not telling Philemon what exactly he is imploring Philemon to do. Instead, Paul deems it important first to establish the framework from which he implores Philemon. By setting aside his right to issue a command and by instead issuing an appeal, Paul divests himself of the aura of apostolic authority in order to come alongside Philemon and address him as a peer in Christ. In other words, Paul does not want Philemon to receive this letter as if Paul is dictating from high in a pulpit down to him in the lowly pew; instead, Paul wants Philemon to receive this letter as if Paul is sitting across from him in a coffee shop, looking in his eyes and conversing with him as a person. This is not a one-sided directive, it is a two-way conversation; this is not a command, it is an appeal. Paul makes known his own thoughts and opinions on the matter, but in such a way that he also invites Philemon to think for himself and to determine for himself the proper course of action he will take.

The Power of Contrast

Throughout this section, Paul ornaments his rhetoric with several dramatic contrasts to drive home his appeal. These include command versus appeal (8–9), useless versus useful (11), sending versus keeping (12–13), compulsion versus free will (14), for a while versus forever (15), and slave versus beloved brother (16).

Paul further establishes this personal framework for his appeal by describing the personal and humble manner in which he comes alongside Philemon. He comes "being this kind of person" (τοιοῦτος ὢν), namely as himself, "as Paul" (ὡς Παῦλος), just an ordinary guy not unlike Philemon. Paul then describes himself in two ways, both of which serve to humanize Paul and bring him alongside Philemon. First, Paul is an "elder" (πρεσβύτης). He is quite literally an old man, so that if he were present with Philemon, Philemon would see the marks of age upon Paul—the wrinkles on his face, the gray in his hair, the stiffness in his steps. But in the church, age brings with it dignity and honor, especially for those whose character has been so shaped in accordance with Christ that they now hold the office of an elder and are worthy of double honor (1 Tim. 3:1–8; 5:17). Second, at the present time (νυνί) Paul is also a "prisoner of Christ Jesus" (δέσμιος Χριστοῦ Ἰησοῦ). This humanizes Paul in his suffering, for to sit with Paul at this moment would mean looking upon the chains with which he is bound and seeing the sores and the wounds that now afflict him. But in the church, such chains also demand respect, for Paul, like the apostles before him, has been deemed worthy of suffering for the sake of Christ Jesus (Acts 5:41).

When we put these pieces together, we see the posture of Paul as he approaches Philemon on this issue. In verse 8, he sets aside his right to assume the posture of authority as an apostle and to issue commands to Philemon. Instead, in verse 9, he assumes the posture of a fellow Christian who comes alongside Philemon with all the humanity of an old man and with all the humility of a prisoner, and yet also with all the wisdom, dignity, and honor that properly belong to a faithful old-timer who now suffers for the sake of Christ. It is from within this framework that Paul invites Philemon to pull up a chair, to sit across the table from him, and to have an open and honest conversation in which Paul will set forth his appeal and Philemon will open his ears to hear and open his mind to consider the proper course of action on the basis of love.

Onesimus's Conversion (10–11)

Paul describes how Onesimus has become a Christian under Paul's ministry and has now been transformed by Christ.

10. Paul continues to move toward his appeal to Philemon, now saying directly to Philemon, "I appeal to you" (παρακαλῶ σε), but Paul still does not give the precise content of his appeal. Further, he labors in verse 10 to delay naming Onesimus for as long as possible so he can first characterize Onesimus on his own terms. In the Greek text, the name "Onesimus" (Ὀνήσιμος) is the final word in the verse.

Most translations have moved his name forward in the verse to make better English (e.g., NIV, ESV, KJV, NRSV, HCSB), but by so doing, they have obscured the literary tension and drama Paul creates in his attempt to mitigate the very real tension and drama in the room by first introducing who Onesimus has become before identifying Onesimus by name. Paul seems to presume that were he to simply name Onesimus, then Philemon and the rest of the church would look upon Onesimus in light of their previous experience with him, where Onesimus is a slave who has run away from Philemon and wronged him. Therefore, Paul takes a proactive approach in seeking to first establish a new way of looking upon Onesimus.

He begins by saying simply and sentimentally that his appeal "concerns my child" (περὶ τοῦ ἐμοῦ τέκνου). In his other letters, Paul frequently describes Christians as his children (e.g., 1 Cor. 4:14; 2 Cor. 6:13; Gal. 4:19), but he uses the term in an especially personal way for his closest disciples and coworkers, namely Titus (Titus 1:4) and Timothy (1 Cor. 4:17; Phil. 2:22; 1 Tim. 1:2, 18; 2 Tim. 1:2; 2:1). As Paul's child, Onesimus has entered into this elite group of those who have become Paul's children through his ministry. "I begot" (ἐγέννησα) him, Paul says, using the language of procreation and childbearing to credit himself with having brought Onesimus to life. Clearly Paul has in view here the new spiritual life that belongs to believers through the gospel, so that through the tutelage of Paul, Onesimus heard and received the gospel, and by faith was united with Christ in his death and resurrection, and now has new life in Christ (see comments on Col. 1:3–8; 2:10–13). Paul now has a special relationship with Onesimus that goes much deeper than simply apostle and convert, for Paul holds Onesimus dear to himself, as his child in Christ. And this relationship is perhaps all the more dear to Paul because Onesimus has become his child during his imprisonment, while he is "in chains" (ἐν τοῖς δεσμοῖς), so that Onesimus serves as proof that God continues to work through Paul even as he suffers.

It is only after these terms are in place and Onesimus has been properly introduced as Paul's child that Paul will finally name the obvious person he has in view, Onesimus (Ὀνήσιμος). By first referring to Onesimus as his child, Paul surely intends for Philemon to hear the tenderness in his appeal, even as a father appeals for his son. Few things are as emotionally moving as hearing a parent appeal for their child on the basis of love—a parent appealing to a judge for mercy as their child is being sentenced, or a parent pleading with a doctor to find some kind of remedy that might ease their child's suffering, or a parent praying fervently for God to intervene and to spare their child in the midst of tragedy. Paul invokes such images and stirs up such sympathies when he casts himself as a parent appealing now for his own child. Paul effectively humanizes Onesimus and ascribes to him all the personhood, value, dignity, and worth a father ascribes to his son, and Paul leans upon Philemon to do the same.

Letter of Pliny

Sometime between A.D. 97 and 112, Pliny the Younger wrote a letter to his friend Sabinianus with an appeal for a slave who has wronged Sabinianus and now seeks intervention. Pliny's letter has many parallels with Paul's letter to Philemon, but one crucial point of departure reveals the uniqueness of Paul's appeal: Pliny appeals on behalf of this slave *as a slave*. Pliny rebukes and threatens the slave as he would any slave, and he asks Sabinianus to receive this slave back as a slave.[1] Pliny does not seek to change the slave's status nor the nature of his

1 Wright explores at length the subversive nature of Paul's appeal to Philemon in contrast to Pliny's letter, particularly in how Paul seeks to effect a change to the fundamental nature of Philemon's relationship to Onesimus in Christ.

relationship with Sabinianus; he aims only to restore the slave to his former condition. Paul, however, will appeal on behalf of Onesimus not as a slave, but as "my child." Paul ascribes to Onesimus a new status that will in turn lead to Paul's appeal for Philemon to receive Onesimus no longer as a slave, but as a brother.

We reprint here Pliny's letter in full to demonstrate this underlying difference:

"Your freedman, with whom you said you were angry, has approached me, and groveling at my feet he has clung to them as if they were yours. His tears were copious, as were his pleas and also his silences. In short, he persuaded me that he was genuinely sorry, and I believe that he has turned over a new leaf because he feels that he has misbehaved. I know that you are furious with him, and I know also that you are rightly so, but praise for forbearance is especially due when the ground for anger are more justified. You were fond of him, and I hope that you will be so in the future; meanwhile it is enough that you allow yourself to be appeased. It will be possible for you to renew your anger, if he deserves it, and you will have greater justification if you have been prevailed upon now. Make some allowance for his youth, for his tears, and for your own benevolence. Do not cause him pain, to avoid paining yourself, for you pain yourself when your mild disposition turns to anger.

"I fear that I may seem to be applying pressure rather than to be pleading with you, if I join my prayers to his, and I shall do this all the more fully and frankly for having rebuked him more sharply and severely, having threatened that I shall never plead with you again after this. That threat was addressed to him, for it was necessary to scare him, and not to you; indeed, I shall perhaps plead with you again, and my plea will again be granted, provided only that it is fitting for me to request it, and for you to grant it. Farewell." (Pliny, *Ep.* 9.21; trans. Walsh, 2006)

11. Paul further describes the transformation Onesimus has undergone with a contrast between the past and the present, between who he "formerly" (ποτέ) was and who he is "now" (νυνί). The contrast here centers around his perceived usefulness, for Onesimus was formerly "useless" (ἄχρηστος) but now has become "useful" (εὔχρηστος). Paul's statement that Onesimus was formerly useless to Philemon is perhaps more an indictment of Philemon than of Onesimus. In other words, this may not necessarily indicate that Onesimus was in fact useless so much as it acknowledges that Philemon regarded him as such. Notably, Paul says Onesimus was formerly useless "to you" (σοι), but he does not say Onesimus was formerly useless "to me" or to anyone else, as he will say about Onesimus's present usefulness. In other words, Paul does not affirm Philemon's assessment about Onesimus's uselessness. We have no indication in the letter to this point that would suggest Philemon is anything other than loving and gracious in his dealings with other Christians, but neither do we have reason to presume he could not have been unfair or even cruel in how he managed his household, and Paul seems to be subtly undermining the critical performance review Philemon has placed upon Onesimus.

The Delicate Dance of Criticizing a Master

In his 1845 autobiography, *Narrative of the Life of Frederick Douglass*, the former slave Frederick Douglass describes the danger inherent to a nineteenth-century African slave in America criticizing their master. He tells the story of a Colonel Lloyd who owned more than a thousand slaves, many of whom had never met their

Wright observes, "Here we see one of the most fundamental differences between Pliny and Paul. Pliny's appeal, we remind ourselves, reinscribed the social dynamics already present. Paul's subverted them" (Wright, 2013, 15).

owner. One such slave happened upon the Colonel without recognizing him as his master, and when the Colonel asked this slave how his master treated him, the slave answered honestly that the Colonel does not treat him well. A few weeks later, this unsuspecting slave was suddenly seized and sold into the slave market farther south, never to see his friends and family again. Douglas opines, "It is partly in consequence of such facts, that slaves, when inquired of as to their condition and the character of their masters, almost universally say they are contented, and that their masters are kind" (Douglass, [1845] 2002, 327–28). This modern example illustrates the delicacy of Paul's appeal, where Onesimus has apparently and to some degree spoken ill of his master by telling Paul that Philemon regards him as useless, and Paul now puts Philemon in a position where he must hear and be chastened by Paul based on the report of his slave. Paul must tread carefully; Philemon must exercise humility and compassion; and Onesimus, by returning, must trust that Philemon will not react by punishing Onesimus for this criticism of his master.

But now, something significant has changed with regard to Onesimus. Where once he was regarded as useless—fairly or not—now Paul appeals to Philemon to see that he has become useful not just to Philemon, but "to you and to me" (σοὶ καὶ ἐμοί). If he was only useful to Philemon, then his usefulness would refer to the new spirit he will bring to his household duties as he now labors for his new Lord, Jesus Christ, even as he serves Philemon (Col. 3:22–24). But his usefulness also to Paul suggests that Onesimus has something to contribute to the work of ministry Paul undertakes as an apostle. At the very least, Paul sees Onesimus's potential for helping him personally during his imprisonment (Philem. 13), but his usefulness suggests that Paul may see in Onesimus the same kind of ministry potential he saw in his other children, Titus and Philemon, and even Mark, whom Paul also calls useful (2 Tim. 4:11). Perhaps Paul envisions Onesimus being discipled and trained for leadership in the church, as a teacher and minister of the gospel. In any case, his usefulness to Paul invites Philemon and the church to look upon Onesimus with new eyes, where Onesimus is no longer the slave who lurks in the shadows attending to household duties as the church meets in his master's house, but Onesimus is now a disciple who actively learns and grows in his faith, and participates in ministry responsibilities and even leadership within the church.

Paul Trusts Philemon to Do the Right Thing with Onesimus (12–14)

Paul concedes to Philemon the right to determine the proper course of action with Onesimus; but at the same time, Paul leans on Philemon to do what is good and right with this slave who has become dear and useful to Paul.

12. Paul continues to speak of Onesimus, who is the subject of the relative pronoun, "whom" (ὅν), with which the sentence begins. Most English translations say Paul is "sending back" Onesimus (e.g., NIV, ESV, NRSV, etc.), but the Greek term here (ἀναπέμπω) most often means to "send up" in a context where a person is sent up "from a lower position to a higher," or sent "on to someone in authority" (BDAG, s.v. "ἀναπέμπω" 1–2, p. 70). It could even be used in a legal context where a person is sent up for trial (Wright, 2013, 14–15). Paul does not merely send Onesimus *back* to Philemon; he sends him *up* to Philemon in apparent recognition of—and even deference to—Philemon's authority over Onesimus.

That Paul "sends up" (ἀναπέμπω) Onesimus to Philemon sheds much light on what Paul is orchestrating in Colossae. It is Paul himself who has been the director behind the scenes, who sent Onesimus to Philemon, and who has orchestrated the scene now unfolding in Philemon's house. Paul deserves all the credit and all the blame—the credit for having sent back the runaway slave and the blame for laying upon Philemon the heavy burden of now determining how to respond. At the same time, by sending up Onesimus to Philemon, Paul gives apparent deference to Roman law and cultural norms that place Philemon in authority over Onesimus as master over his slave. But at the same time, Paul lays upon Philemon the Christian duty to treat Onesimus in a Christ-honoring way in the midst of the entire congregation. No one else can manage this situation for Philemon, but everyone else can watch to see what Philemon will do.

For Paul to send Onesimus up to Philemon is no small thing, for Paul sends up "him—this one—*who* is my heart" (αὐτόν, τοῦτ' ἔστιν τὰ ἐμὰ σπλάγχνα). Onesimus, in other words, has become quite dear to Paul. Notice the emphasis Paul adds here through the redundancy of "him" (αὐτόν) and "this one" (τοῦτ'), so that together they communicate an intensive focus upon Onesimus. Paul essentially says, "*Onesimus* himself, *yes*, this *very* person *who is standing before you*," and then Paul drops the bombshell, that this Onesimus "is my heart" (ἔστιν τὰ ἐμὰ σπλάγχνα). As in verse 7, this phrase can literally be translated "mine own bowels" (KJV), but the metaphorical use here refers to the emotional center of a person, so it is better translated "my own heart" (NRSV; cf. ESV, NIV). Paul draws the closest and most deeply personal connection to Onesimus by saying that Onesimus has not merely had an effect upon Paul's heart, as did Philemon by refreshing his heart (Philem. 7), but Onesimus actually *is* Paul's heart. Paul's emotional well-being has become inseparable from Onesimus's well-being, so that as Onesimus fares, so fares Paul's heart. This truly is the affection of a good parent for their child, where they hurt when their child hurts and they are happy when their child is happy.

Being "Gutted"

In Scotland, to be "gutted" is to have deep emotional disappointment and sadness. For example, when your favorite sports team suffers a crucial loss, you would be "completely gutted."

For Paul to send Onesimus back to Philemon has surely gutted Paul. This has required Paul not only to be separated from his heart but also to send his heart into a perilous situation of unknown outcome. Paul does not know what kind of treatment Onesimus will receive from Philemon, and Paul therefore does not know what the emotional impact will be upon his own heart. At the same time, Paul's statement of affection toward Onesimus raises the stakes for Philemon, for Philemon must now recognize that when he deals with Onesimus, he deals also with Paul's heart. To hurt Onesimus is to hurt Paul, to bless Onesimus is to bless Paul. Philemon's actions will reach beyond Onesimus all the way to the apostle himself.

13. Paul continues to affirm Onesimus by expressing his desire to keep Onesimus with him for his own benefit. This verse begins with the same relative pronoun as the previous verse, "whom" (ὅν), with ongoing reference to Onesimus. Paul speaks of his desire with regard to Onesimus, and the imperfect form of the word (ἐβουλόμην; "was desiring") indicates the ongoing nature of his desire. This is more akin to a longing in Paul's heart to secure Onesimus for himself. What Paul really wants to do is to "prevent" or "restrain" (BDAG, s.v. "κατέχω" 1, p. 532) Onesimus in order to keep him "for myself" (πρὸς ἐμαυτὸν). Paul's aim in keeping Onesimus would not be to protect him from Philemon and the consequences of his previous choices—or at least this is not the aim Paul expresses here—but rather to have some benefit for himself. This underscores the sincerity of Paul's claim that Onesimus has become useful (Philem. 11).

More specifically, Paul longs to keep Onesimus in order that (ἵνα) Onesimus would "serve" (διακονέω) Paul during this time of his imprisonment for the sake of the gospel, while he is literally "in chains of the gospel" or "gospel chains" (ἐν τοῖς δεσμοῖς τοῦ εὐαγγελίου). Notice that Paul uses great care with his words here, as he again avoids describing Onesimus's service with the language of slavery, favoring "serve" (διακονέω) over "serve as a slave" (δουλεύω). Paul sees Onesimus as an asset to himself and a contributor to Paul's gospel ministry, even as Paul suffers in prison. This is a resounding endorsement from the apostle himself that Onesimus has real value not only as a slave, but as a servant of Paul.

Further, and perhaps most startlingly, Paul says that had he actually retained Onesimus; Onesimus would have served Paul "on your behalf" (ὑπὲρ σοῦ; ESV) or "in your place" (NRSV; cf. HCSB, NIV, KJV), as if Philemon would have received credit for Onesimus's service. Paul seems to presume Philemon would have approved of such an arrangement if given the opportunity. This reveals again Paul's confidence in Philemon's overall generosity and his partnership with Paul in the gospel, so that Philemon can be expected to do what will benefit the gospel even at a cost to himself. But, if we take a more cynical view, we could also suppose that Philemon would have approved of Onesimus staying with Paul because such an arrangement would allow Philemon to be done with Onesimus and to avoid the difficult work of receiving Onesimus back and reconciling with him. Paul will not allow Philemon such an easy escape.

Instead, Paul communicates throughout this verse that by *not* retaining Onesimus, Paul has gone against what he himself desires as a solution that would be most advantageous to himself, and Paul has gone against what he presumes Philemon would accept as a viable solution to the entire affair, and Paul has gone against what surely Onesimus would have embraced as an excellent resolution. This would have been a win all the way around, had Paul simply kept Onesimus with him and notified Philemon of his decision. Why has Paul rejected such a winsome solution, even at the personal cost of losing Onesimus's assistance? At the very least, it is because Paul thinks highly enough of Philemon that he will not presume upon Philemon's generosity, nor will he snatch away from Philemon the opportunity to choose for himself to do the right and good thing. Further still, Paul will not allow the situation to resolve with anything less than genuine Christian reconciliation that can only be accomplished with a transformation of all the hearts involved, so that Philemon and Onesimus are brought together as brothers in Christ.

14. In contrast (δέ) to Paul's desire to retain Onesimus in verse 13, Paul also has a desire to do nothing apart from Philemon's approval. The former desire (ἐβουλόμην; Philem. 13) was in the imperfect form, indicating Paul's ongoing longing to keep Onesimus, while the latter desire (ἠθέλησα; Philem. 14) is in the aorist, perhaps suggesting a willful decision that Paul has made, or a resolution, to solicit Philemon's approval (Harris, 2010, 228). Apparently "the will stepped in and put an end to the inclinations of the mind" (Lightfoot, 1981, 341). In this case, Paul has determined "to do nothing" (οὐδὲν . . . ποιῆσαι) so long as he lacks Philemon's consent. This "consent" (γνώμη) can mean simply approval in the form of a decision or declaration, so that a person could give such approval against their own judgment, if other factors prevailed upon their decision. But the word can also refer to "a viewpoint or way of thinking about a matter," where a person has entered into a particular "opinion" or "way of thinking" (BDAG, s.v. "γνώμη" 2, p. 202). The latter fits the context better here, for Paul is not looking for Philemon simply to add his approval to Paul's determination, albeit begrudgingly, but Paul aims for Philemon to be transformed in his own viewpoint and opinion, so that he will come to share in Paul's way of thinking and become an eager participant in Paul's suggested course of action.

Has Paul Really Done Nothing?

We might think doing nothing would require Paul to keep Onesimus with him in his current situation until instructed to do otherwise, but for Paul, doing nothing in fact requires that he send Onesimus up to Philemon. This exposes again the inherent differences between the ancient world where slavery was normal and our modern world where slavery is abnormal. From our perspective, returning a slave to their master would be an abhorrent action of doing *something*, while turning a blind eye to a runaway slave and allowing them to continue in their flight would be doing *nothing*. But in the world of Paul, returning a slave to their master is the normal course of action, while knowingly allowing a slave to continue in their flight—even if only to retain their service for oneself—would have been an act of intervention running against the grain of cultural and legal expectations. From this perspective, when Paul sends Onesimus back to Philemon, Paul is not intervening so much as he is "doing nothing."

Paul's resolve to do nothing has a further purpose (ἵνα) with regard to the nature of the good thing he anticipates Philemon will do. Paul uses the article "the" with the adjective "good" (τὸ ἀγαθόν) to communicate the particular and substantive idea of "the good thing." The question underlying Paul's statement is not the question of whether or not Philemon will undertake such a good thing, but it is the question of what will motivate Philemon to do this good thing. Again, this may reveal Paul's confidence that Philemon will in fact do what is proper, but Paul's presumption of confidence may also only thinly veil the implicit pressure he is laying upon Philemon to follow a particular course of action. By suggesting there is a particular good deed to be done, and by suggesting before the entire church in Colossae that Philemon will follow this good deed, Paul places Philemon under immense pressure to discern and to undertake this good deed.

But at the same time, and with great irony, Paul states that his purpose in having orchestrated the scenario in which Philemon now finds himself is actually to position Philemon with the freedom to determine for himself what he will do. Paul expects that Philemon can now choose to do this good thing not by compulsion but by free will. To act "by compulsion" (κατὰ ἀνάγκην; ESV) would mean acting "out of obligation" (HCSB) or doing "something forced" (NRSV) or "of necessity" (KJV). It is being backed into a corner and feeling your options have been restricted, so that you have no choice in the matter but must take the only course of action afforded to you. On the other hand, to act "of your own accord" (κατὰ ἑκούσιον; ESV) means the action is "voluntary" (NIV, NRSV), "of your own free will" (HCSB), or done "willingly" (KJV).[2] Paul empowers Philemon with the freedom to determine for himself what he will do, even as Paul seeks to influence Philemon to share in Paul's way of thinking and to identify and embrace the particular course of action that is good. For Paul, "to assist someone in reaching

2 Such compulsion can be a complicated thing, even as Paul can say he preaches the gospel under "compulsion" (ἀνάγκη; 1 Cor. 9:16), and yet at the same time he says he preaches "voluntarily" (ἑκών) in his ministry, so that he can have his reward (1 Cor. 9:17). His preaching is simultaneously compelled and voluntary, and he would have it no other way.

what must remain his own decision is not to enslave him, but to set him free" (Wright, 1986, 184).

Paul refuses to manipulate Philemon, and he refuses to abandon Philemon; he will not back Philemon into a corner nor will he leave Philemon alone to figure this out on his own. Paul does not coerce Philemon into behavior modification, so that Paul can simply have the outcome he desires, but he leads Philemon toward heart transformation, so that Philemon will adapt Paul's viewpoint as his own.

The Divine Purpose behind This Conflict (15–16)

Paul ponders whether God might have superintended this entire situation in order to radically reorient Philemon's relationship with Onesimus as brothers together in Christ.

15. Here Paul enters into speculation and suggestion rather than declaration and instruction. He continues in his appeal now with further explanation (γάρ; "for") as he wonders whether "perhaps" (τάχα) there might be a bigger story not yet discovered that would bring purpose to this entire situation with Onesimus, and Paul ventures to offer his own speculation regarding what "the reason" (διὰ τοῦτο) might be. But before Paul gives this purpose, he first describes the situation at hand in the softest terms possible. He uses the passive voice to say Onesimus "was separated" (ἐχωρίσθη) from Philemon, which in a roundabout way absolves Onesimus of the responsibility of his action and suggests Onesimus was not in control of his departure but was being carried along by an unseen hand. Further, Paul downplays his absence by referring to it within the limitations of time, as he was gone only "for a time" (πρὸς ὥραν), perhaps a day or an hour or a season, but certainly not indefinitely or forever.

Paul's speculation regarding the divine purpose contrasts sharply with this temporary absence, for perhaps the purpose is in order that (ἵνα) Philemon might have Onesimus back "forever" (αἰώνιον). This is the classic scenario of enduring a short-term loss for the sake of a long-term gain. If Philemon can come to see this divine perspective, then he will no longer obsess over what he has lost in this time, but he will take advantage of the opportunity to embrace and to lock in a gain that will last for all eternity. To do this will require action on the part of Philemon; he must receive Onesimus as if he is receiving "in full what is due" him (BDAG, s.v. "ἀπέχω"1, p. 102).

Before we move on to the nature of this reception in the next verse, we must pause for a moment and fully realize the nature of Paul's appeal. His language here invites Philemon to ponder together with Paul how his separation from Onesimus might be construed from a divine perspective. What if God has been superintending this entire debacle and working out a bigger purpose than may be immediately apparent? This language recalls the experience of Joseph, who was the victim of great violence at the hands of his brothers and became separated from his family for decades, but later could declare to his brothers, "As for you, you meant evil against me, but God meant it for good" (Gen. 50:20). He does not excuse his brothers for their evil action, but at the same time he embraces the sovereignty of God by which God has accomplished something of far greater good through their evil actions.

Paul's appeal to Philemon runs along a similar line. In our modern conscience, we might wonder what claim Philemon could have to victimhood, since he is the evil slave owner and master. But when we enter into the framework of the first century, where slavery as an institution was the normal course of affairs, then we must realize that from Philemon's perspective (and from the perspective of most others in that world), Philemon has been the victim of Onesimus's flight in terms of the lost income and respect that were due Philemon. We might compare this to a loss an employer would suffer should their employee miss work for weeks on end and negatively impact the company's productivity. Such an employer might have a hard time accepting this situation as nothing more than a temporary separation. However, whatever loss has been realized in the short-term might be mitigated if there is a long-term gain to be made because of the separation. In Paul's estimation here, the temporary loss to Philemon may have been financial, but the eternal gain is deeply personal. He has lost income and credibility, but he stands to gain a brother, and this eternal reward more than offsets the temporary costs.

16. Paul's appeal reaches its crescendo in verse 16 as Paul describes the kind of person Philemon will receive back as the result of this divinely superintended separation. He will no longer receive Onesimus as a slave. The "no longer" (οὐκέτι) implies that Philemon has received Onesimus "as a slave" (ὡς δοῦλον) up to this point, but this formerly acceptable routine has now reached its terminus. We must note that this is the first and only time that Paul ever identifies Onesimus as a slave. Indeed, were it not for this statement, we would have no way of knowing this crucial element of Onesimus's story. In all other instances, Paul goes to great lengths to avoid calling Onesimus a slave, preferring instead to call him our brother (Col. 4:9; see comments on 4:7–9) and my child (Philem. 10). Even now, when Paul finally recognizes Onesimus as a slave, it is only to dismiss this as the way in which he should no longer be received.

Instead, Philemon must now receive Onesimus as "more than a slave" (ὑπὲρ δοῦλον). The preposition Paul uses, when followed by an accusative as it is here, means to go "beyond," even excelling and surpassing (BDAG, "ὑπέρ" B, p. 1031). There is a higher way to receive Onesimus than as a slave, and that is to receive him "as a beloved brother" (ἀδελφὸν ἀγαπητόν). Such a reception would require Philemon to recognize Onesimus's familial status within the body of Christ. Not only is Onesimus a child of God alongside all other believers, and thereby a full and genuine brother to them all, but Onesimus is a child of the apostle Paul (Philem. 10), as is also apparently Philemon (Philem. 19), making them children of the same spiritual father, and therefore brothers together all the more. But Onesimus is not to be received merely as a brother in status—he is to be received as a brother with affection, as a *beloved* brother. This is the same affection Paul has already expressed toward Philemon as his beloved fellow worker (Philem. 1), and Paul routinely describes his other coworkers as beloved (see comments on Philem. 1). Onesimus, too, now joins the ranks of Paul's beloved dignitaries, including Timothy (Rom. 16:21; 1 Thess. 3:2), Titus (2 Cor. 8:23), and Epaphroditus (Phil. 2:25).

Slavery and Dehumanization

Again, Frederick Douglass proves insightful in his *Narrative of the Life of Frederick Douglass*. In the following quote, he observes that the institution of slavery depends upon slaves who are content in their position, and this in turn requires the dehumanization of slaves: "I have found that, to make a contented slave, it is necessary to make a thoughtless one. It is necessary to darken his moral and mental vision, and, as far as possible, to annihilate the power of reason. He must be able to detect no inconsistencies in slavery; he must be made to feel that slavery is right; and he can be brought to that only when he ceases to be a man" (Douglass, [1854] 2002, 384). Paul, therefore, undermines slavery as an institution when he refuses to dehumanize Onesimus as a slave but instead insists upon humanizing him as a man, and more than a man, as a beloved brother.

Next, Paul pushes the rhetoric two steps higher with a superlative ("most of all") followed by a comparative ("how much more"). First, Paul builds upon his previous use of the comparative term "more than" (ὑπέρ), where he described how Onesimus was to be received as more than a slave (Philem. 16); now, Paul adds the superlative "most of all" (μάλιστα) to say Onesimus is a beloved brother "most of all to me" (μάλιστα ἐμοί). Paul puts his money where his mouth is, and he does not ask of Philemon anything he is not willing to do himself. As far as Paul is concerned, Onesimus is a beloved brother to himself, and Paul receives him as such. This should not come as a surprise at this point in the letter, since Paul has already demonstrated great affection for Philemon as his child and heart (Philem. 10, 12). Then, Paul presses even higher than a superlative by adding another comparative, now asking Philemon to consider "how much more" (πόσῳ . . . μᾶλλον) Onesimus is a beloved brother "to you" (σοί), that is, to Philemon, than he is even to Paul, to whom he is a brother most of all. By stacking a comparative on top of a superlative, Paul ratchets up the rhetoric higher than grammar technically allows to emphasize the complete, robust, and elevated nature of Onesimus's brotherhood.

Not only is his brotherhood exalted, but it is also comprehensive. Onesimus is a brother to Philemon *both* in the flesh *and* in the Lord. These two phrases denote two different dimensions to their relationship. The first phrase, "in the flesh" (ἐν σαρκί), refers to the human sphere where relationships follow the pattern of the world; it is the "outward and human level" of relationship (Harris, 2010, 232). For Philemon and Onesimus, this is their relationship as master and slave, whereby Philemon is Onesimus's master "according to the flesh" (κατὰ σάρκα; Col. 3:22). The second phrase, "in the Lord" (ἐν κυρίῳ), refers to the spiritual dimension where relationships are ordered according to their union with Christ; it is "the inward and spiritual level" of relationship (Harris, 2010, 232). For Philemon and Onesimus, this is their relationship as brothers in Christ.

So their relationship is two-tiered—it is both earthly and heavenly, both human and spiritual. Philemon, therefore, has the opportunity now to welcome Onesimus as a beloved brother not only in the Lord but also in the flesh. How easy would it have been for Philemon to recognize Onesimus as a brother in the church on Sunday without any change to their relationship when the work begins on Monday? But Paul leans upon Philemon to take Sunday home with him throughout the week and to embrace Onesimus as his beloved brother at all times and in all places, including as Onesimus works as a slave in Philemon's house under the oversight of Philemon as his master. Paul stops just short of outright requesting manumission, but he goes all in by asking for such a radical and comprehensive transformation of every aspect of their master-slave relationship.

Manumission and Abolition in Pauline Interpretation

Perhaps not surprisingly given its indirect nature, Paul's appeal to Philemon has a complex interpretive history, as demonstrated by Demetrius Williams (2012). At times, Christians have used the letter to Philemon to justify the status quo of slavery in their own day. In one example, a minister preaching to African American slaves on a plantation in 1833 used Philemon to exhort the slaves to fidelity and to condemn running away, but half the slaves walked out and denied that such a letter could exist in the Bible (Williams, 2012, 36). Such pro-slavery interpretations may reflect the interpreter as much or more than Paul himself, given that a lineage of Christians throughout history have worked toward manumission of slaves and even abolition of the institution of slavery itself (Williams, 2012, 27–35). As early as the second century, churches were collecting funds to purchase freedom for slaves, with some believers even selling themselves into slavery in order to ransom others (*1 Clem* 55:2), and further examples can be found throughout Christian history

(Horsley, 1998, 190–94). These believers embraced Paul's theological emphasis on the freedom all believers have in Christ, whether slave or free, and they sought to restructure their social world accordingly (Horsley, 1998, 170–76, 190). In this vein, many interpreters today see manumission as the necessary implication of Paul's appeal to Philemon (e.g., Moo, 2008, 425; McKnight, 2018, 98). Witherington states it directly: "Unless Onesimus becomes at least a freedman, he cannot legally or socially be regarded as Philemon's brother. Manumission, then, is the key that opens many doors here" (Witherington, 2007, 81). Perhaps Paul's appeal for Onesimus's manumission was not so veiled after all, and if the manumission of individual slaves is a moral imperative, then surely abolition of slavery must be as well.

As a brother, then, Onesimus is in no way deficient; he does not occupy a lower status of brotherhood, he does not reside beneath Philemon or any other saint, nor does his brotherhood ebb and flow depending on the time of week. He is fully and completely a beloved brother to Philemon in every way and at all times with all the concomitant rights and privileges and dignity. Perhaps, Paul suggests, God has orchestrated this scenario in order that Onesimus would come to Christ and become a brother, and Philemon would thereby be granted the opportunity to welcome him as a beloved brother. If so, then Philemon's welcome of Onesimus must reach upward higher and higher until the welcome is befitting of Onesimus's status as beloved brother, and his welcome must reach outward farther and farther until it encompasses every sphere of life, not only in the church, but also in the household.

"Brothers don't shake hands; brothers gotta hug!"—Tommy (played by Chris Farley), in *Tommy Boy* (directed by Peter Segal, 1995)

THEOLOGICAL FOCUS

The exegetical idea (Paul appealed on the basis of love for Philemon to do the proper thing toward Onesimus, for God had perhaps superintended the entire situation, so that Philemon would embrace Onesimus no longer *merely* as a slave, but as *more than* a slave, as a beloved brother) leads to this theological focus: Believers must recognize the work of Christ in one another's lives and thereby come to no longer view one another in worldly terms, *merely* as objects to be utilized or rejected for personal gain, but they must learn to embrace one another as *more than* such objects, as beloved brothers and sisters in Christ.

In these verses, Paul humanizes and dignifies both Philemon and Onesimus, and he entrusts to them the sacred responsibility of brotherhood. When Paul sets aside his authority to command Philemon and instead makes an appeal based on love, Paul affirms Philemon's freedom and ability to make Christ-honoring decisions even in a very difficult situation. And when Paul appeals for Onesimus as his own child and his very heart who ought to be embraced not as a slave but as a beloved brother, Paul elevates Onesimus and recognizes his full participation in Christ and his full rights as a brother in Christ. Paul thereby places all three primary actors—himself, Philemon, and Onesimus—on the same plane in Christ. All three are equal as humans and as Christians, and they must treat one another as such.

Paul's approach to humanizing both Philemon and Onesimus runs against the cultural grain of our world today, where we have found countless ways to dehumanize one another. We may rightly reject the dehumanization that comes with slavery, but we embrace dehumanization in countless other forms. We see people merely in economic and utilitarian terms according to what they can contribute to us and to society as a whole. We see people merely as dollar signs to contribute to our bottom line. We see people merely as sets of data to be mined, extracted, and sold to the highest bidder. We see people merely in terms of winners and losers, or success and failure, according to what they have achieved (or not achieved) on the socioeconomic ladder. We see people merely through the filters of social media and seek their approval. In our culture, people have become digitized and monetized, and we reject and dispose of them when they no longer prove useful to us.

But the church stands against such trends of dehumanization. As Christians, we expose and reject such ways of knowing one another, and instead we embrace a new kind of relationship with one another where we move beyond the "merely" of dehumanization and instead embrace the "more than" of humanization. We no longer objectify one another and see one another *merely* as objects to be exploited for personal gain, but we see one another as *more than* such objects, as *more than* slaves, as beloved brothers and sisters in Christ.

And how do we do this? Paul sets forth the roadmap in this text. It begins when each one of us, like Paul, recognizes our own humanity and humbles ourselves, setting aside whatever rights we might have to command and to lord our authority over one another, and we instead come alongside one another in weakness and love. Then, we must recognize the work of Christ in our brother or sister in Christ whereby they have become children of God. They too have a story of how they learned about the gospel message and responded by surrendering their lives to Christ in faith, and they too are experiencing new life and transformation in Christ. If we would only take the time to hear their stories and to see the work of Christ in their lives, we would see the immense value they now have as persons belonging to Christ and we would realize that we are indeed brothers and sisters in Christ, for the work of Christ in our lives is no different. Finally, when other Christians irritate and provoke us, so that we experience conflict, we must embrace the possibility that God in his providence might be at work to teach us to do the good thing, even though it may be the hard thing, by embracing one another as beloved brothers and sisters in Christ.

PREACHING AND TEACHING STRATEGIES

Exegetical and Theological Synthesis

Having established his warm relationship with Philemon in the first verses of the letter, Paul turns to his main purpose: persuading Philemon to treat his runaway slave, Onesimus, as a brother. While Paul does not say so explicitly, he implies his desire for Philemon to release Onesimus from slavery. Up to this point, Paul has avoided outright command (vv. 8–9), even though he had authority as an apostle and used it at other times. Paul also chooses his words carefully, calling Onesimus his "child" (v. 10), and his "very heart" (v. 12); Paul requests consent rather than imposing compulsion (v. 14); and he speculates on the purposes God may have orchestrated in what seemed to be jumbled circumstances and relationships (vv. 15–16). The heart of Paul's persuasion was the theological truth that in Christ all things are new (2 Cor. 5:17). A person who was formerly perceived as useless should now be seen as useful, and though one may be a slave, in Christ he should be seen and treated as a brother.

Preaching Idea

Before believing, we were "merely"—but now we are "more than."

Contemporary Connections

What does it mean?

What does it that before believing in Jesus we were "merely," but now we are "more than"? The enigmatic phrase refers to the shift in perspective that Paul was attempting to instill in Philemon. Onesimus was not *merely* a "slave," or a "runaway," and should not be perceived as "useless." All three of those designations were true, but they were not the more important truth that he was a "brother," "beloved," and "useful." Onesimus was more than his past mistakes. Christ had made all things new and Paul was helping Philemon and the house church to recognize this and act on it.

To bring the preaching idea alive, it might be helpful to offer cultural background on slavery. The sidebar featuring the letter from Pliny may be useful, and the sidebars with quotations from Frederick Douglass's autobiography illustrates a more recent experience of slavery. See also the material on slavery in the commentary on Colossians 3:22–4:1 (e.g., Aristotle, Columella, Harriet Beecher Stowe, Seneca, etc.). Another cultural factor may be missed by modern listeners: honor/shame culture. The Roman world was fully immersed in this. When Onesimus ran away, it would have been natural, almost inevitable, for Philemon to see him as *merely* someone who caused financial loss and shame. When Paul appealed to the leader of the house church to receive Onesimus as a brother, it is possible that Philemon gulped and flushed. Keep in mind that the appeal was made in front of the whole church as the letter was read aloud. Yet Paul confidently appealed to Philemon's better nature to do the right thing based on Onesimus's new identity in Christ. Onesimus was more than his past mistakes and sins. The same is true today when anyone places their faith in Jesus. We are buried with him in baptism and raised to new life (Rom. 6:4). We are more than our past.

Is it true?

When we have been hurt, is it possible to move from a "merely" mindset to "more than"? Is it possible to forgive? After all, the English proverb says that revenge, not forgiveness, is sweet. David Chester and Nathan DeWall studied the brain science of revenge and verified the truth of the proverb. A person who is demeaned or rejected feels emotional pain, but when the person takes revenge, the nucleus accumbens fires, the part of the brain associated with pleasure, and masks the pain. (Hogenboom, 2017.) The motorist who is cut off in traffic knows this if he or she takes revenge with words, gestures, or tailgating. Shakespeare alludes to the pleasure of revenge when one of his characters counsels another: "Think therefore on revenge and cease to weep" (*Henry VI, Part 2,* 4.4.3)

Lashing out when shamed may be natural, but God calls us to live by supernatural realities: forgiven sinners receive a new nature, and in the church we focus on the new nature, not the old transgressions. After his resurrection, Jesus did this with Peter and the disciples (John 21). Peter had denied Jesus three times and everyone except John had run away, but Jesus didn't dredge up the past. Or rather, he *did* recall the past with a charcoal fire, but he did this to restore, not deprecate.

Underlying the shift in perspective from "merely" to "more than" is belief in the power of God. Paul displayed that when he speculated in verses 15 and 16 that God was the stage manager of this little drama involving Onesimus and Philemon. God had used the runaway's pain and brought him to Paul. There God turned Onesimus from *merely* a runaway slave into *much more,* a brother. God was changing Philemon too. Paul hoped that the wealthy patron of the house church would not demand his rights as a shamed slave owner. Revenge might be sweet, but Christians leave vengeance to God. The old law of *lex talionis,* an eye for an eye, is not Jesus's way (Matt. 5:38–42).

Now what?

What practical implications arise from the principle that followers of Christ are not "merely" but are "more than"? First, we might suggest that in the church we must be careful with our language. Words are a mighty force for good or evil (Prov. 18:21). Labeling someone with a demeaning term creates a self-fulfilling prophecy. As the English proverb says, "Call a man a thief, and he will steal." Thankfully, labeling someone with a positive term also creates a kind of prophecy. So, Paul was very careful with his language, calling Onesimus "beloved," "brother," "child," and "servant" (*diakonos*). One time he does refer to him as a "slave" (*doulos*), but that designation is placed late in the argument after the first set of terms has done its work. Paul took pains to describe Onesimus in ways that would help Philemon see Onesimus according to who he was in Christ. Paul's labels for himself were also skillfully chosen. He is an "old man" and a "prisoner." Furthermore, both Philemon and Onesimus were Paul's "children," again emphasizing their equality. When we experience conflict, we will want to follow Paul's example with careful use of language.

Another way to apply the preaching idea is to exercise faith when viewing negative circumstances. Adopting a "God's-eye" view of a situation helps us see people not as "merely" but as "more than." Paul saw God orchestrating the events that culminated in Onesimus's transformation (vv. 15–16). Those events could have been seen as random or generated only by the will of a runaway, but Paul saw the hand of God. Joseph saw the same thing in his own painful circumstances: "You meant evil against me, but God meant it for good" (Gen. 50:20). A question may help listeners develop a God's-eye view of difficult circumstances: *what is God inviting you into?* This question is based on the belief that God is sovereign and intends hard circumstances as opportunities for good. When adult children have conflict with their parents, they can ask what God is inviting them into. More patience, empathy, or love? When an angry parishioner starts a whispering campaign about the youth pastor, the youth pastor might be receiving an invitation from God to enter into the sufferings of Christ, or to consider if the faults the parishioner identifies are true.

Creativity in Presentation

As recommended in the previous preaching unit of the commentary (verses 1–7), the intensely personal nature of this epistle could be recreated by structuring the sermon as a narrative. For an example of a third-person narrative, where the preacher serves as the omniscient storyteller, see Haddon Robinson's masterful sermon "Put That on Master Charge," available through the Center for Preaching at Gordon-Conwell Theological Seminary. For a first-person narrative, the story might be told from the perspective of Onesimus who is standing outside of the room where the house church is meeting. He can hear the letter being read and in a series of flashbacks, he might narrate how he has gone from "merely" to "more than."

For a remarkable story of forgiveness and transformation, watch Marcus Doe's TED Talk, "I spent 18 years plotting a murder. Here's why I chose forgiveness." Doe grew up in Liberia, West Africa, and in the Liberian civil war his father was murdered. Doe became a refugee and ended up in Massachusetts. For eighteen years he plotted murder on the person responsible for his father's death, calling him in his mind "General X." Doe says, "Alone at night, I'd sit across from an empty chair and interrogate the man who killed my father." He then imagined himself back in Liberia, and he would plunge a machete into the man's ribs, and with a pistol plant a bullet in his brain. But then Doe read Jesus's words: "If you forgive other people when they sin against you, your heavenly father also will forgive you." They changed his life. Doe says that forgiveness "is not naïve; it's courageous. . . . And it's not simplistic. . . . Because forgiveness frees people like me from living a life clouded by anger and revenge." Marcus returned to Liberia not for revenge but to offer forgiveness. After discovering the real name of General X, he also found out that the murderer was dead. "But I had already forgiven him, and so

I was free," Marcus states with sincerity. The internal work of transformation was already accomplished.

Perhaps a baptism service could be planned in conjunction with a sermon on this passage. People might share using this prompt: "I was merely . . . but now in Christ am more than that."

A scene from the film *Paul, Apostle of Christ* (directed by Andrew Hyatt, 2018) might help capture the circumstance, physical condition, and mood of Paul (played by James Faulkner), the old man who was a prisoner. Although the incarceration depicted in that movie is not the one behind the book of Philemon, the circumstances are similar. Start at the scene that shows the Mamertine Prison.

Personal stories of how Jesus has turned someone from "merely" to "more than" might be provided by a teenager who is learning to overcome feelings of inferiority, a childless couple who are finding joy in God, or a former felon who is now using his hands to serve others. Some churches have had people write their testimonies in a phrase on plain poster board. One side the board says: "I was . . ." and the other side says, "I am . . ." For this sermon, one side might say "Merely . . ." and the other side, "More than . . . ". The key idea to convey deals with identity before and after we believe in Jesus. A person like Onesimus would be easy to overlook and denigrate, but in Christ all such people are much more than they used to be. We should see them that way. Before believing, we were "merely"—but now we are "more than."

- Before we believed, we may have been seen as "merely" (11a).
- After we believed, we became "more than" (11b).
  - Child (10)
  - More than a servant (16a)
  - Brother/sister (16b)

DISCUSSION QUESTIONS

1. Describe the circumstances behind Paul's appeal to Philemon. Who was he and who was Onesimus? How did Paul meet Onesimus?
2. Do you identify more with "merely" or "more than"?
3. What things keep you stuck in "merely"?
4. What lessons can we learn from Paul's persuasion of Philemon? How might you implement one or two of those ideas in the coming week?
5. If you are in a difficult situation right now, what might God be inviting you into? What would a faith-filled perspective show you about that situation?

Philemon 17–25

EXEGETICAL IDEA

Paul instructed Philemon to welcome Onesimus as if he were Paul himself, and if Philemon will embrace Paul's theological vision and do what Paul asks—and more!—then Philemon will have refreshed Paul's heart and prepared the way for Paul to visit Colossae, so they could have fellowship as mates together in Christ.

THEOLOGICAL FOCUS

When believers develop a Christ-centered theological vision through which they see the world, then they are equipped not only to obey the direct commands of Christ but also to discern how to honor Christ in every situation, so that they are mutually refreshed as they welcome one another as mates together in Christ.

PREACHING IDEA

Let's refresh one another by welcoming one another.

PREACHING POINTERS

Paul wraps up the letter to Philemon by finally delivering some imperatives. The old apostle has taken a long on-ramp to these imperatives, but in this passage he pulls into the fast lane with four commands in quick succession: *welcome* Onesimus (v. 17), *charge* his debts to my account (v. 18), *refresh* my heart in Christ (v. 20), and *prepare* a room for me (v. 22). Welcome Onesimus? Easier said than done. Onesimus had shirked his duty, broken their relationship, and shamed his master in the process. But the command was still given: welcome him as you would welcome me. Grace like that would refresh the old apostle.

In the church there are no Greeks or Jews, barbarian, Scythian, slave or free (Col. 3:11). Today we might say that in the church there are no employers or employees, young or old, male or female, Filipino or Japanese, British-Canadian or French-Canadian. Every member of Christ's body is there because of grace, not merit, and all members love and fear the Lord, our master in heaven (Col. 3:22–4:1). That theological vision is the basis of Paul's command to welcome Onesimus who has become part of the body. So, let's refresh one another by welcoming one another.

Today in our polarized culture, welcome is offered to people we agree with—those who vote the way we vote, scoff at the things we scoff at, and dress the ways we dress. But to be part of the church, one does not need to know the "secret handshake." One simply has to confess that Jesus is Lord. That is the basis for why we welcome one another to the family.

WELCOMING ONESIMUS (17–25)

LITERARY STRUCTURE AND THEMES (17–25)

This final section of Paul's short letter to Philemon begins with the transitional "therefore" (οὖν), indicating that what Paul will write now is inferred from what he has already said. In the previous section (Philem. 8–16), Paul developed his appeal to Philemon, but he carefully avoided issuing any commands. Now, in verse 17, Paul delivers the first imperative in the letter that serves also as the apex of his petition to Philemon: "welcome him as me" (προσλαβοῦ αὐτὸν ὡς ἐμέ). This leads to three additional imperatives that round out Paul's appeal and lead toward the closing of the letter: "charge" it to me (ἐλλόγα; Philem. 18), "refresh" my heart (ἀνάπαυσόν; Philem. 20), and "prepare" a guest room for me (ἑτοίμαζέ; Philem. 22). Each of these command focuses Philemon's attention on how his conduct impacts not only Onesimus, but also Paul himself. Philemon has the opportunity to bless and refresh the apostle Paul by how he welcomes Onesimus.

- ***Paul (Finally) Appeals Directly to Philemon (17–20)***
- ***Paul Affirms His Confidence in Philemon (21–22)***
- ***Letter Closing (23–25)***

EXPOSITION (17–25)

Paul saves the climax of his appeal for the closing words of his letter, as he instructs Philemon to welcome Onesimus as he would welcome the apostle Paul himself (Philem. 17), for Paul's heart has become so intertwined with Onesimus that to harm Onesimus would be to harm Paul himself (Philem. 12). Such an appeal was virtually unheard of in their historical context. Philemon would have never seen a slave treated in this way, where such an esteemed person as Paul elevates a lowly slave to his own level and make him a peer. Further, Paul expresses confidence that Philemon will do even more than Paul asks (Philem. 21), thereby placing upon Philemon the additional responsibility of developing the kind of theological thinking that will enable him to discern an ongoing course of action with Onesimus that will honor Christ in ways Paul himself has not yet envisioned. Paul asks a lot of Philemon, but he also comes alongside Philemon in the task, reminding Philemon of their ongoing partnership together in the gospel (Philem. 17) and of his hope to soon be a guest in Philemon's home (Philem. 22). Paul does not appeal to Philemon from a position of authority over him but from a dear relationship as mates walking together in Christ.

Paul (Finally) Appeals Directly to Philemon (17–20)

Paul commands Philemon directly to welcome Onesimus, and Paul bases this command in his own relationship with Philemon and he backs up this command with his commitment to personally pay the costs associated with Philemon's obedience.

17. Paul begins with the following conditional statement that will lead to his first imperative of the letter: "If therefore you have me *as* a partner" (Εἰ οὖν με ἔχεις κοινωνόν). The word Paul uses for "partner" is *koinōnos* (κοινωνός) and it comes from the same root word as *koinōnia* (κοινωνία) in verse 6. The word indicates a person with whom one shares *koinōnia*, and we previously described *koinōnia* as mutual participation in the gospel resulting in believers being mutually identified with one another (see comments on Philem. 6; cf. Wright, 1986, 176). People are *koinōnos* with one another when they have "common interests, common feelings, common work" (Lightfoot, 1981, 343). We might regard such a person not merely as a "companion" or a "partner" (BDAG, s.v. "κοινωνός" 1, p. 553) but as someone with whom we share a much deeper bond and alliance. They are "comrades" (Fitzmyer, 2000, 116) or mates. By making this phrase a conditional statement, Paul invites Philemon to consider whether and to what degree he regards Paul as such a close mate in the gospel, but at the same time, Paul uses a first class condition ("if" [εἰ] followed by an indicative verb) in which the statement should typically be presumed to be true for the sake of the argument (Wallace, 1996, 692–94). He wants Philemon to answer this question for himself, but Paul clearly expects Philemon to answer in the affirmative. "Yes, Paul and I are mates together in the gospel."

On the basis of this personal relationship with the gospel, and in light of all that Paul has already said in the letter, (note the "therefore" [οὖν] early in this verse), Paul finally delivers his imperative to Philemon, "welcome him as me" (προσλαβοῦ αὐτὸν ὡς ἐμέ). The brevity of this command stands in stark contrast to its gravity. All is at stake in the manner with which Philemon welcomes Onesimus into his home. Christians have "an elemental Christian duty" (Bruce, 1984, 219) to welcome one another in the same way in which Christ welcomes us (Rom. 15:7); and now that Onesimus is a Christian, such a duty extends even to Philemon, though Philemon is his aggrieved master. But even more than this, Paul commands Philemon to welcome Onesimus "as me" (ὡς ἐμέ). Philemon must envision how he would welcome Paul should Paul show up at his door—Paul, who is the apostle himself, who has not sinned against Philemon, who is in good standing with Philemon, who has had profound spiritual influence upon Philemon. Surely Philemon would welcome Paul with the warm embrace of a mate, and he would extend to Paul the honor and respect due him as an apostle. In Paul's estimation, Onesimus deserves no less a reception than this, both in Philemon's household and in the church.

The Limits of Welcoming One Another in the Church

If the Christian welcome to one another extends even to Philemon welcoming Onesimus in this situation, then we might wonder whether there is ever a time when Christians should *not* welcome one another. In 1 Corinthians 5, Paul scolds the church in Corinth for overextending their welcome to a man purporting to be a Christian but who is actually living in perpetual and scandalous sin by having adulterous relations with his father's wife. The Corinthians are proud that they could welcome even such an immoral person as a brother, but Paul rebukes them and commands them to cast such a person outside their fellowship, both for the sake of that person's soul, that they might come to repentance, and for the sake of the church, that such immorality might not become widespread among them. Paul then instructs them to judge one another within the church in order to determine who should be welcomed, and they must not extend welcome to those who claim to be brothers but who continue in their sin rather than demonstrating repentance and a new life in Christ (1 Cor. 5:9–13).

Paul's logic, therefore, takes a turn of implication. We can follow the natural logic of a statement such as, "If you regard me as a mate in the gospel, welcome me." But Paul's logic is, "If you regard me as a mate in the gospel, welcome *him as me*." Paul elevates Onesimus and grants him membership as a mate together with Paul and Philemon. They are all three mates in the gospel, and Philemon must now welcome Onesimus as such, for Onesimus is no less a mate to Philemon than is Paul.

18. Paul now anticipates Philemon's potential objection to this command, for how can Philemon welcome as a mate a person who has been anything but a mate up to this point? The mutual participation of *koinōnia* must be mutual, after all, and Philemon has not yet experienced such mutuality with Onesimus, who was not a Christian when he left and may have even wronged Philemon. These are hardly the actions of a mate in the gospel, and such offensive actions must be resolved first if they are to become mates. Thus, Paul next seeks to resolve whatever wrongdoings and debts might remain outstanding between Onesimus and Philemon.

Verse 18 begins with another first-class conditional statement ("if" [εἰ] followed by an indicative verb; cf. Philem. 17), where the statement is presumed to be true for the sake of argument, now suggesting the parallel ideas that Onesimus may have wronged Philemon and owe something to him. First, Paul raises the possibility that Onesimus has wronged Philemon in some way. To "do wrong" (ἀδικέω) may refer generally to treating someone in an unjust manner, or it can refer more specifically to mistreating someone or even causing them injury (BDAG, s.v. "ἀδικέω" 1–2, p. 20), and it may even refer to theft or poor work (TDNT 1.161). Paul does not define the nature of this wrongdoing, but he uses the indefinite pronoun (τὶς) to speak generically of "some" manner of wrong, whatever that wrongdoing might be. Second, Paul points to any potential outstanding debt that Onesimus might "owe" (ὀφείλω) to Philemon, but again, Paul does not describe the nature or size of that debt.

Paul cannot quite bring himself to state explicitly that Onesimus has committed such a wrong, but by using a first-class condition, Paul indirectly suggests such a wrong may well have been committed and such a debt may likely be outstanding, whether Paul knows specifically the nature of that wrong or simply presumes it probably exists, and he knows such wrongs almost certainly do exist in the eyes of Philemon. At the same time, by stating this as a conditional sentence, Paul at least leaves open the possibility that Onesimus has committed no wrong, or at least Onesimus could legitimately reason himself to have committed no wrong, especially if he only left Philemon for the purpose of seeking out Paul's help. Thus, Philemon could surely build a reasonable case that Onesimus has committed serious wrongs, while Onesimus could likely build a reasonable case defending himself against some or all of these charges. But Paul cleverly uses a conditional statement to avoid adjudicating the issue. He sees no need to bring them to agreement regarding whether or not Onesimus has committed wrongs, and of what nature and to what degree, let alone to consider the wrongs Philemon may have committed.[1]

Is Onesimus a Fugitive?

If Onesimus left Philemon only for the sole purpose of seeking out Paul specifically for help in resolving his difference(s) with Philemon, then Onesimus may not have technically been considered a fugitive in the eyes of Roman law, and

1 Here we see another distinctive difference between Paul's approach and that of Pliny in his letter to Sabinianus (Pliny, *Ep.* 9.21; see sidebar on Philem. 10). Pliny reasons that Sabinianus should show mercy to his runaway slave on the basis of the slave's remorse for his wrongdoing. In so doing, Pliny effectively prosecutes the slave and renders him guilty, and he views the slave as having adequately paid for his own wrongdoing by his remorse, so that now Sabinianus would be justified in showing him mercy. Paul, on the other hand, does not admit directly to Onesimus's guilt, nor does he pass along any expression of remorse from Onesimus. Instead, Paul appeals for the price of Onesimus's wrongdoing and debts to be charged to the apostle, not to Onesimus, and only *if* and to whatever degree *Philemon* regards Onesimus as guilty and indebted. Paul does not give Philemon the satisfaction of validating his grievances as legitimate; he simply pays them so they will go away.

therefore he may not have technically committed wrong against Philemon by his departure. In the first century A.D., a Roman jurist named Proculus made just such a ruling that would protect a slave from being labeled a "fugitive" (Latin *fugitivis*, designating a runaway slave) if he had departed for the sole purpose of seeking out a friend to intercede for him:

"The same [Vivian] says that, when Proculus was asked about one who had hidden at home in order to find an opportunity to escape, said: although he could not yet be seen to have run away, being still at home, he was nonetheless a fugitive; but if he had hidden only until his master's anger abated, he would not be a fugitive, just as the one who, when he realized that his master wanted to whip him, betook himself to a friend whom he induced to intercede for him."[2]

Instead, Paul simply acquiesces to Philemon's judgment in this regard, and he insists on paying whatever cost Philemon deems necessary to make right whatever injustices and debts he claims to have endured, whether such claims are in fact legitimate or not. Paul holds forth to Philemon the apostolic credit card and commands Philemon to "charge" (ἐλλογέω) all of Onesimus's bills and wrongdoings to his account. Paul's concern, in other words, is not to sort out who has done what to whom in the past, or who has the greater claim to harm or grievance, nor does Paul seek to have the consequences of the wrongdoing fall back upon the wrongdoer (cf. Col. 3:25); instead, Paul's sole concern is that their relationship be reconciled in such a way that they embrace one another as beloved brothers and mates together in the gospel, and toward this end Paul himself is willing to pay whatever price is necessary.

In so doing, Paul becomes like Christ, who took upon himself the cost of reconciling people to God (Col. 1:20, 22). For Christ, the cost of reconciliation was his life, as his blood was shed on the cross; for Paul, the cost here may not require his life, but it may still be a large expense.[3] We have no way of knowing what kinds of injustices Onesimus may have committed, nor do we know how much debt he may have incurred, whether by theft or otherwise, even before depriving Philemon of his labor after his departure. Paul is not concerned with the cost, for the reward of their reconciliation is worth any price to him. Perhaps Paul also hopes Philemon and the rest of the Colossian church will follow his example and be willing also to sacrifice for the sake of reconciling believers, whether in this situation or in future situations down the road.

19. Paul now doubles down and insists upon repaying. He likely anticipates Philemon's objection to billing such a debt to the apostle Paul, when Philemon would know that he himself has greater means for paying such a debt than does Paul, whose imprisonment has likely drained what meager financial resources he may have had. Nevertheless, Paul is determined that this debt will not linger but will be repaid. He points to his own handwriting with which he writes, saying "I, Paul, am writing with my own hand" (ἐγὼ Παῦλος ἔγραψα τῇ ἐμῇ χειρί). He uses the first-person pronoun, "I" (ἐγώ), followed by his name (Παῦλος), then the first-person verb, "I am writing" (ἔγραψα; epistolary aor.), and finally the first-person possessive pronoun to say, "with my hand" (τῇ ἐμῇ χειρί). This repetition emphasizes his personal attestation to the guarantee of repayment he is making, as if Paul is attaching his own signature.

2 Justinian, *Dig.* 21.1.17.4; Mommsen, et al., 1985, 2.606; cited by Fitzmyer, 2000, 20

3 On the other hand, "we might muse that since one possible punishment for a badly behaved or runaway slave was crucifixion itself, Paul may even be alluding to that: if he deserves the cross, then I'll take it for him!" (Wright, 2013, 19).

Paul uses just two words in Greek to say, "I will repay" (ἐγὼ ἀποτίσω). The Greek word here is straightforward enough, meaning "to make compensation" or "pay damages" (BDAG, s.v. "ἀποτίνω," p. 124). But the simplicity of the statement is emphatic, as if Paul utters each word slowly and forcefully: *I . . . will . . . repay.* There should be no question in Philemon's mind about Paul's determination to repay the debt. Paul is not presuming upon Philemon by asking Philemon to place the debt on Paul's tab but—wink, wink—we all know Paul does not intend to repay the debt and Philemon should not expect to collect the debt, resulting in Paul posturing himself as the hero while Philemon carries the tab. After all, everyone knows—Paul included—that Philemon would never send the apostle to collections no matter how justified he might be in so doing. But Paul is not playing this kind of game. Paul *will* repay.

However, Paul follows this with a rhetorical game of sorts. He uses a Greek phrase that literally says "in order that I *may* not say" (ἵνα μὴ λέγω), but that functions here as an idiom meaning "not to mention" (Campbell, 2013, 91). The irony here is that Paul goes on to mention that which he says ought not to be mentioned.[4] This is a rhetorical sleight of hand where he says the very thing he says he will not say, but by first saying he will not say it, he softens the audacity and effrontery of what he will in fact say. In this case, Paul highlights another debt that remains outstanding, the debt Philemon "still owes" (BDAG, s.v. "προσοφείλω," pp. 883–84) to Paul. But Philemon's debt is not financial, it is personal in a literal sense, as Paul says Philemon owes "yourself" (σεαυτοῦ) to Paul. By this, Paul does not mean that Philemon owes his physical being to Paul, as a slave belongs to their master, but Paul seems to mean that Philemon owes his spiritual life to Paul, as if Philemon would not know Christ were it not for Paul's generous ministry to Philemon. We can only speculate regarding how Philemon came to be influenced by Paul. Perhaps Philemon encountered Paul in Ephesus and was evangelized and/or discipled directly by Paul, or perhaps Philemon has indirectly benefited from Paul through the ministry of Paul's letters or his coworkers, perhaps including Epaphras (on this latter option, see Dunn 1996, 340). Regardless of how it was accrued, the debt Philemon owes Paul remains outstanding.

Why would Paul mention this debt at this point in his appeal for Onesimus? We might read Paul's words as if Paul is entering into the world of reciprocity, where debts are held out and favors are called in, but though Paul reminds Philemon of his debt, Paul does not draw upon that debt or pressure Philemon for repayment. It seems, rather, that Paul is actually exposing systems of reciprocity as endlessly circular and ultimately incompatible with Christ. Where does it all end, if every deed, whether good or evil, is quantified and entered into ledgers as debits and credits toward one another? How can the spiritual debt Philemon owes to Paul be quantified? And how can the financial debt Onesimus owes to Philemon ever be traded against such a debt? Paul brings the spiritual debt of Philemon into view not to call for payment against the debt, as legitimate as such a call would be, but to highlight that though he *could* operate in this way, he chooses *not* to. Instead, in the body of Christ, does not love require the elimination of record-keeping (1 Cor. 13:5), and are not all believers called to forgive whatever they might have against one another (Col. 3:13), and should not the only debt that remains outstanding be the debt of loving one another (Rom. 13:8)? If Paul can operate in such a way toward Philemon, then the implication is that Philemon should act in the same way toward

4 This rhetorical ploy is technically called "paralipsis," where "a writer pretends to pass over . . . a matter he actually mentions" (Harris, 2010, 238, 267).

Onesimus, even though Paul is determined to pay the cost of Onesimus's debt himself.

20. Nonetheless, Paul reaffirms the potential Philemon has to engage in a new kind of spiritual transaction, no longer counting debts and payments against debts, but now engaging in the open market of blessing one another with kindness and generosity. "Yes" (ναί), Paul begins, thereby identifying his current instruction as an "emphatic repetition" of what he has just said (BDAG, s.v. "ναί" c, p. 665; cf. Harris, 2010, 239). He then speaks directly to Philemon with the vocative, "brother" (ἀδελφέ), a form of address common to Paul but perhaps unexpected here since Paul just described himself effectively as the spiritual father of Philemon. By again calling him a brother (cf. Philem. 7), Paul levels the playing field and stands alongside Philemon as a peer not only of Philemon, but also of Onesimus (cf. Philem. 16).

It is as a brother that Paul now expresses to Philemon his personal desire to be blessed by Philemon. Paul uses two personal pronouns, the first person followed by the second person, to say, "I *from* you" (ἐγώ σου), and then he uses an optative verb (ὀναίμην) to express his desire to receive a benefit from Philemon. The verb itself refers to being "the recipient of a favor or benefit, or to "enjoy" something (BDAG, s.v. "ὀνίνημι," p. 711), and the optative mood expresses this as "an obtainable wish" (Wallace, 1996, 481–83). Thus, Paul is wishing to receive benefit or joy from Philemon for himself. It is surely no coincidence that this verb (ὀνίνημι) comes from the same root as the name Onesimus (Ὀνήσιμος) and it appears only here in the New Testament. The benefit Paul desires is inherently connected to Onesimus, and this benefit would come "in the Lord" (ἐν κυρίῳ), which is to say, as brothers who share life together in the same Lord Jesus and under his authority.

Paul's desire then turns into exhortation in the form of an imperative: "refresh my heart in Christ" (ἀνάπαυσόν μου τὰ σπλάγχνα ἐν Χριστῷ). The language here clearly reflects Paul's affirmation of Philemon in verse 7 that he has refreshed the hearts of the saints. Paul uses the same verb, "refresh" (ἀναπαύω), and the same object, "heart" or literally "inward parts (σπλάγχνον), but now he speaks of his own heart. The location of the word "my" (μου) early in the phrase makes it emphatic in order to underscore that Paul believes "it is now *my* turn to be refreshed" (Wright, 1986, 189). Paul wants for himself the same benefit Philemon has extended to the saints. Philemon has the opportunity to bring rest, relief, and renewed vitality to the inner disposition of the weary apostle who suffers in the chains of imprisonment. Notice, again, that Paul has moved far beyond something as trivial as calling in a debt; he appeals to Philemon as a brother in Christ, with a deep longing in his heart and a weariness in his soul, and he calls for Philemon to act once more out of the same love and generosity that has already refreshed the hearts of many saints, in order that Paul's own heart might again be refreshed.

How will Philemon refresh his heart? By heeding Paul's appeal on behalf of Onesimus, who is Paul's very heart (Philem. 12). If Philemon would just welcome Onesimus as he would welcome Paul, and embrace Onesimus no longer as a slave but as a beloved brother, and no longer count Onesimus's debt against him but charge it to Paul's account, and if Philemon would do these things not out of compulsion but out of his own free will, then how could Paul's heart not be refreshed? There is nothing so refreshing to the heart of a servant and minister of the Lord Jesus Christ than to see the people of Christ "get it" and learn to live in the way of Christ by showing extraordinary love and mercy and kindness to one another as they forgive one another and embrace one another as brothers and sisters in Christ.

Paul Affirms His Confidence in Philemon (21–22)

Paul expresses his confidence in Philemon and hints that Philemon might do even more than Paul asks, even as Paul desires to visit Philemon soon.

21. Paul now brings his appeal to its conclusion. He expresses confidence in Philemon by saying that he is "convinced of your obedience" (Πεποιθὼς τῇ ὑπακοῇ). The perfect form (πεποιθως) of the verb Paul uses means "to be so convinced that one puts confidence in something" (BDAG, s.v. "πείθω" 2, p. 792), but in this case, Paul has not become convinced through direct conversation with Philemon but through the indirect persuasion of Philemon's established character. Philemon is Paul's beloved fellow worker (Philem. 1), his love has encouraged Paul and refreshed the saints (Philem. 5, 7), Paul anticipates his goodness (Philem. 14) and regards him as a partner (Philem. 17), and they have a bond whereby Philemon owes his faith in Christ to Paul (Philem. 19). These traits exhibited by Philemon and evident to Paul are sufficient to convince Paul of Philemon's obedience.

Word Study on "Obedience"

The word Paul uses with regard to Philemon's "obedience" (ὑπακοή) appears frequently in Paul's letters but not necessarily with reference to obeying a particular command. Instead, the term refers more broadly to "a state of being in compliance" (BDAG, s.v. "ὑπακοή" 1, p. 1028), or to what Paul calls the "obedience of faith" (ὑπακοὴν πίστεως; Rom. 1:5), which is the totality of a life shaped by the gospel into Christian maturity (e.g., Rom. 6:16; 15:18; 16:19, 26; 2 Cor. 10:16). In 2 Corinthians 7:13–16, Paul commends the Corinthian church for proving Paul's boasting regarding their faith to be true when by their "obedience" (ὑπακοή) they received Titus in such a way that Titus's spirit was refreshed by them. As with Philemon, the Corinthians are not necessarily heeding a specific command, but they are being obedient insofar as they are embodying the character of Christ in how they receive Titus. Paul is confident Philemon will demonstrate the same kind of broad obedience to the Lord Jesus with regard to Onesimus.

But how can Paul describe Philemon's response to this letter as "obedience" (ὑπακοή) when Paul explicitly said he would not command Philemon (Philem. 8)? We must remember that though Paul began his appeal by forgoing commands and instead appealing on the basis of love in verse 8, he went on to use imperatives commanding Philemon to receive Onesimus (Philem. 17), charge his debts to Paul's account (Philem. 18), and refresh Paul's heart (Philem. 20). These commands seemingly arise not because Paul views himself in a position of authority over Philemon but because he sees Philemon standing under the authority of the Lord Jesus. Even as Philemon strives to live a life of obedience before the Lord, so also Philemon is obligated to discharge his duty before the Lord in this situation, and Paul has done his best to guide Philemon in how this ought to be done. Thus, in Paul's estimation, Philemon must *obey* the Lord Jesus by heeding Paul's *appeal*, and Paul is confident he will do so.

Paul ends this verse with one of the greatest teasers in all of Scripture. Even as he "writes" (ἔγραψά; an epistolary aorist translated in the present tense) this letter to Philemon, Paul says he knows Philemon will do "above what I am saying" (ὑπὲρ ἃ λέγω). The vagueness of this tantalizing statement invites all sorts of imaginative conjecture. Perhaps Paul wants Philemon to send Onesimus back to Paul as an assistant and disciple of Paul. Perhaps Paul wants Philemon to emancipate Onesimus. Perhaps Paul wants Philemon to renounce slavery on the whole and to start a movement of abolition. Paul opens the gate and sets free our imaginations to run wild and to explore new frontiers of obedience to Christ.

And this creativity seems to be precisely what Paul intends to spark—creativity centered in Christ and discovering how the ways of Christ should be lived out among the people of Christ. It is fitting, then, for us to engage at this point in some imaginative speculation of our own regarding Paul's intention. If we grant that Paul wants to see Philemon go beyond Paul's words but to stay within the spirit and trajectory of Paul's appeal, then it would be strange for Paul to intend for "going beyond" to mean sending Onesimus away to work with Paul or emancipating Onesimus to live out his freedom apart from Philemon. Instead, given that Paul appeals for Philemon to welcome Onesimus as a brother in Christ, it makes better sense that Paul wants them to go above and beyond their initial embrace as brothers and to imagine what it would look like to *continue* living alongside one another as brothers in Christ, both in the household and in the church.

Perhaps Philemon and Onesimus will learn to forgive and to be ruled by peace in their relationship with one another (Col. 3:15). Perhaps they will grow alongside one another, teaching and admonishing *one another* (Col. 3:16), so that Philemon humbly allows Onesimus to teach and admonish him too. Perhaps they will set an example for the church in what it means for there to be neither slave nor free in the body of Christ, where Christ is everything (Col. 3:11). Perhaps they will become partners in the gospel, working together to lead the church and to proclaim the gospel in Colossae. These vistas of brotherhood appear farther down the very path Paul charts in the letter, if only their imaginations can carry them so far in Christ.

The Boundaries of Christian Imagination

Paul encourages Philemon to imagine what it would look like to go beyond what Paul asks, but can such imagination be applied to other situations such as homosexuality? In his book *Slaves, Women and Homosexuals: Exploring the Hermeneutics of Cultural Analysis*, William Webb develops what he calls a "redemptive-movement hermeneutic" whereby biblical texts should be carefully interpreted in light of the trajectories or movements they establish with regard to cultural engagement (Webb, 2001). Or, stated differently, our imaginations should be constrained by the Bible's redemptive movements regarding particular issues of cultural relevance. His careful analysis leads him to conclude that while Scripture on the one hand confronts ancient culture by embracing slaves and establishing trajectories for emancipation and abolition, on the other hand, Scripture confronts ancient culture by standing against homosexual practice as sin without ever presenting trajectories whereby homosexuality would be embraced. He finds a more ambiguous middle ground regarding women, where Scripture in some ways stands against cultural patriarchy while at other times affirming that God has established forms of patriarchal order within creation. Therefore, our Christian imaginations should lead us toward abolition of slavery but not toward affirming homosexual conduct.

22. Paul winds down his appeal now with an instruction that comes "at the same time" (ἅμα) and is in some way related to his confidence in Philemon's obedience from the previous verse. He tells Philemon to prepare a guest room for Paul. The Greek term often translated "guest room" (ξενία; e.g., NIV, NRSV, ESV, HCSB, etc.) can refer more broadly to the hospitality and entertainment properly shown to a guest, or more specifically to the lodging or room in which the guest will stay (BDAG, s.v. "ξενία," p. 683). Either meaning would work here, but the broader implications of hospitality align better with the instructions Paul has already given to Philemon regarding how he should welcome Onesimus as he would Paul (Philem. 17). Paul intends for Philemon to show hospitality to Onesimus far beyond merely preparing a guest room, and it stands to reason that Paul now leans upon Philemon to prepare to give such a warm welcome for Paul himself. Thus, the proper response "would doubtless be a hospitable reception in Philemon's house" (Lightfoot, 1981, 345).

But Paul's imminent visit is in no way certain; Paul's hope is contingent upon the providence of God. Paul explains that the hospitality should be ready "because" (γάρ) Paul "hopes" (ἐλπίζω) to travel to them. His hope is less the confident expectation of what has been promised by God for his people (e.g., Col. 1:5; cf. Rom. 8:23–25) and more the wishful optimism of what God may or may not grant. He assumes that not only Philemon, but also the entire church, is praying for him, for it will be "through your [pl.] prayers" (διὰ τῶν προσευχῶν ὑμῶν) that Paul hopes "I will be given to you [pl.]" (χαρισθήσομαι ὑμῖν). Paul requested prayer in the letter to the Colossians (Col. 4:3) but not specifically toward this end. He presumes Philemon and the Colossians desire a visit from him despite the appeal he has delivered in the letter, but he also acknowledges the providence of God in determining whether or not Paul would be delivered from his chains and enabled to make a visit, even as God purposed and superintended the scenario with Onesimus (Philem. 15–16) And should it happen, it would be a gift (χαρίζομαι is the verbal form of χάρις, meaning "grace" or "gift") from God and should be received by them as such.

Paul's desire to visit, therefore, is not so much about applying pressure to Philemon, whether as a form of accountability or a thinly veiled threat, though such a desire cannot help but be heard with a tone of warning. Rather, Paul's desire to visit arises from his confidence that Philemon will do the right thing, so that Paul desires to visit in order to share in the joy of reconciled brothers and a church that has offered a full and gracious welcome to Onesimus. Such a visit would further refresh Paul's heart and lead to encouragement and strengthening for all involved. His visit would not be a perfunctory duty of oversight; it would be a final exclamation point upon the gracious work of God among this circle of brothers in Christ.

Letter Closing (23–25)

Paul closes the letter with a short list of greetings and a final blessing upon the entire church in Colossae.

23. The letter closes with customary greetings, but in keeping with the relatively brief nature of the letter, the greetings are minimal when compared to other letters of Paul that contain greetings. This brevity may further be explained in light of the significant overlap between these greetings and those contained in Colossians 4:10–14. Of the six people named in Colossians, five are repeated here in Philemon (Epaphras, Mark, Aristarchus, Demas, and Luke) and only Jesus called Justusis missing.

The first greeting comes from the well-known Epaphras, who "greets you" (ἀσπάζεταί σε). Note that the greeting is directed singularly (σε) to Philemon rather than to the entire church. Epaphras is well-known to the Colossians and surely to Philemon, since he is the one who first brought the gospel to Colossae (Col. 1:7). Therefore, here as in Colossians, Epaphras receives the most extended commentary within the greetings (cf. Col. 4:12–13). Paul calls him "my fellow prisoner" (ὁ συναιχμάλωτός μου) in Christ Jesus. This is the very same way Paul described Aristarchus, who came first in the greetings in Colossae (Col. 4:10), but now Aristarchus is mentioned without being called a prisoner. Perhaps Paul uses this word literally, as if various members of his coworkers are being arrested and released on occasion (Wright, 1986, 191). But more likely he is describing those who are close to him in his imprisonment, perhaps even taking turns in voluntary staying at his side in prison (Dunn, 1996, 348). Thus, Epaphras the native Colossian, who loves Colossae and longs to return, should be held in highest regard by the Colossians during his absence, for he is serving and suffering alongside the apostle Paul.

24. The rest of the greetings are simply a list of names followed by a comprehensive description of them all as "my fellow workers" (οἱ συνεργοί μου). Paul earlier designated Philemon as his beloved fellow worker (Philem. 1), so that these are coworkers not only of Paul but of Philemon too. They all share together in Christ and in the work of the gospel, and Paul invites Philemon to see himself as part of this team. Perhaps Philemon already does know these folks, since Paul sees no need to further commend them, but Paul does provide further commentary on them in Colossians 4:10–14 that can be summarized briefly here. Mark once had a falling out with Paul but was then reconciled, and when he arrives in Colossae, the church must welcome him (Acts 13:13; 15:36–40; Col. 4:10). Aristarchus was at one time Paul's fellow prisoner (Col. 4:10). Demas is with Paul at this time, but Paul does not commend him in either letter, and Demas would one day choose to love the world and to abandon Paul (Col. 4:14; 2 Tim. 4:11). Finally, Luke is the doctor who traveled extensively with Paul and remained with him to the end (Col. 4:14; 2 Tim. 4:11). All are coworkers who stand with and alongside not only Paul, but also Philemon.

25. The letter closes with a final benediction of grace, as Paul wishes upon the spirits of all in Colossae (note the plural μετὰ τοῦ πνεύματος ὑμῶν; "with *all* your spirits") that "grace which belongs to the Lord Jesus Christ" (Ἡ χάρις τοῦ κυρίου Ἰησοῦ Χριστοῦ). All of Paul's letters, with the exception of Romans, conclude with a blessing of grace (e.g., 1 Cor. 16:23; 2 Cor. 13:14; Gal. 6:18; Eph. 6:24; Phil. 4:23; Col. 4:18; 1 Thess. 5:28; 2 Thess. 3:18; 1 Tim. 6:21; 2 Tim. 4:22; Titus 3:15)—even as all of his letters, including Philemon, begin with a blessing of grace and peace upon the recipients (Rom. 1:7; 1 Cor. 1:3; 2 Cor. 1:2; Gal. 1:3; Eph. 1:2; Phil. 1:2; Col. 1:2; 1 Thess. 1:1; 2 Thess. 1:2; 1 Tim. 1:2; 2 Tim. 1:2; Titus 1:4). In the letter to Philemon, these blessings at the beginning and end are the only explicit mentions of grace; otherwise, this most important of Pauline themes is strikingly absent. Nevertheless, the concept of grace has undergirded the entire letter, as Paul's appeal rests upon the grace of Christ and calls upon Philemon to demonstrate that same grace toward Onesimus by forgiving, reconciling, and embracing him as a brother in Christ. Philemon's compliance will demand an extraordinary measure of grace; and the church too needs grace in abundance, as does Onesimus, and even Paul. Thus, for Paul, there is no better final word than to wish upon them that which is most essential for them as they walk this path: the grace of the Lord Jesus Christ abounding in their spirits.

An Epilogue?

The story of Onesimus and Philemon may be one of the greatest cliffhangers in all of Scripture, for we have no further indication in the Bible for how Philemon responds to Paul's letter and what becomes of Onesimus. Paul's confidence in Philemon would suggest a favorable outcome, as also does the fact that the letter was retained and canonized by the church. But perhaps the most tantalizing clue comes in a letter written about fifty years later (ca. A.D. 110) by Ignatius of Antioch, wherein Ignatius mentions an Onesimus who is at that time the bishop of Ephesus. Ignatius commends this Bishop Onesimus for his great love, and Ignatius even encourages the church to become like their excellent bishop (Ignatius, *Eph* 1:3; cf. 2:1; 6:2).[5] Before we jump to conclusions, we must

5 Bruce finds in this section of Ignatius's letters evidence that Ignatius was familiar with Paul's letter to Philemon, and for Bruce, this strengthens the case that this is the same Onesimus (Bruce, 1984, 201).

acknowledge that Onesimus was at that time a very common name, and by the time of Ignatius's letter, the slave Onesimus would have been advancing in years if he was still living, so this may very well not be the same Onesimus.

But what if this *is* the same Onesimus? Then we can surmise that Philemon not only embraced Onesimus as a brother in Christ, but somewhere along the way Onesimus also grew in Christ and was entrusted with leadership in the church, perhaps first in Colossae and then throughout the broader region as a bishop. Could there, then, have been a time when Onesimus and Philemon were leaders alongside one another in the church? And could there even have been a time when Onesimus was a leader in the church *over* Philemon his master? If so, then whether or not Philemon ever emancipated Onesimus, he certainly gave Onesimus the freedom and the resources that would allow him to flourish in Christ and to grow into and even to surpass the potential Paul saw in Onesimus for service in gospel ministry. *Bishop* Onesimus—perhaps *this* was the result of Philemon's imagination leading him to do even more than Paul asked.

If indeed this was Philemon's response, then Philemon truly did go far beyond the cultural norms of his day as represented by the response of Sabinianus to Pliny's appeal for a runaway slave (see sidebar on Philem. 10). Pliny writes a second letter to Sabinianus in which Pliny commends Sabinianus for how he has forgiven and welcomed back his slave, and Pliny appeals for Sabinianus to continue to treat his slaves in this manner in the future, but we see no evidence that Sabinianus has done anything beyond restoring their past relationship as master and slave

Pliny's second letter reads as follows: "It was commendable of you to restore to your home and affection the freedman who was earlier dear to you, after my letter had guided him back to you. Your gesture will be of service to you; at any rate it is gratifying to me, first because I see that you are sufficiently amenable to be able to accept guidance when angry, and secondly because you repose sufficient trust in me either to follow my authority or to be open to my pleas. So you win both my praise and my thanks, but at the same time, my advice for the future is that you show yourself ready to forgive the misdemeanours of your servants, even if there is no one to plead for them. Farewell" (Pliny, *Ep.* 9.24; trans. Walsh, 2006).

How great is the contrast, then, for Philemon and Onesimus, if indeed their newly inscribed relationship led to Onesimus the bishop.

THEOLOGICAL FOCUS

The exegetical idea (Paul instructed Philemon to welcome Onesimus as if he were Paul himself, and if Philemon will embrace Paul's theological vision and do what Paul asks—and more!—then Philemon will have refreshed Paul's heart and prepared the way for Paul to visit Colossae, so they could have fellowship as mates together in Christ) leads to this theological focus: When believers develop a Christ-centered theological vision through which they see the world, then they are equipped not only to obey the direct commands of Christ but also to discern how to honor Christ in every situation, so that they are mutually refreshed as they welcome one another as mates together in Christ.

In these final verses of his letter to Philemon, Paul's appeal reaches its crescendo. This is the culmination not only of what he writes in this letter but also of what he has written in the letter to the Colossians, as Paul brings all of the theology of Colossians—with its extraordinary description of Christ, and of union with Christ, and new life in Christ—to bear now upon Philemon's imagination, so that Philemon would not only receive Onesimus as he would receive Paul himself, but Philemon would also discern what it would mean to do even more than Paul asks. This kind of imagination requires Philemon to be guided by a theological vision through which he sees this situation and determines the proper course to obey Christ.

Richard Lints describes a theological vision in the following way: "A theological vision seeks to capture the entire counsel of God as revealed in the Scriptures and to communicate it in a conceptuality that is native to the theologian's own age. A theological vision invites one to commit to a peculiar 'way of thinking,' and this involves discovering as well as recovering the revelation of God and then understanding how that revelation affects the way one thinks and lives" (Lints, 1993, 9). For Philemon, such a theological vision requires his thinking to be transformed by the peacemaking work of Christ through which all kinds of people have been brought together within the body of Christ, where anger and wrath must be replaced by forgiveness, love, and peace (Col. 1:20–22; 3:5–15).

When Philemon sees the world with this kind of vision, then his view of Onesimus is transformed from Onesimus being merely an estranged and indebted slave to him now being a beloved brother whose debts must no longer be held against him, even if this requires charging his debts to Paul. This theological vision must also guide Philemon in envisioning Onesimus as a beloved brother, so that he will extend to Onesimus the kind of welcome appropriate for all who belong to Christ, including the apostle Paul himself. For Philemon, this theological vision begins with hospitality extended to all who know Christ, but it does not end there. Paul lays upon Philemon the command to do even more than this, as Philemon's theological vision continues to sharpen its Christological focus and to guide him even farther down paths of obedience to Christ.

What might happen among Christians today if we would develop a robust theological vision centered upon Christ and allow it to be the lens through which we see the world around us and determine how we will treat one another in the body of Christ? If we would take the theological lessons of the book of Colossians and apply them to our vision, then we will be transformed along with Philemon and empowered with the clarity and imagination we need to find our way down paths of Christian faithfulness. Along the way, we will learn to forgive one another, to reconcile with one another, to embrace one another as beloved brothers and sisters in Christ regardless of our background, to welcome one another with hospitality, to experience *koinōnia* together in the gospel, and to do even more than this together in Christ, all in the name of Christ and all for the glory of Christ. Such is the high calling of the church, and toward this each Christian strives—even charging the costs to their own account!—and by this each Christian's heart is refreshed, when every believer develops a Christ-centered theological vision that guides and compels them to walk faithfully in the ways of Christ in every situation, both now and forevermore.

PREACHING AND TEACHING STRATEGIES

Exegetical and Theological Synthesis

In the last section of Philemon, Paul finally makes a direct appeal with the first imperatives of the letter. Up to this point, Paul has been setting the stage, but now he calls his leading actor to the stage—Philemon—to give stage directions: "welcome him [Onesimus] as you would welcome me" (Philem. 17), "charge it to me" (Philem. 18), and "refresh my heart" (Philem. 20). In a final word, Paul adds one more imperative: "prepare a guest room for me" (Philem. 22). Paul expected a lot from Philemon, but he was confident in his fellow worker's character and in their brotherly relationship. In fact, their relationship was also father-son, for Philemon owed his spiritual life to Paul (Philem. 19). Thus, Paul believes that

Philemon would do even more than merely welcome Onesimus (Philem. 21). What Paul had in mind is not spelled out. He left it up to his friend to determine how to act upon this tantalizing hint. Paul then closes in the same way he used in nearly all of his epistles with greetings and a final blessing (Philem. 22–23).

Preaching Idea

Let's refresh one another by welcoming one another.

Contemporary Connections

What does it mean?

What does it mean to refresh one another by welcoming one another? For Philemon it meant that he should overlook the "crime" of his runaway slave, Onesimus, and receive him back into the household. With providence and grace, the Lord had brought Onesimus under the ministry of Paul even while Onesimus was on the run, and he had been converted. Now Paul was starting to graft him into his evangelistic team. Onesimus was formerly perceived as useless, but now he was very useful to Paul, especially as an aide while the old apostle was in prison. But Paul sets aside his own needs, sends Onesimus back to Philemon and the house church, and commands: "welcome him as you would welcome me" (Philem. 17). To make the task easier for Philemon, Paul issues a second imperative: "charge anything he owes you to my account" (Philem. 18). And then a third imperative fills out the meaning of "welcome": "refresh my heart in the Lord" (Philem. 20). When church members extend grace to one another, church leaders take heart. Seeing the body of Christ operate as God intends, by welcoming one another, is water in the desert for an old apostle or a young pastor.

It is water for parents also when they see their children love one another. As the apostle John said, "I have no greater joy than to hear that my children are walking in the truth" (3 John 4). It is also water for leaders of small groups, managers of offices, deans of faculties, and coaches of teams. Welcoming someone because Jesus has welcomed us into his family is one of the most beautiful and inviting actions we can take as Christians and it refreshes us.

Is it true?

Should Christians really welcome one another? The whole of Scripture, what Lints calls a "theological vision," answers yes. The book of Romans is representative: "Welcome one another as Christ has welcomed you" (Rom. 15:7). "As for the one weak in faith, welcome him, but not to quarrel over opinions . . . for God has welcomed him" (Rom. 14:1, 3). Even people who have not heard of Christ can extend grace by welcoming destitute people (Acts 28:2).

Welcoming one another is motivated by the fact that God has welcomed us. Grace fuels the engine of the church. The Pharisee in Jesus's parable who despised the tax collector didn't understand this (Luke 18:9–14); neither did the crowd that grumbled outside the house of Zacchaeus (Luke 19:1–10); neither did the dishonest manager who choked the fellow who owed him a small sum, having forgotten his own enormous debt forgiven by his master (Matt. 18:23–35).

But are there limits to welcoming? Yes. False teachers who deny Christ are not to be welcomed into the assembly (2 John 11–12). Church members who live in flagrant sin and make the church laughable in the eyes of unbelievers should not be welcomed (1 Cor. 5:9–13). But when such people repent, we must reaffirm our love for them (2 Cor. 2:5–11). Placing limits on welcoming may be a hard truth for some listeners because "tolerance" seems to be the highest value pluralistic societies can agree on. But tolerance today connotes something beyond harmonious coexistence. More and more it demands celebration as when the church is pressured not only to tolerate same-sex sexual relations, but also to support and celebrate them. Anything less is seen as judgmental, hateful, and repugnant. So, Christ-followers must be as wise as serpents and as innocent as doves (Matt. 10:16) as we "walk in wisdom toward outsiders" (Col. 4:5).

Now what?

How might we refresh one another by welcoming one another? Cards, gifts, warm words of hospitality, sharing meals, opening our homes for long- or short-term stays, and giving rides or loaning cars are practical ways to welcome and refresh. In church services, some assemblies ask visitors to stand and be recognized. Other assemblies have decided that this embarrasses newcomers and alienates, not welcomes, them. However we decide to implement the command to welcome people to the family, it should be based on the theological vision of grace. In his book *The Five Love Languages*, Gary Chapman (1992) describes how people express and give love differently, so they appreciate receiving love in the same way.

Five Love Languages from Gary Chapman

- Words of Affirmation
- Quality Time
- Receiving Gifts
- Acts of Service
- Physical Touch

Baptism services are an ideal time to welcome new members into the family. Some churches applaud when a new believer is immersed or when a baby is sprinkled. Perhaps a reception and meal could be planned following the baptism. Meals are nonverbal acts of welcome, and the letter in Revelation to the church in Laodicea uses that metaphor to talk about the fellowship Jesus extends to us: "Behold, I stand at the door and knock. If anyone hears my voice and opens the door, I will come in to him and eat with him, and he with me" (Rev. 3:20). When one pastor began his ministry in a new church, his first sermon series was called "Meals with Jesus" (the stories of Zacchaeus in Jericho, Matthew at his collection booth, etc.), and in conjunction with the series, families were encouraged to open their homes to share meals with church members, newcomers, and outsiders.

The importance of the "welcome team" at churches can hardly be overestimated. The initial impression made on visitors, and even on long-time members, influences how they perceive the words and events that follow. A theory from psychology and interpersonal communication suggests why the initial welcome is so important. The theory is called the "halo effect." An initial positive experience with a person or organization has a trickle-down effect on succeeding perceptions. If the greeters wear a "halo," the one greeted tends to perceive the rest of the service in positive terms. Starting well is half the battle!

The command to welcome each other may be especially pertinent in a day of unprecedented migration and immigration. Hundreds of thousands, if not millions, of refugees crowd the camps and cities of Europe, and the United States is not far behind. The "new world" has always held out a beacon to immigrants (see the sidebar below), but in a day of increasing nationalism, the beacon may have dimmed. The church can respond with simple yet profound measures as we live out our theological vision. The documentary *Jesus in Athens* (directed by Peter Hansen, 2019) shows how evangelical churches in that city are living out the vision of grace with beautiful acts of hospitality, and those acts are opening hundreds of doors for gospel proclamation. The churches depicted in the film are truly walking in wisdom toward outsiders.

"The New Colossus" by Emma Lazarus

In the harbor of New York City stands Lady Liberty. She holds a torch in one hand and a tablet in the other. On a bronze plaque inside the Statue of Liberty is inscribed the text of the poem "The New Colossus," composed by Emma Lazarus. The final lines state:

> Give me your tired, your poor,
> Your huddled masses yearning to breathe free,
> The wretched refuse of your teeming shore.
> Send these, the homeless, tempest-tost to me,
> I lift my lamp beside the golden door!

Philemon's example of refreshing the saints by offering hospitality is a great reminder and model for us. Here are some ways to extend hospitality:

- Don't wait until everything is perfect. If you have a 1,200-square-foot apartment, that is a stewardship that can be used to refresh insiders and outsiders.
- Use your spiritual gift for your own kind of hospitality (1 Peter 4:10). Hospitality does not have to be formulaic. If your gift is teaching, open your home for Bible study; if it is administration, organize a welcome party for immigrants; if is encouragement, take your hospitality on the road to the hospital or "shut-ins."
- Recognize the difference between hospitality and entertaining. The first seeks to bless but the second seeks to impress. Martha may have been caught up in the first, but Jesus would have been satisfied with just one dish (Luke 10:38–42). Entertaining fixates on things like perfectly matched table settings recently purchased from Pinterest, but hospitality focuses on the people. Chicken soup and crusty bread is just fine. It doesn't have to be prime rib.
- Check your heart. In 1 Peter 4:9, the apostle Peter speaks candidly: "Offer hospitality without grumbling." Too often we play the role of host or hostess, but it is just a role and we can't wait until people leave. Guests can sense this.
- Pay attention to cultural ceremonies related to greeting and departing: things like removing shoes, kissing on the check, bowing, and thanking the hosts.

Creativity in Presentation

An illustration from current events may suggest how paying others' debts is a way to extend grace and provide refreshment: a generous Uber passenger helped the driver finish her college degree. Latonya Young, a hairstylist who moonlights as an Uber driver, says: "That one ride changed me." Young picked up Kevin Esch outside of a stadium. As they chatted, Young mentioned that she recently withdrew from college because of an unpaid student account. In her words, "Every time I got ready to pay the money, my kids needed something." A few days after the ride, the Uber driver was surprised to receive word that she was eligible to register for classes at Georgia State University. Esch had paid her $700 debt. Esch told CNN, "There was something about Latonya that resonates with me. . . . I could've bought new clothes or I could've helped someone out. And what has come back to me has come back a hundredfold and I would do it 1,000 times over." [You might say that he was "refreshed" for this act of grace.] In December, Esch attended the graduation ceremony at Georgia State University to see Young receive an associate's degree in criminal justice (Hughes, 2020).

A live illustration could convey the concept of a debt being canceled. A volunteer, perhaps a child, could draw a dollar sign on an Etch-a-Sketch or write it with vanishing ink, and then the symbol could be erased or fade away. Perhaps a Clorox stain stick could serve the same purpose as it eliminates a stain. A record of sins could even be burnt or nailed to a cross because Christ's substitutionary atonement is the supreme example of paying someone else's debt.

The theme of extending grace through self-sacrifice has received treatment in many works of literature such as the final scene in *A Tale of Two Cities* by Charles Dickens (1859). One character, Carton, takes the place of another, Darnay, at the guillotine. Another well-known scene comes from Victor Hugo's *Les Miserables* (1862). A newly released prisoner, Jean Valjean, is turned away from all inns because he is a former convict, but Bishop Myriel takes him in. At night, Valjean steals Myriel's silverware. The police apprehend him and bring him to the bishop, but the bishop pretends that he has given the silverware to Valjean. He even presses him to take two silver candlesticks, claiming that Valjean had forgotten them. The police scratch their heads but leave. Bishop Myriel tells Valjean that his life has been spared for God, and that he should use the money from the silver to make an honest man of himself. That act of grace transforms the thief. The novel has been adapted many times for stage and screen, and many clips of the scene are available.

A scene of self-sacrifice can be found in *Star Trek II: The Wrath of Khan* (directed by Nicholas Meyer, 1982). As Spock (played by Leonard Nimoy) dies, he speaks the memorable line, "The needs of the many outweigh the needs of the few or the one."

As recommended in the previous preaching units of this commentary on Philemon, a narrative sermon could help bring the background, relations, and dramatic tension alive. Perhaps *Bishop* Onesimus (see Exposition sidebar) could recount his story from many years ago.

Whatever form we use for the sermon, make sure it serves the main teaching: Let's refresh one another by welcoming one another.

- To welcome each other, we might cover expenses (18–19).

- To welcome each other, we might offer hospitality (20–22).

DISCUSSION QUESTIONS

1. What commands does Paul give Philemon? (There are four.)

2. Why do you think Paul delayed in making those commands?

3. Why did Paul leave this statement open ended: "Knowing that you will do even more than I say" (Philem. 21)? Use your imagination to think about how Philemon might have gone beyond the letter of the law with Onesimus.

4. Do you need to forgive someone? Can you pay someone's debt?

5. Knowing the importance of welcoming people to the family of God, what are some ways your church can upgrade this?

6. Besides welcoming people to church services, how might you extend grace to people in your own sphere, perhaps extended family, or coworkers, or in your social circles?

REFERENCES

Abbott, T. K. 1897. *A Critical and Exegetical Commentary on the Epistles to the Ephesians and to the Colossians.* ICC. Edinburgh: T&T Clark.

Aletti, J. 1993. *Saint Paul: Épître Aux Colossiens.* Etudes Bibliques. Paris: Gabalda.

Arnold, C. E. 1995. *The Colossian Syncretism: The Interface between Christianity and Folk Belief at Colossae.* Tubingen: J.C.B. Mohr.

Arthurs, J. 1997. "Performing the Story: How to Preach First Person Narrative Sermons," *Preaching* March/April: 30–35.

______. 2012. *Devote Yourself to the Public Reading of Scripture.* Grand Rapids: Kregel.

Augustine. 1997. *On Christian Doctrine.* Oxford, UK: Oxford University Press.

Barclay, J. 1987. "Mirror-Reading a Polemical Letter: Galatians as a Test Case." *JSNT* 31: 73–93.

Barclay, W. 1963. *The All-Sufficient Christ: Studies in Paul's Letter to the Colossians.* Philadelphia: Westminster Press.

Barna, G. 2019. "State of the Bible 2019: Trends in Engagement," Barna Research, April 18, 2019 https://www.barna.com/research/state-of-the-bible-2019.

Barone, J., 2017. "A Symphony Breathes Life into 400 Broken Instruments," *The New York Times*, Dec. 4. https://www.nytimes.com/2017/12/04/arts/music/philadelphia-david-lang-symphony-for-a-broken-orchestra.html.

Barrett, Kurian, and Johnson. 2001. Oxford, UK: Oxford University Press.

Barth, M., and H. Blanke. 1994. *Colossians: A New Translation with Introduction and Commentary.* Translated by A. B. Beck. AB. New York: Doubleday.

Bates, M. W. 2017. *Salvation by Allegiance Alone: Rethinking Faith, Works, and the Gospel of Jesus the King.* Grand Rapids: Baker Academic.

Bauckham, R. J. 1975. "Colossians 1:24 Again: The Apocalytpic Motif." *EvQ* 47: 168–70.

Baugh, S. M. 1985. "The Poetic Form of Col 1:15–20." *WTJ* 47: 227–44.

Bauer, W. 2000. *Greek-English Lexicon of the New Testament and Other Early Christian Literature.* 3rd ed. Revised and edited by F. Danker. Chicago: University of Chicago.

Beale, G. K. 2007. "Colossians." In *Commentary on the New Testament Use of the Old Testament,* edited by G. K. Beale and D. A. Carson, 841–70. Grand Rapids: Baker Academic.

Beard, Mary. 2015. *SPQR: A History of Ancient Rome.* New York: Liveright Publishing Corporation.

Beasley-Murray, P. 1980. "Colossians 1:15-20: An Early Christian Hymn Celebrating the Lordship of Christ." In *Pauline Studies,* edited by D. A Hagner and M. J. Harris, 169–83. Grand Rapids: Eerdmans.

Beetham, C. A. 2008. *Echoes of Scripture in the Letter of Paul to the Colossians.* Biblical Interpretation Series. Leiden: Brill.

Bennett, J. 2019. "When Did Everybody Become a Witch?" *The New York Times,* October 24.

Betz, H. D., ed. 1986. *The Greek Magical Papyri in Translation, Including the Demotic Spells.* 2nd ed. Vol. 1: Texts. Chicago: University of Chicago Press.

Bird, M. F. 2009. *Colossians and Philemon: A New Covenant Commentary.* NCC. Eugene, OR: Cascade Books.

______. 2013. *Evangelical Theology: A Biblical and Systematic Introduction*. Grand Rapids: Zondervan.

Blackwell, B. C., J. K. Goodrich, and J. Maston, eds. 2016. *Paul and the Apocalyptic Imagination*. Minneapolis: Fortress Press.

Blass, F., and A. Debrunner. 1961. *Greek Grammar of the New Testament and Other Early Christian Literature*. Translated by Robert W. Funk. Revised edition. Chicago: University Of Chicago Press.

Bonhoeffer, D. 1954. *Life Together*. Translated by John W Doberstein. New York: HarperOne.

Bridges, J. 2004. *Growing Your Faith: How to Mature in Christ*. Colorado Springs: NavPress.

Brown, F., S. Driver, and C. Briggs. 2003. Originally published 1906. *The Brown-Driver-Briggs Hebrew and English Lexicon.* Peabody, MA.

Brown, R. E. 1997. *An Introduction to the New Testament*. New York: Doubleday.

Bruce, F. F. 1977. *Paul: Apostle of the Heart Set Free*. Grand Rapids: Eerdmans.

______. 1984a. "Colossian Problems Part 2: The 'Christ Hymn' of Colossians 1:15-20." *BSac* 141: 99–111.

______. 1984b. *The Epistle to the Colossians, to Philemon, and to the Ephesians*. NICNT. Grand Rapids: Eerdmans.

______. 1985. *The Pauline Circle*. Grand Rapids: Eerdmans.

______. 1988. *The Canon of Scripture*. Downers Grove, IL: IVP Academic.

Bujard, W. 1973. *Stilanalytische Untersuchungen Zum Kolosserbrief Als Beitrag Zur Methodik von Sprachvergleichen*. Göttingen: Vandenhoeck und Ruprecht.

Bultmann, R. 1951. *Theology of the New Testament.* Translated by K. Grobel. 2 vols. New York: Scribners.

Burroughs, J. 1988. Originally published 1659. *The Saints' Happiness, Together with the Several Steps Leading Thereunto, Delivered in Divers Lectures on the Beatitudes; Being Part of Christ's Sermon on the Mount, Contained in the Fifth of Matthew*. Morgan, PA: Soli Deo Gloria Publications.

Butterworth, G. W. 1919. *Clement of Alexandria*. LCL. Cambridge, MA: Harvard University Press.

Cadwallader, A. H. 2011. "Refuting an Axiom of Scholarship on Colossae: Fresh Insights from New and Old Inscriptions." In *Colossae in Space and Time: Linking to an Ancient City*, edited by A. H. Cadwallader and M. Trainor, 151–79. Göttingen: Vandenhoeck & Ruprecht.

______. 2012. "Honouring the Repairer of the Baths: A New Inscription from Kolossai." *Antichthon* 46:150–83.

______. 2015. *Fragments of Colossae: Sifting through the Traces*. Hindmarsh: ATF Press.

Campbell, C. R. 2012. *Paul and Union with Christ: An Exegetical and Theological Study*. Grand Rapids: Zondervan.

______. 2013. *Colossians and Philemon: A Handbook on the Greek Text*. Waco, TX: Baylor University Press.

Carnegie. D. 1932. *How to Win Friends and Influence People.* New York: Pocket Books.

Carter, J. 2019. "4 Reasons Christians Should Ban Porn." The Gospel Coalition, Dec. 14. https://www.thegospelcoalition.org/article/4-reasons-christians-ban-porn/?mc_cid=379d2493d8&mc_eid=1076878034.

Chapman, G. 1992. *The Five Love Languages: The Secret to Love That Lasts.* Chicago: Northfield Publishing.

Colson, C. 1983. *Loving God.* Grand Rapids: Zondervan.

Copenhaver, A. K. 2014. "Echoes of a Hymn in a Letter of Paul: The Rhetorical Function of the Christ-Hymn in the Letter to the Colossians." *JSPL* 4.2:235–55.

______. 2018. *Reconstructing the Historical Background of Paul's Rhetoric in the Letter to the Colossians*. LNTS 585. London: T&T Clark.

Craig, W. L. 2008. *Reasonable Faith.* Wheaton, IL: Crossway.

Crouch, A. 2017. *The Tech-Wise Family: Everyday Steps for Putting Technology in its Place.* Grand Rapids: Baker.

Dana, H. E., and J. R. Mantey. 1927. *A Manual Grammar of the Greek New Testament.* New York: The MacMillan Co.

Darwin, C. 1911. *Life and Letters of Charles Darwin.* New York: D. Appleton and Co.

Dawkins, R. 2006. *The God Delusion.* New York: Bantam Books.

D'Andria, F. 2001. "Hierapolis of Phrygia: Its Evolution in Hellenistic and Roman Times." In *Urbanism in Western Asia Minor: New Studies on Aphrodisias, Ephesos, Hierapolis, Pergamon, Perge and Xanthos*, edited by D. Parrish, 96–115. JRASS. Portsmouth, RI: Journal of Roman Archaeology.

D'Angelo, M. R. 1993. "Colossians." In *Searching the Scriptures 2: A Feminist Commentary*, edited by E. S. Fiorenza, 313–24. New York: Crossroad.

DeMaris, R. E. 1994. *The Colossian Controversy: Wisdom in Dispute at Colossae.* JSNTSup. Sheffield: JSOT Press.

Dibelius, M. 1975. "The Isis Initiation in Apuleius and Related Initiatory Rites." In *Conflict at Colossae: A Problem in the Interpretation of Early Christianity Illustrated by Selected Modern Studies*, edited by F. O. Francis and W. A. Meeks, Revised, 61–121. Missoula, MT: Scholars Press.

Dill, S. 1956. *Roman Society: From Nero to Marcus Aurelius.* New York: Meridian Books.

Douglass, F. 2002. Originally published 1845. "Narrative of the Life of Frederick Douglass." In *The Classic Slave Narratives*, edited by H. L. Gates, Jr., 299–404. New York: Signet Classics.

Duke, A. 2020. "How Sex Became King." The Gospel Coalition, Jan. 8. https://www.thegospelcoalition.org/article/sex-became-king.

Duman, B., and E. Konakçi. 2011. "The Silent Witness of the Mound of Colossae: Pottery Remains." In *Colossae in Space and Time: Linking to an Ancient City*, edited by A. H. Cadwallader and M. Trainor, 247–81. Göttingen: Vandenhoeck & Ruprecht.

Dunn, J. D. G. 1996. *The Epistles to the Colossians and to Philemon.* NIGTC. Grand Rapids: Eerdmans.

Earley, J. 2020. "5 Habits to Practice the Presence of God at Work." The Gospel Coalition, Feb. 10. https://www.thegospelcoalition.org/article/5-habits-work.

Elliott, N., and M. Reasoner. 2010. *Documents and Images for the Study of Paul.* Minneapolis: Fortress Press.

Ferguson, E. 1993. *Backgrounds of Early Christianity.* 2nd ed. Grand Rapids: Eerdmans.

Fitzmyer, J. A. 2000. *The Letter to Philemon: A New Translation with Introduction and Commentary.* AB. New York: Doubleday.

Foster, P. 2016. *Colossians.* BNTC. London: Bloomsbury.

Foster, R. 1998. *Celebration of Discipline.* San Francisco: Harper.

Fowl, S. E. 1990. *The Story of Christ in the Ethics of Paul: An Analysis of the Hymnic Material in the Pauline Corpus.* JSNTSup. Sheffield: Sheffield Academic Press.

Fowler, H. N. 1921. *Plato: Theaetetus, Sophist.* LCL. Cambridge, MA: Harvard University Press.

Frame, J. M. 2013. *Systematic Theology: An Introduction to Christian Belief.* Phillipsburg, NJ: P&R Publishing.

Francis, F. O. 1963. "Humility and Angelic Worship in Col 2:18." *ST* 16: 109–34.

______. 1975. "Humility and Angelic Worship in Col 2:18." In *Conflict at Colossae: A Problem in the Interpretation of Early Christianity Illustrated by Selected Modern Studies*, 163–95. Missoula, MT: Scholars Press.

Francis, F. O., and W. A. Meeks, eds. 1975. *Conflict at Colossae: A Problem in the Interpretation of Early Christianity Illustrated by Selected Modern Studies*. Missoula, MT: Scholars Press.

Friessen, Garry. 2004. *Decision Making and the Will of God*. Colorado Springs: Multnomah.

Gagnon, R. A. J. 2002. *The Bible and Homosexual Practice: Texts and Hermeneutics*. Nashville: Abingdon Press.

Gamble, H. 1995. *Books and Readers in the Early Church: A History of Early Christian Texts*. New Haven, CT: Yale University Press.

Gathercole, S. 2015. *Defending Substitution: An Essay on Atonement in Paul*. ASBT. Grand Rapids: Baker Academic.

Getz, Gene. 1976. *Building Up One Another*. Wheaton, IL: Victor Books.

Golding, W. 1953. *Lord of the Flies*. London: Faber and Faber.

Gottmann, J. 1995. *Why Marriages Succeed or Fail*. New York: Simon and Schuster.

Graf, N. 2019. "Key Findings on Marriage and Cohabitation in the U.S." Pew Research Center, Nov. 6. https://www.pewresearch.org/fact-tank/2019/11/06/key-findings-on-marriage-and-cohabitation-in-the-u-s.

Greidanus, S. 1999. *Preaching Christ from the Old Testament: A Contemporary Hermeneutical Model*. Grand Rapids: Eerdmans.

Grudem, W. 1994. *Systematic Theology: An Introduction to Biblical Doctrine*. Grand Rapids: Zondervan.

Hall, R. and D. Moore. *Same Kind of Different as Me*. Nashville: Thomas Nelson.

Harris, M. J. 2010. *Colossians and Philemon*. EGGNT. Nashville: B&H Academic.

Hauerwas, S., and W. H. Willimon. 2015. *The Holy Spirit*. Nashville: Abingdon Press.

Hawkins, G. L. and Parkinson, C. 2008. *Follow Me*. Barrington, IL: Willow Creek Association.

Helyer, L. R. 1983. "Colossians 1:15-20: Pre-Pauline or Pauline?" *JETS* 26:167–79.

Hemer, C. J. 1986. *The Letters to the Seven Churches of Asia in Their Local Setting*. JSNTSup. Sheffield: Academic Press.

Hogenboom, M. 2017. "The Hidden Upsides of Revenge," BBC.com. April 3, 2017.

Holcomb, J. S. 2014. *Know the Creeds and Councils*. Grand Rapids: Zondervan.

Holmes, M. W. 2007. *The Apostolic Fathers: Greek Texts and English Translations*. Second edition. Grand Rapids: Baker Academic.

Hughes, M. 2020. "An Uber Driver Got a College Degree after One of Her Passengers Wiped Out Her Debt." CNN.com. Jan. 1. https://www.cnn.com/2020/01/02/us/uber-driver-debt-paid-trnd/index.html.

Hunt, A. S, and C. C. Edgar. 1932. *Select Papyri: Volume I: Private Documents*. LCL. Cambridge, MA: Harvard University Press.

Hurtado, L. W. 2016. *Why on Earth Did Anyone Become a Christian in the First Three Centuries?* Milwaukee, WI: Marquette University Press.

______. 2017. *Destroyer of the Gods: Early Christian Distinctiveness in the Roman World*. Waco, TX: Baylor University Press.

Ingraham, C. 2014. "Thee Quarters of Whites Don't Have Any Non-White Friends." *Washington Post*, Aug. 25. https://www.washingtonpost.com/news/wonk/wp/2014/08/25/three-quarters-of-whites-dont-have-any-non-white-friends.

Jones, A. H. M. 1963. "The Greeks under the Roman Empire." *Dumbarton Oaks Papers* XVII: 3–19.

Käsemann, E. 1964. "A Primitive Christian Baptism Liturgy." In *Essays on New Testament Themes*. Translated by W. J. Montague, 149–68. Philadelphia: Fortress Press.

______. 1971. "Justification and Salvation History in the Epistle to the Romans." In *Perspectives on Paul*. Translated by M. Kohl, 60–78. Philadelphia: Fortress Press.

Keller, T. 2009. *The Reason for God*. New York: Penguin.

______. 2012. *Center Church: Doing Balanced, Gospel-Centered Ministry in Your City*. Grand Rapids: Zondervan.

_______. 2016. "5 Reasons to Host a Q&A after Your Worship Service." The Gospel Coalition, July 27. https://www.thegospelcoalition.org/article/5-reasons-to-host-qa-after-worship-service.

Kim, S. 1997. "God Reconciled His Enemy to Himself: The Origin of Paul's Concept of Reconciliation." In *The Road from Damascus: The Impact of Paul's Conversion on His Life, Thought, and Ministry*, edited by Richard N. Longenecker, 102–24. Grand Rapids: Eerdmans.

Kittle, G., and G. Friedrich, eds. 1964–76. *Theological Dictionary of the New Testament*. 10 vols. Grand Rapids: Eerdmans.

Koehler, L., and W. Baumgartner. 2001. *Hebrew and Aramaic Lexicon of the Old Testament*. 2 vols. Leiden: Brill.

Koester, H. 1990. *Ancient Christian Gospels: Their History and Development*. Philadelphia: Trinity Press International.

Kraabel, A. T. 1968. "Judaism in Western Asia Minor under the Roman Empire with a Preliminary Study of the Jewish Community at Sardis, Lydia." PhD Diss: Harvard Divinity School.

Lake, K. 1959. *Eusebius: The Ecclesiastical History*. LCL. 2 vols. Cambridge, MA: Harvard University Press.

Lane Fox, R. 1986. *Pagans and Christians in the Mediterranean World from the Second Century AD to the Conversion of Constantine*. London: Penguin Books.

Lavin, Talia. 2019. "Age of Anxiety." *The New Republic*. Feb. 26, 2019. https://newrepublic.com/article/153153/age-anxiety.

Lee, H. 1960. *To Kill a Mockinbird*. New York: Popular Library.

Lewis, C. S. 1949. "The Weight of Glory." In *The Weight of Glory and Other Addresses*, 1–15. Grand Rapids: Eerdmans.

______. 1952a. *Mere Christianity*. New York: Macmillan.

______. 1952b. *The Voyage of the Dawn Treader*. New York: Macmillan.

______. 2011. "Introduction." In *St. Athanasius the Great of Alexandria: On the Incarnation*. PPS. Yonkers, NY: St Vladimir's Seminary Press.

Liddell, H. G., R. Scott, and H. S. Jones. 1996. *A Greek-English Lexicon with Revised Supplement*. 9th ed. Oxford: Clarendon Press.

Lightfoot, J. B. 1981. Originally published 1875. *St. Paul's Epistles to the Colossians and to Philemon*. Revised. Lynn, MA: Hendrickson Publishers.

Lincoln, A. T. 1990. *Ephesians*, edited by B. M. Metzger. WBC. Waco, TX: Word Books.

Lints, R. 1993. *The Fabric of Theology: A Prolegomenon to Evangelical Theology*. Eugene, OR: Wipf and Stock.

Lohmeyer, E. 1953. *Die Briefe an Die Philipper, an Die Kolosser Und an Philemon*. KEK. Göttingen: Vandenhoeck.

Lohse, E. 1971. *Colossians and Philemon: A Commentary on the Epistles to the Colossians and to Philemon*, edited by H. Koester. Translated by W. R. Poehlmann and R. J. Karris. Hermeneia. Philadelphia: Fortress Press.

Lohse, E., and J. E. Steely. 1976. *The New Testament Environment*. Revised. Nashville: Abingdon.

Longenecker, B. W. 2005. *Rhetoric at the Boundaries: The Art and Theology of the New Testament Chain-Link Transitions*. Waco, TX: Baylor University Press.

Luther, M. 1892. Originally published 1532. *Commentary on the Sermon on the Mount*. Translated by C. A. Hay. Philadelphia: Lutheran Publication Society.

MacDonald, M. Y. 2000. *Colossians and Ephesians*. SP. Collegeville, MN: Liturgical Press.

Macro, A. D. 1980. "The Cities of Asia Minor under the Roman Imperium." *ANRW* II.7.2: 658–97.

Maier, H. O. 2013. *Picturing Paul in Empire: Imperial Image, Text and Persuasion in Colossians, Ephesians and the Pastoral Epistles*. New York: T&T Clark.

Marshall, I. H. 2007. *Aspects of the Atonement: Cross and Resurrection in the Reconciling of God and Humanity*. Colorado Springs: Paternoster.

Mayerhoff, E. T. 1838. *Der Brief an Die Colosser, Mit Vornehmlicher Berücksichtigung Der Drei Pastoralbriefe Kritisch Geprüft*. Berlin.

McGowan, A. T. B. 2012. *The Person and Work of Christ: Understanding Jesus*. Milton Keynes, UK: Paternoster.

McKnight, S. 2018. *The Letter to the Colossians*. NICNT. Grand Rapids: Eerdmans.

McLaughlin, R. 2019. *Confronting Christianity: 12 Hard Questions for the World's Largest Religion*. Wheaton, IL: Crossway.

Meeks, W. A. 1983. *The First Urban Christians: The Social World of the Apostle Paul*. New Haven, CT: Yale University Press.

Mehrabian, A. 1968. "Communication without Words," *Psychology Today* 2 (September).

Mellink, M. J. 1987. "Archaeology in Anatolia." *AJA* 91: 1–30.

Metzger, B. M. 1994. *A Textual Commentary on the Greek New Testament*. 2nd ed. Stuttgart: Deutsche Bibelgesellschaft.

Mommsen, T, and et. al., eds. 1985. *The Digest of Justinian*. 4 vols. Philadelphia: University of Pennsylvania Press.

Moo, D. J. 1996. *The Epistle to the Romans*. NICNT. Grand Rapids: Eerdmans.

______. 2008. *The Letters to the Colossians and to Philemon*. PNTC. Grand Rapids: Eerdmans.

Morris, L. 1965. *The Apostolic Preaching of the Cross*. Third Edition. Grand Rapids: Eerdmans.

Moule, C. F. D. 1962. *The Epistles of Paul the Apostle to the Colossians and to Philemon*. Cambridge: Cambridge University Press.

Mounce, W. D. 1993. *Basics of Biblical Greek: Grammar*. 1st ed. Grand Rapids: Zondervan.

Mullins, T. Y. 1984. "The Thanksgivings of Philemon and Colossians." *NTS* 30: 288–93.

Murray, J. 1955. *Redemption Accomplished and Applied*. Grand Rapids: Eerdmans.

Newbigin, L. 1989. *The Gospel in a Pluralistic Society*. Grand Rapids: Eerdmans.

O'Brien, P. T. 1977. *Introductory Thanksgivings in the Letters of Paul*. Leiden: E. J. Brill.

______. 1982. *Colossians, Philemon*. WBC. Waco, TX: Word Books.

Ortberg, J. 1997. *The Life You've Always Wanted: Spiritual Disciplines for Ordinary People* Grand Rapids: Zondervan.

Osborne, G. R. 2016. *Colossians & Philemon: Verse by Verse*. Bellingham, WA: Lexham Press.

Owen, J. 2006. Originally published 1656. *The Mortification of Sin: A Puritan's View of How to Deal with Sin in Your Life*. Ross-shire, Scotland: Christian Focus Publications.

Packer, J. I. 1984. *Keep In Step with the Spirit*. Grand Rapids: Baker.

Pao, D. W. 2012. *Colossians and Philemon*, edited by Clinton E. Arnold. Grand Rapids: Zondervan.

Perrin, B. 1918. *Plutarch Lives: Dion and Brutus, Temoleon and Aemilius Paulus*. LCL. Cambridge, MA: Harvard University Press.

Perrin, N. 1974. *The New Testament: An Introduction*. New York: Thomson Learning.

Peterson, E. H. 2000. *A Long Obedience in the Same Direction: Discipleship in an Instant Society*. 2nd ed. Downers Grove, IL: InterVarsity Press.

______. 2011. *The Pastor: A Memoir*. New York: HarperOne.

Pinsker, J. 2019. "Are McMansions Making People Any Happier?" *The Atlantic*. June 11.

Plato. *The Republic*. http://classics.mit.edu/Plato/republic.html.

Porter, S. E. 1992. *Idioms of the Greek New Testament*. Biblical Languages: Greek. Sheffield: JSOT Press.

Preisendanz, K., ed. 1928. *Papyri Graecae Magicae: Die Griechischen Zauberpapyri*. Preisendanz. 2 Volumes. Leipzig: Verlag und Druck B.G. Teubner.

Prince, M. 2002. "The History of Mary Prince, a West Indian Slave." In *The Classic Slave Narratives*, edited by H. L. Gates, Jr., 231–63. London: Signet Classics.

Rackham, H. 1932. *Aristotle: Politics*. LCL. Cambridge, MA: Harvard University Press.

______. 1934. *Aristotle: Nicomachean Ethics*. LCL. 2nd ed. Cambridge, MA: Harvard University Press.

Rainer, T. n.d. "Preaching and the Breakout Church." *Preaching*. https://www.preaching.com/articles/preaching-and-the-breakout-church-an-interview-with-thom-rainer.

Raymond, E. 2020. "How to Exasperate Your Children." The Gospel Coalition, Feb. 18. https://www.thegospelcoalition.org/blogs/erik-raymond/how-to-exasperate-your-children-2.

Reicke, B. 1970. "Caesarea, Rome, and the Captivity Epistles." In *Apostolic History and the Gospel: Biblical and Historical Essays Presented to F. F. Bruce*, edited by W. W. Gasque and R. P. Martin, 277–86. Exeter: Paternoster Press.

Reuters. 2019. "Rugby: Tattooed Samoans Don Skin Suits to Avoid Offending Japanese Hosts," September 17, sec. Oddly Enough. https://www.reuters.com/article/us-rugby-union-worldcup-wsm-idUSKBN1W216S.

Richards, E. R. 2004. *Paul and First-Century Letter Writing: Secretaries, Composition and Collection*. Downers Grove, IL: Intervarsity Press.

______. 2008. "Letter." In *The New Interpreter's Dictionary of the Bible*, edited by K. D. Sakenfield, 3:638–41. Nashville: Abingdon Press.

Ritti, T., and P. Arthur. 2006. *An Epigraphic Guide to Hierapolis (Pamukkale)*. Istanbul: Ege Yayinlari.

Robertson, A. T. 1998. *A Grammar of the Greek New Testament in the Light of Historical Research*. Nashville: Broadman Press.

Rocca, F. X. 2019. "Pope Francis, in Christmas Message, Says Church Must Adapt to Post-Christian West," *The Wall Street Journal*, Dec. 21.

Runge, S. E. 2010. *Discourse Grammar of the Greek New Testament: A Practical Introduction for Teaching and Exegesis*. Peabody, MA: Hendrickson Publishers.

Schaff, P. 2006. Originally published 1858–1910. *History of the Christian Church*. 3rd edition. 8 vols. Peabody, MA: Hendrickson Publishers.

Schlink, B. 1997. *The Reader*. Translated by C. B. Janeway. New York: Pantheon Books.

Schultze, Q. 2002. *Habits of the High-Tech Heart*. Grand Rapids: Baker.

Schweizer, E. 1982. *The Letter to the Colossians: A Commentary*. Translated by A. Chester. Minneapolis: Augsburg.

Shelton, J., ed. 1998. *As the Romans Did: A Sourcebook in Roman Social History*. 2nd edition. New York: Oxford University Press.

Shigematsu, K. 2018. *Survival Guide for the Soul*. Grand Rapids: Zondervan.

Shimer, D. 2018. "Yale's Most Popular Class Ever: Happiness," *The New York Times*, Jan. 26.

Showalter, B. 2018. "Witches Outnumber Presbyterians in the US; Wicca, Paganism Growing 'Astronomically,'" *The Christian Post*, October 10.

Silva, M. 1988. *Philippians*. WEC. Chicago: Moody.

Smallwood, C. 2019. "Astrology in the Age of Uncertainty," *The New York Times*, Oct. 21.

Smith, I. K. 2006. *Heavenly Perspective: A Study of the Apostle Paul's Response to a Jewish Mystical Movement at Colossae*. LNTS. London: T&T Clark International.

Smith, J. K. A. 2009. *Desiring the Kingdom: Worship, Worldview, and Cultural Formation*. Cultural Liturgies, Volume 1. Grand Rapids: Baker Academic.

Starhawk. 1979. *The Spiral Dance*. San Francisco: Harper.

Steinbeck, J. 1974. *The Pearl*. New York: Viking Press.

Stirewalt, M. L. Jr. 1991. "The Form and Function of the Greek Letter-Essay." In *The Romans Debate*, edited by K. P. Donfried, 147–71. Peabody, MA: Hendrickson Publishers.

Stowe, H. B. 2005. Originally published 1852. *Uncle Tom's Cabin*. New York: Barnes and Noble Classics.

Sumney, J. L. 2008. *Colossians: A Commentary*. NTL. Louisville: Westminster John Knox Press.

Taylor, J. 2015. "17 Ways to Meditate on Scripture." The Gospel Coalition, May 15. https://www.thegospelcoalition.org/blogs/justin-taylor/17-ways-to-meditate-on-scripture.

Thielman, F. 1995. *Paul & the Law: A Contextual Approach*. First edition. Downers Grove, IL: IVP Academic.

Thompson, J. W., and B. W. Longenecker. 2016. *Philippians and Philemon*. PCNT. Grand Rapids: Baker Academic.

Thompson, M. M. 2005. *Colossians and Philemon*. THNTC. Grand Rapids: Eerdmans.

Thornton, T. G. C. 1989. "Jewish New Moon Festivals, Galatians 4:3-11 and Colossians 2:16." *JTS* 40: 97–100.

Tolkien, J. R. R. 1954. *The Fellowship of the Ring*. New York: Ballantine Books.

VanderKam, J. C. 1998. *Calendars in the Dead Sea Scrolls: Measuring Time*. London: Routledge.

Volf, M. 2000. "The Social Meaning of Reconciliation." *Int* 54: 159–72.

Vos, G. 1948. *Biblical Theology: Old and New Testaments*. Grand Rapids: Eerdmans.

______. 1979. *The Pauline Eschatology*. Phillipsburg, NJ: P&R Publishing.

Wallace, D. B. 1996. *Greek Grammar Beyond the Basics: An Exegetical Syntax of the New Testament*. Grand Rapids: Zondervan.

Walsh, P. G. 2006. *Pliny the Younger: Complete Letters*. Oxford: Oxford University Press.

Walton, J. H., and D. B. Sandy. 2013. *The Lost World of Scripture: Ancient Literary Culture and Biblical Authority*. Downers Grove, IL: IVP Academic.

Webb, W. J. 2001. *Slaves, Women, and Homosexuals: Exploring the Hermeneutics of Cultural Analysis*. Downers Grove, IL: IVP Academic.

White, J. E. 2014. *The Rise of the Nones*. Grand Rapids: Baker.

______. 2019. "The Year of the Witch," *Church and Culture*, vol. 15, no. 85.

Wilken, J. 2014. *Women of the Word: How to Study the Bible with Both Our Hearts and Our Minds*. Wheaton, IL: Crossway.

Wilkin, J. 2019. "How to Help Your Teen Study the Bible." The Gospel Coalition, Jan. 15. https://www.thegospelcoalition.org/article/teach-teenager-study-bible.

Wilson, B. R. 1967. "An Analysis of Sect Development." In *Patterns of Sectarianism: Organisation and Ideology in Social and Religious Movements*, 22–45. Heinemann Books on Sociology. London: Heinemann Educational Books.

Wilson, R. McL. 2005. *A Critical and Exegetical Commentary on Colossians and Philemon*. ICC. London: T&T Clark.

Wink, W. 1984. *Naming the Powers: The Language of Power in the New Testament*. The Powers. Philadelphia: Fortress Press.

Witherington III, B. 2007. *The Letters to Philemon, the Colossians, and the Ephesians: A Socio-Rhetorical Commentary on the Captivity Epistles*. Grand Rapids: Eerdmans.

Wright, N. T. 1986. *The Epistles of Paul to the Colossians and to Philemon: An Introduction and Commentary*. TNTC. Downers Grove, IL: IVP Academic.

______. 1990. "Poetry and Theology in Colossians 1:15-20." In *The Climax of the Covenant: Christ and the Law in Pauline Theology*, 99–119. Minneapolis: Fortress Press.

______. 1997. *Jesus and the Victory of God.* Minneapolis: Fortress Press.

______. 2013. *Paul and the Faithfulness of God.* Minneapolis: Fortress Press.

Yinger, K. 2003. "Translating Katabrabeuet ['Disqualify,' NRSV] in Colossians 2.18." *BT* 54: 138–45.

Yonge, C. D. 1993. *The Works of Philo: Complete and Unabridged.* Revised. Peabody, MA: Hendrickson Publishers.

Zerwick, M. 1963. *Biblical Greek, Illustrated by Examples, English Edition, Adapted from the Fourth Latin Edition by Joseph Smith S.J.* Scripta Pontificii Instituti Biblici 114. Rome.